# PANJAB

## Journeys Through
## Fault Lines

### AMANDEEP SANDHU

PENGUIN BOOKS

An imprint of Penguin Random House

PENGUIN BOOKS

USA | Canada | UK | Ireland | Australia
New Zealand | India | South Africa | China

Penguin Books is part of the Penguin Random House group of companies
whose addresses can be found at global.penguinrandomhouse.com

Published by Penguin Random House India Pvt. Ltd
4th Floor, Capital Tower 1, MG Road,
Gurugram 122 002, Haryana, India

First published by Westland Publications Private Limited in 2019
Published in paperback by Penguin Books 2022

ISBN 9780143459316

Typeset by SÜRYA, New Delhi

www.penguin.co.in

PENGUIN BOOKS

# PANJAB

**Amandeep Sandhu** was born in Rourkela, Odisha. He completed his Master's in English Literature from the University of Hyderabad. He worked as a journalist and later as a technical writer. His first two books were autobiographical fiction: *Sepia Leaves* (2008) and *Roll of Honour* (2012). For the past few years, he has written for the media and contributed to anthologies. He now lives in Bengaluru, Karnataka.

*Panjab: Journeys through Fault Lines*, his first non-fiction book, was originally published in 2019 to great critical acclaim and reception.

*Je ho ji tu samjhe mahiya,*
*Oho ji main hain nahin …*

What you know of me, my dear, I am not that.

—Aman Rozi, Akhara Baba Kala Mehr,
Village Mahesri, District Moga, Panjab
March 2016

*Dedicated to Lakshmi Karunakaran*
*Who sees Panjab with new eyes …*

# Contents

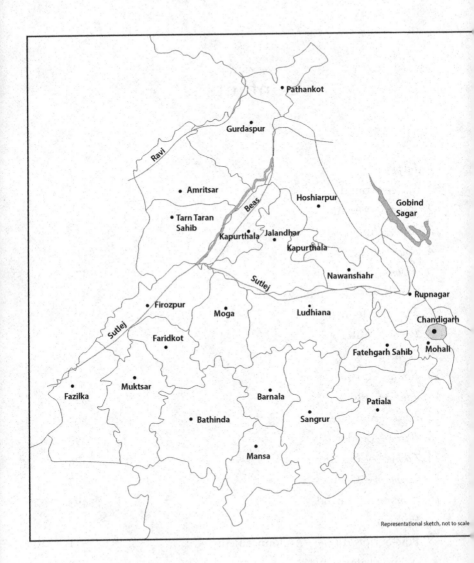

Representational sketch, not to scale

# Preface

'If you want to understand Panjab, be ready to count its corpses,' said the photographer as he reached for the drawer in his desk. On that spring afternoon, Satpal Danish and I had met at his shop in the Brahm Buta Akhara, near the Guru Ram Das Serai, next to the east gate of the Darbar Sahib complex in Amritsar.

As spiritual centres go, I believe, Amritsar is a call. At one stage in my life I did not visit Amritsar for eighteen years. Then I visited the city seven times in two years, bringing my teacher, friends, and once my beloved and later wife on her maiden visit to Panjab. This time I had come to Amritsar weary from roaming Panjab over the past few months. I was journeying fifty years after the state was formed, twenty-five years after the militant guns had fallen silent. I wanted to know if peace had returned to the turbulent land.

Danish is one of the few photographers who, with his camera, has closely observed and documented Panjab politics from the mid-1970s to date. Over the past few decades, especially in what is called the 'dark decade', which is actually a decade and a half (1978–93), when separatist militancy created *dehshat*—a reign of fear and silence—in Panjab, his pictures acquired and distributed by Associated Press travelled all over the world and appeared in major publications. Informally, he was also the personal photographer of Jarnail Singh Bhindranwale whom the nation's discourse portrays as the chief protagonist of the Khalistan separatist movement.

In his shop, from an old translucent plastic bag, Danish pulled out his collection of photographs. He showed me pictures of young boys with guns in their hands in front of Darshani Deodi at Darbar Sahib—their eyes smiling, faces innocent, looks resolute and hands easy on the guns they held. For someone who does not know Panjab, the guns could look threatening. However, given the land's geography and history, resistance and rebellion are central to it and its people. Sikh lore is full of warrior legends. I am sure that, until the violence became targeted, such a scene did not raise Panjab's eyebrows. In the beginning of the movement, the militants were in fact called *bhau*, *khadku* and *munde* which translate to brothers, rebels and boys.

Danish took that iconic picture of a smiling Bhindranwale, the one of Bhindranwale standing wrapped in a grey *loi* (shawl), symbolic spear in hand, and the one of Bhindranwale tying his turban. These pictures came to define the man to the world outside Panjab. As one looks at the many photographs, one can see a dramatic change in Bhindranwale's face from 1979 to 1984—its gradual hardening reflects the many ways in which the central government and Prime Minister Indira Gandhi were blocking his way and the Akalis were weakening in their stance.

There were pictures of Bhindranwale along with Harchand Singh Longowal, the Akali leader who had led the Save Democracy Morcha during the Emergency, and with the head of the representative body of the Sikhs—Shiromani Gurdwara Prabandhak Committee (SGPC)—Gurcharan Singh Tohra, with a hand-held speaker in front of a crowd.[a]

---

a. The SGPC is a constitutional body responsible for the management of historical gurdwaras in the three states of Panjab, Haryana and Himachal Pradesh and the Union Territory of Chandigarh. Its members are elected and a president then chosen from among the members. The control of SGPC came to the Badal family at the turn of the century when the Sikh community was celebrating its tercentenary. That was when the long-standing President Gurcharan Singh Tohra was ejected and for the first and only time, a woman, Jagir Kaur, handpicked by Parkash Singh Badal, was installed as president of the SGPC.

There were two specific pictures that fascinated me for how they were seemingly similar, but actually were a counterpoint to each other. The first picture was from October 1982. Bhindranwale and Longowal were sitting on a *manji* (hand-woven cot), in front of a bolted door. Now, almost three and a half decades later, one can read the bolted door as the doorway to the Indian nation and both these leaders—one emphatic, the other moderate—stood outside the door. It is almost as if they were discussing how to open the door so that Panjab's issues could become part of the nation's discourse. Bhindranwale's sharp probing eyes were on Longowal's passive face and lowered eyes. Their shoulders were relaxed and they seemed to be at ease.

The second picture was from late winter, 1982, a few months later. Bhindranwale and Longowal were sitting wrapped in *lois* on a *manji*, sipping milk from *battis* (big wide steel bowls). It was a warmer picture than the earlier one—a shared ritual of food and camaraderie. Yet, it had a tense undertone. Bhindranwale's sharp eyes were focussed on Longowal's face, while Longowal's eyes were lowered to Bhindranwale's *batti*. The picture spoke volumes on how the equations were changing between the two leaders. A resolute Bhindranwale, ready to engage with the Indian state, was in a commanding position. Longowal, willing to compromise with the Indian state, was subdued.

On the white table-top, Danish placed another picture. It was from the day in mid-June, 1984, when, for the first time post Operation Blue Star, ordinary people were allowed entry into the Darbar Sahib complex.[b] Though what the picture depicts is massive, it stuns me through what it does not show but points at. Like how silences sometimes speak louder than words. In the picture, people

---

b. Operation Blue Star was the code name of an Indian military action carried out between 1 and 8 June 1984 to remove militant religious leader Jarnail Singh Bhindranwale and his followers from the buildings of the Harmandir Sahib (Darbar Sahib) complex in Amritsar, Panjab.

have climbed on to the top of the 156 feet Ramgarhia Bunga on the east of the Darbar Sahib complex and are peering down in all directions. Unsurprisingly, given the inherent patriarchy of Panjab's society, all are men. I count twenty-one adults, all with heads covered as mandated in the Sikh tradition—many with turbans and some with another cloth. Some are probably Hindu—the Darbar Sahib is revered by all faiths. There are four early adolescent boys in the picture, about the age I was when Operation Blue Star took place. I feel I am one of the boys. One person is pointing at something specific, showing it to two of the boys.

To me.

The Bunga, one of two such structures in the Darbar Sahib complex, is a three-storey watchtower originally built in 1755 when the Darbar Sahib was attacked twice by Ahmad Shah Abdali or Durrani, an invader from Afghanistan. Its domes had been displaced after an earthquake at the turn of the previous century. Now, the Indian Army had shelled it and its body bore the marks. From their vantage point, the people standing on top of the Bunga can see the blown-off crown of the supreme Sikh seat of justice, the Akal Takht. The magnificent marble structure, lit by xenon lamps from Vijayanta battle tanks, was shelled from armoured personnel carriers, but stood defiant. Finally, as the rays of the morning sun began to peep, two tanks blasted seventy-five 105 mm high-explosive squash head artillery shells and the Akal Takht was reduced to a rubble skeleton.[1] The people can also see the plundered, looted, burnt hollow shell of the Sikh Reference Library. Holes, gaping holes on every building.

The people suspended mid-air look like they are on a boat. A popular Sikh *shabad*, hymn, says, *Nanak naam jahaz hai, chade so utre paar.* The Lord's name—truth—is the boat and the one who gets on board will get across the *bhavsagar*—the sea of emotions or the ocean of life. The world has receded: aptly, the background is hazy, everything is dimmed, covered by a bubble of hallucinatory smoke.

As I see the picture, I feel not only these people, not only the whole of Panjab, but even I have been sitting on one such Bunga in my mind, looking at Panjab over the last few decades with rising bewilderment. Except for the other Bunga, there are no other structures as tall as these towers in the vicinity. That means, from a distance, the people could also be seeing the inner city of Amritsar. A top angle view of the inner city of Amritsar is remarkably similar to the ventral view of the human brain. Its maze of narrow, winding, entwining by-lanes, *katras*, *akharas* and bazaars are akin to the grooves between the frontal, parietal, occipital, temporal lobes, the cerebellum, the basal ganglia and the brain stem. The Darbar Sahib is at the centre of the inner city as is the corpus callosum in the middle of the brain. The way the corpus callosum connects the two hemispheres of the brain and integrates the motor, sensory and cognitive performances, the Darbar Sahib connects the *Miri-Piri* (temporal-spiritual) aspects of the Sikh faith.

When the picture was shot, the onlookers could not have known the number of combatants and non-combatants killed, injured or imprisoned in the army Operation. Yet, they knew the attack took place when the Darbar Sahib complex was unusually crowded with pilgrims who came from far-flung villages for the 378th martyrdom anniversary of Guru Arjan, which fell in the week of the attack. Operation Blue Star was a watershed historical event precisely because it was an attack by a nation state on the symbol of faith, the corpus callosum of the Sikh community. Since the attack, I have wondered how people keep faith that the nation state they believe in would defend them, their article of faith and their religion? Where, in the human brain, is the organ that creates faith located?

As a new generation has grown up and the nation has gone through a tailspin in terms of its politics, time has exacerbated the wound. The multiple narratives that arise from the event have hardened and lacerated the land and its people, turning it into a landmine. One never knows which stone could explode under one's mis-step. I travelled through this chequered Panjab to address my bewilderment, to learn how to keep faith and how to trust.

Along with the map of present-day Panjab—partitioned in 1947, rendering gory and bloody the birth of India as a modern nation, trifurcated in 1966, shrinking Panjab to a heart-shaped state, one-seventh its original size, that divided the speakers of a common language, Panjabi, and tore asunder the common culture of *Panjabiat* by hardening the identities of people into Hindu, Muslim and Sikh— this picture hangs framed in my study, in front of my writing desk. As I draft this book, I sense the men in the picture, while looking at the Darbar Sahib complex, are now also looking at me, pointing at me.

Their gaze unsettles me.

I ask myself if I am ready to count Panjab's corpses.

## Chapter One

# *Satt* — Wound

'Tired?' asked Satnam when on that humid August morning in 2013, I walked up to his two-bedroom blue home near a dry canal in Ranjit Nagar, on the outskirts of Patiala. 'When I was your age, I could walk miles without even water to drink.'

I remembered Satnam's kindness from a long time back in Delhi and was sure he intended no malice. Then, upon learning that an Adivasi nanny had brought me up in Rourkela, Odisha, he had spoken to me about his experience with Adivasis in Bastar. The memory and warmth of that meeting was what had brought me to him after all these years. Perhaps his comment was even loving, an elder's joke with a younger. Yet, its directness pricked my heart. It made me conscious of my sedentary urban middle class life in Bangalore—the comforts of the car and pucca roads, of the English language and the glib, neat theories that look for easy cause and effect to understand all that is happening in the world and in Panjab.

Guided by his smile, I stepped into his drawing room. Satnam emptied the cane chairs of clothes, newspapers and magazines and went off to ready tea. His comment had pricked deeper in my heart, reminding me of the void at the core of my relationship with Panjab. Unlike people born in Panjab who have a direct connection with, and hence a memory of, the land, I have no liminal or tangible marker of belonging to Panjab. While my family did hail from Panjab, I was neither born here, nor do I live here. I have no address, bank statement, Aadhaar card, passport or land ownership to prove my connection with Panjab.

In the steel town where I grew up, thousands of kilometres from Panjab, as a child, I had smelt and touched Panjab through the bedsheets, the quilts, the durries and the *khes* (cotton blankets), in the tin trunks where they were stored. I had touched Panjab through the brass vessels with Mama's or Baba's name engraved on them in the Gurmukhi script that I could then not read. I inhaled Panjab in the desi ghee bursting in the frying pan in the kitchen as Mama added *tadka* (seasoning) to the daal. I ate Panjab in the pickles and *murabbas* (jams and fruit preserves). I saw Panjab in the photos of Guru Nanak, Guru Gobind Singh and Bhagat Singh in our drawing room, in Baba when he tied his turban every day, in Mama wearing her salwar kameez and covering her head with the dupatta. These were meaningful but partial, for the objects were artefacts and not the whole of Panjab. They rendered my understanding of Panjab limited to a set of fragmented sensory perceptions.

When we talk of a deep connection or belongingness to a place, we recall the bank of a river, a favourite tree, the memory of how our mother prepared a certain dish, how our father took us to a certain shop and so on. We remember the stories and the aural experiences that fill the sensory gaps. I believe, whoever we are, wherever we live, we live in stories. When the world echoes back our stories, we feel at home. When it does not, we feel uprooted. The issue I have with Panjab is that its stories are all entwined, knotted and confusing. I do not know where I belong in them.

A child begins to learn the world in the mother's lap. Mama— diagnosed with schizophrenia—was incoherent in her speech and thoughts. The Panjab I heard in her lap came out rambling. Its love and war legends splintered and turned into a volley of abuse. When

Baba realised this, he made a pact with me. Every day, at 8 p.m., we would sit down on the stone sill in our veranda and I could ask Baba any question, and he would try his best to answer. If Baba could not, he would ask for time to come back with answers.

In my adolescence, when I went to Panjab to attend boarding school during the period of *dehshat*, violence and mayhem were all around: Operation Blue Star, the assassination of Prime Minister Indira Gandhi, the anti-Sikh pogrom in Delhi and other cities in the cow-belt of the nation, the thousands of innocent Hindus and Sikhs being killed, the thousands of enforced disappearances; and personally: guns being pulled on me, the police picking me up, our larger family facing ransom demands, and so on. I would come home during mid-term vacations and ask Baba questions. I realised even Baba's stories trailed, splintered and got entangled, and he left them incomplete.

That is why, perhaps, wherever I have lived, however I have been, I have always sensed a hole in my heart, an emptiness about matters Panjab. That is why I also remain shy about my views on Panjab, about jumping to conclusions about the land or forming ideas about its people. I had now come to Panjab to make sense, to recreate my meaning-making sessions with Baba, to find experiences in lieu of the word, the label, and to complete or at least understand the multiple stories.

'Black tea,' said Satnam as he handed me a steel glass. 'I hope that is okay? I am out of milk.' He also presented delicious homemade *matris* (salty gram flour snacks).

Picking up one, I asked, 'How are you these days?'

'*Vehla* (free).' He then paused to light a bidi. 'After her studies, my daughter went off to work in your Bangalore. When she came back, like any other father, I was a bit worried about her marriage. We just finished the ceremonies a while back. Now I am *vehla*.'

I knew a political and social activist like Satnam could not be *vehla*. For the past few years, every two or three months, a magazine named

*Sulagde Pind* (Burning Villages) that he produced with contributions from friends and readers would reach my home.

'Congratulations!'

'The boy was of her choice. I am happy,' Satnam answered shyly. 'I was for a civil registration. I told my *saathi* (comrades) that I have no money to pay for the wedding. They took care of everything, didn't allow me to spend on anything,' he paused again to take a long drag. 'Come, some of them will be at a rally. Let us go there.'

Amidst a raging dust storm common in Panjab during the summer, we walked up to the main road and boarded a share-auto. Fare: Rs 10 for a few kilometres. People were packed like sardines not only on the back seat, but also on the middle iron barrier between the driver and the backseat. In addition, two people sat on each side of the driver. A vehicle for three was carrying thirteen of us, including four women. Satnam told me the rally had been organised by farmers opposed to the policies of the incumbent Shiromani Akali Dal (SAD) government whose leader, five-time Panjab Chief Minister (CM) Parkash Singh Badal, had built his seven-decade long career on the grandiose claim of being the 'saviour of farmers'.

We got down in front of Gurdwara Dukhniwaran Sahib in the heart of the city and walked to the grain market. I soon found myself in a sea of white kurta pyjamas and green turbans. There were no blue Akali turbans or pastel Congress turbans. Captain Amarinder Singh, the then opposition leader, former CM, and the scion of the royal house of Patiala, had not come. Who then were these people if not affiliated to either of the two dominant parties in Panjab?

The grain market had a large concrete floor, partly covered by a slanted tin sheet. It was unlike the kacha grounds I remembered from my childhood. Beside the shed, the rally was supposed to take place under a huge white shamiana, a cloth tent that could accommodate a few thousand people. Preparations were underway—a stage made with wooden planks and covered with white sheets, durries spread and some chairs laid out for the old and infirm. Around us were kulfi and ice cream sellers on handcarts. Roving masala peanut vendors beckoned. Someone was selling Ayurvedic concoctions which guaranteed relief from constipation and gas. Tall wooden poles displayed colourful plastic animals and wooden toy tractors and trucks. Two mobile bookshops were selling books published by the Tarksheel (Rationalist) Society, biographies of Mao Zedong, Stalin, social realist novels, progressive poetry, works of Sahitya Akademi Award winners, and a number of local publications, many of them magazines similar to what Satnam brought out. It was a *mela* as they call it in Panjab.

Small clusters of men had formed towards the back of the crowd, away from the stage. Farmers were greeting each other. Every hand I shook—and being Satnam's 'friend from *Bunglor*', I shook a lot of hands—was rough and hardened from working the earth. The faces were creased. There were conversations about availability of labour, rates of urea and seeds, schools which had just reopened and so on. There were smiles and greetings, but they were all rather understated.

The inflow of people was continuous. Rural folks had travelled hours on tractors, in trolleys, on a small truck called 'chhota haathi' and on bikes, buses and by foot. They carried with them sacks of wheat flour, daal and vegetables and shared them in the *langar*, the common kitchens set up to cater to the crowds. In a separate enclosure, under the tin shed, firewood was stacked near the huge makeshift *angeethis* (traditional stoves). Both men and women were at work. The men stirred the big vessels full of gravy while the women rolled dough and made rotis.

When the programme began, I went towards the stage, parallel to the small women's section, to listen to what the speakers were saying. The speeches were direct, without mincing words and with no recourse to tall tales. Speaker after speaker said the same thing: 'When India was hungry, we fed it. Now we are dying of thirst and India does not look at us.'

When the first speaker said it, I dismissed it as exaggeration. Panjabis are loud and given to flamboyance in speech and gesture. When another speaker said the same words, I paid attention. When speaker after speaker said the same words, I frowned. Was this a prepared script? Why were these non-party people raising a political issue? As an organiser escorted us to a room near the makeshift kitchen, I turned to Satnam, 'Is this true? Thirst?'

'Don't you believe it?'

'But Panjab is the land of five rivers. How can it be thirsty?'

'Is this Panjab still the land of five rivers?'

'Well, no, but …'

'That is the error. You imagine a Panjab of the past—strong and resilient, its history of bravery.'

'But …'

'It is a perception. We are locked in the perception of being strong. Neither India nor we realise that the strong can also be vulnerable.' I noticed his use of the term 'India'. It was in keeping with the refrain of the speeches. Was it common for Panjab to call out India by its name—as if India were another entity?

Through the simple lunch of rotis and bottle gourd curry, friends and activists, all *saathis*, left Satnam with no time to himself. After we left, the downpour started just when we crossed the Thapar Institute of Technology in the auto-rickshaw. Satnam said, 'The south-west monsoon winds hit the Himalayas really hard. Panjab squeezes what is left of the moisture in the air. Then it floods here. We are a land of extremes—summers, winters, monsoons!'

We reached our stop next to the now clogged canal. I hesitated to get down. Satnam pushed me from behind. 'Just a little rain. You are not made of salt.'

When the municipality had laid the lane to Satnam's house, they had done so with interlocking bricks and forgotten to build drains. Thanks to that, the lane was now a shallow river. I removed my shoes, held them in my hands and rolled up my denims. We reached Satnam's place and dried ourselves. Satnam gave me a pair of dry pyjamas and went off to change. I looked at his collection of books in the drawing room: Marx and communist literature from before the *perestroika* days of the erstwhile Soviet Union, also the Bhagavad Gita and the Mahabharata and European travel and testimonial writings.

In between the rows of books was Satnam's travelogue of his experiences in the Bastar conflict zone, written in 2004—*Jangalnama*. The English translation of the book, published in 2010, had renewed interest in the Bastar region where—in the name of development—state-protected mining companies and industries have been trying to take over the *jal, jungal, zameen* (waters, forests, land) that belong to the Adivasis, the original, indigenous people of the land. The para-military forces are engaged in a battle with Naxalites and Maoists who claim to be fighting for the rights of tribals. Through the conflict between the state and the Naxalites, the Adivasis have borne the greatest burden of violence. I pulled out the travelogue, browsed its pages, and wondered if books solved anything.

Satnam called me in, to the bedroom. He was sitting cross-legged on his cot. He waved me to the chair. 'What brings you to Panjab?'

'Wounds.'

'Wounds?'

'Let me share a recent experience. A few weeks back an institute in Bangalore called me to talk about Panjab. I asked the participants to give me the first word that came to their mind when they heard the term "Panjab". I wrote them on the board.'

'And?'

'A strange word-picture emerged. Its edges rough, at war with itself ...'

'What did they say?'

'The participants gave words like: Sikh, bhangra, Sufi, terrorist, gurdwara, *langar*, Khalistan, Green Revolution, soldiers, Dalit, tandoori chicken, Gurus, Partition, dhol, salwar kameez, mehndi, Bhindranwale, five rivers, *deras*, butter chicken ... and so on.'[c]

'Isn't it nice that people know Panjab in so many ways?'

'At one level it is. But it is also problematic ...'

'Why?'

'I felt it is like the world wants my hand but not my arm; my feet but not my legs; my face, but not my mind; parts of my body, but not the whole self. None of these words give a central idea about Panjab. Placed next to each other, they confuse. How does "*langar*" sit with "terrorist"? How does "Sufi" sit with "Bhindranwale"? If the Sikh religion is supposed to be equal and just, why do we have the highest per centage of Dalits in Panjab? What are *deras*? Why female foeticide? Why does the breadbasket of the nation have the highest number of per capita farmer and labour suicides? Why do only half the children in government schools pass matric? Is Panjab on drugs? What is this new and renewed talk of Khalistan? I feel lost in these micro-worlds.'

'What is Panjab to you?'

'I was thinking about that when you were making tea in the morning. Panjab is a hole in my heart that I want to fill.'

---

c. The Green Revolution in India refers to a period when Indian agriculture was converted into an industrial system due to the adoption of modern methods and technology for farming, such as the use of high yielding variety (HYV) seeds, tractors, irrigation facilities, pesticides and fertilizers. This was part of the larger Green Revolution endeavour initiated by Norman Borlaug, which leveraged agricultural research and technology to increase agricultural productivity in the developing world. The Green Revolution within India commenced in the early 1960s and led to an increase in food grain production, especially in Panjab, Haryana and Uttar Pradesh.

'You have come to ruins to look for phantom palaces,' said Satnam and got up to go to the front room. 'This evening needs some lubrication ...'

The usage of the word 'phantom' struck me. Yes, Panjab was a phantom presence in my life. The Panjab I had learnt about in my early childhood was the land 'back home' that stood for an idea of heroism, equality and justice. The Panjab I experienced in my adolescence in a military school in Panjab in the 1980s was hurtling through violence, torn, as it was, by guns and separatist sentiments. The Panjab I now encountered evoked contradictions. I tried but no book, no article, no film gave me a clear and complete picture of current Panjab. When Satnam returned, I said, '*Daal dus khaan shehar Lahore e ander, bai kinnein boohey tay kinnian barian nein?* (Tell me, in the city of Lahore, how many doors and windows are there?)'

'Wah!' said Satnam, smiling, standing with a half-bottle of Antiquity whiskey. 'When you check for windows and doors, do look inside the rooms. Check which pillars still stand.' He was playing on the poet's lines.

Satnam placed the bottle on a stool and beckoned me to follow him to the back of his house, towards an empty plot. 'A mud artist is visiting me soon. From Bastar. He will stay with me for a month. We will make small sculptures here. Join us.'

'Do they come often? These artists?'

'Not often. But I have a special corner for the tribals from Bastar. Living with them changed me as a person. Yours is a *shabd di satt* (the wound of words). It is often more cruel than physical wounds. Physical wounds heal, but words bewilder. The only way you can handle your bewilderment is by unpacking these words.'

'What do you mean?'

'Your participants mentioned food, right? Look at food. Tell me, how much of the food you get in Panjabi restaurants around the world is also cooked in our homes?'

'Well, most recipes are tandoor or chicken or daal or paneer …'

'The reality is that tandoors are gone now, even in the villages. The maximum you will find is an *angeethi*. Also, about two-thirds of Panjab is vegetarian.[2] But that is not the case with Odisha, Karnataka, Kerala and other states. Most of what you get in their restaurants, they also cook at home.'

Satnam was right. The Panjabi restaurants that have come up in most places are in the lineage of the dhabas that came up after Independence and Partition to support the enterprising Panjabi truckers. They do not serve home food.

'It does not mean that the menu is in any way less Panjabi. Panjab owns it, it is Panjab's past and there are innovations. Just that the restaurant sphere does not overlap much with the domestic sphere. The food we consume at home and the food that we promote are different—there is a gap between reality and representation.'

I smiled.

'Learning this difference between reality and representation is key to understanding Panjab. It is the same with music.'

I knew Satnam was correct. Panjabi music is of various types: folk, classical, religious and so on. One strand goes into Bollywood, another to YouTube. Today, both are played all around the world. I have heard Panjabi music in a tiny town called Krynki in north-eastern Poland—the song *Kajra Re*. On a small island called Iz on the Adriatic Sea in Croatia—*Mundeyan ton bach ke*. A German friend once told me how big MC Panjabi was on dance floors all over her country and in England. Satnam added, 'Yet, in most of Panjab's popular music, the lyrics celebrate patriarchy and the regressive caste system. I am glad the world does not know the meanings of those songs. This is again the gap between reality and representation.'

'But that is not true of clothes, at least womenswear.'

'You are right. The salwar kameez is now ubiquitous around the nation. Though not the Patiala style, with many pleats,' said Satnam.

He continued, 'I have heard south Indian weddings now have mehndi and ladies sangeet ceremonies. Much of this is through Bollywood, the movie industry influenced by Panjab's culture, *Panjabiat*. You see, Panjab's imprint has always been much larger than its footprint.'

'That is true even for the word Panjab—the idea is far bigger than its physicality.'

'You got it!' exclaimed Satnam.

For many millennia the Panjab region extended from the Spin Ghar mountains in modern Afghanistan where the Khyber Pass is located, through Peshawar and Lahore in modern Pakistan to the banks of the Yamuna where Delhi is located. In *Avesta*, the sacred text of the Zoroastrians, the Panjab region was known as Sapta Sindhu, seven rivers. In Sanskrit, the name was Panjnad. To the Greeks, this region was Pentapotamia, an inland delta of five converging rivers. In the Persian Emperor Darius' time (around 500 BCE), Herodotus, considered the father of history, talks about how the Greek explorer, Scylax of Caryanda, took a boat down the River Indus in the service of Darius. Herodotus reported in his text *Histories* what Scylax heard on the eastern banks: that Indians have gold mixed with sand in their land.

In the fourteenth century, the traveller Ibn Battuta from Tangier, Morocco, at one end of the Sahara Desert arrived weary from his long journey across the Red, Black, Caspian and Aral Seas to the north of the Indian subcontinent. On this leg of his journey he had seen the River Nile and learnt of the Amu Darya. He considered both these rivers among the five great rivers of the then known world. When he arrived, Ibn Battuta had crossed the Kyzylkum Desert of modern Uzbekistan, the rocky mountains of Afghanistan and the snow-laden Hindu Kush range. He set eyes on the River Indus in 1393 and the abundance of water struck him—five rivers feeding into the mighty Indus. In his travel memoir, *Rihla*, written in Arabic, Ibn Battuta named the land 'Panj Ab'—the land of five waters.

The words are Persian. The land was Panjab, which I spell with an 'a' from the original Persian.

I said, 'This Panjab is no longer the land of five rivers. It has just a bit over two rivers. Why do we not call it something else? For that matter, why do we not call Pakistan India? After all, more than two-thirds of the River Indus, from which India gets its name, flows through that country now ...'

Satnam interjected, 'And call India what? Bharat? The Sanskrit name would make Tamilians unhappy. But coming back to the point: when you seek to know Panjab, you will need to know the barrier that frames your understanding—the formation of the modern nation state. The current truncated Panjab is an appendage of the Indus Valley Civilisation forcefully grafted on to the Gangetic Valley and the valleys of the rivers Brahmaputra and Narmada. Through a national boundary, East Panjab remains cut from its umbilical cord—the Indus Valley Civilisation.'

'Shall I pour some whiskey?'

Satnam continued, 'Fascinating sites: Harappa, Mohenjodaro, Ropar, the new one, Rakhigarhi, many on the western coast. The civilisation existed in and beyond what we now call Panjab. It was very advanced: the great bath, brick-lined roads, organised housing. But the sites do not tell us why the civilisation disappeared.'

'Is it because no one has been able to decipher the Indus Valley script?'

'I do not know. The oral texts of the later Vedic Age—the Vedas, Panini's grammar, Bharata's *Natya Shastra*, Ramayana and Mahabharata are fantastic, sublime. They are the foundation of our land's cultural and religious imagination. But notice, even they do not tell us how the Indus Valley Civilisation disappeared or how the Vedic Age transitioned to ancient, medieval and modern times.'

'Scholars and propagandists now fight Aryan-Dravidian battles. Was there an Aryan invasion? Did Aryans push the Dravidians down south?'

'That is what. Right from its inception, the history of larger Panjab remains unclear. We do not know what caused the civilisation to vanish—a flood, an earthquake …'

'The current theory is a 900-year drought …'

'In the grand sweep of history, we are headed towards such times once again. Studies have shown 112 out of the 132 blocks of Panjab have become dark zones. We have hit the third-level aquifers. We have smuggled out the sand and gravel. The Thar Desert is advancing upon the fertile plains of Panjab. Districts in the south-west are waterlogged. Global warming is melting the snow in the Himalayas. If we have a great flood or if the Bhakra Dam collapses, we will perish. There will be no record.'

Even as it was getting late, our mood was getting darker still. Satnam loved conversations, and he was also lonely.

'How do you feel?'

'About what?'

'Living like this, alone?'

'Well, I have friends, they visit. Like you have come.'

'Still …?'

'I feel as if I am caught in a noose. This Panjab, in which I live, which you have come to learn about, is in a double-bind. The Centre, Delhi, squeezes it. Its own people tear it apart. I feel claustrophobic. It is not only me. Everyone these days wants to run away from Panjab, students, older people, even government employees. The intent to escape defines this Panjab. Seriously, what have you come to look for here?'

'Doors and windows,' I joked.

'Pillars,' said Satnam.

I went to lie down on the three-seater sofa in the front room. Sleep wasn't easy. What the farmers had said at the rally kept coming to my mind: we saved India, now India has abandoned us. Satellite images of Panjab's water table deficit corroborated their experience and Satnam's data on black zones. The crises the farmers mentioned was not only social or political or economic, but ecological, and threatened Panjab's very survival. The farmers were lamenting India's lack of attention to their woes. I wondered how different these complaints were from early years of militancy, the lead-up to violence—the Neher Roko Morcha (Stop Canal Morcha) launched in 1982 over river waters being directed to Haryana through the Satluj Yamuna Link (SYL) canal. Was Panjab heading towards those times again?

It was late. I put on a song on my mobile phone. It was by the thirteenth century poet Fariduddin Ganjshakar or Baba Farid who is considered the father of the Panjabi language. Pakistan Panjab's singer Nusrat Fateh Ali Khan sang:

*Uth Farida sutteya, duniya wekhan ja*
*Shayad koi mil jaye bakhsheya,*
*Tu vi bakhsheya jaen.*
*Turia turia ja Farida, turia turia ja …*

Wake up O sleeping one, go see the world
You may find a blessed one,
and be blessed in return
Keep walking Farid, keep walking …

The next morning, over a functional breakfast of bread, butter and black tea, Satnam said, 'Panjab will test you and beguile you. It has forever beguiled its seekers. That is because those who seek to define it are often in haste. They want control. But Panjab rebels—it breaks definitions ascribed to it. Your journey here will be incomplete if it is not a journey towards your own self.'

This is what the song had meant last night. For a moment, Satnam sounded like Baba at the 8 p.m. ritual of my childhood. 'Take some time off from your life. Travel Panjab. You may learn some things, like I did in Bastar. At least you will learn to question. Come back and we will discuss more.'

Satnam had given me the tool: study the gap between the many realities and representations of Panjab.

I bid him farewell. I knew his home was open to friends.

## Chapter Two

# *Berukhi*—Apathy

Living in Bangalore as I do, but being interested in Panjab—two and a half thousand kilometres away—has its pluses and minuses. The minus was lack of ease of access. I could not do weekend visits. The plus was, when I did travel, it was for a stretch of time. After my initial meeting with Satnam, it took me a while to plan my visits. In the meantime, an expected but drastic development took place in the country: the Bharatiya Janata Party (BJP), a right-wing political party, came to power in the 2014 Lok Sabha elections.

A friend bitterly remarked, 'If this was to happen, I wonder why the Sikhs fought against Khalistan in the 1980s.'

He was right. In the 1980s, Sikh grievances with national politics had led to the separatist struggle for a theocratic, independent Sikh nation—Khalistan. The movement did not deliver because it lacked a clear sense of purpose and vision of a nation, a lack of a structure of a state for the people which is necessary to create a nation, the fact that the separatists were trapped in internecine rivalries, and the reality that guerrilla warfare does not succeed in flat lands. The Indian state—which supposedly stood for secularism—eventually prevailed by coming down heavily on the separatists, and in the process, committed many human rights violations—such as killing innocents. Panjab's Hindu-Sikh society rejected the idea of a single religion-dominated nation, which constituted the essence of Khalistan, and had chosen to stay with supposedly secular India. Per the dictionary, secularism means the state is disconnected from the religion of its citizens. In practice, at least in India, secularism means all its citizens, irrespective of their religions, are equal.

In the 2014 elections, the BJP played the Hindutva card and through the support of its parent organisation, the Rashtriya Swayamsewak Sangh (RSS), used ballots to come closer to achieving what the Sikh separatists had not been able to achieve through guns—turning a secular nation into a theocratic state, a *Hindu Rashtra*. In a nation where Hindus are in an overwhelming majority, the call to usher in *achhe din* (good days) was based on two premises: huge anti-incumbency and allegations of corruption against government officials, and appeasement of minorities by the Congress coalition government in power; and the mirage of progress and development that the BJP promised. The election had a strong communal element, but it was masked by the rhetoric of combating corruption and ensuring development and progress. The educated middle class, grown rich on the fruits of neo-liberal policies, chose to downplay the BJP's communalism and voted it into power. Yet, communalism is also corruption, albeit without a numerical figure associated with it. Communalism is a corruption of the idea of diversity, of equality, and of secularism. The 31 per cent population who voted in BJP probably did not care for such nuances.

The BJP projected Narendra Modi whose direct message was, 'Your vote for the BJP symbol—the lotus—is a vote for me.' This turned a parliamentary democracy into a pseudo-presidential election. People imagined Modi would deliver, as he had supposedly done in Gujarat for thirteen years. In the run-up to the elections, all discussions centred around whether one supported Modi or not. The BJP victory—an independent, absolute majority in the Parliament—also upturned the three-decade long phenomenon of coalition governments when a big party was supported by various small, regional parties. A coalition government has many minuses in terms of efficiency of governance, but equally, it does not centralise power in a few individuals or a single party. It is perhaps a better representation of the federal nature of our nation and the diversity of its people. This changed with the BJP by itself, as a single party, coming into majority in the Parliament, and with its allies, creating a brute unassailable majority.

When the results came, I discovered that Panjab echoed my dissident sentiment. Panjab is the only region in the world where a minuscule minority religion, Sikhism, is in the majority and yet the region is part of a larger nation. Having borne the pain of a separatist struggle and paid the price for it through extensive loss of human life, Panjab had eschewed the divisive politics that had been on offer in the 2014 election campaign. In Panjab, Modi in real or as a hologram was a negative factor. The reason was that Panjabis recognised that the post-Godhra 2002 rise of Modi was modelled on the Congress-supported pogrom of Sikhs in 1984 after Indira Gandhi was assassinated and the subsequent rise of Rajiv Gandhi. In keeping with its audacious nature, Panjab, with its heart in its hand—rather, fingertip—elected four out of its thirteen Members of Parliament from the fledgling Aam Aadmi Party (AAP)—that had emerged from the 2011 Anna Hazare-led India Against Corruption movement whose avowed agenda was transparency in politics and public accountability. Nowhere else in the country did AAP win a single seat. Unlike the rest of India, Panjab did not look at the BJP or Hindutva for succour from the Congress. It stood alone, an outlier, in calling out the bane of elections and their inherent corruption, usually financial, but in this case, communal as well.

As the mood of the country became strongly anti-Congress, I was stunned to discover the rank opportunism among those who I had grown up believing to be secular journalists, thinkers, academicians, film stars, opinion-makers and social and political leaders. These were those who had, during Panjab's dark days—faced with the prospect of Sikh separatism—informed my idea of India as a diverse, multi-religious, aspiring-to-be-egalitarian nation. They had now turned coat and were supporting the BJP which had been bankrolled by prominent business houses—crony capitalists.

I wondered if this change opened up a space to talk openly about Panjab's experience with the Congress whose—pre- and post-Independence—vote bank soft Hindutva politics had glossed over centre-state relations and portrayed Panjab as a problem area and Sikhs as separatists. Panjab knew that through Hindutva politics the BJP was merely following the path the Congress had paved in Panjab from the 1950s to the 1970s. At that time the Congress had collaborated with the Jana Sangh (from which the BJP originated in 1980) to impose the Hindi language and soft Hindutva politics on Panjab. The difference with the BJP this time was only in degrees—brazen and unapologetic—but the ideology was the same. This time the Muslims and not the Sikhs were once again the new 'other'. As India was entering a tailspin in its politics, I could see its present was echoing Panjab's past. Then perhaps, the only way to get a hint of the nation's future was to look at Panjab's present.

In September 2015, the cotton fields of south Panjab were devastated by the whitefly infestation. Farmers started agitating against the state government demanding compensation. I asked: how is the government responsible for crop failure through natural causes—in this case, a pest attack? That is when an old friend from my college days, who had studied agricultural sciences, but later sold toilet cleaners for a living, who now worked with a media group and was also a right-wing apologist, put up a status on Facebook:

The cotton crop disaster due to the White Fly infestation is a fiction the lazy farmers of Panjab are creating because they did not spray pesticides on the crops in time and the disease has struck. They did not listen to the university and expert recommendations. The lazy farmers are trying to blackmail the government for compensation over their failed crops. Haryana, the state adjoining Panjab, does not have a single incidence of the illness. It shows the Panjab farmers are a rotten lot accustomed to subsidies.

Within a few days, the farmers and farm labourers had launched a *rail-roko* (train blockade) to press home their demands. This protest was a chance for me to understand both what was going on in the food basket of the nation and why the farmers were repeatedly blaming the government.

Panjab became the food basket of the nation in the mid-1960s when India faced dire food crises. In an earlier famine in Bengal in the early 1940s, 4.3 million people had died of starvation. For a fledgling new country, its enemies were not only external, but also internal—poverty, hunger and the need to be self-reliant. That is when the central government chose tiny Panjab, with one and a half per cent of the nation's land, as the cradle of what came to be known as the 'Green Revolution'.

The central government's reason to choose Panjab was because the British had created the conditions for such a revolution. The British had defeated the Sikh Empire and conquered Panjab after the second Anglo-Sikh War of 1849. After that, they had rapidly developed the region: laying down train tracks up to the border with Russia, linking rivers to create canal colonies, and encouraging internal migration by offering land for agriculture.

In the early 1960s, though the canal colonies Montgomery, Rawalpindi and others were now in Pakistan, and east Panjab was left with sandy tracts and hillocks, the state again became the nation's agrarian laboratory. A mere four lakh hectares of the total forty-seven lakh acres of cultivable farmland was irrigated. The state had just 1,973 tube wells of which only 325 had electricity connections, while the rest were diesel motor-driven.[3] The enterprising Panjabi farmer flattened the lands and began growing the Mexican dwarf wheat as the rabi crop (sown in winter and harvested in early summer). The kharif crop (sown in the summer and harvested in early winter) was rice and it became the mainstay even though rice or paddy was a non-native crop and found hardly any place in Panjab's dietary habits. With a majority of Panjab's population devastated through Partition, the consolidation of land holdings by the then CM Pratap Singh Kairon provided scope to limp back to a semblance of economic normalcy.

In the last five decades, the wheat production has increased by eight times and rice production by thirty-three times.[4] Nearly 85 per cent of Panjab's land is under cultivation. Nearly two-thirds of Panjab's population is directly or indirectly connected to agriculture.[5] Since the land is cultivated twice a year, the cropping intensity is nearly 200 per cent. The increase in production has taken place by making farming more efficient: mechanisation through tractors and combine harvesters; hybrid seeds; chemical fertilisers; pesticides and weedicides; and extensive use of water, from rivers and pumped from underground. The Green Revolution was a major success story.

En route to Panjab to witness at first hand the protests post the whitefly infestation, I reached my cousin Minnie's place in New Delhi. Until a few years ago, Minnie, an only daughter, was a successful professional in the United States (US), climbing the corporate ladder. She came back to India when her aged parents fell ill. She re-located her parents from their village Chaklan in Ropar district to Noida near Delhi, close to her workplace, and became their primary caregiver. From Minnie's place, I called up an acquaintance in Bathinda and sought directions to the location of the protest. The acquaintance asked me to reach village Pathrala, near Mandi Dabwali. I also asked, 'Could you suggest a hotel or guest house within my modest budget?'

Bibiji, Minnie's mother, my father's sister, struck by Alzheimer's, was lying in the same room. She overheard me and asked, 'What kind of a call was that?'

'I don't know where to stay.'

She answered, rather innocently, 'You will stay with whomever you are meeting.'

'Bibiji, times have changed. It is no longer like the old days. Those people don't know me. Why would they host me?'

'But when you meet them, they will know you.' I kept quiet, amused by her understanding. She continued, 'When they know you, they will keep you.'

She spoke from how she knew Panjab from at least eight decades earlier when her father, my Dadaji, was still around. She launched into a long, repetitive description of how Dadaji would leave home for political meetings and not return for days. She mixed up names of places, friends and relatives as she told me tales long-forgotten.

Trains were out of the question. In the middle of the night Minnie dropped me outside the New Delhi Inter State Bus Terminal whose outer walls were still soaked in urine as during my adolescence. Once you enter the recently renovated interiors, the terminus looks like a modern airport. Wary that a Panjab Roadways bus could be stopped on the way by protesters, I opted for a Haryana Roadways bus to Bathinda.

Early in the morning, Delhi flyovers are free of dense traffic. We passed the shell of an abandoned Air India aeroplane near Rohini where the bus left the city ring road to embark on the highway. The vista now changed to green fields where paddy was growing, like it does in Panjab. After a few hours I noticed, contrary to my friend's expert opinion on social media, the cotton fields in Haryana too were all black and shrivelled up. The whitefly has struck Haryana too, I wrote back to the friend on social media. He did not answer. After a few hours, I noticed he had blocked me. Apathy is so easy; long friendships dispensable.

We reached Mandi Dabwali by 10 a.m. With the bus still waiting for the driver who had taken a tea break, I called my contact at Pathrala village. He asked me if I was in a Haryana long-distance bus. I was. He sounded relieved and told me the police were not allowing the short distance Dabwali-Bathinda buses to stop at the villages. 'Ask the driver to slow down near a statue of Bhagat Singh at the old bus stop and jump off.' He said he would make sure someone picked me up.

When I requested the conductor, he sensed I was not a local but nodded in the affirmative. As the bus started, I stood at the door. After a few kilometres, it slowed down near the weather-worn statue. The conductor nodded at me and I jumped off. As I touched ground and looked up, I noticed a police picket ahead. Two constables now started to walk towards me. I was about to pull out my phone when a motorbike emerged from a dirt road and its driver gestured to me. Wordlessly, we played our roles in a subversive pantomime. I sat on the pillion. Even as the policemen shouted at me to stop, the driver sped, and soon we were out of earshot.

We literally played out the stereotype: with police, keep a distance. Be neither friends, nor enemies with them. How easily and unconsciously I had slipped into the cat-and-mouse game familiar to me from my years in a military school in Panjab when seniors or authorities attempted to discipline us. My motorcycle driver, Gurpreet, was accustomed to this game. In the days of *dehshat*, an unknown enemy forever lurked in the background—a random militant gun could kill you or you could be arrested, even made to disappear, in a random police raid. This was especially true if you were a young man. The militant gun was no longer a threat but a random police arrest was still a possibility.

We drove about two kilometres, part of it through the village. Gurpreet and I talked about where I was from and why I was interested in the protests. Would I make a news item out of the protest? Which newspaper had sent me? Gurpreet wanted to see the news travel far and wide. I did not know how to explain I was just a writer, merely a witness, not the journalist he was expecting to meet and for whom he had taken a risk.

Between the railway tracks and the village Pathrala train station, the protest site was a sea of green and yellow Bhartiya Kisan Union flags in the hands of thousands of men, women and children, young and old alike. Next to the railway tracks were cotton fields laid waste by the whitefly—the waist-sized plants were shrivelled, the leaves had turned black and the cotton buds were dead. Was the choice of the protest location deliberate? I wondered if the organisers had chosen Pathrala as one of the six sites of protest because of its proximity to the reason for the protest. I was trying to invent a metaphor to talk about the protest—a way to represent the reality. Through the day if I learnt one thing it was that the protest needed no metaphor. The protest was a lived reality of the farmers and workers of the over three lakh acres of devastated crops[6] per government sources, over eight lakh acres per media reports[7] or about ten lakh acres per farmer and labour unions.[8] In a good season, a farmer harvests about ten quintals of Bt cotton per acre.[d] This time the yield was less than ten kilograms of useless cotton per acre.

A makeshift shamiana was erected on the rail tracks with women seated under its shade and the men sitting or standing outside. A tractor and trolley were parked a bit ahead. The front of the trolley served as the stage from which speakers were addressing the people. The back of the trolley had equipment for the microphones and loudspeakers. I expected the protestors to be sombre or angry, but they were not. They were upbeat.

I learnt from Gurpreet that for the first time in the history of Panjab, eleven farmer and worker unions from all over the state had unitedly organised the protest. In the southern belt of Panjab (Malwa) the protest was about the cotton failure and the state's response. Bhagwant Mann from the AAP who represented Sangrur, and the union minister for food processing, Harsimrat Kaur Badal from the SAD who represented Bathinda in Parliament, were both from Malwa.

In the north Panjab belt of Majha, the protest was against the drop in the Minimum Support Price (MSP) of Basmati rice—one of India's biggest exports to Europe.[e] Captain Amarinder Singh of the Congress represented Amritsar from this region. In central Panjab, the Doaba, between the rivers Satluj and Beas, in Nawanshahr, the protest was against the closure of sugar mills, the dumping of sugarcane and the non-payment of previous bills. No leader or political party was supporting the protest. Yet, the strike had paralysed the state. The loss from the stoppage of over 850 trains and their subsequent cancellation

---

d. Bt cotton is a genetically modified organism (GMO) or genetically modified pest-resistant plant cotton variety, which produces an insecticide to destroy bollworm.

e. The Majha today comprises of the districts of Amritsar, Tarn Taran, Pathankot and Gurdaspur and is considered the 'religious belt'.

and diversion to other routes had cost the railways upwards of Rs 100 crore. It was also affecting the transport of hosiery and garments from Ludhiana and Jalandhar, the industrial hubs of Panjab.

At Pathrala, speaker after speaker exhorted the protesters to remember the stories of Bhagat Singh, Kartar Singh Sarabha and Udham Singh from the time of the freedom movement. They then drew parallels between the struggles against British imperialism and a current issue that dominated the headlines then—Modi's failed Land Bill.[f] Amidst the warnings against corporate imperialism, the speakers related stories of Guru Gobind Singh and Banda Bahadur who had fought against injustice.

Every age has its battles between the right and the wrong, the just and the unjust and the weak and the powerful. In today's day and age, while the battle plays out as it has in every other age, one dimension has changed: there is now a tussle between the powerless and the powerful over the icons of the past. Until now these icons were the heroes of the weak and the oppressed. Now the powerful have appropriated the icons—stolen them from the people's narrative and made them the state narrative. If appropriation of an icon by contrarian political forces is indicative of the person's popularity, nationally, perhaps Bhagat Singh stands on top of the historical figures of modern India.

Bhagat Singh was the young revolutionary who had made famous the Maulana Hasrat Mohani slogan *Inquilab Zindabad, Samrajyawad*

---

f. According to the 2013 Land Acquisition law passed by the UPA-II government, if a company wanted government permission to acquire a large swathe of land for a new project, it needed to show that it had the consent of at least 80 per cent of the owners of the land. It also had to conduct a social impact assessment and was prevented from acquiring—beyond specific limits—irrigated, multi-cropped agricultural land. Under the amendments proposed by the Modi government in 2015, key projects in defence, rural infrastructure, affordable housing and industrial corridors were exempted from these rules. Ultimately, most provisions of the 2013 Act were retained as a result of large-scale opposition.

*Murdabad*. (Long live the revolution, down with imperialist forces.) Bhagat Singh's short but striking life is a lesson in the eclectic societal makeup of Panjab. Bhagat Singh was born in a Sikh family, though his father leaned towards the revisionist Hindu sect Arya Samaj. During his time, one of the major figures in Panjab politics was Lala Lajpat Rai, lovingly named 'Panjab Kesari' (the lion of Panjab) who was active in the farmer politics in the newly established canal colonies. Post the division of Bengal, and as a response to the formation of the Muslim League in 1909, Lajpat Rai formed the Panjab Hindu Sabha which led to the formation of the right-wing Hindu Mahasabha. On 14 December 1924, he proposed the two-nation theory in *The Tribune* stating the need for 'a clear partition of India into a Muslim India and a non-Muslim India'.[9]

He protested against the Simon Commission in 1928 and was injured in the lathi-charge which led to his death two weeks later. Bhagat Singh, Chandra Shekhar Azad and RajGuru assassinated John Saunders, mistaking him for the British police superintendent, James Scott, whom they had intended to assassinate. After the killing, Bhagat Singh was on the run for many months until he surfaced in April 1929 along with an associate, Batukeshwar Dutt, inside the Central Legislative Assembly in Delhi where they exploded two bombs, threw leaflets and allowed themselves to be arrested. The Saunders case was then re-opened. Awaiting trial, Bhagat Singh joined fellow detainee Jatin Das in a hunger strike, demanding better prison conditions for Indian prisoners. It ended in Das's death from starvation in September 1929. Bhagat Singh was convicted and hanged in March 1931, aged twenty-three.

Though Bhagat Singh stood up to avenge the right-wing Lala Lajpat Rai, he himself was socialist and had penned the seminal essay titled *Why I Am an Atheist*. The essay still inspires Panjab's youth to take up cudgels against the oppressing forces and to join the 'Naujawan Bharat Sabha', a left-oriented organisation to which he once belonged. In his time, the 1920s, it comprised of Hindus, Muslims and Sikhs. In the 1980s, during the Khalistan movement, the religion-neutral popular picture of a clean-shaven, moustache twirled, blue hat-wearing Bhagat Singh that also hung in our drawing room was appropriated. On the basis of a picture showing him with long hair before his hanging, supporters of Khalistan recast him in a yellow turban with a flare and made him part of the counter-state narrative. Now, the BJP puts out advertisements on his birthday and yoga mascots-turned-businessmen use him to sell dubious Ayurvedic products in the name of 'swadeshi'. Bhagat Singh suits the right-wing narrative because he had ideological differences with Mahatma Gandhi, though the differences did not mean he endorsed the fascist powers from which the right wing draws its motivation. The right wing does not care because it seeks to control not only power but also narratives and icons.

While Bhagat Singh has become a national figure, locally, Banda Bahadur is another tall figure of the people's narrative. In 1708, Guru Gobind Singh met Banda Bahadur at Nanded, in the south, where he eventually passed away. Banda Bahadur was born Lachman Das, who had become an accomplished tantrik, horseman and wrestler. Guru Gobind Singh instructed him to go to Panjab and fight against the injustice of the Nawab of Sirhind. In the name of the Guru, Banda brought the dispersed Sikh forces together and defeated the nawab and avenged the killings of Guru Gobind Singh's younger sons Zorawar Singh and Fateh Singh.[g] As his influence grew, in a short time, Banda and his forces came to occupy the region between the Yamuna and the Beas, cutting off Mughal communication between their capital Delhi and the capital of Panjab, Lahore. He established the first Sikh kingdom, issuing coins marking his capital Lohgarh in the lower reaches of the Shivalik. Yet, his greatest reform was

---

g. Captured post a battle between Mughal and Sikh forces in 1705, the two young boys, aged nine and six, had been walled alive.

socio-economic: removing corrupt officials, abolishing the zamindari system, and giving the farmers proprietorship of their land—so that they could live with dignity and self-respect.

Three hundred years later, the farmers and labourers were fighting for their dignity all over again. The irony is that while the farmers were fighting against modern-day zamindari, the incumbent Shiromani Akali Dal-BJP government celebrated Banda Bahadur by taking its oath of office in its second consecutive term in 2012, at the Fateh Burj memorial commemorating Banda Bahadur, at Chappar Chiri near Chandigarh. Later, in a projection of extreme vanity, the government celebrated the 300th anniversary of Banda Bahadur's martyrdom in Delhi on a stage named after his slogan *Deg Tegh Fateh* (Victory to Charity and Arms) and thus fixed him in the state narrative that oppressed the very farmers for whom he stood.

The treatment of both Bhagat Singh and Banda Bahadur point to the gap between the reality and its representation and the distance between the state and people's narrative. This is the robbing of language, of its meaning, and of denuding a vocabulary of its import. A government, supposed to safeguard people, has, in fact, robbed them. Instead of strengthening people, it impoverishes them. It is an exercise in truncating history and indulging in memoricide.

The speakers urged the protestors to remain peaceful, non-violent, and to not do anything to give the police a chance to break the strike, arrest people and give the government a chance to clamp down upon the agitation. In between speeches, local villagers sang songs, highlighting the issues: agrarian crises, rural indebtedness, spread of drugs, conditions of schools and hospitals, corruption and nepotism of the government. Whether it was speech or song, they concluded with slogans, 'Long live farmer-worker unity', 'Long live the fight against injustice' and my favourite: '_____, *Teri soch te, pehra deyange thok ke!*' (We shall guard your thoughts with our lives!)

Depending upon the protest, the protestors fill in the blank with the appropriate name of the thought leader, who could be a popular one like Bhagat Singh, a local leader, a person facing an injustice around whom the protest is organised and so on. The key word is *pehra* or guarding. Much before Modi made being a *chowkidar* (guard) and his duty (*pehra*) popular and fashionable through election speeches, Bhindranwale used the word *chowkidar* to describe his role vis-a-vis the Sikh community.

In Panjab, *pehra* is an especially loaded world. For many millennia, Panjab, by virtue of its geographical location, between Central Asia and the Arabian Sea, between the mighty Himalayas and the burning Thar desert, between the east and the west, between the Orient and the Occident, has been the gateway through which Central Asia and beyond sought to reach the Indian subcontinent. Ethnicities that now make up around twenty-five modern nations: Persians, Greeks, Mongols, Scythians, Afghans, Huns and Turks, have all passed through Panjab. After Alexander, the Kushanas—Heraios and Kanishka, the White Huns, the Delhi Sultanate—Afghans and Turks, and then the Mughals, ruled the land. These were not the only ones to come. People from other parts of the subcontinent also came to Panjab: the Mauryas, the Guptas and Harshavardhana from the east—rulers of modern Patna, Allahabad and Kannauj respectively—and also flourished here.

Panjab has been a gateway, defined by its major river Indus and its tributaries, whose job, by historical compulsion, has been to guard. Though today this civilisational space, more than fifteen hundred kilometres in width and three thousand kilometres in length, is lacerated by political boundaries, broken into two chunks which are a part of two different nation states and are divided by identity politics, its people carry historical memory. That is why the story of the gate,

Panjab, is different from the story of the house it currently lives in, the nation state India.

The people who came to Panjab in various ages did not all go back. Many settled, built lives here, and then united to prevent others from coming in, turning Panjab into one of the most diverse gene pools in the world—a veritable melting pot, a cauldron of humanity. The Persian language that came from modern-day Iran has had a great influence on Panjabi and Urdu. Not only are the land revenue terms used in Panjab a legacy of Persian, the word 'pehra' is itself Persian.

The Sikh religion, grounded in the idea of the Khalsa by Guru Gobind Singh when he raised an army to defend the society from the unjust oppressors, both Hindu and Mughal, was based on the principle of *pehra*. One of the greatest stories of *pehra* is the martyrdom of Guru Tegh Bahadur who went to Delhi to appeal to Emperor Aurangzeb that he allow Kashmiri Pandits to practise their religion, and sacrificed his life.[h]

In this land of constant political and social upheavals, the farmer or the merchant has always had to guard his belongings from nature, from rivals and from bandits. Being vigilant therefore is a way of life. However, this time, the vigil by farmers and farm workers that I was witness to was against a duly elected government, not a tyrant king. In this vigil, the response from the people to the oppression by the government remained the same, though the composition of society had changed from a feudal, monarchical Panjab to a so-called democracy.

---

h. A group of Kashmiri Pandits had requested the Guru for his assistance stating that they were being forced to convert to Islam by Mughal officials.

Escorting me to the *langar* organised by the protestors, Gurpreet said, 'They say even an ant can't move in the state without Badal (Parkash Singh Badal, the then CM) knowing about it. Here we are, protesting. Can't he see us?'

I asked why the village gurdwara had not organised the *langar*. Gurpreet told me, the village gurdwara was aligned with the SAD–BJP government.[i] His words shattered an idea that not only I, but even my father-in-law, and by extension, the world at large, carried of the institution of *langar*. As I was leaving from Bangalore, a few days ago, Lakshmi's father had said, 'If you ever feel stranded and do not have a place to sleep, just go to a gurdwara. They will take you in.' I was touched by the faith he—a Malayalee—had in the Sikh religion and its institutions, and I nodded. His faith came from anecdotes he had heard as a child of the role the Akalis had played in the Vaikom Satyagraha, 1925. That is when they had provided *langar* to the agitators gathered under the leadership of Narayan Guru, E.V. Ramaswamy (Periyar) and Mahatma Gandhi.

The protestors had therefore pooled in to start their own *langar*. I, city-bred, had carried my bag of snacks to the venue. The local villagers, community-minded as they were, had brought *dolus* (covered buckets) of milk and trolleys of wheat flour and vegetables. Then they had made small monetary contributions for tea leaves, sugar and salt. The food was more than sufficient, as was the spirit. Drinking my glass of lassi, I walked up to a group of women preparing rotis over a wood fire. In theory, the Sikh religion recognises no distinction, in the tenets, between men and women. Yet, in some gurdwaras, in *langars*, there are separate seating arrangements for gents and ladies. In feudal-minded Panjab, men dominate public spaces and women run kitchens and homes. The

---

i. The SAD and the BJP ruled Panjab from 2007 to early 2017 in a coalition government. Since the end of militancy in the early 90s, this was their second stint in power. The first was between 1997 and 2002.

women participating in the protest were breaking the feudal and patriarchal rituals and divisions. I sat on my haunches near an old lady making rotis. It was safer that way instead of approaching a younger woman who was anyway impossible to approach without someone to introduce us.

'Mataji, have you been here on all days?'

'Yes, what else is there to do?'

'Even the others?'

'We are all together. Earlier, we were not so active. Now we must stand with the men. They have tried for long. What came of it? What else can we do? Either the government will kill us or poverty will—we have to protest!'

Another woman joined in, 'Nothing is left now, *putt* (son). The fight has sharpened. The government has to do something.' More women started talking to each other. I sat almost forgotten, grateful to listen to the clarity with which women had approached the protest. Not only had small and marginal farmers and labour come together, but this time even the women were at the forefront of the agitation. It seemed Panjab was revealing its warts and wounds.

By mid-afternoon, I stood out in the milling crowd—the only one dressed in loose cargoes. A diary in my hand, I was taking notes. The speakers relayed information that the police had detained groups of people coming from the nearby villages of Khuddian and Faridkot Kotli. The speaker urged caution and asked people to come through the fields, to avoid detection. Then he said, 'We know there is one person from the CID (Crime Investigation Department) amongst us. The government will try its best to incite violence, to create a rift among us. Make sure you stay cautious. Beware of outsiders.'

Intrigued, I looked up from my notes to find all the protestors staring at me. As a reflex I raised my hand and walked up to the makeshift stage and told the organisers who were all members of the Bhartiya Kisan Union (Ugrahan) and Panjab Khet Mazdoor Union (PKMU) that the state secretary of the PKMU had asked me to come there and that I was a writer. No one understood what a writer did. They understood *patrakar* (journalist), that too not for English newspapers but for *Ajit*, the Panjabi newspaper. I told them I was a Panjabi *patrakar*. One man folded his right arm, pointed his elbow at me and asked, 'Where is your "this"?'

I did not understand.

He patted his folded arm, elbow pointing towards me. '"This"?'

Someone said, 'Camera.'

'Oh! I don't have one. Just writing. Story.' The man lost interest.

Another man said, 'We have to be cautious. Outsiders have always harmed us. Agencies!'

Panjab, anxious about security, accustomed to *pehra*, now uses the word 'agency' for anyone it cannot easily slot. An agency is a plant by external forces that gnaws at a system from the inside, like a termite, weakening it, making it vulnerable and susceptible to attacks. The term 'agency' is both age-old and current. It goes back to the treacherous generals of the armies who made the Sikhs lose the two Anglo-Sikh wars and surrender the Sikh empire to the British. Its current understanding dates back to the dark days of militancy when, at its peak, Julio Francis Ribeiro was the director general of Panjab police. Ribeiro wrote in his autobiography how the police infiltrated the ranks of militants first, with smugglers and criminals, and later, with policemen who volunteered. These moles passed information on targets to the police.[10] No one knew who the barrel of the gun was pointed at. Whom could one trust?

*Vishwas* (trust) in Panjab, the land of saints and Gurus, is not a liberal moral science topic; it is a stark choice between life and death. The period of militancy tore loyalties asunder as separatists preyed on the people and the police preyed on the militants and the people. Finally, those who survived either bear lifelong scars still not addressed by the state or turned opportunist and joined the state. In Panjab's history of invasions and battles, trust has been a coin tossed again and again. In a land of survivors of countless attacks and wars, trust does not come easy.

Would it then be easy for people to trust me? Who am I? Why do I want to understand the farmer and labourer story and join their daily struggle for a day? What will I do with it? What would the book, then merely an idea, do for them? What if I was from a state agency and reported on who made speeches, who organised the protests and so on? The police could then target the ones I pointed out.

Later that evening, there was an announcement for the *patrakar* from Delhi. The PKMU secretary Lachhman Sewewala had called for me. I had asked him for an interview and he had agreed to make time later. He said I was not to worry about accommodation. I remembered what Bibiji said about Dadaji—in his activism days, he stayed where he reached. I joined the people sitting on the railway tracks. They were curious about the *patrakar* who did not leave like others, with the news byte, was dressed curiously and looked different—*shehri* (urban). They tested my Panjabi by asking me to curse. I performed, they approved.

I empathised with the protestors over the devastation and asked how the government was responsible. The response was succinct: whitefly is an old pest, but earlier it could be contained through pesticides. When the fly struck this time, the scientists at the Punjab Agricultural University (PAU) had suggested a second spray of Ethion.

It too failed. PAU's own cotton crop on their experimental farms had failed that season, devastated by the whitefly. The cotton seeds approved by the government had also proven to be non-resilient to the whitefly.

In April that year, before the cotton sowing, in a regular anti-drugs barricade, not far from the protest site, a Deputy superintendent of police had stopped a jeep and found it to be carrying Rs 65 lakh as bribe, allegedly for a senior government figure in the agricultural ministry. Locals called the payoff 'goonda tax', a term that cropped up repeatedly in the coming months in relation to illegal sand-mining, road construction, questionable land deals, and so on. The matter was widely reported, but the government took no action. Later, the Agriculture Department acquired pesticides worth Rs 33 crore without due tenders and made it available for farmer purchase. The bureaucrat who sanctioned the purchase was remanded to judicial custody and barred from media contact.

Later, a farmer accidentally gave his bull a bucket of pesticide mixed with water. Unexpectedly, the bull survived, an indication that the pesticides were fake. Reports on tests of samples at Central Fertiliser Quality Control and Training Institute, Faridabad, varied greatly. The Rajasthan police found hundreds of bags of pesticide, purportedly fake, dumped in the Indira Gandhi canal that flows through south Panjab into Rajasthan. Rajasthan ministers accused the Panjab government of contaminating their drinking water. It all seemed to point to a cover-up.

I wanted to understand how the unions had arrived at the figure of the compensation—Rs 4300 crore. The farmers explained: at the rate of Rs 40,000 per acre for farmers and Rs 20,000 per acre for workers. The average farmer spends about Rs 21,000 per acre on getting the field ready, sowing, pesticides and insecticides, harvesting and transporting the produce to the mandis (markets). These are the input costs. Together, the farmers listed out the names of seeds, pesticides, cycles of sprays, and all that it took to get a cotton crop ready for harvest.

The difference in rate of compensation between farmers and farm workers caught my attention. 'Rs 18,000 is the average *theka* per season,' answered Gurpreet.

*Theka* is the rent on leased land. Most small and marginal farmers do not own much land. They lease lands from the land-owning Jutts and zamindars who do not cultivate their lands by themselves any longer.ʲ Many Jutts, members of Panjab's most powerful caste, have moved to the cities, to states outside Panjab and abroad. Their next generation, accustomed to working in other trades and slaving as corporate employees, have never put their hands to the soil. They are the *Kakajis*—a feudal term of respect which has now become a pejorative on the tongues of landless tenant farmers.

There are around eighteen and a half lakh farming families in Panjab and around 65 per cent of them are small and marginal farmers.[11] This is a ballpark figure because data on land division within families can never be absolute. This points at how the division of lands through inheritance laws is making more and more farmers small and marginal, and at the institutionalisation of *theka*. *Theka* is sacrosanct. *Kakajis*, wherever they may live, rarely give up the claim. Often, given the rising cost of living, they, too, are dependent on it. The existence of an unregulated, mostly verbal agreement-based system poses challenges to the government in terms of record-keeping, and deciding compensation if it ever agreed to pay it. Yet, the government has never intervened, and the parallel economy of absentee landlordism remains in practice.

---

j. I have gone with 'Jutt' which is closer to the way it is pronounced in preference to the more common Jat. The Jutt Sikhs of Panjab are an agrarian community who own most of the land and dominate the political and social life of the state. While similar to the Jats of Haryana, UP and Rajasthan, they are not entirely the same.

I asked how many among the thirty-odd people around me had to repay loans. All hands went up. I then asked how many owned the land they cultivated. Less than half the hands went up. A state-created agrarian system, corrupted and crumbling, feudal land ownership patterns and *theka* are responsible for the plight of the farmers, especially when the crop fails.

An old man sat down near us, listening. After a while he said, '*Mukdi gal kawan?*' (Shall I have the last word?)

'*Das Babeya, tu das de*,' someone from the group said. Yes, revered old man, you speak.

'All this is …,' said the old man, '*chaurasi da geda* (the circle of 84).' I do not understand. Does he mean the year 1984 or the Hindu concept that each one of us is trapped in the cycle of eighty-four lakh or 8.4 million births and deaths? I ask him again, '*Eighty-four da geda?*'

The old man replied, 'That is what I understand. I am now a grandfather many times over but I was young in 1984. For the first time, I went to Chandigarh to protest. We gheraoed the governor's house. The police were everywhere. It was a huge mela.'

'What were the issues?'

'The same as now. Enhanced electricity rates, better prices for wheat. What is our lot? This! What will be our issues? These!'

Just then a boy came with the message that the president of BKU-Ugraha, Joginder Ugrahan, was looking for me. My head buzzing, I left the conversation midway to meet Joginder Ugrahan.

When I approached Joginder Ugrahan, he was telling a young volunteer, 'You have to find the bolt. We shall do no damage to property.' He looked at me and said, 'A bolt in the railway tracks has gone missing …'

The mild-mannered, soft-spoken Joginder Ugrahan who was in his sixties apologised for being supine on the railway tracks, head resting on a rail and legs dangling on the other one, 'It has been a long day. If you won't mind ...' He gave me a happy childlike smile. I asked him if they would achieve the purpose of the strike. 'The protest will take us to the negotiating table but the government will try to fox us.' From his long experience in strikes, he could sense the outcome. Yet, the strike continued.

Joginder Ugrahan looked me in the eye, his face a picture of studied seriousness. 'Yet, the purpose of this protest is different. We have achieved it. We wanted to tell the politicians, those who take us for granted, that we are not theirs. It is a fight for self-confidence, for respect—to be able to look into the eyes of the leaders.'

'How are these protests different from the Akali protests in the 1970s and 1980s? Those days, Badal stood for farmers and Akalis agitated for river waters.'

Joginder Ugrahan sat up, animated. 'Those days, there were two distinct styles of protest. During the Emergency, the Akalis protested peacefully, non-violently. But once they came into power, their protests changed. The strike for river waters, the Dharam Yudh Morcha in August 1982, caused destruction of public property and was the trigger that led to the state being engulfed by militancy. The BKU, since the 1980s, has struggled non-violently. We are not cutting trees, not damaging buildings. It is just our bodies—unarmed people against the armed state and its policies.'

'What was it about the bull at the rally?'

He was amused. 'You know about the bull?'

I nodded. 'The news was quite striking.' A few weeks before the *rail-roko*, the farmer-labour protest in front of the deputy commissioner's office in Bathinda had to be abandoned because a bull had entered the protest arena.

'You see, the police have many tactics. The bull was *mastya* (intoxicated). Who knows what they fed it and led it to the rally?

This happened in front of the deputy commissioner's office. First, the police placed a cordon of young women constables. It was the worst defence because we, the protestors, were mostly men. How could we jostle with women? We talked to them. We told them they were our daughters. Wearing a uniform cannot break our relationship. They worked for a salary and we were agitating for survival. The women police constables understood and let us pass. We gathered again. Next, the police set the bull loose.' He paused a moment, 'Throughout the protest we have allowed the Cancer Train to pass, but the government is not running it. It is to discredit us.'

The president was referring to the train that now carries hundreds of cancer patients each day from Panjab to Bikaner in Rajasthan—a dire aftermath of the Green Revolution which has bred disease and illness through pesticides, insecticides and fertilisers over the last four decades.[k] He reminded me that the last sustained *rail-roko* in Panjab was in the year 2000 by the Akali Dal. It lasted seventy-two hours.

'The one that is underway right now has long since crossed that, having already exceeded four days. Now we have extended it to two more days. In the last thirty-eight years of my activism, I have never seen so many youth coming together. It is a new phenomenon. The youth are restive. This opens up new challenges for us. The youth come because they are now aware, but they are also difficult to control. The challenge is to keep them focussed on change, on compelling the systems through mass pressure to work and fight for pro-people changes.'

Joginder Ugrahan has been an activist for almost as long as my age. It tells me something: that the Panjab I knew when I was a child, the Panjab I romanticised in my mind all my life, also had deep issues which I had not noticed or acknowledged. 'We have stormed the citadels of the Badals and those of every political party's major

k. The Cancer Train runs from the Malwa region in Panjab (the southern part of the state), which has some of the highest cancer rates in the world, to Bikaner in Rajasthan where cheap cancer treatment is available.

constituency. They come to us seeking our votes. Then they exploit us. These protests are to tell them we are not theirs. That is our achievement,' he concluded.

After the meeting with the president, the secretary of PKMU Lachhman Sewewala and I left on an old and creaking Bajaj scooter. Night-time had set in. Two young men on individual motorbikes followed us through the dark for a few kilometres across three villages. We stopped at a house and were offered water. It was a modest household, barely a room and a half, no cattle, no tractor. The man of the house asked if he should serve tea. Lachhman refused, citing it would cause acidity at that hour. The real reason was that we were very hungry, but he did not state it. The man returned with two full-to-the-brim steel tumblers of milk. I asked Lachhman about the men following us and where they had disappeared. 'They are for protection.'

'From?'

'Police, Akalis, *dhanaad* Jutts (rich land-owners).'

The secretary moved out to talk to the man. It struck me how in this time and age farmers and workers asking for mere compensation was considered an illegal and subversive act. How I had now associated myself with those whom the state hunted. My wanting to know the truth had made me a pariah. Soon, we left the house. With our scooter headlights off, we drove through the inner lanes of yet another darkened village. In the next village we reached a home lit by a single bulb. The gate was partially open. We entered and sat in the drawing room.

Over the next months I would notice a pattern in how guests were treated in rural Panjab. At an average Jutt home, either the person you want to meet, a male child or an older man opened the gate and escorted you in. Most village homes in Panjab have rooms in a row, with a drawing room and bathroom bunched together on one side and the kitchen and usually a cattle-shed opposite. In between the two wings is an open space, a courtyard where people park vehicles and tractors.

If you intend to wait for the person you have come to meet at lunch hour, a meal is always on offer. If you opt for it, a young man or boy serves a simple meal comprising of daal, vegetables, sometimes a bowl of curd, rotis and salad in the drawing room. You hardly see the women of the house unless she is a matron or a very young girl. Yet, you can hear them calling out to the man or boy serving you.

In Dalit households, in the *vedah*, the sloping side of the villages where Dalits live, the gates are often open or absent. The kitchen is usually open. In the absence of the person you want to meet, the woman greets you and serves you tea or a meal. It is the same in most Hindu households. Preventing guests from seeing the women is more prevalent among Jutts than others.

After a few minutes, a young man brought food. Soon his mother came in to ask if we needed anything else. We were in the front bedroom, next to a makeshift temple with pictures of Lord Shiva, Durga and Guru Nanak, indicating that it was a Hindu household. The family were Banias, belonging to the trading community.

Over a dinner of chapattis and daal with onions, green chillies and lemon pickle, Lachhman said, 'Labels like Green Revolution, granary of India and so on don't help. In fact, they misrepresent the conditions. The Green Revolution brought a boom in agricultural produce but devastated the farmers. The expenses on agriculture have increased and profits have decreased. In spite of all claims by the government, all the policies, the procurement and marketing boards, the agricultural university, and everything that the politicians say, for the last half century the system has miserably failed in creating a farmer-friendly framework for agriculture. The input cost of agriculture remains higher than the output.'

The protest had brought small and marginal Jutt farmers, labourers, Dalits and women together. It had certainly created a caste realignment, but caste hadn't disappeared. Poverty had forged a bond. Lachhman continued, 'In its real sense, a farmer is one who derives his living from farming, with or without land. A small farmer and a landless labourer actually have the same issues: employment, price rise, sustainable agriculture, loans and recovery, suicides and so on. In this post-Green Revolution phase, while the farmer suffers, the labourer also suffers greatly. The labourer's sustenance from land and his relationship with it has changed. They no longer get fodder for cattle, straw for cooking fires, free vegetables and so on. That is why we need to fight together.'

'Is it the first time that traditional rival voters are fighting together on this scale?' Historically, the voting pattern in Panjab has by and large been the Jutts voting for the Akalis, urban Hindus voting for BJP, Dalits and other castes voting for Congress, though for a while, among the Dalits, the Bahujan Samaj Party did make some inroads.

'On this scale, yes. We have collaborated earlier over the compensation for farmer suicides, over reduction of electricity bills, but not in this manner. Until now the political parties managed to create a rift among us. The government tried to divide us again this time. Badal asked us to drop the labour part of the compensation. Our coming together has had them worried. How come these poor, backward people are united without support from any political party? We did not stop politicians from joining us. But we told them to come in their individual capacity and that they could join the crowd at the back—no mic, no stage. This strike is beyond labels like Akali and Congress.'

'Do you feel you will succeed?'

'Compensation is one issue. The larger gain is that we demonstrate our resistance, raise our voice against injustice and make the powers realise they should stop taking us for granted. Our solidarity is our real gain from the movement.'

It struck me that both Joginder Ugrahan and Lachhman Sewewala had the exact same criteria to evaluate the success of the protest. It showed how well prepared they and the cadre were for the long battle ahead.

Next morning I woke up to a babel of *kirtans* and *paath* from different gurdwaras in the village. Lachhman had left. I asked about the multiplicity of sounds and was told that it was a common feature across villages. Each village has many gurdwaras whose *granthis* are not in sync with each other. Rural Panjab wakes up early, there is cattle to attend to and housework to do. I asked Pankaj, the young man who had served us dinner and made our sleeping arrangements, why Lachhman had come there the previous night. He told how a few years back the PKMU had helped the family during a property tussle with their Jutt neighbour, an Akali supporter.

When Sukhbir Badal, the deputy CM, son of Parkash Singh Badal, took over the reins of the Shiromani Akali Dal, the second-oldest political party in the country, he introduced a new level into governance by creating the *halka* (constituency) in-charge. He made the police and bureaucratic machinery in each constituency subservient to the local *halka* in-charge—a political position accorded to a prominent local Akali Dal leader. The *halka* in-charge called the shots in the constituency even if it had a Congress candidate representing it in the Assembly.

Right from ordinary people to the village sarpanch, justice—instead of going to courts—became a matter of cosying up to the *halka* in-charge. If a Jutt, through his filial networks, sought to usurp a small Hindu Bania's land, what choices did the Bania's family have? It could either give up the claim or sell. That is where PKMU played a role. It stood outside the paradigms of Akalis and Jutts. It wielded influence because it could stop labourers from working in the Jutt-owned farms. The family had since remained obliged. This is how people's movements cultivate relationships. In the coming months I saw many farmer, labour, industrial and thermal employee unions at work. They would perform skits and songs to galvanise support over people's issues. Everywhere, in every big or small meeting, everything moved through a sense of camaraderie and solidarity—'*Naal khade ne!*' (They stand with us!)

I moved to Faridkot, Muktsar and Fazilka districts to meet other leaders, activists, ordinary farmers and labourers. The roads were all lined with vast black cotton fields. Many farmers had uprooted the crop to sow wheat. Near towns I saw abandoned large godowns whose roofs had blown away. These used to be cold storage units. In many large plots stacks upon stacks of gunny sacks full of wheat or rice lay exposed to the vagaries of the weather, at some places covered with mere tarpaulin. This was the grain procured by the Food Corporation of India, but not yet moved out. The system could barely provide safekeeping for fifty lakh metric tonnes (LMT) of grains.[12] The rest was all under cover-and-plinth storage. In 2018, Panjab's Central Pool contribution was estimated as 122 MT for wheat and 190 MT for rice.

Alongside godowns, on the roads I saw large flex banners with many stamp-sized pictures of individuals. All men. These banners were put up as thank you messages by political party loyalists who were newly appointed heads and members of cooperative, civil supplies and marketing agencies like PUNSUP (Punjab State Civil Supplies Corporation Limited) and Markfed. Since 1965 when the State Agriculture Marketing Act and Mandi Board came into existence, Panjab has developed a network of about 1850-plus procurement centres—grain markets or mandis—but put together they do not manage to cover the farm produce supply chain. Half a century since Panjab was made the nation's food basket through the Green Revolution, the processes of production, procurement, payment and placement of produce remain leaky and fraught with issues. This is systemic apathy.

The apathy is also in how the Centre treats Panjab. Neither in the 2007 central rehabilitation package of over Rs 15,000 crore for southern states, nor in the special package to Vidarbha, nor even in the dry-land package for water-deficient areas did Panjab receive any aid. In 2008, out of the sanctioned Rs 71,000 crore to finance the national agricultural debt waiver, Panjab received only Rs 608 crore. While debt waiver itself is not the solution, the fact is that the Congress-led UPA-I government was in power at the Centre while in Panjab the SAD–BJP combine held the reins of power, and the neglect from the Centre suited Badal's agenda as it fit the age-old narrative that the Centre was apathetic to the plight of Sikh farmers. When the central government changed in 2014, Badal's old partners, the BJP came to power in the Centre. Yet, nothing came from the Centre for Panjab. Even the PM's farmer insurance scheme and soil laboratories scheme did not work in Panjab because the government had not adopted it. This was the double bind in which Panjab found itself entangled.

In the ongoing whitefly protest, against a demand for Rs 4,300 crore, the Panjab government offered a paltry Rs 600 crore for farmers and Rs 64 crore for labourers. In effect, Panjab's government was doing to its people what the Centre had done to Panjab. Parallely, to weaken the momentum of the strike, the government began offering compensation to farmers it identified as long-standing party supporters. The ordinary protestors could not wait indefinitely for the government to assess the damage. In any case, the records for who planted what and in how much land were hard to uncover through the *tehsildars*, the village land record-keepers. Any protest, especially a critical *rail-roko*, has a period in which it can be kept in check and steered towards a purpose. After six days, that time was up. Though the meeting with the CM was inconclusive, the unions withdrew the strike.

The irony: the protestors, much more than the government, seemed to feel a sense of responsibility about the people, the society, and the state.[1] That is how I learnt that when the farmers in Pathrala or Patiala said India, they did not mean Bharat Mata, the buzzword which the right wing uses to whip up polarised nationalism. For the small farmer or farm labour, India means the state apparatus that dictates how they should deal with his land—what to grow and where to sell the crop. Their lament against India was not a call for separatism, as it was in the 1980s, but a plea to the system to hear and acknowledge them.

In the evolution of human beings, a major change occurred when they moved from being hunter-gatherers to settling down with agriculture. It is this primary sense of being one with nature that one feels when one waters a plant and sees it bloom, more so if one

---

1. The farmers and workers planned a major gathering in village Raike Kalan near the chief minister's village Badal in the end of January 2016. In spite of this being an era of communication and its attendant snooping and spying, and there being spies and intelligence agents spread out, like I was doubted to be one, the police did not get a clue of what was going to happen. In this era of social media and WhatsApp messages, the Kisan Morcha organisers did not use any of these new-age devices to relay the message that the gathering had been advanced by two days. The police were taken aback when thousands of protestors, especially women, suddenly descended upon the village. However, again, nothing came of it.

maintains a garden. At my wife Lakshmi's parental home in north Bangalore, her parents maintain both a front and a kitchen garden. The kitchen garden is 10 feet by 30 feet. It has two coconut trees, a jackfruit tree, a lychee tree, a guava tree and a banana tree. Besides these, the plot is home to chillies, tomatoes, coriander, tulsi and other plants. Amma also just planted an avocado and a dragon fruit sapling. We joke, all that is missing is black pepper and rubber, for all of Kerala to be at her doorstep.

When the roses, dahlias, marigolds, jasmine and chrysanthemums blossom in the front garden, I see the joy on Amma's face. This joy is underpinned by the fact that by following the cycles of the seasons when planting new saplings or sowing fresh seeds, she feels she is in harmony with nature.

In Panjab, the green basket of the nation, where nature should play the most vital role, the scale of agriculture aided by brute technology—both mechanical and chemical—has thrown everything out of balance. The industrial nature of agriculture and the duress of the market economy has driven a wedge between the farmer and his land, society and nature. The aftermath of the Green Revolution is the proverbial elephant in the room. Everyone has an idea about it, but no one knows its full extent.

Since the 1990s, when India opened up its economy to neo-liberal practices, the nation has focussed on attracting investment for industry. Not only did neo-liberalism ignore agriculture, even though more than half of the national population was dependent on the sector, it created the conditions for many companies who dealt in agricultural equipment, seeds, fertilisers, pesticides, insecticides, farm produce and processing to enter the market. Besides the Gross Domestic Product (GDP) and the Human Development Index (HDI), it prioritised whether we, as a nation, were doing well by superimposing the gods of the temple of Mammon on our understanding—the Sensex of the Bombay Stock Exchange and the Nifty of the National

Stock Exchange. In the last decades, industrial growth has increased, stocks of agriculture-based companies have galloped, the speculative commodities market has peaked, but their base—the farming sector—and its contribution to the GDP has shrunk.

At the same time, at forty-five quintals of wheat and sixty quintals of rice per hectare, Panjab's food production per cropping area is among the highest in the world. Panjab contributes 40 per cent wheat and 30 per cent rice to the central pool.[13] But at what cost? From around three lakh hectares in the 1960s, the area under rice—grown for the central pool and not local consumption—has gone up to twenty-eight lakh hectares. In arid Panjab, paddy is cultivated using double the amount of water that it needs in Bihar and Bengal. Paddy fetches a high price, but takes a toll on the land and water aquifers. Though farmers prefer to stop paddy cultivation, the system does not provide alternate frameworks or employment. It does not create an income guarantee structure to adequately pay the farmers. A panel report tabled recently in Parliament says instead of an ideal nitrogen, phosphorus and potassium combination of 4:2:1, in Panjab the ratio is 39:9:1, thus indicating how the fertile lands of Panjab have been saturated with chemicals.[14]

The imbalance is not only about land or water or resources, it is also about earnings. Consider a leading agrarian expert and my school senior, Devinder Sharma's explanation. Per the 2016 Economic Survey Report, the average income of a farming family in Panjab was Rs 3,500 per month. In 1971, in the earlier days of the Green Revolution, the MSP of wheat was Rs 76 per quintal and the paddy price was Rs 21 per quintal. In 2015, the MSP on wheat was Rs 1,450 per quintal—nineteen times the price in 1971. The MSP on paddy was Rs 1,400—sixty-seven times the price. In the same period, the basic salary plus dearness allowance of government employees had gone up 120-150 times, of college teachers 150-170 times, of school teachers 280-320 times, of corporate employees of the general manager rank 300 times, of a vice-president and above, 1,000 times. If we were to create income parity between farming and any other trade, the wheat price should be Rs 7,600 per quintal and paddy should be Rs 5,100 per quintal.[15] On the surface it might look like an argument to increase the price of food, but it is more complicated. If the food prices increase, the worst-hit will be the ones who already miss out on benefits in the neo-liberal economy—the have-nots in the cities, the small and marginal farmers and labourers and artisans in the villages.

What we have presented above still remains in the domain of the farmer. Let us explore our role in this tragedy. Look at farming from our dining table point of view: What do we pay for the wheat flour and what do the farmers get for the wheat they grow? The MSP for wheat in 2015 was Rs 1450. But that does not mean every farmer sells his produce for that much. Or that the MSP is a commitment to buy. It means the MSP is a guidance figure. Though the heavily mechanised farming process in Panjab aspires to work with factory-like precision, the quality of wheat or paddy, the time of sowing, the watering of fields, the sprinkling of chemicals, the time of harvesting, the rainfall, the moisture content, the probability of disease, the grade of produce, all play a role in how the rates of grain are fixed. The wheat could vary in moisture content and quality. The produce could even be rejected for being surplus, for lack of funds, or because private players corner produce and do not release it to government agencies. In the farmer's ecosystem, money rarely changes hands, as almost everything is through a system of slips and credits, and rotates around the *arthiya*, the commission agent, who serves as the farmer's conduit to the market and the local bank, extending loans and credits, often at short notice. Calculating backwards from Rs 1450 would mean Rs 14 for a kilogram, much lower than the Rs 45 per kilogram of wheat flour that we pay—three times lower. In this gap of what the farmers earn and what we pay lies the ordinary man's complicity in the disaster of the agrarian sector.

The argument thus is not about increasing the price of food but understanding where the Rs 31 (the difference between Rs 45 and Rs 14) goes. It is this Rs 31 per kilogram that we pay for agro-processing industries located in other states, transportation across the country, above the basic procurement price of wheat that gives the corporates control on governments by bank-rolling political parties. Governments, usually beholden to corporates for election funding, remain under the influence of the World Trade Organisation (WTO) which pushes for a free market, thereby complicating any possible government-subsidised arrangement for the farming sector. This is not a crisis of Panjab or India alone. In the last few years, in South America, Europe and Africa, farmers have been protesting the lack of state support—an indigenous system to maximise their trade potential.

For the last decade, political parties have been talking of implementing the Swaminathan Commission report on the basis of which they will ensure that the MSP doubles by 2022.[16] But the report also calls for land reforms by redistributing ceiling-surplus land, substantial investment in irrigation through canals, drainage and the million well scheme, soil testing laboratories, a cap on interest rates levied on farm loans, primary health centres and suicide prevention facilities, and a food guarantee programme through local self-help groups, and so on. This second set of proposals is rarely spoken about. Whether it is professors, thinkers and commentators, everyone is clear: small and marginal farming is untenable as it does not produce enough income. It needs to change, but to what form? Should corporates or landlords buy the land and dispossess the farmers? There are no clear answers.

It is no wonder then that activists and ordinary farmers and labourers consider Panjab the 'food-producing colony of the nation' faced with myriad problems that barely register on the national consciousness. This non-listening, non-acknowledging violence of the state through colonial capitalist practices based on neo-liberalism has paralysed Panjab's agriculture.

There were two main critiques of the protest—one overt, another silent. One was that well-off union leaders were exploiting the sentiments of the poor farmers and labourers, which I checked and found to be untrue. The second was that Panjab was used to protests and knew that they were always stonewalled by governments. Many acknowledged the injustice of the agrarian system but were loath to support the unions because they assumed nothing would come out of these protests.

I saw the fire in the eyes of the protestors, their will to fight non-violently and their calmness and preparation. I also saw in their struggle that the neo-liberal system, perpetuated by opportunistic politics, had usurped the tools protesters could employ—religion, *langar*, language, icons, and so on—rendering it a vastly unequal tussle. On the one hand, the march of progress continues, in spite of often inclement weather, as Panjab continues to deliver bumper harvests, contributes to the central pool and the agricultural marketing and supplies companies continue to reap the benefits. I asked myself, a product of neo-liberalism's burgeoning urban middle class, whom do I stand with?

Panjab's agrarian crisis, like that of India's or even the world's, is not only about external systems. It is about whether the small and marginal farmer and the landless labourer feel they are part of the system, supported by the state, or whether they feel isolated and on the brink of annihilation. It is about our collective conscience that allows the *annadata*, the producer of our food and the nourisher of our society, to perish. Is there a way I could do something to prevent one farmer or labourer from giving in to darkness and succumbing, because he is not up to standing *pehra* on life? The question is, therefore, simple: how can the political will be turned towards the agrarian cause?

## Chapter Three

# *Rosh* — Anger

On 11 October 2015, at Fazilka—close to the border with Pakistan—I had a special night reliving one of my favourite childhood spectacles: an earthy Ram Lila performance under strobe lights, in a tacky, colourful tent. The episode that day contained the famous line, '*Pran jaye par vachan na jaye!*' (I shall defend my promise with my life.) The line is very popular and has such moral and cultural resonance that it is sprinkled liberally in more than one Ram Lila episode. It was fun to watch how the histrionics and gaffes of the mostly Sikh actors with natural long hair endeared them to the audience. Nothing much had changed since childhood, except that the mics were stereophonic and the smoke from a device on stage often blurred the action on it. There were also more stalls to gorge on chaats, pooris, pakodas and fruit salads.

Next morning, the farmer and labour unions were to meet the CM in Chandigarh. I checked my mobile phone for the news when I spotted a few WhatsApp messages that said: in village Bargari near the town of Kotkapura, on the Faridkot-Bathinda road, villagers had woken up to find the pages of the Sikh scripture—the Guru Granth Sahib—strewn on the lanes of the village.

The news of the *beadbi* (sacrilege) of the holy text spread among hawkers, shopkeepers, rickshaw wallahs and at the tea shop. Those who know Panjab, the stories of Partition and the period of militancy are familiar with stories of a cow's tail in a temple, the pig's carcass in a mosque, and other provocative actions carried out to foment trouble. Too many times in history, those seeking to provoke or insult the Sikhs have attacked the Granth Sahib and the gurdwaras. It happened during Partition and it happened in 1981 when the police chasing Bhindranwale over the alleged killing of Lala Jagat Narain—owner of the *Hind Samachar* group of newspapers—burnt two busloads of Sikh scriptures in the village of Chando Kalan in Hisar in Haryana. During Operation Blue Star, the Granth Sahib in the Durbar Sahib was inadvertently pierced with bullets and the Akal Takht was destroyed. In the 1984 anti-Sikh pogrom in Delhi and other cities, 175 gurdwaras were destroyed and hundreds of holy texts were torn and burnt. In 1986 in Nakodar, after incidents of sacrilege of the Granth Sahib, four innocents were killed in police firing. *Beadbi* always touches a raw nerve. Its occurrence now was ominous, especially because it was timed with the farmer-labour meeting with the CM.

By around 11 a.m., since no direct bus was going to Kotkapura, I took a bus to Bathinda. I reckoned, if I got late, I could stay back in the town. On social media I saw a statement by the farmer and labour unions condemning the sacrilege and calling it a distraction from the *rail-roko* protest which was called off the previous night. I reached Bathinda bus station to find that no bus was going towards Kotkapura. No driver or conductor wanted to go out, risking the safety of the passengers and the bus. The trains, stopped by the farmer-worker protests, were still not functional.

Hoping for a ride in a passing car, I walked to the road junction where on a pedestal stands a life-like, gaunt, black statue of a soldier with his left leg beginning to break into a run, as if ready for action. This junction is locally called the Fauji Chowk and the statue is of the Victoria Cross and Maha Vir Chakra recipient, Naik, later,

Jemadar or Naib Subedar Nand Singh. Naib Subedar Nand Singh won his Victoria Cross (VC) in World War II, on the Maungdaw-Buthidaung Road, in Burma (now Myanmar). He led his section up a steep knife-edged ridge under very heavy machine-gun fire to recapture a position gained by the enemy. Later, as a Jemadar in the post-Independence Indian Army, he led a 1 Sikh platoon in Jammu and Kashmir operations in 1947 to repel Pakistani raiders. He was mortally injured and his VC ribbon gave the Pakistanis an indication of his identity. His body was rumoured to have been taken by Pakistan soldiers and paraded in an open truck in Muzaffarabad. He was posthumously awarded the Maha Vir Chakra. A few months ago, a construction company had taken charge of repairing the chowk. The platform they built crumbled quickly. Yet, given its prominent location, private companies now displayed buntings and advertisements at the spot.

It was late now. Reaching Kotkapura seemed difficult. There was the additional matter of where I would stay. I had no contacts and was unsure of hotels. I went to the Teacher's Home, a prominent activist meeting place in Bathinda next to the Fauji Chowk and learnt that the union meeting with the CM had ended in a stalemate. I stayed back in Bathinda at an activist's home. This is how I learnt first-hand how the transport system was gentrified in Panjab. The air-conditioned Mercedes Benz or Volvo buses that plied between Delhi international airport and the cities of Panjab were all owned by the various interlinked subsidiary companies of the then-ruling Badal family.[17] The lucrative local routes were also owned by the Badal family. When the Akalis came to power for the second consecutive time in 2012, they manipulated the transport policy, adjusted licences, ran more buses per licence and created several transport companies—Dabwali, Orbit, Taj, Jhujhar and so on, to beat the system that was designed to prevent a monopoly. They adjusted the route timings, kept peak hour routes to themselves and adjusted the vehicle tax structure in their favour. The income of Panjab Roadways, the public sector undertaking, fell by 93 per cent, translating to losses of over Rs 500 crore per annum. This was merely one instance of the involvement of the Badal family in shady business deals. As I was to learn later, there were others as well.

By that night, a plethora of YouTube channels, run by diaspora Sikhs, were reporting that missionary Sikh leaders had reached Kotkapura. Based outside Patiala, Ranjit Singh Dhadrianwale is a sharp-tongued, baby-faced preacher, in his mid-thirties. In Kotkapura, he and another leader Panthpreet Singh organised a procession with the torn pages of the holy book. They addressed a huge rally in which they urged the Sikh protestors to unite against the sacrilege. In their speeches, they forewarned that outsiders could infiltrate and vitiate the atmosphere. The fear was—akin to the farmers and workers—of 'agents' and outsiders penetrating the movement and destabilising it. The police arrested Ranjit Singh post-midnight. I rued missing going to Kotkapura but recognised that I neither had local hosts there, nor any contacts. I headed back towards Chandigarh, hitching a ride in the car of a kindly Panjabi University professor on his way home to Patiala.

On 13 October, the police lathi-charged the protestors in village Buttar Kalan and fired in the air. On 14 October, the police fired in the air and dispersed the crowds gathered at the Kotkapura crossing from where roads went to Bathinda, Patiala, Muktsar, Ludhiana and Amritsar. A few hours later, people were gathered in silent protest near village Behbal Kalan on a road from Kotkapura to village Bargari. The police lathi-charged the protestors and opened fire. Two protestors died: Gurjeet Singh and Krishan Avtar Singh. More than a hundred were injured. The blame for the killings rested on the superintendent of police, Charanjit Singh Sharma, but he was obeying someone's orders. Whose? No one knew and the government did not tell.

The situation then got out of hand.

The state media reported nothing on television, and reportage in print media was thin. Panjab has a history of news censorship and there were other issues in terms of media ownership and control too. In 1984, during Operation Blue Star, the media was driven away from Panjab due to state censorship. The All India Radio did not give adequate news. In Rourkela, Baba and I had then tuned into the British Broadcasting Corporation (BBC) for news. Later that year in November when Indira Gandhi was assassinated, newspapers in Panjab carried blank pages with the word 'censored' written across their front pages. I was then studying in a military school in Panjab and remember waiting seven weeks until Baba could physically come all the way from Odisha to take me home on vacation. Baba told me the steel town administration had ensured that he and Mama and hundreds of other Sikh families had found refuge in a gurdwara for a week. He had tried calling me and sending telegrams, but no means of communication had worked.

Then there was a kind of censorship enforced by Khalistani militants through targeted killings—of Ramesh Chandra, the chief editor of the Jalandhar-based *Hind Samachar* group of newspapers; Sumeet Singh, the editor of the literary journal, *Preet Lari*; Sukhraj Singh, the editor of the journal *Chingari;*[18] the director of All India Radio, Rajinder Kumar Talib.[19] Fifteen newspaper agents and hawkers were also gunned down by separatists.[20] Most of these killings were over how the media ought to address the militants: should they be called terrorists or extremists or militants or separatists? The implication was that a 'terrorist' or 'extremist' seeks to disturb a national narrative but a 'separatist' or 'militant' seeks to create a new nation. The former is a law and order issue, the latter is a political one. The separatists sought to legitimise their struggle by asserting their position in the political discourse. They killed famous poets Avtar Singh Pash, Ravinder Ravi and the left-leaning poet and activist Jaimal Singh Padda. The singer Amar Singh Chamkila who was known for his ribald songs was also killed, though the killing is sometimes attributed to internal rivalry. The lack of a definite version keeps the waters muddied.

Under the Badals now, the media faced a different kind of censorship: financial muscle hiding behind the mask of technology.[21] *The Tribune*, the state's oldest and largest-selling English daily, was denied government advertisements. In the recent past, NDTV channels were blocked during the state elections of 2012 as was the BBC. Aaj Tak was blocked for a month in 2012 because it showed the deputy chief minister enjoying a movie while the Ferozepur floods raged. Zee Punjabi ran into trouble when it dared to criticise the government. A well-regarded channel, Day & Night News, run by senior journalist Kanwar Sandhu, had to wind up operations in 2013. In metropolitan cities, direct-to-home (DTH) service providers operate, but outside these cities, cable operators control close to 75 to 80 per cent of the market. These operators charge their customers for their services, but they also charge TV channels between Rs 2 to Rs 5 crore per year as carriage fee depending upon which band the channel chooses to relay its signal through. Day & Night News's issues started when Manpreet Badal, Parkash Singh Badal's nephew, left the Akali Dal and formed his own People's Party of Punjab before the 2012 elections. The channel then reported his activities extensively, but soon began noticing interruptions in their transmission.

When Day & Night News took up the issue with cable operators, they got the usual replies: non-availability of slots and infrastructure issues. Finally, they were told to tone down their criticism of the government. When they stood by their content, operators bumped the channel off their cable network. In the course of their investigation, Day & Night News found out that most cable operators were actually a front for one company, namely Fastway Transmissions Private Limited. The Cable Television Network (Regulation) Amendment Act did not provide for any redress in case the cable operator defaulted on the agreement.

While a TV channel had to get permission from various authorities in order to begin transmission, cable operators needed no permission to beam numerous local in-house channels to their select audience (the subscribers of their network). Fastway broadcast *kirtans* from local gurdwaras and temple ceremonies which were local content based on demand from customers. The Cable TV Network Act is, typically, silent about what and how much cable operators are allowed to broadcast.

Also, in Panjab, the deputy chief minister, who also held the home portfolio, had a stake in the PTC and PTC News channels, as declared in his nomination papers. With an in-house TV channel at its disposal, the government did not advertise on any other TV channel. PTC also got the rights to beam the Kabaddi World Cup, the NRI Sammelan, Vidhan Sabha proceedings and other prominent local events that were deemed good publicity for the government. This is how nepotism works, how people are kept away from news, and how protest is curtailed.

The easy accessibility of the internet had, however, changed the game. Given the large presence of the Sikh diaspora in Canada, US, Australia and Britain, their social media campaigns and websites have become accessible through the internet on mobile phones. Post the *beadbi* incidents, detailed coverage of the events from villages and towns began surfacing on the internet. The incidents of sacrilege too reached surreal proportions as if Panjab was being carpet-bombed— not only the Granth Sahib but also the Holy Quran, the Gita and the Ramayana.

Soon, Sukhbir Singh Badal, deputy chief minister and scion of the Badal dynasty, announced: '(The attack is) sponsored by certain forces who want to sow the seeds of communal tension in Panjab and take the state back to the turbulent times of militancy.'

Quickly, without enquiry or probe, the administration had reverted to the 'terrorist and traitor' rhetoric of the dark decade to instil fear in people. The intention of the state's narrative was to threaten people with the violence that the society had braved and fought. The Akalis hoped that remembering those days of extreme hardship, the people would not speak. The phrase 'take the state back to turbulent times' in the state narrative, coming from the deputy chief minister of the state and going out into the wide world through official media channels shaped the perception of the world: Khalistani militancy was back! Panjab had returned to the dark days!

On the ground, in Panjab, Sukhbir Badal's rhetoric did not work. Protests continued as people spilled out on the streets with black flags in small and big towns and on highways. Panjab's demography is such that Sikhs are a majority in rural areas and Hindus in most urban areas. However, social media does not discriminate. A huge number of social media profiles displayed a black flag which said, 'Rosh'. *Rosh* translates as both angst and fury. The strikes were the people's narrative invoked by the failures of the government that had been unable to stop the incidents of sacrileges. Panjab curled up in its *rosh*.

Village, town and city gurdwaras and *jathedars* galvanised the protests. They mobilised people, often by consent, but sometimes by force. During this period, I was to meet a *palledar* (one who carries sacks of grain on his back in the mandis) near Moga. He called up and said, 'Don't come. Young boys in saffron *parnas* (small turbans) are roaming on motorbikes, asking everyone to join the protests. They are carrying sticks, swords and guns. They have gone crazy. They could erupt anytime and create a nuisance.'

The words were certainly alarming, but was this undue alarm? Weapons are common in Panjab, as part of its attire and gesture, and are a part of its narrative. The show of arms and the accompanying posturing is not unusual. Much about the Khalsa identity is about the right to bear arms. What intrigued me in the call was the word 'crazy'. What could it mean? Were the youngsters truly crazy or had they become unpredictable, and so people feared them? Where does one draw the line with an angry mob? The *palledar* must have thought such display of arms and angry attitude and the borderline violent attitude, ready to spill over, would be unacceptable to me.

In any case, I could not have gone. Given the Badal family stranglehold on the public transport sector, the only way I could have made the trip was if I had a personal vehicle. No buses were plying. When I tried taking a taxi, no driver was willing to venture out. People cut down trees and blocked roads, schools and colleges closed, markets downed shutters, vegetable and milk supplies stopped, chemists closed their shops, fuel stations went empty, and in spite of the paddy harvest season, grain markets wore a deserted look. Panjab was at a standstill. Thousands of protestors gathered on the Hari ke Pattan bridge, next to the Nanaksar Gurdwara, at Harrike, where the Satluj and Beas meet before the Satluj turns to Pakistan and the Indira Gandhi canal flows to Rajasthan. Another group gathered on the bridge over the Beas near Rayya. For about a week, the Majha region of Panjab was cut off from India.

However, in spite of the posturing and some instances of hooliganism, this was not a repeat of the decade and a half of militancy. The militancy period was a breakdown of law and order. It began with a grouse against the state but became an opportunity for some people to indulge in violence and kill innocents. In these current incidents Panjab had gone into an angry curl and the state and administration had abdicated their responsibility. As a direct rebuff to Sukhbir Badal's view, even the lower-level functionaries of the SGPC came out in protest against their leaders. Panjab clearly was not crazy—it was in solidarity.

These instances of *beadbi* were related to a gross banality—the shroud of which had fallen on Panjab for at least a whole decade. Soon after the Baisakhi of 2007, a religious head, Sant Dr Gurmeet Ram Rahim Singh Insaan, of a sect known as the Sacha Sauda, located at Sirsa, in Haryana, on the border of south Panjab, had teased the Sikhs. Gurmeet Singh's moniker is a pun on his claims of multi-religiosity to manipulate the socio-cultural divisions within society and endear himself to all, at least literally. Even the name of the *dera* is from an episode from Guru Nanak's life. As a young boy, Nanak's father lent him money to trade, which Nanak used to feed the poor instead. When Nanak's father asked him if the *sauda* (deal) was done, Nanak's reply was that he had concluded a *sacha sauda* (a true deal).

Gurmeet Singh's rise remains shrouded in mystery and there are rumours of his association with Khalistani militants and their assistance in his takeover of the *dera*. In 2007, he purportedly imitated the tenth Sikh Guru Gobind Singh's clothing and ritual of *Khande di Pahul* (initiation into the Sikh faith) while conducting the initiation rites for the followers of his cult, the Dera Sacha Sauda. He wore a long knee-length full-armed pink kurta with a sky-blue waistband and in a large *karahi* (wok), prepared a pink liquid concoction that resembled milk mixed with a synthetic rose essence. This reminded me of summers from my childhood when we would visit Panjab and prepare this mix of milk, ice and rose essence in large quantities for the joint family. The colour could also have been from Rooh Afza, the famous north Indian summer drink.

The act provoked Sikhs because the religion does not permit representation of Gurus. The Sikh religion shuns iconography and idolatry, is focussed on the *shabd* (the word) and considers the Granth Sahib, the text, as the eleventh and eternal Guru. At that time, I wondered how either Gurmeet or anyone else, for that matter, knew the details of the Guru's physical appearance and how he dressed or looked. There are no reference pictures. There are no records. The Sikh doctrine prohibits visual representation of Sikh Gurus, since it is considered idolatry. Yet, though there were earlier paintings of the Gurus, the look that has been understood to be the look of Guru Gobind Singh was formalised by the painter Sobha Singh in the early twentieth century. His depiction of Sikh Gurus came to dominate calendar art which has now translated into idols that adorn homes, businesses and even car decks. Most gurdwaras also now have pictorial representations of the Gurus. The self-styled godman Gurmeet Singh parodied this representation of Guru Gobind Singh. Pink is a gaudy colour and newspapers prominently featured the pink dress and the pink amrit concoction.

The gesture was a caricature of the original event when Guru Gobind Singh had raised an army—the Khalsa—to fight against injustice, and led to major unrest in south Panjab. The *dera* followers, called *premis* (lovers), were soon involved in several tussles with Sikh groups. The police stepped in and curfew was imposed. Offended and ridiculed, the Sikh community did not know how to respond effectively. Should they seek a legal remedy? Should they take the law into their own hands and do what their history told them to do: *sodha*—discipline through force of arms, which was illegal in a democracy? The Akal Takht, the highest seat of justice in the Sikh community, summoned Gurmeet Singh, but he never appeared.

In the decade that followed the events of 2007 till his conviction for rape in August 2017, Gurmeet Singh's banality knew no bounds. He parroted messages of peace and harmony while leading a degenerate life. He amassed Guinness world records for the largest vegetable mosaic, the highest number of birthday greetings and the highest

number of retinal scans and blood donation camps. His biography
listed over fifty talents in the arts and sports. His atrocious self-
promotional movies succeeded at the box office, with generous help
from his followers. Owing to his reach in the political constituencies
of south Panjab and Haryana, political parties of all hues—the Akalis,
the BJP and the Congress—patronised him. He was said to control
around thirty-eight Assembly seats in the Malwa region. He seemed
above the law—a power only unto himself.

Three weeks before the incidents of sacrilege of 2015, in time
for the release of Gurmeet Singh's latest film, *MSG 2: The Messenger*,
an unsigned letter supposedly written by him to the Akal Takht
emerged, seeking an apology for the events of 2007. Under pressure
from the Badals, especially Sukhbir Badal, the SGPC requested the
Akal Takht to pardon him.[m] The pardon was granted. When Sikh
groups criticised the decision, the SGPC brought out advertisements
in local newspapers justifying their decision. Yet, the Sikh community
was not placated. There were talks of a non-Akali Sikh leadership
planning a meeting in Ludhiana. A week or so before the sacrilege
incident at Bargari, posters had appeared on village walls. The posters
demanded a smooth release of the movie. Else, they threatened *beadbi*.

The anger that the people of Panjab felt was over the possible
involvement of Dera Sacha Sauda in sacrileges and the complicity
of the SGPC—supposed to be the custodian of the Sikh faith—in
the pardon of Gurmeet. The general opinion was that by pardoning
Gurmeet, the SGPC had rendered the Sikh community voiceless.
The historical parallel to the current incidents of *beadbi* goes back
to an incident that marked the beginning of militancy in Panjab. On
Baisakhi day, 1978, the leader of the Sant Nirankari sect, a splinter

---

m. While the SGPC is a constitutional elected body, the Akal Takht located at
Amritsar is a religious body. The *jathedar* (leader) of the Akal Takht is the highest
spokesperson of the Sikh community and is meant to be a spiritual leader
without control or influence from any outside politically motivated sources.

group of the original Nirankari sect, Gurbachan Singh, had mocked the Sikh scriptures. This resulted in an armed encounter with a Sikh sect, the Akhand Kirtani Jatha, in which thirteen Sikhs and three Nirankaris were killed. Later, in 1980, a carpenter, Ranjit Singh and his accomplice Kabal Singh, shot dead Gurbachan Singh. Ranjit Singh surrendered soon after but was freed twelve years later when he was appointed the *jathedar* of the Akal Takht by the Sikh community.

As the nation watched and perhaps even expected, Panjab did not burst into flames, and communal harmony stayed intact. The protests against the *beadbi* moved to a three-hour block each day and then dwindled. Many videos of ordinary villagers chasing away the SGPC members and politicians from sites of protest emerged. The state tried to use the media by giving out details of suspects arrested— two *granthis* who claimed greed, a woman who claimed payment and two brothers who had collected the first set of torn pages, one of whom was subject to a severe police beating. Sukhbir Badal's version was that foreign agencies had funded them, which proved to be a red herring as the said foreign contact refuted the charges. The state had no defence, and as the sacrileges increased, it was clear that it was completely ill-prepared and abjectly incapable of providing administration.

If Panjab was returning to the dark days, as was Sukhbir Badal's claim, it was more in terms of the state administration's inefficiency. As a face-saver, the government shunted out the director general of police, Sumedh Saini. In the post-militancy phase, Sumedh Saini was one of the most notorious names in Panjab. He was the inheritor of the legacy of K.P.S. Gill, who was much lauded nationwide, but in Panjab was known for the disappearance of thousands of young men in the militancy period. While Saini was a president's medal awardee, he also had cases of kidnapping and murder pending against him, and had been close to both the Congress and the Akalis. He was, at the time of the incidents of 2015, Sukhbir Badal's blue-eyed boy.

I was amazed at how—as with the farmer labour union protest—the religious protest too had hit a wall of apathy. The Badal regime had stonewalled both the protests.[22]

Over the subsequent months and years, until the completion of this book three years later, I remained amazed that the Panjab that went through so much a quarter century ago—whose Darbar Sahib was attacked, whose Akal Takht was destroyed, which lost so many lives to militancy and enforced disappearances—had now dug in its heels to seek justice over *beadbi* and the killing of two young men.

To me it seemed odd that a religious community that considers the *shabd* as its Guru should get riled up over the sacrilege of the external, physical manifestation of the *shabd*—a text, the Guru Granth Sahib. Yet, to believe that the religious community should let sacrilege pass is also an error. For the text, the Guru Granth Sahib, embodies the reverence and faith the people place in the symbol.

The monotheistic Sikh religion, founded by the iconoclast Guru Nanak, shuns blind rituals and idolatry and propagates equality among all people irrespective of class, caste, gender and other differences. While its central idea is to stand against injustice, its stated goal is *sarbat da bhalla* (the welfare of the entire world). The core message of the religion is aural: *Ek Onkar, Sat Nam* (There is one God, thy name is Truth). The conception of God is in the mind, in one's imagination, as *Akal Purakh*—the timeless one. The word *Sikh* comes from *shishya* (learner). Nine Gurus followed Nanak, and the religion is codified around their ideas. The Granth Sahib is a collection of verses by the first five Gurus and a number of other saints, both from Panjab as well as other regions. It has been set to music as per the classical ragas.

The sixth Guru, Guru Hargobind, bestowed the concept of

*Miri-Piri* upon the Sikhs, the temporal-spiritual struggle, symbolised by the twin dagger that has become a prominent Sikh symbol. Every Sikh is supposed to walk the twin paths of struggle against injustice in their time and seek spiritual elevation. The tenth Guru, Guru Gobind Singh, created the Khalsa, a fighting army, a sub-sect of the Sikhs, which has the nomenclature Singh (lion) for men and Kaur (princess) for women. Since the Khalsa was an army, it had the visible symbols of long hair (*kesh*), a comb (*kanga*), iron bracelet on arm (*kada*), a dagger or sword (*kirpan*) and long shorts (*kacchera*)—a uniform. He decreed that after him, his followers must consider the sacred text Granth Sahib as the eternal living Guru. That is why the Sikhs consider the Granth Sahib as the embodiment of the living Guru—an anthropomorphism. This makes the text both a powerful and a fragile symbol.

Though the religion was against ritualism, in all gurdwaras—the term means the door to the Guru—now the Granth Sahib is roused in the mornings through the ritual of the *Prabhat Pheri*, seated on a high platform, prayers are conducted all day long, and the Granth Sahib is put to sleep at nights through the ritual of the *Sukhasan*. Special prayers are held from time to time: *Sehaj Paath*—easy recitation, *Akhand Paath*—marathon recitation in forty-eight hours, followed by *Ardas*—communal prayers. Inadvertently, this led to the Granth Sahib now being treated as a symbol or icon. No wonder then the commonest phrase I heard those days was: 'Someone has torn the limbs of our Guru', the pages of the text being the *ang* (limbs).

To comprehend the events surrounding the *beadbi*, we need to step back and look at the theme of *dharam da sankat* (crisis of religion) in the history and narrative of the Sikh religion right from its inception. 'Dharam da sankat' is a constant refrain in the Sikh community. But it is unlike the much-touted present-day 'dharam ka sankat' that we hear from Hindutva groups. Hinduism is a widely practised religion in South Asia. About 80 per cent of the Indian population is Hindu.

Still, to deliberately excite and aggravate a polytheistic religious community, Hindutva forces remind followers of perceived historical wrongs, mostly from the Mughal period, propagate statistics, proven false by Census reports, on the rise of the Muslim population to convey that Hindus are dwindling in comparison. It serves a political end. Right-wing forces gain electorally. It is not like that for the Sikhs. The Sikhs are a miniscule minority in India. At 2.6 crore, two-thirds of whom live in Panjab, the Sikhs comprise barely 2 per cent of the Indian population. At the same time, in Panjab the Sikhs are in majority at around 56 per cent. The Sikh sentiment that their religion is in danger raises the question if the perceived sense is real or comes from a sense of paranoia. The incidents of *beadbi* demonstrated that the sense was not imaginary. The repeated *beadbi* was one type of *dharam da sankat*. There were others too, not mutually exclusive of each other.

One—in its initial phase, the Sikh religion drew followers who were born Hindu or Muslim and of different castes, from the Panjab region. When they joined the new faith, they brought the cultural practices of their religions and their allegiances to a certain form of God—a certain shrine (*jathera*), a family elder, the clan to which the person belonged, and so on. The need was that the followers of the Sikh religion discard all those allegiances and follow the religion that advocated equality and justice. This had not entirely taken place.

Two, the idea that the Granth Sahib is a guiding force but is not a Guru. Sects and *deras* have come up around one living Guru or another. These Gurus consider themselves as those who can understand and interpret the Granth Sahib to lay people, their followers. The followers are often those who feel slighted by the mainstream Sikh religion mostly over issues of inequality.

Three, from those in the Hindu religion who continued to deny the Sikhs an independent identity and considered the Sikh religion as part of the larger Hindu religion and the sword arm of the society. This argument seeks to appropriate the Sikh religion.

Let us take a closer look at the reasons listed above. For a society besieged by social differences of religion and gender, the inception of the Sikh religion and the idea of being a Sikh was radical. The Central Asian invader and founder of the Mughal dynasty, Babur, plundered Panjab in Guru Nanak's lifetime. As the Sikh religion coalesced, Mughal rule firmed up in Delhi and eventually grew to become a powerful empire. Two Sikh Gurus—Guru Arjan and Guru Tegh Bahadur—were executed on orders from the Mughals. These executions created a narrative of extreme oppression, and Sikh history is full of legends of great heroism. Here are a few incidents of assault on the Darbar Sahib just after the period of the Gurus.

In 1737, Zakriya Khan, the governor of Panjab, invaded the Darbar Sahib. He tortured and killed Bhai Mani Singh, scholar, scribe, soldier and the caretaker of Darbar Sahib, and installed the Mughal official Massa Ranghar. It was less an act of loot, for the Sikhs were not very well-off then, and more an attack on the Sikh power centre. Massa Ranghar desecrated the gurdwara and the *sarovar* (the holy pond) by allowing free consumption of alcohol, tobacco and drugs in the sacred space and converted the shrine into a brothel. Two Sikhs, Bhai Sukha Singh and Bhai Mehtab Singh disguised themselves as Muslim tax collectors, arranged a meeting with Massa Ranghar and cut off his head in full view of guards and soldiers. Soon after, Mir Mannu, the general of Lahore, first clashed with the Afghan ruler and invader Ahmed Shah Abdali and later joined him. Mannu was vicious towards the Sikhs and killed thousands. A saying of that time goes:

*Mannu saadi datri, assi Mannu de soye,*
*Jeon Mannu wadh da, asi doon swaaye hoye.*

Mannu is our sickle, we are Mannu's grass,
As he kills us, we return in twice the number.

In October 1757, Ahmed Shah Abdali, on his fourth invasion of Panjab, destroyed the Darbar Sahib and filled the sarovar with debris and animal carcasses. The Sikhs later liberated the sanctum sanctorum under the leadership of Baba Deep Singh. On 5 February 1762, an Afghan army numbering 150,000 soldiers under Abdali fell upon a large gathering of Sikh men, women and children at village Kup Rohira near Malerkotla. They killed over 30,000 Sikhs in the *Vadda Ghallughara* (The Great Holocaust) and once again, Abdali had the Darbar Sahib blown up and the *sarovar* filled with refuse and the entrails of cows and bullocks. In December 1764, Abdali yet again marched on Amritsar and launched a sudden assault on Darbar Sahib with an army of 30,000 men. Facing him was a small contingent of thirty highly committed Sikhs under the leadership of Baba Gurbaksh Singh. The Sikhs shocked the Afghans with their bravery and inflicted heavy losses on the enemy. Abdali once again blew up the Darbar Sahib. Abdali's invasions were so brutal that a saying became popular:

*Khaada peeta lahe da, baki Ahmed Shahe da.*

All you have is what you consume, Ahmed Shah loots the rest.

The values of pragmatism and fatalism ascribed to Sikhs as character traits have roots in this bloody history and legacy. Under Maharaja Ranjit Singh (ruled from 1801—1839) and later, until Operation Blue Star, the Darbar Sahib remained untouched.

The contest over the Guru remains central to the Sikh religion and the various sects that have sprung from it. It started early, just after the first Guru, Nanak. When Guru Nanak appointed his successor Guru Angad from a Hindu Khatri family as the second Guru, his own son, Sri Chand, felt slighted at being ignored. Sri Chand broke away from the mainline Sikh religion to form a sect that came to be known as the Udasis. Even as Guru Angad collected Guru Nanak's verses and propagated them, Sri Chand spread Guru Nanak's ideas far and wide through his followers. The Udasis remained in close contact with later Sikh Gurus, playing a key role in rediscovering and identifying places visited by Gurus, participating in battles along with Guru Gobind Singh and being custodians of Sikh places of worship in Anandpur Sahib and Nanded. They established centres of learning such as the Brahm Buta Akhara, next to the Darbar Sahib, and dug the canal that brings water to the *sarovar* at the Darbar Sahib. Yet, the core difference between Sikhs and Udasis remained: Sikhism as a pragmatic religion based on equality and justice did not believe in renunciation as a stage of life, while many Udasis were ascetics, even celibates.

The idea of the Granth Sahib as the Guru was also challenged soon after Guru Gobind Singh by the very person sent by the Guru to defeat the oppressors in Panjab: Banda Bahadur. After he overthrew the Mughals, he sought to declare himself in the lineage of Guru Gobind Singh. A group of Sikhs, the Tat Khalsa, the pure ones, opposed Banda Bahadur's move. The split in Banda Bahadur's army as a result of being besieged by Mughal forces in the Lohgarh fort near Gurdaspur resulted in the Sikh forces weakening and Banda Bahadur being captured and eventually, put to death.

In the second half of the nineteenth century, by the time the British took over Maharaja Ranjit Singh's kingdom, there were even more sects: Nirmalas who traced their origins to the five scholars Guru Gobind Singh had sent to Benares to learn and study the classics in Sanskrit; Namdharis, a sect founded in the mid-nineteenth century by Baba Ram Singh who believed in himself as a living Guru and the Nirankaris, another nineteenth-century movement founded by Baba Dyal Singh.

At this time the Tat Khalsa re-emerged. This was necessitated by two major factors. One was the British taking complete control of Panjab, laying down train tracks, building canals, creating canal colonies, relocating populations, appointing officers and administrators right up to the border with Russia, and trying to evangelise Panjab by opening schools and setting up churches. While many of these moves were to consolidate the land and develop the land of the five rivers as a food-growing region to serve the Empire, the British assault on the region's education was deliberate. Per historians, the education level in Panjab under the Lahore Durbar ruled by Maharaja Ranjit Singh was far more advanced than that of Britain or Europe at that time.[23] Many women in Panjab were literate and the education system was organised through schools attached to religious institutions. *Tehsildars* (land revenue officials) were the custodians of the *Qaida*— the language primer.

After the events of 1857, the British searched every home in Panjab to seize the primers and burnt them in big bonfires. In the 1850s, there were 300,000 registered students. The numbers fell steeply in the next few decades. The Hindus, the Muslims and the Sikhs eventually rose up to the British design. The Hindus started the Dayanand Anglo-Vedic schools and colleges, the Sikhs started the Khalsa Missionary schools and colleges, the Muslims, many of them followers of a sect called the Ahmadiyyas based at Qadian, also started their own schools and colleges.

However, the British understood the value of faith in religion. While engaging with Panjab—having burnt their fingers with the infamous pork-cow fat issue that had led to the Sepoy Mutiny in 1857, the British maintained a core principle: do not force the Panjabis (including Hindus and Muslims) into a template. The British, who recruited Sikhs into the army in large numbers asked them to fight in the name of the eternal living Guru—the Granth Sahib—and nourished the faith by allowing Sikhs to set up temporary gurdwaras and observe the birthdays of Sikh Gurus. It was common to see the Granth Sahib being carried before a marching Sikh battalion to the front lines of battles. They also encouraged the use of Sikh weaponry—kirpans, quoits and sabres—along with gunpowder, guns and cannons.

Those who frown upon the role of religion in social life may call it indoctrination, but the tactic worked for the British and was first used to extend imperialism in Africa and the Middle East and later in the two World Wars to free Europe from the Axis powers. In the two World Wars, about a quarter of the British Indian Army, about 300,000 soldiers, were Sikhs. 83,005 Sikhs were killed and 109,045 wounded. Sikhs participated in campaigns in China, Afghanistan, Iran, Iraq, Palestine, Turkey, Malaysia, Singapore, East Africa, Eritrea, Ethiopia, Italy, Belgium and France. They were labelled a 'martial race' along with the Gurkhas and Kodavas.

In the 1870s, a Gujarati, Dayanand Saraswati, a Hindu leader, as alien to Panjab as the British, came to Panjab. Dayanand Saraswati had, through his studies and journeys, come to believe in the futility of the ritualism of Hindu practices and idolatry and begun to lean towards the ancient Vedas as the true fount of knowledge. He established the Arya Samaj (the noble society), a Hindu reform movement that promoted values and practices based on the infallible authority of the Vedas. Arya Samajis believe in one God and reject the ritual worship of idols. When Dayanand Saraswati reached Panjab, he learnt of Guru Nanak and his teachings, which were on similar lines as far as idolatry and ritualism were concerned. Guru Nanak had moved beyond the Vedas and borrowed ideas even from Islam to propose the idea of one God and create a syncretic faith. Dayanand Saraswati viewed Guru Nanak's influence as a matter of losing Hindu followers to Sikhism. This insecurity prompted Dayanand Saraswati to unflatteringly and disparagingly criticise Guru Nanak in his work, *Satyarth Prakash*.

In order to appropriate the Sikhs or not let them go out of the fold of the Hindu religion and establish their independence, the Arya

Samaj began calling the Sikhs the sword arm of the Hindu religion—the militant ideal of the Hindu. The ploy was simple: assimilate those who seek to define themselves as an independent identity and take over their discourse. This is how the discourse that Sikhs were created to save Hindus from Muslims began to gain currency. It is a completely false idea because historically, none of the Gurus nor any of the later Sikh leaders conceived of the Sikhs as the saviour of Hindus alone.

In time, this view of Sikhs as the sword-arm was appropriated by right-wing groups and is now a popular notion among Hindutva forces. This idea that Sikhs are the protectors of Hindus is similar to the appropriation of Bhagat Singh and Banda Bahadur by Hindutva groups and the Akalis. The Arya Samaj spawned the Jan Sangh, the forerunner of the current-day BJP. The Sikhs were the earliest community the right wing attempted to appropriate and it is now a battle that is a century and a half old.

Very early in this battle, in the late 1870s, with the formation of the Tat Khalsa and the Singh Sabhas, the Sikhs sought to define themselves as an independent religion, distinct from Hinduism, with independent customs and traditions and a history dating back to the fifteenth century. In 1898, the lexicographer Kahn Singh Nabha wrote his book *Hum Hindu Nahin* (We Are Not Hindus). Nabha attempted to formalise the Sikh identity: not cutting body hair, shunning halal meat and use of tobacco, believing in the Granth Sahib and the ten Gurus, and having no other religion. The Tat Khalsa adopted this as the religious boundary.

An important reason to draw the boundary was that at the turn of the twentieth century, the traditional caretakers of gurdwaras, the Mahants, started playing a mischievous role. The Mahants placed idols in many gurdwaras, especially the Darbar Sahib. The loyalty and interests of the Mahants were in serving the colonial masters and appealing to Hindu religious sentiments, rather than to uphold Sikh traditions. A gurdwara, like any other place of worship in another religion, is not only the repository of the community's faith but also garners donations and is a keeper of the community's monies. Controlling a gurdwara and its finance is to control the community in the name of faith.

When the Jallianwala Bagh massacre took place in 1919, the Mahant of the Darbar Sahib honoured Brigadier-General Dyer, the perpetrator of the massacre. The gesture was widely seen as provocative. The Sikhs rallied together under the banner of Akali Dal and launched a movement in the 1920s to liberate the gurdwaras from the British-appointed Mahants. It was a peaceful, non-violent struggle in which more than 40,000 Akalis were arrested and more than 7,000 slain. The huge success in the multiple Gurdwara Movements at Jaito, Nanaksar and the Darbar Sahib led to the Sikh Gurdwaras Act of 1925, and the creation of the SGPC.

The national leadership had keenly watched the Gurdwara Movement, and upon the success of the movement, Mahatma Gandhi telegraphed Baba Kharak Singh, the Akali Dal leader, 'First decisive victory of the forces of nationalism.' Jawaharlal Nehru too wrote a letter in which he stated, '... The Sikhs are the finest soldiers of the nation. I earnestly hope I shall prove worthy of their high tradition and fine courage blended with compassion.'

While Sikh participation in the national struggle in the next three decades was deep and abiding, the identity of Sikhs is not independent in the Indian Constitution.[24] Article 25 that provides for 'freedom of conscience and free profession, practice and propagation of religion', mentions in Explanation 2 under Section B: 'Reference to Hindus shall be construed as including a reference to persons professing the Sikh, Jaina or Buddhist religion'. This posits the Sikh religion as part of the Hindu religion and not as an independent religion with personal, property and marriage laws like Islam or Christianity.[25] It also became the reason to rally against the laws, like by then Panjab

CM Parkash Singh Badal who burnt the Constitution in front of Parliament House on 27 February 1984, a few months before Operation Blue Star.

However, the drawing of any boundary cuts both ways. The Gurdwara Act of 1925 led to Udasis and Nirmalas stopping the display of the Guru Granth Sahib in their Deras and premises. Increasingly, the Nirmalas, the Udasis and the Namdharis found themselves out of the Sikh fold. Ironically, Bhai Kahn Singh Nabha, the man who had codified Sikh identity, was himself a Nirmala Sikh. This resulted in the mainstream Sikh religion becoming a smaller, albeit purer one, by some arguments, than what it could have been if the sects had been included. But the consequence was also an exclusive Sikh religion bereft of the inclusiveness that had marked the religion's beginning when Guru Nanak emerged from meditation and pronounced: *Na Koi Hindu, Na Musalmaan* (There is no Hindu or Muslim). Guru Nanak's message was that all of us are one as human beings.

Guru Gobind Singh, on the other hand, in response to his circumstances, established a fighting army, well-marked by symbols. Drawing the line turned the Sikh narrative from an inclusive one in the time of Guru Nanak to an exclusive one with the supposed approval of Guru Gobind Singh. The boundary shrunk the immense spectrum of Sikh thought contained in the Granth Sahib and tilted towards a narrower vision.

In current times, the recent controversy over the depiction of Guru Nanak as an animated moving character in the film *Nanak Shah Fakir* has brought out all the nuances of this line of thinking. The SGPC sought to prohibit a moving visual representation of the Guru and consequently, the film did not show in Panjab, though it showed in the rest of India and abroad.

Today, quotes from the Granth Sahib adorn the walls of schools and colleges, calendars, are a part of mobile messages and posts on social media, and are, of course, quoted ad libitum. Where, then, is one to draw the boundary on purity of the text and its desecration? What if the paint on a wall which contains a quote peels off and a couple of words go missing? What if a calendar on which quotes are printed becomes dated and its pages used for purposes other than what was originally intended? Would that still be desecration? The real question is: doesn't the fulfilment of any Granth (text) finally lie in the meaning it creates and the message it delivers? The core idea, the return to the *shabd*—the word and its meaning—is lost. If all Sikhs were to follow the Granth Sahib and live by its tenets, we would actuate a wider sphere of influence than by prioritising symbols alone.

The question then is, how to understand and follow what has been written? For that, just like Hindus, the Sikhs too have their own *pracharaks*, *jathedars* and *sants* who compete with each other on who is the purest of all. The need to look up to an elder, to seek guidance, to be able to believe in a leader is part of Panjab's social psychology.

The unintended consequence of prioritising symbols is that they make the community vulnerable. That is why the 183-plus desecrations and sacrileges of the Granth Sahib, the Gutka Sahib (an abridged version of the Granth Sahib), gurdwaras, the Holy Quran, the Bhagavad Gita and the Ramayana in October-November 2015 showed that they were deliberate and pre-planned.

The instances of *beadbi* began on the morning the farmers and labour unions were to meet the chief minister over compensation for the whitefly epidemic. This raises the obvious question: was the religious issue a well-planned distraction from the *rail-roko* and the economic crisis? *Beadbi* had ruptured old scars and raised questions on the role of the representatives of the Sikh religion, the Akalis.

Unable to leave Chandigarh during the Bargari sacrilege incidents and thereafter, I met with my friend, film-maker, journalist and translator,

Daljit. Besides being a journalist and making documentaries, Daljit works with the Panjab Digital Library that has over the past decade digitised more than a billion pages of text. By doing so they have brought technology to bear on a riddle set by Guru Gobind Singh when he declared the Granth Sahib as the future Guru.

Since the Sikhs believe the Granth Sahib is a living Guru and have ascribed rituals of the living to the text, they also believe that after a certain age, every text should be consigned to flames, like human beings are, upon death. The Sikhs cremate their texts at two prominent gurdwaras—both named Angeetha Sahib—located in Ludhiana and Dehradun. By doing so, the community loses the cultural reference of the text—the calligraphy, the physical, tangible beauty and markers of history. Digitising the texts has preserved their legacy, though the physical remnants are destroyed. It was, to me, an exquisite effort at record-keeping, documentation and creating historical records.

Daljit informed me, 'A Sarbat Khalsa has been called. It hasn't happened since 1986.'

In 1986, after Operation Blue Star, there were two Sarbat Khalsas: one when the community decided to raze the Akal Takht built by the government and build a new one through kar sewa (voluntary service), and another in which Khalistan was formally declared. After Operation Blue Star, the central government, through the then Sikh minister Buta Singh, had enrolled the Nihang Singh leader Santa Singh to rebuild the Akal Takht.

Traditionally, Nihangs are considered soldiers of Guru Gobind Singh. Over the last three hundred years they have freely maintained the form of the Guru's army and practised a nomadic lifestyle on horses, spreading the word of the Sikh religion. Now they were roped in for a state agenda which did not go well with the community sentiment. The reason to raze and rebuild the Akal Takht was that the Sikhs, angry and hurt by the government, did not want its highest temporal seat, the Akal Takht, rebuilt by those who had destroyed it. The Sikhs saw the government-sponsored Akal Takht as a shoddy attempt to placate the community while not addressing why they had razed it during Operation Blue Star.

Daljit added, 'The decision on Khalistan was taken in a second Sarbat Khalsa, on 29 April. Ours is such a short history but we have forgotten to plot a timeline.'

'Who has given the call this time?' I asked. 'Who can claim to represent the Sikhs?'

'It isn't clear yet. Many factions of Sikhs are calling for it.'

When Guru Gobind Singh ascended the Guruship, he began a system called the Sarbat Khalsa which provided for a set of checks and balances on decisions taken by its leaders. It is a system of direct democracy started decades before the modern concept of democracy evolved after the French Revolution. Per the Sikh system, the gathering of Sikhs elects five members, *Panj Pyara* (the chosen ones), who take their seat in the presence of the Granth Sahib. People raise issues on which the *Panj Pyara* deliberate openly and reach conclusions. When a set of conclusions are reached, they are approved and adopted as the *Gurmata* (resolution in the name of the Guru).

According to accounts of travellers[26] in the post-Guru period, Sikhs gathered twice a year, on the occasions of Baisakhi and Diwali, at the Akal Takht to take stock of the political situation, to devise ways and means to meet common dangers, to choose men to lead them in battle, and so on.[27]

In an attempt to allow his progeny to succeed to the throne unhindered, Maharaja Ranjit Singh ended the practice of the Sarbat Khalsa. After the Gurdwara Reform movement that led to the Gurdwara Act in 1925, the SGPC came to be considered the voice of the Sikhs and the Sarbat Khalsa was put on hold. The events of 1984 changed that. Neither the SGPC nor the Akalis managed to prevent Operation Blue Star. In January 1986, the All India Sikh Students

Federation (AISSF) called for a Sarbat Khalsa to reject the government-built Akal Takht. Emboldened by the support of the community, in a second Sarbat Khalsa, held a few months later, the Panthic Committee appointed by the AISSF declared the formation of Khalistan—a term which has been invoked in Panjab politics time and again over the past few decades.

The reality of Panjab was that in spite of the hundreds of incidents of sacrilege, Panjab's Hindus and Sikhs as well as its tiny Muslim and Christian communities had remained peaceful. It is a lived reality but does not make for news because it defies the 'othering' that is highlighted about Panjab.

The fact is that both realities co-exist in Panjab; the gurdwara-going Sikhs also tie red threads on their wrists from a dargah; the Hindus go to gurdwaras; pictures in shops and both Hindu and Sikh homes display both Gurus and Hindu Gods; there have never been large-scale communal riots in the state in the last seventy years, since Partition; yet in theory and in action too, identity politics has played a big part in Panjab's landscape, during Partition and the Khalistan movement, but has not percolated to the level of mutual animosity. Despite all the churning of history, this remains the eclectic nature of Panjab.

On 25 October 2015, an *akhand paath* was organised to honour the two martyrs of the police firing at village Bargari. That day saw a huge crowd gather under the leadership of Baljit Singh Daduwal who heads the group, Panthic Sewa Leher. Sikh missionary leaders,

and members of other factions which are considered radical groups because they continue to harbour a tilt towards the idea of Khalistan, attended the meeting in the ground between the two village schools. The speakers spoke about misgovernance, corruption, sacrilege and political intervention in religious institutions. A day before the sacrilege, Narendra Modi had described Parkash Singh Badal as the Nelson Mandela of India, owing to his terms of imprisonment for various political reasons. Modi's remarks had initiated a series of advertisements from Akali leaders in print and online media, congratulating Badal. The meeting at Bargari lampooned the idea and instead compared Badal with Babur, Ahmed Shah Abdali and Mir Mannu. Speakers raised the demand for an inquiry into the instances of sacrilege, the arrest of the culprits, the filing of cases against police officials, and the withdrawal of cases against the implicated Sikh youth.

The dominant sentiment was that the *Granth* (text) and the *Panth* (the Sikh community) were not safe in Hindu India and hence the need for Khalistan. Bhindranwale's statement before Operation Blue Star, 'The day the Indian Army steps into Darbar Sahib the foundation of Khalistan will be laid,' was used to imply that he had laid the foundation and it was now time to build the roof of Khalistan. Opposition Congress leaders, fishing for opportunity, were on stage while these announcements were being made. The AAP also sent its representative, Sangrur MP Bhagwant Mann. Someone claimed to have smelt liquor on his breath and he was consequently shooed away. People were split over whether or not he was drunk and if he had insulted the ceremony. The ayes and nays once again distracted from the main purpose of the ceremony.

Daduwal read out an eight-point agenda. He called for a Sarbat Khalsa and a Black Diwali. Traditionally, Diwali is celebrated with great pomp and gaiety, especially at the Darbar Sahib. Guru Amar Das, the third Guru, had accepted the festival as part of the Sikh calendar.

Later, the festival had been associated with Bandi Chhor Diwas (Free Prisoners Day) because the sixth Guru, Guru Hargobind, was released from Gwalior Fort where the Mughal emperor Jehangir had imprisoned him.

The upcoming Sarbat Khalsa was a pointer to the lack of faith people had in the Akali government. It also perhaps signalled a rejection of the system of the modern state which has emasculated the community's idea of justice from the just use of the sword to an ink mark on the finger and ballot paper—electoral democracy. It was a loud message and both the Akalis and the Centre panicked.

Under pressure from the government and for reasons of mutual incompatibility, as Sikh organisations joined and left the parleys prior to the Sarbat Khalsa, two factions—the Shiromani Akali Dal (Amritsar) led by Simranjit Singh Mann and the United Akali Dal led by Mohkam Singh—remained in the fray.[28] The Panjab government cited various reasons to render the Sarbat Khalsa illegitimate: not been convened through the Akal Takht, not being held at the Akal Takht, and that it did not have approval of the *Panj Pyara*. The reasons did not hold water because the Akali-controlled SGPC runs the Akal Takht and the SGPC would not have given permission for such a gathering. The government's final ploy was to remind the public that the organisers were radical Sikhs—hardliners who supported Khalistan.

On 10 November, the day of the Sarbat Khalsa, at village Chabba, near Tarn Taran, Amritsar, the crowds were overwhelming. Since the police had been stopping private vehicles and buses, attendees had walked many kilometres and reached the site the night before. The site is of historical importance: Guru Hargobind fought one of the

battles for Amritsar against the Mughal troops at this place where there is now a historical shrine called Gurdwara Sangrana Sahib run under the auspices of the SGPC. The reason the organisers chose the spot was the presence of Nihangs at Gurdwara Naudh Singh on the Tarn Taran road. The Gurdwara Naudh Singh is named after the *meet-jathedar* (administrative head) of the legendary Sikh leader Baba Deep Singh who had liberated the Darbar Sahib three centuries ago.

The crowds had turned out in saffron and black turbans. The women were proportionally lesser than at the farmer and worker rallies. Images of Bhindranwale, Major General Shabeg Singh who fortified the Darbar Sahib, Amrik Singh, the former president of the AISSF who had been killed during Operation Blue Star and others appeared on the gates to the venue and on the boards and walls of the tent for the Sarbat Khalsa. Representatives from around a hundred Sikh organisations, many from around the world, spoke on the stage. Yet, given the traditionally patriarchal and feudal nature of the Sikh society, only one woman, also belonging to a Sikh right-wing outfit, addressed the congregation.

The discourse was largely repetitive: how the current political powers had laid waste the community, the state, and had hijacked Sikh institutions. Speakers emphasised the idea of sacrifice that underlined Panjab's narrative. Occasionally, references to Bhindranwale, to Khalistan, and to the 1984 pogrom came up. These are now an inalienable part of Panjab's bruised experience and always elicit emotional responses. The call of the organisers was: liberate the Sikh religion, its institutions and its ethos from the hands of its current guardians.

At the end of the meeting, while Simranjit Singh Mann, the chief organiser, absented himself citing health reasons, the other organisers read out a set of resolutions (*Gurmata*). No discussions transpired or were even initiated. No views were sought. Once passed with *jaikaras*—chants or calls—of '*Jo bole so nihal, sat sri akal*' (blessed are those who say god is supreme), from the entire congregation, the *Gurmata* becomes binding on the entire Sikh community. The call is common to Sikh gatherings and is used to express a wide variety of public emotions. The organisers used it to garner assent of the Khalsa: once the *jaikara* is made, no dissent and no alternative point of view is admissible. The deliberations were private and behind the scenes.

The resolution dismissed the current *jathedar* of the Akal Takht—high priest—and nominated Jagtar Singh Hawara as the *jathedar*. Hawara is currently lodged in Tihar Jail, Delhi, because he is one of the accused in the assassination of former Panjab Chief Minister Beant Singh in 1995. The organisers had played an old trick. By nominating Hawara as *jathedar* of the Akal Takht—like in the case of Ranjit Singh in the late 1990s (as discussed earlier in this chapter)—the organisers were again trying to undermine the law in the name of religion. The organisers revoked the awards to Parkash Singh Badal, and also sought to constitute a global Sikh parliament, seek Vatican-like status for Amritsar, and added, almost as an afterthought, a call for an end to segregation at gurdwaras and cremation grounds on the basis of caste.

The last point is significant because it shows another double bind in which the Sikh religion is caught today. Even as its institutions have been hijacked by the Akalis, caste discrimination within has torn the community apart. Panjab has the highest percentage of Dalits, at 31.9 per cent per the 2011 Census. The prevalence of caste should have prompted genuine concern from the organisers. But that was not the case with the Sarbat Khalsa. The next day, the Darbar Sahib did not celebrate Diwali. As demanded, it was a Black Diwali.

The day after, the Badal government moved in to arrest the organisers of the meet on charges based on the British-era sedition law. The charge was false and misplaced because the agenda of the meet was the Sikh community and its issues. While Khalistan was mentioned and human rights discussed, the Sarbat Khalsa did not make any anti-India statements. When the major leaders were arrested, the support of the lakhs of people who had assembled for the Sarbat Khalsa evaporated. People seemed to have sensed that like political parties took their votes and did what they wanted post elections, the organisers of the Sarbat Khalsa too had taken their assent to do what they wanted, without actually bothering to consult the community. At present the Sikh community has two sets of *jathedars* at the three important shrines located in Panjab—one nominated by the SGPC and the other by the Sarbat Khalsa.[n]

Meanwhile, Hawara was still in jail. While the Sarbat Khalsa raised a larger question of how to reach a consensus in a large gathering, the hasty *Gurmata* of 29 April 1986 and the muddled one of 10 November 2015 compromised the hoary tradition of the Sikh community. The first, by imposing a perennial question mark on the community's loyalty to the nation and providing it no structure, system or state mechanism to actualise Khalistan. The second, by evoking the discontent of the people but proving how splintered the community was and proposing no ways out. All that the disappointments on both sides—electoral democracy that resulted in the Akali government and the hasty Sarbat Khalsa declaration—did was push the people towards *rosh*.

---

n. The Sikh community recognises five Takhts—at Amritsar, Anandpur Sahib and Talwandi Sabo in Panjab, at Nanded in Maharashtra and Patna in Bihar.

*Chapter Four*

# *Rog* — Illness

As I travelled within Panjab in late 2015, I frequently returned to what residents and the local media called the 'City Beautiful'— Chandigarh. The city was built as a replacement for Lahore, the capital of greater Panjab, lost in the Partition. The brutal modernist red and grey square city was designed by Swiss-Frenchman Le Corbusier in the shape of a human body with its head being the Capitol Complex—housing the Vidhan Sabha, the high court and the secretariat. The complex also features the city's symbol, an open hand which per Le Corbusier stands for 'Peace and Reconciliation. Open to give and open to receive.'

Chandigarh's shoulders are the homes of top politicians and bureaucrats. The Jan Marg is its central spinal cord. Sector 17 has the shopping arcade and bus station which is its heart. The industrial area and Panjab University are its two arms. Each sector in Chandigarh is 1.2 kilometres long and wide-fitting on a grid that contains uniform housing and many gardens, theatres and museums.

The relics in the Government Museum and Art Gallery, Sector 10C, trace the city's lineage back to the Indus Valley Civilisation. Yet, through its architecture and style, it now stands alienated and disconnected from the history and civilisation of the land around it and is distant from Indian sensibilities. Unlike any Indian city, and

I grew up in another modern city planned by Germans when they built the steel plant in Rourkela, Chandigarh is completely bereft of local landmarks that define addresses to us Indians—for instance, the blue temple at the corner, opposite the old dharamshala, next to the tin market.

Its wide, long roads offer no shortcuts and are clearly meant for cars. Due to lack of public transport, autorickshaws are expensive. It is a city for the rich and affluent. Early mornings, in its many parks, it is common to see smartly dressed men, many of them bureaucrats or baton-wielding retired military officers, their well-set moustaches turned upwards, turbaned, taking their walks with a long leash at the end of which is tied a Pomeranian, a Lhasa Apso or a Maltese, barking away at all and sundry.

As a joint capital of Haryana and Panjab, Chandigarh is a fortress at the edge of the two states, Panjab and Haryana. Instead of moats, it is buffered from the states by satellite towns to which it provides a huge incentive in land prices: from Haryana through Panchkula; from Panjab through Zirakpur, Mohali and Kharar. The state assemblies, the courts, the secretariat and the government offices are shared between the two states. The big hospitals and the local English news media headquarters are also located in Chandigarh. Which is why the bureaucrats often settle here post-retirement, away from the socio-politico-economic morass they helped create in the states they administered, thus keeping the dusty states and their problems at arm's length. Matka Chowk, the traditional protest space, is now no longer available, through government orders, and the new venue for protests is near the cremation ground in Sector 25 on the outskirts of the city. I was safe in Chandigarh, but to me the City Beautiful was an open prison, disconnected from Panjab.

I find Chandigarh's motto—'peace and reconciliation, openness to give and receive'—ironical at two levels.

One, when it was being built, Chandigarh was supposed to be the capital of Panjab, but for the last five decades, it remains the contested capital of both Panjab and Haryana. In 1966, Panjab was reorganised and Hindi-speaking Haryana was carved out. In 1969, a senior Akali leader, active in the Gurdwara Movement, a freedom fighter and Panjabi Suba activist, Darshan Singh Pheruman, fasted unto death demanding Chandigarh for Panjab, but the Centre did not budge on fulfilling its own promise.

Within a year of Operation Blue Star, the new prime minister of India, Rajiv Gandhi, signed the Panjab Accord with the Akali Dal leader Harchand Singh Longowal. The Accord promised to look into long-standing issues like the inclusion of Panjabi-speaking areas of neighbouring states, the transfer of Chandigarh as a capital to Panjab, the SYL canal, and so on. The Accord did not go down well with the Sikhs who were aghast at Longowal signing away more river waters to Haryana, and questioned his authority to sign the Accord as he was not an elected representative. Longowal was subsequently assassinated, the SYL was stalled and has been for forty years, and the Accord was not implemented.

Now, half a century later, Chandigarh has changed even further from what it was when it was established. Above 73 per cent of the city's mother tongue is Hindi while Panjabi is the mother tongue of 22 per cent.[29] Per the 2011 Census, in 2001, Hinduism was the religion of 78 per cent of the people and in 2011 it moved up to 80 per cent. Sikhism decreased from 16 per cent to a distant second at 13 per cent.[30] Most of its settled population have grown up in the city and are distant from Panjab.

Panjab remains obsessed with Chandigarh but Chandigarh's people neither linguistically, nor demographically, and not even emotionally want to be a part of Panjab. This is how a post-Independence India's historical connection and a Panjab trying to lift itself up post-Partition's dream have soured because there is estrangement on the ground. The issue has been pending for half a century with no solution in sight, adding to Panjab's disenchantment with the Indian state.

Secondly, while the states squabble over ownership of Chandigarh, we need to remember that the city was built by razing twenty-nine villages. They never found reconciliation with the new brick-and-mortar city. They lost their homes and then got lost labouring to build the city.

Now, the city has yet another set of people—migrants to the city, many of whom were born in Bihar and Uttar Pradesh. Many of them are second-generation migrants whose families have been in the city for close to three or four decades. Many of these migrants work as drivers, house help, construction and factory workers and are located in eleven slums which are often relocated, as the city advances, squeezed between its sectors, between its satellite towns, and hostage to a bewildering variety of building rules and regulations, which are strictly implemented when compared to many Indian cities. Every few years, these slum dwellers lose their homes, have to get new identity papers, find schools for their children and look for work.

The pattern of inner migration is clear: as the city advances, the slum colonies move where new construction is taking place, new apartment complexes are being built, in a clockwise movement from the industrial area, to the south of the city, and most recently, to the lands acquired from Panjab's farmers for New Chandigarh on the west. These slum demolitions continue to take place despite inhabitants having all papers—ration cards, voter identity cards, even passports. The brutal bulldozers break the promises made by politicians and leave the inhabitants bereft of home, papers and livelihoods. Many people just disappear. The 'City Beautiful' is blind to the sufferings of those who maintain the beauty. I wonder how Chandigarh will resolve even its brief history or if it will remain in denial of its very motto.

After the Black Diwali of 2015, during the course of my travels, I saw that many villages in upper Malwa had put up boards at the entrance of their villages proclaiming, 'Neither Akali, nor Congress, not even AAP leaders are allowed entry to the village.'

I wondered what Panjab would do now. The people's stance defied the very basis of the society we now inhabit—electoral politics.

In Bathinda, I met a young but seasoned lawyer who often took up people's issues. We spoke about what happens to democracy when people are not interested in any political party.

'What are people saying?' I asked.

'Exactly what they are saying,' he replied. 'Why can't we take them at face value?'

'Because the implication is unsettling.'

'People are saying they have seen through the greedy politicians and cannot choose them to be their representatives.'

'Yes, but how can that be possible?'

'Point is: it is possible. You have been travelling, you have seen the disenchantment.'

'But, how will we organise the state without elections? Without political parties?'

'That is for the state to decide.'

'But the state is the people!'

'Is it? Then ask why the people are unhappy. They obviously do not trust the parties.'

'Well … so, will it be NOTA (none of the above)?'

'What is the point of a vote if it won't change anything?'

'It will send out a message. Say if 5 per cent is NOTA.'

'Who will hear the message? Act on it? The people or the political parties?' He was dismissive about NOTA.

The NOTA option in elections came into effect in 2013 through a Supreme Court ruling. It was on the basis of an Election Commission request which was opposed by the ruling UPA government. Finally, a non-governmental organisation, People's Union for Civil Liberties (PUCL), filed a public-interest litigation and the Court decided in favour of NOTA.

I tried to remind the lawyer, 'In the 2012 elections, the Congress in Panjab lost by a 1.5 per cent vote margin. Are we sure even 1.5 per cent or so of the people would not have voted NOTA? You see, it could have been a crisis.'

'Do you think the politicians are really interested in people?'

'But something has got to give! If there is a significant percentage of NOTA votes, it will be a crisis.'

'Isn't what is going on a crisis—the strike, Sarbat Khalsa? It is always the powers that decide what is a crisis and what is not.'

The logic was simple but it opened my eyes to the idea of who determined what was a crisis.

'In 1992, Panjab held elections to prove democracy worked and that militants were no longer strong. The Akali Dal boycotted them. Still, with only one main party and some independents, the elections were held. A government was formed. The turnout was 23 per cent, officially. In reality, it was even lower. The central government did not want to acknowledge the reasons for the low turnout. The Congress was contesting and winning and that is what the Centre wanted. They got what they wanted.'

I tried to dig deeper. 'Would you say that the crisis we see now, the disquiet in Panjab in spite of the guns going silent, is a legacy of this truncated vote?'

'Not only that vote, but also the attitude—the Band-Aid fixes by the state without investigating the reasons for the systemic collapse.'

'Then?'

'Frankly, I do not know. As of now, NOTA is like a steam valve of the pressure cooker that our society has become. It has no other function unless a government arms it. Say, if NOTA is higher than the difference between the number of votes two candidates receive, there will be a re-election. But as long as the "First Past The Post" (FPTP) is how we form governments, NOTA is of no use.'

The reference was to the BJP which had formed a government in 2014 with 31 per cent of the vote, but a historic majority in the Lok Sabha. These days the talk of FPTP has gained currency in the country but the electoral system needs even greater reforms which no party in power would be willing to usher in.

'Isn't even AAP an option?' I asked because in spite of the village boards I could sense a tilt towards a third party in the state which was used to being abused by both major parties—the Akalis and the Congress.

'They lost the people's faith when the Prashant Bhushan and Yogendra Yadav fiasco took place. Now they have suspended two out of their four MPs.'[o]

'Then?'

'I would suggest boycott. The state is very clever. It is devious. It knows how to perpetuate itself and is not interested in people or their issues. That is what electoral democracy has come to now.'

I was trying to wrap my head around the lawyer's suggestion to boycott elections. I was also conscious of something deeper: my own armchair thinking. How easily, benefitting from the systems the state had created—markets, jobs, urban life, police, delivery systems, and so on—I had taken many of the systems for granted. Yet, at the base of all this lay agriculture, food, land and farmers and farm workers. The farmers and farm workers were unhappy with the political system. Yet, I, hiding behind the system, wanted them to maintain the status quo. How easily I had clung to the idea of NOTA. I saw how NOTA was a tool to release angst and to save the system that exploited the very people who ought to benefit from it. In fact, it often helped a candidate or a party.

---

o. Dr Dharmavir Gandhi and Harinder Khalsa had been suspended. Their two other MPs, Bhagwant Mann and Prof. Sadhu Singh, were with the party.

He continued, 'See, we know our work. It is to fight people's cases. We never tell people where to vote. It is their choice. But unless the people change the system and decide who comes into power, these neo-liberal policies will continue. The only solution is to bring down the structure of governance. Then build anew.'

'A revolution? But that is not possible. This is a big country. Say if 10 per cent people vote NOTA, it will send an important message.'

'What will the message do? Do you think any politician will give up their position to listen to the people's voice? There will still be a government. The rule should be—if, say, above 5 per cent people vote NOTA, no government will be formed. But that is not the rule. The only way for people is to challenge the government. The strike paralysed them. The sacrilege protests harassed them. We will harass them in the courts.'

'But even the revolution failed—the Khalistan movement. The state crushed it.'

'What did that movement propose? It did no groundwork and had no alternative system in place. It identified enemies per its ideology and had a list of grievances. Instead of fighting with the government, they were killing our own. That is not a revolution.'

I stayed quiet, listening.

'The issue is not the government per se. The issue is the policies. The neo-liberal policies do not have a solution for the agrarian crises. Neo-liberalism has not even considered agriculture. No one has even read the various committee reports on agriculture, forget about implementing them.'

'What you say is similar to what farmer and labour leaders said a few weeks ago.'

'Yes, that is our understanding from the ground. We face issues, we know what is going wrong. Not only in agriculture, even in education and healthcare. The state is withdrawing, without creating a regulation mechanism on how private parties will enter the space.

That has created the chaos. Instead of people, the politicians have taken over the discourse in the state.'

He paused and then said, 'But the discourse needs to shift to the people. The fire in people's bellies will keep the powers on their toes.'

Given the unpredictability of inter-city bus service and how gentrified travel had become in the state—unreliable buses and dependency on one's own vehicle—a journalist friend suggested I buy a second-hand car. He offered to take me to the Sunday vehicle bazaar. I did not have enough cash. Another acquaintance offered me the use of a cousin's Mahindra Scorpio, a Sports Utility Vehicle. I was touched, but asked, 'Can I park it in a *vehda* and expect people to talk to me?'

He saw the point. SUVs look good in Jutt landlord *havelis*, not in *vehdas*, not in urban slums and not near temporary hutments. Finally another friend, Jasdeep, whom I consider an excellent resource on Panjab and equally helpful to anyone who is interested on working on any aspect of Panjab, and himself a writer and translator, offered me a choice between his Royal Enfield and a eleven-year-old Maruti Alto. The motorcycle was great. I don't think there is a better vehicle than a Bullet to travel in Panjab. When on it, one feels like there is a horse under one's legs, the sound of the motor pumps up your blood flow and the ease with which it negotiates kutcha roads, fields, mounds and sandy banks is unparalleled. It was perfect, but not for me. The Bullet is also a vehicle of privilege, of entitlement and used mostly by Jutt landlords. It defines a gaze, it signals an attitude, and I did not want that.

I chose Jasdeep's car. The bumbling silver beauty's windshield was cracked. During the course of my travels it would suddenly stop, run out of battery power, get punctured, but somehow pull on.

In the year 2015 alone, Panjab recorded 13,089 protests, the second highest in the country after Tamil Nadu. In the car, over the next year and more, I travelled one hundred and fifty nights covering these protests and the build-up to the state elections in 2017. I would do what Bibiji told me about Dadaji: stop at random villages and ask to be taken in and hosted for a night. In all these nights not a single time did I pay for dinner or stay on even for breakfast the next morning. In any conclusion we may reach about Panjab through this book, let it be underlined that this level of warm hospitality towards a near stranger is also at the core of my experience of Panjab. I have a small test for myself about a place I can call home—if I am stuck on a road at 2 a.m., do I feel safe? In Panjab, I did. Every single night and day.

Given my earlier book on mental illness, I knew a few psychiatrists in Panjab. Early on, I went to meet them and they took me to asylums. As a lifelong caregiver to Mama, I was intimate and familiar with psychiatry wards because I feel safest among those the society keeps in its asylums. The hospitals and rehabilitation centres need to remain unnamed because the government had banned visits to them, and prisons—the two places where inmates reveal themselves without pretence.

*

As I sat with a doctor in his chamber at a psychiatric hospital to learn how he diagnosed patients, I noticed that he initiated the conversation with a standard question that went: 'Do you feel *darr* (fear) or *ghabrahat* (anxiety)?'

I asked him later why he had asked that question, and the doctor remarked that Panjab's people were reticent and they hardly talked about themselves. He couldn't say if this was cultural or behavioural. I knew even from my interactions that, barring some exceptions, the use of language is limited in Panjab and replies are often monosyllabic. The doctor was right, especially in the case of men. 'That is why,' the doctor said, 'an open question like "How are you feeling?" does not manage to elicit much of a response.'

People pretend to be happy even when they are not. People in Panjab choose to appear brave. It's a matter of honour for many, it is also an injunction by religion, the need to remain *chardi kala* (high spirited), and most people pretend rather than confess the reality of their situation. And yet, if they were happy, they wouldn't be in the hospital. By posing a question with two negatives— fear and anxiety—the doctor intended to get the patient to either agree or refute the original premises. That usually got them talking. Fear and anxiety—two sides of a coin. Panjab caught in a double-bind.

The patient was an old man, well in his sixties. He wore a blue Akali turban, was dressed in white kurta-pyjama and his beard was open. He was an *Amritdhari* (one who recommitted to the five Ks of Sikhism). The strap that held his six-inch *kirpan* went across his chest. After consultation for bipolar disorder, the man requested for some *afeem* (opium). 'Why, Babaji? You are *Amritdhari*,' said the doctor.

'I took *Amrit* to stop drinking,' said the old man. 'Haven't touched liquor since.'

'Then why *afeem*?'

'To sleep. I can't sleep.' The man's face is the epitome of innocence.

'*Koi na*. These new medicines will help with sleep. Tell me in three weeks if they don't,' the doctor replied pleasantly.

The man realised his innocence wouldn't work. He got agitated. 'We pay fees to you. You do not give what we ask!'

The doctor replied patiently, 'You are free to go to those who give you *afeem*. You come here to take advice. Please follow the regimen.'

The man realised his strongarm move had not worked and became pliant again. He smiled, wished the doctor Sat Sri Akal and left.

★

I walked into a ward where a young man, A, lay on a bed. About sixteen years old, he had just thrown away the drip administered into his arm. The cannula had ruptured and he was bleeding. Drop by drop, the white bed sheet was turning red. The nurse was trying to calm him and adjust the tubes. When she was leaving the room, I asked her, 'What is wrong with him?' She answered, 'He is not eating.'

The act of eating, and mealtimes, are often a ritual. Society and family often insist we cannot skip that ritual. This is how lifestyle, whether agrarian or industrial, mostly defined in roles people need to fulfil, forces itself upon people caught in their distress about the need to conform.

Later, energised by saline, A tried to sit up in bed but collapsed. I asked A why he did not want to eat. A said, 'The food is poisoned.' By whom? 'My mother.' A's psychosis had led him to mistrust a relationship we take for granted, and disrupt a ritual. It was remarkably similar to many people I had met who believed that Panjab suffered because of a conspiracy by the Centre, by *Dilli*. The reference was always to 'agencies'.

I told A that his mother was not in the hospital. 'She is everywhere,' he replied. 'I trust the doctor, but mother has bribed the nurse.'

Similarly, people also feel the political nurses—Akali and Congress politicians—are hand in glove with the BJP and the Congress central command respectively and that bureaucrats have perfected the art of serving their political masters while the police is power unto itself. But they are looking for doctors, for someone they can trust.

★

B, in his sixties, in white kurta pyjama, his turban well-tied, his beard flowing, held my hand and whispered, 'You look familiar.' I nodded.

It was a common response in psychiatry wards. I wonder if those we call mad can sense a kinship with others who have been close to madness. Was this a subconscious tribal behaviour? Are the mad a tribe, pushed away from civilisation based on reason? I smiled, but did not say anything. B stated, 'I tried to commit suicide ... when I came here I wanted them to kill me.'

I asked him why he wanted to commit suicide. *Karza* (loan) was the reply. A common reason now in Panjab. B wanted to disrupt another ritual: of living. The statistics of farmer and labourer suicide show how common this feeling of nihilism is in Panjab. The loss of hope, of dreams, the claustrophobia brought on by the loans one had taken and the image one had cultivated in society—it was a cocktail of events that pushed one to abdicate one's responsibility to oneself, to one's family and to society.

B took me to his room. The lights were off and we sat on cots across each other. 'I could not sleep,' he said. And now? 'Now I want to go home. I will pray.' B was ready for another ritual. In the darkness, I touched his feet. He patted my head. 'Oh! I forgot to put on the light,' he remarked as he pressed the switch.

I was amused as I had assumed B had a thing for darkness. This was how our social systems had changed from when most living was public and one did not assume an off behaviour on the part of another. Instead, one asked questions if one felt something was odd. This ceasing of conversations, this allowing of individuality, often makes us hesitate to reach out to others. 'Tell me to sleep,' pleaded B.

Panjab too seeks someone to tell it what to do, someone it can trust, an elder, a better-informed close one. A doctor.

\*

Nothing had prepared me for the pretty young girl who walked in with her mother. They were smiling. The psychiatrist was confused and asked if all was well. The mother replied, 'Yes, *daktar sa'ab*, we have brought sweets.'

She opened a box of *mithai* (sweets).

'What is this for?' asked the doctor.

'C's marriage has been fixed.'

The doctor was taken aback. 'But she has to finish school.'

'We will allow her to study up to Class X. After that her husband and in-laws can decide.' C was beaming, her eyes cloudy, her mind elsewhere, her shoulders and body rigid.

'Is the boy known to C?'

The mother answered, 'No. But they will know each other after marriage.'

The doctor asked C how she was doing. C's replies were in monosyllables. The doctor prescribed the dosage and called them back a month later for follow-up.

'Bless her, *daktar sa'ab*.'

The doctor asked if the in-laws knew about C's condition. The mother answered, 'Are we fools? Why would we tell them? She will be fine after marriage, I'm sure!'

After they left, the doctor told me, 'C had her first catatonic schizophrenia episode more than a month ago. This is their third visit. She seems to be doing okay.'

The question—why my mother was married when she was unwell and my father's family not told about her condition—has haunted me all my life. A half century after my parents' marriage, I had just witnessed my history being repeated.

'But marriage? Where did that come from? C has to finish treatment, studies!'

The doctor cleared his throat. 'Well … it is really a private decision. I tried to probe if C's family had prevented her from loving someone which triggered her illness, but that wasn't the case. The groom seems to be a stranger. I can't interfere.'

This drawing of lines between the doctor and the patient is not the case when people take someone 'in whom a spirit has entered' to a dargah or a shaman or a *dera*. Until psychiatry arrived in the twentieth century, that practice was very common. In those spaces the priest or godman purportedly removed the 'spells' that had resulted in the condition and also had a say in the decision on whether or not to marry off the girl. Again there was a community elder, vested with religious powers, a wise one and hence beyond questioning, guiding the ordinary folks. In fact, often marriage was prescribed as a solution to the illness.

In C's story, competitive rituals were at stake: C's medication was treatment but its intake was a ritual to prevent episodes of mania. Being a woman in feudal, patriarchal Panjab, C was studying, because we assume we have a system where educated folks advance. However, in lived reality, her destiny was the ritual of marriage, like of most young women. C's illness was set to disrupt this destiny. With her marriage fixed, her family was relieved. It was prepared to hide her illness in the belief that marriage fixes people. This was exactly what my mother's family had decided when my parents married. C was from a poor Dalit family and since it was difficult for them to raise a dowry, they were thankful for an alliance. My mother's family was Jutt, her father, my Nanaji, was a war hero and was awarded the Military Cross in the same theatre of war, Burma—as Jemadar Nand Singh—and also the British Order of Merit in Kohima during World War II. But military merit is not social awareness and my mother never got well. In fact, her condition worsened.

*

The doctor at a rehabilitation centre and I entered the room of a person who had been admitted last evening. D was tall, well-built, well-groomed and fair. I read his details on his file in the doctor's hands. He looked like he was in his mid-thirties but was actually in his late forties. He sat fidgeting on his chair and got up only when the doctor introduced himself. He looked agitated but answered politely.

'Yes, addiction. Yes, finally decided to come over. Yes, two weeks is fine.'

Then he began listing out his queries: 'Can I get a phone? I run three-four businesses; I need to take a status report two or three times a day.'

No, the doctor told him. D's wife had said that she would take care of the business.

'Can I wear my own clothes and not the hospital uniform?'

Why?

'I am not sick.'

The doctor smiled and asked him why he thought so.

'Well, yes, I am sick,' D conceded. 'But not like other illnesses.'

Okay, the doctor allowed him his clothes.

'Can my wife bring me some? I like T-shirts.'

Yes.

'What I really want to ask is … I want to say is … I need your help. I smoke 35–40 cigarettes a day. I want to smoke …'

'Here?' asked the doctor, surprised that someone would ask permission to smoke. 'Here, in the rehabilitation centre?'

'Yes, here.'

But this is a hospital, you have come to de-addict.

'Yes, from heroin. Not cigarettes.'

Well, from everything on which you are dependent.

'No! Not from cigarettes.'

Okay, but ten per day. When you need one, ask the staff to open the back door.

'Thank you, doctor.'

The doctor gave him a time frame: one week. 'Then we will bring it down to five and one less each day. You can't go home from here smelling of tobacco.'

The doctor did not wait for a reply and walked out. I asked the doctor if such negotiations were common. Tellingly, the doctor replied,

'The whole phenomenon of addiction, actually dependency—I do not agree with the word addiction, because of its negative connotation—is based on negotiations.'

'Please explain ...'

'Well, it is all about approach: addiction assumes that one is afflicted and has to be forcefully kept away from a substance. But the substance is commonly available outside. Once he leaves from here, the patient can get it again. Reinforcing the idea of addiction is like creating a forbidden fruit, creating aspiration, even if negative. It is a stigma, it makes the patient or user or consumer a criminal.'

'And dependency?'

'When we call it dependency, we seek to educate the patient that life is possible without it. The drug is finally a crutch. We try to invoke the patient's own strengths to fight the dependence. It is not we who are fighting drugs, it is the patient who is fighting. We are only assisting them with calibrated therapy.'

'Now that is interesting ...'

'See, if the patient owns up responsibility for the condition, he is our biggest ally.'

'You said the dependence is based on negotiations; how is that?'

'It is a regular pattern. Tell me, who does not know that liquor, cigarettes and drugs are bad for health? Yet, we indulge in them. Simply because we believe we can stay on top of them, use them for definite purposes, to get a high or whatever, and then leave them. It is often too late when we realise we are in their grip. We substitute one for another and that one for yet another. We are constantly negotiating them in our heads—one more, half, this last one ... our mind's capacity to negotiate with itself is endless. D made his negotiation public—because we confiscated his cigarettes.'

I made a snide remark, 'Is it because this is a private hospital?' D is, after all, a client.

The doctor did not blink. 'You are right. His bills pay us our salaries. But there is always a case-by-case approach. We assess situations and decide. There are no fixed rules. His getting off heroin is a bigger need than us alienating him over cigarettes. We need to earn his goodwill, convince him we are his friends and help him with his heroin dependency.'

★

At the doctor's clinic, a woman who seemed to be in her mid-forties, wearing a yellow branded T-shirt and white jeans entered the room. She took her seat in front of the doctor's table. The doctor started by asking her how she was doing when she looked at me. It was the first time in the few hours since the patients had been coming that someone had noticed me. The earlier ones talked to the doctor, at the doctor and to themselves. Or they did not talk. The caregiver accompanying them talked. None of them had noticed me. The doctor intervened, 'He is a friend, a writer, observing my sessions. If you feel uncomfortable he can leave.

She looked at me, her eyes paused a while on my face. 'No,' she said. 'It is okay.'

The doctor asked again, 'How are you?' Her eyes dimmed and she smiled. 'No one asks me that. Please don't. I am doing my job. Running businesses, managing two adolescent sons, taking care of my husband's parents. I don't know how I am doing all this but everyone around me is doing fine.'

The doctor remained silent.

'This is not why I had come to India from England seventeen years back. I had never expected to be trapped like this. Forget it. Tell me, will he recover from his illness?'

'Recover from what? He is not ill.'

'Whatever, ill, not ill, he should stop it.' She did not say addiction or dependency. I noticed the use of the word 'sick' in D's conversation and 'ill' in this lady's. I put them together and realised they were husband and wife.

'Since when have you known about it?'

'Well, many years, even before marriage. He promised me he would stop. He stopped. For many years.'

'Then?'

'Then he started again. Then again stopped for six years and now has resumed.'

'Did you take him to a de-addiction centre earlier?'

'No, never. He has good will power. He can just stop.'

'Then why has he come this time?'

'I asked him to. He has to stop now. Enough is enough.'

'Well, maybe he didn't really stop? Maybe he hid it from you?'

'No, he never lies to me. He has been drinking all these years. He never hides things from me. That I am certain about.'

D was in good health, physically. Smoking, drinking, drugs and still he looked young.

'Tell me, how would you look if you spent three to four hours in the gymnasium every day? Not bother about anything but yourself … Eat all those protein diets while your wife is running the whole show, putting on weight and compromising on her health. Then you chase younger women.' I looked at the lady again. She did look older than her husband. I do not know how much older he was to her, but she looked like she had aged faster.

'Does he love you?'

She blushed. 'Yes, he does, but I have no time. All these responsibilities. He has the luxury of love.'

'You said you have adolescent children?'

'Yes, two, brats. And in-laws. Getting old, they need care.'

The doctor sought to end the meeting and said, 'Let us see. Your husband has asked permission to call. He has asked for home clothes. '

'Always something or the other. Hasn't he asked to be allowed to smoke?'

'Yes, he has. We are regulating it, but he can smoke.'

'Thank you, doctor.'

I was tempted to ask her to meet the doctor again. This time for herself. She seemed to have reached breaking point. I held back my words. She already doubted my presence. Of course, she had a right to do that. Before leaving, she nodded at me. I nodded back.

It is a fact about feudal Panjab that when the man goes off the path set for him, the family's responsibilities fall on the woman. In an earlier age, with men gone away as soldiers in the army, as drivers in transport businesses and abroad on work, Panjab's songs and romance centred around waiting and pining for the lover to return. Yet, the woman had space and control in the family. Now when men were unable to handle responsibilities, the shouldering of the family had fallen on the women. She gained voice inside the home but still not in society.

I noticed how it fell upon the doctor to clarify to the husband and wife that addiction was not a crime and the condition needed to be seen as dependence. How he urged family and society to accept the users, not push them away. This was because the pushing away, either tangible or perceived, was what had led the users towards the drugs, as an escape. The import of such usage is how society deems what is right and what is wrong and puts away the wrong ones. Unless that changes, one can't really hope to see users recovering.

*

The man and woman I observed next were well-dressed and in their mid-forties. They looked like they were from a well-to-do business family. The man asked about his son E. 'If E is able to cope with the routine, how is he managing his craving?'

The wife was pragmatic and asked questions about recovery and what they needed to ensure when E was discharged. The man asked to see E. The woman sought to prevent it. The couple had a minor argument and the man didn't insist.

He told the doctor how he had tried everything, including arranging heroin for his son, and how he used to personally take his son for oral replacement therapy. How his son was the only heir to their business but now he worried how the young man would take over in a few years. In fact, he had invited the son to join the business right away, but E was keen on drugs, bikes, music and friends. There had been police cases. He then insisted again that he wanted to see E. The doctor reminded the father that the son was playing on his sentiments. 'No, do not worry. I want to keep him here. I just want to see him,' said the father.

'You can go to his room,' said the doctor.

'No. No, doctor. I can't see him there. I will break. Please call him. Just five minutes.'

Finally, since the father insisted, the doctor called for the son.

E, a young man, about twenty, came in along with two members of the staff. As soon as he saw his father he began to shout, 'Daddy, daddy, take me away from here. I want to come with you, daddy. How can you be so cruel?'

The man tried to placate his son. The staff held E's arms even as he tried to free himself. I sensed a wall between them. Invisible, but very real. The wall between the sane world and the world the sane wanted to correct. The young man was on the other side, trying to break through the wall. He was getting violent. 'Daddy, you never told me these people will torture me. They will not give me food. They will deny me television. You lied to me, daddy, you lied to me.' E never once addressed his mother.

The doctor got up, trying to calm E. He touched his shoulder. E recoiled. 'Don't touch me, don't you dare touch me. You are evil. Evil!' The doctor backed off. I feared the situation would get out of hand. E was struggling hard against those holding him back. The father tried to come close to E. The doctor gestured to him to stay put. 'Daddy, look, look how the doctor, the staff are stopping us from meeting. How they are dividing our family.' The father looked on, helpless. 'Why do you want to keep me here, daddy? What have I done, daddy? Why do you hate me?' screamed E even as the father was reduced to tears.

The doctor asked his staff members to take E out. The staff members were well-built. E was physically weaker but he could shout. 'Daddy, I will never forgive you for this. I will never accept you as my father!' E hollered as he was carried out.

The father was sweating. After a minute of silence the doctor called his secretary. He listened to her, put the phone down and turned to the couple. 'Your son is fine. As soon as he stepped out of the chamber, he relaxed. He told the staff it was just drama. To tug at your hearts. He walked back on his own to his room. He even joked on the way.'

Emotional blackmail is how the consumers have cracked and compromised the primary unit—the family—which ought to prevent the supply of drugs and keep track of consumption patterns, and has instead become an abettor of the habit and begun supporting those trapped in the habit. Once the family became a safe haven, the battle got tougher. E's family kept him at the centre but sooner or later he would leave. Once he did, as long as he viewed the family as the barrier he would continue to fight it to find his fix. Unless E owned up to the habit and desired to cure himself of it, in spite of the family keeping him in the hospital, his situation would not change. Even after he wanted to kick the habit, he would need the family to support him when he wavered, but all the guilt tripping he did weakened the family. E and his family would waste many years in and out of the habit. The termites have hollowed the structures. There are no easy solutions.

A year later, in 2017, on World Health Day, the Department of Psychiatry, Government Medical College and Hospital, Sector 32, Chandigarh, released the report 'National Mental Health Survey: Punjab'. The report showed that one in eight Panjabis or 21.9 lakh people in the state suffered from mental illness.[31] The statistics did not surprise me. My reading was that the number of depression cases would be even higher.

A suicide or a drug-induced death is not sudden. Suicides are often not reported, nor are drug-induced deaths. Such deaths, whose numbers the state government does not have, probably match the numbers of those dead during militancy. Each such death has a history of mental breakdown, not only the individual's but also of the family and peer groups. The death only vacated the individual from the fight against his or her circumstances; it did not solve the issues. This led families into depression.

The ideas of Sigmund Freud who used to be considered the father of psychotherapy are now much contested and critiqued. Especially his views on women. Yet, one of the core ideas that has survived and something subsequent mental health practitioners have been upholding since is that depression is anger turned inward. This is clinically borne out by international studies and in my own interactions with people I met. Claustrophobia, as Satnam said. A noose tightening around Panjab. Yet, apart from breaking into protests from time to time, which too have become ritualistic, Panjab does not know a road forward. Where does it leave an ordinary person? In the grip of fear, anxiety and depression.

Panjab is a mental health time bomb, ticking away furiously.

What I had seen play out in C's illness and imminent marriage jolted me and reminded me of Mama—especially her last days. It is strange how, hurtling through life, you sometimes miss out the obvious but it comes back to you when you look at events in retrospect. I now noticed that in terms of Panjab shutting down, the autumn of 2015 was a déjà vu of the summer of 2007.

In the summer of 2007, we had discovered that Mama, who had been schizophrenic all her life and who, in 2003, after Baba passed away, was diagnosed with cardiomyopathy (an enlarged heart, three times bigger than normal, which found it hard to beat because its muscles had weakened and mass had grown), now had Stage IV breast cancer. When Mama was diagnosed with cardiomyopathy, I had started calling her the big-hearted one, which was a literal truth but a white lie. I did not tell her about her heart's condition. Now I, too, was at a loss. A friend remarked the two worst illnesses were located within six inches of each other in Mama's chest.

Mama had wanted to go to Panjab, to her father's room, to his bed, to where he had passed away. We brought Mama to Mandi Dabwali, to her sister, my Masi's hospital-cum-home. My memory of that summer is of dust storms from the nearby Thar desert. Masi and I had bowed down in *sajdeh*, in supplication, in Mama's bedroom converted into an Intensive Care Unit. Mama was hooked to oxygen and our effort was to keep her pain to the minimum.

Owing to Gurmeet Ram Rahim's antics in Sirsa, forty kilometres from Mandi Dabwali, I could not go to Chandigarh to get morphine for which doctors in Bangalore had written me a letter addressed to the Post Graduate Institute of Medical Education & Research in Chandigarh. As the streets erupted with the anger of Sikh groups and *dera premis*, we followed Mama's palliative care regimen and maintained a steady dosage of the painkiller Proxyvon. It worked, and as the cancer spread to her lungs, stomach and intestine, Mama did not feel pain again.

In a few weeks, Mama's big heart collapsed. While giving her the final bath I saw Mama's naked broken chest—her left breast lumpy from heart ailment, her right breast withered from a deep black, blood-dried hole—cancer. It is now, when I look again at that moment in my mind's eye, that I realise Mama had gifted me an insight into Panjab which I did not then realise.

In her chest, that I had seen then but noticed now, was the map of Panjab devastated by two mis-revolutions—Green and Khalistan. Panjab, too, like my big-hearted Mama, praised and lauded by the nation for being food producers, does not see its dire ailments and continues to believe in myths about itself. These are white lies, like the ones I had told Mama. The super-speciality of the doctors diagnosing Mama's various illnesses, one focussing on the mind and another on the heart, had allowed cancer to creep into her, eventually driving her to death.

In fact, the cardiologist was so happy with Mama living on for four years after the detection of her illness that he took her case to his medical students to show how medicine had helped her left ventricle improve its function, akin to how agricultural scientists demonstrated the benefits of different fertilisers and pesticides to farmers. The super-specialists had failed to view Mama's body as a whole. The experts and politicians of Panjab also approached its many issues individually, applying Band-Aid fixes to some and not acknowledging others. Thereby, they had missed evolving a holistic understanding of what these issues were doing to the whole of Panjab and its people and the larger state, India.

I felt Mama's cancer was like militancy that had taken a great toll on Panjab and solved nothing. This was because the illness itself was created by multiple reasons and led to an uncontrolled growth of cells. This unregulated growth of cells then spread in the body and resulted in the devastation of all the organs.

## Chapter Five

# *Astha* — Faith

In Panjab's case, two of the many reasons that fed into militancy go back at least a century. They were the struggles over the identity of Sikhs coupled with the fact that their population was much smaller as compared to the Hindus and Muslims. These twin reasons played out both before and after the Independence of India and Pakistan and the resultant partition of Panjab.

## *Before Independence*

In 1927, the British appointed the Simon Commission to propose constitutional and political reforms for India. The Commission did not consult the Indian leadership. It was in the 'Simon Go Back' protest that Lala Lajpat Rai was injured, leading to his death, which Bhagat Singh chose to avenge. The Congress responded to the Simon Commission by appointing its own Commission under the leadership of Motilal Nehru. In 1928, the Nehru Report outlined the demand for self-rule through dominion status under the British as was prevalent in Canada and Australia. The committee recommended the abolition of the existing communal representation and urged the government to introduce mixed or joint electorates for all communities. The committee did allow for the reservation of minority seats in provinces having a minority of at least 10 per cent. The committee did not mention anything on reservation of seats for any community in Panjab and Bengal.

The Akali Dal represented by Mangal Singh did not accept the recommendations of the Nehru Committee. The Muslim League under Mohammad Ali Jinnah and the Scheduled Castes under B.R. Ambedkar also rejected the proposal.[32] Though in the initial phase of struggle for the gurdwaras the Akalis adopted the Congress method of satyagraha, soon a tussle emerged between the Congress, representing the larger Indian interest, and the Akalis, representing the Sikh interest. It was akin to the tussle between the Congress and Muslim League representing Muslim interests, and between the Congress and B.R. Ambedkar representing Bahujan interests.

At that time, the Sikh population of undivided Panjab was 13 per cent and Sikhs were a minority in every single district. With such a small and distributed population the Akalis grappled with the question of how the Sikhs would elect their leaders. When the Akali Dal opposed the Motilal Nehru Committee report, Congress leaders Mahatma Gandhi, Motilal Nehru and Jawaharlal Nehru (during the 1929 annual session at Lahore) met with the veteran Akali leader, Baba Kharak Singh, and gave him a solemn assurance that after the transfer of power, no constitution would be framed by the majority unless it was acceptable to the Sikhs. This assurance satisfied the Akali leaders and they expressed their cooperation with the Congress.

When after the Third Round Table Conference, in November 1932, the then-prime minister of Britain, Ramsay MacDonald, instituted the Communal Award, it provided separate representation for the Forward Castes, Scheduled Castes, Muslims, Buddhists, Sikhs, Indian Christians, Anglo-Indians and Europeans. Master Tara Singh, the leader of Akalis, remained critical of the Award since only 19 per cent seats were reserved for the Sikhs in Panjab, as opposed to the 51 per cent for the Muslims and 30 per cent for the Hindus.[33] This, according to Master Tara Singh, was a clear mandate for Muslim domination, and true enough, the Muslim-dominated Unionist Party came into power in Panjab.

In 1942, the proposals of the Cripps Mission granted the principle of territorial sovereignty as a means of communal protection, and consequently, in 1943, Giani Kartar Singh raised the proposal of Azad Panjab. Azad Panjab was a proposal to transfer Sikh, Muslim and Hindu populations to seek balance of demographic power in the undivided Panjab region. But as the possibility of the partition of the Panjab and Bengal grew, the scheme became less and less meaningful and was abandoned.

With Partition looming large, the spectre of Muslim domination was replaced by the fear that the Sikh community would be split between India and Pakistan.[34] The Akali leaders were against the division of India, the division of Panjab, and Partition. They threw in their lot with India as Jawaharlal Nehru and Mahatma Gandhi promised to look into the matter of a Sikh region. However, the blood of Partition drowned the population and its leaders and their words, promises and commitments. Clearly, the Jinnah trajectory had evolved into the creation of Pakistan. The Ambedkar trajectory slowly led to caste consciousness which now informs public debate and politics in India. The Master Tara Singh trajectory—the matter of Panjab and Sikhs—remained unfulfilled.

## *Post Independence*

On the eve of Independence, India inherited a conglomeration of princely states and free regions whose borders had been determined by the British. The new nation had to create new states for smooth administration. Historically, the Congress had favoured the creation of linguistic states post-Independence. The linguistic state proposal was the Congress position in the 1945-46 election manifesto as well. On 17 June 1948, Rajendra Prasad, the president of the Constituent Assembly, set up the Linguistic Provinces Commission (aka Dhar Commission) to recommend whether the states ought to be reorganised on a linguistic basis. Within six months the Commission recommended that formation of states exclusively or mainly on linguistic considerations was not in the larger interests of the nation. The apprehension was the nation's integrity would be at risk if linguistic states were to be constituted. This fear had its origin in the trauma of Partition that had stunned all leaders. The Commission recommended the reorganisation of the provinces on the basis of geographical contiguity, financial self-sufficiency and ease of administration.

The Congress, at its Jaipur session later that year, set up the JVP committee—comprising Jawaharlal Nehru, Vallabhbhai Patel and the Congress president Pattabhi Sitaramayya—to study the recommendations of the Dhar Commission. The JVP committee stated that the time was not suitable for the formation of new provinces on linguistic lines, but also stated 'if public sentiment is insistent and overwhelming, we, as democrats, have to submit to it, but subject to certain limitations in regard to the good of India as a whole.'[35]

On the ground, the frenzy of linguistic division of states was gaining currency all over the nation. The Panjab that had emerged post-Partition extended from Delhi to Amritsar and included an administrative entity known as PEPSU (Patiala and East Panjab States Union which included all the princely states of Panjab) besides present-day Haryana and a few districts that were later included in Himachal Pradesh. It had two major religious communities: the Hindus and the Sikhs, with Hindus constituting above 60 per cent of the population.

In the Panjabi-speaking areas of the state, the language was written in three scripts: Gurmukhi, Shahmukhi (derived from the Urdu and Persian scripts) and Devanagari. In June 1948, Bhim Sen Sachar, then chief minister of Panjab (not including the PEPSU states) presented the Sachar Formula for education. Per this formula, schools in the Hindu-dominated areas would use Hindi in Devanagari as the medium of instruction while Sikh areas would have Panjabi in the Gurmukhi script. The option of parents or guardians opting to switch the language for those who insisted on another language also existed.

Later, in 1948, the Hindu-dominated municipal committee of Jalandhar passed a resolution making Hindi the sole medium of instruction for schools within its jurisdiction. From 1948 itself, a businessman from Lahore, Lala Jagat Narain, had campaigned actively for Hindi, ironically through his newly-launched Urdu newspaper *Hind Samachar* that catered to the urban salaried class. The Senate of the Panjab University in a meeting on 9 June 1949 turned down by majority vote a proposal to adopt Panjabi as the medium of instruction, though the Sikh members were of the opinion that as a concession to Hindu sentiment, it could be written in Devanagari instead of Gurmukhi.[36] As the 1951 Census came up, there was a sustained campaign by the Jalandhar press for the Hindu population in Panjabi-speaking areas to return Hindi as their mother tongue for official records. As a result of these disagreements, the Sachar Formula failed.

Parallel to these events, in a strange development, eyeing political power in East Panjab, on 17 March 1948, the working committee of the Shiromani Akali Dal advised all members of the Panthic Party both at the Centre and in the state to unconditionally join the Congress. It was a brief merger which soon came undone, but two prominent leaders Baldev Singh and Swarn Singh became cabinet ministers in Nehru's Congress cabinet. The result of this merger and separation was that Panjab became a perennial site of one-upmanship between the two parties—the Congress and the Akali Dal, the consequences of which can be seen even now.

In the next few years, Ambedkar lent his voice to a Marathi-majority Maharashtra state with Bombay as its capital. Meanwhile, Potti Sreeramulu demanded the formation of a Telugu-majority state and sat on a fast which led to his death in 1953. This sparked off agitations all over the country with several linguistic groups demanding separate states. The Telugu-majority Andhra state was formed in 1953 even as a major movement started in current-day Karnataka seeking to unify the Kannada-speaking areas. These protests pushed the central government to institute the States Reorganisation Commission (SRC) to recommend the reorganisation of state boundaries. In 1954 itself, while the SRC was still looking into the matter of states reorganisation, the Akalis, led by Master Tara Singh, upon noticing Hindu groups like the Arya Samaj and Jana Sangh and their disdain for the Panjabi language, had begun the struggle for a Panjabi Suba (province).[37] The impetus had come from Sikh leaders meeting Ambedkar who told them that a demand for a Sikh state would be a cry in the wilderness and urged the leaders to ask for a Panjabi-speaking state instead. In effect, it would be a Sikh state.[38]

At that time, the Centre had two choices to tackle Panjabi grievances: either resurrect the Sachar Formula and push the Hindus to accept it or accept Panjabi as an independent language and create Panjabi and Hindi states. Panjab's geography—it being a border state, next to Pakistan—played a role. The Centre was not in favour of a Sikh-dominated region next to a Muslim-dominated Pakistan. In 1955, aided by the Official Language Commission per Article 344 of the Constitution, the SRC recommended that state boundaries be reorganised to form sixteen states and three Union Territories on linguistic lines. Consequently, the States Reorganisation Act of 1956 came into being. The SRC ruled that there were fourteen well-defined languages, but Panjabi was not one of them.

Panjabi, a 900-year-old language, with its own script, literature and cultural cosmology—was deemed grammatically similar to Hindi and not an independent language by itself. By seeking to curb legitimate Panjabi demands, the Centre made it a flashpoint and ended up making language a bone of discord between the Hindus and Sikhs and precipitated a crisis between the two communities which were historically and culturally aligned with each other. In fact, the first person to standardise the Gurmukhi script and print books in Panjabi was a Hindu—Dhani Ram Chatrik—through his Sudarshan Press; one of the greatest Panjabi novelists, Nanak Singh, was born a Hindu, but as was a widespread practice, had begun to observe the tenets of Sikhism and was deemed a Sikh; Master Tara Singh too was born Hindu but practised Sikhism. Religion in Panjab which had been amorphous and flexible was now becoming concretised. By associating Panjabi with Sikhs, which was a partial truth, the Centre made Panjab a language battlefield and sowed the seeds of what would devastate the state in the years to come.

In 1956, when the states were re-aligned, the PEPSU was merged with Panjab and the Centre proposed a Regional Formula on the lines of the Sachar Formula. Per the Formula, Panjab, with PEPSU (but not the areas later ceded to Himachal Pradesh) amalgamated with it, was to be divided into two regions, Panjabi-speaking and Hindi-speaking, each having its Regional Committee consisting of its own share of the state legislators, but not including the chief minister. The state would continue to have one governor, one council of ministers, one legislative body and one high court, but legislation relating to specified matters would be referred to the Regional Committees who were entrusted with fourteen subjects, other than law and order, finance and taxation. Provision was made for the demarcation of the two regions, and it was declared that the state would be bilingual, recognising both Panjabi (in Gurmukhi script) and Hindi (in Devanagari script) as the official languages of the state. The Formula was incorporated in the States Reorganisation Act, 1956.[39] The Akali Dal accepted the Regional Formula in its general body meeting held at Amritsar on 11 March 1956. On 30 December 1957, the Congress Chief Minister Partap Singh Kairon declared, 'In the

Panjab, Panjabi comes after Hindi.' However, Hindu groups assailed it as harmful to their interests and launched a fierce agitation to have it annulled.

Master Tara Singh was not opposed to the Regional Formula but the way the government torpedoed it in practice disillusioned him. At Amritsar, on 14 June 1958, he renewed his demand for a Panjabi Suba.

## Panjabi Suba

For the Panjabi Suba, thousands of Akalis courted arrest like during the Gurdwara Movement. In August 1961, at the Akal Takht, Master Tara Singh declared that he would fast until the Indian prime minister ceded a portion of the Panjab as a Sikh state or until death claimed him. In the early days of the fast, Nehru responded that submission to Master Tara Singh's demands would be against India's secular constitution and unfair to the Hindus in Panjab. Yet, later, he wrote to Master Tara Singh promising to investigate the Sikh demand. Upon the receipt of the letter Master Tara Singh broke his forty-eight day fast. As soon as he broke his fast, the Centre put Panjabi Suba on the back-burner. This incurred the wrath of the Sikh community who punished the colossus who had straddled over five decades of Panjab's history. Master Tara Singh was sacked from the leadership of the Shiromani Akali Dal and Sant Fateh Singh was elected in his place.

Two successive wars followed, one with China under Nehru in 1962 and another with Pakistan under Lal Bahadur Shastri in late 1965. After the 1965 war, when Fateh Singh brought up the language and not the religion issue, the Centre decided to create Panjab as a separate linguistic state.[40]

Yet, in the way the state's boundaries were drawn up, this intention was betrayed. The basis of the boundary decision was the 1961 Census in which many Panjabi-speaking Hindus had declared that their mother tongue was Hindi. On the basis of the recommendation of a parliamentary committee, the Centre proposed the Punjab Reorganisation Act.

Ironically, after such a long struggle, when the Act was announced the Akalis were dissatisfied with how the committee had taken tehsil and not village as the unit for linguistic demarcation. They opposed the Act in Parliament. On 6 September 1966, before the vote, Sirdar Kapur Singh elaborated[41] on the shortcomings of the committee's proposal in the Lok Sabha. But to no avail.

A new state, Haryana, was carved out of Panjab. The northern hilly regions with a majority Hindu population (albeit many of them Panjabis) was merged with Himachal Pradesh.

The Akalis sought to prevent implementation of the Act— actual division of states. The Centre assured them that their demands would be considered but again backtracked. Politically, Panjab with a majority Sikh population suited the Akalis because they were confident of coming into power and they at the time did not satisfactorily pursue the river water sharing formula, the status of Chandigarh, the shared Panjab and Haryana High Court, and the lack of industries. The trifurcation was largely peaceful. But since the formation of a truncated Panjab in 1966, relations between a dominant Centre and a strong state have remained turbulent.

The greatest victim was Panjab's composite culture, its *Panjabiat*, divided by Partition and now by the trifurcation. If the Centre had acceded to the grant of a larger Panjab, the Akalis had not played the religion card, and the Congress had focussed on people instead of power, Panjab would have had a different history. Yet, history is what it is. It bequeaths wounds and illnesses.

Since I was travelling and researching Panjab at my own expense, I applied for a fellowship. When I interviewed for the fellowship, the luminaries on the other side of the table asked me about the linkages between Operation Blue Star and the Green Revolution. I was taken aback. I did not believe they were linked. It was true that the Panjab that fed the nation had also entered a period of separatism, but in my limited understanding I had always seen it as a contradiction. I was thrown off. I bungled my interview and did not get the fellowship.

Researching this aspect while travelling Panjab, I discovered how my growing up in the rest of India, and my sense of faith in the Indian society and its leaders had blinded me to the critical fact that the Green Revolution and Panjab's watershed event Operation Blue Star were indeed linked. In the land known as the land of Gurus and Pirs, a yawning gap had crept in between the bottom and the top words—a lack of faith, a disquiet and a sense of mistrust. The Panjab of my boyhood days was not like that—though its Partition-related tragedies were great, it did not complain, it did not wince and it did not despair. This Panjab does, and every story, whether it is of the systemic breakdown of institutions or a legacy of the militancy years, directly or indirectly links back to the events of the year 1984— Operation Blue Star and the anti-Sikh pogrom. These events remain this Panjab's central watershed moment. To understand these we need to plot the events that built up to it.

A number of strands went into the creation of Operation Blue Star.

After the creation of the trifurcated Panjab in 1966, the governments formed in the first five years—Congress or Akali Dal— remained shaky and hardly lasted even a year each time. One of the people that the political system threw up was a dentist from Tanda, near Hoshiarpur, who had won an Assembly seat on a Republican Party ticket in 1967, served as speaker of the Assembly and later as Finance Minister—Jagjit Singh Chouhan.[42] He lost the elections in 1969, and in 1971, migrated to England. On 13 October 1971, he placed an advertisement in *The New York Times* proclaiming Khalistan as an independent Sikh state. In 1980, at Anandpur Sahib, he declared the formation of a National Council of Khalistan and declared himself the president of the council.

Chouhan's brand of politics constituted one thread of the Khalistan movement. At the electoral politics level, in 1972, the Akali government once again fell when the Bharatiya Jana Sangh—the precursor of the BJP—withdrew support. Thereafter, following their rout in the 1972 Assembly elections and the coming to power of the Congress under Giani Zail Singh (later president of India), the Akalis framed the Anandpur Sahib Resolution.[43]

Over the years and even now, this resolution has come to be seen as a charter of religious demands and separatism and has been much maligned by the Indian state. This is partly because the Akali Dal—the sponsor of the Resolution—is seen as the party of the Sikhs (panthic in local parlance) and partly because of the long preface to the Resolution.[p] Yet, a closer reading of the points of the Resolution (various versions are available) shows that the issues it addressed were both religious as well as economic. Its demands were located in the context of a state experiencing the Green Revolution.

The demands were for attention to weaker sections of the society, industrial growth to create jobs, diversification of agriculture, procurement of farm produce by the state, revision of tax structures, control on the headworks of rivers, improvement of relations with neighbouring countries, and the safeguarding of Sikh religion and identity.[44] It also sought to address the devolution of power from the Centre to the states and was, in effect, a plea for greater federalism. The resolution was against a dominant Centre (read Congress), at a time when the party was unchallenged at the Centre. It did not propose anything against the nation and was not against the secularism of the country. Here we need to note that unlike the

---

p. The word 'panthic' from the word 'panth' is foreign to the English language and does not quite translate into the word 'sect' which has origins in the church. 'Panthic' essentially means representing the Sikh community.

West, in India the word 'secularism' carries a different connotation and does not mean a divorce between religion and the state but the co-existence of various religions in a state.

With reference to the call for greater federalism, Panjab or the Akalis were not alone in raising such demands. In 1969, the Rajamannar Committee report initiated by the Dravida Munnetra Kazhagam (DMK) government in Tamil Nadu sought to shift the balance between the states and the Centre. In 1977, the West Bengal Memorandum too called for a greater federal structure and better distribution of taxes.

In the 1970s, the most prominent opposition leader was the veteran freedom fighter, Gandhian Jayaprakash Narayan, referred to as Lok Nayak or simply as JP. As a political activist, JP was on his own journey from Marxism to socialism to sarvodaya (universal upliftment) to the call for sampoorna kranti (total revolution). At the advanced age of seventy-two, he came out of semi-retirement in Patna in the early 1970s as a result of the growing disenchantment with Indira Gandhi.

Upon losing an Allahabad court case over election malpractices, Indira Gandhi imposed Emergency on the nation on 25 June 1975. In the initial days of the Emergency, when mostly Jana Sangh leaders were being arrested, even though no Akali leaders or cadre were arrested, the Akalis stood up to the draconian Centre. The Akalis convened a meeting at the Akal Takht within a week of Emergency being declared on 30 June 1975 to pass a resolution that stated that the Emergency was 'the fascist tendency of the Congress'. On 7 July 1975 the Akalis launched the Save Democracy Morcha and began courting arrest.

Per Amnesty International, during the Emergency, Indira Gandhi jailed about 140,000 people. Out of these, per historians, 40,000 were

Sikhs from the Akali Dal.[45] Going by sheer numbers, the greatest resistance to the Emergency was from Panjab which otherwise is 2 per cent of India's population. Fearing the Akali defiance might inspire civil disobedience in other parts of the county, Indira Gandhi offered to negotiate a deal that would give Akalis joint control of the Panjab Legislative Assembly. The leader of the protests, Harchand Singh Longowal, refused to meet with government representatives so long as the Emergency was in effect. In a press interview during the Emergency, Longowal made clear the grounds of the Save Democracy campaign. 'The question before us is not whether Indira Gandhi should continue to be prime minister or not. The point is whether democracy in this country is to survive or not. The democratic structure stands on three pillars, namely, a strong opposition, independent judiciary and free press. Emergency has destroyed all these essentials.'

While the civil disobedience campaign caught on in some parts of the country, the government's tactics of mass arrests, censorship and intimidation curtailed the opposition. After January 1976, the Akalis remained virtually alone in their active resistance to the regime. JP hailed the Akalis as 'the last bastion of democracy'. Unlike the RSS who apologised and made pleas for pardon, the Akalis never bent to Indira Gandhi and continued to come out in large numbers every month, on the day of the new moon—symbolising the dark night of Indian democracy—to court arrest. Indira Gandhi lifted Emergency on 21 March 1977. In the elections held later that year, the Janata Party under Morarji Desai came to power, as did the Akalis in Panjab. Beset with contradictions from the inception, the government fell within two and a half years resulting in general elections which brought Indira Gandhi to power yet again.

After the Emergency was lifted, the Akalis ratified the Anandpur Sahib Resolution in 1978. When Indira Gandhi came back to power in 1980, she did not consider the Anandpur Sahib Resolution. With the river water crisis looming large, the Akalis, now out of power, having been dismissed on Indira Gandhi's return, started the Neher Roko Morcha (Stop the Canal protest) over the SYL canal to stop more water from the rivers of Panjab from going to Haryana.

The protest began at village Kapuri, not far from Rajpura on the inter-state border between Panjab and Haryana. Akali leader Harchand Singh Longowal then collaborated with Jarnail Singh Bhindranwale, a little-known religious preacher from the Damdami Taksal. The Akalis shifted the Morcha to the Akal Takht on 4 August 1982. The Morcha also reiterated the demand of Chandigarh for Panjab and the implementation of the Anandpur Sahib Resolution.

In the mid-1980s, the Centre instituted the Sarkaria Commission to look into the Anandpur Sahib Resolution and the Rajamannar Panel Report. The Commission did not favour structural changes and favoured a strong Centre to safeguard the unity and integrity of the nation, though it argued that centralisation of power needed changes in its functional and operational aspects. This is how the curtains were drawn on the demand for a federal India and the Anandpur Sahib Resolution came to be seen as a secessionist document.

Jarnail Singh Bhindranwale belonged to the Damdami Taksal, a Sikh educational institution supposed to have been founded by Guru Gobind Singh (this is disputed by scholars) in order to educate the Sikhs by elaborating on Gurbani and the Sikh way of life. Per Mark Tully, in the late 1970s, Bhindranwale was promoted by Sanjay Gandhi and former Panjab chief minister and then home minister Zail Singh as an alternative voice to the Akalis. This theory is disputed by Bhindranwale's loyalists who believe their hero could not have been planted by a sundry politician.

The Akalis collaborated with Bhindranwale due to his rising popularity post his pro-Sikh stances over the Nirankari episode, his voice against the targeting and extra-judicial killing of Taksal students, his stance against the discrimination of Sikhs during the 1982 Asian Games on the Haryana border, his alleged killing of Lala Jagat Narain who helmed the *Hind Samachar* group of newspapers and his voluntary surrender at Chowk Mehta in Amritsar, the base of Damdami Taksal in September 1981.

Bhindranwale's surrender and subsequent release pushed him to prominence. He started making speeches putting forward the Sikh cause. His language was strong, his words were provocative and his speeches were acerbic. At the same time, the law and order situation in the state was worsening and incidents of violence were growing. Some militants would stop buses, segregate people on religious lines and kill the Hindus. Hindus were fleeing the border villages of Amritsar and Gurdaspur. The central government accused Bhindranwale of extortions, robberies, plane hijacks and stockpiling of weapons inside the Darbar Sahib. A serving police officer—a deputy inspector general in the Panjab police, A.S. Atwal—was gunned down on the steps of the Darbar Sahib in April 1983.

Parallelly, a new group named after an earlier illustrious Sikh fighting unit—Dal Khalsa—emerged in 1978, shortly after the Nirankari incident on the day of Baisakhi. Its antecedents are a little doubtful. Some point at Zail Singh's role in promoting them, but senior journalist Jagtar Singh refutes the idea.[46] Others point to Gurbachan Singh Manochahal as its founder. At its first annual conference held in Gurdaspur in December 1979, the Dal Khalsa passed a resolution demanding that Amritsar be declared a Holy City. The demand was supported by the All India Sikh Students Federation and taken up with the Indian government by the SGPC in 1980. Then processions took place to press home this demand in late May 1981. Parallelly, Hindus marched through Amritsar with cigarettes on Trishuls and placards made out of cigarette packs to oppose this demand and Sikhs marched with naked swords and flags in support of this demand.[q] Yet, these processions skirted the edge of violence and made both communities nervous and anxious. The protests underlined how bland symbolism had replaced the core issue: the promotion of the city as a religious and tourist destination in the manner of many European cities.

The reason Hindu groups opposed the proposal was less about Amritsar and more about how they viewed the Dal Khalsa. On 1 August 1980, the Dal Khalsa had hoisted the flag of Khalistan at the spot where thirteen Sikhs had been killed during the Nirankari clash in 1978. Their activists also raised the flag of Khalistan at various places in the state during Independence Day on 15 August 1980. On 29 September 1981, when Bhindranwale was under arrest, five members of the Dal Khalsa hijacked an Indian Airlines Jetliner (Boeing 737). The plane was taken to Lahore and the demand was for money and the release of Bhindranwale and all other political prisoners arrested in the name of Khalistan.[47] By 1982, the Dal Khalsa and the Khalistan Council were banned. By 7 October 1983, law and order worsened, the Centre dismissed the elected state Congress government and imposed President's Rule and declared the state as placed under the Panjab State Disturbed Areas Act, 1983.[48]

With more and more documentation emerging about that period, what is clear is that much of the violence taking place in those days in the rural areas of the state was beyond the control of any one person or organisation. It was in a sense similar to how provocative speeches work everywhere. When right-wing leaders today make speeches in favour of the 'gau mata', against minorities and so on, they are not

---

q. Declaring Amritsar a 'Holy City' would have meant that cigarettes, liquor and possibly, non-vegetarian food could not be sold in the city. Hence the protest march with cigarette packs.

directly calling for lynching or beatings. Yet, incidents of violence take place.

In hindsight, it is clear that the Akali move to collaborate with Bhindranwale, to take the Morcha to the Akal Takht and to allow Bhindranwale to secure his position in the Akal Takht, was being clever by half. It came from the tendency to shield oneself behind religion, but within the structure of a nation state that pledges to stand by democracy. It also appeared to be informed by the belief that the army would never enter the Darbar Sahib premises. Neither the Akalis nor Bhindranwale expected an operation of the scale of Blue Star or for the Darbar Sahib complex to become a battleground. The army was upbeat on its own sense of bravado and its commanders were on record saying they expected to conduct the Operation in a clinical strike and be done with it in a few hours.

At that time there were six Sikh groups inside the complex: Damdami Taksal, the AISSF, Babbar Khalsa, Dal Khalsa, Akhand Kirtani Jatha and the Akal Federation. The SGPC and government agencies allowed an arms pile-up inside the complex to appease these groups which would break out in internecine turf war with each other. The army had ignored the Panjab Police information on details of arms and had planned the Operation with the view that there were about 2,000 militants inside the complex from all factions, of which about 500 were hardcore.[49] Given the strength and ability of the Indian Army, the fourth-largest in the world, they did not expect to be held back for over four days by the committed fighters.

But, that is what happened.

Though Bhindranwale was the leader of the resistance, the person to train the young Sikh fighters and fortify the Darbar Sahib was Major

General Shabeg Singh. The source of Sikh resistance to the army was not sophisticated armoury but the belief of every fighter that this was a Holy War and their willingness to be martyred in it.

Little is known about Shabeg Singh apart from his involvement in Operation Blue Star. In Amritsar, during my travels, I met Beant Singh, Shabeg's youngest brother, who was able to give me a lot more details about this enigmatic personality.

Major General Shabeg Singh hailed from the Bhangu family whose ancestor Mehtab Singh along with Sukha Singh had avenged the desecration of Darbar Sahib by Massa Ranghar in 1738. In 1942, Shabeg Singh was a tall, lanky and athletic hockey player, selected by the British to join the army. He served on the Burma front and then in Malaya in World War II.

In the 1965 operations against Pakistan, he was in the Haji Pir Sector in Jammu and Kashmir, commanding a Gorkha battalion, and was mentioned in dispatches for the capture of important enemy positions. He was a commanding officer at that time and as the battalion was to be launched into attack, he received a telegram from his mother informing him that his father had expired. His brother Beant Singh told me that upon receipt of the telegram, he asked for a five-minute break. Silently, he paid his respects to his father and resumed operations. No one in his battalion knew that the commanding officer had lost his father on the eve of battle. His mother Pritam Kaur never asked him why he did not return to perform the last rites.

When the political turmoil in East Pakistan (now Bangladesh) began and the Bengalis declared their intention to separate, the Yahya Khan government cracked down on them, forcing them to flee to neighbouring Indian states. India decided to intervene. In 1971, India started the clandestine insurgency operations in East Pakistan—Mukti Bahini. Chief Field Marshal Sam Manekshaw selected Shabeg Singh, then a brigadier, and made him in-charge of Delta Sector headquartered at Agartala. He was given the responsibility of planning, organising and directing the insurgency operations in the whole of Central and East Bangladesh.

All the Bangladesh officers who had deserted from the Pakistan army including Colonel Osmani, Major Ziaur Rehman who later became president of Bangladesh and Mohammad Mustaq who became Bangladesh army chief were placed under Shabeg Singh for training. As a call of duty, Shabeg Singh changed his appearance. The Sikh soldier, proud of his personal family lineage and his religion, cut his hair, took to smoking and began signing his name as S. Beg as part of his undercover appearance.

Since the Mukti Bahini Operation was covert, it has not been documented and not much is known about it. Yet, it is clear from subsequent reports and books and articles that the Mukti Bahini played an important role in the Bangladesh War. Shabeg Singh, having been in charge of a covert operation, was promoted to Major General and awarded the Param Vashisht Sewa Medal in recognition of his services. He was then posted in Jabalpur where the East Pakistan military general Amir Abdullah Khan Niazi and all the 93,000 Pakistan prisoners of war were held.

Parallelly, the JP movement had pulverised Bihar during 1972-73 and became a serious threat to the Indira Gandhi government. The Centre received reports that the police in Bihar were sympathetic towards JP and his followers and decided to seek the army's assistance. Indira Gandhi sent an informal message to Shabeg Singh to arrest JP and take harsh measures against his followers. Shabeg Singh refused. This refusal did not go down well with Indira Gandhi. In order to deny him promotion, he was not given the command of a Division and was posted as the commanding officer of the Uttar Pradesh Area Headquarters (HQs) at Bareilly. The army instituted a court of inquiry stating that Shabeg Singh had accepted a plaque costing Rs 2,500 as a gift on his posting out of Jabalpur Area HQs. The army also brought charges that Shabeg Singh had used army trucks to smuggle teak out of Assam to build his house and had permitted sale of goods purchased from customs in the area headquarters' army canteen. The cases dragged on until a day before his retirement on 30 April 1976 when the army dishonourably discharged him from his duties.[50]

Later, Shabeg Singh fought the cases in civil courts and won. Intending to settle down in Dehradun, Shabeg Singh had built a house there. Yet, drawn to Panjab politics, unlike his peers who joined the Congress, he opted to fight for the Sikh cause by joining the Akalis. He became an *Amritdhari* Sikh, and when the Akalis courted arrest during the Dharam Yudh Morcha (battle of righteousness), he suffered the plight of ordinary prisoners. In a telling last interview, when asked about his role in Mukti Bahini—as becoming a soldier of his kind and given that the operation was covert—he remained silent.[51] When asked about his collaboration with Bhindranwale, he again remained silent.

Beant Singh claims that Shabeg Singh first met Bhindranwale towards the end of 1983 and advised Bhindranwale to vacate the Akal Takht premises. Bhindranwale refused, saying the Morcha would be weakened. Bhindranwale again called Shabeg Singh in March 1984 and agreed that there could be an army attack but qualified his agreement with the fact that it was too late to leave the premises then. He requested Shabeg Singh's help. Shabeg then began fortifying the complex and training Sikh fighters. The soldier who had dedicated all his life to the service of the nation was now preparing to defend his religious institution against the same nation in case it attacked it.

In those days there were intense parleys between the central government, the Akalis and all sorts of intermediaries. The CRPF had already encircled the Darbar Sahib complex. On 1 June 1984 the CRPF had spent eight hours shooting at the complex, testing the preparedness of the fighters inside. 'Three days before the attack,' Beant Singh said, 'Bhindranwale, his personal assistant Rashpal Singh, Shabeg Singh, Amrik Singh, Harminder Singh Sandhu—considered close to Bhindranwale, but allegedly a mole since he surrendered during the Operation—and others met Gurcharan Singh Tohra, the head of the SGPC, at the Akal Takht. Bhindranwale asked Tohra what would happen if he were to leave right away. Could Tohra promise that the army would not attack? Tohra's face fell, he bowed his head and lowered his eyes in embarrassment over his helplessness.'

It was clear that Indira Gandhi was no longer willing to listen to the Akalis. 'Shabeg Singh then instructed his wife and mother to close their annual *chabeel* (cold sweet water stall), a tradition they had maintained for years, and go home.' A lady, her identity withheld, close to the Akhand Kirtani Jatha involved in the Nirankari episode, told me that just a few days before the Operation, her sister had barged into Bhindranwale's premises behind Akal Takht. She saw him sitting amidst huge mounds of currency notes and loads of ammunition being cleaned by his fighters. She confronted him, 'You are a preacher. How have you come this far?'

He said, 'Bibiji, I have been trapped by both the Akalis and the Centre. I cannot betray my promise but I have no way to prevent what is going to happen.' Satpal Danish too met Bhindranwale during that time and his response was, 'I have sworn to fight unto death, performed *Ardas* and now I cannot break my word.'

It was clear that the Anandpur Sahib Resolution—some of whose demands related to the Green Revolution—opposition to the Emergency and the river waters issue had led to major differences between the Akalis and the Centre, but there was yet another

direct reason besides deteriorating law and order, and demand for
Khalistan: farmer protests. Within a decade of the Green Revolution,
issues started cropping up with the system that emphasised massive
productivity to save the nation from hunger and de-prioritised the
concerns of the farmers engaged in the task of producing food.

In the 1970s, farmers in Panjab organised struggles under the
Khetkari Zamindari Union. Some of the important struggles were:
anti-Single Food Zone, 1972; the struggle against power tariff, 1975;
against increasing water rates, increasing commercial tax, 1975; against
defective tractors, 1977 and the diesel morcha, 1979.[52] The initial
criticism of these protests was that they were big farmers crying foul.
In 1974, the word 'zamindari' (landlord) was dropped from the name
of the organisation because there were definite differences between
the issues big and small farmers faced. The union was spreading its
network to reach out to small farmers whose issues began featuring
in their agenda: rates of electricity, water and diesel.

In 1980, the Khetkari Union became part of the Bhartiya Kisan
Union (BKU). Dairy farmers successfully fought the milk agitation
in Moga in 1981 and succeeded in raising the rates of milk. They
launched an agitation against the defective Universal-445 tractors
which succeeded when the government, after a committee review,
ordered parts to be replaced. On 12 March 1984, on BKU's call
for reduction in electricity rates, thousands of farmers reached and
occupied the posh northern sectors of Chandigarh. Conservative
estimates put the number of farmers at twenty thousand but unofficial
estimates place them at one lakh.[53]

It was a symbolic gesture: rural India had occupied urban
and modern India. Village life had taken over the grand modern
showpiece, Chandigarh. The posh and genteel city was thrown out of
gear but there was no incident or provocation of any kind between
the police and the protestors. For a whole week the protest remained
absolutely peaceful.

Farmers from Andhra Pradesh, Maharashtra, Madhya Pradesh, Uttar Pradesh and Gujarat joined in, led by Sharad Joshi of the Shetkari Sangathna from Maharashtra. Devi Lal from Haryana also supported the BKU as did the Akali Dal, Kirti Kisan Union and the Kisan Sabhas of the Communist Party of India (CPI) and Communist Party of India (Marxist). Yet, like some of its factions now, BKU stood by itself as a non-political party. On 18 March 1984, the BKU organised a huge rally in Chandigarh addressed by farmer leaders Mange Ram and Sharad Joshi, but not by politicians. The gherao was a resounding success.

The BKU then launched a three-pronged morcha: *Kanak Roko, Karza Roko, Gaon Roko* (Stop Wheat, Stop Loan Recovery, Close the Villages). In April that year, demanding a better procurement price for wheat which had been increased from the previous year by only a rupee, the BKU asked farmers not to deliver wheat to the markets. Very little grain reached the state mandis. The BKU also asked farmers to not pay back loans and forbade the entry of recovery staff to the villages. Boards came up in villages, announcing, 'Without proper accounting, recovery of loans is illegal. Entry of recovery staff is strictly prohibited without the permission of BKU.'

Negotiations between farmers and the governor's administration went on for a week.[r] Finally, when the administration promised no extra charge in electricity rates for tube wells and postponed the recovery of electricity bills along with a reduction in reconnection charges, the farmers ended their strike, but not their struggle. The farmer unions and the presidential government decided to form a committee under a leading agrarian economist to look into the electricity tariff structure, the principles behind determining the tariff, and the level of service charges to be recovered from farmers. The date fixed for the report was 31 May 1984.

---

r. Panjab was then under President's Rule owing to the disturbances of the militancy period.

On 4 May 1984, the BKU met up with the state committee and asked for an assurance that along with the report they would also get the data on the basis of which the cost of power, staff cost and inventory of the Panjab State Electricity Board was computed. They also asked for data for computation of the cost of production while fixing procurement prices. They said such data would help them understand the merits of the forthcoming report and help them decide to accept or reject it. The committee submitted its report, as instructed, on 31 May 1984. The central government did not make the report public.

That is when the Akali Dal stepped in. It announced from the Akal Takht that it would stop the transportation of wheat to the rest of the country from 5 June onwards. Surprisingly, no one seemed to remember exactly how the call went out. Yet, there was a call. On my re-reading a book I had read long ago, I discovered that was the call Major General Kuldip Singh (Bulbul) Brar, one of the officers who directed Operation Blue Star, mentions: 'The final justification for army action was the announcement made by Longowal that a statewide morcha would be launched on 2 June 1984, to prevent movement of grain from the state.'[54] This call—mentioned a number of times in his book—became the reason for the attack. Commenting on the Operation, General K. Sundarji famously said, 'We went inside with humility in our hearts and prayers on our lips.' But to do what? Secure India's food? At what cost? By inflicting a thirty-five-year long wound on Panjab and the Sikh community which is far from healing even today. This surely was an equation of master-slave, coloniser-colonial subject. Is it a wonder then that Panjab considers itself the food-producing colony of the nation?

The battle of the Darbar Sahib during Operation Blue Star was thus an engagement between the nation state and the fighters of a religion whose very ethos lay in standing up for justice and honour the way they interpreted it. It was a clash between the hubris of

Indira Gandhi based on the arrogance of the Indian Army versus the stubbornness of Bhindranwale supported by the willingness of some dedicated young men ready to die for their religion, trained by a soldier whose own faith in the nation had been split wide open, because its systems had been hijacked by its leader Indira Gandhi.

It was plain to the naked eye that Bhindranwale's followers could not defeat the Indian Army. Shabeg Singh, a keen student of military history, certainly knew this. He also knew the weaknesses and strengths of his own former army. He architected the fortification of the Darbar Sahib complex not to win but to reveal the extent to which the Indian Army would expose itself in its mission to win the battle. He pushed the Indian Army to display the might of the nation state against its own citizens. The army played into Shabeg Singh's plan and wrote its chronicle of blood and destruction. It is all on record—the bloodied conscience of a nation with both sides vastly underestimating each other.

When the Centre launched Operation Blue Star and brought the state under military rule, the army expelled all press persons, stopped all communication from going out of the state and imposed a complete clamp down on media. Everything that really happened in Darbar Sahib complex, in Panjab, thus became a matter of lived experience and anecdotal testimonies, and not of objective record-keeping. Starting with Operation Blue Star, through Operation Woodrose, the army raided thirty-eight gurdwaras all across Panjab. In the countryside, the army was carrying out combing operations, killing and arresting young Sikh men on mere suspicion or for exhibiting the emotional pain of the destruction of their sanctum sanctorum.

The two operations resulted in a massive disruption of the BKU's planned strategy to get justice for the farmers. In July 1984, the BKU again raised the demand for the report on electricity meters that the government was not making public. 54,300 farmers courted arrest. The police arrested all top leaders from their homes. The BKU general secretary Ajmer Singh Lakhowal and secretary Balbir Singh Rajewal went to meet P.H. Vaishnav, the then finance commissioner (development), Panjab. The report was still not available. The secretary, electricity and irrigation, promised to publish the report and asked the unions to hold their peace and not go to press. Still the government did not publish the report. Instead, it started to use force to recover farmer loans and began to disconnect electricity connections. This legacy of government apathy continues until now.

In the last three and a half decades, much has been written and said about the events of 1984. There are books, television series, first-person accounts and commentaries. There are also the State and the SGPC White Paper. They do not agree on something as basic as the number of those killed, injured and arrested. While some works answer the question 'what happened', there is no clear answer as to why it happened and nothing at all addresses the question that now that it has happened, what should be done to help heal the society? When versions of events remain ambiguous, uncertainty pervades the whole system and spreads through the society. It questions the sense of faith a citizen can place in the justice of the system after its sanctum sanctorum, its corpus callosum, has been attacked.

India is a very recent democracy. When we became independent in 1947, we borrowed a lot from the British systems where public opinion was shaped by developments in Europe during its Age of Reason (1685–1815) and in particular by the French Revolution (1789–1799) and the document that was produced during the French Revolution, 'The Declaration of the Rights of the Man and of the Citizen'. This document was influenced by the doctrine of natural rights wherein the rights of man are held to be universal: valid at all times and in every place, pertaining to human nature itself. One of the major thinkers who influenced the Revolution was Jean-Jacques Rousseau through his treatise *Social Contract* or *Principles of Political Right (Du contrat social)* written in 1762, and his views on natural rights.

The social contract view holds that persons' moral and/or political obligations are dependent upon a contract or agreement among the people to form the society in which they live. The theory is associated with the moral and political theory advanced by Thomas Hobbes, John Locke and Jean-Jacques Rousseau.

To quote from a popular website that summarised the ideas of all three:

> Hobbes theorised that the establishment of a monarchy was something agreed between a society and its ruler. Rather than believing in the 'divine right of kings', Hobbes believed that the king got his power because his citizens voluntarily swore allegiance to him. Locke's social contract was between the ruler and the citizens he ruled. For Rousseau, the social contract was amongst the people that formed a society. Rousseau refers to a country's people as the 'sovereign', and suggests they should be treated as an individual person. He argues that although the sovereign was made up of individuals with personal interests, it generally reflects an aggregation of the common will, and strives for the common good. The sovereign only has authority over matters of public interest, and plays no role in personal matters. The key role of the state, therefore, is to reflect the will of the sovereign and ensure liberty and equality through its laws. According to Rousseau, societies collapse when friction builds between the will of the government and that of the sovereign.[55]

Rousseau states that in profit and loss terms what a citizen loses by the social contract is his natural liberty and an unrestricted right to do anything he/she wants and can get. What a citizen gains is civil liberty and ownership of everything he/she possesses. While natural liberty is limited only by the individual's powers, civil liberty is limited by the general will. The faith that we talk about in systems is this transaction between the individuals and the systems. As citizens, we give up on certain liberties when we accept the government created by the general will of society, but we expect the government to protect our rights as citizens. The French Revolution upheld Rousseau's theory and since then it has had much wider ramifications when it spread around nations changing from monarchies into democracies.

Through Operation Blue Star, by attacking the sanctum sanctorum of the Sikhs, the nation effectively breached this social contract between the nation and the community, the citizens of the nation. Religious belief is a part of citizen rights and when the Sikh community witnessed the hoary institution of their belief, the supreme seat of justice, the Akal Takht, blown off, they felt a bewilderment and betrayal which has lasted three and a half decades. The Akal Takht is not just a seat of power and the Darbar Sahib not just another gurdwara, but lie at the very centre of Sikh belief and can be compared to the Vatican in Rome or the Kaaba at Mecca. Operation Blue Star was a fundamental rupture and can only be addressed through a process of addressing the reasons for the Operation and ensuring that future governments respect the systems of belief and institutions of minority communities. To address the issue we need to comprehensively answer the violation of the principle laid out in the Constitution: are the minorities in a diverse Indian nation safe or vulnerable? Do the same rules apply to the majority and the minority? The reason we need to address the Operation is not only because it is about the Sikhs alone but also because it concerns the very idea of democracy we celebrate as a nation.

As citizens of a democratic country we can assume that the government must have maintained records either at ministry level or with the intelligence under the Official Secrets Act. If any government wants to clear the air on the Operation, surely it can bring out those records for study. That has not happened. We have not even answered a simple question: who ordered Operation Blue Star—the council of ministers, the prime minister or the president?

Procedures for civil servants follow a template but are tweaked from state to state. Per protocol, the deputy commissioner or a district magistrate (the same position, but the role changes when one is dealing with taxes or law and order) can requisition an army operation in case his understanding, based on intelligence reports, is that the police cannot handle the situation or cannot be relied upon. While the request can be made by the magistrate, the order for the army to carry out an operation can only come from within the army or its line of command which goes up to the defence minister and finally the president who, per Article 53 of the Constitution, is the supreme commander of the armed forces.

A democracy, a people's government, needs checks and balances so that it protects itself from power being usurped by a particular leader or a cabal with vested interests. Democracies might seem tedious but have a function, akin to a doctor following the procedures of an operation theatre before performing surgery. An operation of the nature of Blue Star could not have been carried out without inverting the protocol. Now, many years after the Operation and with most of the chief dramatis personae dead and at no personal risk anymore, there is no reason why the entire set of papers cannot be made public. Yet, the government does not budge. What this does is obscure the chain of command in a democracy, removes accountability from the system, and leaves those who seek answers groping in the dark, entangling themselves in a web.

The regular story of the Operation is that someone from the Centre, we do not know who, asked the then Amritsar DM Gurdev Singh to call in the army. He is reported to have stated that the situation was not dire and he could arrest anyone in his jurisdiction. He was asked to go on immediate leave. Ramesh Inder Singh from the West Bengal cadre was called in and was asked overnight to take over as the DM. He requested for the army to be called in. Ramesh Inder Singh later rose to become principal secretary to Parkash Singh Badal's government in 1997. In Badal's next tenure in 2007, Ramesh Inder became chief secretary. Post-retirement, he was appointed chief information commissioner (CIC) of Panjab. He was awarded the Padma Shri in 1986. In a June 2019 interview, Ramesh Inder Singh debunks this story and says Gurdev Singh was slated to go on regular leave and he was already in Panjab since 1978.[56] He says that since Panjab was declared a 'Disturbed Area', the regular protocol was not applicable. According to him, the Panjab Governor B.D. Pande directed the chief secretary K.D. Vasudeva and home secretary A.S. Pooni to issue a letter to request the army to come in aid to civil authority.[57] This applied not only to the Darbar Sahib but also to thirty-eight other gurdwaras in Panjab. The letter was a bureaucratic protocol; the larger question is, who sanctioned the Operation?

The president who was the supreme commander of the armed forces at the time of Operation Blue Star was a Sikh, Zail Singh. While his role in Panjab politics as a Congress CM was not above board, he was most likely kept in the dark about the attack. Does that mean that the nation can employ the army without the knowledge of the supreme commander of the armed forces? What does that tell us about the breakdown in the chain of command through which the system, the government and the armed forces were supposed to function?

Guru Arjan's martyrdom anniversary fell in the week of the attack and thousands of people had gathered at the Darbar Sahib. In May 2017, the courts ruled that there wasn't enough notice given for pilgrims to leave the Darbar Sahib premises before the Operation began.[58] The announcements were made from afar, from where the congregation could not have possibly heard them. That means the Indian Army either wilfully or through neglect, killed many pilgrims. Knowing this, it remains difficult for the Sikh community to repose its faith in India's democracy.

The immediate fallout of the Operation was that the Panjab governor, B.D. Pande, resigned soon after. Author-journalist Khushwant Singh and the founder of the Pingalwara Ashram (a home for destitutes) in Amritsar, Bhagat Puran Singh, returned their Padma awards. Even more disturbing was how the Operation shattered the very ethos of the army, at least for some time. Starting with the 9 Sikh, there were instances of collective insubordination in about one dozen units involving more than 3,000 deserters. The Commandant of the Sikh Regimental Centre in Ramgarh, Brig. S.C. Puri, and his two deputies, Col. Jagdev Singh and Col. H.S. Cheema, were attacked, leading to Brig. Puri's death.[59]

While India is made up of various ethnicities, and its people serve the armed forces, a major reason (which even the British recognised as discussed in the chapter *Rosh*) was the Sikh soldier's loyalty towards the Guru Granth Sahib. Now when his nation had attacked his centre of faith, he responded in the way he had served the army— by standing by his faith. Many deserters were court-martialled and dismissed from service. The issue still rankles because the Indian nation was built through the participation of its diverse ethnicities, and each community's faith is sacrosanct.

Every year on the anniversary of Operation Blue Star, people gather at the Akal Takht. The SGPC head and the Takht *jathedar* make speeches. Groups like Simranjit Singh Mann's Akali Dal (Amritsar),

Dal Khalsa and other assorted Sikh bodies seek a chance to address the congregation. Clashes erupt. Pictures of a sea of turbans, flashing swords and spears become media coverage, and the community bumbles along, upholding the narrative of victimhood which is ironically opposed to the scriptural injunction of accepting God's will with equanimity. The nation watches as if it is a matter of the community alone and it has no role to play in it.

However, this mess should not be Panjab's alone, or merely a Sikh issue. If the nation claims the Sikhs are an integral part of the nation, then the nation needs to come clear on the Operation and adopt the grievances of the Sikhs as its own grievances and look for solutions, not 'other' the Sikhs. For that, the nation needs to find ways to reconcile histories from the various sides involved in the Operation. Even till today, thirty-five years later, the use of words that caused killings of innocents—terrorists, separatists, militants, insurgents—are not defined and their usage has not been formalised, and narratives remain splintered.

The question is: does the nation admit that Operation Blue Star was an internal war situation? If it doesn't, then why was the army called in? If it does, then has the nation followed post-war practices to reconcile differences? This causes ambiguity, for we then do not know how to handle those arrested, the families of innocents who died, the thousands of disappearances and the excesses of the army and the police. If all that was collateral damage, then the question is, whose interest was served and at what cost?

It is the same with prisoners from that time—some awarded life sentences until death. Judicially, there might be no reason to demand their freedom but if the nation was at war with the community, then international protocols of war times, such as the Geneva Conventions, should apply. Yet, the nation maintains a hands-off policy, aggravating the pain.

What happens time and again is that the term Khalistan is raised as a bogey as per each political party's convenience to distract from the issues of the people as for example in the whitefly and sacrilege episodes. Politicians have learnt to milk the emotions associated with the Operation and the militancy period, spin it, use it, but not resolve it.

For example, as a moral step, Captain Amarinder Singh of the Congress quit his party after 1984. He joined the Akali Dal and was part of the party for almost a decade while militancy raged in the state. Even after militancy was over, he and other senior Akali leaders signed the Amritsar Declaration in 1994 which was an intention statement to carry out Khalistan's goals without mentioning the word.[60] After all, the leaders did not know which side the wind would blow.

Once the militancy period was over, the Akalis returned to electoral politics, the Captain found himself rudderless and went back to the Congress. Since then, the Akalis under Parkash Singh Badal have been in power twice, once for two terms, and Congress too has been in power twice, once under Amarinder Singh. Since the Operation and the anti-Sikh pogrom, the Akalis have used the events to campaign against the Congress and milk votes. This, even when the Akalis have been in partnership with the BJP and the BJP has come to power five times in the interim (once for a spell of thirteen days in 1996, then in 1998, 1999, 2014 and 2019). Yet, even a BJP government in the Centre has not addressed the issues arising out of the decade and a half of militancy. They have not even addressed the issues that led to the decade and a half. When in power, leaders and parties talk about Khalistan as if it was the biggest anti-national agenda, and when in the opposition, they use the issue of Khalistan to stoke fires.

A common critique presented is that the Operation should have been conducted like the later Operation Black Thunder I and Operation Black Thunder II in 1986 and 1988. These Operations are cited as models on how to cordon off the Darbar Sahib premises, cut off water, electricity, food supplies and squeeze out the militants. Such arguments are on the basis of hindsight and wishful thinking, oblivious to the arrogance and stubbornness that led to Operation Blue Star. The bigger question is, when after such great effort and destruction, the Darbar Sahib complex was cleared of militants in 1984, then how was it occupied again by the same forces in 1986 and 1988? What were the security forces doing that they allowed the sanctum sanctorum to be garrisoned again?

Those who support Bhindranwale say the Centre engaged the communists to prop up the BKU as an agency to disrupt the Akali Dharam Yudh movement. The contention is that the communists were under the influence of the then Union of Soviet Socialist Republics (USSR). How much the USSR's influence was in fomenting trouble in Panjab remains undocumented and unproven. The biggest evidence is the *Mitrokhin Archive* when a former Komitet Gosudarstvennoy Bezopasnosti (KGB) spy defected to Britain in 1992 and published his notes over three decades. Per these notes, the campaign to attribute the Khalistan agenda to the Sikhs who were protesting for their rights had started even before the Dharam Yudh Morcha, and there was large-scale planting of up to 3,000 stories in the Indian media. The Indian Ambassador to Pakistan was furnished with fake letters of Pakistan's involvement in the hope that they would reach Indira Gandhi. They did. However, the Mitrokhin notes remain disputed. The Indian government has not ordered an inquiry to confirm Soviet involvement.

It is a historical fact that it was the era of the Cold War and the Soviet Union did not want America's base in Asia—Pakistan—to gain power by fermenting problems in India. They created a narrative that Pakistan was directly[61] involved in training and supplying arms to the Khalistan movement.[62] Evidence of terrorists captured did prove the facts on training camps but the arms confiscated had Chinese and Afghan markings. Soviet involvement is also borne out by a statement by maverick politician Subramanian Swamy who met Bhindranwale multiple times and was all praise for him. The issue is Swamy's reliability as he has built his career on being contrarian.

The ones who look at the political economy of Panjab and support the farmers say the Akalis had reached a point of no return in their negotiations with the Centre before the Operation. Many rounds of talk had failed, and in spite of the pledge to 'fight unto death', Akali leaders were at their wits' end. On the eve of the attack, Parkash Singh Badal escaped from the Darbar Sahib premises. Longowal and Tohra surrendered to the army. There was not a single meeting between Indira Gandhi and Bhindranwale in spite of him asking for it multiple times. Yet, a scenario could well have been: all Akali leaders decide to stay in the Darbar Sahib, exert pressure on Bhindranwale and keep their channels of communication with Indira Gandhi open. They respond to Bhindranwale's query for an honourable escape. Would the army then have needed to attack the complex?

The fact is that the Centre and the Akalis had both come to accept that Bhindranwale had gone out of their hands. They abandoned him in the belief that he was ready to declare Khalistan with Pakistan's support. The deeper question is, where was the government, where was the intelligence and where was the police, when arms were being smuggled into the Darbar Sahib complex? The Sikh religion has a code of arms but those arms are kirpans and swords. The gun, the rifle and rocket launchers are modern arms. The state has a system of licences for arms. Did the state not know that the arms being smuggled in trucks carrying rations for *langar* were not against state-issued licences? Did the intelligence not know that one of India's finest soldiers was commanding the Sikh youth inside the Darbar Sahib?

On 31 October 1984, at about 9.30 a.m., Indira Gandhi was assassinated by her two Sikh security guards, Beant Singh and Satwant Singh. By noon that day, the Sikh president Zail Singh's car was attacked by angry mobs at All India Institute of Medical Sciences where he had gone to pay his respects to Indira Gandhi's body. Thus began the four-day macabre anti-Sikh pogrom in which, by official estimates, 2,700 Sikhs were killed (the unofficial number is 8,000) in Delhi alone and many more in north Indian cities from Jaipur in Rajasthan to Daltonganj in Bihar, going right up to Calcutta. The pogrom led to the mass exodus of Sikhs from other parts of the country to Panjab and the belief that Sikhs were not safe in India, which added fuel to the militancy fire in Panjab.

Various news reports, testimonials, commissions and panels have until now named a number of big and small Congress leaders and others who were either involved in or instigated the anti-Sikh violence. Some of the bigger names are: H.K.L. Bhagat, Kamal Nath, Jagdish Tytler, Sajjan Kumar, Dharam Das Shastri and Lalit Maken. Per a government answer in Rajya Sabha in December 2015, a total of 442 people have been convicted for the pogrom, but besides Sajjan Kumar, not a single senior leader has been charged.[63]

Whatever prevented the Congress from cleaning up its ranks—proximity to Congress leadership, ability to raise funds for elections, sheer impunity through stature—is a mark of how much the Congress has compromised and remains guilty unto the Sikh community. This involvement cannot be washed away by appointing a Sikh prime minister, Manmohan Singh, or even his apologising to the community. Any apology is based on an event and an apology means that it is the beginning of acknowledgement and taking ownership of the event. It follows that the apology should lead to a process of justice. Justice demands that it is not only done but also seen to be done, that has been clearly missing over 1984. How then can Sikhs repose their faith in India? To extend the question further, how can any citizen of the nation be assured that the nation will not, and cannot, violate the interests and the belief systems of its citizens?

The 1984 anti-Sikh pogrom was one-sided, so they were certainly not riots. What would we call them? Pogrom, carnage or genocide? For many years now the Sikhs have been petitioning various governments around the world to call them genocide. Some have agreed, but India remains ambiguous—sometimes it calls them genocide, at other times not. While so much needs to be done on the ground, does India want the Sikhs to eternally keep squabbling over these terms?

Today, a whole new generation has grown up abroad bearing the transgenerational trauma of the event and the later pogrom against Sikhs in October-November 1984. These are the next generation of those who left Panjab, many in earlier decades, but many also in the 1980s. Growing up abroad, they hear the stories of state violence, apathy and complicit activities, again and again, and these stories are reinforced in them. Then there are blacklists of those not allowed to enter India. What happens when their children want to connect back with Panjab, with their families in the land, with their history? What do they then think of India?

Like the Operation and the anti-Sikh pogrom, the fact is that today the term Khalistan itself has come to take on different meanings. While before 1984 and Operation Blue Star, it was a quest for an independent nation linked to the idea of 1944 Azad Panjab and Akali-Congress politics before that, post 1984 the term has come to

148 | Panjab

stand for two different aspects:

a) a struggle for a homeland that petered out because of internal contradictions, extreme police pressure and the fact that the Hindu-Sikh connection is like milk and water and cannot be separated

b) a quest for justice, of the wrongs towards the community during Operation Blue Star, the anti-Sikh pogrom, years of militancy in which thousands of forced disappearances and unmarked killings occurred, and the result of all these on families and society

Unless these are sorted out, Panjab will only be treated with Band-Aid fixes, not long-term solutions.

That is why groups like the World Sikh Organization and Sikhs for Justice hold anniversaries of Khalistan and slap cases in foreign courts on Panjab and Indian politicians. The Indian media, fed on nationalism, calls these groups fringe and radical. They might well be, but there is a huge question mark here on India: its lack of accountability leading to the alienation of the diaspora and local Sikhs.

Over the last few years, revelations of secret files in England show that the British were involved in the planning of the Operation.[64] This has caused considerable churning in the Sikh diaspora. Recently, the British courts have passed orders to make their Blue Star-related files public. Yet, nothing has changed in India.

This generation faces a plethora of narratives and spin-offs from those who support Bhindranwale and those who oppose him. Meanwhile, in Panjab, Bhindranwale has himself become a Che Guevara-like figure. He adorns T-shirts and the windshields of cars and his posters are all over Panjab. There is a gurdwara inside the Darbar Sahib dedicated to him and another in his village Rode in

Faridkot district. In an era where people have seen politicians of all hues betray the people, display their greed, switch parties and positions for power, the simplest reason for people to valorise Bhindranwale is this: he was a leader who stood by his word. He did not compromise. He took on the might of Delhi and was wilfully martyred. This fact establishes his role in the myth-making growing in the community's imagination and is a huge sentimental draw.

In many homes, shops and public spaces I visited, Bhindranwale occupies a place of pride and reverence. In many homes from where a son has migrated abroad, I see drawing rooms with three pictures on the wall: Bhagat Singh, Bhindranwale and the migrant son. A Panjab sinking into depression through the shenanigans of Centre and state politicians and its own religious bodies feels these are the three heroes who could have, and now can, save it from economic distress. Bhindranwale is now Sant Jarnail Singh Ji Khalsa Bhindranwale Jio.

My reason to feel bewildered is simply this: my grandfather had supported the Indian freedom movement, Baba had heeded India's prime minister, Jawaharlal Nehru's call to build 'temples of modern India' and quit his job at the Bhakra Dam to travel two thousand kilometres away to Rourkela to work at the steel plant, and I had grown up never doubting that India was my nation just as much as my family was my family and its religion was my religion.

When I discovered that the Operation was planned months in advance, that British intelligence was involved, a model of the Darbar Sahib was rigged up at Chakrata in the Doon Valley and the army had been practising there, and a retired army officer, lieutenant general S.K. Sinha, disclosed in an interview that he was superseded and not made chief of army staff because he had refused to carry out the Operation, the news unsettled me and assaulted my sensibilities.

What is even more unpalatable is the fact that the nation launched such a massive Operation against a people and a community, the producers of its food, to protect itself from a food crisis and to ensure its food security. I do not know how to reconcile the fact that the very Green Revolution that had fed the nation had led to grave harm to its base in Panjab.

Besides community faith in the nation, one of the greatest losses during Operation Blue Star was the destruction and looting of the historical records of the community—the Sikh Reference Library.[65] Allegedly, the Central Bureau of Investigation (CBI) was searching for a letter from Indira Gandhi to Bhindranwale. In 185 gunny sacks, the CBI took away all the rare books and manuscripts on Sikh religion, history and culture including handwritten manuscripts of the Guru Granth Sahib, Hukamnamas with signatures of Sikh Gurus and documents relating to the Indian Independence movement. After that, the army burnt down the library building. In its white paper the government says the building was damaged in the Operation, but it has been argued in courts that the building was set on fire after the Operation had concluded. Per media reports, the following texts were taken by the army: 512 handwritten Guru Granth Sahib; 2,500 Sikh scriptures; 12, 613 rare books and manuscripts; twenty to twenty-five Hukamnamas (edicts), signed by the Gurus.[66]

If that one letter was not found, the rest of the valuable heritage could simply have been returned to the Darbar Sahib, but there begins the confusion. On the one hand the army claims they returned the material in seven phases to the SGPC and the Panjab government. However, in 1988, the SGPC wrote to the central government asking for the return of the material taken by the CBI but received only some minor office files. On 23 May 2000, the then defence minister, George Fernandes, wrote to the SGPC secretary, acknowledging that the material was under the government's control. He referred the matter to the ministry of personnel, public grievances and pensions, under whose jurisdiction the CBI falls. He later publicly mentioned that the CBI had destroyed 117 seditious documents but the rest, especially the historical ones, were with the government.

In an order on 26 April 2004, the Panjab and Haryana High Court ordered the central government, the government of Panjab and the CBI to return the 'valuables, books, scriptures, paintings, etc. that were seized'. In February and May 2009, A.K. Antony, defence minister of India, claimed in parliament that the army no longer had any material taken from the library.[67] In June 2019, news surfaced that a rare handwritten Guru Granth Sahib had been sold for Rs 12 crore. This led to a plethora of claims and counter-claims. While Sukhbir Singh Badal reiterated his demand to the Union Government, there were allegations by former Delhi State Gurdwara Management Committee president Manjit Singh GK that he had documents proving that the material had been accepted by SGPC officials.[68]

Whichever community we might be from, our histories, our documents, our ancient texts and our cultural artefacts are our roots to our origins. When the ISIS burnt down the library in Mosul and when the Taliban destroyed the Bamyan Buddhas, we knew a great wrong had happened in our civilisational history. Those events were graphic, tangible, and could be seen and believed.

However, the matter of the Sikh Reference Library has become a matter where people do not know what to believe and whom to believe—whether the loss is tangible or notional. This is how another black hole has emerged in matters pertaining to the Sikh community's history and culture. What it means is that I do not even know if my memoricide is real or phantom. The SGPC decided in June 2019 to constitute a committee to look into the matter. Given that the charges of pilferage were against the SGPC's own officials, and the faith in SGPC being what it is, there is no guarantee that the matter will find closure. What needs to happen is that the state produces full evidence of it no longer being involved in the loot of the Sikh Reference Library. Then it will be up to the community and how it chooses to make its members accountable. Else, this is a memoricide.

If the Operation was a Himalayan blunder, the lack of accountability and answers that have followed since have now created an abyss in our democratic system which has given rise to right-wing Hindutva forces who never accepted the nation's systems and are out to change it. The bias showed when Bhindranwale was termed a secessionist for his acerbic speeches but Bal Thackeray who had done the same in Mumbai in the past—engineering riots to throw out Biharis and south Indians in the name of 'Marathi Manoos'—was given a free hand because he had rowdy street power. Thackeray formed the Shiv Sena which later fought elections, won and formed governments. When he died, Thackeray got a state funeral: draped in the tricolour, and the who's who of the nation turned out in attendance.

The bias shows when the head of the Goraknath Mutt—which, in its history and tradition, can be considered a parallel to the Damdami Taksal—is anointed chief minister of Uttar Pradesh after the 2017 Assembly elections. The head, Ajay Mohan Bisht, known as Yogi Adityanath, also founded the Hindu Yuva Vahini, a far-right militia organisation involved in killings, riots and incidents of arson. Cases have been filed against it and against Adityanath, but his political career has only grown. It shows up when in Maharashtra and in Madhya Pradesh religious leaders get cabinet rank and privileges. The question is not a 'what about' but a serious examination of how is it wrong when Sikhs—Bhindranwale or the Akalis—invoke religion in politics, but condoned when majority groups do the same. These days we see the right wing openly conduct armed training camps; its leaders show the army down by bragging about their efficiency and the nation does not even whimper against them.

I now understand what Danish meant when he said: to understand Panjab, you have to count its corpses. Still, if the Sikhs and Panjab continue to retain faith in India, still produce food for the nation even at their own ecological and economic cost, its people at the borders stand up to defend India from enemy attacks, it is because they have not let the crises of faith consume them. Yes, they struggle, like I saw in two sets of protests—the whitefly and the anti-sacrilege—but they continue to hope the nation does not take them for granted.

Our diverse nation is held up by each of our citizens feeling that they belong to India and the Constitution that we have adopted. If we do not address the breach of the Constitution by Indira Gandhi and the Centre, the weakening and compromise of our systems, the causes and effects of what happened later, including the 1984 pogrom on which the Godhra riots of 2002 were modelled, we have really made our minorities—Sikhs, Muslims, Christians, Jains, Dalits, Adivasis and any other group—much more vulnerable. Panjab presents the nation an opportunity to display it can make amends. It presents an opportunity to overcome the breach in faith and rebuild it.

## Chapter Six

# *Mardangi* — Masculinity

The ritual of democracy—embodied most of all in the process of elections—is such that it imposes itself, irrespective of how people feel or no matter what they seek. As 2015 moved into 2016 and with political parties getting into election mode, the earlier talk about forbidding political parties from entering villages and the idea of NOTA seemed to be receding into the background. Panjab, on the brink, restless, buzzing, once again sought direction through the familiar ritual of democracy—elections. It was a chance to see how people's issues were once again sidelined, this time through the traditional stereotype of the land—its image of masculinity.

In late 2015, many months before the Assembly elections, which were due in February 2017, from conversations with people on my travels, at least outside of the areas which were forbidding political parties from entering their villages, it was clear that Captain Amarinder Singh was the most acceptable face as the next chief minister. At the same time, given Panjab's anguish with the Congress owing to its past role in the state and alongside extensive Akali propaganda against them, people did not completely tilt towards the Congress. Still, Captain Amarinder had a sense of his appeal and threatened the central Congress leadership that he would leave the party and form his own party if he were not appointed leader. The central Congress leadership buckled, ended the party's long-standing internal feud and appointed Captain Amarinder Singh as the leader of the party. A rival contender, Pratap Singh Bajwa, was made a Rajya Sabha member.

One traditional Congress vote bank, the urban Hindu voter, had in recent elections supported the BJP, who were in alliance with the Akalis. The other traditional Congress vote bank, the Dalits and other lower-caste communities in villages, were now under the influence of *deras* such as Sacha Sauda, Ravidassia and others. Manpreet Badal, the former finance minister of Panjab, nephew of Parkash Singh Badal, who had disagreed with Akali government policies and quit the party to found the Panjab People's Party (PPP) in 2012, merged his party with the Congress. The musical chairs were a comedy: in the 2012 elections, when Congress had lost to the SAD–BJP combine by 1.5 per cent votes, the PPP had not won a single seat but gathered 5 per cent votes. If the PPP had joined the Congress alliance in those elections, the state would not have had to bear the devastation it was now undergoing in the second SAD–BJP term. However, this time there was the new kid on the block, the AAP, which had won four seats in the 2014 Lok Sabha election from Panjab. Sukhpal Singh Khaira and Aman Arora, well-entrenched leaders in the Congress, now jumped ship along with many others to join the AAP.

Each political party was now peddling its wares, and all of them played on the discontent of Panjab. The Congress addressed the drug menace in the state. In a dramatic move during the election campaign, near Damdama Sahib in Bathinda, Captain Amarinder Singh placed a *gutka* (the Sikh holy book containing chosen hymns from the Granth Sahib) to his forehead and swore an oath to 'break the back of the drug menace within four weeks of coming to power'. In its earlier incarnation, before militancy, the Congress had played the soft-Hindutva card. Now it was playing the religious Sikh card.

Towards the end of every year, the Sikhs and Panjab mark arguably the greatest story of bravery, defiance and martyrdom in their history.

It is a story of the martyrdom of the younger sons of Guru Gobind Singh. More than 300 years ago, when Guru Gobind Singh left Anandpur, he entrusted his mother Mata Gujri and two younger sons Zorawar Singh and Fateh Singh, aged nine and six, to the care of his household cook named Gangu. Gangu brought Mata Gujri and the two Sahibzadas to his native village of Sahedi. Bribed by the Mughals, he turned over the three members of the Guru's family to the *faujdar* (garrison commander) of Morinda. They were then brought to the Nawab of Sirhind, Wazir Khan, who offered them safe passage if they converted to Islam. They refused and it is said that they were bricked alive. The three-day annual Jor Mela is held at Gurdwara Jyoti Swarup which was built on the site of the martyrdom. While the first day is religious in nature, the next two are usually political.

Over the last couple of decades, political parties have been using the Jor Mela to assert their presence. In 2015, the situation that had been building up since the Sarbat Khalsa ensured that the Jor Mela would be more eventful than usual. The *Panj Pyara*, who, as representatives of the community, could have a say in the matter of the Akal Takht granting pardon to Gurmeet Singh, had summoned the *jathedars*, the custodians of the Sikh institutions, but they had failed to appear before them.[69] The *Panj Pyara* then directed the SGPC to replace them. The deadline for this replacement was 2 January.

On 28 December, the last day of the Jor Mela when Avtar Singh Makkar, the SGPC *jathedar* took the mike, the congregation began shouting *jaikaras* and did not allow him to complete his speech. It was a spontaneous defiance by the community of its highest institutional structure. In deference to the congregation's anger, Giani Gurbachan Singh, the *jathedar* of the Akal Takht, one of the five seats of power in Sikhism, and informally, the most important one, decided not to address the congregation.

Though the Sarbat Khalsa had not worked out, the people's defiance continued and the Jor Mela demonstrated that Sikhs were calling for reforms within their religious institutions. This time the congregation used the same *jaikara*, recited at the end of the *Ardas*, subversively, by shouting out Makkar. The act stung. Rattled by the public defiance and under the influence of the Badals who controlled the SGPC, on 1 January 2016, in an unprecedented move, the SGPC sacked four of the *Panj Pyara*: Satnam Singh, Tirlok Singh, Mangal Singh and Satnam Singh Khanda. The fifth *Panj Pyara*, Major Singh, had anyway retired the day before. The SGPC stated that the *Panj Pyara* were paid employees, and the supreme Sikh body could terminate their services for violation of their jurisdiction and for issuing decrees to the SGPC.

It was a clear indication that, if questioned about its functioning, the Sikh body would suppress the community with a heavy hand. However, by doing so, the prime religious institution of the Sikhs had turned its back on the community instead of standing by the people who continue to believe in the Granth Sahib and the Sikh religion. It was a volte-face, a complete turnaround by the Akalis. In the Nehru era, the Akalis had represented a kind of popular politics which the people were practising now without a credible leadership and the Akalis had shown up to have morphed into a pale shadow of their former self.

In 1953, Prime Minister Nehru had dismissed the nation's first non-Congress Akali government of PEPSU led by Gian Singh Rarewala. This was after Nehru had kept the Panjab Assembly in suspension for nearly ten months in 1953 to help the state Congress government get its act together. Master Tara Singh had then given a call to not allow Nehru to speak at the Jor Mela, which he was scheduled to attend.

When on 27 December 1953, Nehru was about to take the mike, Tarlochan Singh, then a young student of Mahindra College, Patiala, forcibly removed the mike. Nehru was left confused. The police charged Tarlochan Singh and his eight accomplices, all members of the All India Sikh Students Federation, with attempt to murder. They were kept shackled for thirty-six days, until Master Tara Singh prevailed upon Yadvindra Singh, the Rajpramukh at that time, and got the sentence commuted.[70] Later, not only Tarlochan Singh—who rose to become President Zail Singh's press secretary, a Rajya Sabha member and vice-chairman of the National Commission for Minorities—but even his accomplices rose to eminent positions within the Akali party. It was the beginning of the Akali and Congress tussle to obtain power in the state. This time the events showed the distance the Akali Dal and the SGPC had travelled between when they had stood for the community and now when they sought to control the community by force, if necessary.

It was tiring. It was as if it was a repeat of all that we had seen earlier. The land of rivers had itself become an eddy, turning and turning in a quagmire. Panjab was making me feel cold and angry and my mood was darkening. I asked my cousin Minnie if I could stay at her village home for a few days. Since the home had been locked for a while, she requested her cousin Bhola, who lived in the village at Chakklan, caring for his bedridden father, to set up the place for me.

Bhola, a male child, born after seven girls, is an example of Panjab's fascination for the male child. Being the apple of his mother's and sisters' eyes, he was pampered when young and in spite of his father being a school headmaster, he never completed his Class X. As he grew up idling, his mother protected him from all criticism and prompts to make something of his life. Now his mother was dead, his sisters were married, while he and his wife—with whom he often argued over his love for the bottle—took care of his ageing and infirm father on whose pension they subsisted. Recently, he had pushed himself to begin farming on his land that he had previously leased out and taken Phuphadji's (Minnie's father) small patch along with some others on *theka*.

Minnie's house was on the road from Morinda to Chamkaur Sahib. If the government decided to acquire land to widen the road, half of her house would come under the axe. The road-widening scheme had been pending for a couple of decades. In the militancy era, this state highway was one of the bloodiest roads in Panjab with many encounters on it between the police and the militants. It had prompted a then-young Minnie's parents to send her away to Rajpura for studies. She never really returned to the village after that. Years later, when she came back from the US to take care of her parents, she took them away to Delhi where she worked.

A few years earlier, when Minnie was still in the US, I had gone down to be with Phuphadji and Bibiji on the occasion of Diwali. Frail Phuphadji and I had slowly walked to his farm and lit a lamp at his tube well. Then we had gone to the well associated with *Shaheedan*, the martyrs of the village in an ancient battle no one clearly remembered, and lit a lamp. After that we went to the village pond, to the *samad,* the grave of an ancestor. It was marked by a trishul on a mound and was full of lamps from the village—a de-facto temple of sorts. After that we walked to one of the three gurdwaras in the village. The prayer hall was upstairs and Phuphadji found it hard to negotiate the steps. He gave me a Rs 100 note and asked me to offer it in prayer. We went home and lit a lamp in front of Goddess Lakshmi, the benefactor of wealth, and Bibiji recited the *mool-mantar* from the Granth Sahib, after which we partook of *prasad* (sweets in this case). We did not cook non-vegetarian food that evening, but later in the night, Phuphadji opened his bottle of whiskey and we had a drink. This multiplicity of rituals—the nonchalant crossing of religious borders, the animistic worship of the well, the reverence for land, martyrs and an ancestor—this syncretism seemed wholly organic to the ways of life of the people of Panjab. It was a warm memory.

This time I was surprised that near the *samad* there was now a gurdwara. Earlier the *samad* was on the bank of the pond. Unless the village panchayat had sold the pond land, which it couldn't have, it meant the gurdwara, funded with money from the diaspora, had encroached upon it. I asked around and found no one even remotely inquisitive about the question I had in mind. The response was: what is the harm in having a new gurdwara? I asked why not a temple. After all, the *samad* with a trishul had looked like a Shiv temple.

The *samad* certainly did not look like I remembered it. When I was a kid it used to be a mound, and near it were a pair of wooden slippers and a *chimta*, a musical instrument with long tongs and with metallic discs attached to each of the tongs. These two objects were rumoured to have been left behind by the seer who lived in the area and had one day disappeared into thin air. Anyone who made fresh jaggery would come here to make an offering. When a buffalo began lactating, the first milk or colostrum would also be offered here. Sometimes, if the rains were delayed, people would light a prayer fire at the location. Don't the Valmikis come here anymore? I asked. Valmikis were, of course, Dalit Hindus. I was told they did, and when the Sikhs went to the gurdwara they first bowed their head at the *samad*. In fact, the gurdwara itself is called Samadwalla Gurdwara.

Bhola and I set about dusting and cleaning the house when Bhabhi (Bhola's wife) came in and scolded us, 'Is that a man's task?' Bhabhi had also brought along Jeeto who worked in the house. She and Jeeto went about setting up the front room, the bathroom and a rudimentary kitchen. They pulled out rugs and quilts from the boxes. Bhabhi told me that meals would come from her place and that Jeeto would bring them. That night I went down to Bhabhi's place for a dinner of *sarson ka saag* and rotis, a staple meal in most rural Panjab homes in the winters. The sound of trucks on the main road made sleep impossible. I made my way to an inner room and decided to buy a heater.

The next morning, there was no electricity. Minnie had renovated her home a few years earlier, pulled down the old beam roof and got a concrete roof put in, modernised the bathroom and fixed a geyser. But the water pressure was never enough for the water from the sump to reach the overhead tank. When I was figuring out how to heat water, Bhola came in carrying cow dung cakes. From the store, Bhola pulled out a double-barrel water boiler.

The boiler had two cylinders, one inside the other. When one poured water, it settled between the cylinders. The firewood, old beams from the roof, were placed inside the inner cylinder. The heated water rose as steam and would be poured out into a bucket through a metal pipe. Bhola told me a full firing could churn out eight to ten buckets of hot water. This indigenous geyser with no name definitely beat the electric ones. From then on, for the few days I stayed, we heated water at night and enjoyed the bonfire and bath.

When I stepped out, neighbours greeted me and asked about Phuphadji and Bibiji. That evening, fair, cat-eyed, long-bearded Bira Uncle and another friend came home with a bottle of Bagpiper whiskey and some snacks. Minnie had told me that he had some land and a car which he used as a taxi to ferry village folks who lived abroad to Chandigarh or even to Delhi to help them catch their international flights. I casually asked Uncle about the Mazhabi Sikhs (lower caste Sikhs) in the village and if they had their own gurdwara. The friend told me they had one, in the back of the village. Uncle then said that another gurdwara was coming up near the canal—the

Shaheedan Gurdwara. I remarked, 'For about a total of 1,300 residents, the village has four gurdwaras, a *samad* and a martyrs' well! Such great religious fervour should make for an extremely pious society …'

The men laughed. 'A way of making money, certainly. Not many young boys find jobs locally. About a hundred families in the village have one or more person abroad. The masons, the carpenters, the plumbers are all *bhaiyas* now—migrant labourers from east India.'

'Do they marry locally?' I asked. Uncle went silent but the friend said, with sadness, 'Some have, to Sikh girls.'

I was amused by the double standards. To marry the foreigner, the *gori*, the *mem*, the white woman, was such an aspiration for the youth and even older men. Yet, when migrants came here and found love or convenience and got married locally, we frowned. As we were pouring drinks, Jeeto came in with my dinner. Suddenly, the behaviour of the men changed. Eyeing Jeeto, they tried to act sophisticated. They asked her to cut some onions and chillies. I saw the two men watching her like hawks, measuring her up. It made me uncomfortable and I quickly sent her away.

Jeeto was married not so long ago and was the mother of a small child. Her husband was a factory worker who doubled up as a *palledar*. These two men were probably older than her father, but their patriarchal and predatory attitude towards the Dalit woman unsettled me. I wanted them to leave but couldn't say it directly. I made their pegs larger. After they were sufficiently drunk, I escorted them to the gate. They parted, saying, 'Now your turn to get some alcohol. For tomorrow.'

Early next morning, the dissonance of the multiple mutually mistimed recitations of the Gurbani from the four gurdwaras woke me up. I wrapped a shawl around myself and walked up to them. While the main and the Mazhabi Gurdwara had a *paathi* reciting from the Holy Book, the NRI Gurdwara and the newly-built Shaheedan Gurdwara were playing pre-recorded Gurbani. The *paath* wasn't live. Reason: lack of staff, shortage of *granthis* and *paathis* because most trained *granthis* now sought fortunes abroad, where, among the diaspora, gurdwaras were proliferating.

That afternoon, Bhola and I walked up to Phuphadji's one and a half acre land holding in which wheat had been sown. The crop was about two feet tall. The sight of greenery, the sense of growth, the freshness in the air was soothing. But we noticed the leaves had a faint yellow stripe and some yellow powder collected on them. As we walked through the crop, the powder fell on the lower part of my jeans. I touched the leaves and the soft powder came on my fingers. Bhola seemed worried. He was aware of the *peeli kungi*—the striped or yellow stripe rust disease had come on early that year. 'I have been to Chamkaur Sahib and Morinda; I am not getting the medicine,' said Bhola. 'Medicine' referred to Propiconazole concentrate to prepare the fungicide. 'I do not even have money to get it.' Bhola had three acres of his own and had taken another five on *theka*.

Per the university instructions, at the rate of one litre Propiconazole per acre, to be mixed in 200 litres of water and sprayed, Bhola would need anything between rupees five to fifteen thousand to buy the concentrate. The Sygenta version, Tilt, was priced at Rs 1,600 per litre. Pikapika at Rs 700 and Teer and Avtar were somewhere in between. It was for better yield that the farmers over another twenty-five lakh hectares in Panjab had sown wheat variety HD 2967. Ironically, the yellow stripe rust disease affected this variety the most.

Over the next few days, an anxious Bhola went to the *arthiya* (the commission agent and moneylender), who would have given him credit but even the shops in the commission agent's network did not have the pesticide. If the crop failed Bhola would have another one lakh rupees as loan on top of the five lakhs he already owed to banks and the *arthiya*. The *theka* does not relent. If he got the pesticide he would be down rupees fifteen thousand which would be most of his profit from the produce.

Finally, Bira Uncle contacted a shop in Samrala where Propiconazole was available. The *arthiya* arranged credit and went with Bhola to purchase the chemical. The *arthiya* bought in bulk but still paid a black market rate. He rationed Bhola's supply and would sell the rest to other farmers in the village. When credit is king, the relationships in the villages are enmeshed. The ones with whom you want to keep distance are also those who could help you when in dire straits.

In the dense fog of the next morning, we carried the five litres of Propiconazole and a large plastic drum to the fields. The spray machine was tied to Bhola's back. Bhola mixed the concentrate with half the prescribed water, saying, 'This will double the dose. We are already late.' He also mixed Admire Imidacloprid and Fen from Bayer and Bhoocare in the fungicide. These were insecticides for the crop. As the fog lifted, Bhola sprinkled the fields. It took him the whole day. I was concerned that we had made a mistake in preparing the spray. But Bhola was desperate and could only double his efforts; in this case, chemicals. The larger question was why was Propiconazole not available? Why did the government not step in when the disease had been detected in Nurpur Bedi, in another part of Anandpur Sahib district?

When I called Bhola after about two weeks he told me the spray had not worked. The disease was still consuming the plants. The disease had spread to more villages. After the whitefly on cotton had devastated south Panjab, the yellow stripe rust was going to push debt-laden Bhola along with many other farmers of eastern Panjab into further misery.

By the end of January the weather changed dramatically. The yellow stripe rust proliferated in the cold moist season. It rained, then the sun came out for a few days and the fog disappeared. In the next week or so, the disease went away but not without creating a large hole in Bhola's pocket. Now he had to continue tending to his and the leased fields knowing that he would perhaps earn nothing for his work and would perhaps not sink into further debt until another calamity arose—rains during the harvest and sale and the lack of storage facilities. The anxiety in Bhola's eyes haunted me, for this was what the hardy, jovial farmer had been reduced to: panicking, facing the vagaries of the weather, and trying to keep ahead of disease mostly by his own efforts and networks and with no support from the system.

Aligning the ritual of democracy with the ritual commemoration of a historic event, at the Maghi Mela in Muktsar, on the day of Lohri (13 January), the Akalis and the Congress arranged huge rallies. Many folks made use of the Akali-arranged buses and vehicles to reach the venue but did not attend the Akali rally. Instead, they walked off to the parallel AAP rally. Guru Amar Das had declared Maghi (winter solstice) as one of the three important festivals of the Sikhs, with the others being Baisakhi and Diwali. By the time of Guru Gobind Singh, Maghi took on an overt religious hue because of the story of the forty liberated ones, *mukte*. These forty Sikhs had given a memorandum to the Guru and deserted him in his battle at Anandpur Sahib. An upright lady, Mai Bhago, pointed out their cowardice to them and exhorted them to fight for the cause. They joined the Guru at the battle of Kidhrana and all forty of them laid down their lives. Before his end, their leader requested the Guru to cancel the memorandum. The Guru tore it up, pardoned them, conducted their final rites, and declared them *mukt* (free). The town close to the scene of the battle was now called Muktsar—the pool of liberation. It is a story of desertion, penance and return.

Symbolically, Arvind Kejriwal's return on Maghi Mela was a poetic and religious message. Kejriwal was atoning for the trouble that had erupted in the party the previous year when he had sacked two of his important co-founders: Prashant Bhushan and Yogendra Yadav. Along with them, two elected Members of Parliament—Dr Dharamvira Gandhi and Harinder Singh Khalsa—from Panjab had been suspended. There was no talk of taking them back or placating them. It was similar to the apology Kejriwal had made to the people of Delhi for having resigned in their first term because they did not have a majority. It had worked in Delhi and AAP had won big time in the 2015 Delhi Assembly elections.

The festival of Lohri is connected to the folklore of Dulla Bhatti, a Robin Hood-like figure from the time of Akbar.[71] AAP sought to fit the story tropes of Muktsar and Lohri. AAP claimed that its entry to Panjab was nothing short of the beginning of a revolution which would take a year to fructify, i.e., at the next elections in February of 2017.

When he came on stage, Kejriwal was dressed in a yellow turban, held a sword and the atmosphere was replete with slogans: *Bole So Nihal, Sat Sri Akal* symbolising Panjab's religious side and *Inquilab Zindabad* symbolising Panjab's leftist or socialist side. AAP sought to reclaim the space the Left had lost due to its role during the Emergency when it supported Indira Gandhi and because of its being avowedly against the Khalistan movement. AAP, promising a revolution, sought to feed on both: the disenchantment the Sikhs had with the traditional parties and their socialist sentiment.

Given the political, economic and social morass of current Panjab, and the identification of the destroyer, the enemy, the slogans implied: rout the Badals, the Akalis, free the land and reclaim it. Kejriwal swore to get those responsible for the sacrilege of the Guru Granth and the kingpins of the drug syndicate including Bikram Singh Majithia, the brother-in-law of Sukhbir Singh Badal, arrested within four weeks of coming to power.

About a year back Majithia had been accused of running the syndicate by the wrestler, former Arjuna awardee and police officer, Jagdish Bhola, who had turned to drug smuggling. Majithia had then been questioned by the Enforcement Directorate. A few days later, the ED had transferred the investigating officer, deputy director Niranjan Singh, to Kolkata. The Panjab and Haryana High Court revoked the transfer but later the officer flip-flopped over resigning from service. In between he got his daughter married for which he invited popular music stars Diljit Dosanjh, Miss Pooja, Gippy Grewal and Jazzy B which attracted the court's attention due to the expenses incurred for the wedding which were not in line with Niranjan's income, and he was quizzed. The Majithia issue went on the back burner though AAP and Kejriwal repeated the claim that they would arrest Majithia many, many times in the next year.

Since I was seeing Panjab as my mother's chest, as any caregiver I expected if Panjab had to survive, it needed an accurate diagnosis of its issues, a plan to provide healing, time for recovery, and perhaps some amputation. That would be its treatment. Yet, with AAP, new to Panjab, new to its people, new to politics even, without its own independent study or understanding, Panjab was already in solution mode, focussing on the low-hanging issues—drugs and sacrilege. Sacrilege was no doubt a current issue, but drugs, to me, was a symptom of all of Panjab's problems—not a disease in itself. AAP's language scared me. Their militaristic purpose—promises to solve Panjab's issues—enticed a bewildered and beleaguered Panjab. The political posturing was akin to a doctor who declaimed solutions even before knowing the full extent of the illness. The language with which AAP started and the bravado and overconfidence did not seem to fit the mood of what was needed to understand and work with Panjab to heal its wounds. It seemed violent.

Perhaps it was needed. Perhaps as a political party it needed to catch people's attention. Yet, it betrayed a discomfort which had to do with its own recent conduct—suspension of its elected leaders. In Panjab, rhetoric has been done to death. Whether it is through diktats of elders to buck up, perform better, be a man, never cry, not grieve, or through the cheap posters in drawing rooms with scenes of the Alps or the Rocky Mountains and positive slogans that accompany them—Be Happy; Honesty Best Policy; Never, never, never give up and so on—or through the public stereotypes about the valorous Panjabis and their tendency to be over-achievers. In keeping with the flamboyant spirit of Panjabis and their do-or-die attitude, AAP was stoking their fires. I wondered how AAP would take on the mantle. Would AAP rise above the morass of the two established parties, the Akalis and the Congress who had fortified Panjab with language and then battered its people? That seemed unlikely, for it, too, like the other two parties, was using religion and rhetoric to further its propaganda.

The representative phrases about Panjab that are often bandied about—soldier and farmer, traitor and terrorist—conjure up ideas of male figures, usually the macho man. Panjab celebrates the alpha-male masculinity of the farmer-feeder and the soldier-defender of the nation. Some even celebrate the identity of the terrorist-killer, and the traitor-rebel. If Panjab is macho land its best expression should come out—in the absence of war—on the field, in sports.

The Kila Raipur Sports Festival is known the world over as the rural Olympics. The first Kila Raipur games were held in 1933. Since then, the games have survived a world war, the Partition of India, and the era of militancy in the state. They have encouraged many other villages to host such games. They have created players who have competed at the world level, especially in hockey where players from

Panjab still comprise about half the national team. Besides hockey, sports like kabaddi and equestrian events have benefitted from the Kila Raipur Sports Festival.

On the morning of 4 February, my birthday, I headed south from Ludhiana towards the Grewal Stadium, the venue for the annual Kila Raipur games. The games are an annual three-day sports festival in Kila Raipur village. They include sports that sound quaint but are still played in villages. *Tirinjen, kikli, khidu* and *kokla chhapaki* are games popular with young girls and involve singing and swirling and catching each other. *Gilli danda* is a rustic version of cricket, played with a long stick and another shorter one tapered at both ends. *Kidi kada* or *stapoo* is a kind of hopscotch. In *ghaggar phissi* one boy is weighed down by other boys until he can carry them no more. The games also feature *akharas* where wrestlers grapple with each other, and kabaddi matches. The Nihangs join in with equestrian fare. Hockey remains a big sport, but the centrepiece is the bull racing events.

On the way to the venue, I found no signboards leading to the stadium. Was the event so big that it needed no publicity? Panjab is not like that. Here the obvious is stated in many different ways. Had the games been called off? Upon reaching the stadium, I noticed that many residents of Kila Raipur seemed unenthusiastic about the event. Their disinterest piqued my interest.

The gentle sun was out and a group of villagers played cards at the village *sathh* (meeting point), typically a platform under a prominent tree, as an announcement glorifying MRF, the tyre company sponsoring the event, played in the background. Its announcements clashed with announcements from the local gurdwara. Finally, the stadium speaker went silent for a while, letting the gurdwara one finish. A huge poster declared that these games had the blessings of Adesh Partap Singh Kairon, then minister for excise and taxation, food and IT. Kairon was from the famed Kairon family and a grandson of the ex-chief minister of Panjab, Partap Singh Kairon. Through a political marriage that reminds one of the kings of yore, and is a reality of today's Panjab, he is the son-in-law of Parkash Singh Badal, once Kairon's rival, albeit a junior one, and later, chief minister, and is also the brother-in-law of Sukhbir Singh Badal. Additionally, he is the nephew of Harcharan Singh Brar, an ex-chief minister who took over when his predecessor Beant Singh was assassinated in 1995.

'The poster is to announce that control of these games has moved from Bikram Singh Majithia to Kairon,' the reporter who gave me a ride in his car told me.

'It is still the same family,' I said.

The reporter replied, 'Within the greater Badal family, but moved from the Majithia family to the Kairon family. The nuances of ownership matter.'

Some camels and horses, dressed in colourful shawls, stood on the far end of the ground. I went to see them, and as we approached, a drummer started beating the drum, making the animals dance—a vigorous leg and body movement. Soon after that the drummer asked us to pay up. A languid hockey match was on in the main ground. But even as the game was on, the audience criss-crossed the field at will, forcing the players to make adjustments in the middle of their run. The speaker kept requesting people to clear the ground. Nobody listened.

That day and the next, I never saw a crowd of more than two and a half thousand people. It was a far cry from the tens of thousands who usually attended every year from across the country, and beyond. The Grewal Stadium abuts another open ground which hosts the small food and toys fair and the parking lot. People mostly gathered near the makeshift stalls selling pakoras and tea. Winter was waning and people came to bask in the sun and not really to watch the games. At the sugarcane juice stall, Brij Lal, originally from Uttar Pradesh, who had been coming there for four decades, told me, 'A glass of juice used to be Re 1, now it is Rs 20. Yet, I made more money then.'

Amidst the hockey matches, there was a show of strength—a man pulled a car with his beard. Another carried a cycle placed on a wooden bar between his teeth. A third lifted huge stone weights. People rushed to the ground to catch a glimpse of these displays and shot videos on their mobile phones. I wondered where the wrestling *akharas* were. I could not spot any of the children's games either. I asked around and no one seemed to know. Some people were playing kabaddi but spectators were barely interested. Young boys and girls ran 100- and 400-metre races on the track. I looked for the *bazigars*— the iconic community known for their acrobatic skills. They were absent. Taekwondo had replaced them like western athletics had replaced indigenous games.

A series of dog races started in the afternoon on the far side of the ground. Once people surrounded the dog tracks, the ones seated in the stadium could see nothing. The well-kept canines chased fake rabbit skin. Their names were all Western: Bullet, Ford, Lucy, Bravo and Computer—a bullmastiff, a great dane, a boxer, a golden retriever and an ordinary mongrel respectively. The Nihangs on horses hardly participated, except for ceremonial purposes—a round of the field, a bit of trotting, and they were done. On the first evening, a lackadaisical *gatka* troupe from the Eik Onkar Akhara displayed some feats but the mock fights and drills were deflated. I asked my journalist friend about the bull races. He said, 'Oh! They are banned.'

'But were they not the highlight of the games? Why were they banned?'

'Jallikattu ban. Don't you know?'[s]

---

s. Jallikattu is a traditional spectacle in which a bull is released into a crowd of people, and multiple human participants attempt to grab the large hump on the bull's back with both arms and hang on to it while the bull attempts to escape. It is popular in Tamil Nadu.

The decreased popularity of the games was a result of the 2014 Supreme Court ban on bullock races. The 103-page judgement clubbed with a number of pending high court cases and passed a nationwide ban on any event that included exhibition of or performances by bulls, in compliance with Sections 3 and 11 of the Prevention of Cruelty to Animals Act. The judgement discussed the anatomy of the bull, and stated that the animal was unfit for racing. The judgement does not specifically mention Panjab even once, nor does it contain any references to the bull races in Kila Raipur. It explicitly cites the jallikattu event in Tamil Nadu and the bullock cart races in Maharashtra. Nevertheless, the Grewal Sports Association, the organising committee for the games, complied with the orders and dropped the races (the jallikattu events were later temporarily allowed by the BJP central government earlier that year, following which the Supreme Court issued a stay on the government's order, and upheld the ban). Since 2015, the Kila Raipur games have featured a horse race as a substitute. A week before the games were due to begin, for a day or so, bull owners in Panjab protested the Supreme Court ban, but their voices fell on deaf ears.

For seven years before the races were banned in 2014, Jagjit Singh Jaggi's bull won a spot in the top three five times. 'Just like among dogs we have strays, those with smelling prowess, and hunting packs, among bulls we have those which carry loads and those which run,' he explained. 'Our bulls are Nagori, well-known for their agility.'

The National Dairy Development Board affirms Jaggi's contention. On the Dairy Knowledge Portal, an informational initiative by the board, Nagori bulls are identified as a 'famous trotting draught breed of India' generally appreciated for 'fast draught activity'. The post notes that Nagori bulls are famous as trotters and are used in Rajasthan 'in light iron-wheeled carts for quick transportation'. The famous bull races at Kila Raipur fit the description given: they are a race among bulls, with a light cart upon which the bull owner stands.

I brought this up with Manilal Valliyate, the chief veterinarian of People for the Ethical Treatment of Animals (PETA), which had been the initiator of the case that led to the jallikattu ban, but he did not agree. 'How can a bull be induced to run without fear or provocation?' he asked. 'If owners are doing that, they are being cruel to the animal. Can they get the bulls to run without sticks or whips, by a tug at the noose or harness?'

'Yes, we can,' Jaggi countered, when I told him about Valliyate's concern. He added that he would welcome any animal rights activist or journalist who wished to ascertain his claim, to his farm. 'If you line up a few Nagoris, ready them in a position to run, upon release of the harness, they compete with each other.' After speaking to Jaggi, I contacted various animal rights organisations to find evidence of cruelty against bulls in the Kila Raipur games. No one was willing to go on record. There was no evidence.

Dr Kirti Dua, a senior veterinarian who works at the Guru Angad Dev Veterinary and Animal Sciences University in Ludhiana, averred that he had seen many bull owners spend more than Rs 500 per day in caring for their bulls. 'Many of them may or may not remember their children and families, but they remain updated on how the bull is doing every half an hour,' he told me. Dua added that he had yet to come across an instance of owners sending their bulls for slaughter even in old age. In the event of a bull's death, he had seen owners perform the last rites, or host a *langar* for the village, a practice commonly followed in Panjab following the death of a family member. He conceded, however, that incidents of cruelty, such as steroid injections or using spiked clubs, were known to have occurred in the past. 'But that was more from ignorance than from greed,' Dua said, before adding, 'What the courts need to do is frame criteria to test the bulls. The whole reason for demonstrating the best bull is social recognition. Tell me, which owner would risk his reputation? A blanket ban does not help at all,' he concluded. 'In fact, it risks the pedigree of bulls, and breaks a tradition.'

While it is difficult to establish beyond doubt whether the animals are treated with kindness or cruelty, the politics of the ban on the bull race involves more than just animal rights. In 2012, the Bhartiya Gau Raksha Dal—an organisation that works for the protection of cows—registered a petition against the use of bulls in these games. The Panjab and Haryana High Court combined the petition with two others, one by the Malwa-Doaba Bulls Welfare Association and another by the Rural Hult Race and Welfare Association, both of which claimed that the Kila Raipur races did not constitute a violation of Section 11 of the Prevention of Cruelty to Animals Act, as the races did not qualify as performance or exhibition. The court ruled in favour of these two petitions and allowed the races. The presiding judge observed, 'At the cost of repetition, it is observed that the bulls, which are being used for the sports, are well looked after, well-nourished and are not treated with any cruelty.' This order constituted a defeat of the right-wing voices, until the 2014 Supreme Court order.

When I asked Nikku Grewal—the spokesperson of the Grewal Sports Association (GSA)—why the association didn't challenge the ban, he was candid. 'Laziness. We thought the Malwa-Doaba Bull Welfare Association would pursue the case; they thought we would do it. Neither of us did.' Since the games used to pull in a lot of people and the state elections were due, political parties appeared to be interested in leveraging the games to their advantage. In the absence of bulls, Amarinder Singh of the Congress was slated to be a big draw, but he failed to show up. Even Ravneet Bittu, the MP from Congress who was supposed to have come, finally did not arrive. 'It was a chance to involve the AAP,' Grewal said. 'After all, H.S. Phoolka contested the 2014 Lok Sabha polls from Ludhiana. We could have used him to plead our case. But we didn't. We are disappointed.'[t]

---

t. H.S. Phoolka is a senior advocate known for his lifelong work to secure justice for the 1984 anti-Sikh pogrom victims in Delhi, and used to be a member of the AAP.

All the state needed to do was remind the Supreme Court of the high court order and get an exemption, but it did not do that, and through this negligence reduced the value of the games and Panjab's heritage.

By the second day evening, the singer and actor Gurdas Maan arrived to promote his new film. The famous poet Surjit Patar accompanied him. Since they were in a hurry, the games were stopped temporarily for announcements pertaining to the film launch. Maan did not even sing, and left. The games that were originally conceptualised to showcase the glory of Panjab now served as a forum for film promotions. I was more disappointed than surprised. These games had given Panjab so much, yet the state was allowing them to die.

There was yet another twist. A twist I found in many stories and testimonials of Panjab, which is why I showcased this story. When we wish an aggrieved party—here the GSA—should pursue justice, there is a reason that prevents it from following through. The twist is such that it would implicate the supposed aggrieved party as an offender in a situation of injustice. This holds good for both individuals and groups, for the lowly and the mighty. For example, Captain Amarinder Singh whom the Congress has declared as their leader has decade-old cases of corruption in Ludhiana and Amritsar Improvement Trusts against him.

Captain Amarinder Singh's son Raninder Singh, president of the National Rifle Association of India, and wife Preneet Kaur, former union minister, allegedly have Swiss bank accounts where they siphon off money. The dynamic Akali-baiter MLA from Atam Nagar, Ludhiana, Lok Insaaf Party (LIP) president Simarjit Singh Bains has a decade-old case of assault on *tehsildar* Major Gurjinder Singh Benipal over fake stamp papers. BJP's aggressive motormouth, former cricket player Navjot Singh Sidhu has a three-decade old case of assault and murder on him. This is how rivals have the tails of these leaders in their grasp and can anytime use state institutions like police and investigative agencies to tighten the screws on them when their criticism becomes uncomfortable.

Similarly, the GSA is locked in a battle for the land on which the games are held. In 1997, Surinder Singh Grewal, a retired senior army officer, filed a case in the local court. According to him, the GSA had wrongfully appropriated Kila Raipur village's common land in 1985 through the then District Development and Panchayat Officer. The land, he argued, had originally been given to them for the three days of the games, but they controlled it through the year. In a recent judgement, the local court upheld Surinder Singh's petition. The hearing revealed that the GSA accounts had never been audited. The court ordered the GSA to give the land back to the village by mid-February. It didn't, and the games still take place at the stadium.

The most likely reason for the Kila Raipur fiasco was that the Akali government did not want to disturb its status quo with the BJP government, even at the cost of the heritage and reputation of its own people. The bull in the race was not just an animal but symbolically a mascot of masculinity.[72] While Panjabis are known to fight for personal honour, they have failed when it comes to preserving their symbol. In the last few years, jallikattu has been allowed in Tamil Nadu but bull races have not restarted in Kila Raipur. Even if they do, I doubt the games would regain their position of pride.

As a child, when Mama was in her schizophrenic mania in Rajpura, the male members of the family assumed all she needed were a few good slaps. The slaps would shut her up. That is when my eldest cousin used a word for Baba that made me curious, and when I understood the meaning, it pricked me: *namard*—you are not a man. In the masculine, patriarchal and feudal language-scape of Panjab, the word *namard* asserted the negation of a quality that the society feels is important for its being and survival—masculinity. The message at the core of masculinity is: when men are good in bed, their families are under their control.

I learnt the word from billboards and crudely painted wall banners in Panjab's towns and villages that said: *namardgi to milen*—if you suffer masculine weakness, please meet. This time, travelling in Panjab, I saw even more of them—many more than I have seen anywhere in the country. I decided to visit some of those shady-looking shops, mostly painted white, with half-open doors. I called the sex doctors from numbers given on advertisements to seek an appointment: Dr Zail Singh Rajput, Dr Waryam Singh Rajput, Sablok Clinic, Dr Bengali, Dr Momi, Dr Yogi and so on. Most of them had a bachelor's degree in Ayurveda, medicine and surgery. All of them were curt.

'What is there to talk?'

I tried to be inviting. 'No one talks about it. Should we not?'

'Do you want treatment?'

'No.'

'Then don't waste our time.'

Finally, I made contact with an allopathic doctor, a rarity. To my surprise, even on the phone, he was encouraging. 'The big issue is we don't talk about it. Please come.'

I went to his shop-cum-office (SCO). SCO is a typical Chandigarh address wherein shops are on the ground floors of markets and offices on the floors above. It was early evening when I climbed up the narrow steps wondering how much time he would be able to give me in the peak consultation hours. When I pushed open the door to the clinic, I was surprised that except for the receptionist the clinic was empty. At the far end behind a ground glass door sat the forty-year-old doctor. He was mild-mannered. He looked well-suited for a job where the client had to trust the doctor enough to share his deepest 'secrets'. Assuming I was from the media, the doctor allowed me ten minutes. By the time we finished, it was late night.

The doctor told me his business had been on the rise since he had started in the late 1990s and had grown hugely after the advent, in the last decade, of the internet and mobile phones. 'The desire of the society reveals itself in this clinic: men from eighteen to eighty years; women too. Cases of homosexuality, of bisexuality, heterosexuality, and incest: daughter-in-law with father-in-law; sister-in-law with brother-in-law; cousins; even siblings. I have dealt with mothers and sons, fathers and daughters, you name it. People seek guidance on extramarital sex, even group sex. Then there are massage parlours. There are no boundaries or limits.'

'That must be a lot of business …'

'We have a simple revenue model: in Panjab men go around with big moustache curls and their cars declare them to be proud landowners. Yet, there is no worse humiliation for a man than his partner kicking him out of bed because he could not perform. He will spend any amount of money to get back his lost masculinity.'

I was aware of this kind of peer pressure—right from my school days. Even now, in meetings with young men, the topic used to come up—whether it was one asking how someone started taking drugs, or why someone joined a gymnasium and began body-building or participating in kabaddi and wrestling matches. One time a young man asked me for help with his visa application and I asked him why he wanted to leave if he was married. His answer had saddened me: I am unable to please my wife. I now wanted to know the statistics. How many people, what demography?

'There are no studies, but at least 20 per cent of Panjab's males suffer from some problem or the other. Mostly, it is just a crisis of confidence. You see, sexual dysfunction is subjective. There is no standard. You can't count or measure it. On a scale of one to ten, you might be satisfied at three, someone may be unhappy at ten. But we can't make a normal person super-normal. The biggest issue is ignorance—lack of sexual and reproductive education. It is our loud culture, our focus on masculinity measured in fertility and being soldiers and farmers. We learn them from our alpha-male image and our songs. Then, when at the time of copulation something does not work, as can happen to any of us, people suddenly doubt themselves. This doubt, this having to live up to an image, leads to dysfunction.'

'What else besides confidence and knowledge?'

'In gymnasiums, use of drugs like Nandrolone and Deca Durabolin and injections like testosterone and Sustanon affect that single organ which no medicine can help. Fertility goes down and so does sexual prowess which may be non-recoverable and non-treatable. You know how male child-oriented we are. At some point, the focus of sex life became children, not enjoyment, and fertility, not pleasure. Even the educated elite classes have made masturbation such a big cause for guilt.'

'But do people know what is an orgasm?'

'Men know it is linked to ejaculation. I have found more than 90 per cent people do not know what an orgasm is like for a woman. But now more women are speaking up in bed. Men realise they are unable to make their women reach orgasm.'

'And how does diet link to sexual issues? All these chemicals in food?'

'In Panjab how can you escape chemicals? There has been a drop in sperm count. From 60 million sperm per millilitre a few decades ago to 15 million sperm per millilitre now. Then there is the dairy industry which has grown in parallel to the Green Revolution.'[73]

'What about it?'

'Pesticides in dairy fodder increase your estrogen levels. Cattle owners often inject cows and buffaloes with Oxytocin to increase production of milk. It increases estrogen levels in the male body. Estrogen is a female hormone. Our bodies have a balance of estrogen and testosterone. When estrogen intake increases, the balance goes haywire. The huge consumption of milk, milk products and chicken is responsible for the decrease in libido.'

'What else?'

'The lifestyle change in our society, all these desk-bound jobs, the high-flying careers in information technology and business processing outsourcing are taking their toll now. People don't have time for each other, for intimacy, for relationships and for sex. One partner is travelling, then another partner is travelling. In some ways Panjab has had this problem for long, with so many men in the army and now abroad as migrants. But it has become acute now. I get so many cases which need no medicine and no cure. All they need is time together. The sexual health in villages is still better, but there, in joint families, people have issues with space. If everybody lives together and sleeps together, where can couples go?'

'But I also feel there is a category called asexual, which is just not recognised ...'

'Absolutely. A huge number of people are genuinely asexual or do not have the kind of drive the images of sex want them to have. Libido differs from person to person. Sex is natural but it is also a construct. So much of everything in our life, birth, marriage, family and relations revolves around sex. So, people try to fit each other into roles. No one really recognises the asexual, like they did not recognise homosexuality a few years back. Even now it is a very reluctant topic.'

'Do you treat homosexuality?' I asked, because a few years back an Indian-American anthropologist film-maker had featured me and some others in a film on masculinity.[74] One of the others was a gay activist, Dhananjay. He had spoken about being gay but he was in a heterosexual marriage, with children. His story had touched me and I had met him and his friends to understand the sub-culture. His friends were a riot, but Dhananjay also presented some data which had stunned me.

Dhananjay was working with an NGO that provided HIV and STD prevention kits to men who have sex with men (MSM). He said he had around four thousand registered clients and around a thousand incidents occurred in Chandigarh alone each night. When I asked about the villages, he had said, 'Every village has a tempo or two.' Tempo meant a gay bottom for public use. In fact, homosexuality was a taboo area but at the same time very prevalent in society.

The doctor said, '*Ardhanareshwar* is an Indian concept. It is society which has drawn rigid lines. Once you are in the bedroom, all lines crumble, or should crumble. No one knows who you are. There are those who perform four times, six times in a day but they may not enjoy sex even once. They are just counting their ejaculations. Panjab does not admit to homosexuality because they relate it to maleness. The notion of a man is that he can make male babies. The stance against homosexuality is that no babies come from it. Often, homosexuals or bisexuals get into trouble once they get married. After marriage if they are not indulging in sex with their wives it causes discord and becomes a matrimonial dispute. I know a homosexual man who married four times until he found a poor girl who had no choice but to stay with him. Patients come to me asking me how to go about anal sex—to treat injuries to the penis or anal tissue tears. I teach them through diagrams and counselling. To me sexuality is sexuality, it is not gendered.'

The doctor opened his drawer that had a huge number of syringes. 'Many people, because of lifestyle or age or food, do not get enough strength in their penis or want to maintain erection for long or they want medication through intra-penile injections.'

'You mean you inject them? Steel so close to the organ?'

'Not close, inside. Poking the organ,' replied the doctor. 'These syringes and injections, used for intra-penile drugs, can sustain erections for four to eight hours. I have boys who bring girls, park their partners downstairs, run up the steps, get the injection, run down and take their partners to a hotel or a secret place for sex. That is how desperate they have become.'

'Injections in the penis?' I asked, stunned.

'We have two types of injections: one does not work in stress and the other works in any situation. People in Panjab use the second type on their first night because the phobia of the first night is huge. The penile injection is like a diabetes insulin injection. It is a bi-mix or a tri-mix. I mix different medicines and tailor them to the patient's needs. That mix is my secret. There are auto-injectables too. For those I recommend the dosage. One injection costs Rs 7500. If someone needs to store the medicine and auto-inject, I charge a lot more. People pay. In some rare cases, for patients of injuries or accidents, we go in for penile implants—the kind used in pornographic movies.'

'Has access to pornography over the internet and mobile phones affected sex lives?'

'Yes, hugely, again by building false images. There are youngsters into modelling or part of the fashion industry who sometimes become gigolos. They have to perform with both males and females. One person in the morning, another in the afternoon and then another at night. They ask me for medication which will give them an erection. There are also youngsters who come to me asking for medicine to curb their sexual thoughts because they have college exams or are preparing for competitive exams.'

'Do women also come for consultation?'

'We have a lot of visits from call girls. They come for vaginal washes due to sex with multiple partners and the fear of infection. Some come to learn how to do non-penetrative sex, oral sex or anal sex. Some come to know about sexual massages. The big change now is that women talk, but men are still unable to express themselves. That is why when patients come to me, I always insist on both partners. In fact, half the time the wife drags her husband to the clinic.'

'But there is also good sex, healthy reciprocal sex?'

'Oh! That! I call it poetic sex. Foreplay, afterplay, attention to the mood of the partner. Of course, it is there, but I feel at least in north India it is rare.'

'What is your own life like?'

'For one, my wife has many friends who send questions through her. She is a hit in her kitty parties. I am happy about that ...'

'But ...'

'Lonely,' said the doctor, emotional for the first time. 'Not one client of mine would go out in public with me. In marriages, even in bazaars, people always avoid me. But a while back, my kids' school called me to speak on sexual health. That was when my son told me, "Daddy, until now I always hid what you did. Today you made me feel proud." I felt such relief! I am helping the world; no one should be ashamed of me.'

The doctor told me about some of his high-profile clients and I felt, amidst the immense jostling in this land, where people seek anchors of power—the ones who can bend rules—this doctor, and those like him, are the most powerful people in Panjab. After all, who is more powerful than one who knows the real secrets, solves one of the core problems of the society and helps people keep up their image and encourages 'poetic' sex?

Panjab's affiliation with cows predates its current status as an agrarian society. It goes back to the time when its people were pastoralists and herders and then settled down in villages. In a pre-industrial age, the cow was the centre of the village life and economy. The ox ploughs the land, the cow gives milk, the dung is used to plaster walls, and the urine has medicinal qualities. In many cases, people who do not have a religious taboo against it, unlike the Sikhs and Hindus, consume its meat. Beef or carra, buffalo meat, is the best source of protein at that price range, and our society's greatest issue is poverty, especially the below-poverty-line nutrition. The cow or ox benefits people even in death: its hide is leather. In these days of mechanised agriculture and a booming dairy industry, besides Jutts, Dalits in villages too keep cattle to supplement income and to arrange for home milk.

The economic disparity between medium and big Jutts and small and marginal Jutts and Dalits is huge, and it is precisely because of this that the poorer folks pay more attention to cattle. The recent Hindutva attempts to resurrect the cow have their roots in this identification of the cow as an economic fulcrum. It is just that the ideas are now dated, but *gau rakshaks*—armed squads of lumpen elements who stand to protect cows—now use the animal to vilify and lynch Muslims and Dalits.

Historically, in Panjab, the cow stood for another idea: resistance. The Namdhari sect among the Sikhs was among the earliest in modern times to take up cudgels against cow slaughter. The Namdhari sect originated when, in 1857, Baba Ram Singh began his mission of seeking to restore the values of the Sikh religion after the Sikhs had lost their territories in the Anglo-Sikh wars, and Panjab had been colonised. Baba Ram Singh gave a call for a social, economic and institutional boycott of British goods, services and institutions, thus setting in motion a people's movement against imperialism—a method Mahatma Gandhi later adopted through his Satyagraha.

The Britishers had established cow slaughterhouses adjacent to the Darbar Sahib. The Namdharis confronted the butchers at Amritsar, Raikot and Malerkotla and rescued the cows. The British came down with a heavy hand, hanging to death many, blowing off others by cannons. They deported Baba Ram Singh to Burma (now Myanmar) on 18 January 1872. They banned gatherings of more than five Namdharis, their properties were attached and a police outpost was established outside the gates of Sri Bhaini Sahib—the main Namdhari shrine—for the next thirty-five years. The cow was thus a metaphor for the precursor of India's Independence movement. The Namdharis are strictly vegetarian, the Sikhs in general do not eat beef either, but are big in the dairy business.

With the advent of *gau rakshaks*, and given the fact that once a cow stops producing milk, it cannot be sold or sent to the butcher, Panjab has a huge stray cow issue. Very few owners have the financial capacity to continue taking care of cattle until their natural death. Though there are emotional bonds, preventing the end stage of the cattle is disrupting their life cycle. While the state has 472 *gaushalas*, it has around one lakh stray cattle and they are everywhere, on roads, on grounds, and even in the fields. Around a hundred people lose their lives to stray cattle each year.[75]

Yet, when you visit the cattle fairs, the mandis where cattle are bought and sold, which used to be teeming with cattle, you see a sudden decline in numbers. The numbers of Indian breeds, Gir and Sahiwal, were already losing out to milk-rich foreign breeds like Jersey and Holstein Friesian. Now the fear of the *gau rakshaks* the cattle owners sense is palpable. There is no saying where the lumpen will pop up, claiming to be *gau rakshaks*.

The SAD–BJP government has imposed a 2 per cent cow cess on essential services: electricity bill, property registration and so on.[76] The cess and revenue does not seem to show any results. There are no records available with reference to funds or their utilisation.

One of the most famous *gaushalas* is the one on the road where my uncles' bungalows stand in Rajpura. Its owner, Satish Kumar, also runs the Gau Rakshak Dal and is infamous for posting online videos of drivers and owners of trucks carrying cattle for slaughter from Panjab to other states being thrashed. Soon after, several drivers accused him of abducting, robbing, beating them up and even sodomising them.[77] He went absconding only to be arrested later in Vrindavan.

While this is the scenario with the cattle trade, it is the daily living of ordinary farmers that has suffered the onslaught of cow protection. In some villages such as Tamkot in Mansa district villagers now employ horsemen to prevent the stray Amriki cattle from entering the fields. Each villager pays up to Rs 300 per acre, and a village's contribution could be as high as Rs 6 lakh per year. It is reminiscent of a medieval Panjab when feudal warlords were evolving into *misls* and villagers would pay *rakhi* to protect their property and produce. Three centuries later, the practice of *rakhi* is back in southern Panjab, but in a slightly different version. The plunderer is not a rival feudal warlord, but an 'Amriki'—a foreign cattle breed, now abandoned.[78]

Panjab's famed masculinity has shrunk. Its over-reliance on external means—chemicals—has affected the image of the valorous farmer, soldier and sportsman.

*Chapter Seven*

# *Dawa* — Medicine

After the initial euphoria of the AAP deciding to enter the electoral arena for the Panjab Assembly elections had settled down, they launched a series of dialogues with local communities called *Bolda Panjab* (Panjab Speaks) led by senior journalist and AAP member, Kanwar Sandhu. The issues raised in these dialogues were supposed to inform the manifesto that AAP would present before the elections. It was on the lines of how the party had sought public opinion in Delhi before the elections there. There could have been no better way for a party to commit itself to work for people. There could have been no better forum for me to listen to Panjab as I researched what would be this book.

As I attended a couple of such dialogues, I noticed that AAP had become a sort of flying squad that travelled from city to city, town to town, and to some important villages, gathering oral commentaries in all of these places. The issue with *Bolda Panjab*, indeed, with any such effort, is that when we set up a platform to hear the people, we lose the spontaneity of life, of being, to the performative act of showing, revealing and doing. Besides, AAP was also on the hunt for candidates and volunteers, and these dialogues became a forum for recruitment of a sort. *Bolda Panjab* spaces became more theatre than life, with people vying with each other to present a face to the people they met. Soon I began to stay away from these meetings. I sought to experience Panjab first-hand by myself—to see and feel its disparity, to smell the stench of its drains, visit its hospitals and sugar factories and have a meal and sleep on sagging cots in ordinary homes.

The loudest hysteria everywhere I travelled was around drugs, and I wanted to understand what the narrative meant. As far as I could recall, opium and alcohol had always been part of Panjab's culture. What was with these drugs that had become so big now? I asked this because I was perhaps three years old when we once went to meet Nanaji. Baba had later told me that as Nanaji opened his bottle in the evening, he asked me to open my mouth and poured in a cap full of his rum. It had tasted bitter and I had cried. He had frowned and said, 'A fauji's grandson cannot cry. Now you are inducted.' Upon hearing the story from Baba, I wondered if it was a rite of passage.

I was perhaps five years old when one evening Baba and Phuphadji were having a peg and I had a toothache. Baba said to Phuphadji we must touch some rum on my tooth to put the *keeda* (insect) to sleep. Those days we used to believe that toothaches happened because a mite or some other insect had got into the tooth. I got excited. Phuphadji responded, 'What if the *keeda* starts doing the *bhangra*?' It put paid to my plans.

Later, when I was an adolescent, Baba told me: if you want to drink, drink with me. Don't hide. That simple gesture drove out the forbidden and hence tempting notion of alcohol from my mind. In that itself I had stood out from most of my friends from other states and backgrounds. I assumed the openness was part of Panjab's culture.

My memory of a handsome Sikh man is of a grand-uncle who was related to our family. Baba, his brothers and Bibiji would call him Rumiwale Mamaji. He was my Dadiji's brother, probably a cousin. We also called him Mamaji. He was not very tall, perhaps only a few inches over five feet. He had green eyes, was fair, stout and well-built, with rippling muscles even at seventy. He always wore a cream *kurta* and wrapped a colourful *chadra*, an unstitched wraparound like a *dhoti*, and a checked turban—brown and beige. When he came home to Rajpura, it was always for a night. He would reach early evening, pull out a bottle of liquor and occupy a place of pride on the *manji* (jute woven cot) on which he would settle down upstairs.

He would keep the bottle on the table in front of him. It was an open invitation to anyone who would dare to ask for a sip. No one ever did. He would pour a Patiala peg—four parallel fingers deep—and ask me to fill the glass to the brim with water. I must have been seven or eight years of age, and as the youngest one, my job was to keep his supply of walnuts, groundnuts, cashews and chicken going. I loved the opportunity to serve because it was my chance to watch him in deep discussion with my Dadaji and sometimes my elder uncle and eldest aunt who would always sit with her head covered with a *dupatta*, not facing him directly—the way good Panjabi women should behave. Over the evening his cheeks would get redder and redder.

At some point, after a couple of drinks, he would need to go to the toilet and he would ask for my hand for support. My small hand would get lost in his big, thick paws, but he would stand up and I would pass him his stout walking stick. He would ask me to hang from his upper arm muscles. They were bigger than my two-hand grasp. Then he would hobble away to the toilet. It would give me time to arrange his dinner on a stool next to the *manji*.

After I had helped him wash his hands outside the room by pouring water from a jug and offering him the towel on my shoulder, he would sit down for his meal. A pile of rotis with a *batti* or two of *daal* and another *batti* or two of dry *subzi* along with mango or lemon pickle. Then he would retire. The next morning, he would wake up early and it would be my job to take *dudh-patti* (milk boiled with tea leaves) for him in a wide-mouthed but necked brass pot and an empty glass. He would pour his tea and then pull out a dense black paste from his pocket. He would roll it into a small round ball between his palms and gulp it down with his tea.

A cousin said it was *afeem*. 'See how his cheeks are red!' That is how I learnt the secret to his good health. Yet, the way my cousin said it, with disdain, and aunts mentioned liquor with derision, it seemed like *afeem* and liquor weren't very good things. But Rumiwale Mama-ji was the handsomest and strongest man I knew.

My favourite uncle was a mechanical engineer, an agrarian scientist, who researched and taught at the Panjab Agricultural University. He would take me to our fields on his cycle. It was a sublime experience jumping, dipping, floating, frolicking, bathing and swimming in a large cement tank in our fields. A silvery, frothy stream of water gushed into the tank from a four-inch-wide iron pipe. The pipe extended into the brick-walled well, with ringed footrests, deep into the earth.

When I dared to peep in, I could spot a motor at the bottom of the well. It came alive with a roar when I pressed a red button in a dusty lime green box. I would spend hours in the tank, playing in the gurgling water. The availability of water at the press of the button was such a different experience from how we got water in Rourkela for one designated hour in the morning and one in the evening. In Panjab, water was abundant.

Uncle was a visionary. He told me he was working on a concept that tube wells could work on air and didn't need electricity. His theory was: 'Air rises, so all we need to do is create an endless stream of bubbles in the water. Since air wants to escape, it will rise through the pipe and push water out.' He would give me a straw and set me the task of creating bubbles in the water. He would ask me to record how many times I created bubbles, how long each exhaled breath was and log the data from my experiments in a notebook. Then he would be gone for long into the guava orchard. After a while, the farm hands would bring our buffaloes to drink water from the tanks and we would together give them a wash. The farm hands and I would then milk the buffaloes. By evening uncle would come back, I would show him my notebook, he would encourage me to try longer exhaled breaths the next time and we would head home. Sometimes on the way back home he would feel sluggish and it would be hard for him to cycle with me on the front rod or carrier.

At home, members of the joint family kept all their medicines together in one tin box. The medicines would be for blood pressure, asthma, body pains, heart problems, fever and gastric issues. Suddenly, a cousin would discover a whole strip of Crocin or Brufen or Calmpose missing. It took me a while to learn that uncle's disappearing in the guava orchard was to do with medicines disappearing from the home medicine box. While I was experimenting with air and water, uncle was experimenting with tablets. I learnt later that as a student at the Thapar Institute of Engineering and Technology, uncle had sought to sleep less so that he could study more. He had asked a doctor for tablets that would help him. The doctor had not given the names of the tablets but had powdered them and given him a few doses. Since then, uncle was used to consuming random medicines, that too in bulk.

When the Panjabi movie *Sarpanch* was released in 1982, uncle took me to the Alps Cinema in town. A song from the movie was a big hit: *Eik gal das bottle kaminiye, main tainu peena haan ki tu mainu peeni hain?* (Tell me, you mean bottle of alcohol, do I drink you or do you drink me?). I do not remember much else from the movie, written and directed by Veerendra, a cousin of Dharmendra, the Bollywood star. Veerendra was later shot dead, perhaps by militants, though some maintain that it was on account of personal enmity.

It dawned upon me how, knowing fully well the effects of alcohol, the writer attributed notions of othering to the bottle, thus opening up an unending engagement. The line was a mantra for my uncle whenever he wanted to have a drink. He would mutter the line to himself as he hit the bottle, forbidding anyone from preaching to him.

There were many such songs: *Adhiya hor mangade*—'get me another half bottle' by Gurdial Nirman Dhuri and Harwinder Biba; *whiskey di botl*—'a bottle of whiskey' by Yamla Jatt; *Jatt Ho Ke Sharabi*—'When the Jutt gets drunk' by Kuldip Manak. A song like *Amli nu chah* included opium in the ambit. These popular songs reinforced the image of the drunkard and elevated drinking to a stage of progress—of having arrived. I was in my mid-adolescence when uncle passed away from a heart attack. By then he had stopped consuming medicines and had become an occasional drinker. Yet, it was too late.

The assertion that opium and poppy husk, along with home-brewed alcohol, have been an age-old phenomenon in Panjab is authenticated by folklore, folk songs, anecdotes, popular culture and academic studies. Much of the labour-intensive farming and small-scale industrial growth of Panjab in the 1970s was a result of the hard work put in by the slightly stoned migrant labourers from UP and Bihar.

During my school days, when I would come to Rajpura during the holidays, one of my tasks in the wheat harvest season was to carry from home the materials to make tea in the fields where the labourers were at work. When we set up the fireplace in the fields and started boiling the water and milk and sugar and tea leaves, another uncle of mine would pull out a packet of black powder-like substance and pour it into the mix. Years later, in Sanghria in Rajasthan, near Mandi Dabwali, at a government-approved opium outlet, I savoured similar tea and learnt that the black powder was *bhuki* (poppy husk). It is also consumed by *palledars* who carry heavy sacks of wheat or rice on their backs to load trucks and trains. The *arthiyas* (commission agents) and *banias* (shopkeepers) or even grain procurement managers manage the supply of intoxicants. Poppy husk is banned in Panjab but comes from Rajasthan. The Green Revolution was in part based on the accepted and prevalent aid of intoxicants for back-breaking productive work by migrants and Jutts.

When combine harvesters journey across the country to Maharashtra, Tamil Nadu and Madhya Pradesh, their drivers take opium to stay awake. This opium is supplied by the owners of these machines. Opium and poppy husk used to be common to another profession in which Panjabis participated extensively in the early decades of the formation of the nation—truck-driving and transportation. Around two-third of the nation's inland freight travels over roads and highways is through trucks and lorries.[79] The industry relies on opiates to carry on delivering for the betterment of the nation.

Since I was somewhat familiar with Panjab's drug culture, I was stunned by Rahul Gandhi's remark in 2012 and how it shaped public perception.[80] Speaking at a Congress-affiliated National Students Union of India rally at Panjab University campus, he said, 'What is happening to human resources in Panjab? Seven out of ten youth have the problem of drugs.'[81] This turned Panjab's 'drug problem' into breaking news. In Panjab's militancy phase, the youth were labelled traitors and terrorists; now they were labelled drug addicts. The label has changed, but the demonising stays: Panjab is unruly and creates problems for the nation, a pariah.

I live in Bangalore and I am aware of the drugs issue in my city. In many social gatherings, someone or the other has cannabis on them and people casually smoke up. I am aware of rave parties in Delhi, of drugs, HIV and Hepatitis C incidents in the Northeast, but Panjab has been labelled the drug state.

If 70 per cent of Panjab's youth were on drugs, I would have seen hazed, glassy-eyed young men and women on roadsides, in bus stands, in markets, in fields, in factories, in schools, in hospitals, in homes, literally everywhere around Panjab. Yet, that was not the case. It made me pause and try to understand the phenomena.

In 2012 itself the Akalis immediately responded to Rahul Gandhi's statistics. They pointed at how in 2009 they had submitted to the high court that Panjab was on the edge of the Golden Crescent—Afghanistan, Iran and Pakistan—that produces 90 per cent of the world's opium.[82] The usual route for opium export in the 1980s was from Afghanistan through Iran into the Balkans or north through the erstwhile USSR. The Iran-Iraq War in the 1980s, the Soviet invasion of Afghanistan, the splitting up of former Yugoslavia and the wars that followed between the new nations impacted the Balkan route. When the Soviet occupation of Afghanistan ended, the Taliban encouraged opium cultivation in Afghanistan. This opium, smuggled through Pakistan, started crossing into Panjab on the way to Delhi and Mumbai for supply to other parts of the world. Pakistan and the Indian border states, especially Panjab, because of its topography—parts of the border are riverine and it has a road network to Delhi—made for a good transit route.

The production of opium in Afghanistan in the last two decades has gone up nine times (from one thousand metric tonnes to nine thousand metric tonnes).[83] To escape the hardship of their economic conditions and the ravages of a four-decade war, Afghan farmers are bringing more and more land under opium cultivation. The only way to get the opium out so that it reaches Europe, the Americas and Africa is either through Pakistan and then India or towards the north through Central Asia.

This was borne out when I met smugglers from an earlier era in Gurdaspur, Dera Baba Nanak and Tarn Taran. They spoke about the flourishing inter-border trade from the 1950s to the 70s. For people on both sides of the border—which was anyway considered to be a political encumbrance—it was simply trade. The border lay amidst brambles and jungles and was hardly patrolled. For a few years after 1947 there was great demand for white handkerchiefs from Delhi Cotton Mills because Pakistan had still not started producing enough skull caps for *namaz* (prayers). Later, the objects traded were the *goti* borders of chunnis and dupattas, alcohol, gold, even televisions. Every smuggler worth his salt wanted to go to Heera Mandi, Lahore's fabled red-light area, and also wanted to enjoy the culinary delights of Pakistani Panjabi cuisine. An eighty-year-old smuggler I interviewed said he had stopped working when the business shifted to opium, arms and ammunitions, but if I wanted to, he could arrange for me to cross over. In fact, for old times' sake, he said he himself would take me across the River Ravi which is shallow and wide at many points and easy to cross.

The Akalis submitted to the court that since the international border with Pakistan was the Centre's responsibility and the Border Security Force (BSF) was deployed there, it was the Centre's responsibility to check the smuggling. That the smuggling is extensive is borne out by the regularity with which the BSF seizes drugs at the border. Locals who chose to stay anonymous were of the view that the security forces disclose only part of the captured consignments being smuggled. Now Haryana towns and villages on the path from Ambala to Delhi and districts in north Rajasthan are increasingly showing higher instances of addiction, especially among the youth. It is the same with Pakistan. Even a cursory look at the United Nations Office on Drugs and Crime (UNODC) data shows that the nation has 6.7 million drug users, out of which 4 million are addicts.[84]

However, in the last few years, the narrative is that Pakistan, especially the Inter-Services Intelligence, is pushing drugs into India to destabilise Panjab. In the absence of proof, I am sceptical about it because of two reasons. One, this is a familiar old story going back to the time of Indira Gandhi's 'foreign hand'. Two, business is business and it always grows when money is to be made, in spite of a state agency. Everything might just be correct: Panjab a transit route, Pakistan-based smugglers or even the army itself promoting the drug smuggling, the Indian forces not able to man the border effectively, and the involvement of local smugglers. But that Afghanistan is not hauled to account or the Amercians are not questioned about the effects of Operation Enduring Freedom is puzzling. How is it possible to solve an international issue by focussing on the local alone, that too, negatively—as hysteria? How is it also possible to blame Panjab for smuggling and addiction when the borders of the nation are manned by Central forces? Then is it the role of the Panjab Police in local raids, in not destroying, and circulating apprehended drugs? If cases on police officials are any evidence, then they point to direct involvement of officers. Why then do political parties blame each other and the people when the larger security system is broken?

Rahul Gandhi's statement and numbers were so staggering that they completely omitted the context of the study. In 2007, the governor of Panjab requested Amritsar-based Guru Nanak Dev University to do a study on drug addiction. Professor of Sociology, Ravinder Singh Sandhu, spent about six months on the study, for which he chose a sample group from different villages and urban areas. His sample group was controlled, as in, all 600 people in the survey were addicts. Of these respondents, he found that 73 per cent were between the ages of 16 and 35.[85] That explains the seven in ten youth conclusion. But clearly, the conclusion Rahul Gandhi or his team had drawn was erroneous.

Another study on drug abuse was commissioned by the Institute for Development Studies (IDS) and conducted four years later by the Department of Health and Family Welfare in the border districts of Amritsar, Tarn Taran, Gurdaspur and Ferozepur. The study conducted by Prof. R.S. Verma and Vaishali chose two border tehsils from each district and was based on interviews and information generated from a sample of more than 1,500 drug addicts. Similar results emerged that seemed to indicate that over 70 per cent of the people surveyed were youth who were addicted.[86] Again, in this study, the sample group was 100 per cent addicts.

This is not to say there is no addiction. Of course there is addiction. We met some cases in a previous chapter (*Rog*). Those stories are not only from rehabilitation centres. They are everywhere in Panjab, in many homes, in localities, villages and towns. I met many scores of addicts. I had to seek out addicts at lonely tube wells, around hospitals and rehabilitation homes, inside big, lonely, abandoned mansions whose owners were abroad, in lonely street corners, inside abandoned godowns, outside factories, outside colleges and institutes, public and private, and the like—in short, they frequented places away from the public eye. This is because, all said and done, addiction is still looked down upon by society. It is frowned upon by religion, especially the Sikh religion. Yet, the incidence is nowhere close to what is projected.

In recent decades, Panjab has lost its youth in four ways: one, during militancy, when the youth either joined the ranks of militants or were illegally abducted by the police, tortured and murdered in extra-judicial killings; two, through farmer and labour suicides;

three, to drugs; and four, through migration abroad either as students hoping for residency or as labourers in the meat and dairy industry in Europe, truck drivers in North America or field workers in Australia.

Each of these losses have their own kind of silence around them. The families of those lost to militancy are tired of pleading to the system. The families of those who migrate remain a little wary of sharing information because there could be issues about their ward's citizenship status abroad. However, there is a commonality between suicides and drugs—a stigma, shame and a reluctance to expose oneself.

While we will focus on other kinds of losses elsewhere in the book, let us understand the silences in drug-related instances here. When I asked families of addicts across the spectrum of society—rich to poor—how the habit started, the commonest response was denial. 'No, it does not happen in our kind of families.'

If a family has accepted their ward to be an addict, they choose to downplay it, understate it and somehow keep a shroud of decency. I noticed Panjab places such a premium on what others would say— neighbours, relatives, society, community—that families are inclined to push the addiction under the carpet and remain stoic and silent in the face of it. Such behaviour only ends up enhancing the stigma against drug addicts. They end up being considered criminals of the system.

When I asked the addicts what led to the habit, they were more open. This was the gap between those who felt responsible to keep up a face—the families—versus those who had touched the nadir. *Pathar chaat ke aa gaya*—'has licked the wall and returned' was a common phrase among addicts who survived. The commonest answer to what led to the habit was peer pressure, followed by laments of how education had failed them, parents had pressured them to perform either at studies or find a job, but they faced a severe lack of jobs or opportunities to earn a living, and in some fantastic cases, they thought a dose could help their sex lives. The underlying theme was always sadness, frustration and despair.

Many addicts narrated stories about how they hated begging from their families and supported their addiction through underhand means: sometimes even beating up family members, selling off utensils, jewellery and property. Almost every addict said he or she knew they were doing a wrong thing by consuming drugs. Each of them pleaded to be saved and said they were unable to kick the habit because their body needed it, their mind was enslaved to it and their will power was compromised. On the one hand they suffered being under the control of drugs, on the other there was the guilt associated with mistreating family members and loved ones, betraying their faith. Together, the overwhelming sense of weakness of not being able to break the tweezer grip of addiction and guilt over wrongdoings spirals the addict downwards into a bottomless well. Drugs have destroyed families, broken relationships, emptied coffers, ruined health and even caused death.

The IDS report states that one-third of the drug addicts were Jutt Sikhs, another third were Scheduled Castes and the last third were upper castes and other backward castes. Religion-wise, almost two-thirds were Sikhs, one quarter Hindus and the rest were Christians and Muslims. It concluded that agriculturists preferred alcohol, opium and poppy husk while the labour class preferred tablets and capsules.

Now this is also problematic because the definition of what is a drug itself is not clear. To study drug addiction, one has to decide if all intoxicants are to be called drugs. Intoxicants are of various types: alcohol, tobacco, cannabis, opiates—meaning opium derivates, pharmaceutical products, synthetic drugs and concoctions.

Out of these, alcohol and tobacco are legal, sold by the government, taxed and a huge source of revenue. The government quota of liquor in the state was increased from 2.76 crore proof litres in 1980-81 to 18.35 crore proof litres in 2017-18. This is an increase of six and a half times, whereas the growth of the population is less than double. In spite of this increase, in spite of the stereotype of the Panjabi drinker, in spite of the notion of the Patiala peg four fingers high, the state is nowhere in the list of the top alcohol-consuming states in the country. Panjab is tenth in a nationwide ranking. It is the same with tobacco, with about one-fifth of the state consuming it. All this is legal, but the rest of the others are drugs.

The need is for an effective categorisation of addiction to identify the problem. In 2015, the government of India's ministry of social justice and empowerment and the department of health, Panjab government, conducted a study by an organization called Society for Promotion of Youth and Masses, supported by AIIMS, Delhi. The Punjab Opioid Dependence Survey (PODS) commissioned by the ministry of social justice and empowerment, conducted across ten districts in the state, found that even though 80 per cent of the addicts had attempted to break their habit, only 35 per cent were able to obtain help. There are a number of de-addiction centres in the state, many of them run even by non-registered doctors, with the support of muscle-men. Families pay for their addict sons to be picked up in the middle of the night and they are confined in these units. The addicts are denied drugs and thrashed when they ask for it. When released, they go back to the habit. It is self-defeating.

Though this report has still not been published, the state government, in its eagerness to throw numbers and show reduced incidences, put up a six-page summary of the twenty-seven page report. The report was based on a study in ten districts of a sample size of 3,620 opioid-dependent users. The report extrapolated numbers and concluded that Panjab had exactly 232,856 opioid-dependent people. An upper and a lower limit were also projected to make it sound even more authentic. However, upon reading the fine text of the report, it was clear that the method used to arrive at this number was the number of people who had visited rehabilitation centres in 2014 multiplied by something called 'reverse of proportion of the sample reporting that they were admitted to the same centre in 2014'. If this does not make sense to you, rest assured it does not make sense to me either, and perhaps even the central government—that is why it withdrew the report.

The issue is, what a statistician will call the confidence level in the sample used and the methodology. This sample too is of only opioid-dependents and it is an all-male sample, while the fact is that many women have also taken to drugs. Per this report, the number of dependents turns out to be 1 per cent of Panjab's population. Even if we consider, from other surveys, that users are generally four times the dependents, the number comes up to around ten lakh, which is about 3 per cent of Panjab's population. The gap between this 3 per cent and Rahul Gandhi's 70 per cent is vast. What Rahul Gandhi's irresponsible and misleading statement did was that it sensationalised the drugs issue in Panjab and brought a lot of adverse publicity. This led to a political volleyball between Congress and Akalis. The SAD-BJP government became cagey and the focus moved away from actual ground work that could solve the drugs issue.

A few months later, the state police conducted tests for drug use on another controlled group: aspirants for jobs of police constables. About 4.7 lakh young men applied. On the first day of the recruitment process, 7,800 people were tested for drugs. Of these, 3.7 per cent, or 294 young men, tested positive for either performance-enhancing drugs or habit-forming ones. One would expect that young men who apply for a job which involves physical fitness tests would all be clean. Yet, even in this sample, 3.7 per cent were substance abusers, almost equal to the number of fully opioid dependent people earlier surveyed.

The lack of evidence-based analysis of the situation reminds me of the Akbar–Birbal story where Akbar asks Birbal how many crows lived in the city of Agra to which Birbal gives an exact number. When quizzed on accuracy, Birbal talks about how at a particular time some crows could have flown away, visiting other cities, or new ones could have come to visit Agra. The truth appears to be that no one knows how many addicts of what kind live in Panjab. Yet, for the people, the families who suffer, drug addiction is a gory reality beyond any statistics. It needs to be solved. The question is, what should be our approach? The state seeks a 'discipline and punish' attitude by using police, nabbing addicts, throwing them in jails and rehabilitation centres. There are now a plethora of news reports telling us how drugs are easily available in jails, and the police is complicit in the trade. Obviously, this approach fails.

Pick up any book on pharmacology and the first adage you learn is: the dose makes the poison. This adage is by the fifteenth century Swiss pharmacist Paracelsus, birth name Theophrastus von Hohenheim, who is considered the father of toxicology. The full observation is: 'All things are poison, and nothing is without poison, the dosage alone makes it so, a thing is not a poison.'

This means that everything we consume, even water and oxygen, can potentially be harmful. This has been stated even in our systems of Ayurveda and Unani medicine which, too, advocate a moderation of diet, aligning it to our body characteristics and our nature. The desired state of body and mind is a balance which can be skewed by indulgence.

Opiates are an extract from the poppy plant. The juice from the flowers is opium and the dried and crushed flowers is poppy husk, locally called *dode* or *bhuki*. Traditionally, Panjab has used opiates in various ways, as part of food, or medicine, for a high. The kings of yore even extracted revenue from it. Even now, the government allows it to be grown in a controlled manner in Rajasthan and Madhya Pradesh and supervises its use for medicinal reasons. Morphine, which I needed for Mama, is an extract of opium. Heroin is further purified morphine, stronger and more addictive. Heroin in pure form is white in colour; in street form, it is brown.

Any alcohol is basically ethanol. Ethanol is a compound distilled from sugar water. Alcohol is of three types: *angrezi*—foreign, *desi*—country, *ghar di*—home-brewed. The popular *angrezi* liquor is Indian Made Foreign Liquor (IMFL), which is certified, and on which the government levies taxes and sells from *angrezi daru thekas,* outposts or shops. Country alcohol, too, is certified and sold from *desi daru thekas.* Home-brewed is not formally sold, and requires no tax payment. Whether it is home-brewed alcohol, or country-made, with brand names like Santri or Khasa, or IMFL, all have the same molasses base. Very often, the country manufacturers provide the alcohol base to the IMFL producers who then caramelise it, treat it through one or more round of distillation, standardise the alcohol-by-volume (ABV) percentages, package them better and sell it at roughly three times more than *desi daru*. In terms of the Bureau of Indian Standards (BIS), both country and IMFL varieties are certified Grade 1.[87]

An excise inspector took me to a major IMFL bottling unit near Pathankot. An average worker—mostly temporary, migrant—enters the workplace sober in the morning; by evening the worker has inhaled the equivalent of four pegs and leaves drunk. I saw seven major brands, that belonged to one manufacturer, being packaged. The huge hall had many assembly lines. Long pipes fitted with taps, liquor flowing from huge barrels in the back, drains under the pipes, workers seated or standing next to each other on the sides of the pipes, then the cap area, the label area, the sticker area, and so on. On these conveyer belts, alcohol flows in pipes, the bottles are inspected and filled, the filling is checked and the cap affixed, the sticker pasted, the label glued and the bottle sealed. The bottles are then inverted, checked for leakage and gathered in trays.

I watched, fascinated by how this was an almost foolproof system of one of the most desired products of human consumption. When we were done with our rounds, the inspector picked up a bottle and handed it to me. I wondered if he was gifting me the alcohol. He asked around for a spanner-like instrument which, instead of an open end, had a ring affixed to one side of the bar. He gave it to me. I asked why, and he shrugged his shoulders. I tried putting the ring on the neck of the bottle and did not succeed very well. The inspector called a worker and gave him the bottle and spanner. The worker slipped the ring onto the neck, bent the bottle a bit and yanked the ring, and off came the whole cap. The whole of it, seal, sticker, lock, everything intact.

The inspector said this was how alcohol was adulterated. 'Never buy a bottle under a Rs 1,000 range; all have at least one-third adulterated stuff.' The cap had fallen on the ground. The worker picked it up and handed it to the inspector who fixed it back on. No one would ever be able to make out that the sealed bottle had been opened, the liquor could be adulterated, and sealed again with none the wiser. It is clear that consumers do not really know why they pay extra for a mere false assurance that the liquor they consume is not as damaging to health as country liquor or the home-brewed variety.

Home-brewed *desi daru* can range from what is called moonshine to a very sophisticated but undistilled variety that I saw being produced one afternoon in central Panjab by a farmer who has been experimenting with producing alcohol for many years now. Brewing alcohol at home is a common feature in many villages and farmhouses in the countryside. Of course, the government holds all of it to be illegal, and the joke is that to start producing alcohol the one skill needed is the ability to bear the lathis of the police.

The difference between what intoxicant is allowed or not allowed depends on the government and its laws and not really on what the product is all about. One reason for the government ban on home-brewed alcohol is health concerns. After all, the mix is not standardised. A bad mix or early methanol fumes could be hazardous to health. The other reason is simply taxation. The government does not earn from it.

A psychiatrist explained to me—and I authenticated it with other doctors and police officers—how, about a decade and a half ago, the quality of opium and poppy husk available in the state began to deteriorate. Earlier when you opened a packet the whole room smelt of it. Now there is no smell. People need to consume more to get a high. That led to a shift in consumption patterns. Earlier, *bhuki* was consumed by the load on a visiting card boiled with tea—a load or two boiled with tea or water. Now a consumer needed three to four cards, and prices have shot up. This had led recreational users and addicts to look for alternatives.

Those who were used to opium and home-brewed alcohol started using medicines which have alkaloids and produce some kind of intoxication, for common illnesses. For example, Glycodin is an age-old drug and contains codeine. Codeine in large quantities has the effect of morphine. Many users began by using these pharmaceutical products. A few years back, city parks, tube wells and outhouses would often have huge stashes of empty cough syrup bottles such as Corex, Glycodin, and so on. In time, users moved to Schedule-H drugs— which technically cannot be purchased without a prescription—such as Lomotil, which is used to treat diarrhoea; Tramadol, an opioid pain medication and Fortwin and Phenergan injections, which are also used to treat pain.

When the government began to regulate the supply of these drugs, chemists stopped stocking them, causing a grievous deficiency of painkillers for surgeons and operation theatres. The government did allow doctors to procure drugs, but there was always a risk posed by the police. The chemists too need to keep bill copies in triplicate and send them for regular audits. All this proves too much, and the lack of genuine painkillers continues to plague medical services while the same drugs are also available in the black market.

The space thus opened up for players who could produce synthetic drugs—base chemicals such as ephedrine, pseudoephedrine, acetic anhydride and others. Many of them were either Panjab-based chemicals manufacturers or pharmaceutical companies based in Baddi in Himachal Pradesh close to the Panjab border, but some also came from as far away as Chennai and Mumbai.

Over time, some of these producers have been caught diverting these chemicals to illicit synthetic drug manufacturers on a large scale. These multiple concoctions are also called *chitta* and are cheap and easily available—a hazardous cocktail. The issue is not only that pharmaceutical companies supply the drugs but that they are mixed by addicts at random. Generally there are two families of drugs: stimulants and depressants, or uppers and downers. Both act on the central nervous system, but in radically different ways. Stimulants send the central nervous system into overdrive, increasing heart and breathing rates, suppressing appetite, and causing a spike in blood pressure. They make users feel supercharged with energy, a rush of euphoria, especially if they're taken via common abuse methods like snorting, smoking or injecting. Depressants are more varied and work by inhibiting the central nervous system, slowing the heart rate, and the respiratory and gastrointestinal systems. This brings about a feeling of relaxation, peace, sleepiness, and produces an intense euphoria.

Common stimulants are: caffeine, nicotine, cocaine, methamphetamine (ICE) and MDMA (ecstasy). Common depressants are: alcohol, heroin and other opiates, Codeine and other cough syrups, and painkillers. While these are the categories, in Panjab most of the original is mixed with subtances and made potent. Dr Piare Lal Garg, former registrar, Baba Farid University, says, like *dalda* is mixed with ghee, sugar with honey and synthetic chemicals with milk, drugs like heroin, cocaine or methamphetamine are also mixed with cheaper substances.

For heroin, it could be sweet soda, sugar, arrowroot, talcum powder, dry milk, detergents, etc. For methamphetamine, it could be lithium, salts, iodine, chemical fertilisers, etc. For cocaine, it could be dish-washing powder, boric acid, caffeine, Benzocaine, Lidocaine, Phenacetin, Chloroquine, Aspirin and so on.

This is what creates *chitta*, which can be consumed intravenously through injections. A kit is commonly available for Rs 35 from *paan* and cigarette shops. Each kit has a lighter tinfoil and a hollow pipe. Syringes are also commonly available from any druggist. Many a time, addicts share syringes, increasing the chances of passing on HIV, Hepatitis C and other dangerous diseases. Panjab is a virtual chemical laboratory and each addict who survives is almost an alchemist. Yet, the threat to life or health is not only from the uppers and downers but also from their completely unorthodox mixtures.

As I hung around with addicts, I saw the apotheosis of what we call *jugaad*—a local fix, a hack. *Jugaad* is an intelligent low-cost solution to any problem, a way to think constructively and differently about innovation and could refer to a workaround, a solution that bends the rules, or a resource that can be used in such a way and is used to make existing things work or to create new things with meagre resources. Every farmer, every worker who knows how to innovate knows *jugaad*. It is part of life in Panjab and north India or actually anywhere where mechanical technology needs to be tweaked to create local solutions. It works for chemicals too.

There is yet another layer to the addiction. Owing to its martial history—the soldier, the wrestler, the sportsman—Panjab remains massively trapped in the alpha male macho image. The focus on the body, on vitality, the legends of Gama Pehalwan and Dara Singh, prompt youngsters to take up physical activities. Panjab's original tradition was of *akharas* where young men used to build their bodies and wrestle. The diet was ghee, milk, a home-made wheat-flour based, multi-dry fruit sweet called *panjiri*, soaked overnight black gram, and herbal concoctions.

In a post-Green Revolution society, the quality of food has deteriorated, but in keeping with that image, I found hundreds of boards and banners announcing local kabaddi matches in villages, between villages, even at the tehsil and district level. This is a result of the Deputy Chief Minister Sukhbir Badal glamorously starting the World Kabaddi Cup in 2010. This is kabaddi all right, but is actually a version of the game—popular in Panjab as circle kabaddi.[88] The rules of the game are different from the international style kabaddi played now in the Asian Games or in the Pro Kabaddi league created for television audiences. Circle kabaddi is a more vigorous version of the game and involves one-to-one confrontations as opposed to the teamwork required in international style kabaddi.

The World Kabaddi Cup soon took wing, attracting a lot of youth, villagers, international teams and the diaspora. They served as a channel of interaction between Panjab and its diaspora and as a major boost to the ruling party before the elections of 2012. In its very first edition,[89] many players were caught doping—thirteen out of twenty-nine.[90] The numbers of drug incidents kept piling up as the games proceeded, year after year. There were accusations based on police reports that some from the diaspora were aiding and abetting the drug trade and encouraging the use of opiates and steroids among participants. Every kabaddi season, reports in national and international media would appear, naming some new people, but would fall on deaf ears.[91] After the fourth year, Nirmal Singh Bhangoo of the Pearl group who had been sponsoring the games since its first edition was arrested for having defrauded ordinary people to the tune of Rs 45,000 crore by running a Ponzi scheme.

The Kabaddi World Cup thus became a juggernaut, attracting interest and participation, fuelled by corrupt money, abetting and creating the mayhem of dietary supplements, steroids and drugs, and yet gaining more limelight with each passing year until the 2015 Sarbat Khalsa, when it was called off.[92] Though foreign teams participated, India won each time. There were complaints, but they fell on deaf ears.[93] In effect, Panjab had once again created a pseudo atmosphere to keep up its macho reputation.

The kabaddi tournament came on the back of another sunshine industry in the post-militancy years. Property prices went up, leading to a mushrooming of real estate developers and property brokers who often employed local toughs for eviction and protection. The need for muscled young men who were bulked up and had big biceps grew. The traditional *akharas* were replaced by gymnasiums and body-building centres. There is also the culture of youngsters who do not know enough, relying on an elder, a brother figure who could be a village or locality senior, the gymnasium instructor, or a chemist, for advice on what to consume and how to exercise. Registered medical practitioners and chemists supply shiny, glossy, neatly packaged whey, protein mixes, amino acids, and other laboratory-produced edible supplements.

The core of this new approach was the same as that of the Green Revolution—chemicals. The shiny, attractive packaging is similar to the one on fungicides, insecticides and pesticides. The lure of the foreign, the looking down on the traditional and local thus proliferated, and there was little or almost no control by any agency. The focus on big biceps and broad shoulders led the youth to steroids like nandrolone, testosterone-based Sustanon injections. Many were willing to use these chemicals for increased body strength. They believed what they could do with land, they could also do with their bodies and make them yield more.

The essential check—the Food Safety Act, 2006—is anyway outdated by more than a decade since all these synthetic supplements have started dominating the market. Most manufacturers do not register with the Food Safety and Standards Authority of India (FSSAI). Fakes proliferate in the market, most branded 'Made in USA'.

In 1985, a few years after discovering that his son Sanjay Dutt had become an addict, Member of Parliament Sunil Dutt proposed the Narcotic Drugs and Psychotropic Substances Act (NDPS). It was approved by parliament and got the presidential nod. This law banned all narcotics. Narcotics, per definition, are extracts of plants which make for addictive drugs, affecting mood or behaviour, and induce drowsiness, stupor or insensibility, and relieve pain. Tobacco and alcohol and caffeine also do the same but are legally not considered narcotics.

The answer to what is dangerous and what is not, what is allowed and what is not, thus lies in law, is linked to taxes, and is not about the substance itself. A point in context: when the NDPS law was framed, India had already been under immense pressure for a quarter century to consent to a US-sponsored worldwide law called the Single Convention on Narcotic Drugs. Its roots lie in the American Prohibition of the early twentieth century, a move that led to bootlegging and the rise of cocaine. India too followed the 'discipline and punish' approach to deal with the drug problem in total negation of its own long tradition.

Whether it was the Akalis arresting thirty thousand young addicts and preparing First Information Reports from a template—or the society deeming drugs to be its enemy and political parties wooing people with the 'discipline and punish' approach, no one wanted to understand the phenomenon.[u]

I have some experience of addiction. One of my biggest embarrassments in journeying through Panjab was the fact that I smoked. It was difficult to do so when I stayed at the homes of people who welcomed and hosted me. From personal experience I know how hard it is to quit smoking. The desire is Janus-faced: on the one hand it builds as a body craving, an intense need, but on the other hand it propagates a myth that you need it only once and not more than that. This creates a mistaken belief that you could actually control the habit, if you have a strong will power. Until the next time the desire rises. The desire keeps coming back, in the first few days after quitting, but for weeks, for months, even years. The mind tricks you.

To quit is to play another mind game. You recognise your limitation in handling your addiction and start believing that in spite of how the body craves, how the aches rise, the muscles cramp, the chest burns, the mind becomes foggy, not giving in to the habit, to addiction, will not kill you. Often those who quit their addiction are prompted by a strong motivation to quit because something better lies beyond their addiction. That is why the only real motivation to quit addiction is to know that not giving in to temptation will give rise to confidence, a belief that one is stronger and fitter, more agile than when one is drugged. Once one is out of the control of the craving, one will neither be exploited nor exploit others—it is a matter of dignity.

Yet, if one is an addict, this is the hardest learning of all because the inadequacy one feels turns one extremely selfish—driven to only be focussed on how one can score the dose. To quit, one needs to break that pattern and focus on self-confidence which turns one to be concerned about family and relationships. Among those forces

---

u. Most FIRs spoke of arrests near traffic signals, mentioned the seizure of 5 grams of heroin from the left pocket and other such copycat information.

who quit, I saw that quiet sort of change, the awareness that they were no longer squandering money and assets on the addiction, being underhand—basically becoming and realising one's humanity. The writing is on the wall if the state would want to read it: the state approach should create a system using doctors and social services where addicts find a purpose to quit, which is higher than their addiction. This purpose could be a promise to a loved one, a religious oath, a goal, an occupation, or simply the need to clean up. Yet, it needs a purpose that will restore the dignity of the addict. The least that the state can do is create job opportunities to serve as a purpose. My purpose was to not smell any longer of cigarette smoke. It worked.

Later in 2017, Dr Dharamvir Gandhi, MP from Patiala between 2014 and 2019, proposed to table a private member's bill to amend the NDPS Act, 1985. The bill proposed that the definition of 'narcotics' and 'psychotropic substances' in the act, which currently includes all drugs, be classified into 'soft' drugs—which are naturally grown, such as opium and poppy husk—and 'hard' drugs—which are synthetic compounds and laboratory or industry-made chemicals. The proposed amendment also suggested that the possession of soft drugs be decriminalised, and its growth and sale be regulated by the government. 'We are seeking a classification of drugs so petty drug users are not unnecessarily penalised,' Gandhi, who is a heart specialist and has practised for over thirty-five years in rural Panjab, told me when I met him in Patiala, at his clinic, which was teeming with patients, that the regulated supply of opium and poppy husk for medical and personal use would be crucial in providing relief to drug users and to 'rid society of dangerous unsupervised medical and synthetic drugs'. He added, 'No one has ever died of natural drug use.

People have been consuming opium for centuries but there are no recorded fatalities.'

Gandhi's proposed amendments mark a radical departure from the approach that the police and governments have historically used in their attempts to curb the drug menace—primarily, to discipline and punish drug users. In its present form, the NDPS act and its implementation fail to pursue the real perpetuators of the drug business—the financers and the suppliers. The blanket banning of narcotic and psychotropic substances has resulted in the propagation of a ban-smuggle-promote model, where a banned substance is brought back into the market through illegal smuggling, and promoted by dealers looking to ply their wares. Gandhi's proposed change could transform how the consumption of drugs is dealt with throughout India, especially in states such as Panjab, Manipur, Mizoram and Himachal Pradesh, where drug use is widespread and has become a significant public health risk.

In September 2015, Kiren Rijiju, the union minister of state for home affairs, had admitted in Parliament that since 2014, fifty-three policemen from various departments in the Panjab Police were arrested for being implicated in drug-related cases. The police in the state commonly uses *chitta* (smack) as a threat to subdue citizens, to settle scores, and even to implicate fellow policemen. News reports have repeatedly confirmed that even in jails, drugs are easy to come by. In a note explaining the objectives of the bill, Gandhi noted that only 2 per cent of those arrested are financers and suppliers of drugs, while nearly 88 per cent of the arrested are either users or addicts. It is here that Gandhi's reform becomes key—the proposed changes to the NDPS would establish drug users as victims and not perpetrators of drug abuse, and protect them from undue stigmatisation.

'The reporting is less than real consumption because the patients are scared of NDPS,' a medical professional who is in charge of a government-run National AIDS Control Organisation de-addiction clinic in Panjab told me. He added, 'We can't solve the issue through rhetoric, slogans, goodwill messages and jails.' The medical professional is a strong supporter of harm reduction by way of decriminalisation of addicts, and Opioid Substitution Therapy (OST) by which an addict or abuser of opioids—heroin, brown sugar, poppy husk or any other—is put on a calibrated dosage over a period of time to wean them away from their addiction. The drugs used are a combination of opioid modulator Buprenorphine and opioid antagonist Naloxone. The drugs work in reducing the cravings for opioids such that even when a user tries to take an opioid while on treatment it does not give a high. 'We must reduce harm by prevention of sharing syringes to prevent HIV and Hepatitis C, accidents, health expenses, family distress and loss of jobs.'

However, the twist in Panjab's drug story is that treatment remains patchy—government hospitals either run out of the OST dose or lack of resources means a lack of supervision—and now OST medicines have themselves become a form of abuse. In several de-addiction centres I visited, addicts swing between heroin or smack and OST drugs. On the other hand, the OST drugs have also found their way out of regulated hospitals into the open market and now there is a market for these tablets. In short, the medicine, the cure, has itself become an addiction.

In the past, various nations have flirted with different approaches to curb drug trade, but few have succeeded in doing so by punishing drug users. That prohibition is ineffective is well-known: in America in the 1920s, prohibition of alcohol spurred rampant bootlegging and the rise of an underworld, and was eventually repealed. Closer home, the prohibition in states such as Bihar and Gujarat has been widely criticised and has led to the development of large, unregulated black markets. Recently, prohibition was declared illegal by the Patna High Court.

The war on drugs in the US, which began with the former US President Richard Nixon's declaration of drug abuse as 'public enemy number one', has cost the US billions of dollars every year and has widely been proclaimed a failure. Its focus on incarceration has resulted in the disproportionate targeting of people of colour—especially young black and Hispanic men—and profoundly affected its relations with South America. Over the past few years, the US government has softened its stance on natural drugs—in nearly half the country's fifty states, regulations on marijuana growth, sale and use have been enacted, which include both decriminalisation of possession and legalisation of growth for sale, and personal and medicinal use.

Decriminalisation is different from legalisation. With the former, the emphasis is on eliminating jail time for drug users, while dealers are criminally prosecuted. Bolivia, which, until a few years ago was notorious for coca—used to manufacture cocaine—has emerged as a success story in the war on drugs. In the past four years, it has reduced its coca production by 34 per cent. It did so by first expelling the US Drug Enforcement Agency, in 2008, and then by promoting economic development in rural areas that produced coca, and allowing farmers to cultivate coca for personal use and to sell in authorised markets.

But perhaps the grandest story is that of Portugal, which cleaned up its act through a fifteen-year period of reform in which it decriminalised all drugs. Portugal did not respond as governments usually do, with zero-tolerance legislation and an emphasis on law enforcement—instead, it focussed on prevention, education and harm reduction. Today, more than twenty European and South American countries have removed criminal penalties for the possession of small amounts of certain—and in some cases, all—drugs.

There is no doubt that any proposition to amend the NDPS and decriminalise drugs will find resistance among political parties. This is especially true in Panjab, where the drug problem is rarely seen as a complex issue that requires careful consideration and where it has been refashioned by every party to suit their platform for the upcoming Assembly elections. In October 2016, at a press conference in Chandigarh, Sukhbir Singh Badal, then deputy chief minister in the ruling Akali government, asked the media to treat the drug issue as 'a closed chapter'.

Panjabis can often be heard saying that the simplest solution to any wrongdoing—to mischief, to not studying well, to any deviation from what is understood to be the correct path—is a few tight slaps. Disciplining by punishment is ingrained in the state's cultural ethos, but it has been unsuccessful in tackling its drug problem. Gandhi's proposed change, which can regulate opiates and make them available to addicts, could serve as a first step to axing synthetic drugs from the system. Opium policies prescribed under the NDPS already allow farmers to grow opium legally, albeit only for sale to the government. To expand this system and allow natural drugs to be sold for personal use will not be possible overnight, nor will it occur by just a change in law. But by considering Gandhi's proposition, and by treating drug proliferations as a public health issue instead of one of policing and vigilantism, the parliament can push the state to bring empathy to the care of its citizens. Decriminalisation for petty users and the re-classification of drugs is the need of the hour. Sadly, Dr Gandhi's proposal, in spite of being cleared by the committee, was never tabled in the parliament.

Yet, even if the Bill were to be passed, it alone would not have solved the drugs issue because addiction is the symptom, not the disease. The disease is Panjab's socio-economic-cultural meltdown. For decades, Panjab has been encouraged to break all records of agricultural productivity by relying on technology and chemicals, but what message does that send to its people? Simply this: that its land and water resources can be exploited. Now the people are doing the same to their minds and bodies. The addict believes that like the hardy farmer who increased the productivity of his land, he, too, will be able to maximise the potential of his mind and body by skewing the dosage. How else can the people deal with situations like having forty lakh unemployed young men and women—one-sixth of its population, the breakdown in social structures due to nuclearisation of families, the lack of support networks, yet the need to look strong while being eroded from inside?

Nearly all addicts spoke about two things: one, they felt slighted by the system, whose insistence on treating them as criminals robbed them of a dignified method of getting help and treatment. Two, the prevalent business model through which the cycle of drug abuse is perpetuated: once a person is hooked and runs out of money to support their addiction, their dealers encourage them to find five or ten new recruits to whom they can sell their product. The addict thus becomes the supplier. Not only does the criminalisation of addicts and users fail to tackle the root causes of the patterns of drug habits as they stand currently—such as the reduction in the availability of natural drugs—it also compounds the stigma that is already associated with drug use.

Panjab's drug issue stems from the real crisis—despair—within each addict. The only way to recover from where drugs is pushing Panjab is by solving the state's social and economic issues and giving its people a sense of purpose. Historically, Panjabis respond best when their purpose is clear. Solving the drugs problem means we open the energies of the people of Panjab to reclaim their place in the world, in their own history, and stand up for themselves—with dignity.

Until the governments realise that drugs are not the disease but the symptom, Panjab will continue to chase the dragon's tail—the curl of smoke that rises from the spoon when *chitta* is inhaled. As of now, the tail has Panjab in its vice-like grip where the addicts continue to beat the system while the police and the state have not understood their plight and innovated their approach to help the addicts out of addiction.

## Chapter Eight

# *Paani* — Water

Hope is such a mirage. AAP's 2016 Maghi Mela performance had sent a current through Panjab. As the fog lifted, the green wheat turned to gold, winter turned to spring and Kejriwal and AAP started to seem like a real possibility. AAP had come to Panjab riding on the superb performance of winning sixty-seven seats out of seventy in Delhi. Its leaders started to say that Panjab would be 100 per cent—all 117 seats. I wondered if AAP would be able to maintain the tempo and harness the energy it had unleased. Or was it a flying saucer the people had loved but did not know how it would land?

Since it was a new party, AAP had the task of building a cadre. AAP appointed around fifty observers, two to three per district, on the ground. All these people were from Uttar Pradesh and Bihar. AAP had appointed Sanjay Singh as in-charge of the state unit of the party. It sent Durgesh Pathak to prepare the organisational setup and chose an old Panjab hand, from the days of Jarnail Singh Bhindranwale, Sucha Singh Chhotepur, as party convenor. By doing this, AAP forgot what had given the party a buy-in in the state in the 2014 elections. Then, Panjab had taken AAP's anti-corruption vision at face value and voted them in. Now, after the suspension of two of its MPs, with its first line cadre having fallen, AAP tried to rebuild its presence through what it knew: NGO style. After all, besides being an IITian, an ex-IRS officer and now an anti-corruption crusader, Kejriwal's claim to engagement with people's needs is running his two-decade-old NGO named Parivartan that had at one time solved the drinking water issues of people in north Delhi.

This method ignored a basic understanding of how Panjab looks at its relationship with Delhi, not only now, but since medieval times—it looks askance at what it called and understood as the 'Delhi Darbar'. The reasons for this view are rooted in history, but have also found resonance in Delhi's post-Independence role vis-a-vis Panjab. In medieval times when Delhi was the seat of the Mughal empire, Panjab's tussles with Delhi were many, and are well-recorded in Sikh history. Delhi was also the place from where the British ruled and annexed Maharaja Ranjit Singh's empire north of the Satluj after his death. Post-Independence, for two decades, Delhi denied Panjab a composite state, recognition as a distinct linguistic community and even when that was achieved, Panjabis came into possession of a truncated entity. Since then, relations between Delhi and Panjab have never been smooth, especially because of Delhi's role in fermenting trouble in Panjab in the 1970s over river waters which later led to the Khalistan movement and militancy in the region.

When the British East India Company annexed Panjab in the mid-nineteenth century, the armies, both infantry and cavalry they brought to fight the Sikhs, were from the Bengal presidency.[94] Through their classic divide-and-rule policy, the British sowed the seeds of contempt between the Panjabis and the *poorbis*—easterners, the *chawl khanas*—rice eaters. Later, the British evaded Panjabi censure by developing Panjab's canal colonies and offering jobs to Panjabis in the military, but the prejudice against the easterners stayed in Panjab's psyche. The Akali Dal and Congress used this bias against AAP and *poorbis*.

The other term of disdain was *topiwallas*—the Gandhi cap, made popular in the recent past by the Anna Hazare anti-corruption agitation in 2011 from which the AAP sprang, but before that by Mahatma Gandhi during the Independence struggle. This was another bias: the Sikh majority state was anxious that if the AAP won, a Hindu could become chief minister. Except for two former chief ministers who were from a different caste—Gurmukh Singh Musafir and Zail Singh—since the formation of this Panjab in 1966, all its chief ministers have not only been Sikhs, but Jutt Sikhs.

Though the Jutts constitute only about 25 per cent of the population in the state, they are the dominant caste, politically and economically. A change in that status quo was a matter of anxiety. While earlier Bhagwant Mann, the most popular leader, and for a while Suchha Singh Chhotepur were considered as possible CM candidates, closer to the elections, Kejriwal's name began to be bandied about as a choice. This was a matter of major consternation in political circles as well as among Sikhs.

Another perceived difference with the AAP lay in the rural–urban divide. India and Panjab are a million different interlinked ecosystems. While they differ from region to region and people to people, yet, there are discernible patterns on the basis of location, caste, religion and gender. While the other patterns are power-hegemonic, the location factor is simply about political economies. In that sense Panjab stands apart from Delhi, which is where AAP had a foothold. Panjab is overtly an agrarian economy and I wondered how a new and predominantly urban party would grapple with rural issues.

One simple way to define an insider and an outsider: intention. Does AAP intend to serve Panjab? Or does it intend to step into India through Panjab—replicate the land's historic role as a gateway? The test came soon enough.

In my adolescence our train from Delhi to Panjab would cross the Panjab border in the early hours of the morning. We would wake up to the sound of it crossing a bridge on a partially dug, incomplete canal, and we would start moving our luggage to the door of the compartment. This canal was the SYL canal.

Two hundred and fourteen kilometres of the SYL canal pass through Panjab from Ropar to the village Kapuri where the Haryana border begins. I have seen it run parallel to the British-created Bhakra mainline canal which carries water from the Satluj to the south of Panjab and passes by near Bibiji's village—Chaklan—close to Chamkaur Sahib. The two canals, one full, one incomplete, one unlined, another lined on its sides but its concrete slabs incomplete and broken, have remained in my mind as parallel narratives of the land. The gash on the earth has existed since after Panjab was made an independent state. The canal became the reason for the Akali-organised Dharam Yudh Morcha in 1982, and later for the militancy.

The last time the SYL issue had come up, Amarinder Singh, the former CM from Congress, had scored, while the original instigators of the issue—the Akalis—had missed the boat. In 2004, Amarinder Singh helmed the Panjab Termination of Waters Agreement Act, 2004. The Act annulled all earlier accords and awards on the apportionment of river waters between Panjab, Haryana and Rajasthan. Neither Sonia Gandhi, the Congress president, nor Manmohan Singh, the PM, intervened in this matter.

The Constitution mandates that any act or law passed by the State Assembly has to go to the governor for a nod. Over the last decade, the Act had merely moved from the Panjab governor's table to the president's table. The president had sought the advice of the Supreme Court. The Act had not been formally passed, since the final constitutional authority had not given his assent. Amarinder Singh had then scored a political point over the Akalis. This time, the Akalis, who were on the backfoot over the incidents of sacrilege and corruption and large-scale dissonance among the people, sensed an opportunity to get back into the perception game. AAP, seeking to project itself as the saviour of Panjab, fell into the trap.

As the matter of the Act was coming up for hearing again, the Badal government seized the initiative and passed the Panjab Satluj-Yamuna Link Canal Land (Proprietary Rights) Bill, 2016. This Bill promised to return to the farmers the 5,376 acres of land the government had acquired in the late 1970s for the proposed SYL canal and redeem the image of the Akalis.[95]

The governor did not sign the Bill but the idea was that once the farmers re-occupied their lands, it would need police action to evict them. That would become a human rights issue and the courts and the Centre would attempt to negotiate a compromise. The Congress, not to be left behind, highlighted the Termination Act that it had championed. AAP then unearthed posters of Congress leader Captain Amarinder Singh welcoming Indira Gandhi to the ground-breaking ceremony for the SYL on 8 April 1982. The Akalis were happy to amplify this new development.

Arvind Kejriwal now declared, 'The SYL should not be built. Panjab does not have water to spare.' Kejriwal hailed from Haryana and was now the Delhi CM. His current stance was contrary to his position in both these states. The Akalis and Congress reminded Kejriwal that during the Delhi elections in 2015 he had supported the SYL canal project, for it promised to bring water to Delhi. In the courts, the AAP counsel Suresh Tripathy, representing the Delhi Jal Board in the ongoing hearing of a presidential reference in the matter, informed the court that Panjab had gone beyond its legal competence in unilaterally passing the Panjab Termination of Agreement Act, 2004, echoing Haryana's stand on the issue. It appeared that the AAP supported SYL in Delhi and opposed it in Panjab.

I was about nine years old when I became conscious of the fact that water was also political. One hot summer afternoon, Baba and I were walking through the Baradari—the erstwhile royal gardens of Patiala. The sun was blazing and I was very thirsty. Baba spotted a rubber hose lying on the lawns, water gushing from it into flower beds. He asked the gardener's permission to drink water. The gardener was curt, 'Water is free. It is your right. Why ask me?' When we finished drinking, the gardener said, prophetically, as it turns out, 'The day water is no longer free, this land will end.'

During my childhood I could spot hand pumps everywhere in Panjab, including one right opposite the home where Baba's extended family lived. In our fields, three in the city market, more in the old town, one between the railway station and the bus stand, hand pumps were a part of the locality. Not anymore. Now packaged drinking water is everywhere. In the eighteenth century legend so often sung all over Panjab, valiant and love-struck Sohni drowns in the River Chenab while her lover awaits her on the other bank because the pot she is using to keep her afloat and take her across the river is made of unbaked mud and cannot withstand the pressure. Metaphorically, the river is the world while the pot is the truth. What Sohni considers true turns out to be a lie and she is duped. She drowns and her love remains unrequited. In the religious sense too, water is the sea of emotions. A popular song goes:

*Je bhavsagar langna ni, jindadiye pad Satgur di baani …*

(If you intend to cross the sea of emotions, read the writings of the True Lord.)

Perhaps the most chanted text by Guru Nanak is the beginning of the final *shlok* of Japuji, a part of the Guru Granth Sahib:

*Pavan Guru, Pani Pita, Mata Dharat Mahat*

(Air is the Guru, water is the father, the earth is the eminent mother.)

Water defines Panjab—the land of five rivers. Water is the lifeline of Panjab which has no other mineral or resource. The issue of waters has also snared Panjab for the past half century since the state was formed.

In this context it is important to note that the five rivers and the sixth where the five merge—the Indus—form the entire river basin which has now been divided between India and Pakistan, east and west Panjab. In 1960, the two national governments reached a United Nations-mandated treaty on the use and sharing of waters of their rivers—the Indus Water Treaty. It is one of three most significant river water treaties in the world agreed upon by nations in conflict. There is much war rhetoric that regularly surfaces in India and Pakistan but it has not touched this almost six-decade-old treaty. It is only now, under the current right-wing dispensation, that India has made some noise over it.

Even this noise is wholly out of place and impractical. To abrogate the treaty and retain all of the water in India, which is the right-wing dream, close to three hundred small dams have to be constructed on the Indus, Jhelum, Chenab, Beas and Ravi that flow in the Indian territory. This is a near-impossible exercise, given the amount of displacement that it would entail or the costs that would have to be incurred. The treaty has continued to be honoured. Yet, within India, as far as Panjab's relations with Haryana, Rajasthan and Delhi are concerned, the matter of river waters has been infinitely contested.

I decided to travel the last leg of SYL from Banur, south of Chandigarh, which, due to constant media reports, is also the most public part. In March 2016, Jasdeep and I traversed the fifty-odd kilometres along the length of the canal on his Bullet motorcycle a day after the Supreme Court-designated team had been there to inspect the canal. Jasdeep was driving the Bullet. From close to Banur, at the bridge over the SYL canal, we left the highway and turned east. The canal under the bridge was full of water hyacinth growing in a

feet or so of stagnant water. We climbed the embankment and drove
a bit more to find the kacha road leading to a village.

At Thuha, the first village we entered, I asked for the *sathh*, an
informal meeting point found in most Panjab villages. The three
villagers I asked, one after another, looked at me as if I had lost my
mind. 'We don't have the *sathh* in this part of Panjab. For *sathh*, go
west. That is where Badal is from. That is where he has diverted our
waters. Go!' But Badal had recently given back the canal land to these
people. Why were they still angry?

We spotted an older man and I asked, 'Aren't you happy you got
your land back?'

'Shall I beat my head with it? What use is the land to me?' replied
Shamsher who I found out was a block samiti member.

'I am sorry. I don't understand.'

'Did we raise the demand for a canal? Did we ask for it? We never
wanted it. Forty years back Badal forced it upon us because of his
friend Devi Lal. The government acquired the land, dug it up, and
then stopped any further work. All these years we have been waiting
for water to flow in the canal. It has never come. In the meantime,
the ground water table has gone down from 70 feet to 500 feet. This
canal is the bane of our lives!'

Soon, a number of villagers gathered around us. They asked who
we were and what we were doing. They told us that TV channels
came, shot footage from the road and disappeared. No one entered
the village, talked to them or sought their views. The team from the
Supreme Court had also done the same thing—their cars slowed
down on the bridge, the people never got down from the vehicles,
took pictures and sped away without talking to the crowds.

'Crowds?'

Amarjit Singh replied, 'Our sarpanch is the Akali leader Baljinder
Singh. He made the announcement from the gurdwara: water will be
released, rush to the canal. We went in big numbers. Then some Akalis

in blue and black turbans came in front of us facing the road, carrying banners and flags. The Supreme Court team would have thought the whole crowd was Akali, and people wanted their land back.'

'So it was all a frame-up?'

'Yes,' they replied together. 'The gurdwara lied.'

'Our lands were never very fertile. Yet, in the last few decades, Badal has made a desert of east Panjab. Now they tell us to take the land. What will we do with the land? Some of us gave half an acre, some one acre in two parts, and so on. What will we do with it if it is returned?' Shamsher explained, 'How wide is the canal? Only that much land was acquired, through the length of the canal. Yet, how deep is the canal? More than 10-12 feet. How will we fill it and reclaim the land? It will cost us three to four lakhs, maybe more, to just get it levelled. Are we that rich that we can afford it? Do you know how much a JCB costs per day, plus the mud? Where will we get mud from? Our own fields, the topsoil? There should be some logic!'

An almost angry Avtar Singh joined in the conversation. 'Sister fuckers! We don't care whether you want to give water to Haryana or not. Keep sorting it out. You already have a barrier built in at the end of the canal at Kapuri before it goes to Haryana. Just close it. Give us the water. Don't even lay concrete in the canal. We need *sem* (waterlogging) in our fields.'

'But *sem* is a huge issue in the south-western districts,' Jasdeep said, 'where the Indira Gandhi canal flows. In Fazilka and Faridkot.'

Avtar retorted, 'It is, there! We need our water table to come up. Give us *sem* for a few years. Give us the water!'

They asked us to join them for tea. We refused politely. Shamsher told us that the local villagers even held a press conference on 11 March. No media reported it. 'We are Jutts, landowners. Now we do daily labour. But what can we do for water?'

We took their leave and proceeded along the canal wherever

we found the embankment clear enough for a ride. I hollered, 'I am amazed, Jasdeep!'

He screamed back, 'Why?'

'Farmers in Panjab kill for inches of land. They cultivate everywhere, even under electrical grid towers. Yet, here they are not willing to take back their own land.'

Jasdeep merely said, '*Garibi*.'

'What?'

'Poverty! They don't have money to level the land, what use is it to them?'

I went silent. Poverty indeed! Through Badal's seven-decade long career—he became the sarpanch of his village in 1947—he had played politics like a game of chess. This time round, the poverty he had ushered into Panjab had betrayed him. Before the canal digging started, there were mango orchards in the area. We don't find any clusters of trees any longer. The land is dry, parched, broken and pale brown. Brambles grow on the embankment.

'California, said Sukhbir,' remarked Jasdeep. 'I will make Panjab into California.' Indeed, the landscape is a desert.

At Surajgarh we stopped at a small *dhaba* next to a *theka*—a local liquor shop. Five men were seated on wooden benches. Cut and salt-sprinkled boiled eggs lay on newspapers and dirty plastic plates. A bottle of *santri*, a local liquor, stood on the small table with plastic glasses around it. We ordered for some *bhurji* (scrambled eggs). The responses to our questions were the same, albeit more flowery, full of abuses for the Badals and other politicians and the politics of the SYL. I noticed that the glazed eyes were sad and lifeless. Wheat fields stood opposite us. In one of them a cow munched away at the wheat stalks. No one stopped it. No one seemed to care any longer. When a government, a system, a state has not been able to care for its people, the people too stop caring.

At village Nanhera we stopped at a *tikki chaat rehri*, a food cart. School children had gathered around it. I asked the *thelawala*, a Bihari who had migrated there thirty years ago, if there was anyone in the village who had a large piece of land returned to him from the canal. A man at the *thela* overheard us and said Paramdeep from the village was a big landowner and was getting back eleven acres. We asked for Paramdeep's number or the way to his house. As we sat there chatting over a glass of tea, the students came with the number. I called up Paramdeep and asked him if he intended to take back his land. Paramdeep apologised for not being able to meet us as he was away but agreed that he stood to benefit from the land and so was opting for it.

'But how are you getting so much land back?'

He told me his property was still in joint ownership. The brothers had not yet split. Together, the three bothers owned around forty acres of land, and now, with eleven more, they would have a good chance of managing it.

'But the expense of making the land cultivable will also be around twenty-five lakhs. Plus, where will you get water?'

Yes, he agreed the expenses would be high. They were thinking of getting a new bore—submersible pump—in addition to the two he already had. Between the three pumps there should be enough water.

'Do you have the cash?'

He laughed and asked which Jutt would have so much ready cash, and said he was thinking of a loan. I thanked him and put the phone down. This was how a farmer who was out of the debt trap would come under it. The idea that eleven extra acres would be useful would have been valid if the lands were fertile. They were not. There were hardly any customers, too, for the fallow land, if he were to sell it. Yet, the desire to own more land would force Paramdeep to take a loan.

We reached the National Highway 1 (NH 1), crossed Shambu, and spotted a police post near the railway line. The post was a makeshift red brick and mortar room, a resting place for police constables, next to the railway bridge of my adolescence before Rajpura. It felt strange to see on ground this bridge I had seen all my life from the train, announcing the arrival of my destination. The constable offered us water. I asked, 'Since when have you been here?'

Constable Lal Singh replied, 'You mean me or this post?'

'Well, both ...'

Constable Harpal Singh said, 'I have been here for six years. Lal has just been here a few months. But this post has existed since the issue of the SYL came up.'

Jasdeep asked, 'Which bridge are you monitoring? The one on the Ghaggar river or SYL?' That is when I realised there were two bridges one following another. Strange, in spite of being on them hundreds of times, I had not noticed that.

Lal Singh told us that the Ghaggar bridge was three-fourth with Haryana and one-fourth with Panjab. The SYL was completely with Panjab. 'We are in charge of the SYL bridge.'

'Why isn't the Railway Protection Force monitoring it? The tracks belong to the railways.'

Harpal retorted, 'Why do you wish we lose our jobs? We are anyway temporary.'

'Still?'

'I get just Rs 12,000 per month. The matter is in the court. That is why we home guards are deputed here. It is easy, home is at Rajpura.'

'For how many hours of work?'

'Well, it is between Lal and me. Day and night. Twenty-four hours.'

I asked Lal and Harpal what they thought they were protecting: the tracks, the trains, the passengers, or something more—the law of the land made by selfish politicians? Lal answered, 'I haven't thought so deeply. I just know if something happens, we will lose our jobs. We are just doing our duty.'

Harpal pitched in, 'What law are we talking about? Even the courts and judges have not understood the law. *Siapa hai ji, siapa*—it is a lamentation. We will continue to do our job and hope that we become permanent (employees). Tell us if you can do something for us.'

We proceeded towards Kapuri, the now infamous village where Indira Gandhi had broken ground for the construction of the SYL and crossed the seasonal Ghaggar. It looked like a large drain with black sewerage at its bottom. Villagers say the black waters were sewerage from Chandigarh, thirty kilometres away. Was this where the sewerage of big cities went? Like the sewerage from Jalandhar's tanning industry went into the Chitti Bein, the white rivulet, next to the Mughal Sarai near Nakodar. Like the sewage that emptied from hosiery and dye factories of Ludhiana into the Budda Dariya.

Farmers had installed scores of pumps to raise the black waters to their fields. The black muck was irrigating the crops. It was toxic. Farmers knew it was wrong. But what could a small farmer do? Instal submersible pumps? At what depth? Along the way we heard people in different villages claim, from their own experience, that water was to be found at a depth of 700 feet, at other places at 1,000 feet. The only choice was to abandon farming, take on another profession and eventually sell the land which, too, was priced much lower than land elsewhere in Panjab. Yet, there were few buyers. For decades, due to its being a border state, the Centre had not created heavy industries in Panjab.

On the way to Kapuri we stopped at the sluice gates of the SYL canal. Tall concrete pillars, huge iron gates now stand rotting in the midst of a small thorny jungle. The villagers were right. For forty years the government could have supplied water in the canal to east Panjab, and still stopped it from going to Haryana. In the process of making the SYL a rallying point for Panjab's right on its waters, the government had made a desert of the whole area. It had served no one's interest.

We then reached the Narwana canal, which broke from the Bhakra main line at Mandour and supplied water to Haryana. The crossing of the Ghaggar with this canal is a feat of modern engineering—one over the other. We carried on to the Sarala Head Works where part of the water from the Narwana canal was diverted to the Haryana part of the SYL canal. A car full of youngsters arrived and parked itself amidst some families of idle picnickers and opened beer bottles. Oblivious to their surroundings, they got busy talking and joking with each other. The picnicking families moved away.

We came back to Kapuri. It was now getting late. We sat down at a small tea shop. People gathered, and the villagers told us how Indira Gandhi's helicopter had landed and she came close to the village. They showed us the field where the Akalis had gathered about two kilometres away. The police had prevented the Akalis from going near the spot of the ground-breaking ceremony. They told us how Bibi Rajinder Kaur, daughter of Master Tara Singh, made a speech and then crackers were burst. Indira Gandhi assumed that guns had been fired and hastily left.

Initially, the Akali numbers were in hundreds, but gradually the numbers dwindled. That year, in August, the Akalis shifted the protest—from Neher Roko Morcha to the Dharam Yudh Morcha—to Amritsar. The villagers rued that no one ever paid them compensation for the destruction of the standing crop or for loss of paddy the next season. No one had paid them, whenever protests had taken place in the village in the last four decades. An old man, Kishan Chand, remarked, 'We are a peaceful sort. We don't even shoo away dogs. But worldwide we are known as a terrorist village.'

Kapuri is now infamous.

In Panjab, the work on the canal first stopped when thirty migrant labourers were gunned down on the site in 1988, and later when Avtar Singh Aulakh, a superintendent engineer and M.L. Shekri, the chief engineer, were killed in 1990 in Chandigarh. Since then, this canal had remained incomplete and unresolved.

'So how much water is at stake?' I screamed at Jasdeep from behind the bike.

'About 5 per cent,' he screamed back, but because of his helmet his voice was muffled. The night traffic was haphazard and we maintained silence until we reached his place. The matter of the SYL, its court cases and documentation can bewilder anyone trying to understand the issue. To understand more, I sought help from a senior journalist and told him about our trip. He said, 'All that is left now is to let water in the canal and block it at Kapuri. The Panjab government could run a fish farm—pisciculture. The world's longest fish farm!'

All the five rivers that comprise Panjab originate in the Himalayas. They start from the territory of Tibet which is currently under Chinese occupation, move through Jammu and Kashmir and Himachal Pradesh to Panjab and then into Pakistan. Water is a finite natural resource. Since it is a finite resource, it has rights, duties and consequences associated with its use. There are two internationally accepted criteria for river rights: riparian rights and basin rights.

The rights around water usage from a natural source such as a lake, pond, river or stream are known as riparian rights. Riparian rights determine who can and cannot use the waters. The word 'riparian' comes from the Latin word 'ripa' which means the bank of the river. As an adjective it stands for the legal rights of the owner of the land on a riverbank, such as fishing or irrigation. The basin is a surface which feeds the river, from where surface water from rainfall seeps into the rivers. Those regions also have rights on the rivers.

Look up the current maps of India, Tibet, China, Kashmir, Pakistan Occupied Kashmir and Pakistan. Then zoom into the maps of current Panjab, Haryana, Rajasthan and Delhi. The state boundaries are clear proof that neither the Satluj nor the Beas flows through any state except Panjab, and before that through Himachal Pradesh when it enters India from Tibet. The Satluj flows a hundred kilometres, the Beas two hundred kilometres and the Ravi three hundred kilometres from the Haryana border and even more from Delhi and Rajasthan. The facts on the ground tell us that no other state but Himachal Pradesh, Jammu and Kashmir and Panjab have riparian rights on the waters from the rivers Satluj, Beas and Ravi. That is why the SYL issue is unlike the Cauvery water issue or the Mahadayi issue in Karnataka or the Narmada issue in Gujarat in which cases the rivers flow through multiple states who are in conflict with each other.

If, in a leap of fancy, the Centre or states were to argue that Haryana and Rajasthan form part of the Indus river basin, per the Indian Water Resources website, the Indus river basin is over eleven lakh square kilometres.[96] The basin includes not only the Himalayas but also China, Tibet, Haryana and Rajasthan. But Haryana, Rajasthan and Delhi do not feed the Satluj or other rivers in any way. They do not form part of the three lakh plus square kilometres of the Indus, Satluj or Beas catchment area. In fact, the altitude difference between the Himalayas, Panjab and Haryana means that water will percolate downwards and not upwards into the Satluj. That is why, when in the last few decades, while floods have taken place in Panjab, Haryana and Rajasthan have borne no consequences. If, for some reason, the 226 metre-high Bhakra crumbles and the Gobind Sagar lake wrecks mayhem, it is Panjab that will bear the consequences, not Haryana,

Delhi or Rajasthan. That is why, neither on the riparian basis nor on the basin basis do these states have a claim on the waters of Panjab and Himachal Pradesh. That should ideally sort the matter out.

But it does not. Haryana claims a previous map. It is a map of Panjab before 1966 when the state was trifurcated. In that map Haryana does not exist, nor does some parts of Himachal Pradesh. The entire region is largely Panjab. This map has the Yamuna flowing through what is now Haryana towards Delhi as the eastern border of Panjab. In 1966, when Haryana was created and parts of Panjab ceded to Himachal Pradesh, Panjab's waters too were divided through Clauses 78, 79 and 80 of the Panjab Reorganisation Act. In this division, however, the water of the Yamuna was not considered. Until date there is no reasonable answer to why it was not considered. Since the total quantum of water was not considered, one can conclude that the division too was arbitrary. The clauses deal with the rights and liabilities with regard to Bhakra-Nangal and the Beas Projects (Clause 78), the Bhakra Management Board (Clause 79) and the Construction of the Beas Project (Clause 80).

Specifically Clause 78 states:

> Notwithstanding anything contained in this Act but subject to the provisions of sections 79 and 80, all rights and liabilities of the existing State of Panjab in relation to Bhakra-Nangal Project and Beas Project shall, on the appointed day, be the rights and liabilities of the successor States in such proportion as may be fixed, and subject to such adjustments as may be made, by agreement entered into by the said States after consultation with the Central Government or, if no such agreement is entered into within two years of the appointed day, as the Central Government may by order determine having regard to the purposes of the Projects: Provided that the order so made by the Central Government may be varied by any subsequent agreement entered into by the successor States after consultation with the Central Government.[97]

This is legalese, but notice the time frame: two years.

It is now year fifty-two. Is there anything that can explain this delay except a lack of will on the part of the central government? To solve the river waters issue, one would have to answer the question: on what basis are the successor states deemed as rightful stakeholders of the waters? There is no parallel to such contestation of water rights by non-riparian, non-basin successor states. On the other hand, the phenomenon of predecessor and successor states takes place often over land in Panjab. When fathers divide land among children, or when they pass away, each child is a successor. Each successor gathers what he or she gets at the time of division and begins life. It is disingenuous on the part of the Centre to not make a clear division, ambiguously define the terms of division, not meet the time criteria set, and make the states squabble for decades. Since 1966, Panjab and Haryana have been paying the price for the Centre's mistakes.

However, let us go further and understand the status of water as a subject. Is water a state, central or concurrent subject per the Constitution of India? Though water is a State subject per Clause 17 in List II (State List), it is tied up with Clause 56 in List I (Union List) which deals with inter-state rivers. Clause 262(1) and (2) hold that in case of conflict between states over river waters, the decision of the parliament will overrule the court or even that of the Constitution. Clause 257(2) states that in the case of inland waterways, water becomes a central subject. We need to recognise here that when the Constitution was written, water was taken to mean river water and always referred to as inter-state waters, anticipating that conflicts would be inter-state. Wells, ponds and ground water were not considered. The case of Panjab vis-a-vis Haryana, Rajasthan, and Delhi is different because the rivers under dispute do not flow through these states.

The waterways clause is the reason for a new fable to come up: not only will SYL provide the much-needed drinking water to south Haryana, it will also eventually become a grand inland waterway on which small ships will be able to carry goods, through the Yamuna onto the Ganga and upstream. This canal was therefore going to connect east and west India. The nation would save the time and cost that it currently expends when ships circumnavigate the subcontinent through the Arabian Sea and Bay of Bengal. The delay in construction of this short canal is the only impediment in unimagined prosperity and development of the nation. There can't be a bigger fable than this about the canal and the interlinking of rivers.

Let us step back a bit and consider a few basic terms at play here: water as a resource, the act of sharing and the phenomena of ownership. There is no doubt that water is a precious resource and Haryana, Rajasthan and Delhi also need water. However, what can be shared is what is available or in surplus. One can't share if one is oneself deficient. A couple of decades back water was abundant, but modern farming and people's needs have created a shortfall of water. This brings us to the question of ownership or its reverse—appropriation. Unless it is resolved that Haryana, Rajasthan and Delhi are not natural owners of the rivers, things cannot move forward.

Whether it was Indira Gandhi threatening the then Panjab Chief Minister Darbara Singh or another chief minister, Zail Singh, playing to please Delhi, the Centre has ridden roughshod over Panjab's rights. Since then, Parkash Singh Badal and Devi Lal have played their games. When the Akalis raised the issue which aggravated centre-state relations, it led to Operation Blue Star. Later, when the Panjab Accord was signed, the Akali leader Sant Harchand Singh Longowal capitulated for no good reason. But all these are distractions from the moot question: who has the rights on water?

Coming back to resources, one could deem them national and not state, and move it accordingly in the Constitution to the central list. Water is a need, but so is oil for machines and vehicles, coal for power plants, stones for building material and so on. What logic can

Delhi offer to Panjab that its water is a national need and hence should be shared, but the other needs of Panjab can only be fulfilled through payments that Panjab makes to states that own oil, gas, coal, stone and the like? If water is to be divided, it is only fair to ask for other resources to be divided with Panjab free of cost.

Rajasthan's case is even more peculiar because before Independence, the king of Bikaner used to pay for the water Rajasthan received from the Satluj. This is water from the earlier Ferozepur and now Harrike Barrage where the Beas meets the Satluj before it flows to Pakistan. Per the Indus Water Treaty, India has the rights to use the water and it diverts the water to the Indira Gandhi canal. Over years and stages, the canal has been expanded, which has led to the Thar desert being irrigated, but the structure of the canal is such that it causes wetness (*sem*) in the south-western districts of Panjab. The excessive dampness renders the soil not very good for agriculture and small canals have been built to drain out the *sem*. While that is an issue, the moot point is, why has the payment for the water Rajasthan used to pay stopped since 1955 when the Government of India promised it would be taken up separately?[98] The irony is that through desertification in the east and dampness in the south, Panjab is helping other states become green while it perishes itself.

Panjab has incurred a loss of Rs 32 lakh crore since it has been giving its river waters for free to the non-riparian state of Haryana, the Union Territory of Chandigarh and the non-riparian and non-successor states of Rajasthan and Delhi. Addressing a press conference, ex-AAP MP Dr Dharamvira Gandhi stated: 'Sections 78, 79 and 80 of the Panjab Reorganisation Act are violative of Articles 162 and 246(3) of the Constitution as irrigation and hydel power are the state subjects under entry 17 of the state list.' He demanded the setting up of an independent authority for calculating the cost of river water in terms of its monetary value.

In 1956, the government passed the Inter-state River Water Disputes Act which sought to regulate how water is shared between states but never formed the board to implement the Act. Counsel for Gandhi, advocate Rajvinder Singh Bains, said that Section 14 of the Inter-state River Water Disputes Act 1956 was unconstitutional because it was not implemented.

Subsequently, a team of lawyers and the former MP from Patiala, Dr Dharmavira Gandhi, backed by the Panjab government, have filed a petition in the Panjab and Haryana High Court. They are demanding that at the symbolic rate of one paise per litre, Rajasthan pay Rs 80,000 crore to Panjab, and terms for further use be laid out.[99] The petition is yet to come up for hearing.

In recent times, an even more fantastic fable is turning real by the day. This has gained currency since the new wave of Hindutva was visited upon us by political and social forces in the country—the search for the great hidden river of Indian antiquity, Saraswati. It has been the belief that Prayag in Allahabad is the confluence of the rivers Ganga, Yamuna and Saraswati and that is why the Maha Kumbh is organised there. Prayag is therefore a revered place in the sacred geography of Hinduism. Allahabad has recently even been renamed Prayagraj. The Rigveda mentions the river Saraswati forty-five times. The Ramayana, Mahabharata and Puranas also talk of the Saraswati. The river is also called Brahma's sacred daughter Ikshumati—the greatest of mothers, rivers and goddesses.

The most likely explanation is the Saraswati was lost due to the tectonic movement of the earth plates. Based on American satellite imagery that showed traces of water channels that had disappeared long ago, academic references proposed that the Saraswati was the Ghaggar-Hakra river (Ghaggar in India and Hakra in Pakistan) and was the lifeline of the Indus Valley or Harappan Civilisation (between 3,500 and 1,900 BC).[100]

On this basis, the Bhartiya Janata Party government in its previous term (1999 to 2004) ordered archaeological diggings to ascertain the presence of the river Saraswati. The findings of this project are mixed. In some places like Yamunanagar and Kurukshetra in Haryana they have found water not very deep below the earth's surface. That does not mean that if a river has been lost, it has to be re-created.

Yet, that is exactly what the current BJP government wants to do. They are actually trying to recreate, alongside the Ghaggar, the lost river, Saraswati, from Himachal Pradesh, flowing towards the Rann of Kutch in Gujarat. Archaeological teams in Haryana are digging up a canal which will connect the Satluj to the Arabian Sea. The canal will divert the water from the Satluj through headworks proposed in Himachal Pradesh at Haripur, Lohgarh and Adi Bari. That means the Satluj will reach Panjab empty. However, per international riparian laws, this will be illegal. The Convention on the Law of Non-Navigational Uses of International Watercourses, 1997, adopted by the United Nations (UN) clearly states that riparian states can use water per their needs and not change the courses of rivers. Yet, given how religion and ancient mythology now play an important role in Indian politics, there is no guarantee that Hindutva forces will let the matter rest.[101] This will complete the desertification of Panjab.

A few days later, I was alone, driving Jasdeep's silver Maruti Alto to understand Panjab's double bind. While division of river waters is a fundamental issue, I was curious to check another phenomena: the Satluj creates a distributary on which Panjab's biggest city and industrial centre Ludhiana—known as the Manchester of the East—is located, and after a hundred kilometres or so again becomes a tributary to the Satluj. Before the city, the distributary is called Budda

Dariya—the old river—and after the city the tributary becomes Budda Nalla—the old drain.

Phuphadji and Bibiji worked in the education department at one of the holiest cities called Chamkaur Sahib. Phuphadji was a block sports officer and Bibiji was a Panjabi teacher. They had a cute red official flat, the last in the lane, next to a huge ground. That is where, during my vacations in childhood, Phuphadji would prepare chicken curry and offer it to me with a peg of gin or vodka. 'Should not smell,' he would whisper. Phuphadji was fun. To get the chicken we would go to the town market where everyone would greet him. The clothes store would invariably give me cloth for a new shirt. The young boys and girls, his students, would discreetly nod at Phuphadji. He was important and could get them a selection in the school, village, district and perhaps, state teams. Phuphadji personally preferred athletics, hockey and basketball.

The wide market road led to Gurdwara Katalgarh Sahib—the fort of murder. This is where the older sons of Guru Gobind Singh had fought against the mighty Mughal army and attained martyrdom. This is also where the first *Panj Pyaras* had asked Guru Gobind Singh to leave the fort. The story tells us how a leader would not only order but also obey. The *Panj Pyaras* had waited for the Guru to signal about his safe escape and then plunged into battle. The Guru signalled from a place now known as Tali Sahib—the gurdwara of the honourable clap.

When I was a kid, Katalgarh Sahib was a red brick structure, part of which was even rumoured to be original. Tali Sahib was a small room, much visited but not ostentatious. Then SGPC took over Katalgarh Sahib and raised money for renovations from the congregation by bringing in *kar sewa wale Babas*—elders who build marble gurdwaras and often, secretly pocket the earnings from the congregation. They destroyed original, older structures, wiped clean the real histories, and imposed their template, making everything look uniform. Katalgarh Sahib is now a white marble gurdwara which resembles other gurdwaras but has lost the original essence of the fort where Guru Gobind Singh had planned his attacks, and sacrificed his sons.

Sikh history has an elaborate version of the route the Guru took when he left Anandpur Sahib and crossed the river in spate, was separated from his family, and traced his way to Talwandi Sabo—the Guru Gobind Singh Marg. However, current Panjab hardly resembles the Guru's Panjab. For instance, the Neelon canal which now passes by Chamkaur Sahib, and the Sirhind canal which now passes a few kilometres from Ludhiana, were not in existence in the Guru's time.

On the misty, winter night on 7 December 1705, how did the Guru reach the jungles of Machhiwara and find the Mahant's home where he rested briefly? With Mughal forces around, he wouldn't even have been able to carry a lantern. I am guessing he would have done what humans have done through history—followed a river or rivulet, especially if he knew it went somewhere he wanted to go. It is my hunch that he might have followed the Budda Dariya.

I set out to trace where exactly the Budda Dariya left the Satluj. No one knew. I reached Bela and asked around. Under a pipal tree I met Sukhcharan who was a Bahujan Samaj Party worker and hopeful now of a ticket to fight the elections from Chamkaur Sahib. He said he could help me find the rivulet, jumped into my car, and asked me to drive west towards Machhiwara. I sensed something was wrong. Sukhcharan wanted me to see the rivulet. I wanted to see the origin of the rivulet. We had to be heading north-west, towards the Satluj. We stopped at a decrepit tea stall to make enquiries, and the shop owner turned us back. I offered to drop Sukhcharan at Bela but he refused to get off and said he would come with me to the Satluj.

On the way we spotted a huge red vehicle that looked like the chassis of a truck with nobody on it. It was at least 20 feet long, standing in the middle of a field and had smothered part of the still green wheat leading up to its location. A tall, thick iron pillar lay half buried in the ground, pumping away like a piston. Mud was flying around. It was a dual-rotary machine digging a well. The owners had probably invested about half a crore rupees in getting the machine to Panjab from Europe or the US. Upon seeing us, Ram Kishan, the driver manning the huge machine, stopped the machine and came up to us. When I asked him how deep he would dig, he said, 'At least 500 feet, no good water before that.'

'Even with the Satluj so close by?' I asked.

'Everything is dirty, the land, the water, full of chemicals, sewerage.'

I asked the farmer in whose land the well was being dug, since when they have had tube wells in the area. 'Since the '80s. Before that the water was either through *khaal* (smaller canals dug in the '70s), or hand-dug wells for *mitha paani* (potable water). Now canal water is not enough to grow paddy. We need tube wells.'

'Did you take permission to dig the well?' asked Sukhcharan. The farmer did not know who we were and said, 'Yes, yes. Shall I show papers?' Sukhcharan turned to me and said, 'Earlier people were free to dig tube wells but now they need permission from the government. They need power lines. There is also some deposit.'

Ram Kishen said, 'I have been digging bores for three decades. We used to make up to five bores before we found water. With these machines failure is less.'

'How less? The machine is expensive.'

'The rate is almost one in two, or 50 per cent.'

Divining for water is perhaps the hardest guessing game one can play, and human beings have been playing it since civilisation began. It was still okay when a group of people, perhaps fellow villagers, joined together to dig a well by hand. Water in the vicinity would trickle down. Now it was one deep bore—individual effort, but no social participation.

Ram Kishen was back to work and I saw how the machine plummeted into the earth, sending concrete rings inside. Sukhcharan said, '*Bhaaji*, the problem is not only the bore but the expenses of the bore. Earlier, one tube well was good for twenty acres of land. Now a farmer with even five acres wants a bore.'

'But why? The water from the tube well has not reduced.'

The farmer answered, 'I have just four acres. My neighbour refuses to lend me his tractor or take water from his well.'

'It is all about being a Jutt. The idea of ownership. "My" tube well. "My" tractor. Who knows they may want "my" combine harvester too,' Sukhcharan said sarcastically.

'What are the expenses to dig a well?'

The farmer said, 'I spent one lakh for power line and poles. Another one and a half lakhs on the bore. Then one lakh for a 15 HP submersible pump. Earlier people bought second- or third-hand motors and got a test report by paying bribes. Now it has to have the ISI mark and can be only from few companies. The motor alone costs Rs 50,000. Plus wires and pipes. The earlier bore was at 250 feet, with a four-inch pipe and concrete slab. Now it starts at 500 feet.'

That was the bore I knew from my childhood. It was a *kacha*, well, non-concrete. We kept a fan on the slab placed first at 20 feet, then at 40 feet. Then came the era of mono-block motors, then the submersible ones. I remember how my uncle had said with neighbours going for submersible, we had no choice. The water had gone deep. 'So, overall Rs 3.5 lakhs if the bore succeeds, else, Rs 4.5 lakhs,' said the farmer.

'Do you have that kind of money?'

'With four acres? Are you joking? I mortgaged one acre. Took a loan.'

'How long will it take to dig the well?' I hollered at Ram Kishen.

'It will be done by night.'

'And how many wells a month?'
'Normally fifteen to twenty.'
I wished him the best and thanked the farmer.

The governor of Panjab, in his address to the Panjab Assembly in the 2016 Budget session mentioned that Panjab, which supposedly was abundant in water resources, now supported 79 per cent of its irrigation through tube wells. The number of tube wells had risen from 28,000 to 13.5 lakh between 1980-81 and 2016-17.

Per Professor Malkiat Singh, retired from Panjab University, Panjab had another twenty-three lakh submersible pumps which provided water to towns and cities. In total, since the 1960s, Panjab had drained out 132 cubic kilometres of water.[102]

The greatest property of water as a substance is that it can take any shape but cannot be compressed. This makes water an excellent foundation for the ground surface. But what happens when water is drained out?[103] It creates a gap, filled with air or even vacuum. Panjab is thus now standing on vacuum under its surface. As the pressure of multi-storeyed buildings increases, the earth's surface will give way and Panjab will start submerging.

To extract this water Panjab uses 1,150 crore unit electricity per annum. Four thermal plants produce this electricity and use 43,800,000 tonnes of coal. One-fourth of this coal becomes fly ash which flies in the air. This fly ash is full of toxic metals—uranium, mercury, chromium, arsenic and selenium. The metal particles blow in the air, fall on the ground, mix with earth and water. Per nuclear physicist Dr Hardev Singh Virk, the average value of uranium is in the range of 2,109 ppb (parts per billion) to 2,277 ppb in certain pockets of Hoshiarpur district against the permissible limit of 60 ppb or microgram per litre set by the Bhabha Atomic Research Centre (BARC) and the 15 ppb limit set by the World Health Organisation (WHO). The average value of uranium in the state was 115 ppb, which is double the BARC limit and almost ten times the WHO limit.[104] These metals enter crops and food systems. They cause cancer and this explains how the presence of fluorides has led to a huge incidence of arthritis and the necessity for knee replacement operations. To purify this water for drinking, many homes and hotels use the RO filter that wastes three-fourths of the water, which it drains out.

In the land of perennial rivers, this is an unending cycle of water scarcity, fulfilled by drawing water from the ground, causing air and land pollution because of the coal used for electricity to run the tube wells, and then wasting water by treating it through machines. These circumstances are causing Panjab to become not just a desert, but a wasteland.

The question is: why does Panjab, with an average of five hundred millimetre annual rainfall grow high-yielding paddy varieties that need an average of eleven hundred millimetre annual rainfall? An average kilogram of paddy needs five thousand three hundred litres of water. That is why Panjab's contribution to the central pool is not just the final produce (rice), but also the water needed to produce the rice. Panjab's per annum water export to the nation—while the land itself goes dry—is 48,105 million cubic metres.[105] Who will compensate Panjab for the loss of water?

We moved on towards Bela. In the next village, Attari, Sukhcharan proudly told me this was the village of the jailed scamster Nirmal Singh Bhangoo, who was now in jail. Then he asked why I believed that Guru Gobind Singh would have taken the Budda Dariya route.

'That is just my imagination,' I replied. In Panjab it does not take time for a rumour to become a fact and I almost regretted that I had revealed the reason for my pursuit.

'I know, I know. But it is worth exploring.'

'How can we explore it?' I asked. 'We can only explore the rivulet.'

The car went through a well-canopied but broken road. There was a mud canal of sorts next to the road but I wasn't sure if it was the rivulet. The air was becoming cooler. Sukhcharan asked, 'Do you know why this road is broken?'

I shook my head. 'Sand smuggling. Many trucks pass by this road in the night. Carrying sand from Satluj's banks to construction sites in Chandigarh, Mohali, Panchkula. The rates have gone up from Rs 2,000 for a truck a few years ago to Rs 15,000 or even Rs 20,000 now. All illegal.' Now I understood why in the village Chaklan, on the same road, I was disturbed by truck noises at night.

We crossed village Wadda Daudpur, and before Chhota Daudpur, reached a landing space on the riverbank. We noticed a concrete gateway for water on our side. Some water had gone from it to form a stream that sort of got lost in the overgrowth and thick shrubs. Was this the beginning of Budda Dariya? It was such an anticlimax. However, the place had two quaint aspects: a boat that was making its way across the Satluj, to the immense sand banks across, with three motorcycles loaded on it; and a handpump from which we drank liberally.

I realised I could not follow the Guru's path. If this was the origin of the Budda Dariya then it soon became a swamp and the only way one could find out its origin was by using the instruments a geologist would employ. However, I wanted to check if the villagers knew the rivulet passed by them. I dropped Sukhcharan off at Bela.

While getting down he asked me to also go to Dera Ballan, near Jalandhar. He said he was a follower. His wanting to know Sikh history struck me as odd, with him being a practising Ravidasia, but this is the eclectic nature of Panjab.

I had no intention of questioning the popular history of the Guru. I couldn't even say how the rivulet would have moved in three hundred years or where in the section of the Satluj bank that was cemented was the origin of the Dariya at the Guru's time. I took the road to Machhiwara but not the designated Guru Gobind Singh Marg because I wanted to explore the villages. I stopped at Rampur where I saw a mud canal utterly choked with water hyacinth. Yes, this was the Budda Dariya, a farmer told me. In the monsoon, it got water. In fact, people used its water to cultivate small patches of vegetables. This was the wheat season and the dry rivulet was not in use. It had big snakes, said a son of a farmer. What kind? I asked. Mostly rat snakes. I was glad to have sighted the rivulet, on which, across the road, there was now a rice sheller. Nature has its laws, its terrain, which humans have now forgotten.

At Sehjo Majra the rivulet was visible. It was dry, grass grew in it, but it was uncluttered. As I approached Machhiwara, I saw water in the rivulet and lo and behold, I found three boys fishing in it near the bridge that went to the Gurdwara Charan Kanwal (lotus feet), where the Guru had rested.[v] I stopped by to check if it was the rivulet I was chasing. I asked the boys where it was coming from and they did not know. They said it started close by and there were fishes in it. Small ones. These banjara boys—nomads—lived in tents on the banks of the rivulet.

---

v. It was from Machhiwara that two horse traders, the brothers Ghani Khan and Nabi Khan, Rohilla Pathans, took the Guru—disguised as a Muslim *pir* of Uchch, an old seat of Muslim saints in south-west Panjab—in a palanquin across the Mughal lines, towards Damadama Sahib.

Unlike most canals that have a road next to them, the Budda
Dariya had fields and I could not take my car through them. I took a
link road to Manewal, again spotted the dry rivulet bed and realised
I needed to get to a place where the rivulet started filling up. I drove
to the Neelon bridge. From Katani Kalan I turned towards the village
Kot Gangu Rai.

The Dariya was still bone dry until I reached Koom Kalan where
another channel met it and the confluence was a spread of water
hyacinth. I continued alongside the dry rivulet to Dhanasu towards
Tajpur Road, on the outskirts of Ludhiana. As I crossed the garment
factory, I saw its drains vomiting coloured effluents into the rivulet
and it was flowing now with rust brown liquid.

In my adolescence I would stay with my uncle who taught at
the Agricultural University—the same one who used to consume
entire strips of tablets—and visit the woollen and hosiery markets in
Chaura Bazaar, which ironically seemed to be the narrowest streets. I
would buy shawls and sweaters that I would sell for pocket money in
Rourkela. Even in those days, the industry that once traded with the
Soviet Union and Eastern Europe had fallen on bad days. Years before
*perestroika* and *glasnost*, the economies of those nations had shrunk,
precipitating the break-up of the Imperium—the Union of Soviet
Socialist Republics (USSR), the fall of the Iron Curtain and affected
business in this far corner of the world.

Now tall mounds of garbage and the stink of rotting vegetables,
decayed fruits and industrial dyes were everywhere. Tajpur Road was
one of the biggest urban slums where lakhs of temporary industrial
workers lived in run-down, crude, congested concrete homes amidst
mounds and mountains of piling garbage. Amidst these houses, what
to me was a sacred Budda Dariya now turned into a Nalla, a sewerage
channel. In 2015, the central government adopted Ludhiana as one
of its pioneer Smart City projects. The idea was to turn Asia's biggest
bicycle manufacturing city into a bicycle user city. However, even

the National Highway through the city remains incomplete and congested. On the crammed roads I counted more than two score types of vehicles—hand-pushed carts to tractor trolleys to large public carrier autorickshaws called Marutas, to bicycles to motorbikes and cars, including Audis and Mercedes-Benz, and sports utility vehicles, Toyota Fortuners and Mahindra Scorpios. Ludhiana's flyovers were narrow and dusty; its factories worn out.

After the dyes-filled water leaked into the Nalla, there was a huge dairy farm area dumping all its muck into it. The water flowed, carrying urine, dung and plastic and fodder waste. Solo pipes projected from houses in the slums that lined the Nalla, ejecting home and toilet waste into it. The water was turning black, putrid and a stench was rising from it that could render one unconscious, but the people who lived there were accustomed to it. The Nalla had no lights and no boundary wall.

A small shopkeeper told me that a few months back, a child and his mother collided with an ox on its bank in the Shivpuri colony. The child slipped, fell into the Nalla and drowned. The divers found another child's corpse along with this child. At Krishna Chowk near Har Gobind Market I saw a shop selling fish. The fish lay on the trays, mouth open, eyes fixed at the skies. I asked if they were from the Nalla. The shopkeeper smiled and said no. I did not believe him. At Valmiki Nagar I saw women washing clothes in the setting sun and it is anyone's guess how clean the clothes would find themselves post the wash. By now, I was unable to bear the stench, and the sun had also set.

I went to a friend's place for the night. I told the friend and his wife I was trying to understand how the Budda Dariya had become Budda Nalla. The lady warned me, 'Be careful tomorrow. Sidhwan Bet has a reputation. Addicts stretch wires across the road. Motocyclists fall and then the addicts loot them.' More fancy stories! This might have happened with some, but had now become a legend.

Next morning I missed the turn on the Jagraon Bridge and drove down the confusing national highway. I turned to Sidhwan Bet from after the toll tax point on the Satluj on the way to Jalandhar. I took the road to Hambran parallel to one next to the river that quaintly hosted the Borlaug Institute for South Asia in village Ladhowal. I stopped to have a good look at the board because I was amused about how personalities had become brand names and continued to hold institutional sway over governments, get funding, run institutes, while people crumbled, following the very policies these names had formulated. I have often asked myself why Norman Borlaug—who had passed away in 2009—did not relook at his policies when Panjab started protesting the Green Revolution and showing its after-effects. I realised it took great courage to turn away from what was deemed successful, to interrogate it and to accept the blame of its flip side. Perhaps he remained unaware, perhaps he was not interested.

I reached Hambran where a distillery ejected its waste into the Nalla and turned right towards Budda Nalla and the Satluj. Given Panjab's increase in liquour consumption, now there were distilleries everywhere. I sought directions from an old man. He said, 'The Nalla has been put in the river near village Manewal.'

I asked who had put the Nalla in the river.

He answered, 'The government. That is why we have problems.'

'But it is nature that makes rivers meet. The nalla was dariya before Ludhiana. Nature willed it to meet the river here ...'

The old man did not believe me. He said, 'The government is punishing us.'

'Punishing?'

'Yes, my daughter died of *kala pelia* (black jaundice). It was from the water. My son-in-law has Hepatitis C. The government has even closed its hospital.'

The ugliness of the Nalla was all along the route. Its water cut through the loamy black clay, enhancing its blackness, its surface shining with chemicals and paint waste. Its stench was pervasive. I drove through the deserted streets of Manewal village. I could see the Nalla on my right, with tall grass on its sides. Hardly any birds flew over. Finally, beyond the Nalla I could see the river Satluj. Its water was blue in the beige sand mounds. It spanned a vast area, trucks standing in it. I remembered sand—smuggling from near Bela. For a few kilometres the black Nalla and blue river ran parallel to each other. A bridge on the Nalla had crumbled. I went ahead and climbed Satluj's embankment, driving towards where the Nalla met the river.

The meeting of waste and water was eerie—one heavy from its garbage and toxic waste, another light and cheerful. The river surface now changed colour. For a few hundred metres the two bands appeared distinct but then they mixed, and far away, the Satluj looked black, contaminated by the Nalla. I had earlier seen at Harrike Patan where Satluj met the Beas that its water was black from the Budda Nalla and the tanneries of Jalandhar. The pristine white Beas, flowing down from the Himalayas, took on darker shades after the wetlands before flowing to Pakistan and Rajasthan.

A decade back environmentalists were pleasantly surprised to see a number of Indus river dolphins in the Beas. Since then, the thermal plant at Goindwal had put them at risk. Harike used to be the biggest migratory bird sanctuary in north India, but now the number of species are dwindling. Bird watchers reckoned that seventy-two species of birds had already disappeared from Panjab. How long before the people too started to flee?

I noticed an old man and three buffaloes ahead on the path where I parked my car. I walked up to Ajmer Singh. His small hut was beside him. He sat on a cot bare-chested, his skin withered. I asked him if he lived there. He said he did so during the day. His house in the village did not have space for cattle. He used to come there when the Nalla was cleaner, and now he was used to it. He went back to the village at night. I asked him how long he had been there. 'I came back from the army twenty years ago. The river turned black in the last decade.'

'Why don't they clean it?'

'The government made two treatment plants. They don't work. Who can tell big factory owners? Who can tell Ludhiana to not let its sewerage into the Nalla?'

He offered me a glass of water. He noticed me hesitate and said, 'It is safe, from 500 feet below. See that hand pump?' I noticed the hand pump, like I noticed it at the beginning of the Budda Dariya. I drank the glassful of water.

In an era of fake god-men like Gurmeet Ram Rahim, Asaram Bapu and Rampal who were all now in jail over charges of rape and murder, a Guru of the Nirmala Sikh sect, Guru Balbir Singh Seechewal, pulled off an ecological miracle about two decades back. Seechewal belonged to the sect that owes lineage to Guru Gobind Singh and has its *dera* at Sultanpur Lodhi.

Initially, Seechewal guided people to flatten the sandy mounds around their villages to reclaim agricultural land and make paths and roads. Then he shifted attention to the Kali Bein—a much abused rivulet but associated with Guru Nanak's meditation. The Bein then gathered industrial waste, was overgrown with shrubs and water hyacinth, full of waste from home-brewed liquor factories on its banks, and was almost a dead rivulet. Its banks were illegally occupied by villagers.

Seechewal decided to clean up the 160-kilometre-long rivulet. He started by plunging into the rivulet and cleaning it with his own hands. Soon, volunteers from about forty villages joined him. Together, the team cleaned up the rivulet, made banks around it, planted fruit trees, and opened it up to visitors and tourists. The issue still was that villages along its banks were letting their sewerage run into it. That is when Seechewal devised a cheap, local method to clean the wastewater and use it for irrigation in the fields. With Seechewal's team I visited one of his main project sites in a nearby village.

Most Panjab villages have open drains and pools and puddles of wastewater. In no village until then had I seen a clean pond without the green algae cover. However, in this village, the drains were all covered and the familiar stench that marked villages was absent. Seechewal's approach was two-pronged: cover village drains or make underground ones and collect the water from bathrooms and kitchens in a big tank. Let the water flow through three interconnected wells, each with a different inlet and outlet. The first well collected water and the trash rose to the top. The second well filled from below, which caused the water to rotate. The churn freed up the plastic and other waste that rose to the top. These were picked up using big nets. In the third tank, water was let in from the top so that heavier waste settled at the bottom. This water was let out so that farmers could use it for irrigation. It was not drinking water but good enough for farming. This solved not only a huge problem of the Kali Bein pollution but became a model for other villages to follow. Sadly, not many Panjab villages follow the model, but I saw people from Uttar Pradesh and Madhya Pradesh visiting.

While Seechewal has been awarded the Padma Shri and has been in more than many discussions with ministers and various state governments, his method is yet to be adopted on a large scale. Three years back, village Khassan in Kapurthala district won a World Bank award for water conservation.[106] Two years back village Man Aspal in Mansa district won the national award for water conservation.[107] These awards and recognition are much celebrated and in that celebration we forget that we also need to replicate and implement them in other villages and towns. A decade back Seechewal walked the Budda Dariya/Nalla to assess how to clean it up. Till date nothing has happened.

Travelling through the land, I was amused that places as far as Lehra Gaga and Faridkot advertised that cars were washed using RO water. Service stations near Abohar and Fazilka provided canal water to clean cars. There was a distillery at Sangat Kalan in Bathinda district and a bottling unit less than forty kilometres away at Jhanduke. Such pressure on the ground water, no wonder the crisis loomed large. While earlier borewell water in Panjab was sweet, now even deep submersible pump water is tasteless. Then there was brackish water in south Malwa, causing waterlogging and marshes. Near Jalalabad and Muktsar one could see small canals made to dry out the fields of excessive water. If this was the case, why did the ecological concern not play a role when experts were designing the Indira Gandhi canal? No doubt deserts need water, but even the World Bank team in the 1950s had advised against ruining Panjab's lands to benefit neighbours. I am amazed at how, through decades, Panjab has remained blind to its own crises and they have now gained such proportions.

The SYL canal, though politically a huge issue, a rallying point with decades of history as baggage, with even greater ramifications, is actually just one instance of Panjab's water issues. It is Panjab's urgent need to take steps to solve its acute water crisis. It is the Centre's urgent responsibility to help Panjab avert more such crises. Yet, even in the election year of 2016–17, none of the political parties featured water on their agenda.

In 1995, Ismail Serageldin, the founding director of the Bibliotheca Alexandrina, had said that the wars of the twentieth century were fought over oil but the wars of the twenty-first century would be fought over water.[108] In Syria, one sees both these wars. While the Arab Spring, Assad's politics, ISIS, it being a battlefield between

America, its allies and Russia, are well-known, one of the triggers for the wars was also its water crises. The well-documented water depletion of Syria, Iraq and Yemen's water tables in the last decade is comparable only with north India, especially Panjab. The prolonged drought forced a large-scale exodus of its rural, agrarian people to urban centres and added to its refugee crisis.[109]

Given Panjab's geo-political location—on India's border with Pakistan, with China's interest in the region, in Balochistan, and the One Belt One Road project—water is all it has, and it will be doomed if it does not conserve it both internally and by negotiating with the Centre so that it can take full advantage of its rivers.

*Chapter Nine*

# Zameen — Land

A few years back, at the time of our wedding, Lakshmi asked me for a gift. She wanted to visit Baba's birthplace—the village Manawan, near Moga, in Panjab. I was both amused and surprised. Why would Lakshmi, born 3,058 kilometres away in Kodungallur, Thrissur, Kerala be interested in Manawan? In my four plus decades I had never been there myself. If she wanted to go to Panjab, we could go to Rajpura, where my grandfather (Dadaji) had later settled. From where first Baba and a few decades later, his brothers—my uncles—moved after selling their land. Where they still owned a *kothi* (bungalow) each.

Why Manawan?

When I asked Lakshmi the reason, she reminded me what had dulled in my memory over the last decade—Baba's last wish. Before he passed away in Bangalore in 2003, Baba had wished to go to three places in Panjab: Anandpur Sahib, where in 1699 Guru Gobind Singh had formed the Khalsa; Amritsar, where the Sikh community has its sanctum sanctorum—the Darbar Sahib; and Manawan where he was born. He had managed the religious pilgrimages but had taken ill for the personal journey and his wish had remained unfulfilled. As a tribute to Baba, Lakshmi wanted to start life with me from his village by completing his story.

Towards the end of that winter, Lakshmi and I, along with my cousin Minnie who too had never been to Manawan, took a road trip to our ancestral village. We left very early in the morning from Delhi and drove down NH 1. NH 1 is an ancient road. In Ashoka's time it was called Uttrapatha—the north road connecting Taxila near Islamabad in today's Pakistan with Patna (Pataliputra) in Bihar. Sher Shah Suri, the fifteenth century Pathan king who, after defeating Humayun, ruled for five years during the time of the Mughals, upgraded the road, extending it from Peshawar to Chittagong, built *serais* (rest houses) on it, built the Kos Minars at approximately every three kilometres to inform people of the distance and called the road Sadak-e-Aam. The British called it the Grand Trunk Road.

With the sun rising on our back window, we covered Haryana in about three hours and were at Ambala by daybreak. Rajpura, our hometown and Panjab's first town on the highway, was next. When I was a kid, at the Focal Point chowk outside Rajpura, there used to be a huge cement statue in the shape of a canister of hydrogenated vegetable oil—Gagan Dalda. It was our signal to turn into town. Rajpura had since expanded to include a thermal plant where coal comes from Sambalpur—the district in which I was born—the concrete canister had vanished and made way for a flyover. The simple Eagle Motel, the farthest limit of the town, which my cousins frequented to drink beer, had become a flashy, multi-storey hub where long-distance buses lined up.

A new traveller on this road, bewitched by the idea of Panjab, taken in by its greenery, its fields dotted with marble gurdwaras, its roadsides with prosperous-looking *dhabas*, amidst five deep rows of eucalyptus or poplar trees, could miss the now faded blue, dilapidated, wood and glass wreck which used to be the floating restaurant on the Bhakra Main Line canal before Sirhind.

Next on the route came the town of Mandi Gobindgarh. A town full of chimneys from hundreds of iron smelting industries, most of them now smokeless and padlocked. The escalating price of electricity had robbed them of business. The same electricity that the

Akalis under Parkash Singh Badal made available free to the farm sector in 1997.[110] The irony is, this subsidy favours the big and rich farmers and the small and marginal ones continue to protest their domestic bills.[111] Yet, it has locked them into dependence on the state. For a number of years, the system instituted sixteen to twenty hours of load-shedding all over Panjab until the Akali government signed Public-Private Partnership agreements with coal-based power suppliers, prioritising their power over the state-produced thermal power and thus skewed the system, causing industry to move out, on account of the huge bills.

On a government tourism department board we spotted the state tagline: *India Begins Here.* I showed it to Lakshmi and she smiled. The Arabs and the Europeans first came to the subcontinent we now call India through Kerala, not Panjab. The Persians and the Central Asians came through Panjab, but the Panjab they entered lay beyond the border, in Pakistan. The tagline sought to appropriate the idea of an earlier Panjab and impose it on the modern truncated Panjab while erasing the memory of the laceration of Panjab through Partition.

Ludhiana, the industrial hub of Panjab and the state's biggest city, arrived in another hour. Knowing that the city would be crammed, we skirted it by taking the under-construction road next to the Sidhwan canal which breaks at Doraha from the Sirhind Main Line canal. The road from Ludhiana through Moga to Ferozepur is not a national highway. Yet, the army will use the road if there is reason to quickly reach Ferozepur Cantonment close to the border with Pakistan. Like the national highway, this road too has been under construction for over a decade. We crossed the famous Nestlé factory on the left and soon after it saw what looked like UFOs—the huge silos constructed by the Adani group to store wheat. The eleven silver-coloured silos were meant to address a grave need: better storage facilities for farm produce. Clearly, storage too was now privatised.

'Kot Isse Khan is three *kos* (one *kos* is about two miles) from home,' Bibiji had said. 'Turn on the Zira road. Don't go off to Makhu.

That used to be our railway station.' We traced our route with help from Google Maps and broke into a smile when behind the neem leaves on a white board next to the road to Zira we found written in black paint on a white iron board—Munava. The board spelt the name differently from how Google Maps spelt it, but in line with how we pronounced it in Panjabi.

As we approached the village, Lakshmi asked, 'Where did you hear the word "manawan" first?'

I wasn't sure.

Was it in these Baba Bulleh Shah lines?

*Kanjri banya meri izzat na ghatdi,*
*mainu nach ke yaar manawan de*

I don't mind being called of loose morals,
if I can dance and please my friend

Or was it nostalgia from Baba's or Bibiji's lips?

The Panjabi word 'manawan' means 'to placate'. It has a ring of endearing fights between lovers, sweet nothings to please the annoyed partner, and the flavour of a love that strengthens. Lakshmi had come to Manawan to pay homage, I had come to bond, to be assuaged. We passed a concrete gate with white marble tiles on which was inscribed in blue font the name of Dadaji's enemy—Sodhi.

All through my childhood, Dadaji—my paternal grandfather—was a tall, lanky man who always carried a long thick stick. He wore a deep blue turban and a beige or brown kurta-pyjama and *jutti* (open shoes). When, as a kid, I first visited our fields near Rajpura with him, near the cattle shed, he made me sit on his shoulders. Perched high above the ground I asked till where our fields extended. 'Till wherever you can see,' he replied. I thought that was quite grand. Now, here I was, to understand how he lost his original land.

The story I had heard of him from my family is based on an old photograph of his in which he is sitting disguised as a *sadhu* (mendicant), in front of Nabha jail, for an unknown assignment, under a thick, curved neem tree trunk, which still exists. In his youth, Dadaji was a sub-inspector in the British Indian police. Family sources tell me he was a *jasoos* (spy). They don't use the real word. He was actually a mole. He leaked information from the British to armed Indian revolutionaries and carried information from the revolutionaries back to the British. Thrice, he helped the revolutionaries raid the police station and steal armaments. He was the kind of person Panjab calls 'agency'. He also loved the bottle.

I do not know the real reason for his discharge from service: family sources claim he was prompted by Mahatma Gandhi's call 'Do or Die' during the Quit India movement in 1942. The 'Do or Die' bit seems improbable because in those days, the tallest Sikh leader of the Akalis, Master Tara Singh, was opposed to Mahatma Gandhi and supported the British efforts to mobilise young men to fight its wars in Europe. At that time, Dadaji was close to Master Tara Singh and not the Congress. Baba told me about Dadaji's insubordination to his senior, about his being suspended and not reporting back at work. Bibiji tells me that in 1942 he was in jail along with later Congress chief minister of PEPSU, Colonel Raghubir Singh, under whom he had once served when in the police. Later, along with Zail Singh, he clashed with the Maharaja of Faridkot, and went underground. Zail Singh appears in photographs taken at my parents' wedding.

Baba told me in the early 1950s, in Manawan, Dadaji asked farm workers to claim the land they maintained for their landlords and instigated a peasant revolt against the Sodhi landlords. The Sodhis curbed the uprising. They instructed the village folks to boycott our family: not to supply us rations and milk or work in our fields. Eventually, Dadaji was forced to leave the village. He sold his land, about sixteen acres, and later, his house. He moved to Bathinda, then Patiala and finally to Rajpura where he had several years earlier taken land on lease from a Pandit family who wanted to leave their village, Devinagar, and settle in Varanasi.

When Dadaji came to reclaim the land, the tract was overgrown with shrubs and brambles and neighbours had encroached upon large parts of it. Dadaji found supporting hands from the political work he had been doing for the past few years. There were pitched clashes with the locals. By the end of these clashes he could retrieve less than one-fourth the land he had originally leased. A decade later, he paid the Pandits in Varanasi in full. This story, I suspect, glamorises reality which families sometimes do. Did he really pay the Pandits?

Lakshmi had asked for the trip, but my reason to go to Manawan was to winnow the wheat of Dadaji's story from the chaff. I was trying to trace what parts of the story were not hagiographic.

Raising dust on the broken gravel road, we reached the outskirts of the village. Under a banyan tree some old men were playing cards at the *sathh*. Panjab has extreme temperatures which vary up to 20 degrees in a day, in summer and winter. Farm work is typically done in the morning and evening. Afternoons are idled away. In the afternoons the men meet at the *sathh* to while away time, playing cards, take a nap, or discuss issues. We asked the men if they knew Dadaji's home. They could not recollect the name of Baldev Singh (my Dadaji). We asked if they knew the Sodhis. They remained silent. 'The village gate says his name,' I offered. One of the men said, '*Pata nahin ji.*' (We don't know.)

'Why? Aren't you from this village?'

'We are. But we are new.' That was a blatant lie. Migration in Panjab is either to towns or cities or abroad, hardly ever to other villages. In any case all the old men could not be new to the village.

The men murmured among themselves and turned their backs on us. Was it because of a kind of othering deep-rooted in Panjab, as we looked to be city folks? *Shehri* and *pendu* is a distinction Panjab makes between the city and the village, between the urban and the rural, between the market and the farm, between what Panjab culturally considers the superstructure and the base of its economy. The *pendu* disdains the *shehri* and vice-versa—ways of othering.

Minnie changed track. She asked them for the house of the subedars. Our great-grandfather Thakur Singh was a subedar in the British Army. As soon as Minnie took my great-grandfather's name, an elderly man gave me his mobile phone and asked me to search for a number and dial it. A jeep arrived and we got into the car to follow. The driver went over the village *phirni*, the outer road that circles villages, and entered the lane from where the house was most easily accessible. In terms of physical infrastructure Panjab's villages are well-developed: lanes are brick-layered, with drains either in the centre or on the sides. The issue is with maintenance. Most drains are open and clogged. The rotting smell in the streets is of dry and wet sewerage and water from bathrooms and kitchens, but thankfully not from toilets. Earlier, most homes had pit-type latrines, now they have modern ones with septic tanks. Jutt homes have wide gates to allow tractors and trolleys to enter along with cars, jeeps, scooters and motorbikes.

We parked our car in the lane and stood tentatively in front of a large wrought iron gate of what was once our home. The jeep driver opened the wicket gate and we entered to a view of *chandini* (crape jasmine)—a green flowering tree with small white flowers. It was like moonbeam after a long dark night of half a century.

The building in the plot was newer than the house Baba and family would have left behind. It was more like a city *kothi* with a large veranda in front and empty space behind. The rough painted pale blue windowpanes were broken. Its doors were weather-beaten.

Its cream paint was peeling off the walls showing patches of a garish purple. It was in a state of disrepair. On it, in fading deep blue letters was written: Guru Har Gobind English Medium Public School.

We stood in the veranda and a boy emerged with water in a red plastic jug and steel tumblers. In an earlier time the jug would have been steel, the tumblers would have been brass. We heard a middle-aged lady call from inside. The boy went in. In a minute or so both returned. The woman asked Minnie about the purpose of our visit. Unlike the story of loss of many Panjabis which goes back to Partition, our family did not lose our home to that political event. We lost our home to Dadaji's political action in the interest of the daily wage farmworker.

All the lady knew was that the plot was sold twice after our family left the village. It now belonged to someone from Amritsar who tried to run a school. A few years back they had bought land outside the village and shifted the school there. Since then the building had not been in use. The mother and son lived there to take care of the three buffaloes. We had no interest in seeing the school premises from the inside and approached the cowshed. The lady told us that the back wall of the cowshed was probably from when our family lived there. I put my palm to it and kept it there for a long time. It felt warm and reassuring. The wall was the only physical reminder of our ties with the plot of land and the home my family lost.

We thanked the family and proceeded towards the village school about which Bibiji had told us: how since she was older and helped out Dadiji—my paternal grandmother—she would get the brothers ready for school; she had talked about her teachers and about how lessons were on *phattis* (wooden boards) and on slate with chalk. As we turned the car at the end of the lane we noticed the grand piece of furniture—*takhtposh* (a platform with legs)—that all my family talked about. On which the home *sathh* used to take place. I had never seen a *takhtposh* in public or private spaces in any other village in Panjab. At the end of the street stood another lonely *takhtposh* made of wooden planks now discoloured by rain, its steel legs rusted—a reminder of the camaraderie and togetherness that once was part of the culture of the villages of Panjab and was now eroded.

The school was behind the gurdwara, but it was a Sunday and the gates were closed. We turned to the gurdwara which was being expanded. In the last couple of decades Panjab has seen immense emigration to England, Canada, the US, Australia, New Zealand, Italy and now to East Europe and the Middle East. Unlike engineers from Bangalore who find jobs in the software industry or people from Kerala who go to the Middle East to execute projects or as nurses in the healthcare industry, the Panjabi migrant is usually a labourer, in the construction and food industry, or finds work as a taxi driver or a factory worker. Still the money they earn in dollars seems big in Panjab. The diaspora, apart from upgrading their homes, starting with bathrooms and toilets, renting expensive cars, flashing fake designer clothes, also donate money for reconstruction of village gurdwaras. The gurdwara places a plaque in the name of the migrant son— enshrining him within history.

The local gurdwara management was building a six-storey minaret—dedicated to Guru Har Gobind, the sixth Guru. In the whole of the upper Malwa region, village after village is building minarets so as to tower over and above the settlement around them. Ironically, the holiest of holies, the Darbar Sahib in Amritsar, whose foundation stone was laid by Sufi saint Miyan Mir, is the lowest gurdwara. It is lower than the city of Amritsar around it. But humility is no longer a value we would associate with the organised, institutionalised and corporatised Sikh religion.

'You don't look local,' interrupted the elderly man as we partook of *langar*. We told him Dadaji's name and his face crumbled. He looked at me, asked if I was Rashpal's son. I said, 'Yes.' He had tears in his eyes. 'I thought you were some *bhaiya*.'

The comment did not prick. Instead it asserted a moniker I have heard all my life in Panjab, from family and friends. When I was an adolescent and would come home to Rajpura from the hostel after the annual exams, the larger family would be busy harvesting the wheat. Through the seven years at school, I remained the youngest working hand in the family. It was a pre-combine harvester age. My uncle would assign me roles like bringing tea, food, carrying back sweaty clothes and such. Walking over the dry, parched ground, with remains of wheat stalks, sharp as nails, jutting out, was an ordeal. The wheat thresher would bellow flakes that settled everywhere, including the hair on the head and the insides of clothes. In these fields I discovered the migrant labour who, under the charge of the *numberdaar,* would manually harvest the wheat, carry it to the thresher, collect the grain and sift the husk. The original term numberdaar relates to the land revenue system. The *numberdaar* was a collector of revenue. In the farmer-migrant labour context, it was used to address the one who interfaced with the farmer and handled the labourer's payment. Without access to language, dependent on what little Panjabi the *numberdaar* could understand, the labour gang was mostly clueless about how to work. Upon learning that I was from their side of the country and I could speak to them in Hindi, they were relieved. I became a fixture, constantly ferrying messages in Hindi and Panjabi between the labourers and uncle. This earned me the *bhaiya* moniker at home.

*Bhaiya* is what Panjab calls the migrant labourers from Uttar Pradesh and Bihar. *Bhaiya* is a way of othering the east Indian labourer, fixing them in a label and not acknowledging their individuality. *Bhaiya* is what the Panjabi labourer is abroad but there they fight for rights. I was amused, but Malkiat Singh was embarrassed.

Malkiat Singh sat us on cots and told us about his friendship with our elder uncle and his visits to Rajpura. How he, being in the police, used to lend his regulation gun to my uncle to shoot partridges and doves. How he had attended my cousin's marriage and my younger uncle's funeral. All through his narration he was unable to look into my eyes. I was the son of the toddler he used to take to school. He told us he had *gharelu mamle* (family disputes). He felt his daughter-in-law was too modern—she sometimes wore jeans—and his son neglected him. I wasn't sure if he felt closeness to us or if he wanted to share intimate details and evoke our sympathy. He said he got a pension which he saved and had found work—salary and a place to sleep—at the gurdwara and decided to move there. He went home for food, though. Why not partake of *langar*, I wondered silently.

We were interested in confirming Dadaji's back story. I asked him if Dadaji had indeed instigated a peasant revolt. Malkiat Singh said he did not know. He was barely two or three years older than Baba, which meant he was fifteen or sixteen in the 1950s when the incident took place. It was not possible that he did not remember anything. But if he did not want to speak, what choice did we have? We asked him if anyone in the village would know. He was not sure anyone older than him was alive or remembered. He took our phone numbers and promised to call if he found anyone. Despite his urging us to stay, we left. As was the custom, I bowed to touch his feet and also said to him: even if I were a *bhaiya*, your religion teaches you equality.

On our way back from Manawan to Rajpura, I told Lakshmi my Dadiji's story. I had not seen her. She had passed away before I was born. Bibiji and Baba told me how, through the years of family struggle, she bore everything in stoic silence. When necessary, when Dadaji was away fighting for India's freedom, she begged and borrowed to feed her children but she did not complain to her husband. However, over the years, especially when the family moved to Rajpura, she spoke less and less to him.

There was a distance, as was expected in old-fashioned Panjabi families. No one in the family remembered asking her how she was, how she felt about all these changes of home and means of sustenance. She was always the reliable one, the quiet one and the silenced one. She was the one who kept a warm meal ready for family and friends. Yet, she once had an outburst.

In 1971, the Government of India decided to honour Dadaji with a 'Tamra Patra' given to freedom fighters. When the news of the award came, Dadiji responded with neither joy nor sadness. When Dadaji came back after receiving the award from the president of India and handed Dadiji the copper plate, she held it in her hands and a wail escaped her lips. She threw away the award, composed herself and said, as if grunting, 'All our life, for this?' Then she walked away. A few months later, she died of a heart attack. Rather, a broken heart. The loss of my grandmother, whom I never saw, is how I became aware of what happens to silenced people; what happens to people who dedicate themselves to causes in which they find themselves trapped and pay the price.

At Rajpura we stopped in front of my uncles' locked bungalows— one light green, another peach—which mark our family's connection with the town. I wanted to see the land which was ours once.

For about four decades our family tried to work the land while my uncles and aunts also took up jobs in the government. The eldest uncle was an excise and taxation officer. In the 1990s, Baba decided to sell his landholding in Rajpura. His larger family tried to stop him, but he did not listen. He had lived away all his life in Rourkela. I had left Panjab. He did not find much use of the land and sold his share. His brothers followed. Bibiji wilfully did not want a share in the land.

I saw it as a counterpoint to Mama all her life asking for her share in Nanaji's land, but being denied that right.

The new owners of our land in Rajpura installed a rice sheller. Initially, they did not do well. Then one of the family members dreamt that at some earlier point the land was hallowed by the long meditation of a holy man. Dadaji, my uncle and my cousins had also dreamt of a white stone in the guava orchard. Our educated family ignored the dreams. We never questioned why the dream reoccurred. The prompt to the new owners was to mark the place. As we stepped into the guava orchard our family had planted, we noticed the new owners had now built a structure: something between a shrine and a gurdwara, with a Sikh flag—the Nishan Sahib. The owners had marked the cremation spots of my paternal grandparents. Their business was doing well. I felt land was not just soil. It also had *sanskars*—its own memory and rituals.

Driving back from Rajpura I asked Lakshmi how she felt. She said she was glad she could physically complete Baba's journey. Minnie felt disappointed that we did not make much headway on Dadaji's story but she was happy she had fulfilled Bibiji's wish: that she should visit Manawan once in her life. I was satisfied I could step into the plot where our family had stayed. I was thankful that the new owners of the land in Rajpura had marked my grandparents' cremation spot. I realised what I had held against Baba—his selling away his share of the inherited land, which would have been mine—was perhaps not such a bad thing after all. For more than two decades I had felt he had deprived me of my entitlement but through that act he had freed me to chart my own path in the world and allowed me the freedom to come back to Panjab on my own terms.

We discussed if we were arrogant to believe that we could just barge into our ancestral village and get our family's story. Did we imagine the village waited for us or had itself up on offer? It was certainly not that. Yet, I must confess, I had hoped for some clues. We had even met the right man—Malkiat Singh. But he either did not know the story or was not telling us. Hence, I could not piece together the story of the exile and that remains a black hole in my heart.

Do I believe Dadaji was a Robin Hood or, to use a Panjabi reference, a Dulla Bhatti-like figure? All we have is a Tamra Patra which affirms Dadaji's contribution as a freedom fighter, a few photographs and Bibiji's memories which can't last very long, since she suffers from Alzheimer's.

During my travels in 2016, trying to understand the role of the Left in Panjab politics, I met an old-time communist who was now a doctor among the poorest of the poor. He told me Manawan had become a big flash point in the 1990s. That was when Amarjit Sodhi, the son of the Sodhi who had thrown Dadaji out of the village, was killed. I confirmed the story from other activists. The version seemed to run as follows:

In his time, Sodhi was a terror. He held kangaroo courts and had accused two of his labourers Rupa and Teja of stealing farm fertilisers and hens from his farm. He tortured them, beat them up and then fed them poison. The police postmortem revealed no foul play. The beatings were with sugarcane stalks which don't leave much of a mark. The death was from poisoning.

In and around the village, Sodhi was very powerful. In order to investigate the matter, the farm workers formed an action committee. A great many people gathered—mostly small farmers and farm workers—and decided to file a case against him. The police arrested him, courts granted him bail.

On bail, while Amarjit Sodhi was at the Moga grain market, two young men arrived on a motorcycle and gunned him down at point blank. The youth claimed they were from the Naxalite Guerrilla Force, part of the Revolutionary Communist Centre who believed that Indian courts would not give justice and the only way to pursue justice was through guns.

The farmers and farm workers condemned the murder. The police arrested those who belonged to the Naxal group and tortured them. A case followed and jail terms were announced. The assassins went to jail and were released after a few years.

I went to Manawan again. This time by myself. I met Malkiat Singh again, outside his home. I asked him for the Dadaji–Sodhi story again. There were no answers, though there was an invitation to tea. I refused tea and went to the *vehda* side of the village—where the Dalits lived—to enquire about Teja and Rupa's family.

The villagers introduced me to Rupa's brother—a gaunt-faced man, now in his late sixties but still a daily wage labourer. He had the hands and body of one who has lived by hard physical labour all his life. In spite of my repeated but polite and empathetic questioning, all he kept saying was, 'Rupa died of poison. The Sodhis gave him the poison. *Mitti pa* (bury it)!'

He did not speak about the beatings. He did not speak about how his brother owed money taken on loan and was indebted and hence served as almost a slave to Amarjit Sodhi. He spoke no more. The villagers filled me in on the details. The villagers told me, after Amarjit Sodhi's murder, the Sodhi family left the village. Having leased out their land, they hardly even came to check on it. They too, like Dadaji, had been forced out of the village.

I looked at Rupa's brother's face again. His face was dim and his eyes blurred. I could see the veil. I could see that he had many stories in him but he wouldn't speak. These stories were in probability about discrimination, debt, caste and of structural violence. His self-respect prevented him from sharing them with me. I respected his silence. I knew I could not reach him. *Mitti pa!*

A villager asked, 'You came from the other side. Who did you meet there?'

'Malkiat Singh.' I mentioned my family's connection with the village and with Malkiat Singh. I told him I had checked with him a few years back on any family of Rupa or Teja still in the village. He had denied any knowledge.

'Never trust him,' said the villager. 'He won't answer. No one would, actually, without specific names, without you knowing about the case.'

'But how can I know if no one tells me?'

'Well, we have to live here. How can we speak?'

That was the issue: lives are linked and interests are entwined. The truth can wait. A few months later, I told Bibiji about Amarjit Sodhi's murder. She snapped out of her Alzheimer's, let out a sigh. 'Killed? Amarjit and his brother Mandeep were your father's best childhood friends. They all went to school together.' She did not remember that our family had to leave Manawan because of the Sodhi family. *Mitti pa!*

'This is not a *chitti-patti* road,' said the young Panjabi teacher, Pargat, accompanying me in the car. *Chitti-patti* roads are state highways marked in the middle with white paint like the stitches on our clothes. We were on a link road. The kind that connected villages to grain markets. 'Driver side,' said Pargat. I turned right. Over the past many weeks I had learnt about 'driver side' and 'conductor side'. That is how villagers in Panjab gave directions. It made sure that one never confused left and right. The irony was: Panjab was itself driver-less and conductor-less for a few decades now.

We were thirty kilometres from Lehra Gaga on our way to the village Kishangarh in Mansa district. Pargat made a sweeping arc towards the green, unripe wheat fields and said, 'This whole area used to be dunes and hills. People flattened it with their ox ploughs and later with tractors.'

The one-lane road was quite bumpy and difficult to drive on. Then there were the tractors and their overladen trolley as also combine harvesters. The hay-laden trolleys were huge—the load swelling up to three times the size of the trolley, sticking out a couple of feet on both sides of the plastic gunny sacks stitched together to make a cover and tied with ropes, leaving just about a foot or two of room between the road and the field next to it, which was usually a bit lower than the road. How could one get ahead of such a vehicle? One had to back up to a culvert, or a little broader stretch. Often a motorbike or a cycle got in between. It was a constant act of juggling.

Government propaganda claims thousands of kilometres of road were built in the last nine years since the Akali government came to power. Those were inter-city roads—the highways. This network of link roads between Panjab's 12,500 plus villages were a legacy of a chief minister who served a little more than eight month in office in the 1960s, Lachhman Singh Gill. They were as elaborate as a spider's web and also now, through neglect over the last few decades of staying untarred, as fragile.

The difficulty in keeping the glass windows rolled up was that the car became stuffy. If you kept them open, within a minute the car would fill up with dust. Fine, silky, black dust rises all over Panjab but especially in the south of Panjab, the Malwa region, which is on the edge of the Thar Desert in Rajasthan. On the bumpy road, we reached the village and were surprised it did not have its name outside it. That was uncommon.

At the *sathh* we asked if this was Kishangarh.

'Which Kishangarh,' asked an old man, smiling, 'Muzara or suicides?'[112] I had come to see the site of the big land occupation movement that took place in the middle of the last century and also acknowledge that the very same village had now, for many years, had the highest number of farmer and labourer suicides in Panjab. 'Both,' I answered. The man asked us to turn driver side to a memorial being built by the former sarpanch, Kulwant Singh, next to the *haveli*.

Through the brick-lined streets of the village, I noticed shops selling fertiliser and pesticides alongside an unusually large number of clinics, many run not by doctors but by Registered Medical Practitioners (RMPs) who are mostly chemists. A few cots were stacked on the sides but upon need could be spread out in the brick lanes. A nebuliser, a drip of saline with standard antihistamines or other medicines is not so hard to administer. We went past a blue and yellow structure that looked like a fancy lavatory but actually was a Seva Kendar—service centre for all documentation needs of citizens which the Badal government then said would be functional by the time its term ended. Only half of them finally became functional, plagued as they were by a shortage of trained personnel.

We drove to the site to see the *haveli* being renovated. We asked an old man supervising the work from his cot about Kulwant. He gave us a number and Kulwant said he would be with us shortly. In front of the *haveli* was an obelisk, red in colour, the colour of the Left. What the obelisk commemorated—the Muzara movement—had turned Leftwards, but did not originally start as a Left movement.

The old man told us the earlier structure had crumbled. Since we were awaiting Kulwant and could spot a gate to the village at about half a kilometre, we walked up to it. We realised that though a village is open from all sides, often two or three roads approach it. We had entered the village from the opposite side. This one being closer to the *haveli* had a modest gate, two red and white pillars, and a tin board that announced: 'Dedicated to the memory of martyrs of PEPSU-Muzara movement, who fought against feudalism and monarchy.'

Kulwant arrived on his old Bajaj scooter of indeterminate colour. Slightly built, middle-aged, he approached us. 'Looking for me?'

'Yes, we came to see the memorial,' I replied. 'Are you building it by yourself?'

'Through small contributions,' he replied. 'We are rebuilding it. It will house an office, a library and a room for travellers.'

'But it is such an important landmark. Why would the state not want to build it?'

'One can't expect state support,' said Kulwant in a deadpan voice. I realised my naivete. 'People's history is not the history the state wants to showcase. In fact, they want us to forget it.'

This was the issue of agrarian Panjab's political economy, the issue of land. Today, even the records of the land movement are not available in the government archives.[113] As another generation passes on and memory dims, this gate dedicated to the memory of martyrs of the PEPSU-Muzara movement draws our attention to the most important people's movement in Panjab over the last century.

When the British ruled the subcontinent, the political landscape was of two kinds: territories which were directly under the British; and the princely states which were free to rule as they wished as long as the princes vowed loyalty to the Crown and paid the British in cash and kind. In Panjab's case, the British direct rule was west of the Satluj—the erstwhile kingdom of Maharaja Ranjit Singh annexed after the two Anglo-Sikh wars in the middle of the nineteenth century. The princely states were east of the river Satluj: Patiala, Nabha, Faridkot, Kapurthala, Jind and Malerkotla. Over a period of time, the people directly ruled by the British earned some rights to participation and representation, but the people of many princely states did not have those rights.

In the 1870s, the Maharaja of Patiala implemented the *biswedari* system, which appointed *biswedars* as local authorities of agrarian villages. The *biswedars*, mostly government officials and close kin of the Maharaja, gradually took full possession of lands and reduced the original owners to the status of *muzaras* (tenants). *Muzaras* had to pay *batai* (share rent) to their landlords, consisting of half of their crop, though landlords often overestimated the crop yield to justify taking a larger share. This led to considerable unrest among the *muzaras*.

As the *biswedars'* influence grew in the administration, for they collected revenues to give to the kings who in turn gave it to the British, they started claiming proprietary status like the *zamindars* of the British-ruled areas. They relegated the entire body of the cultivating proprietors—who tilled the land and paid revenue to the *biswedar*—to the position of occupancy tenants and tenants-at-will. These tenants in turn regarded the new landlords as parvenus, who had no legitimate right to the land which had belonged to them for generations. This usurpation of their lands was not in the manner in which a traditional tenant might regard their old, established, feudal landowners, whose right to the land had acquired a certain social legitimacy by virtue of its antiquity.[114]

The people in princely states opposed the British but more locally they opposed their rulers on account of such draconian laws. At this time, across the Indian subcontinent, in many princely states, the Praja Mandal Movement had begun to articulate the grievances of the people in the princely states. In the 1920s, the Indian National Congress, wisening up to the people's movements, had included the idea that any opposition to the British must include the people's demand in both British colonies and princely states.

In Panjab, Sewa Singh Thikriwala, known as Kirpan Bahadur, began organising tenants in several *biswedari* villages, encouraging them to withhold payment of *batai* to landlords. In 1928, the Akalis, fresh from the victory in the religious sphere through the Gurdwara Reform Movement, organised the people of the princely states of Panjab. On 17 July 1928, at Mansa, the Panjab Ryasti Praja Mandal

Movement (PRPM), which was part of a larger All-India States' People's Conference, came into being and established close contact with the Indian National Congress.

The PRPM Movement was against the Maharaja of Patiala Bhupinder Singh's despotic rule in the Bathinda district which included Barnala, Mansa, Maur, Sunam, Bhawanigarh and other regions. Bhupinder Singh was the grandfather of Captain Amarinder Singh, the current chief minister of Panjab, and he governed the state under the paramountcy of the British Raj.

Sewa Singh Thikriwala, Master Tara Singh and Baba Kharak Singh denounced the maharajas and demanded that autocracy be replaced by democracy. Jaswant Singh Danewalia, PRPM president, also made the same demand. He termed the Chamber of Princes (a lobbying body which represented princely interests to the British) as dacoits whose ring leader was Bhupinder Singh. Bhupinder Singh arrested Sewa Singh Thikriwala and forty other Akalis.

A few years before that, former members of another illustrious formation—the Ghadar Party—had returned to India from North America after World War I. Located at San Francisco, the Ghadar Party was a pan-Panjabi movement, with some Bengalis and leaders from the Hindu, Muslim and Sikh communities. Its ideology was based on a coming together of Sikh ideas and the growing influence of Marxist socialism. Once the Gurdwara Movement had succeeded non-violently and the Babbar Akalis, who endorsed violence, were crushed by the state, the Ghadarites joined the land rights movements alongside the PRPM which was already aligned with both the Congress and the Akalis. The goal was freedom, not only from colonialism but also from economic bondage.

In August 1929, following a huge public outcry, Bhupinder Singh was forced to release Thikriwala and the Akalis. Thikriwala undertook an intensive tour of the Patiala state. Thikriwala's tour culminated in the first PRPM session in Bradlaugh Hall, Lahore, on

27 December 1929. Hundreds of workers from different East Panjab states attended the session which was addressed by leaders of the All India States People's Conference and the Panjab Provincial Congress Committee.

In May 1930, tenants in the two villages of Rajomajra and Bhadaur in Patiala began refusing payments of *batai* to their landlords. Over the next few years, tenants in several other villages began refusing to pay landlords, and landlords increasingly had to rely on police force to collect *batai*. Some tenants destroyed their own crops in order to avoid paying their landlords. Police systematically repressed tenants, forcibly confiscating their crops for *batai* payments, and imprisoning resisting tenants. When Bhupinder Singh, as chancellor of the Chamber of Princes, was chosen as the sole representative to the First Round Table Conference, the PRPM stepped up its activities and even wrote to the Viceroy of India. Protests followed in Amritsar, Ludhiana, Shimla and Delhi.

In 1931, Bhupinder Singh issued a *hidayat* (instruction) to counter the PRPM and ban all political activities in the region. In spite of the law, tenants continued to organise and meet in secret or across state borders. In January 1933, Seva Singh Thikrivala was arrested under the provisions of the *hidayat* and sentenced to six years in prison. In jail, he undertook a hunger strike against the treatment meted out to prisoners. On 20 January 1935, he died in Patiala Jail in solitary confinement.

This is when Master Tara Singh entered into an agreement with the maharaja and freed the remaining Akali leaders. After this, the Akalis withdrew from the Praja Mandal Movement and began focussing more on Sikh identity politics. The Congress too let go of the land rights movements and started focussing on the freedom struggle. Clearly, the Gandhian non-violent methods of ahimsa and satyagraha, which the Akalis had adopted in the Gurdwara Movement, did not work for the Muzara Movement. To persist in one's struggle while receiving police blows is one kind of agitation. To actually have your fields looted, crops burnt and people killed in the course of your struggle is another kind. Satyagraha could work with the British where there was at least a pretence of a human conscience. It would not work with maharajas who only wanted to plunder and subjugate. However, with the death of prominent leaders and the withdrawal of Akali and Congress leaders, the movement did peter out to an extent. Yet, its ideas remained.

A violent confrontation took place between the police and tenants in November 1937 in the village of Qila Hakima. Three hundred to four hundred tenants were peacefully protesting, asking the police not to take away their crops when the police and landlords opened fire, killing several tenants. The state made an official inquiry into the incident. The state magistrate condemned the tenants for their defiance of authority and exonerated the police of all charges of excessive use of force.

In response, the Praja Mandal formed a counter committee to investigate the issue and came to the conclusion that the tenants were unarmed and peaceful, and landlords had illegally participated in the shooting. The Praja Mandal aided the *muzaras* in printing and distributing pamphlets on the Qila Hakima incident. Following the Qila Hakima incident, a group of *muzaras* went to Master Hari Singh, leader of the communist Kisan Committee, to ask for support in their struggle.

The death of Maharaja Bhupinder Singh in 1938 and the coronation of a young inexperienced ruler Yadwinder Singh strengthened both the Praja Mandal and the tenants' resolve to continue in their struggle. In 1938, tenants from villages across the state formed the Muzara Committee to further the movement in villages. By early 1939, the tenants decided to form a Kisan-Muzara Committee to plead their cases. The committee gave a call at Jethuke in the Rampura Tehsil of Bathinda district for total stoppage of the payment of *batai*. Tenants then moved crops to their homes. The government took it as a challenge to its authority and let loose its repression. In the face of increased police action, the campaign ebbed in 1940, and the *muzaras* remained relatively submissive until 1942. This is when the *muzaras* began to align themselves with the communist Kisan Party. In one incident, the former President of India Zail Singh spearheaded a *muzara* rally in May 1946. Dadaji was with him. When the Maharaja of Faridkot tied Zail Singh to a jeep and had him dragged, the same treatment was also meted out to Dadaji.

When India gained its Independence in August 1947, the Maharaja of Patiala was the first prince to join the Indian Union. Yadwinder Singh announced constitutional reforms in January 1948 and became *rajpramukh* (governor) of the newly formed PEPSU. Gian Singh Rarewala, the uncle of Yadwinder Singh, became the first chief minister (actually, he was designated the prime minister) of PEPSU in 1947, 1948, 1949, and then again in 1952. He led a United Front government which included the Akali Dal. Colonel Raghubir Singh from the Congress punctured his tenure twice and became the chief minister.

Meanwhile, the *muzara* struggle was growing. Yadwinder Singh, isolated by the opposition of all political groups, launched severe repression on the *muzaras*, leading to appeals to the Ministry of States in Delhi on behalf of the tenants, now backed by the Congress and influenced by the communists. The PEPSU state was unable to assert its authority and the situation was increasingly beginning to resemble a civil war in which the contending classes or political groups were left, by and large, to settle the issue between themselves as best they could. Landlords began to use armed gangs which led the *muzaras* to raise their own armed wings. The decision to organise an armed volunteer corps was given concrete form by the formation in 1948 of the Lal Communist Party, by Teja Singh Swatantar—a breakaway group of Panjab Communists, mostly belonging to the Kirti group which had its origin in the Ghadar movement and had an uneasy relationship with the Communist Party of India.

On 16 March 1949, at Kishangarh, a battery of more than hundred policemen tried to evict the tenants but failed. Three days later, on the orders of Yadwinder Singh, cannons started bombarding the village. Tenants fought back. They were arrested, tortured and jailed. The movement spread to more than seven hundred villages.

In Col. Raghubir Singh's first term as Panjab chief minister he set up the Agrarian Reforms Enquiry Committee to study the issue and make recommendations. Till the time the legislation could be enacted, the PEPSU Tenancy (Temporary Provision) Act was to be promulgated in January 1952 to protect tenants against eviction. This was while the committee continued to search for a more permanent solution, but the government fell. Rarewala came back to power but again did not pass the Bill. When Rarewala's government fell and president's rule was imposed, the PEPSU Occupancy Tenants (Vesting of Proprietary Rights) Act (1953) was enacted.

Under this Act, occupancy tenants could become owners of their land by paying compensation amounting to twelve times the land revenue, an amount which, given the post-war, post-Partition inflation and the fact that land revenue continued to be assessed at the pre-war rates, was not too large. The communist parties affiliated with the tenants were not too happy with this solution because it required tenants to compensate the landlords. Tenants, however, found this agreement acceptable. PEPSU acquired eighteen lakh acres of unworked, potentially rich wheat land for distribution to landless peasants, irrespective of their caste.[115]

This move did benefit a lot of tenants and there was a lull in the movement for a few years. Yet, many tenants were still left out of the ambit, and when the students' movement galvanised in the late 1960s, the Naxalite movement started in West Bengal, and it echoed in Panjab as well in the early 1970s. But in the absence of support, the Naxalite movement waned.

As member of the Lal Party, in the Teja Singh Swatantar period, post-Independence and before the PEPSU Occupancy Tenants Act, Dadaji had urged the tenants to stand against the Sodhis. He had not acted alone, but was part of a larger wave. It is a matter of chance that Dadaji's battle failed and led to his exile from Manawan. My brief reading of this long but forgotten history reveals that Dadaji had participated in the land rights movement because it was a people's movement. The Congress and the Akalis had abandoned the movement. Each played their own cards and finally, the farmers were left to fend for themselves.

Standing for the tenants cost Dadaji his place in his native village. He chose to stay away from both the Congress and the Akalis. The people I saw at the rally to which Satnam took me in Patiala were people like Dadaji—non-political. Non-political, however, is itself a huge political stance. It means you stand with people, not parties.

Dadaji, in his youth, was a mole. A mole, if prompted by ethics and not money or petty gains, owes loyalty to principles, not to notions of political parties or political states. While Sikhs, by being part of the British Army, were actually fulfilling the colonial agenda, the police was perpetuating injustice by serving the maharaja and the big landlords.

Amidst this, Dadaji shed his police uniform, became a freedom fighter, then a tenant rights fighter, and finally, was exiled. Given a choice, I'd take an erratic, fighter, drunk grandfather than one who was a stooge to royal or political power.

'The *haveli* belonged to landlords. The state can claim it,' I said to Kulwant just to get his response.

'Dare they do it!' On his mild face, Kulwant's eyes shone. It was clear that the custodians of the Muzara movement would not let the last vestige fall into the state's hands.

'So tell me, how come this important village is now famous for suicides?'

'The after-effects of the Green Revolution. Both farming and the village culture have been affected.'

'But your village was different.'

'What is different? Yes, a historical event happened, but we are also like the others. We do not live in isolation from what is happening in Panjab, actually worldwide. You must have seen the chemists and RMP doctor clinics. Before the Bt cotton came, when the American bollworm used to wreak havoc, farmers and labourers had to do twenty to thirty sprays. Everyone would take ill and need help with breathing. The Bt cotton was okay for a few years but now again it has disease. It is an unending cycle. Science develops pest-resistant seeds while pests develop greater tolerance of insecticides and pesticides.'

'But why the suicides?'

'The issues are economic but they lead to others. Three or four decades back the new type of farming, what we call Green Revolution, for which Panjab was chosen, brought in better incomes. Those created needs: clothes, education, vehicles, social life, expensive marriages, and so on. Expenses started increasing. Then incomes peaked and started sliding down, especially for small and medium farmers. The needs did not decrease. There were fights at home, loans to be repaid through more loans even as the expenses on agriculture kept mounting. Now agriculture is not profitable for most people except the rich. There are no jobs and there's nothing in sight. What will people do? Insecticide is easy, it is available everywhere … Land consolidation has begun. Sooner or later, most small farmers will have to move out of agriculture. It is not profitable anymore. The expenses are higher than income.'

This is exactly what I had learnt during the whitefly agitation. Yet, knowing this made me question the history of the land movement once again: no doubt it was a necessary movement to stop the exploitation of the tenant farmer, but in the long run how wise was it to create small tracts? Of course, the *muzara* did not then know about the Green Revolution or its aftereffects, but now these small tracts were even further divided through inheritance laws and had become the big issue. I wonder what it is that Panjab should do now to be ready for the post-Green Revolution phase. The other aspect is to notice the effect of the Akalis walking out of the land movement. The Akalis certainly foregrounded identity politics over the political economy—land. Ironically, this had major consequences when it was land that was divided during Partition.

We must note here that the land rights movement was mostly in the south of Panjab, among small Jutt tenants. The Akali leadership in the early and mid-twentieth century was from Majha, the north of Panjab which anyway was under direct British rule. Also, initially, the Akali party was dominated by the trading class Sikhs. Those Sikhs were distant from the farming class Sikhs—the Jutts.

This changed only in 1972, when Gurcharan Singh Tohra became the head of the SGPC and remained at the helm of affairs for the next twenty-seven years and brought in Malwa Jutts into the organisation. This was because Tohra's own brush with politics started with the Praja Mandal Movement where he was arrested for agitating in Nabha in 1945. The current epicentres of Panjab politics are Bathinda, to which five-time chief minister, Parkash Singh Badal, belongs, and Patiala to which Captain Amarinder Singh belongs. Both Badal and Amarinder own thousands of acres of land. They are unlikely to give up their personal interests for the people.

The post-Partition period was an opportunity to redistribute land, but it did not take place. The reason was again the trauma of the Partition that was so sudden and so brutal. Close to five million Hindus and Sikhs moved from West Panjab to East Panjab. Among them, the Sikh farmers were granted land on what were previously Muslim holdings in India on the basis of their holdings in West Panjab. The bureaucrat, Mohinder Singh Randhawa, was in charge. He and his team of officials carried out the task with efficiency. Yet, a lot of chicanery took place in the process which helped farmers escape the land ceiling. It is common to find big farmers who got land as replacement, having registered it in the names of other family members, the labourers on the farm, and even in the name of cattle. If the Partition were not so traumatic and the state had really focussed on creating some kind of equitable distribution of land, at least this could have been prevented.

That is the reason the Swaminathan Commission recommendation, which mandates land ceiling for big farmers, has been gathering dust for the last decade. Which politician will implement it in Panjab against his own interests—Badal or Captain Amarinder?

Post militancy, from the mid-1990s, when the guns fell silent, with rapid urbanisation, Panjab saw a steep rise in land prices. With agriculture in a stalemate, many farmers near towns and cities were trying to cash in by selling farmland to real estate developers. In the villages set to be acquired near what is touted as New Chandigarh, to the west of the city, a sarpanch asked me if Hesarghatta near Bangalore was a good location to invest in land. I was surprised at the reach and knowledge of farmers.

When Phuphadji wanted to sell a small piece of land, two kanals across the road from his home in village Chakklan, I saw the papers at the *tehsildar's* office. The land had had forty-two owners in the past. Fortunately, it was a clear title but most land is not such. Around two to three thousand property-related cases enter Panjab's police stations and courts each year.[116] They make up more than half the cases in the courts. These cases take up to three decades to be solved.[117]

When the title is not clear or there is dispute or confusion of land deeds, on the one hand are tedious courts and on the other are property dealers who groom organised gangs that step in between the factions and buy the land at the expense of both parties. This property dealer gang creation has led to a mushrooming of the gymnasium culture to churn out able-bodied men who, in turn, become prey to performance-enhancing food supplements and drugs. At a restaurant, I checked with the bouncer about his day job. That led me to spend two days with gangs that are on hire to landlords, to real estate agents, to politicians and to ministers—all of this under police patronage.

The land that diaspora Panjabis own, from which they continue to get *theka* (rent), and that is often usurped by relatives or neighbours is a Pandora's box. These landholdings remain the central concern of those who have emigrated out of Panjab or abroad. At the state's NRI Sammelan, which was held for a few years in an attempt to connect to the diaspora, the maximum queries were about land issues and feuds, marriages of convenience for citizenship of foreign countries and the issue of overseas husbands abandoning wives back home. So much so that the government appointed an inspector general in the police to look into these matters. Yet, the cases remain stuck because revenue officials and police are complicit, biased and can be bribed. The most common answer I got when I asked NRIs about why they don't invest in Panjab is that they can't trust the system because they themselves are facing land issues complicated by the courts.

'We have to get to Gobindpura,' I said. 'There the issue is different, I hear.'

'Yes. It is not very far. The government acquired land and now five years are up. They have not even begun building the power plant.' Kulwant smiled darkly. We exchanged phone numbers.

When a project comes to a village it is usually good news and there is the anticipation of money. That is what happened with Gobindpura in 2010. The government decided to set up a 1,320 MW thermal plant there and in two neighbouring villages to be set up and run by Poena Power Company, a subsidiary of Indiabulls Infrastructure Ltd. It then requisitioned for land.[118]

We drove down around fifteen kilometres when we started noticing cement poles about 5 feet high marking barren land. At the village we met the sarpanch Gurlal Singh who was allied to the Congress. He asked us to meet his son at the village school. The son was chatting with a few villagers but they made way because they saw Pargat and me as journalists from Delhi.

The son, a young man with cheeks as red as his father's, told us that the issue was that the government wanted 860 acres of land but got about 700. The owners of the rest of the land from this village were not willing to sell because the compensation at Rs 23 lakh was less than the market rate which, at that time, was around Rs 30 lakh. With the help of Bhartiya Kisan Union and Pendu Mazdoor Sangh, they had agitated, and got the compensation increased to 26 lakh plus a job per family. The protests had thousands of farmers demanding better rates, thousands of policemen picketing the lands and lethal clashes between them.[119]

The current issue was that five years had passed, the land issue had not been resolved, and the project had not started. By law, the government must return the land, but the farmers had no money to pay back to the government. Also, the villagers discovered that a new list of landowners had emerged in the meantime, entitling them to jobs. The new owners owned as little as 0.01 marla land (2.72 square feet). This entitled the family to a job. *Tehsildars* and *patwaris* had changed the papers overnight. The deputy commissioner was transferred and the new one pleaded innocence. Yet, the papers remained as they were.

We surveyed the land and saw that the *khaal*—narrow water canal—was broken and never repaired. This led to lands further up going bereft of water. It could not be repaired now because the land was under government occupation. A private security guard, employed by the IndiaBulls company, told me that he has been there for the last couple of years. He got a monthly salary of Rs 4,000 for twelve to fifteen hours of work—guarding the land from its erstwhile owners. The water table in the village varied from 120 feet in the south to 750 feet in the north. Yet, the land acquired was in the south. How did this happen?

Gurlal Singh tells me this was on account of machinations of the former Akali Dal sarpanch, Balwan Singh. In the previous term, the sarpanch post was reserved for a Scheduled Caste woman. The trend in the village had been to rotate the seat between the two parties. In the village gurdwara meeting Balwan Singh proposed the name of a lady to be elected unanimously. The Congress-oriented folks left the premises. After which Balwan Singh introduced another lady, his house help. She was elected the sarpanch of the village. Balwan then had the acquisition managed through her. She signed where he asked her to sign. The Akali members of the village got their land sold to the government. That is what led to clashes: the land to be sold was in the north but what was sold was in the south.

'Now with all the money, the owners have bought guns, vehicles and have reinvested the money where land is cheaper. Near Abohar and Fazilka. Our village has the highest density of guns in the district. Most of them unlicenced.'

Gurlal offered us tea and I asked him about his journey to becoming a sarpanch. Earlier in the village, a villager had told me

Gurlal had done time in jail. There were two other men in his drawing room and he looked at them and smiled. 'Even they won't know it. They are now inviting me to join the AAP,' he said.

Gurlal's journey was an archetype for most local and state-level leaders in Panjab. As a young man in the 1960s, seeking solutions to the issues of injustice around him, he joined the Naujwan Bharat Sabha. He became active during the Naxalite Movement in 1969-70 but quickly joined the Akalis. In the 1990s he shifted his allegiance to the Congress. Now he was contemplating joining the AAP, in case they assured him a ticket to fight the Assembly elections. When I got up to leave, he reminded me: 'The land is to be used to construct a thermal plant only. I will resist every move the government makes to change its proposal. In fact, now that five years are up, the government should return the land free of cost. I will fight for it with my life.'

As we were leaving the village, I asked for the former sarpanch, the Dalit lady's home. We parked the car a little away from the gate and entered what seemed to be a two-room set with space in front and asked for Karamjit Kaur. The lady said she was not at home. I told her I was willing to wait. She gave me a number to call. I called it and a man responded. I asked him about Karamjit Kaur and he said he would be with me in five minutes. Time passed.

After waiting for about half an hour, the lady finally said, 'I am Karamjit. Tell me.'

I was taken aback. Why had she pretended otherwise? Just then two men entered and started asking me why I was there. I told them I wanted to speak to the former sarpanch and that I wanted to know about Balwan Singh. The lady said, 'He is no longer in the village. He does not live here anymore. He has shifted to Sangrur.' The man hushed her up, asked for chairs to be drawn, tea to be made and invited us to sit down.

'Ask me anything you want to know,' said one of the men. 'I am her husband.'

I knew better than to challenge his authority but still said, 'You must be proud your wife was a sarpanch. Surely she can talk for herself.'

There was an awkward pause. I continued, 'I just wanted to know about Balwan and the land deal.'

'There is nothing to say. Balwan was good. Helped us get a plot of land, build this house. He is gone now.'

We sipped tea. 'What do you think about the deal?'

'We don't know anything,' replied the man but I could make out from his tone that he wanted us to leave.

'But *bhenji* (sister) signed the papers.'

'I am illiterate,' Karamjit burst out.

Since I had her attention, I now addressed her, 'Bhenji, I don't know if I can ask you: would you do things differently if you were re-elected?'

'What has happened has happened. I will never be sarpanch again,' she said impassively, but the weight of her words and her disappointment showed.

While tracing Dadaji's story, learning about the people's struggle, or understanding the land issues in Gobindpura, the conclusions were the same: it was always people versus the state, the people's narrative versus the state's narrative. The 73rd Amendment to the Constitution—empowering the Panchayati Raj—was meant to disseminate power to the ground level. Yet, as we saw, one person,

Balwan—with the help of his political party—had beaten the system. This kind of misuse of powers was widespread as I saw in the rural employment guarantee scheme and funds that came in from the government to develop villages.

While land remains contested and fraught with issues and its woes do not seem to have a chance to end anytime soon, discovering how people create their voice and tell their stories in opposition to the state narratives—the pamphlets distributed by the Praja Mandal after the Qila Hakima episode—taught me the value of documentation. Interestingly, the name of the village Qila Hakima translates to the 'fort of physicians'. Yes, physicians is what we need for Panjab.

In an age where government hides data, politicians distract from the real issues, hardly any media is neutral and post-truth dominates the discourse, it is to hear the voices from the ground that Satnam's magazine *Sulagde Pind* had drawn me to meet him. The same spirit prevailed in other people's organisations as well when they collected data, prepared reports and made knowledge available to the world. The state abhors such reports, pamphlets and documentation. Yet, they persist.

In the future, this story too would be told.

## Chapter Ten

# *Karza* — Loan

The Panjab government's revenue officials had decided that on 26 April 2016 they would evict Baljit Singh and his family from their house and land in village Jodhpur, district Barnala. That morning, at around 11 a.m., so confident was the *arthiya*, Teja Singh, from the nearby Cheema village that he came to the site to evict Baljit and family even before the police and revenue officials who would oversee the eviction had reached. Teja, a former policeman, was accompanied by his sons, Jaspreet Singh Jassa and Manpreet Singh Manna, as well as two other men, one of whom was his nephew. Armed with the *kabza* warrant—possession order—to evict Baljit Singh, they barged into Baljit's house.

In 2002, Baljit's father, Darshan Singh, a small farmer, had borrowed Rs 1.8 lakh from Teja to meet agricultural expenses. For this loan, he mortgaged his land—roughly two acres—on which his house was also located. Darshan was unable to pay back the loan, and after he died in 2012, his debt was transferred to his son. Due to extreme poverty and changing interest rates on the loans, Baljit too had been unable to pay back the debt for many years.

That morning, Teja demanded that Baljit and his family vacate the premises and hand over the land. Baljit pleaded with him for a little more time, but Teja did not relent. A scuffle broke out between them. Meanwhile, dozens of policemen, with revenue officials—the *tehsildar*, the *patwari* (the land-record clerk) and his supervisor, the *kanungo*—also turned up.

The Panjabi word *kurki* is a terror among loan takers and defaulters. It is a word loved by moneylenders and land sharks. It means attaching the land with the original owner, now a defaulter, losing rights on it and the new owner, by assumption, free to use it or auction it. Over a hundred activists from the Bhartiya Kisan Union (Dakonda) were also present at Jodhpur that morning. Members of the BKU told me that, over the last fifteen years, they had prevented over 2,000 cases of *kurki* and auctions. This time it was different.

'Jassa is a district office holder of the Student Organisation of India (SOI),' said Manjit Singh Dhaner, the state vice president of BKU (Dakonda). SOI is a student body which the head of the Akali Dal, Sukhbir Badal, has patronised for use as musclemen to take on political opponents, as rallyists to govern gatherings and programmes and to fight elections in Panjab University, Chandigarh.

According to an independent enquiry by the Bathinda-based Association for Democratic Rights, Panjab, when in 2003, Baljit's father Darshan failed to pay back the amount, Teja got him to sign blank papers—a common tactic by moneylenders. In 2007, Baljit moved the civil court on his father's behalf, accusing Teja of adding interest on the loan amount in an arbitrary manner. His petition was turned down, and Teja then sought to take possession of the property. He got the land attached, conducted a dubious auction and reportedly got the land registered in the name of another Baljit Singh, said to be his business associate.

When Darshan died in 2012, the *tehsildar* issued a possession warrant in favour of the new owner. In Baljit Singh's case, the BKU prevented the possession on fifteen different occasions. The BKU also mediated four rounds of talks between Baljit and Teja, even offering a deal by which Teja could leave the house and a third of the land and take the rest, but Teja refused to budge. Baljit then filed a case in the high court. In February 2016, the high court dismissed Baljit's suit and issued orders for him to evict his home and hand over the land. It also asked for a reply on its orders by 6 May. This was the reason for the revenue officials' and the police's haste in evicting Darshan's family from the land. The superintendent of police for Barnala, Swarn Singh Khanna, stated, 'These are court orders. The police have to perform its duty according to law and procedures. We had to take action.'

When BKU activists tried to prevent the eviction, they were arrested. Baljit then ran to the roof of his small home, with a bottle of pesticide in his hand. Villagers milled around his house and pleaded with him to come down, but he gulped down the contents of the bottle, and collapsed. When his mother Balbir Kaur saw him drinking poison, she too consumed poison. The police and villagers rushed the mother and son to the civil hospital in Barnala. Balbir Kaur was declared dead on arrival. The doctors referred Baljit Singh to Rajendra Hospital, Patiala, but he died on the way. The suicides were dramatic and they caught attention. Otherwise, in rural Panjab, suicide is sadly not big news. It is not that the newspapers do not report the suicides. It is not that the government does not know about them. With minor details like name, place and method being different—like in this case of double deaths—most suicides are a copy of one another. Panjab is saturated with such news. Death is a dance in Panjab, farm and labour-related suicides a pantomime.

Cases were registered against Teja, his sons and the others who accompanied him, under Sections 306, 452, 148 and 149 of the Indian Penal Code: abetment to suicide, trespass, rioting and being armed with deadly weapons, and they were jailed. The BKU (Dakonda) and the villagers initially refused to allow the bodies of Baljit Singh and Balbir Kaur to be cremated.

Buta Singh Burjgill, BKU (Dakonda) president, said, 'Charges have to be filed against all who are complicit: the government and police officials too.' On 26 April, the day of the suicide, farmer activists sat in protest and refused to allow the bodies to be taken for post-mortem and cremation until the Barnala district authorities agreed to pay Rs 6 lakh in compensation to Baljit Singh and Balbir Kaur's family, provide one member of the family with a job, and waive off the loan. The only survivors of the family were Baljit's younger brother, Manjit Singh, who, until now, had earned his living by grazing goats, and his wife and children. Once the bodies were cremated on 28 April, the *arthiyas*, supported by political leaders from the SAD and BJP, entered the SP's office and demanded that the police file cases against the BKU leaders.

Referring to the recently passed Settlement of Agricultural Indebtedness Act (2016) to regulate the credit in the farm sector, Parkash Singh Badal explained the suicide away with a cryptic statement: 'The government can't bring the water level up all of a sudden.' This implied that the *arthiya*-farmer issue which had puzzled everyone for decades now could not be solved overnight. Entrenched in political manoeuvres and given to protecting powerful *arthiya* groups, successive governments have not shown the inclination to take measures towards making this critical relationship a fair one for all.

Soon, the Congress and the AAP, both of whom were attempting to gain political ground, also jumped into the fray. Captain Amarinder Singh from the Congress said, 'Aggrieved by helpless farmers committing suicide as police watch. [If elected] I will outlaw land auctioning of indebted farmers.' The village fell under the AAP MP Bhagwant Mann's constituency. Initially, the AAP did not speak on the matter, but on 1 May, Mann announced that since Baljit was unmarried, Delhi chief minister and AAP leader Arvind Kejriwal would adopt the farmer's brother, Manjit's children. AAP did not talk about what it intended to do about the families of the other farmers who had taken their lives.

The wheat procurement season was ongoing, and the Panjab *Arthiya* Association, many of whom were traders who bought the wheat from farmers and sold it further, threatened to go on strike in order to secure the release of Teja's sons and file cases against BKU leaders. On the other hand, the farmer unions decided to start protests in front of the Barnala District Magistrate's office to demand loan waivers for all debt-ridden farmers in Panjab.

Any suicide is a complex matter, but at the heart of this particular one—and many others like it—is the fear the farmer has of the loss of land, often the only source of income available to him, often even more than the loss of his dignity in society, being declared bankrupt, which, because of the image of a hardy farmer, is an assault on his idea of masculinity.

Commonly, lenders follow a three-step process when a farmer is unable to repay a loan. First, they get the assets of the farmer attached—they approach the courts and obtain an order banning the farmer from being able to sell the land. Then, if the farmer is still unable to pay, they conduct a public auction. Though this auction is supposed to be conducted at the site itself, this is rarely done—the lenders often conduct the proceedings within the court, and many times in the presence of their acquaintances or relatives, and sell the land to them. Finally, the court allows the new owners to evict the farmers, and take possession of the land. But this process is rarely transparent or fair.

Maharashtra, Andhra and Karnataka, being much larger states, dominate the number of suicides—about three lakh in the last two decades. Coming to Panjab, the government data records very low numbers—from 2013 to 2016 the government says only 542 farmers committed suicide.[120] Answers to questions in parliament state that there was at least a 118 per cent growth between the year 2015 and 2016.[121] However, a door-to-door survey conducted by three of Panjab's universities places the number of suicides at above 1,000 per year in the last fifteen years—a total of 16,006 plus suicides, making Panjab the suicide capital of the nation in per capita terms.[122] The central government has not disclosed figures in two years. To not record the reality of Panjab is the shrouding of the reality of its political economy—the unfolding of its memoricide.

In most families I spoke to, the reason why their earning member who defaulted and committed suicide took the loan was: *'Kheti laheband nahin rahi!'* Farming was no longer profitable, hence, to meet expenses of various kinds, a loan had to be availed.

'Children's education.'

'Bribes.'

'Getting a roof made.'

'Building a new room in the home.'

'Daughter's marriage—dowry!'

'Buying a tractor or a motorbike.'

'Digging a well.'

The reasons tumbled out one on top of another—a card game every family knows it has lost. How can one determine which expense was 'important' and which was not?

When I talked about the ease of dying, the deadpan answers, like family members swatting flies, stayed with me:

'Sulphas is so common.'

'Every farmer has plenty of pesticides—aluminium phosphide is usually available.'[123]

'Then there is hanging. There is no dearth of tube wells or cattle-sheds.'

'Mine did not opt for trains. Too much blood spill.'

'Canals are graves.'

Panjab is veined with canals which also serve as graves.

Inderjit Singh Jaijee, the chairman of an NGO, Movement Against State Repression (MASR) has been documenting farmer and labour suicides for over two decades. Some years ago, he released a video of human bodies floating in the Bhakra Beas canal suicide spot where the canal splits at village Khanauri Barrage in Sangrur district on the Panjab-Haryana border. The irony of the video is it was shot five years after the Panjab and Haryana High Court, on an earlier petition by MASR, had instructed that for easier notice of bodies, underwater lights should be installed at the barrage. The government had simply not acted on it.

Jaijee said the reason most suicides were not reported was because they were a matter of shame. They exposed the poverty of the family. Sometimes, the government tried to explain away the causes of suicides as having been committed for non-agrarian reasons.[124] Speaking about how the state responded to suicide cases, he said the questions asked were: 'Are you sure it is suicide from being unable to pay back loans? Did the person not have family fights? Was he an alcoholic? Was he depressed? Was it a heart attack? Did a personal rivalry cause it? Where is the post-mortem? The hospital is just fifty kilometres from your home, why did you not take the body there? Did you register a First Information Report? Where is the police report? Where is the bank letter? Who is the moneylender, did he say something? The labyrinthine state machinery works fantastically well when it comes to denying compensation to the family of the dead. In the process, deaths go unreported. After all, there is shame.'

The issue was also with the official definition of a 'farmer suicide'—it was only labelled so in the case of landowners and was not even an option for tenant farmers or farmworkers. Having witnessed the whitefly agitation and after meeting suicide-affected families, I realised that these protests were not only against the government, its policies and its neglect. I now saw each farmer and labourer standing in solidarity against his own weaker self, his own sense of nihilism and his own tendency to fatalism in the face of overwhelming odds which the state ought to ease, but made harder and unsurmountable with its policies and their implementation. The protest was against depression, against breaking down and against giving into societal and family pressure. The protest I was witness to, and every such protest, in my experience, was a last stand against suicide.

Panjab's culture that eulogises the martyr and frowns upon suicide is fatalistic in both ways: in creating heroes and in denouncing failures. This fatalism can also swing both ways: if it finds a cause, it can create a martyr, if helplessness takes over, it can lead to suicide. The self that feels weak and battered, the self that feels shame and despair, the self that prompts one to take the final step—suicide.

The reason Parkash Singh Badal had spoken in the metaphor of 'water and well' about Baljit Singh and his mother Balbir Kaur's twin suicide was because the SAD–BJP government passed the Settlement of Agricultural Indebtedness Act (2016) to regulate the credit in the farm sector. This bill had been first introduced in 2001 and had then taken the government fifteen years to revise. That itself is a mark of the apathy which cost Panjab 16,006 lives. In any case, this was the government's admission that a huge issue with rural indebtedness did exist. In his intention statement, the then Panjab agriculture minister Tota Singh wrote, 'This legislation provides for a framework for regulation and settlement of agricultural debts.'

Bathinda-based advocate, Narinder Jeet, who had been defending cases on behalf of small farmers and farm labourers for several decades and who had studied the problem of rural debt was dismissive. 'The Bill was supposed to address farmers in debt but actually takes the burden off the courts and benefits the *arthiyas* by assuring them a double return on the money they have lent,' he said.

For instance, Clause 2(H) of the Bill, which defines 'debt' does not cover loans other than rural indebtedness. But, needless to say, loans are often taken by poor farmers for activities other than agriculture and livestock. In Malwa—known for having some of the highest rates of cancer in the state—many loans are for health reasons, for building a room in the house to store food grain, for starting businesses and so on—activities that are not unrelated to the farming trade. Clause 4 of the Bill, which specifies how the interest will be calculated, does not put a cap on non-institutional interest rates. Instead, it proposes that the government would decide the rate annually. But a floating rate cannot work for non-institutional loans, and will certainly not assuage farmers.

One of the crucial clauses in the Bill is Clause 5, which suggests a settlement forum, and includes an *arthiya* instead of an official or expert, along with a retired member of the judiciary and a farmer representative in the forum. It does not, however, specify how these members will be chosen, nor does it guarantee any means for transparency in the process. Clause 8 states that a decision of the forum would be effective even if there was a vacancy. Simply put, decisions can be passed even in the absence of the farmer representative.

The Bill also glossed over the recovery mechanism. By doing so, it bypassed the most contentious of the recovery provisions: seizing a farmer's movable and immovable assets. Clause 24 mandates that the orders of the forum are to be executed by the civil court as if it were a decree or an order of that court. This takes the problem back to square one—the police and revenue officials will remain involved in ensuring repayment, and the debtor's land and possessions will be attached, auctioned and possession will change hands. The Bill also makes no mention of curbing processes such as forged promissory notes, tampered accounts, false witnesses—all of which are common practices employed by *arthiyas* to hold the farmer to ransom.

The Act therefore fell way short of providing any actual relief and was a face-saver for the government which faced elections the next year.

Panjab is neither a cash economy, nor a cashless one. It is an economy of unending credits and debits. I learnt this as a young boy when I helped with farm work in my school holidays. I remember in a harvest season I climbed the trolley in which we carried wheat to the mandi. I sat on the piled-up wheat and our *siri* (permanent farmhand), Bhagta, sat with me. A few migrant labour *bhaiyas* also sat atop the wheat at the far end of the trolley. My uncle drove the tractor that pulled the trolley. To me the travel from field to town seemed like a king's procession. From my geography books I knew this wheat would reach faraway Odisha and Kerala. My uncle was the good king who served his people, fed them and saved them from hunger.

It took us a whole day to unload the wheat, get it weighed, store it in sacks, sew the sacks, arrange them in order, and count them twice over. All day I helped where I could, mostly in picking up the fallen grains and putting them in sacks. Later, in the evening, my uncle and I went to meet the merchant uncle who had bought the wheat. He offered us tea and biscuits and then started getting lentils, sugar, tea leaves, soap, talcum powder and so on loaded in the tractor trolley. He even got me an additional ice cream. After this ritual he opened a big, thick red cloth-bound register and wrote down a figure, then asked my uncle to check and sign. He gave us no money. This was unlike Baba, who, after a month's work in the Steel Plant in Rourkela, would go to the bank with me and withdraw money. Money that we would take to the market and buy lentils, sugar, tea leaves, soap, talcum powder and so on. I, who started the day feeling

like a king, now even with the items in our trolley, felt like a pauper
without any money in hand.

On the way back, I sat next to uncle on the tractor, on top of
its big back wheels. I did not want Bhagta or the *bhaiyas* to hear our
conversation. In a low voice, though the tractor is a noisy vehicle, I
asked my uncle, 'Did we get a fair price?'

'Yes,' he answered.

'Then why didn't we get any money?'

'That is how it is. *Arthiyas* keep our accounts. Do you need
anything we did not get?'

I could not get the experience out of my mind and compared it
with how in the last vacations Baba had given me a home course on
how money came into being and the barter system was discarded.
Yet, this seemed like barter system to me. That was my surprise: how
come in my own lifetime, in the same country, we had two systems—
cash and credit? Salary and barter?

When we reached home, uncle, who was also a science teacher,
took out a chart paper. He folded the chart paper into two. On the
left side of the fold he drew a patch of land and a man next to it.
To this initial picture, he added a tractor, diesel container, water in a
canal, a tube well, electricity, seeds, fertilisers, pesticides, labourers, a
sickle and also the combine harvester which then was a new product.
Against each of them he put the rupee sign.

On the right side he drew a grain market like I had seen that
morning, part of it covered by a shed with shops all around, weighing
machines, sample grain, mounds of grain bags, godowns, labourers,
tractors, trucks, factories, shellers for rice and *atta chakkis* (flour mills)
for wheat. Then he drew rail tracks, distant cities, more bags, more
shops, homes, kitchens, rotis, children sitting around a dining table,
and their mother cooking.

In between the two parts of the paper, on the fold, he put a
question mark: who connects them? It is the *arthiya*, he told me. This

is how the *arthiya*, commission agent, fits into the agrarian system and is in fact the pivot on which both the farm and the market rotate.

Depending upon the Minimum Support Price—available only on wheat and paddy—the *arthiya* procures the crop. He also procures maize and vegetables and basmati rice, whose prices fluctuate from mandi to mandi, and sugarcane which goes directly to the sugar factory. His payment from the market is not certain and could take any amount of time and is often delayed for various reasons: bureaucratic reasons, the state's fiscal health, rice shellers and sugar industries, who were the *arhtiya's* customers, not being able to market the produce and so on. However, the farmer needs immediate resources to carry on with the next crop cycle. The *arthiya*, through his logbooks and guided by his sense of the farmer's finances—previous loans, credits, other expenses—advances the money to the farmer.

The complex market system involves multiple stages of which the government has barely regulated a few: seed, grain testing, pricing and godowns. Even these fluctuate depending upon the produce and are often manipulated by the merchants. The Food Corporation of India and the Panjab agriculture marketing boards like Marketing Federation (Markfed) and Panjab Supplies Corporation (PUNSUP) are supposed to inspect the yield, but inspectors in Khanna, Asia's largest grain market, told me that they continue to rely on the *arthiyas*, their relationships with the clients and their ability to test the yield. Since seeds, pesticides, insecticides and fertilisers are all the needs of farmers, *arthiyas* have deep networks with their suppliers and because of the credit that is extended to them, farmers are forced to tap into those networks, thereby binding them very closely with the *arhtiyas*. According to a survey published in January 2016 by Panjabi University, Patiala, 89 per cent of Panjab farmers are under debt.[125] The outstanding debt in rural Panjab stood close to Rs 70,000 crore, of which about one-fifth was from loans extended by private moneylenders—*arthiyas*. Panjab has 20,000 *arthiyas* and the extent of farm indebtedness has doubled in the past ten years. Each *arthiya* works with around 300 farmers. While the *arthiyas* are strengthened by their position on the right side of the law, support for farmers and labourers remains scarce.

With greater privatisation, the state seeking to step out of the flawed agrarian and agricultural market structure and corporates looking to step in at various stages of the process, the need actually is of a giant political will to set up the terms of trade to regulate Panjab's 1850-plus grain markets. The farmers' need for resources continues to be their primary concern. The farmers also have other basic domestic and familial needs for which they need money. Like in the case of the striped rust disease when Bhola suddenly needed money to purchase fungicide. Which bank would have advanced him the money without guarantee? How long would that have taken? He had to go to the *arthiya*—who is both a flexible bank and a brutal recovery agent. The *arthiya* charges an interest of anything from 12-18 per cent in south Panjab to 18-24 per cent in north Panjab, on the money he advances.

Even the big farmers, owing to their social class which has taken a wholly materialistic turn—big weddings, posh cars, palatial houses, an unending desire for land, either agricultural or a property in a town or a city—are often under debt to the *arthiyas*. This affliction ails the small and marginal farmer too, albeit not at the same scale. It is a social peer pressure. It raises the question why a poor person is not entitled to what Panjabis are otherwise celebrated for around the world—living it up. Of course, the larger question is if such pomp is even necessary.

The Panjabi farmer, especially small and marginal, but also a big one, is always at the edge of fiscal sufficiency. Loans and debts go down generations, yet he remains optimistic. If you ask any farmer, big or small, he will tell you that he will somehow repay his loan: a better crop, a better price, a better season. But it isn't easy. A single spell of rain before the wheat crop matures by the end of March can devastate the crop. Rain and strong winds before the paddy harvest in October can flatten the fields. Then there are diseases, illnesses, and all sorts of pest attacks. How does this kind of life—without any assurance of returns, without any guarantee of income for a whole season of work—shape the mind of the farmer?

It wears down his patience. It makes him prone to emotional decisions. What logic or reasoning can we present about the rain or wind or pest that devastates the crop? A farmer can only respond to the vagaries of nature. He can't control them. It is an unending fight where the only let-up is if nature remains kind. When it doesn't, and the cycle of debts entangles him, to keep his honour, in the absence of state systems to keep him going, he just goes down—commits suicide.

The critical difference between a farmer's life and that of a salaried person or a businessperson is that salaries come on timely intervals, recoveries happen in weeks or in a couple of months, but a farmer has to wait a whole season (which stretches to about six months), and that too at the mercy of the weather. The *arthiya* is the pivot of the system because the state has failed to nuance itself enough to truly aid the farmers and meet their needs. Where it does meet the needs and the farmers fail, their pictures are pasted on the walls of banks as if they are criminals, recovery agents are sent to threaten them at their homes, the police and legal machinery get involved, and there is widespread public shaming. The shame that this brings leads to suicide.

From my meetings and interviews with *arthiyas* in mandis, I learnt that while many are just *arthiyas*, the reasons why some of the current *arthiyas* seem to be predators are that earlier, when *arthiyas*

were Hindu *banias* and Hindu-Sikh *khatris,* they had little interest in acquiring the land and in farming it. They were powerful, as in they dictated terms to Jutts, but it was a symbiotic relationship. That demography of *arthiyas* has changed over the last two decades. A few years back, the economist Professor Sukhpal's research highlighted that more than one-fourth of all *arthiyas* today are Jutts.[126]

From my loose observations, I place the figure now at one-third of all *arthiyas.* Jutt *arthiyas* understand the farmer very well because of their common caste background. While many of them remain symbiotic with farmers, some don't. This is where the stories of *kurki* and exploitation come to the fore. Unlike the *arhtiyas* of yore, a Jutt *arhtiya* is more than capable of farming the land. Hence, he has no qualms in acquiring it. The other reason is the boom in the price of land, as we saw in the previous chapter. The simple fact is that owning land is more lucrative than farming it. The additional reasons are not the failure of the state in broad policy terms but have to do with how corruption and political patronage has grown over the past few decades.

The *arthiyas* I met also told me stories of how corruption and demands from politicians hamper the system.

'The inspector assigns a price to the grain and demands money from us. They take one rupee for every sack weighing fifty kilos. If your shop receives 30,000 sacks of grain, then they'll ask for Rs 30,000,' said one.

'But he can't just pocket the money?'

'The income tax officer demands money, the sales tax officer demands money ... Politicians understand how the system is functioning.'

'Are politicians also receiving money?' I asked, wondering if I would get a reply.

'Yes, of course.'

'How?'

'Through district magistrates in charge of food at the district level. They send money to the local MLAs and ministers.'

How well-oiled the process is!

'There must be bribes for posting?'

'Yes. I have heard that it could go up to Rs 50 lakh. The entire system is compromised. If someone says that suicides are just because of *arthiyas*, it is false.'[127]

Most *arthiyas* are now either pro-Akali or pro-Congress. When either is in power they blame the other group for treating farmers badly. But the fact is that the entire process is compromised and the *arthiyas* have enormous influence over what lawmakers decide.

In 2013, the government decided to reform the Agriculture Produce Market Committees to help farmers bypass middlemen and directly sell to the purchaser. However, these reforms were never operationalised as the government did not amend the Agriculture Produce Market Committees Act in order to allow this to happen. In the same year, when the government chose to enact a Contract Farming Act to clip the wings of commission agents, the law did not usher in any significant changes, though it helped private supermarkets buy produce from farmers directly.[128]

One cannot wish the *arthiyas* away from the system. One has to find ways of incorporating them into India's diverse market systems. The modern banks, even co-operative ones, with their Kafkaesque processes of forms and guarantees, come nowhere close to the efficiency of the local *arthiya*. The question really is: if the *arthiyas* are such an important link between the farmers and the markets, why hasn't the state, in the last half century since the Green Revolution and since becoming a state, acted and created laws that make the atmosphere conducive for both *arthiyas* and farmers?

The crisis is not only of Panjab. It is a national agrarian crisis. The reason Panjab is relevant is that this was the original laboratory of the so-called Green Revolution that later spawned the White (milk), Blue (fish), Golden (honey and fruits), Pink (onion), Silver (eggs), Red (meat and tomato), Yellow (oil seeds) and Round (potato) Revolutions. These are revolutions that encompass the entire rural agrarian sector which is more than half of our nation's population. As we hear more voices from the field, we now know every revolution has had its after-effects. Why could the nation not learn to correct itself from Panjab, the original laboratory, and in the process not let Panjab slide?

It begets the question: is what we call the Green Revolution really a Green Revolution? In political terms, a revolution is when the people overthrow the apparatus of power. But owing to the nomenclature of the industrial revolution belonging to Europe, which was about changing the means and modes of production, the term revolution is now applied to other spheres as well. No doubt the revolution that helped the nation battle hunger was a huge change from earlier agrarian practices, but was the change in scale or in the means and modes of production?

When one looks at the development of Panjab as a hub of agriculture one notices the means and modes of production in agriculture in Panjab changed not in the 1960s but much earlier— when the British created the canal colonies. What we call the Green Revolution was actually an agriculture of steroids, a boost, a creation of a factory for farm produce in which we neglected the core component—nature.

In 1879, the British constructed the Upper Bari Doab canal to draw water from the Chenab river and take it to Lyallpur (now in Pakistan and renamed Faisalabad) to set up settlements in uninhabited areas. Promising to allot free land with several amenities, the government persuaded peasants and ex-servicemen from Jalandhar,

Amritsar and Hoshiarpur to settle there. Peasants from these districts left behind land and property, settled in the new areas and toiled to make the barren land fit for cultivation.[129] The Chunian Colony in the southern part of Lahore district with an allotted area of 103,000 acres was the next project. Eighty per cent of the land was allotted in the form of small holdings of up to 50 acres, known as peasant grants. It was with the opening up of Chenab Colony (now in Pakistan) that agricultural colonisation assumed significant importance. This was the largest of the canal colonies, with an allotted area of over two million acres.[130]

This habitation of Lyallpur was the original Green Revolution. As soon as the hard-working farmers had made the land fertile, the British government enacted new laws to declare itself master of this land, denying the peasants the right to ownership. These laws reduced the peasants to sharecroppers; they could neither fell trees on these lands, nor build houses or huts or even sell or buy such land. If any farmer dared to defy the government diktat, he could be punished with eviction from the land. The new laws decreed that only the eldest son of a sharecropper was allowed to have access to the land tilled by his father. If the eldest son died before reaching adulthood, the land would not pass to the younger son, rather it would become the property of the government. This created discontent among the peasantry and also created the undue interest in the male child that Panjab still prefers, causing a huge skew in its gender demographics from which it is only now emerging.

In 1907, in Lyallpur, Ajit Singh Sandhu—also Bhagat Singh's uncle—spearheaded the movement that articulated the farmers' discontent. In his autobiography, Ajit Singh wrote: 'I had deliberately selected Lyallpur … because it was a newly developed area. This district had attracted people from all over Panjab and was especially populated by retired soldiers. I was of the view that these retired army personnel could facilitate a rebellion.'

Indeed, his hunch proved to be true. There was a great deal of attraction and sympathy for the Pagdi Sambhal Jatta movement within the army. The catchy slogan, *Pagdi Sambhal Jatta*, the name of the movement, was inspired by the song by Banke Lal, the editor of the *Jang Sayal* newspaper. When a contingent of over two hundred Sikh soldiers attended a meeting in Multan, the direct fallout of this was that soldiers at many places refused to obey the British government's orders to fire at the protestors at the peasant rallies. Seething anger at the repression unleashed by the British government erupted in riots in Rawalpindi, Lyallpur, Gurdaspur, Lahore and many other towns and villages. The agitated protestors ransacked government buildings, post offices, banks, overturning telephone poles and pulling down telephone wires.

It was then that Lord Ibbottson, the governor of Panjab, dispatched an urgent telegraph to the viceroy, Lord Hardinge. He wrote, 'Panjab is on the brink of a rebellion being led by Ajit Singh and his party. Arrangements must be made to halt it.' Just prior to this, on 29 August 1906, the viceroy Lord Minto had written to the then India Minister in Britain, Lord Macaulay: 'Ground is being prepared for a rebellion in the armed forces. Literature of a certain kind is being distributed among the soldiers and this will no doubt result in a rebellion.'

Ajit Singh's travels through the central and western provinces of India during the massive famine of 1889-90 which left one million dead, and later, during the floods and earthquakes in Srinagar and Kangra, had shaped his ideas and firmed his resolve to fight to overthrow the British. His means went beyond the moderate Congress means of petition, prayers and protest. He believed in agitation, strikes and boycotts. In 1903, when the viceroy Lord Curzon had invited all kings and princes to declare their allegiance to the Raj, Ajit Singh and his brother Bhagat Singh's father Kishan Singh came to Delhi. They secretly met many kings and urged them to build up another revolt on the lines of 1857. All they got were formal assurances of support but no real support.

In 1906, Ajit Singh participated in the Congress session at Calcutta, to seek out and forge links with patriots who wished to go beyond the Congress's methods of petitioning the British rulers. Upon returning to Panjab, these patriots founded the Bharat Mata Society called 'Mahboobane Watan' in Urdu. It was an underground organisation. Kishan Singh, Mahashay Ghasita Ram, Swaran Singh and Sufi Amba Prasad were some of its trusted lieutenants and active members. Their main objective was to prepare to re-enact the revolution of 1857 on its fiftieth anniversary in 1907.[131] In May 1907, the British police arrested Ajit Singh and another prominent leader, Lala Lajpat Rai, and sent them to Mandalay. While the national leadership of the Congress threw its full might behind Lala Lajpat Rai, they maintained a complete silence on Ajit Singh.

On the ground, the Pagri Sambhal Jatta movement had spread from the peasants to the army. The government had withdrawn its laws and later returned ownership to the peasants. Considering these, they released Ajit Singh, who received a hero's welcome in the state. However, soon after his release, curbing his newspaper, *Peshwa*, the British passed another warrant with the clear intent of securing a death sentence for him when he escaped India from Karachi. He travelled to Iran, then to Europe and South America. He spent around four decades abroad. During World War II, from the Indian soldiers fighting for the British captured by Italy, he raised a cadre of 10,000 soldiers for the Azad Hind Fauj. Yet, with Partition imminent, he was heartbroken. Keeping his frail health in view he was sent to Dalhousie where he breathed his last on the morning of 15 August 1947—the day India became independent.

The reason Ajit Singh Sandhu's story is important is because it has to do with how Panjab was being turned into a British factory enterprise to export wheat for British soldiers in Europe. Another important early twentieth-century figure was Sir Chhotu Ram (1884–1945). Born near Rohtak, in present-day Haryana, Sir Chhotu

Ram's contribution to the legal aspect of peasantry has been largely ignored. Sir Chhotu Ram resigned from the Congress in 1920. Along with Sir Sikandar Hyat Khan and Sir Fazli Husain he launched the Unionist Party to represent the interests of Panjab's large feudal classes: landed gentry and landlords.

This was in response to the British-sponsored Panjab Land Alienation Act of 1900[132] which defined land ownership in terms of 'agriculturist' and 'non-agriculturist', thus affecting the moneylenders who were mostly Hindu and could no longer attach the properties of the peasants. Though Muslims were a majority in the Unionist Party, Sikhs and Hindus also supported it. The Unionists supported the British Raj in the 1920s and 1930s. They contested elections to the Panjab Legislative Council and the Central Legislative Council when Congress and the Muslim League boycotted them. As a result, the Unionist Party dominated the provincial legislature until India's independence and Partition through a later pact between its leader Sir Sikandar Hayat Khan and the Muslim League leader Muhammad Ali Jinnah. The Radcliffe Line divided more than a region; it also obliterated the challenge to Congress that existed in Panjab since most Unionist leaders belonged to, and their landholdings lay in, what became Pakistan.

Sir Chhotu Ram, as revenue minister of Panjab, enacted a number of laws to regulate the agrarian sector. Among them was the Restitution of Mortgaged Land Act, 1938. It terminated all old mortgages existing before the Panjab Alienation of Land Act. It offered statutory extinguishment of mortgage of agricultural land, after the mortgagor had paid an amount twice or more of the principal amount. This law helped to restore agricultural land to almost three lakh sixty five thousand poor peasants taken over by moneylenders using earlier laws.

Another law, the Registration of Moneylenders Act, made it mandatory for a moneylender to obtain a licence before doing business. Conciliation Boards were set up and the majority of its members were farmers. The Agricultural Produce Marketing Act shifted the grain market from the control of moneylenders by forcing them to get registered. The registration of mandis began by the formation of Mandi Regulation Committees, with two-thirds of the representatives having to come from the farmers and one-third from moneylenders. These laws favoured the farmers over the moneylenders and went a long way in regulating the procurement and marketing of agricultural produce.

Another significant law was the Relief of Indebtedness Act, 1934, which offered settlement between the debtor and creditor through debt conciliation boards, which were quasi-judicial bodies. The Debtors Protection Act, 1936, was a law under which the decree holders (the person who has a court order to take over/sell off somebody's property as mentioned in the court order, for the debt/recoverable dues from that person), the majority of which were moneylenders, were restrained from taking over or selling off the essentials of the peasants and farmers. For example, house, fodder, standing crop, bullock cart, milch cattle, cow shed.[133]

Clearly, the 2016 Rural Indebtedness Bill owed a lot to Sir Chhotu Ram's laws but sadly did not improve upon them. Between Sir Chhotu Ram's time and now, the Panjab Agricultural Indebtedness (Relief) Act, 1975, was the only other law which addressed this issue by providing for discharge of the debt of farmers and release of mortgaged property if a sum exceeding or equivalent to one and a half times of the principal amount of the debt had been paid. This Act was never implemented.[134] Clearly, Panjab's *pagdi* (the turban), the symbol of its dignity, has not been steady on its head for over a century now.

At the heart of the idea of the modern nation state is the fact that a society, any society, seeks safety and protection. While democracy has come to Panjab in the last few decades, as we discussed earlier (in the chapter *Mardangi*) the practice of *rakhi* (protection) by *misls* has been at the core of the Sikh religion spreading post the Guru period. While democracy's spread in Panjab has been uneven, the idea of *rakhi* has been kept alive by many of Panjab's leaders to their own advantage. I had a chance of witnessing *rakhi* firsthand in Ludhiana, one evening, when I went to meet an independent maverick politician Simarjit Singh Bains at his Atam Nagar office.

In 2012, Bains won an Assembly seat with support from the Shiromani Akali Dal (Mann). He then came close to the ruling Akali Dal but left it before the 2014 Lok Sabha elections. He fought the elections as an independent candidate but lost. He and his brother Balwinder Singh Bains remained MLAs and later started their own Lok Insaaf Party.

Their rise to power has been ambiguous. There are accusations of land deals, of electricity pilfering and so on, but the most publicised was the case in 2009 in which Simarjit Singh Bains allegedly attacked a whistle-blower *tehsildar*, Major (retd.) Gurinder Singh Benipal, who exposed the shady land deals of the Akali councillors in Ludhiana.[135] The charges on Simarjit Singh Bains are of attempt to murder. The case drags on but Bains has also been voicing strong contempt against government officials, the land mafia, the cable TV mafia and toll taxes.

I was interested in knowing how, on the one hand, the Bains brothers rallied against the government machinery and on the other hand used the democratic electoral system where people elect them to office. It was late by the time I had jumped off a share auto at Gill Chowk and taken another one towards Atam Nagar. I told the driver to drop me where the Bains' office was closest from. The driver turned respectful and dropped me at the beginning of the lane and told me it was a bit of a walk from there. He was apologetic that his autorickshaw could not enter the lane, as it was too narrow. I walked, asking for directions. Once people learnt I was going to the Bains brothers' office, everyone helped. It was a two-kilometre walk through the migrant labour colony: extremely narrow bylanes which only two-wheelers could enter, houses located cheek-by-jowl, the markets on the narrow street busy, and temples and gurdwaras abutting each other.

Finally, I reached the office. Comfortable cushioned chairs lined the room, a water dispenser was available, there were toilets, and the wood and glass cubicles gave the office the look of a medical diagnostic centre. Many people were sitting and television screens were showing a cricket match. The people looked to be the poorest of the poor. I learnt that if the Bains brothers were in town, the office started to get crowded around 9 p.m. I took a seat. It was 9.30 p.m. and there was no sign of the brothers. Yet, the office work was going on, people were going into one of the three offices, gathering forms for rations card, for the Aadhaar card, discussing and paying electricity bills and sharing their grievances, with the workers of the Lok Insaaf Party helping them out.

Much of the talk was in a mixture of Hindi and Panjabi because the people were from Uttar Pradesh, Bihar and Odisha. I approached a worker and he asked what task I had at hand. I mentioned that Simarjit Singh Bains had called me. He escorted me to yet another waiting room, smaller but more elegant, and with sofas. I was alone there. I soon came back to the main waiting room to be among people. There was a certain kind of smile one could spot on faces when their long-pending grievances were solved. It was a sigh of relief and the thanks of a prayer fulfilled. I had occasion to see many such relieved faces that night.

By 10 p.m. the brothers arrived. Simarjit Singh Bains asked me to join him in yet another room where yet another set of sofas were laid out and a meeting was in progress on whether to join the AAP or not. A young municipal councillor, from a Hindu trading family, who had studied in boarding schools in Himachal and served a short stint abroad, had come from Moga to meet Bains and pledge his support.

Soon, more people who wanted to meet the brothers in person started to trickle in. Someone had a wedding that he wanted to invite the brothers to, someone a land dispute, someone needed money for treatment of an illness. Bains directed the disputes to be logged with a party worker who took down details. He asked for calls to be placed to the police, the *tehsildar* and the *patwari* the next morning. He handed over bundles of money—Rs 10,000, even Rs 20,000—to those who sought treatment. No one asked any questions or set any terms. This was a fiefdom—small, but cogent. It addressed people's issues. This got them votes irrespective of their ideology or party. People want a guardian, someone who can get their minor and major jobs done; the Bains brothers did it and earned their loyalty. The brothers were popular and invincible in their constituencies—direct democracy both outside and inside the system.

It was 11 p.m. Bains apologised for keeping me waiting. He asked me if I would mind joining him as he attended marriages and *jagratas* in his constituency. Bains and his entourage, that now included me, piled into three SUVs. A burly man, I learnt later that he was one of the three assistants, brought up a list to Bains. Bains discussed the schedule with him and marked the route. He selected seven functions that night from a list of fifteen or so. He discussed the others too, though, and gave instructions: send flowers, send a senior member to bless, send some money, and so on.

In our vehicle Bains was on the front passenger seat and his father-in-law was with me on the back seat. I leaned ahead to interview Bains, ask him about his protest against illegal sand- and gravel-mining. On his phone he showed me an email he had received from someone in England who sought his help to make a documentary on the issue. 'I studied the issue. Who are the people involved, what is the revenue leakage, which are the sites—in Ropar, Hoshiarpur and Pathankot. I decided to make teams to film the issue. I was surprised that the amount is Rs 90 to 95 crore every day. There is no law on the ground. It is just "might is right" and at the core is the Badal family—Sukhbir and Majithia.'

He went on, 'Post my protest the truck rates dropped by one-third. But investigations must still be conducted.' I asked him to share the papers with me and with the filmmaker too. That is the only way we can build a voice, I said. 'The problem is also language. They want everything in English. But I will share. We need a Commission to look into it. Once a Commission is created I will share everything I have collected. But give me your email address. I will share everything with you.'

'Is the matter sub-judice?'

'Yes, it is, but the police has really taken the high court on a merry-go-round. It has produced so much misleading documentation that I am not sure the court will be able to wade through it. Do you have any material?'

The material I had was personal experience. I had gone to Pathankot which stands at the border of Panjab with Himachal Pradesh and Jammu and Kashmir. It has a huge army cantonment and its economy revolves around the defence services. In the mid and late 1980s, this was where both Kashmiri Pandits from Kashmir and Hindus fleeing militancy in Amritsar and Gurdaspur districts had found temporary shelter.

Ironically, literally, one of the main colonies set up for these refugees of communalism was called Dhakka Colony, in other words, 'Push' Colony, probably referring to how the people came to stay there—by virtue of being 'pushed' from their previous location. It had been more than a quarter century since that, and life had moved on. I met a school friend there who introduced me to his friends, all former residents of the Dhakka Colony. These new friends connected me to the owners of crushers.

At the mining sites, all the work was being carried out by migrant workers. It was illegal but not entirely. The owners did have licences but were mining far greater quantity of gravel than they were permitted to. The word that came up most often was *parchi* (chit). A *parchi* was an illegal gate pass issued against a bribe of Rs 5,000 or so to overload the truck, to pass more trucks than allowed, to mine outside the regulated mine area, to break rules and not be caught. I told Bains about the *parchi*. I did not say what my friend had said one morning, pointing towards the Shivalik ranges. 'We are eating up the hills. Soon we will gobble the Himalayas.'

We got down to attend a wedding. Bains ate almost nothing. His father-in-law, who regularly accompanied him—as did other relatives, his personal army—told me that discipline was necessary. 'Food is simple *daal-roti* at home.' It was late and we could see the remnants of the extravaganza of a Sikh marriage. Men drunk, bottles lying around, immense amounts of food wasted, tents in disarray. The family was beholden to Bains for marking his presence. We moved on after the bride and groom photo-op. The next stop was nearby, a night-long *jagraata*—singing of songs in the name of the Goddess. It was less than 200 people in a *basti* on the outskirts of Ludhiana. The whole tent came out to receive Bains. They were very happy and offered *prasad*—sweet semolina mixed in milk. Bains spoke a few words and we left.

On his aligning with the Badals earlier, he said he regretted it. 'In fact, it was my biggest mistake. People still ask me if I will go and sit with the Badals. I tell them no. I am done with them. But the positive is, if I had not seen how corruption works in the CM house, I wouldn't have taken to the battle against corruption. I learnt a lot from my experience.'

Before dropping me at the Parker Guest House in the Panjab Agricultural University, he asked me my opinion on the debt that Panjab owed the Centre. This was a claim Parkash Singh Badal often made: Panjab owed a debt of Rs 2 lakh crore plus to the Centre. This debt was making it impossible for the state to address the needs of its farmers, labourers, teachers, nurses, industry and all other expenses that the state should meet. Without waiting for my reply, Bains said, 'About a lakh crore is debt incurred during the time of militancy. They say it was the cost of bringing in paramilitary forces to occupy schools and dispensaries to combat militancy. Why was Panjab fighting against militancy if not for India? We incurred the loss of life, our society suffered, and yet we now owe money to the central government? What kind of justice is this?'

India as a nation is based on the idea that all its regions, states and their people are equal. We all have contributed in our ways to making this nation. That is why it feels odd when the nation holds a monetary figure on a state as debt it owes to the Centre. If this was debt, then would the Centre compensate Panjab for being the food basket of the nation, for its historical role as the gateway to the subcontinent and even its current role of sending in one of the highest per capita numbers of soldiers to protect India?[136]

I later learn there was a similar debt on Assam which too went through a militancy period in the 1980s. Kashmir, where the military and paramilitary forces are still deployed, also had a similar debt.

The fact is that when Panjab-born I.K. Gujral was prime minister, he had waived off the loan incurred since 1984 upto his term in 1997.[137] The Badals, however, say when it came to implementation, only the outstanding balance on that date was waived.[138] We bid farewell and Simarjeet Singh Bains asked me for my opinion on him joining AAP. I smiled and said nothing. It was 1.30 a.m.

In any case, the Bains email never came. I doubt Bains even responded to the filmmaker. Many times on my probing among various other people who had highlighted the Badals' misgovernance, claiming to have fought court cases, and were now thinking of joining the AAP, I noticed similar grand talk which was never followed by sharing the details of their work—actual proof. I am sure they knew a bit, but they wanted to keep the information to themselves to use it as arsenal against the government in the election campaigns. Even in its misery, the truth of Panjab was that everything remained at the level of a turf war. It showed that Panjab's plunderers and saviours were both equally territorial.

As I continued my travels, I kept thinking of going and sharing my observations and notes with Satnam. Yet, considering him a constant, I kept postponing meeting him. He was so close, so available, that I believed I could go whenever I felt like it. Why not make the most of my travels, learn some more; I will then be better prepared, I thought. That is why I did not even call him.

Towards the end of April 2016, while I was following the story of the twin suicide, the journalist son of Satnam's dear friend Darshan Pal called me to say that Satnam was no more. He had committed suicide.

I did not know what to say. I thanked the friend and put the phone down.

Claustrophobia. At that moment, I was reminded of the word Satnam had used to describe Panjab—claustrophobia. He had said, 'The intent to escape defines this Panjab.'

Now he had escaped.

'I feel as if I am caught in a noose,' he had said, simply, easily and honestly. Yet, I could not fathom the depth of his honesty. In his death, Satnam had once again proved it to all of us, his well-wishers, that we had not been able to understand him well.

I felt numb. Bereft of the guidance I had received to undertake my study of Panjab. I realised I had to write down my experiences and understanding—complete this book. I owed it to Satnam.

## Chapter Eleven

# *Jaat* — Caste

It was a simple long dusk-time shot of the sun setting over the lush green fields. We thought we would climb the minaret of the gurdwara at Randeep's village, Maddoke, and he could shoot to his heart's content. A few weeks back when I had met Randeep to learn of his experience of caste in Panjab, he had asked me if I could spare a few days to accompany him as he went about shooting his documentary on caste and land-related issues. I agreed because it was an opportunity for me—a Jutt, of upper caste, blind to discrimination—to witness Panjab through Randeep's eyes. Pargat also joined us.

Caste in Panjab plays out differently as compared to other parts of India. It is subtle, and hence more invisible. There is also an unwilful blindness, a sort of lens that an upper caste person tends to wear while looking at the reality of how caste discrimination plays out in society which has to do with the political economy of the land. To my mind it is also a legacy of the Gurus who sought to establish an equal society. Though the society is not equal, since the Granth Sahib says it is or should be, people tend to hide behind it and not acknowledge caste. At least, for a while, this was the case with me. I had not grown up in Panjab and though I was not blind to caste, I was blind to the fact that Sikhs who believed in the Granth Sahib could be practising caste and not be obeying the Granth Sahib.

The origins of the Jutts goes back to the Scythians and White Huns. The term 'Jutt' probably comes from the Gatae (Thracian tribes) and Massegatae (Iranian) people. There is a belief that Jutts were around in the times when the Ramayana and the Mahabharata were composed, and so on, because they find mention in texts like the Rigveda.

There is no clarity on where the Jutts fitted in the varna system, but some scholars maintain they are lapsed kshatriyas which would technically mean they are *shudras*. The answer to how Jutts climbed the varna system to become landlords lies in the eleventh century or so; the advent of Sufis into Panjab with their religious rituals and music. The Sufis set up base in the Panjab region, and marked their presence by tombs—the dargah or mazar—of revered Sufis. These shrines attracted crowds, and by the fourteenth century, the state, wary of their popularity, sought to incorporate them into its structure. This was done by offering them land grants in the name of the shrine, but in effect to the spiritual inheritors of the shrine—the Sajda Nasheen.

The Sajda Nasheens in turn invited pastoralists from the south of Sindh and from Multan and settled them in these lands, asked them to till it, and collected revenue from them. The Sajda Nasheen thus became an intermediary between the farmers and the state. When the Persian well was invented, it further propelled these pastoralists to becoming sedentary cultivators—Jutts.

Many Jutts gradually converted to Islam. Many later converted to the Sikh religion. All over the geographical region of Panjab, today split between India and Pakistan, there are many common surnames among the Jutts. In the village economy, with little mechanisation, most farmers were Jutts. There were other communities too: *silkigars* were nomads but skilled in making weaponry, and a favourite of Guru Hargobind, the *lohars*—ironsmiths, the *tarkhans*—carpenters, the *cheemba*—calico printers and later, tailors, the *chamars*—leather workers, the *chuhras* or *bhangi* among Sikhs and *valmikis* among Hindus—scavengers, and so on. Regarding *mazhabis*, the story goes that when Guru Tegh Bahadur was killed by the Mughal King Aurangzeb in Delhi, three lower caste men recovered his dismembered body from a Muslim crowd and brought it back to his son, Guru Gobind Singh. In recognition of their bravery, Guru Gobind Singh named him 'Guru ka beta', the son of the Guru and gave them the name *mazhabi* (the faithful). Yet, these castes were segregated against, with restrictions on movement and separate living spaces—the *vehdas*.

Neither their centrality to religion nor the social and economic importance of their respective professions brought them equality in the Sikh faith. Whether it was in Maharaja Ranjit Singh's time when the armies he raised from them were discriminated against by the Jutt armies or when the British raised armies and created separate divisions such as the Sikh Light Infantry which recruited only lower castes, the other castes are still being discriminated against in Panjab.

When the Green Revolution came and suddenly the income levels of Jutts shot up, the gap between them and other castes widened and created enormous social and economic disparities. If, earlier, a village had around a quarter population of Jutts owning almost all the land, small fractions of each of the other castes also contributed to farming and formed part of the village economic and social ecosystem. Now, with tractors, combine harvesters and tube wells, the need for ironsmiths, carpenters and leather workers has dissipated. The labour too comes from other states. When the Jutts, especially the wealthier ones, became richer and less dependent on other castes, they left their villages, found employment in towns and cities and shifted their base to them. This aggravated caste discrimination.

As I travelled with Randeep, he narrated story after story of the discrimination he had faced right from early childhood. He had worked as a Left party volunteer for many years and was now critical even of them, showing me how even the Left ideology, in practice, perpetuated caste: marriages in the same caste, religious ceremonies, and so on. Randeep's stories had upset me because they questioned how I had experienced Panjab. They showed me how, once I had learnt that the Sikh religion preached equality between castes and gender, I had suspended observation and failed to pay attention to experience. My sense of what being a Sikh meant—a believer in equality and justice—had blinded me to the reality of caste.

It was still afternoon and we had planned the shoot for 5 p.m. As we turned from the Ludhiana-Ferozepur road, at Ajitwal, towards Randeep's village, Maddoke, we stopped at village Duddike. Duddike is famous for its son, the eminent freedom fighter, nationalist, Hindu leader Lala Lajpat Rai. We roamed the village streets a bit. There were several large palatial houses whose owners had moved abroad and left behind caretakers in their homes. The caretakers were mostly *bhaiyas*, from Uttar Pradesh or Bihar, besides a few from Odisha.

When I started speaking in Odia to one of those caretakers, something shifted in Randeep. Until now, for a few days, he had spoken forcefully against the Jutts. Deservedly so, for the Jutts practised discrimination. Randeep realised I wasn't fully a Jutt too. I told him I was actually a *lohar* since my father had worked in a steel plant. I also told him that owing to Mama's condition I had been brought up by an Adivasi nanny. Randeep and I then discussed how society was a matrix and caste and class were its two axes. The Left's focus on class struggle alone, and Jutt Sikh blindness to issues of caste, had both sidelined the reality of society. After that, I sensed Randeep develop a new warmth for me.

In Duddike, we went to see Lala Lajpat Rai's memorial. It was a small park with many statues and plaques of Ghadar Party heroes and other Indian nationalists. It seemed hagiographic. We then proceeded to the gurdwara at Maddoke. It was a fairly simple task: climb the minaret, point in the direction of the setting sun, shoot. As we parked and pulled out equipment, Randeep wore his cap. As we crossed the gate, an old man sat up in his cot and asked us, 'Where are you going?'

Randeep replied, 'Babaji, we want to shoot some scenes from the minaret. Where is the office?'

'Who are you?'

'I am from the village, Babaji.' Randeep remained polite. 'Where is the office?'

'You say you are from the village. Don't you know where the office is? In any case, you also need my permission,' said the old man with a hint of arrogance in his voice. 'Which family's son are you?' It was not stated, but what was clearly meant was: which Jutt family?

'My father used to bring you food, Babaji ...'

'Food? Who was your father? *Achha*, are you so and so's son?' It was a reference to the sarpanch of the village, a Jutt.

Randeep grunted. 'No.'

The old man caught his tone, rudely asked, 'Who then?'

'You have forgotten who carried your lunches and dinners from Jutt families?'

'I don't remember,' said the old man dismissively.

'I am so and so's son. *Vehde-walle*.'

'Oh! That Mazhabi!' The old man waved his hand and turned his face away and grunted, 'Go on ...' In that dismissive wave of the hand and the accompanying grunt I saw centuries of violence. As we walked ahead, the old man muttered loudly, 'The kind of people who carry big cameras nowadays ...'

We all heard the snide remark. Randeep was seething but did not say anything. He proceeded towards the minaret without even entering the sanctum sanctorum. I went in to *maatha tek* (bow my head) to the Granth Sahib. The Bhaiji had seen us talking to the old man and did not offer me *prasad*. Pargat told me how once, years ago, in the peak of summer, he had gone to the gurdwara to collect leftover rotis and *kacchi lassi*, made from milk, for home and how the

Bhaiji had mocked his poverty. Pargat had thrown the rotis and *lassi* in front of the Bhaiji, and consequently, was beaten black and blue. Through school, college and university, he had avoided going to gurdwaras.

By the time we reached the top of the minaret through the narrow steps with the equipment, Randeep had composed himself. We must have spent another hour shooting, but we did not talk about the incident at the gurdwara gate. I wondered what the point of the minaret was, given that it was full of dust and pigeon shit. The gurdwara *golak* (cash box) was loaded with donations from the village diaspora but it could not attract volunteers to clean its minaret.

The famous Panjabi novelist and man of letters Jaswant Singh Kanwal is also from Duddike. His oeuvre is also a reflection of the different eras of Panjab from being Left reactionary to pro-separatist and Khalistan-oriented. I have been curious about intellectuals who shift stances. On hindsight it does look opportunist, like I saw when many intellectuals shifted stances with the coming of the Modi government. I had planned to meet Kanwal, perhaps interview him after Randeep's shooting of scenes at the gurdwara was complete. Yet, the experience at the gurdwara had soured us and we did not go down to Kanwal's home. A few weeks later when I went to meet him, his son told me that he was a bit indisposed and I marked him down in my diary as an incomplete journey.

However, the real question Kanwal's work evokes is: should a writer sort out his or her ideology before he or she begins writing or should it change as per the politics of the time? Those who turned coat in the first Modi government term had done so because they sensed which side their bread was buttered. Kanwal, I would deduce from his work, did so because he was wedded to the idea of rebellion—a very Panjabi trait—but in Kanwal's lifetime the rebellion had shifted from Left ideology that wanted to change the structure of society but remain loyal to the nation state to militancy which sought to dismantle the nation state. Perhaps his politics always was rebellion and in that sense he was the quintessential Panjabi.

While there are stories of everyday atrocities on Dalits, the reason I was with Randeep was to track a land movement that the Dalits had initiated over the last few years. In a predominantly agrarian society, land is a necessity, not only for producing crops, but also as a source of fodder for cattle, for creating manure, for dry wood and straws to light *chulhas*, and in many cases, for ablutions in the absence of toilets in homes. In most villages, the Jutts maintain an oppressive stronghold over a majority of the farmland, often through fraudulent practices and violence. Many Dalits who either work on Jutt-owned land or collect fodder from it are subjected to abuse. Women from lower caste communities often face verbal, physical and sexual abuse at the hands of the landowners—an ordeal many of them would be less likely to face if they could own or work on their own land.

In 1961, the government of yet-not-trifurcated Panjab decreed per law that one-third of the village common lands had to be given to Dalits to cultivate via public auction.[139] The Dalits, who are 32 per cent of the total population of Panjab—the highest percentage in the country—are now waging a land movement reminiscent of the Muzara movement. Today, these common lands come up to nearly 51,000 acres of Panjab's 1.4 lakh acres panchayat land. Since only members of Scheduled Caste communities are allowed to bid during the auctions of the panchayat land reserved for them, Jutt farmers regularly hire Dalit villagers to act as their proxies, often in collusion with revenue officials and the panchayat, whose responsibility it is to oversee the process. Given that most Dalits are unable to afford the high land rates, these candidates win the auctions on behalf of the farmers from the Jutts, the dominant caste. Once the candidate has been assigned the land, the Jutts take it over, often employing Dalit villagers to work as serfs.

In 2008, young Dalit men from Benra—a village in Panjab's Sangrur district—mobilised the village's 250 Dalit families. They pooled in money to enter a bid—for an auction that was due later that year—for a nine-acre tract of land. The families came together under the banner of a farmers' collective called the Kranti Pendu Mazdoor Union (Revolutionary Farm Workers' Union). In late 2008, when the auction was held, even though the authorities in Benra did not extend any help to the Dalit collective, it managed to secure the bid for the land. The collective also succeeded in forcing the administration to grant it a cut in land rates. Since then, the families that formed the collective have been farming on the land together, growing wheat and paddy along with fodder for their cattle.

In 2014, Dalits from the village Seekha in Barnala district wrested control of the seven acres of land that was reserved for them from the upper-caste farmers who had been occupying it. In this effort, they were helped by members belonging to the Panjab Students' Union, a collective of student activists. The activists and the farmers picketed the office of the block development officer and held protests until the administration agreed to hand the land over to them.

In 2014, inspired by Benra, a group of eight Dalit girls in Matoi, a small hamlet outside the Muslim-majority township of Malerkotla, stood up for themselves.[140] Sandip Kaur, Gurmeet Kaur and their friends, all college students, formed the Ekta Club on Ravidas Jayanthi. The villagers ridiculed them, mocked them and mockingly asked them to go home. Yet, they persisted. After clashes with the police, the auction failing two times in 2015 and arbitrary rate hikes, they won the lease for seventeen bighas (3.4 acres) of land. This was unprecedented in Panjab's feudal and patriarchal society.

Again, in 2014, in village Baupur in Sangrur on the southern border of Panjab, the demand for twenty-seven acres of land by about 105 Dalits led to a social boycott by the upper-caste Jutts.[141] The upper castes cut off the water supply to the Dalit part of the village, fields and sheds. They announced over public loudspeakers that anyone employing a Dalit farm labourer would be penalised. They stopped Dalits from selling vegetables in the village, forced them to close their small shops and forbade Dalit children's entry to the village school and hospital. Yet, the Dalits persisted and got the land and have begun cultivating it. Hearing this story, I was reminded of what my family would have undergone in Dadaji's time. But, I was also conscious that we were Jutts and we had found a way to move on—after all, we did own land near Rajpura. Rupa and Teja's families had not moved on. They were left behind and killed. Caste is economic, caste is networks. Upper caste is mobility, upper caste is escape. Dalits often have no escape.

There was general excitement in the lane in Baupur as Randeep recorded the views of the villagers and their leader Krishan Jassal. Suddenly, there was a power cut. Filming is dependent on electricity: the camera charge, the microphone, and the lights. Since the shooting was indoors, the work stalled.

As we took a break and waited for the power to be restored, I asked a few children if they would also continue the fight for land rights. The children didn't seem very keen. They were interested in studying and getting jobs. Yet, for high school they had to travel to Sunam, twenty kilometres away. I asked how many had studied and got jobs. The answer: no one they knew about.

Then they told me about the land for which the Dalits were struggling. There were three majority Dalit castes in the village and each of them was demanding one-third of the land. While getting into the car, Pargat, who is a Banjara—nomad—by caste, though now settled for two generations, said 'Baiji, that means I will still be without land?'

He was right. While the Dalits, mostly Mazhabis and Valmikis, had united to wrest the land that belonged to them per law, when they had split internally, those Dalit castes that were still a minuscule minority were left nowhere. Each of the communities that owned land began to replicate the behaviour patterns of the Jutts.

Yet, I also recognised that this battle for land was on the edge. It was true that the Dalits had split in Baupur, but in many villages they had stuck together. As matters stood, it was important for Dalits to stick together and wrest their lands, become successful cultivating them and educate their children to seek opportunities elsewhere, even perhaps away from their land.

The power didn't get restored and we decided to leave. Once we had driven off towards village Balad Kalan for another shoot, Randeep got a call on his mobile from the Dalit leader at Baupur. The electricity had apparently been restored within five minutes of our leaving. They had figured out that the Jutts had asked the electricity department for the cut. Not only would Jutts deny the Dalits their rightful ownership of land but they would also not let the stories be recorded to go out to the world.

At Balad Kalan, we stayed in the house of a marginal farmer, an old-time communist leader, Bhola Singh. In June 2014, 143 Dalit families from Balad Kalan came together to ensure that an ongoing auction of the 121 acres of panchayat land would not be subverted by upper-caste villagers or the revenue officials.[142] The villagers were met by nearly 500 riot policemen, who lathi-charged them and beat them up severely. The police charged forty-one men belonging to the Dalit community under various sections of the Indian Penal Code, including an attempt to murder. The men were incarcerated without bail for fifty-nine days. Protests broke out throughout the state, and continued until the state administration and panchayat agreed to surrender control of the land, in late August.

Next morning, we went down to the side of the village where Dalits rested during the day, after field work. Randeep tentatively asked if he could talk to the women—after all, they were the ones who suffered the Jutts' eye and lust. The leader, an older man, readily called for the women. This was completely different from how Jutts in villages would deal with the women. The openness was in complete contrast to Jutt feudal behaviour.

As we awaited the women, we talked about how getting the large tract of land, almost one acre per family, had revolutionised the status of Dalits in the village. The Dalits now planned to acquire two tractors to till the land and even rent combine harvesters to cut the crop. The best part was they had no shortage of labour. In the season, all families sent one or two members to work on the fields, and work which would take a week now took a day.

The Dalit women arrived in a group. Marching down to the location, they were a wave of energy. Jaspreet Kaur, whom the police had hit with lathis on her head and who had been in a coma for three weeks, led the troop. Now recovering, but not one to show it, she took the front portion of the platform where Randeep seated them to capture them on camera. The older man, the leader, tried to intervene, 'Look at the camera and speak …'

She retorted brusquely, '*Budheya* (old man), keep quiet. I know what I have to do. Don't interfere.' In her matter-of-fact tone. I noticed how thousands of years of patriarchy had been trampled upon. Then she turned to Randeep and asked, 'Are you from TV?'

He shook his head. 'This is for film.'

'Okay. One, you will ask all questions in Panjabi. No other language. No English *ghit-pit*. Second, you will record all that I have to say. No cutting my lines.'

If this was what the Dalit Land Movement could create, then all that it and its Jaspreets needed was our unflinching support and not interference or guidance which even the good-hearted upper castes were often willing to dispense. This was history being created in front of our eyes. While parting, the leader asked me for my name and number. I gave the first name and he added, 'Kumar?' I was embarrassed and said, 'No. Sandhu.' He lifted his head from his notepad and looked me in the eye. He did not say anything. He noted down my phone number. In his silence, I heard the echoes of what the Jutts had done to the Dalits for many generations.

To distract myself, as Randeep was completing his shoot, I walked up to a group of men in the corner of the ground, next to the fields. They were sitting around, playing cards and smoking, some doing so even in their turbans. They were marginal Jutts.

As we talked about landholdings, a man remarked, 'They have shrunk. In one generation we have come down from ten acres to three. Even we can't make a living out of it. Write that too somewhere.'

He gestured towards another man. 'Look at him. Neela. Oye Neele, come here,' the man called out to a friend in a grey kurta pyjama and a checkered black and cream *parna* on his head. The man came closer to where we stood. His eyes were blue, beard brown, face with plump cheeks, round and fair. 'He and his brother own two and a half acres of land. That is why he did not even get married!'

I turned to Neela and asked, 'Is it to avoid children? To not have the land divided further?'

'Yes. My brother already has two children. His wife is Purbi.'

'Why Purbi?'

'No one in our village or the neighbouring ones was giving him his daughter. We are small landowners. We don't have any other job.'

Purbi means from east India. 'Did he buy her?' The wife was most likely bought and brought to the village and married to the brother.

'Who are you?' Neela asked, suddenly worried that I could be from the police or could leak the information to authorities. If the brother had two children, the marriage had to be at least a few years old. Yet, the fear of human trafficking hadn't left him. But my concern was different. It was about Neela's life. 'I am just a writer. I came here to understand the land movement. Are you single? No kids, no wife?'

'Just that nothing suited me. It is fine. I am fine. My brother's kids are like my kids.'

'But still the body has needs.'

Neela took my elbow and pulled me away from the men.

'It gets adjusted in the family,' Neela now said in a low voice. 'My brother and I work together, earn together, spend together; it is my family. My Bhabhi is a good woman. We are fine. There is nothing more to say. Now leave me alone.'

I left him alone. I realised I had no right to probe further. Pargat later said to me, 'Bai, you can write a whole chapter on the single men of Panjab, from all castes and religions. There is an acute shortage of women.' The gender equation of Panjab at 889 girls for every thousand boys was skewed. A decade back it was 837 girls.

Next day, we went down to the village of Jhaneri in Sangrur district whose sixty Dalit families had bid and obtained about thirty acres of land. They had borrowed close to Rs 4 lakh from an *arthiya* and pooled in their resources to raise the Rs 7 lakh for the bid. When I enquired about the impact of the Employment Guarantee scheme (MGNREGA), Surjan Singh, the leader, showed us registers of the project. The papers recorded names, the number of days of work and the payments made. Work meant for the whole village was actually going only to Jutts and not being allotted to Dalits.

However, now with the possibility of the land lease, there appeared to be hope, but a new issue had come up—the construction of a *gaushala*. The panchayat had decided to build a *gaushala*, and since a part of the panchayat land was going towards the project, the expectation was that the Dalits too would give up proportional land, which came up to seven acres. It was a tricky bait. Many Dalits eked out a living from their cattle. How could they refuse a Jutt panchayat's demand for a *gaushala*, especially in a time of cow cess, when the cow was being propagated as mother? Yet, losing seven acres was a very big deal. We walked up to the land being considered to be given off. It was already being flattened. On the yellow JCB, right between the lights, on its forehead, so to speak, was written: *Naag di Bachhi*— Cobra's Daughter. Indeed!

News of the action in Benra and Balad Kalan spread through many districts, and inspired other landless Dalits to rise in protest. Janhastakshep, an activist coalition that included professors from Delhi University and Jawaharlal Nehru University, conducted a fact-finding mission on the caste conflicts in villages in Panjab. In June 2016, Ish Mishra, a member of Janhastakshep and a professor at Hindu College in DU, published their findings on his blog. Mishra stated that in about sixty-five villages in the Malwa region in Panjab, Dalit residents had been agitating for their right to panchayat land, and that they had succeeded in as many as sixteen villages in Sangrur district alone. In April 2015, the Zameen Prapti Sangharsh Committee (ZPSC—a committee to fight for land rights) organised a Mahapanchayat to discuss how such collectives across Panjab could be strengthened. A report published on the website of the Communist Party of India (Marxist-Leninist) noted that in 2016, Dalits in forty-four villages launched protests to obtain their share of panchayat land. In nearly forty villages, the report stated, the agitators had managed to secure the land.

Late in 2016, Lakshmi joined me briefly in Panjab. That is when we got news of a huge caste clash in village Jhaloor, near Sangrur. Against the backdrop of a long-standing dispute over agricultural land in the village, the Jutts had mounted a brutal assault on Dalits.

On 11 October 2016—the day Dussehra was celebrated that year—Lakshmi and I drove down to Jhaloor but initially stopped at Sangrur to meet Sukhwinder Pappi, a member of the ZPSC who had participated in the struggle at Balad Kalan. Pappi told us that the post-harvest calculations conducted by the organisation showed that in whichever village the Dalits bid and got the land, each Dalit family had earned close to Rs 10,000 from the land each season. This was not a very considerable sum, given the violence, being in jails, and hospitals. The greater reward, he said, was one that could not be quantified: dignity.

We wanted to meet Pappi's colleague, the founder of the ZPSC, Mukesh Malaud. He was underground. Pappi guided us to the village Jhaloor but could not join us for obvious reasons—fear of the police. He was also of the view that as an independent writer who had no language issues, I needed to meet the villagers directly to get their version. 'Too many news stories are planted. They serve no purpose. They are just one version against another.' I later learnt that Pappi was himself a poet, besides being a farmer who was going organic, and an *arthiya*.

We reached the village at about 3 p.m. Upon our arrival, we enquired about the attack at a local tea shop located next to a rest house—the Ravidas Dharamsala—in the *vehda*. Within a few minutes, a group of nearly forty men and women from the community had gathered around us. One of the men suggested that we move into the closed courtyard of a nearby house. I later found out this was because we stood at the site of the attack. The men and women were nervous because we were in plain view of the police, many of whom were milling about the rest house in the aftermath of the attack.

In the courtyard, the men told me in detail how the Jutts had beaten up Dalits and vandalised their homes—breaking windows, household appliances and water pipes—and even injured cattle and pets. The Jutts had groped, molested and beaten up Dalit women. Over forty Dalits were severely wounded: nine had suffered head injuries; one villager's arm was broken, while another's jaw was dislocated. Their community was being subjected to an informal social boycott: the Jutts had refused to buy milk from the Dalits, leaving the latter unable to procure fodder for their cattle. The Jutts also forbade doctors from treating those who had been wounded in the attack. The Dalit villagers said that their milk and food supplies were fast depleting. Fearing another attack, several families belonging to the community had locked their homes and fled Jhaloor, while many others had sent their young daughters away to relatives in other villages. A few farmers with small land holdings, who had supported the Dalits in their clash against the Jutts, had also left.

Amidst this narration, a boy emerged, carrying a tray with two glasses of milk and a packet of biscuits. My tears welled up and I stepped back. Lakshmi handled the situation by asking for two empty glasses. She poured out the milk for two children in the group and we both took two half glasses. Not drinking the milk would have been an insult but drinking the whole glass would have been criminal while hearing stories of how the victims of the beating were suffering the social boycott. We then distributed the biscuits among all of us.

Over the next hour, as the men told me what had transpired on the day of the attack, I noticed many Dalit men were wearing a similar locket. The locket had a blue background on which was a gold number, 1, which also looked like the alphabet I. DSSO was etched underneath. DSSO stood for Dera Sacha Sauda Organisation. The 1 or I stood for one God and also for Insaan—human. They all believed that Gurmeet Ram Rahim was their saviour and belonged to the Dera Sacha Sauda.

Meanwhile, I realised Lakshmi was missing. I looked beyond the group I was talking to and saw her emerging from a house. There, she met several women from the gathering, one after another. Later, she told me, 'Each woman took me indoors and stripped to show me big marks on their bodies—purple and blue blood clots under their breasts, on their backs, buttocks and inner thighs.' The women told Lakshmi that their husbands were in jail, they did not have medicine to treat themselves, or buy milk for their children. They had not spoken about their wounds, because they were ashamed. 'These are *gupt-chot* (hidden wounds). They are deliberate, so we can't expose them to police or doctors or activists who are normally always male.'

Though Lakshmi understood Panjabi, her ears were tuned to a more urban variety. Obviously, she could not understand everything the women were saying. Yet, there was an understanding that was beyond language. It was the space of empathy, of nakedness and of being bare in your pain. Lakshmi understood that space of empathy.

Although 250 of the 600 families residing in Jhaloor belong to the Dalit community, they do not own any of the 2,300 acres of land in the village. Most Dalits in Jhaloor eke out a living by tending to cattle and selling milk, working for Jutt farmers, or through other petty trades. The panchayat land in Jhaloor is nearly 50 acres. The 16.5 acres of land reserved for the Scheduled Caste community is split into three parts, of which only one part—about six acres large— is cultivable. The other two plots, of 6 and 4.5 acres each, are located at quite a distance from the village and are not cultivable. Relying on the villagers I met, as well as a report that was released by the Association for Democratic Rights (AFDR), a Panjab-based human rights watchdog organisation whose members had visited Jhaloor a day before us, I pieced together an account of the events that led to the violent attack the Jutts had launched on 5 October 2016.

On 10 May 2016, after the revenue officials and administration at Jhaloor failed in three of their attempts to conduct auctions because of protests led by the ZPSC, they decided to hold a forced auction of the six acres of cultivable land reserved for those belonging to the Scheduled Caste community. The auction was conducted in the presence of police officials. Jugraj Singh, a Dalit, won the six acres for Rs 2.62 lakh. Jugraj later told the AFDR team that Harvinder Mangu—a Jutt landlord—had lent him the money to buy the land. He also said that he had no prior farming experience. According to the account he gave the AFDR team, Jugraj did not own a tractor or any agricultural implements either—he was planning to borrow all of these from Gurdeep Babban, another Jutt landlord. Effectively, Jugraj had stood in the auction as a dummy candidate for Babban.

According to the report, when the administration handed over the land to Jugraj, many Dalit residents of the village, aware that Babban would control it, had camped on it for a month in protest. In the second week of June, the police had forcibly evicted them. Subsequently, Jugraj, with help from the Jutt landlords, planted paddy on the land. A few weeks later, the Dalit villagers uprooted the paddy seedlings.

In the meantime, six members of the Jhaloor panchayat wrote to the additional deputy commissioner (ADC) of development, asking for a revocation in the decision to allot the land to Jugraj since he was a dummy candidate. They received no response. The ADC later denied receiving any such letter. Members of the ZPSC said they had submitted multiple memorandums to the block development and panchayat officers as well as the sub-divisional magistrate (SDM), requesting that the false bid be cancelled. Several Dalit villagers recounted that they had protested in front of the office of the block development officer on 10 and 11 August. The members of the community repeatedly demanded the cancellation of the bid. In spite of all this, by late August, Jugraj had planted paddy on the land again.

Till 29 September, the outcome of the bid remained unchanged. That day, the Dalits uprooted the unripe paddy once again. For this, the police booked several members of the community under Section 452 of the IPC—trespassing with the intent to harm. On

2 October, a group of Jutts attacked the ZPSC leader Gurdas Singh's family in Jhaloor and injured the son of Prakash Singh, a Dalit member of the village panchayat. They also beat up two other members of the community and vandalised their homes. The victims were hospitalised, but the police did not register a complaint against the Jutts.

On 5 October, the ZPSC organised a rally outside the office of the SDM in Lehra, a town nearly ten kilometres away from Jhaloor, to demand that the land be handed over to the Dalits in the village. Members of the community in Jhaloor and neighbouring villages attended the demonstration. According to Nirbhay, a Dalit man in his thirties who had stayed back in Jhaloor that day, at about 2 p.m., while the protest was ongoing, the village gurdwara's loudspeaker crackled. The repeated announcement was: 'Jutts should gather with arms and reach the Lehra SDM office.'

About fifty Jutts—drunk and armed—arrived at the venue of the protest. Afraid that the Jutts would attack them, the Dalit villagers expressed their apprehension to the police. The police officials told AFDR that they had asked the group of Jutts to go back to Jhaloor. The *tehsildar* assured the villagers that the police would protect them, and arranged for a few policemen to escort the protestors back to the village. Four policemen—three constables and a station house officer (SHO)—escorted the seven vehicles that were ferrying the villagers back. However, the SHO did not continue beyond Moonak, a village located just before Jhaloor. Several villagers told me that the constables did not enter the village either.

Nirbhay told me that the protestors, including those from other villages, had arrived in Jhaloor at about 4.30 p.m. 'The announcement being made on the gurdwara's speakers then changed. It now said: "The Dalits have killed Gurdeep Babban. A thousand Dalits are coming to the village," and, "We must teach them a lesson." Upon reaching Jhaloor, the Dalits saw around 250 drunken Jutt men, young and old, had climbed the rooftops of the houses around the Ravidas Dharamshala.

The men were armed with stones, bricks, scythes and rods. As the 200-odd Dalit women and men entered the village on their *chhota hathis* (a mini truck fashioned out of old motor parts), the Jutts launched an attack on them. They pelted stones on the unarmed villagers climbing down from the vehicles and broke seven *chhota hathis*. The Jutts broke open doors and windows, entered the houses and beat up whomever they could lay their hands on: women, children, cattle and domestic pets. They broke household objects and electric meters, cut open water tanks, and plucked out taps and pipes.

ZPSC members called the police but officials took more than an hour and a half to reach from Lehra—a journey that usually takes about fifteen minutes on a motorbike. Even after the policemen reached, they waited outside the village while the attack continued. ZPSC leader Balwinder Singh was specifically targeted. A group of Jutts entered through the roof of his house and beat up the members of his family. Gurdev Kaur, Balwinder's mother, who was of frail health, was lying on a cot in her courtyard and was unable to move. The Jutts attacked her with axes, almost severing her leg. She went into shock and was later admitted to a hospital in Chandigarh.

The attackers, it seemed, were looking for Balwinder Singh's brother, Balbir Singh, of the Panjab Farmers' Union. They also ransacked the trunks in the house and stole Rs 30,000, which was kept aside for the newborn girl of the family. The Dalit women told Lakshmi the Jutts uttered obscenities to women and stripped naked in front of them and asked, 'Will you join the protest against us?'

Jaspreet Kaur, who worked as a sweeper in the village school, said that while the Jutts beat them, they repeatedly said that they wanted to put the Dalits 'in their place'. She added that when the attack was ongoing, several Jutt women helped Jutt men identify the houses that belonged to Dalits.

According to the ZPSC, over 100 Dalit villagers were trapped in Jhaloor. Late in the night, upon the SDM's assurance, the men and women came out in groups of five and seven. The police took them to the hospital, but arrested several Dalits the next morning. Although close to forty people were injured and in need of medical attention, many did not go to the hospital for fear of being arrested. Some among those who were receiving medical care left the hospital without the doctor's consent.

According to a police officer, eighty-six cases were registered after the attack. Of these, only eighteen were against the Jutts. On 6 October, the police took fifty to sixty Dalit men into custody and illegally detained them.

The Dalits, under the aegis of the Jhaloor Kand Jabar Virodhi Action Committee (a committee to protest the Jhaloor action), organised a massive rally on 21 October at Lehra Gaga, a set of twin towns near Jhaloor. Close to 5,000 people attended the demonstration. Members of the ZPSC, the Bhartiya Kisan Union (Ugrahan) and the Panjab Khet Mazdur Union, which mobilises landless workers, among others, attended the protest to express their solidarity with the Dalits' cause.

The silence from the political machinery in Panjab was astounding, but unsurprising, especially when one considers the relevance of Sangrur, the constituency in which Jhaloor falls. Various union leaders and villagers—both Jutt and Dalit—told me that Gurdeep Babban was Dhindsa's man—referring to Parminder Singh Dhindsa, the minister for finance and planning in the Akali government in power then. Babban's proximity to a prominent minister would explain the inadequate measures taken by the police to ensure the safety of the Dalits. Rajinder Kaur Bhattal, a former chief minister of Panjab and a member of the Congress, belongs to a village called Changali Wala—less than fifteen kilometres from Jhaloor. Several people told me that Bhattal had visited Jhaloor on 3 October, and expressed solidarity with the Jutts. She left without even meeting the Dalit villagers. Bhagwant Mann, a member of parliament who belonged to the AAP, was elected to the Lok Sabha from Sangrur in 2014. Mann, too, remained silent on the issue of panchayat land.

On 7 October, Rajesh Bagga, the chairman of the Panjab Commission for Scheduled Castes, ordered an inquiry into the violence by constituting a committee comprising the Lehra Gaga SDM, the superintendent of police and the deputy superintendent of police. The ZPSC rejected the formation of the committee, alleging that Bagga had only met the Jutts who had instigated the attack, and that he went to meet those who were injured and being treated at the civil hospital, even though it had not admitted the Dalits. Till date, the commission has not met any of those who were attacked. Gurdev Kaur died from her wounds and was cremated on 28 November. In her death, she became the face of the Dalit movement for land. Lakshmi remained silent for three days. I wondered what kind of Panjab I was showing her. Was this the land and people of which I was proud?

Two symbols stayed in my mind from Jhaloor: one, the Jutts had used the village gurdwara to make divisive announcements, rally their men and prepare for attacks on Dalits. It was similar to how the Akali sarpanch at village Thuha on the SYL had misled people from the gurdwara. On the one hand Panjab was battling incidents of sacrilege of holy texts, on the other the Jutts and Akalis were misusing the gurdwaras, supposedly places of truth, justice and equality. Second, the locket on the necks of the Dalits, partly because of the incidents revolving around Ram Rahim during Mama's death in 2007 and his alleged involvement in the sacrilege incidents of 2015 and also given the fact that he was considered the king of bling. The locket was not only an assertion of caste, it was also as if the Dalits were declaring their distance from both mainstream Sikhism and Hinduism.

The word 'dera' derives from the Persian word 'derah' or 'dirah', which literally means a camp, abode, monastery or convent. The phenomenon of the dera as a sectarian institution is not new in Panjab. It is older than the Sikh faith. Deras in Panjab, before the Sikh faith, belonged to Sufi Pirs, Yogi Naths and the Sants of the Bhakti movement.

Later, in 2016, I decided to visit not only the Dera Sacha Sauda but also some of the other prominent deras. Scholars aver that Panjab has about nine thousand deras, but the main ones are: Dera Sacha Sauda, Dera Sachkhand Ballan, Radha Soami Satsang Beas (RSSB) and the Divya Jyoti Jagrati Sansthan (DJJS) Nurmahal. The Nirankaris and the Namdharis are two other major sects and have been around for much longer, and much to the chagrin of Sikhs, continue to use the Guru Granth Sahib.

The single distinguishing factor between all these deras and the Sikh religion is that the deras continue to believe in a living Guru while for the Sikhs the living Guru is the Granth Sahib and not a human being. Apart from that, there is a lot of overlap in practice between the deras and the Sikhs. An important aspect of the deras is they attract followers from Dalits, poor Jutt Sikh and Hindu families who feel disenchanted by the Jutt control of the institutions of the mainstream Sikh religion. However, the deras themselves are run by mostly upper caste Sikhs. For example, a Khatri Sikh heads the Nirankaris, a Sidhu Jutt heads the Dera Sacha Sauda, a Dhillon Jutt heads the Radha Saomis and a Brahmin heads the DJJS.

I drove down to Sirsa to visit the Dera Sacha Sauda. At first sight, the ashram is huge or at least seems to be, from the walls around it painted in cheerful colours, depicting nature scenes. I parked and walked to the gate. The security person gave me a form to fill. The form asked for details such as address, phone number and my reason for visiting. I wished I could write *bhakti* (devotion), but I knew it would be wrong. The very fact that I was asked to fill a form meant that the security person did not believe I was a devotee. Many others before me had passed without scrutiny.

When entering, the security person took my mobile phone, handbag and even my pen and notebook. Beyond the filmi fort gates lay a huge ground, on one side of which I saw a massive stage. I moved to the left, towards the office and the restaurant. I hoped to get some tea to relieve me after my long drive. The restaurant was full of haphazardly arranged plastic tables and chairs with their covers worn out. It seemed more like a poorly maintained college café.

Post a cup of tea, I walked up to the stage. On the way, I saw boards with instructions, the kind the secular Indian state issues for social welfare: keep your home clean, throw garbage in dustbins, get polio drops, go for an eye test and so on. It was all benign and safe. This, I later discovered upon viewing Ram Rahim's videos, was the core message of his sermons. All he publicly did was to exhort people to lead superficially stable, clean and healthy lives including undergoing medical tests and eye check-ups—facilities that the state should ideally provide for its citizens.

Gurmeet Ram Rahim's behind-the-scenes activities came to light after he was imprisoned in 2017. The list of atrocities is long. He was accused of rape, plotting murder, forced castrations and gathering wealth through illicit means. He also controlled a sizeable vote bank which political parties coveted. Yet, none of this revealed itself to the naked eye when I walked around his ashram. At the same time, I felt the atmosphere was stilted, and got a sense that the neat and clean ashram was hiding its real face from me.

I went to the other side of the lawn from where the path led to Gurmeet Ram Rahim's *gufa* (cave), but his security personnel did not allow me in. I felt unwelcome and I soon left. I perhaps felt how

Dalits feel in Jutt Gurdwaras—a lack of access, of not belonging to the religion or feeling one with the environment.

Nurmahal is named after Noor Jehan, the wife of Mughal Emperor Jehangir, who was brought up here. The town's main claim to fame was the well-preserved Mughal Serai. Also in Nurmahal is the ashram of a very unlikely religious leader in Panjab—Bihar-born Mahesh Kumar Jha later known as Ashutosh Maharaj—who was the founder-head of the DJJS. On 29 January 2014, he was declared clinically dead by a team of doctors but his followers believe him to be alive and in a state of *samadhi* (deep meditation). For the last five years, no court and no police, despite orders, have been able to prevail upon his followers to give him a funeral. His alleged son too was not allowed to claim the body. At stake is a vast empire that has lined the pockets of many politicians, all interested in its votebank.

I stopped my car near the signboard on the road that pointed to the ashram and asked a lone Home Guard sitting there if I was at the correct place. He motioned to me to park my car on the road and walk to the ashram, which was at a distance, next to an open ground. I could sense that I was being watched. At the entrance booth, the security person opened my bag and upturned it. When I put my things back, he kept it and gave me a token. As I walked on, looking at the preparations for an upcoming programme—tin sheds being erected, ropes being tied, banners being put up—a guide came and ushered me into a room. I first noticed two CRPF personnel in the room, heads covered, without shoes and holding automatic weapons.

I approached the desk manned by a receptionist who subjected me to more than an hour of scrutiny: Who was I? Where was I coming from? If from Delhi, why did I not go to Pitampura? What did I know about DJJS? What was the purpose of my visit? I had very little to say. I was just a traveller. The questions were repeated as were the answers even as the CRPF soldiers watched and stayed on the sidelines. It was an opacity I did not know how to handle. Neither at Sacha Sauda nor here had I expected so much resistance. I was flummoxed.

Finally, when they let me visit the prayer hall, it was with a supposed guide keeping close watch. The prayer hall was a disappointment. Just a huge hall with some men and women sitting in huddles, talking to each other. The observer said that the hall was active only when a senior member led the prayers, which did not happen every day as the maharaj was in *brahm samadhi* and his soul was travelling in the upper reaches of the Himalayas. I spent a few minutes at the curios shop, picking up a few books on the history and philosophy of the ashram.

Ashutosh Maharaj was famous for his cows. But I no longer had much time to visit 'the most beautiful *gaushala* in the world' as advertised in billboards. A lot of my time had been spent in the office, fielding banal questions. I felt a bit angry. Did I really look dangerous? Was being a mere observer threatening? A few minutes later, we proceeded to the kitchen and ordered for some milk. The volunteer who served us was in his early twenties. When the guide was not paying attention, had got up to meet someone, I asked the volunteer his story and all he said was that he was there of his own will. He belonged to a prosperous business family and had a brother, but Maharaj and his father had chosen him to serve here. Now this was his life. I noticed women volunteers looking at us. I knew better than to take my questions to them. The guide gestured to me to leave. I did not resist. Once outside the gates, I let out a sigh. This was claustrophobic.

The Radha Soami Satsang Beas at Rayya, less than forty kilometres from Amritsar, thrived through the militancy years. In fact, it was a safe haven from both the militants and the police in those years. The sect remained impartial and its practice was not in opposition to any religion. It never criticised any other practice, book or God. The pursuit of God, it proposed, was individual, private and unhindered by any religion to which a follower might belong. Its followers were former government servants, teachers, public sector employees and others from the educated middle class around the country. It claims a follower base of four million devotees and has acquired land in about five thousand cities and towns around the country and the world. Across Panjab and other parts of north India, a plot outside habitations, lined with a red brick boundary wall, topped with cream paint, displaying the Radhaswami board is a common sight.

The approach to the ashram was a long, wide road leaving the NH 1 just before the bridge of the river Beas. The road led to a parking lot so huge and divided into so many sections that thousands of cars could be parked there. The registration process was not cumbersome but mobile phones were not allowed. The security person informed me politely, 'You have come for satsang, please do not be bothered about the world. We also do not want you to disturb others.'

Small carts ferried us around the huge premises and took us to multiple meditation halls, temporary residential sheds where scores of thousands could sleep, the gardens being cultivated and the elaborate kitchens with the latest technology where sattvik vegetarian food was cooked. The sprawling grounds and the roads were absolutely clean and the services, whether transportation or food delivery, extremely efficient. A giant building in the back seemed inspired by the Khalsa College in Amritsar—a syncretic architecture defining Panjab. The public buildings were all red and white of the kind I had grown up seeing in a public sector town.

This was indeed the wet dream of every public sector employee and every government official who had worked through the

Nehruvian five-year plans. Perhaps the nation could not improve, but here was one heaven that had come true. Or so it seemed. Permanent life membership was available for the asking, provided one showed that one had means. If one did not, one was free to accept help from the organisation. What else could one ask for in life?

Our guide was excited about a new resident of the ashram— Shivinder Mohan Singh, a billionaire who had stakes in Fortis Healthcare, Religare and Ranbaxy Laboratories. The guide and the other devotees too were of the opinion that such a big man having renounced the world of business and joined the ashram augured very well for the future of the organisation. I kept asking myself: why would such a rich man renounce the world and come here? And the answer that struck me most, and I have heard it elsewhere too, in other *deras*, was: '*Jithe tuhade gyan khatam hunda hai na, uthe sada raah khulda hai*'. Now that was an incontestable position. It meant: where your knowledge ends, that is where our path begins. What could one say to that? It was repeated in all situations and posited the old 'rationality versus faith' paradigm and was a dead end since faith could not be contested with rationality.

Still, after my two earlier experiences, the experience at this ashram was a lot better. It was interesting to see how an educated middle class could create a utopia of sorts.

As I left, I looked at the bridge across the river Beas from the other end. Most rivers in the plains have two sandy banks. However, here the ashram on the west side sat on an elevated land and the riverbank there was virtually non-existent. If you do not consider that a river needs to have two sandy banks, then this *dera*, the Radha Soami Satsang Beas, at Rayya, is indeed a miracle. The west bank of the river is embanked with concrete. The east bank floods every year, causing havoc in the nearby villages. There were serious allegations of the ashram using muscle power to increase its holdings, but the biggest revelation came later.

I kept thinking about the phrase: where your knowledge ends, that is where our path begins. In September 2018, Shivinder Singh and his brother Malvinder Singh said in a joint email response to media questions, 'Today we have lost control of all our key businesses—Fortis, SRL and Religare in our committed effort to repay our debts and also as a result of invocation of pledged shares by the banks. This has ultimately led to insignificant shareholding remaining with us in these businesses.'[143]

The Ranbaxy story is many decades old. It began in pre-independence India in Amritsar. Ranbaxy got its name from two cousins, Ranjit and Gurbax, who started a drug distribution firm in 1937. After failing to repay a loan, they had to forego their company in 1947 to a businessman, Bhai Mohan Singh, who had come to Delhi from Rawalpindi in Pakistan after Partition. Under Bhai Mohan, the company launched its first blockbuster drug, Calmpose, in 1961.[144] The drug is a variant of Diazepam, a drug to induce sleep. This was the drug my Mama took most of her life. Now addicts abuse it. Post the time of Bhai Mohan Singh, his son Parvinder took over the company and took it abroad, setting up plants outside India, and expanded the company's horizons beyond pharmaceuticals.

Following Parvinder's death in 1999, Malvinder and Shivinder who were then very young (twenty-seven and twenty-three respectively) found a surrogate father in Gurinder Singh Dhillon known as Babaji or the Sant of Beas, the spiritual head of the Radhaswamis. Dhillon's father was Charan Singh, the earlier spiritual head for four decades, from 1950 to 1991. His sister Nimmi Singh was the Singh brothers' mother.

In June 2008, the Singh brothers hit gold with a close to Rs 10,000 crore cash deal when they sold India's then-largest pharmaceuticals company, Ranbaxy Laboratories, to Japan's Daiichi Sankyo. However, later, Daiichi Sankyo filed cases against the Singh brothers, alleging they had hidden information about the company during the sale. The case is being tried in Singapore. Meanwhile, with the money received, the Singh brothers paid nearly a quarter in taxes, made previous loan repayments and invested two quarters in Religare and the Fortis hospitals chain. They transferred the last quarter to companies owned by the Dhillon family, his wife Shabnam Dhillon, and companies associated with the Radhaswami sect's senior functionaries. It all came crashing down in the next few years.

Religare and Fortis are examples of reckless expansion, and its consequences, the money transferred to Dhillon and associates—which (with interest) is now estimated to be between Rs 4,000-5,000 crore—remains unpaid to the Singhs because Dhillon invested the money in real estate which first boomed and then crashed and then went into a tailspin. In a decade, the Singh brothers had squandered Rs 22,500 crore, lost control of prized possessions such as Fortis Healthcare, once the country's largest hospital chain, and one of the largest NBFCs, Religare Enterprises. Such decimation of a flourishing and diversified empire within a decade is unprecedented in India's corporate history. The story that has emerged since September 2018 reads more like the Singh brothers sleepwalked in somnolence in the last decade.

The turn of events bring up the many issues about how corporate structures in the country, especially in Panjab, are based on kinship and familial ties and the looking up to an elderly figure, in this case, Gurinder Dhillon. It takes place right across the society from small, poor families to the highest echelons of corporate control. When the one looked up to fails, it leads to chaos. There is also the question of why Dhillon was paid so much money without being made accountable for it. Was Shivinder paying the sect so that he could become its head after Dhillon? There might be a path opening where my knowledge ends but I felt just being head above shoulders could have prevented this corporate meltdown. In any case, Shivinder has now returned from the Radhaswamis to sort out worldly matters, but a door remains open. No one should be surprised if he eventually ends up leading the Radhaswamis. It, too, is a corporate entity.

I drove from Amritsar towards the international border to see a new temple that the Badal government was constructing for the Valmiki community. The same road went to Preet Nagar near Lopoke which, before Independence, was established as an artists' village and was dedicated to literature and the arts. The Partition dealt a heavy blow to the village and later militancy affected it. The centre has now lost much of its sheen, though the founder's descendants continue to courageously bring out the magazine *Preet Lari* and have recently started an artist residency programme.

The temple I was driving to was the ashram of Maharishi Valmiki where he supposedly gave shelter to Sita, where her sons Luv and Kush were born, where they went to school, and where they battled with Lord Ram's armies. The site held my interest for three reasons:

a) The narrative that the Hindutva forces have milked for decades now—the origin of the Ramayana. In oral tradition, the Maharishi Valmiki Tirath Sthal dates back to the period of the Ramayana. The epic Ramayana is considered to have been composed here by Maharishi Valmiki.

b) How the SAD–BJP government was patronising a community on identity lines by giving them a centre of worship, but was basically seeking their votes.

c) An echoing of how the Tat Khalsa streamlined the Sikh religion by censuring sects and practices of the time which later led to the Gurdwara Movement and one dominant narrative of Sikh religion. This is theorised by a Sikh scholar Harjot Oberoi in his book *The Construction of Religious Boundaries,* much panned by the Sikh clergy and community.

As I proceeded to the complex, near the gate I spotted an old foundation stone from 2003 laid by the chief minister of Panjab, Amarinder Singh, in his first term. The name of the builder was Deepak. This was the same builder who was constructing the Jang-e-Azadi memorial near Jalandhar. I spotted another plaque which said former Congress CM Beant Singh had laid the foundation for the Luv Kush *paathshala* (school) in 1993. It had taken the government fifteen to twenty-five years to execute the project.

The reason the Maharishi Valmiki Tirath Sthal had taken so long to build was because of a quarter century-old tussle between Mahant Baldev Giri and Mahant Malkeet Nath. The case of the ownership of the *dhuni* (holy fire) and the *paathshala* (school) went to court. For a long time, in spite of many attempts, the court orders favouring Baldev Giri could not be carried out in spite of police protection. The fears of backlash and violence were too high.

However, by September 2014, the Panjab government, with the help of the police, brokered a compromise between both the parties. The *paathshala* went to the Mahant and the state took over the *dhuni*, but that necessitated the building of the temple. The local MLA Gulzar Singh Ranike had been winning since 1997. He was the head of the Akali Dal Scheduled Caste wing, which was an irony, for the representation admitted the caste faultlines of the Sikh community. In 2016, he was the minister of animal husbandry, dairy, fisheries, welfare of the Scheduled Castes and the Backward Classes. He wanted the temple complex built because the Valmiki community was his vote bank.

As I entered the complex, I saw that the gates opened to a huge pool of water and that an ornate, beige sandstone temple in the shape of a cottage was coming up in the middle. It looked remarkably similar to the Durbar Sahib and the famous Durgiana Temple in Amritsar which was a copy of the Darbar Sahib. It was a temple to Sage Valmiki who predated organised religion by many millennia. Yet, the temple was a copy of a Sikh shrine which had been copied by a Hindu temple and was now copied here once again.

Around the *parikrama*—the circumambulation of the sarovar—there were many small and big temples. One was the well where Sita, daughter of the earth, had supposedly disappeared. Two temples were dedicated to Luv and Kush, and there was a Hanuman temple which had an almost 30 feet tall idol, a replica of Vaishno Devi and Lord Jagannath, and a temple of Shirdi Sai Baba. There was a library dedicated to Sage Valmiki, a small frame of Jesus Christ, many temples with shivlings, and some dedicated to Lord Vishnu (since Lord Ram is an avatar of Vishnu).

To the west of the temple were statues of Valmiki and Ambedkar. While Ambedkar stood straight, with the Constitution in his hand, Valmiki was sitting with Luv and Kush in front of him, aiming their arrows placed on bows. Both Valmiki and Ambedkar were pointing towards different directions, one towards Delhi, another towards Lahore. Were these two different paths to truth? Or were they echoing exactly what was going on in the nation: an aspiration for a utopian Ram Rajya now usurped by right-wing forces dragging us into a divisive politics and crony capitalism and another strain pushing us in a direction we can perceive but are unable to practise—the annihilation of caste? Together the image was of the cyclical nature of narratives which trap us all.

The walls of various buildings were full of slogans. No pillar or parapet was left without being inked with words. To me it seemed something I have always sensed while trying to talk about Panjab—the need to state more and more, to explain—because somewhere I, Panjab, and even more so, the subaltern classes of Panjab feel that we have not been heard and are not understood. The dominant discourse has not provided us space to articulate our own reality.

One slogan was: *kutte da kutta vairi, bhra da bhra vairi, choode da chooda vairi, jutt da jutt vairi.* I was intrigued by the directness of the slogan. I must admit it was quite on the mark: a dog is a dog's enemy, a brother is a brother's enemy, a Dalit is a Dalit's enemy, a Jutt is a Jutt's enemy. What struck me was the use of the word 'chooda' for Dalit. That usage was to my mind now illegal, at least by other castes. But what can one do if a Dalit wants to call himself/herself a *chooda*? Is it offensive, I asked myself, or does it unsettle me? Is there some reality I am burying behind the notion of polite language? I can never answer the question because I am complicit with those who have oppressed Dalits. Another aspect that struck me was the comparison with dogs. Again I asked myself if I was hiding behind normal, polite language. Was this a new syntax of protest: to throw politeness out of the window and confront people with the sheer truth of the Dalit condition?

Another board read: 'Sri Sri 108 Satguru Gyan Nath who was released from Chaki no. 16, Amritsar Jail on 10 February 1967 along with forty-five sadhus after incarceration (of two and a half months). On that day a mela is held every year in commemoration.' This again threw up two questions: one, that this jail term seemed to be completely disconnected from the Panjabi Suba movement which had just enabled the formation of the state of Panjab; two, instead of the birth or death date, the date in which the Satguru's biography intersected with the state discourse became his commemorative date. This again shows us how this Valmiki leader's biography originates from a very different set of perspectives as compared to how normal biographies are enshrined. The fight for recognition of the Valmiki community transcends state narratives, for the oppressed know that though nations become independent, as far as they were concerned, the dominant classes merely exchanged power. The community's subjugation remains unchanged.

Then there was the communal pledge which listed the Valmiki contribution to society through many millennia as its prime warriors and architects and sought the blessing of the colour red. Was the colour red inspired by Marxism? But the Adivasis, which is how the pledge identified the community, are a continuous tradition who go far back into time much beyond any later -ism or configuration.

Yet, it is amidst these contradictions that a new identity is created which pushes out all differences and becomes the lived reality. This reality is represented by the 8 feet tall, 800 kilogram bronze statue, with two kilogram gold plating, armed with a quill and a leaf, of Sage Valmiki in a sitting position on a platform in the centre of the temple. The temple was in the centre of a pool of water. Under the statue was written:

*Jo Bole So Nirbhay/Bhagwan Valmiki Maharaj Ki Jai*

The one who utters will be fearless/Praise to His Highness

Valmiki

The jaikara seems very close in rhyming pattern to:

*Jo Bole So Nihal/Sat Sri Akal*

In any case, the installation is nearly complete and all debates and ownership clashes are for now suspended. It would be fascinating to watch how the statue subsumes all the other narratives that have been persistent around the site for many centuries.

In May 2009, I was travelling in Ladakh when news arrived about violence in Jalandhar. The provocation was the killing of a leader of the Ravidassia sect in Vienna allegedly by Sikhs. The followers of the Ravidassia sect are mostly Chamars, who believe in Bhagat Ravidass.

Bhagat Ravidass's text is included in the Sikh holy book, the Granth Sahib. The Dera Sachh Khand is in village Ballan near Jalandhar in the Doaba region of Panjab. When I heard the news then, I realised I did not know enough to understand exactly what was happening and why.

The killing and later violence led to the Ravidassia sect disavowing its Sikh identity and declaring itself to be an independent religion with its own religious text—the Amrit Bani Guru Ravidass Ji, now installed in the new premises of the *dera*. The Granth Sahib is also installed in the older premises.[145]

The larger question is: why do the Chamars seek an independent identity if Sikhism itself was born out of a need to create social equality and break caste divisions? It serves to remember that the Sikhs themselves came from Gurus questioning the rigidity of caste structure and feeling alienated within the Hindu religion or Sanatana Dharma. The birth and spread of sects and religions end up following the same trajectories. At the heart of all quests is the question of identity, of feeling at home and of dignity. The history of the Ravidassia movement goes back to the 1920s when Ghadar Party member, Mangoo Ram, who had lived for a number of years in the US, came back to the country and started the Ad Dharm movement. In 1931, the identity was even part of the Census records and was contested by the Arya Samaj, the revivalist Hindu sect. However, by the time of independence, the movement petered out, only to be rejuvenated in the 1970s, and is now further re-energised.

When I started for the *dera* from Jalandhar, a city known for its sports goods business where most people from the sect work in the leather factories run by Hindus and Sikhs, I spotted cars and bikes with the slogan: *Proud to be Chamar*. It is a caste assertion, a projection of the self that the community was missing because the religion founded to create equality—Sikhism—had not entirely fulfilled its goal. Yet another slogan competed with it; this was from Jutts, and the slogan on the cars was: *Proud to be Akali*. Panjab, I realised, was not only a battlefield of contesting narratives but even of contesting slogans.

I spotted the Ravidassia Dera amidst green fields. It stood out from afar and looked very much like a gurdwara. The Ravidassia sect calls it a Bhawan to distinguish it from Sikh places of worship. I was struck by the similarity between a gurdwara and this Bhawan. Both were the same shape, which was the shape of Mughal tombs. The difference was that unlike most gurdwaras which are covered in white marble or paint, this one was painted pink.

It was monsoon and the new paddy was fresh in the fields. Luckily it was not pouring. I walked down the narrow road wondering how the big rich cars of the *dera* and its followers take this road when they need to reach the Ashram. On the *dera* gate are inscribed the biographies of the earlier four leaders (Sants) of the Ravidassia sect. The security at the gate frisked me. I noticed he was wearing shoes inside the sacred precincts of the Bhawan.

As I entered the Bhawan, in front of me was the statue of Sant/ Bhagat/Guru/Satguru Ravidass. On the left was seated the current leader, Sant Niranjan Dass. Mounted on a stand in front of him was the open Amrit Bani. Facing him were a few women followers catching up with each other. One of the followers told me that earlier, when the sect still revered the Granth Sahib, it was always displayed at a pedestal lower than the Ravidass statue.

Now that they had their own holy book, they displayed it likewise. In a Sikh environment, in a gurdwara, placing the Granth Sahib lower to any idol or text or human would have been sacrilege. Yet, here I learnt that even when the sect was invested in the Granth Sahib, they didn't worry about the Sikh injunction. They didn't care about the Sikhs dictating to them how to project the text. Religious injunctions are also a function of physical might; inside the *dera* the followers do what they deem is right.

The follower guided me to the community kitchen. I took a seat on the mat with other followers. One of the *sewadars* asked me to get up and move to another mat. I wondered why, but did not question the instructions. I noticed that while the others at the *langar* received rotis and dal, the *sewadar* handed me an empty tray with many small containers. He then brought a big bowl of *kadi pakoda*, a gruel made from curd and yellow rice. The *sewadar* also brought me a glass of water, while others drank from a tap on the side of the hall. A bowl of *kheer* followed once I finished the meal. When I got up to wash my tray, the *sewadar* said it wasn't required. My caste was not the same as theirs. I wondered how he knew.

I became conscious of how the people at the *dera* saw me: wearing jeans, English-speaking, maybe a reporter, certainly urban, or as is the normal belief in all sorts of groups in Panjab, from the intelligence wing of the government—*agency*! The *sewadar* telling me that I was not of their caste was an uneasy reminder. It was not at all a put-off or being viewed suspiciously like in other *deras* but the reverse—a regard for my being from a caste the world considered higher than theirs, a sort of deference. I asked myself if the Ravidassias sought independence from the rigid structure of the Hindu caste system which had carried over into Sikhism, why did they have to regard me as higher caste and not just an equal?

The being viewed suspiciously came soon enough. The central ritual to becoming a Ravidassia is for a follower to be initiated through the ritual of *naamdaan*—an initiative of being given a name, instituted by the current Guru. Diagonally opposite the Bhawan is a large hall which can reputedly seat ten thousand people. I went towards the hall, crossed the main gate to the enclosure and from the glass walls I could see a small group of around a hundred people standing inside. I went up to the door when a turbaned security guard stopped me. He had a revolver in the holster on his waist.

'I want to see the *naamdaan* ritual,' I said.

'Are you a Ravidassia?'

'No, I am just interested in seeing how the ritual is performed.'

'Do you want *naamdaan*? Where is your *parchi* (slip)?' There must have been a slip given to the follower who wanted to be initiated. I had none.

'Go away, I don't want to see you inside that gate,' the guard thundered.

I did not want to annoy him. I came out ruing the fact that if I had not gone to the door I might have been able to see the process from this side of the multiple glass doors.

I had one last query. I wanted to know where the first Sant, who founded the sect, had nursed the pipal tree. The story was written on the gate of the main Bhawan, as is the story of subsequent Sants—Sarwan Dass, Hari Dass and Garib Dass. No one seemed to even know the story I was telling and no one knew what to answer. I noticed the dates on their biographies, like at the Valmiki Mandir, were not birth to death, but the period commemorated—the one in which they became Sants of the community.

In the year 1895, Sant Baba Pipal Dass Ji came all the way from Bathinda, from village Gill Patti. He was well-versed in the Granth Sahib and a person of spiritual leaning. People asked him about his powers and challenged him. They said, here is a dying pipal sapling; if you can revive it, we will know you are special. He nursed the sapling and it grew into a tree. Ever since then, the village, and gradually, the community, began revering the Sant and named him Sant Baba Pipal Dass Ji. I found a middle-aged Sikh gentleman whom I had seen earlier near the gate, near the *langar* hall. He seemed mild and approachable. I asked him about the tree and he drew a blank. I then changed tack and asked to see the original home of the Sant in the village. He agreed to take me there.

On the way, about half a kilometre from the Bhawan, we passed a branch of the State Bank of Patiala. All the earnings from the *dera* were deposited there and I was told that it was the richest branch of the bank. Clearly, it was a matter of pride, though I could see how pride for the *dera* was used to create a contest among followers to donate more. Many Ravidassia followers were from the Doaba region, which had a high migration rate. Most families in Doaba had one or more members abroad, hence, a lot of money came in.

I further asked him how he had become a follower of the *dera*. He said he was a headmaster of a high school in Hoshiarpur. At some point in the 1980s, he visited the *dera* with his family and took initiation. I asked him why. 'You see, if you are a stray dog, anyone can throw a stone at you. But if you have a collar around your neck, people will hesitate. They will think you have an owner. I wanted to belong.'

I asked him, pointing at his turban, 'Isn't that a collar the Gurus gave you?'

He replied, 'No, it is not. It was others with this very collar who harassed me. I was a government employee. I faced so many transfers, so much bureaucracy before I became a Ravidassia. Once I followed the sect no one transferred me or bothered me for the rest of the fifteen years of my service. This collar helps.'

I asked him his name. He said, 'Avtar Ram.'

'Ram!' I said, 'Are you a Hindu?'

'Yes,' he answered. 'In my childhood all my friends were Sikh and wore turbans. My mother encouraged me to tie one.'

I know it is no longer common, but still, it wasn't unusual for Hindus to wear a turban like Sikhs. But I did not expect all three identities in one person: Hindu, Sikh and Ravidassia. Panjab is so much about this fluidity of religious identity and practices. Not only did Avtar Ram wear a turban, he also kept long hair.

We walked the brick-lined path to the centre of the village and reached a massive pipal tree with a platform, the *sathh*, under it.

Behind the pipal tree was painted—white on green—the Islamic holy number 786. Opposite the *saath* was a double-storey light blue-coloured house. This was the original home of the Sants. It was locked. I assumed the pipal tree was the original tree but no one could tell.

An old lady appeared at the gate of the adjoining house. I asked her if I could get permission to enter the Sant's house, but she replied that the keys were with the Sant's family. She told me, the Sant's family had split up recently. One of the brothers, 'the intelligent one who knew how to operate a computer and mobile phone', had gone away to Pune. The story put out was that he had gone to manage affairs in the *dera* at Pune.

'I am more than eighty years old,' the lady told me. 'I have seen these Sants from when they were kids. They used to be sitting around morning, afternoon, evening. One day a sweeper woman came and was picking up cow dung from the streets and they said we will help you. They started helping the poor lady. Gradually, some other people joined. Then the second Sant started giving sermons. People listened. They became big,' she said as if she was herself wonderstruck at their growth. 'People started saying they are great.'

'So, aren't they great?' I asked her if she believed in their powers.

'Now the head is Sant Niranjan Dass. I am like a mother to all of them. To me all are lovable. But tell me, how will a mother feel if her sons fight? Yes, they have become very big now. Bhawan and *dera* and *naamdaan* and everything. But they should also stop more people from becoming addicts, drinking liquor, wasting themselves. Good work starts from home. Doesn't it?'

She was right. I had seen liquor shops open not only in this village but even in the ones on the route as early as 9 a.m. when I had arrived. In Panjabi there is proverb, *dive tale anhera* (darkness under the lamp). It is true, often a new light, a new political identity, signals a change in social configuration and gives dignity to its followers, but the groundwork for the improvement of the community still takes a backseat.

Kanshi Ram, who was from Hoshiarpur, founded a political party devoted to the rights of the Bahujans in 1984—Bahujan Samaj Party. In the 1992 Panjab election, which the Akalis boycotted, the party won its highest ever number of seats with the highest ever percentage of votes—nine seats and 17 per cent. This was lower than the percentage of Dalits in the state, but the pity is that even this dwindled over the next elections. The party has not won a single seat in the last three elections. With Kanshi Ram's passing away, the mantle of the party came to rest on an ex-schoolteacher, Mayawati. She steered the party and it performed its best in Uttar Pradesh. On the basis of votes polled and coalitions, Mayawati herself became a short-lived chief minister of UP three times, until 2007, when her party won a majority and she lasted the full term. Sadly, the BSP has not fared well in Panjab.

Since the *deras*, ashrams and satsangs exert influence among their sphere of followers, they are also hugely patronised by political parties who seek their support in elections. In the summer of 2016, Parkash Singh Badal inaugurated a solar power plant spread over forty-two acres on the Radhaswami premises and the government claimed it was the world's largest single rooftop facility with capacity to produce 11.5 MW electricity. In the winter, Rahul Gandhi and Arvind Kejriwal both visited there. Congress and AAP leaders met with Dera Ballan leaders to influence the Doaba votes with an eye on the Panjab Assembly elections. The Dera Sacha Sauda had supported the Congress in 2007, an election the Congress lost. Now they had tilted towards the Akalis who were busy saving it from flak from the Sikhs.

I took the route to Jalandhar from the cantonment side on the NH 1. I wanted to see how, as the road rises on a flyover, the view sets up a frame that to me depicts the complete irony of Panjab's society and its basic building block—education. On the left side, as if metaphorically, one can see the Desh Bhagat Yadgaar Hall—the Ghadar Party Memorial Hall. It is a fine two-storey structure, with a large hall, library and retiring rooms. It serves as a leftist cultural centre of sorts and is a common meeting place for activists, lectures, symposiums and talks.

Since the early 1990s, it is best known for its cultural programme on the first of November every year to celebrate the birth of the Ghadar Party in 1913. On that day, its own and various other drama troupes from across Panjab perform there in the presence of a huge audience. It is a memorial and a reminder to keep the old promise of synthesising socialism and Gurbani for self-determination, and creating a well-educated, emancipated society. Though that is also problematic to me because since 1984, the Sikhs mark 31 October and 1 November as an anniversary of the pogrom. Even if I do not want to relook at those days, friends on social media send condolences to make sure I remember that the Indian state remains unjust. Yet, the very next day I am supposed to feel uplifted by the Ghadar story for justice in the colonial era. Seesawing between these two emotions for the last three decades takes a huge emotional toll and makes you realise how caught up you are in the world's perceptions of what you must feel and how you must feel.

On the right of the same road, right opposite the Yadgaar Hall, is the MBD Neopolis Mall. MBD stands for Malhotra Book Depot. This mall is a result of the money made from many decades of selling *kunjis* or study guides to students to help them with their exams, for which MBD is well-reputed. The MBD study guides even tell you which questions are important, which answers are to be learnt by rote and vomited in exams to pass them. The mall is a symbol of how education can be compromised by rendering teachers unworthy and schools and colleges unimportant.

MBD guides pre-date what is normally believed to be the core reason for our nationwide and Panjab's failure in a state-sponsored, public education system—neo-liberal policies through which the state pulled out of education and private systems have replaced what was earlier the government's responsibility. Having provided a crutch to students and made their life arguably easier, they have created a society of officers and administration who never invested in real education, and perpetuated their follies.

To me this juxtaposition of two competing ideologies, this nostalgia of the past in the Ghadar memorial and brutal greed in the MBD Neopolis sums up Panjab's deep fault line. Every village I have travelled, every *basti* I have been to, the parents of the oppressed pin such hopes in the edifice of education. They are right. After all, Babasaheb Ambedkar gave the slogan: Educate, Agitate, Organise. Yet, the edifice of education itself has been eaten up by the termites of study guides, what the students learn, how they grow up, find jobs or start businesses and lead lives to pull their families out of the quagmire of poverty and caste prejudice, which have made them dependent on crutches and not on educators. We know how synthetic drugs have ruined the physical and mental health of people. Similarly, these study guides have destroyed the education system and the intelligence of our society.

In such a milieu, where is the possibility of the abolition of caste? The system itself is geared towards keeping people trapped in caste structures, making them identity-conscious and keeping them from creating an equal society. No wonder caste plays such a major role in elections, in society, and the identity crisis looms large over Panjab.

*Chapter Twelve*

# *Patit* — Apostate

'What kind of a Sandhu are you if you do not go for the *jathera?*' asked Jasdeep with a twinkle in his eye. I was at a loss to say anything. 'Go claim your roots,' he said.

An individual's need for a family, a tribe, a community, a society, is basic to living. We all seek warmth, we all seek company and we all seek a familiar network as we tackle the world where we do not want to be struggling alone.

In Panjab's folk cosmology, the universe is divided into three realms: *Akash* (Sky) with its *Dev Lok* (Angels); *Dharti* (Earth) with its *Matlok* (Humans); *Naga* (Underworld) with its *Naglok* (Serpents).[146]

The ritual of ancestral worship and the worship of indigenous gods and local festivals has continued into modern-day Panjab in spite of the advent of the Sikh religion. Sikhism was modern in a sense that it was premised on equality. This meant giving up names which denoted the caste of its followers and adopting Singh (lion) for men and Kaur (princess) for women, as last names. Of course, this was a move to organise the religion, specifically the Khalsa, as a fighting force and served the same purpose as a uniform.

Still, there are many shrines in Panjab villages, which represent its folk religion. A popular one is Guga Pir, saviour from snakes. Then there is Seetla Mata, saviour from smallpox and other childhood diseases. There are *jatheras*—shrines to commemorate a common ancestor of those sharing a surname or gotra and all clan ancestors—all across the Doaba region. Some of them have big gates at the entry point to villages proclaiming their presence, which is an aspect of the caste division.

The one Jasdeep asked me to attend was of Baba Kala Mehar at village Mahesri, not very far from both Jasdeep's native village Joge Wala and my own ancestral village Munawan, in Moga district. When I reached the village in March 2016, it was thronging with people who were all gathered at the almost dried-up village pond. They picked some wet mud from its bed and placed it near its walls. Then they washed their hands and proceeded to a white compound which had two domed structures.

People had gathered around the smaller dome and were bowing in front of it. I peeked into it. On its walls was a crude painting of a yellow-robed headless man on a horse, holding up a sword in his right hand and his head in his left palm. The painting reminded me of Baba Deep Singh—one of the most revered and hallowed martyrs among Sikhs. Was this Baba Kala Mehar or Baba Deep Singh?

With this question in my mind, I crossed a marble floor with a crude *shivling* and many lamps lit around it, wheat grains on the floor around it in a pattern and entered the bigger, more recently built dome. Here there were paintings on the walls and a Plaster of Paris statue of an old man standing, eyes half closed, leaning with both hands on a wooden staff on which he had rested his chin. At many places in the dome, near the paintings, was written 'Baba Kala Mehar'. So, this was certainly Baba Kala Mehar, but then why was Baba Deep Singh painted in the older, smaller dome where people had collected?

Baba Deep Singh (1682–1757) was the first head of Shaheed Misl Tarna Dal—an order of the Khalsa established by Nawab Kapur Singh. Jarnail Singh Bhindranwale's Damdami Taksal claims that he was the first head of their order. Baba Deep Singh was born to a Sandhu Jutt family. He lived in the village of Pahuwind in present-day Amritsar district. He was initiated into the Khalsa by Guru Gobind Singh and spent considerable time with the Guru learning weaponry, riding and other martial skills. From the scribe Bhai Mani Singh, he learnt the Gurmukhi script and the interpretation of the Gurus' words. After spending two years at Anandpur Sahib, he returned to his village in 1702 before he was summoned by Guru Gobind Singh at Talwandi Sabo in 1705, where he helped Bhai Mani Singh make copies of the Guru Granth Sahib.

In 1709, Baba Deep Singh joined Banda Singh Bahadur during the Battle of Sadhaura and the Battle of Chappar Chiri. In April 1757, Ahmad Shah Durrani (Abdali) raided Panjab for the fourth time. While Durrani was crossing Panjab on his way back to Kabul from Delhi, the Sikhs relieved him of his valuables and freed the captives he was taking with him. On his arrival in Lahore, Durrani, embittered by his loss, ordered the demolition of the Durbar Sahib. The shrine was blown up and the sacred pool filled with the entrails of slaughtered animals. Durrani then assigned the Panjab region to his son, Prince Timur Shah, and left him a force of ten thousand men under General Jahan Khan.

Incensed at Durrani's act, Baba Deep Singh, seventy-five years old, emerged from scholastic retirement and marched towards Amritsar. As he went from hamlet to hamlet, many villagers joined him. By the time Baba Deep Singh reached Tarn Taran Sahib, thirty kilometres from Amritsar, over five thousand Sikhs armed with hatchets, swords and spears accompanied him. The Sikhs and the Afghans clashed in the Battle of Amritsar on 11 November 1757. In the ensuing conflict, Baba Deep Singh was mortally wounded, with a blow to the neck. Legend has it that he then held his head with his left hand and, killing soldiers on his way, reached the periphery of Darbar Sahib where he breathed his last. The Afghan army was forced to flee and the Sikhs recovered Darbar Sahib. Baba Deep Singh's fifteen-kilogram double-edged sword is still preserved at the Akal Takht.

I asked folks around if the image of the horseman was there because Baba Deep Singh was a Sandhu. No one knew, but apparently, the headless warrior story was valid even for Baba Kala Mehar. In the pecking order of respect, once the Gurus have occupied the top slots, how much room is there for the other revered? A martyr is a good slot. Communities eager to elevate their ancestor try to promote him to martyr level, but that needs a story.

An old man at the *langar* told me the story. Baba Kala Mehr was a cowherd in the times of Raja Salwan, a semi-historical figure. Baba Goraknath came to save Raja Salwan's son Pooran Bhagat who was confined to a well as punishment. Pooran was confined because he refused the advances of his stepmother Loona who, on being rejected, lied to the king that Pooran had tried to seduce her. The king cut off Pooran Bhagat's limbs and threw him into the well. When Baba Goraknath was returning after saving Pooran Bhagat, he is said to have stopped by near Baba Kala Mehar's fields.

When Baba Kala Mehar asked how he could serve Baba Goraknath, Baba Goraknath asked for a dish of *kheer*. It was afternoon, the morning milk had been consumed and there were a few hours before the evening milk could be gathered from his buffaloes. Therefore, Baba Kala Mehar expressed his helplessness. Baba Goraknath asked him to milk a dry buffalo which was brown in colour. Baba Kala Mehar, with faith in Baba Goraknath, milked the buffalo and miraculously, it produced milk. Baba Goraknath, happy with Baba Kala Mehar's faith, blessed him with prosperity, and soon, the reputation of the buffalo spread far and wide.

This reputation drew the attention of the local Bhatti landlords to Baba Kala Mehar. They requested for the special buffalo and Baba Kala Mehar gave her to them for a few days. When Baba Kala Mehar went back to ask for his buffalo, the Bhattis lied that the buffalo had run away. Baba Kala Mehar then called out to her and she broke her chains and came running. The Bhattis lost face in the village. They sought revenge and asked Baba Kala Mehar's companion Veer Jiwan of the Mirasi community—traditional musician and singers—for the vulnerabilities of Baba Kala Mehar. Veer Jiwan replied that Baba Kala Mehar was the master of sixty-four strengths, well-versed in the scriptures and the arts. He was not bothered by hunger, thirst or sleep, and practised deep meditation.

Following Veer Jiwan's reply, the Bhattis tried to bribe the cook, Kalia Brahmin. Kalia told the Bhattis that often, when grazing his cattle, Baba Kala Mehar leant on his staff and went to sleep. Yet, his eyes remained half open and thieves and enemies believed he was awake. This was the cue the Bhattis needed. They attacked Baba Kala Mehar while his cattle was grazing and beheaded him. Yet, his soul, perfected by years of meditation, did not escape, and resurrected his body. Baba Kala Mehar then mounted his horse, chased the Bhattis and slew them.

The old man telling me the story said, 'Even now you can make out Sandhus from how they sleep. Their eyes are half open.'

I tried hard to recollect Baba's sleeping eyes.

Through the middle ages, the legend of the headless horseman was common in Europe and in parts of India, including Panjab, Rajasthan and Madhya Pradesh. Baba Goraknath is estimated by various scholars to have lived sometime between the eleventh and the fourteenth centuries. That was also the time when the Sufi Sajda Nasheens were granting lands to the pastoralists, and in the process, giving shape to the Jutt community. It is likely that during this time some Jutts, perhaps related through marriages and family alliances, would have formed a tribal kinship and consolidated themselves as Sandhus.

Scholars aver that the surname Sandhu comes from the river Indus or Sindhu. Various historians provide various versions of the origin of the Sandhus.[147]

- V.S. Agrawala writes that the *Ashtadhyayi* of Panini mentions janapada Sindhu during the Mahabharata period which may be identified with Sind-Sagar Doab, the region between the Jhelum and the Indus. The Sandhus, in his telling, are descendants of King Satyasandhu. Sindhu Raja Jayadratha had married Duryodhana's sister and fought for the Kauravas in the Mahabharata.
- Bhim Singh Dahiya contended that the ancient Greeks called the Sandhus Sindi (Sindicar of Herodotus) and located them around the river Bosporus.
- Dilip Singh Ahlawat stated that the Sandhus were one of the ruling Jat clans of Central Asia.
- Ram Sarup Joon believed that about 600 years before Christ, the king of Sindhu helped the king of Cyprus, against Babylonia. But later on, the king of Cyprus, on becoming very powerful, drove them out of Sindh. The Sindhar gotra is a derivative of Sindhu. He also mentions that during a conflict between KhanKesh, a province in Turkey, and Babylonia, they sent for the Sindhu Jats from Sindh. These soldiers wore cotton uniforms and were experts in naval warfare. On return from Turkey they settled down in Syria.
- A copper plate inscription of Gujarat, Chalukiya Pulakesi Raja, refers to Tajikas, i.e. Arabs who had defeated the Sandhus and other tribes in west India. Earlier, in 739 CE, they had defeated the Arabs under their king Punyadeva. In 756 and 776 CE, they twice repulsed the Arab naval attacks.

All these versions were feel-good stories. But I was in no position to confirm which of these was true. Even more deeply, I could not commit to a position or a history because just searching for my own grandfather's back story had proved to be an onerous task. What, then, was one to make of these stories? Even in the folk story involving the Bhattis one can clearly see how the rise of the Nath way of thought—which was at that point contesting the Sufi way of life— had demonised the Brahmin. Many histories are sugar-coated tales of power struggle.

The offerings to Baba Kala Mehar at the smaller dome were alcohol, that too, mostly offered by women. The alcohol was of all kinds—IMFL, desi, country. All offerings were poured into a huge blue plastic tank. A tank would fill up in roughly fifteen minutes and would be moved. In a few hours the filled tanks were all lined up. These tanks were then opened to people who made themselves comfortable near what is called the *akhara*. An *akhara* originally meant a space for a gathering of warriors or scholars. In Panjab, it is used for wrestlers and martial arts practitioners but also for singers who stage performances. Maybe Panjab believes that songs too can be weapons of assault.

Aman Rozi and Atma Singh set the ball rolling:

*Je ho ji tu samjhe mahiya,*
*Oho ji main hain nahin …*

What you know of me, my dear,
I am not that.

The line was so true for not only the lyricist and the singer but for the whole of Panjab. It was about perceptions. It was about how the world perceived Panjab and how Panjab did not conform to any of those silos, labels or columns in which the world sought to slot it. It celebrated Panjab's eclecticism.

The singers sang about the agrarian crises, drugs, visas and female foeticide in the way Panjab likes it—naughtily, a bit raunchily and by landing the embedded patriarchy a punch in its gut.

Patriarchy was all around. In the parking lot, the songs were blaring from the speakers. Men sat in the cars. Harjeet, a friend from

Jasdeep's village, and I had two bottles of home-brewed alcohol. We poured them in glasses, bought roasted *chana* and puffed rice from vendors as thousands of men got slowly and steadily drunk. There were no women in these hundreds of vehicles.

Folks told me this was not the only mela for Baba Kala Mehar. The mela was also conducted at Sikhan Wala in Faridkot, Jhoke Saraki in Ferozepur, Baba Marana in Kapurthala, and other places. It was the same with other Jutt gotras. Baba Jogi Pir was of the Chahals, Baba Kaallu Nath of the Romanas, Baba Sidh Kalinjhar of the Bhullars, Lakhan Pir and Pir Baddon Ke of the Cheemas. Then there were the *jatheras*: Sidhsan of the Randhawas, Tilkara of the Sidhus, Sidh Surat Ram of the Gills and Baba Manna Ji of the Shergills. Ancestral worship was a feature of most folk religions. The sense of ownership was shared and not controlled by a centre as in organised religion that also dictated the terms of engagement.

In between, Harjeet and I took a break and walked up to the grounds where the previous day, a kabaddi tournament had been held. The ground was littered with empty syringes and empty medicine strips. Harjeet, whose gotra was Sangha, asked me how I felt about the Sandhu Mela.

I replied, 'I certainly felt that I would like to belong to the surname to which Bhagat Singh and his uncle Ajit Singh Sandhu of Pagdi Sambhal Jutta fame belonged. Yet, if I were to claim a special bond with them, how could I refuse a bond with the SSP Ajit Singh Sandhu of the enforced disappearance and extrajudicial killings infamy who committed suicide? Sandhus might have a lineage, a historical one proposed by historians and a folk history signified by Baba Kala Mehar. Yet, as for myself, I am just a grandson of a Jutt who lost his land, the son of a Jutt who became an ironsmith, and I'm just trying to find my way around the world.'

Around the same time as my visit to the Baba Kala Mehar shrine, on 12 March 2016, the representative body of the Sikhs, the Shiromani Gurdwara Prabandhak Committee, moved a proposal to effectively disenfranchise about ten million *Sehajdhari* Sikhs from the religion and debar them from voting in the SGPC elections in Panjab. The Rajya Sabha too unanimously, and without discussion, passed the Sikh Gurdwaras Act (Amendment) Bill that changed the 1925 Gurdwaras Act. Later, the president of India gave his nod to the amendment. The law has since come into effect retrospectively from 8 October 2003.

The central pillar of the Sikh religion—the Guru Granth Sahib—does not distinguish between the *Sehajdhari*, the *Keshdhari* or the *Amritdhari* Sikh. The first nine Gurus had names such as Dev, Das, Rai and Kishen. They may or may not have grown long hair, and despite what calendars and art portraying the Sikh Gurus depict, there are no authentic images or records. The changes in Sikh philosophy—its followers taking up arms—came in with Guru Hargobind, the sixth Guru. He introduced the concept of *Miri-Piri*, temporal and spiritual, symbolised by two swords, and instructed every Sikh to follow both paths simultaneously. Feeling the need to defend themselves and rise against injustice, Guru Gobind Singh created a band of armed warriors—the Khalsa, or the pure, as discussed in the chapter *Rosh*.[148] Guru Nanak's vision, though iconoclastic, could be considered as a folk form of the Sikh religion. However, from Guru Hargobind to Guru Gobind Singh, the Sikh religion became an organised religion.

This identity formation, part of organising the religion, has been on since the 1870s, as discussed earlier in the chapter *Rosh*, led to communities like Sindhis and sects like Udasis who believe in Guru Nanak alone being ousted from the religion. It also led to sects like the Namdharis who believe in all the Gurus from Guru Nanak to Guru Gobind Singh but also believe in a living Guru being ousted from the Sikh religion.

In practice, the term for turbaned Sikhs is *Keshdhari*, with *kesh*, or *Amritdhari*, those who are initiated and consciously wear all the five symbols. There are many who do not follow the Khalsa tradition but call themselves Sikhs because of their faith in Guru Nanak and in no less measure in Guru Gobind Singh and all the other Gurus. Just that they do not follow the tenet of long hair or wear the steel bracelet.

Some tie a turban per need—when visiting a gurdwara, on family occasions, or just for style. Then there are Sikhs who do not follow any other sect and believe in Guru Nanak and the Guru Granth Sahib but have cut their hair and so are called *Sehajdharis*. The term '*Sehajdhari*' comes from the 1930s when Kahn Singh Nabha published an encyclopaedia that would come to be integral to the Sikh faith: the Sikh *Mahan Kosh*. In the *Mahan Kosh*, Nabha defined the term *Sehajdhari* as a person who remains at ease with liberal thought, who is an integral part of the Sikh community, does not adhere to the *amrit* and *kach-kirpan*, but believes in the ten Gurus and Guru Granth Sahib and has no other religion.

Nabha's definition was based on the understanding of the term: *sehaj*, meaning ease, and *dhari*, meaning follower. Through his definition, he had kept the religion open to Sikhs who could not follow its strict tenets, as well as those not born into the religion but who wanted to adopt the faith. *Sehaj* stood for an easy adoption and belief in the Sikh faith. But Nabha's *Mahan Kosh* definition—which also became the widely understood description among the Sikh community—was not used when key amendments were made to the Sikh Gurdwaras Act of 1925.

The first of these was in 1944, when two definitions were added to the Act. One of these was that of *Amritdhari* Sikhs. The other was the term *patit*. A *patit* was defined as any *Keshdhari* or *Amritdhari* Sikh who had trimmed his or her hair. *Sehajdhari* Sikhs, however, were not defined in the Act until 1959. The 1959 amendment returned the right to vote in SGPC elections to the *Sehajdharis* and also defined the term. Experts hold that this shift to include *Sehajdharis* in the voter list was an attempt to weaken the *Keshdhari* Sikh (read Akali) dominance of the SGPC.

The Act stated that a *Sehajdhari* who followed Sikh rites and rituals believed in the Granth Sahib, was *patit* if hair was trimmed. This definition, which was not consistent with the *Mahan Kosh*, laid the ground for the SGPC's attempts to exclude *Sehajdharis*. It also shifted the definition of the *patit* from an *Amritdhari* or *Keshdhari* not following the rules to all *Sehajdharis* being *patit* because they were supposed to be born and remain *Keshdhari*. With my hair cut, I am now a *patit* and no longer a Sikh.

Bibi Kiranjot Kaur, granddaughter of Master Tara Singh, a member of the SGPC, who manages the Central Khalsa Orphanage in Amritsar, told me that she believed that it was important to define the Sikh. She shared her experience when she was out canvassing for votes for the SGPC elections in the mid-90s. She visited homes of Sikhs who had cut their hair and smoked cigarettes. 'We asked ourselves, are these people going to vote for us?' Kaur asked. 'If Sikhs cannot keep up their own appearance, what right do they have to decide who will run their religious institutions?'

Yet, during the twenty-seven-year-long tenure of Gurcharan Singh Tohra as the head of SGPC, the *Sehajdharis* were allowed to vote. In 1999 when the Sikhs celebrated the 300th anniversary of the formation of Khalsa, the Shiromani Akali Dal was the political face of the community and the SGPC, under its president, Gurcharan Singh Tohra, was the religious face. The two edges of *Miri-Piri*, the central tenet of Sikh religion, were still distinct. That year, the Shiromani Akali Dal's Parkash Singh Badal finally managed to push out Tohra and gained control of the SGPC. This was the corporate takeover of the organised religion. With the BJP government in power, who were alliance partners of the Akalis, the SGPC soon made a case for barring *Sehajdharis*. The 2016 Bill is clear indication that the corporate Sikh religion needs to keep its voter base small so that it can be manipulated.

Through its labelling of Sikhs who have cut their hair or have touched a scissor to their bodies as *patit*, the SGPC has been doing their best to invert the definition of the term *Sehajdhari*. By declaring the *Sehajdharis* as *patit,* as heretics that have lapsed from the Sikh religion, they choose to interpret the law in letter, but not in spirit. The SGPC has, through the courts and the parliament, polarised the rich and immensely meaningful spectrum of Sikh thought by making followers choose between the legacy of Guru Nanak and Guru Gobind Singh.

In 2001, the SGPC secretary Manjit Singh Calcutta moved a resolution to deny the *Sehajdhari* Sikhs the right to vote in the SGPC elections. About two years later, in 2003, when the BJP was in power at the Centre, it issued a notice accepting the SGPC resolution and debarred *Sehajdharis* from voting. That same year, another Akali Dal faction led by Simranjit Singh Mann filed a case in the Panjab and Haryana High Court against the *Sehajdharis'* right to vote. The Sehajdhari Sikh Federation (SSF) later responded by filing a writ petition contesting the case and asked for a stay on the 2006 SGPC elections. As the case dragged on, the elections took place. The *Sehajdharis* did not participate.

In 2008, the SGPC adopted a resolution stating that they would stick to the definition listed in the Gurdwaras Act. According to them, a *Sehajdhari* Sikh was only someone born into a non-Sikh family but was adopting Sikhism. The resolution made it clear that, according to the SGPC, any Sikhs born into Sikh families who changed their *Keshdhari roop* (appearance) would be considered *patit,* as would be the *Sehajdharis* who, after adopting the faith, cut their hair. Their resolution was condemned by the SSF who said that the definition was against the teachings of the Sikh religion.

Meanwhile, the case dragged on. In September 2011, a little over two weeks before the SGPC elections, the United Progressive Alliance government at the Centre issued another notice withdrawing the 2003 decision to debar the *Sehajdharis* from voting. In December 2011, a three-judge bench of the Panjab and Haryana High Court ruled in favour of the *Sehajdharis*, and restored their voting rights. The decision nullified the 2011 elections. The SGPC approached the courts, asking for the decision to be reversed. Without legitimate elections, the SGPC was forced to carry on with a working committee, and not as a full-fledged body.

'A child born in a Muslim family is Muslim, in a Hindu family is Hindu, and in a Christian family is Christian,' said P.S. Ranu, the national chief of the SSF. 'What if a child born in a Sikh family decides to not grow his or her hair? What will be the religion of the child?'

Ranu has been railing against the SGPC for several years. He considers the SGPC's actions proof of it being influenced by the SAD and the Hindu right wing, which wishes to further dilute the other religious minorities. 'For the sake of their vested interests,' Ranu said, 'the Akalis have played into the hands of the Rashtriya Swayamsevak Sangh.' The RSS interference in Sikh affairs, including the creation of the Rashtriya Sikh Sangh, is a case study on how one right-wing organisation can push another diktat-bound community to take a stand against its own people.

For almost two decades, the *Sehajdharis* have been jostled in and out of the Sikh community, sometimes through challenges to their identity, and other times, through amendments to the Gurdwaras Act. Through most of this time, they have retained the right to vote in the SGPC elections, but have not been allowed to do so. Following the Rajya Sabha decision, and the president's nod, that has changed. The parliament move negated a December 2011 judgement by the Panjab and Haryana High Court that restored the *Sehajdhari* voting right.

This has raised a key question facing the Sikh community: who, exactly, is a Sikh? The term Sikh means *shishya* (student). In the wake of the 9/11 bombings in the US and the consequent attacks on Sikhs, mistaken as Arabs, there is a growing movement to propagate the understanding that Sikhs are a different faith and are recognisable through their turbans and beard (*keshdhari*). Their anxiety is palpable, but what happens to those Sikhs who have cut their hair? Do they become *patit*? Obviously, the sweet definition of Sikhs as learners has no space in the new form of the organised and corporate Sikh religion.

In 2008, the SGPC disallowed Bhai Ghulam Mohammad Chand, a descendant of Guru Nanak's lifelong friend and musician Bhai Mardana—arguably the first Sikh—from singing a devotional song in the Golden Temple because he was not *Amritdhari*. Noted Panjabi writer Waryam Singh Sandhu told the story of Bhai Des Raj from his village Sur Singh. After Baba Deep Singh had reclaimed the sanctum sanctorum from Ahmed Shah Durrani's army, over the next two years the Sikhs collected money and asked Sikh leader Jassa Singh Ahluwalia to lay the foundation stone of the Temple.

The community gave the responsibility of constructing the current Golden Temple to the Gur-Sikh *khatri* moneylender Bhai Des Raj (Gur-Sikh means the person is a Sikh of the Guru even if he is not a practising Sikh). With the current ruling, even Bhai Des Raj wouldn't be eligible to vote. Neither would one of the most famous poets of Guru Gobind Singh's darbar, Bhai Nand Lal, be eligible. Nor would Bhai Kanhaiya, the water bearer in Guru Gobind Singh's battles. There are thousands of such stories of the togetherness of spirit and the syncretic nature of Sikh thought and practice.

To me it is fascinating how, when it came to a crisis of definition, the highest management body of the Sikhs, the SGPC, chose to take recourse to the courts of a 'secular' country. The SGPC and the Sikh community, which remain wounded by the destruction of the Akal

Takht—the timeless seat of justice, at least for its followers—during Operation Blue Star have now for years been going to the courts of a secular nation to get justice, to even define and identify who is a Sikh and who is not. This is when many Sikhs contend that for three decades and a half the courts of the nation have not done justice to the community over the 1984 pogrom. These two and the river water issues are the greatest grievances of the community ever since India became independent, yet it is to this nation's courts that the SGPC scrambles to, whenever challenged. With every victory of identity the SGPC scores in the secular courts, it undoes and divides the community a bit more.

Any community or religion looks to increase its sphere of influence and grow the basis of its thought, and its numbers. While the basis of the Sikh faith—selflessness and service—are widely known, through its diktats and orders and at the same time undercutting the community interests, the SGPC has greatly compromised the religion. In a world which has not been able to shirk off the influence of religion on communities, which often operates through the religious filter, given the fact that the Sikhs are such a miniscule community, further dividing it on the basis of long and short hair serves only the purposes of a few who gain from this division, not the community as a whole. They are the same custodians of religion who often claim that the religion is under threat! It bewilders me how the SGPC is happy to lose more than one-third of its followers on the basis of the definition of a *patit*.

It is also a matter of concern for Indian courts where the destruction of Babri Masjid, which is a religious issue, is masked as a land dispute (which I oppose), or Sabarimala where admission of women to the sacred shrine is a religious issue masked as a rights issue (which I support), or in the case of admission to an SGPC medical college where a religious issue is masked as an education issue (which amuses me). This way we citizens actually use a via media to score judgements in our favour without considering how we weaken our own systems and compromise them.

In the early 2000s, an SGPC-run medical institution, Sri Guru Ram Das Institute of Medical Sciences and Research in Amritsar, denied admission to a young student, Gurleen Kaur, for its MBBS course because she had plucked her eyebrows and was hence 'no longer a Sikh'. The institute enjoyed minority status courtesy a Panjab government notification, which enabled the SGPC to reserve 50 per cent of its seats for Sikh students.

Given the sensitive nature of the matter, the court summoned not only lawyers but also Sikh intellectuals and scholars to deliberate. After listening to an array of views, in May 2009, the Panjab and Haryana High Court ruled in a landmark case on defining Sikh identity. The court concluded that it could take a decision on Sikh identity only according to the Sikh Rehat Maryada—the code of conduct and conventions—and not the scriptures which do not define the identity because the Gurus had set up the religion as an open inclusive space inviting people from all communities to learn, to be shishyas. The judgement reads: '… they all lead to one unambiguous answer, namely, that maintaining hair unshorn is an essential component of the Sikh religion.' It goes on to add:

'… even an act of dishonouring hair is taken as a tabooed practice. An act of dyeing one's hair is treated as an act of dishonouring hair. It would, therefore, not be incorrect for us to conclude, that maintaining hair unshorn is a part of the religious consciousness of the Sikh faith.'

This is how the Khalsa's code became the norm for the larger Sikh community. The decision cost Gurleen Kaur her seat at the college. The diaspora hailed the verdict because worldwide it is engaged in legal cases with foreign governments over the issue of turbans. The verdict also bolstered the SGPC resolve to bar *Sehajdhari* Sikhs from voting in their elections. But most of all the verdict reduced the vast ocean of Sikh thought and philosophy to the presence or absence of hair on one's body. The reductive logic in both cases and the definition by those who manage one of the most modern religions in the world is galling.

The question of the right to vote for the SGPC is relevant only so far as the Sikh community is aware that it is giving up its responsibility of its gurdwaras to factions close to the SAD. In truth, most Sikhs do not care much for the SGPC elections. They visit the gurdwara because of their faith and not to score political brownie points.

Those Sikhs who do not engage in gurdwara politics still contribute to the gurdwaras because per the Sikh tradition one is expected to offer a *dasvand*—one-tenth—of one's earnings for the cause of the community. Not everyone gives one-tenth; some give less, some give a lot more, but the money goes to the Guru's *golak*—funds. However, the control over the contributions to the *Guru ki Golak* (the gurdwara coffers) is with the SGPC.

Now I could see why, during the whitefly infestation *rail-roko*, the striking farmers and labour were denied *langar* by the gurdwara in Pathrala. The gurdwara, named after the Patshahi Dashmi (the tenth Guru), was just forty kilometres from Damdama Sahib, one of the revered Takhts (seats) of the Sikhs and associated with Guru Gobind Singh. Upon my asking as to why *langar* was being denied to the protestors, a *sewadar* replied, 'Orders from above!'

The stance was political. The SGPC, controlled by the Badals, did not want to support those agitating against the Akalis, or really, the Badal government. By not offering *langar* and overturning the institution, the SGPC and the Akalis were abusing their power and in the process sending out a signal that they did not really care about the community.

*Langar*, specifically the *sangat-pangat*, is a fundamental tradition of the Sikhs. Guru Nanak instituted it to create equality among people.

'Sangat' stands for association and 'pangat' for rows. The idea was that in the new religion there would be no discrimination over religion, caste, class, gender, and people would sit in rows to partake of the *langar*.

Most visitors who tell you they have been to Panjab are the ones who have gone on spiritual tourism to the Darbar Sahib at Amritsar. For them and for every Panjabi, one of the biggest highlights of Darbar Sahib is the *langar* that feeds 50,000 to 100,000 people per day. The Britain-based Sikh organisations Khalsa Aid and United Sikhs have now assumed mythical proportions, especially after their service in Iraq, Syria, to the Rohingyas in Myanmar, and during the 2018 Kerala floods.

The popular belief is that if you start a *langar* you will never be short of funds to support it. It proves true time and again. *Langar* is based on the *dasvand*, one-tenth of one's income that each Sikh is encouraged to contribute for the betterment of the community. Though contributions are uneven at an individual level, the total contribution to gurdwaras is still huge. The contributions come from the faith that Sikhs and others have in the institution.

*Langar*, like taxes, ought to benefit the people, directly or indirectly. While Sikhs seem to do well when the need for *langar* arises from natural disasters or wars, the community's response to the agrarian crisis left much to be desired per their own religious injunctions. The community that holds Guru Nanak's teachings as its pillars—*kirt karna*, *naam japna* and *wand chakna* (honest labour, remembrance of God and sharing with others)—was now found wanting. It was because the institution of religion, the gurdwaras, had been usurped by the politics of the SGPC.

The SGPC's declared annual budget is about Rs 1200 crore. They spend it on the upkeep of gurdwaras, on running educational institutions, on hospitals, on salaries for employees and on maintenance work. A small portion of their work is community-oriented. The SGPC has hardly done anything to fix the much larger issues of entire Panjab's crumbling health and education system. While the SGPC could claim that was the government's job, given that the brunt of the crumbling infrastructure is being borne by the community, their intrusion is morally warranted. After all, isn't the true purpose of the Guru's *golak* to help the community and not cover the gurdwaras in marble, which is what it often does?

In the last thirty-five years, the SGPC has done very little to help the victims of the 1984 anti-Sikh pogrom in whose name political parties have been waving flags and gathering votes all these years. The nation state has denied them justice, but what has the community done for them? Isn't the SGPC or the Delhi Gurdwara Prabandhak Committee responsible for their welfare? Isn't the SGPC responsible for helping the families of those who became victims of forced disappearances and extrajudicial killings?

The SGPC runs a forty-acre organic farm near Amritsar and now claims that the vegetables for its *langar* comes from this farm, but what is their participation in alleviating the agrarian misery of Panjab? Have they ever stepped in to prevent the suicides that have taken place in the countryside? Have they helped the families of the victims? No, they could not even allow the farmer and labour agitation in Pathrala to have *langar* at the gurdwara. Has the SGPC not allowed village gurdwaras to be first divided on the lines of the Akali and the Congress under its aegis and then on the basis of caste, again under its aegis? What has it done to make communities that feel they are discriminated against within the Sikh religion bind with the religion? What has it done to eradicate caste divisions? What has it done to stop even cremation grounds being divided on caste lines? The hypocrisy of the top religious body of the Sikhs is apparent.

Even now, the SGPC does not want to admit the corporate hold on the management body. Its apologists and many in the community contend that *patits* and *Sehajdharis* are only banned from voting and that no one considers them lesser Sikhs otherwise. That is doublespeak. The fact is that voting for SGPC is directly linked with SGPC controlling the *Guru ki Golak*. Will the SGPC accept that? Will it accept that children born in Sikh families who do not keep long hair to qualify as Sikhs should not donate to the gurdwaras? Yet, the community, too, is apathetic to how it has been manipulated to serve the SGPC's interests. There was a brief spark against the SGPC's nepotism when the community rose up for the Sarbat Khalsa in 2015, but it dissipated quickly. The fact is the SGPC today is the Mahant of yore and unless the community rises to create a Singh Sabha 2.0, the control of the Akalis on the SGPC is going to leech the community.

In the 2011 Census, Panjab's population was twenty-four million, of which Sikhs comprised fourteen million—about 60 per cent. The 2011 SGPC voter list had fifty-five lakh *Keshdhari* voters—a third of the number of eligible Sikhs in Panjab. The rest of the Sikhs, above seventy lakh in Panjab alone, and approximately one crore worldwide, who have ever touched a scissor to their bodies, are *patits* and non-Sikhs. This satisfies another question that the Supreme Court had asked in January 2016 on another admissions-related case: is Sikhism a minority religion in Panjab? The answer now is yes and that means SGPC will continue to enjoy the benefits owing to its minority religion status; just that it is not only the nation's minority religion but also Panjab's minority religion.

Through this, Panjab, where a religious minority was a majority, has lost its unique status in the world. This reverses the very reason why, in the 1950s the Akalis backed the Panjabi Suba movement which resulted in the truncated state of Panjab. That is how the SGPC has turned its back on the history of its own people. What can be more self-defeatist than the beauty and magnificence of a faith being reduced to a bodily artefact—long hair. This is how the management of the Sikh religion has failed its own people and is not accountable to them.

In 2015, the SGPC pardoned Gurmeet Ram Rahim for the 2007 blasphemy through a Rs 100 crore deal brokered allegedly at actor Akshay Kumar's home in Mumbai. That is when Sukhbir Badal had, without consulting the SGPC President Avtar Singh Makkar, got the Akal Takht Jathedar Gurbachan Singh to issue the pardon. Later on, the SGPC had issued advertisements in leading newspapers, paying Rs 90 lakh from its own coffers, which are really the community's funds for the exercise.

If this is how the SGPC is going to uphold the Sikh community's interests, then I might just be relieved of a huge burden when SGPC throws me out of the Sikh religion. The question of the *Sehajdhari* right to vote is a question of identity. The question is, who defines one's religion? Is it the follower or is it the entity that controls the religious institutions? Is religion a set of rituals or is it the sum of its values? The Durbar Sahib, which is visited by followers of all religions, has gates on all four sides. These gates signify equality: people of any class, caste, gender and religious faith are welcome. Yet, the temple has only one causeway to reach the sanctum sanctorum. As of now, the Badals, through the Akalis, through the SGPC, control this causeway. This is their corporate control of the religion.

Maybe it is just as well that the SGPC has no jurisdiction on gurdwaras outside Panjab, Himachal Pradesh and Chandigarh. Haryana, too, has recently sought its own SGPC. Sikhs from south India and Jammu no longer oblige the SGPC. The Sikh community is divided and it is being manipulated. The community does challenge representations of itself, that it believes compromises its image, by anyone outside the community—be it a movie, a speech or discourses common in the RSS and Hindutva circles. Yet, until it does not reflect on and plug its own internal divisions and its undermining by its own religious bodies and recognise the double-bind in which it is caught, it might fragment further. By continuing to donate to the *Guru ka Golak* the SGPC controls, the community keeps them in power. That is the religion's fault line today.

By the summer of 2016 the people of Panjab had moved past the SYL doublespeak by the AAP and were willing to overlook the outsider label. Sucha Singh Chhotepur, the convenor of the party, had rallied a good number of volunteers to take AAP's cause forward. Though there was cynicism, AAP seemed to be gaining ground. Slogans started appearing on the walls of rural homes: *Kejriwal, saara Panjab tere naal* (Kejriwal, the whole of Panjab is with you.)

The AAP election symbol—the humble broom—was everywhere. Bhagwant Mann, the most eloquent AAP speaker, made enough references to how the broom was not only a symbol but even a metaphor for what the party stood for—wiping corruption and scattering the opposition like the sticks of the broom. Many AAP leaders were now in touch with the diaspora and found enough support, both monetary and moral. Many from the diaspora started influencing their networks and villages and urged relatives and friends to support the AAP. Since the migrant son or daughter is considered the successful and wise one and is respected, the kinship listened.

The AAP announced an early schedule to declare its nominees for each of the 117 seats, to give each ticket holder at least six months to prepare for the election. This was unprecedented and got the people curious. In the beginning of July, in Amritsar, it launched its ambitious, smart and well-crafted Youth Manifesto. The manifesto, launched in Amritsar, whose cover page had the picture of the Durbar Sahib, was a fifty-one point document that addressed most of the youth's concerns quite meaningfully—education, health, drug de-addiction, employment, skills training and so on. It promised action on the supply chain of drugs within a month of coming to power, and twenty-five lakh jobs for the youth. It was ambitious but it seemed that the AAP had come prepared to deliver. People sensed AAP's preparation. It sent a wave of expectation among the people.

But AAP didn't know Panjab's terrain. It knew its rival Akali's strategy even less. The Akalis raised an objection: on its cover page a broom was placed on top of the Durbar Sahib. Indeed, the AAP logo with the broom was right on top, over the text announcing the name of the document, and the Darbar Sahib covered most of the lower half of the page with Kejriwal standing, head covered, hands folded, and another broom on the side. The broom, the Akalis held, was an insult to the sanctum sanctorum. The Akalis said that they had never placed the Durbar Sahib on their election manifesto, not even for the SGPC elections. This caused a flutter. The issue of the broom became the highlight of the manifesto. No one read the manifesto itself. On top of it, the AAP leader Ashish Khetan compared their manifesto to the Granth Sahib, the Gita and the Bible, drawing further jeers from Panjab.

Politics could not get funnier than this, but this was dead serious. The AAP did not know what had hit them. Chhotepur and Sandhu, in charge of the manifesto committee who had worked hard through the Bolda Panjab dialogues to collate people's issues, evaluate them and propose solutions, denied having seen the final manifesto in advance. Kejriwal did a penance of sorts by washing vessels in the *langar*. But once again, the AAP cookie crumbled. So much of our elections is a game of perceptions, but the incident also confirmed my view that AAP had squandered the opportunity to understand Panjab.

The AAP had verbally committed tickets to multiple people in each constituency. They had often claimed they had no money to fight the elections, hence set goals for every aspirant: print posters for Rs 5 to 10 lakh and put them up in a stated number of villages. People who were made promises began spending money, and in the posters started placing their own name and photograph to create the impression that they were popular and a good choice for the ticket. As another step forward to their ambition, many took to the grapevine to spread stories against their deemed rivals in the constituency. Soon the landscape, already a landmine of state and anti-state counter narratives, became an enmeshed jungle of stories. The AAP wave started to waver.

In the first list of nineteen candidates, seven candidates were from other parties who had switched sides and some others were not entirely acceptable to everyone in their constituencies. People realised newcomers had lesser chances of securing nominations. Party politics was feeding the supply of candidates even in a new party. The bickering rose, volunteers and local leaders started using spy cameras and other recording devices to bust rivals. The jungle of stories grew denser, the fear of recording devices caused panic and the people were at a loss. Chhotepur seemed incapable of being able to contain the damage.

By the end of August, Kejriwal sacked him.

Upon being sacked, Chhotepur held a press conference in which he revealed that when the manifesto fiasco had taken place, Kejriwal had asked him to own it up. He had replied that if he did that, he would be sacked from the Sikh *panth*. Kejriwal had responded, 'So what if they throw you out of the Sikh community?'

The revelation met with a huge uproar because it showed that Kejriwal had very little understanding of the dynamics of the Sikh community. Kejriwal, born urban, a non-Sikh, a believer in the Vipassana practice which has Buddhist origins, perhaps a believer in other religious practices, was attempting to establish his political venture in a Sikh-dominated state, but had no clue what it means to a Sikh to remain part of the community. He was too removed from the earth of Panjab, its traditions, its culture and its social psychology. Though the Sikh religion is arguably one of the most modern, its followers place a high value in belonging to the community—a sort of tribalism. The Sikhs consider excommunication the ultimate insult—loss of purpose of life itself.

One can debate this endlessly but in elections people are looking for a party, a candidate, who would root out earlier evils and usher in reforms, but they do not want these at the cost of their deep beliefs or by exposing their insecurities. Kejriwal was dealing with a deeply feudal society, entrenched in religious beliefs. He was a misfit, like the Left had been earlier when they preached irreligiosity and failed to convey their message to the people. There was a vast gap between what the AAP leadership imagined Panjab to be and the reality of Panjab. This gap was never bridged because though they had time, the AAP never got down to learning about Panjab.

That is why in the previous section, I found it hard to accept, to commit in writing, that I was *patit*. I was pained at how the community had so easily, so casually, thrown me and another one crore people like me out of the community. This is not to say that the Sikhs themselves do not break the Rehat Maryada and always follow its strict injunctions.

They break it all the time—cutting hair, some by smoking, some by doing drugs, and in various other ways. All of these actions risk excommunication. Yet, it does not happen or has only happened now, in the case of the *Sehajdharis* being declared *patit*. While I am not a practising Sikh as per how Sikhs should behave or conduct themselves according to the path that the Gurus laid down and that the Granth Sahib calls for, yet, to be thrown out and to be labelled an apostate or a heretic is a bitter pill to swallow.

That is why, whether it was Zail Singh, former president, Surjit Singh Barnala, former chief minister, Buta Singh, former union minister, or even Maharaja Ranjit Singh, the greatest emperor of the Sikhs, they had all wilfully accepted punishment and not risked being excommunicated. That is why the Dera Sacha Sauda chief being pardoned pricked the Sikh community. That is why Sucha Singh Chhotepur, who had, in the early 1980s, sworn a *Marjeevdian di Sounh* (Fight Unto Death) along with Jarnail Singh Bhindranwale, but had not sacrificed his life during Operation Blue Star and had carried the betrayal of his own promise in his heart, could not afford to be excommunicated and lose face.

Over the last few centuries, other religions of the book— Christianity and Islam—have split vertically. Christianity now has many divisions: Catholic, Protestant, Orthodox and others. Islam too has divisions: Sunnis, Shias, Ahmediyas and so on. The way the Jutts have handled gurdwaras, where Dalits and Mazhabis and Ravidassia and others, are discriminated against, resulting in them joining *deras*, the way the SGPC has handled the idea of *Keshdhari*, *Sehajdhari* and *patit*, the day people start asking for the accounts of their *dasvand*, the community could also vertically split into camps. I wonder if that is the goal of the community, if that is what Guru Nanak or Guru Gobind Singh would have wanted.

It is a question the community needs to ponder upon.

The issue with the Sikh religion is not just that it is corporate, but also that it is a bad corporate. In these changing times the SGPC is not interested in growing, in keeping its flock together, in bringing about clarity to those who follow the Sikh religion. Engrossed in the management of gurdwaras, looking for ways to collect more money, the SGPC hardly works towards truly bringing the Gurus's messages to the people.

Though all religions have their strong points, as a religion based on equality and justice, the Sikh religion has a unique voice and unique stories, well-documented in time and place, which could be very relevant to this age where corporate greed and right-wing politics is gaining ground. Yet, in its anxiety to define itself as unique, the SGPC has gone ahead and created further confusions in how history is mapped and events are celebrated.

Most of her life Mama lived far away from Panjab. One of her most tangible connections to Panjab was the *jantri*—the Sikh calendar. In every visit to Panjab she would make sure she got a copy of the new *jantri*. She would map every date of significance, every festival on her *jantri*. So, Diwali was per her *jantri*, Baisakhi was per her *jantri*, the Gurus' birth and death anniversaries too per her *jantri*.

Instead of the Gregorian solar calendar we follow these days, the *jantri* was based on the Bikrami lunar calendar. About two decades back, around the 300th anniversary of Khalsa, a person called Pal Singh Purewal—a Canada-based engineer and calendar expert—decided that the Bikrami calendar was too Hindu and he needed to create a Sikh calendar. There were precendents in the eighteenth century in Banda Bahadur, in the twentieth century in Gian Singh who was the first to use *Nanakshahi Samvats* along with those of *Bikrami Samvats* when he wrote the *Twarikh Guru Khalsa*.

The epoch of the new Sikh calendar was the birth of the first Sikh Guru, Guru Nanak, in 1469, and the Nanakshahi year commences on 1 Chet—that is 14 March in the Gregorian calendar. By denying any history prior to Guru Nanak, the Nanakshahi calendar denies the Sikh religion the context of it being a syncretic space based on whatever religions preceded it from the begining of time, so to say. The Nanakshahi calendar is based on the *barah mah* (twelve months), composed by the Sikh Gurus, and reflects the changes in nature which are conveyed in the twelve-month cycle of the year. Yet, a history devoid of its precedents—with no grounding in the Gregorian calendar and no mention of the Vedic Age and the Indus Valley Civilisation—was the version of history propagated in textbooks in the state and in the Virasat-e-Khalsa museum in Anandpur Sahib.

The strength of the Nanakshahi calendar is utterly pragmatic—festivals fall on definite dates. That is practical, given the confusion created between the Gregorian calendar and the Bikrami calendar due to which our dates of festivals and anniversaries shift every year. However, it contravenes a basic pragmatism which is the premise of the Gurus who spoke against the Hindu life stages of Vanaprastha and Sanyasa—which starts when a person hands over household responsibilities to the next generation, assumes an advisory role, gradually withdraws from the world and then finally seeks spiritual liberation (moksha). The Gurus, who emerged in the time of social and religious turbulence, emphasised that life and moksha were here and now and must be dealt with squarely. I wonder how, by making a religion stand out of the context of its origins, denying the history that precedes it, one could make the religion relevant to this time and space.

In any case, that pragmatism too was not upheld when the Nanakshahi calendar was implemented in 2003. The Sikh community still split between the Bikrami and Nanakshahi calendar—two of five Takhts (Nanded and Patna) followed the Bikrami calendar—wondered when Guru Gobind Singh's birthday was and what was the date that marked the martyrdom of his sons. Traditionally, the Gurus's birthday is in the first week of January and the sons's martyrdom is at the end of December. Amidst all this confusion, Mama just stopped using the *jantri*.

In 2010, the SGPC hit upon a compromise. It moved the start dates for the months so that they coincided with the Bikrami calendar and changed the dates for various Sikh festivals so that they were based upon the Nanakshahi calendar. In 2014 this led to two birthdays of Guru Gobind Singh in January and December of the same year. In 2017, both the birthday of Guru Gobind Singh and the martyrdom of his sons fell on the same day (25 December) which is also Christmas per the Gregorian calendar. In 2018 the SGPC was forced to move the 'Gurgaddi diwas' of Guru Hargobind from 8 May to 7 June, following objections from Giani Jagtar Singh, head granthi of Darbar Sahib. There have been calls by various Sikh factions to move back fully to the Bikrami calendar or to adopt the original Nanakshahi calendar. This has led to confusion within the Sikh community.

It is strange that a religion whose belief is that God is Akal—out of the bounds of time—has so easily slipped into errors on temporal time. Obviously, the calendar needs work, or perhaps should never have been devised. The shifting dates of festivities of the Bikrami calendar that even the Gurus followed was good enough.

Yet, the SGPC perpetuates its errors as a bad corporate purely because the Sikhs remain high on symbolism, but in fact blindly believe the Granth Sahib and the institutions that are under SGPC control. The simple teaching that the Gurus gave was: open your eyes, listen closely, use your senses and think. But it does not seem to have percolated to the masses in five hundred and fifty years.

The real identity battle of Sikhs is not with those myriad Hindutva groups that keep popping up in Panjab to challenge them—Hindu Takht, Hindu Sangharsh Sena, Bajrang Dal, and many that call themselves Shiv Sena of one variety or another. The Shiv Sainiks of

Panjab are not even cognisant of the fact that the term 'Shiv Sena', as coined by Bal Thackeray, is from Shivaji Maharaj, the Maratha hero. They believe instead that they are Lord Shiva's forces.

During my travels, the Shiv Sena declared a Lalkar Rally on the Beas bridge on 25 May 2016. While the Sikhs started gathering the night before, the next day hundreds of Sikhs appeared with naked swords shouting slogans 'Khalistan Zindabad' and '*Bhindranwale teri soch te, pehra deyange thok ke*' (Bhindranwale, we shall guard your thoughts with our lives)! It turned out to be a damp squib because of a no-show by the Shiv Sena activists.[149] Yet, it served the purpose—of showing Sikhs as favouring Khalistan. The same accusations that have dragged on for three decades.

However, almost every year on the Operation Blue Star anniversary there are clashes between Hindutva groups and Sikhs over religious posters being torn and the name of Jarnail Singh Bhindranwale being invoked, with Hindutva groups sloganeering against, and Sikhs in favour. The Hindutva groups celebrate Indira Gandhi, the former CM Beant Singh, General A.S. Vaidya, General K. Sundarji and the Sikhs oppose these celebrations. Often, in these clashes, the Hindutva groups are on one side and the Sikhs on another, sometimes supported by Muslims and Dalits. Though jarring, these are regular and almost predictable irritants to Hindu-Sikh relations of Panjab because the Hindutva groups themselves are on the fringe of society.

The real clear and present danger to Sikh identity is the same as was a century and a half ago: Panjab as the laboratory of Hindutva politics. This was an area that Lala Lajpat Rai and Indira Gandhi too had trodden. The original question on the identity of Sikhs (chapter *Rosh*) keeps changing form, but becomes even more relevant now: are Sikhs a sword arm of the Hindus? A century back, the Singh Sabha-backed Gurdwara Reform Movement could wrest the gurdwaras from the Mahants. Now the Sikh clergy under the auspices of the SGPC and an avowedly Sikh party (the Akalis) are themselves compromised. The Akalis are partners with the BJP and control the SGPC.

As an organisation, the RSS, founded in 1925, is almost as old as the Akalis. Yet, while the freedom struggle was on, unlike the Akalis who were making great sacrifices, the RSS remained obsequious to the British. Hindutva as an ideology has created many threads: the Arya Samaj who, in Panjab, through language politics, opposed the Akalis and the Sikhs; the Vishwa Hindu Parishad; the Hindu Mahasabha; and the nationwide organisation, the RSS. Their visible face now is the BJP, but the RSS is more than the BJP's parent organisation. The RSS is a version of the Hindutva idea that believes it has a right to interfere in every minority community's belief and worldview to destabilise the minority, mould it, and align it with the grand dream of a Hindu Rashtra.

After Operation Blue Star and Indira Gandhi's mis-steps and through its legacy, the RSS knows better than to challenge the Sikhs. So, they do the reverse—they operate subversively in Panjab. They embrace the Sikhs, and through that they seek to appropriate them. By accepting the Sikhs—their Gurus, their belief system and their rituals—the RSS leaves the community with little option to assert themselves as a distinct voice. The idea is to subsume the Sikh religion within the larger Hindu fold. Even at RSS Ghar Wapsi programmes mostly for Christians, the RSS allows them to join either the Hindu religion or the Sikh. After the militancy years, the RSS *shakhas* had dwindled in the border districts, but the RSS has now been on a drive to revive them.[150]

The RSS has also spawned the Rashtriya Sikh Sangat which attracts Sikhs who seemingly are not so bothered about the identity question. The larger push is to dilute the Sikh identity so much that they stop asserting themselves as different from Hindus and fall in line with the grand project of India as a Hindu Rashtra. That is why in 2004 the Akal Takht forbade the Sikhs to associate with the Rashtriya Sikh Sangh. The Sikh clergy needs to realise that mere proclamations and orders do not work on the ground. The lines between the BJP and the RSS are fluid. When Sikhs join or support the BJP, they automatically open up to being under RSS influence and within the RSS propaganda machinery.

The RSS strategy in Panjab is not to get confrontational but facelessly permeate the Sikh ethos in such a way that one can't make out if a phenomena is because of Hindutva influence or because of Sikhs not knowing their own code of religion well, or just plain fashion. For example, in the practices of the idolatory of Gurus as discussed earlier; rituals like Karwa Chauth being celebrated by Sikh women sporting *choodas* (bangles); the question of Panjabi language (as discussed in the chapter *Sikhya*) and many others. Through history, the Sikhs have been known to do well against an enemy with a face. Their whole martial history is built on the opposition being a visible force. Now the opposition—Hindutva thought—has entered the Akali Dal leadership, the working of the SGPC and the very practice and day to day living of Sikhs, and the Sikhs are at a loss on how to deal with this new onslaught.

The Sikhs realise this but are unable to prevent the erosion of their religion. They feel claustrophobic, under covert assault by the RSS. They end up taking law in their hands and killing RSS and Shiv Sena leaders. In the last few years, a number of top functionaries of the RSS and other Hindutva groups have been murdered by suspected Sikh hardliners. Among those killed were RSS state vice-president Brig. (retd.) Jagdish Gagneja; RSS leader Naresh Kumar; president of Mazdoor Sena Durga Prasad Gupta; Amit Sharma, a preacher at Hindu Takht; RSS and BJP leader Ravinder Gosai; Vipan Sharma, leader of the Hindu Sangharsh Sena; Dera Sacha Sauda followers, Satpal Kumar and his son Ramesh Kumar and Sultan Masih, a pastor at the Temple of God church. These attacks have been owned by the Khalistan Commando Force and a new outfit, the Dashmesh Regiment. These killings are an old strategy and solve nothing on the ground. They only revive memories of militancy. The need of the hour for the Sikhs is to engage with the RSS and Hindutva groups who have taken the identity game into play and find ways of preserving their unique identity. It is fine if the Hindutva groups want to revere Sikh symbols and rituals, but they need to be asked to stay away from appropriating the Sikh voice.

The option for the community in these times is clear: resist being appropriated, or perish. Sadly, neither our clergy, nor the Akalis are willing to engage with right-wing forces. Per the Gurus, the line is clear: stay away from empty rituals and focus on the essence of knowledge. Stay away from unnecessary reverence and symbolism, focus on real action—become a learner, a *shishya*, a Sikh, and stand with the oppressed. That is why the community will have to either rise to the challenge of stepping away from decadent practices in the religion or just perish by being appropriated.

*Chapter Thirteen*

# *Bar∂r* — Border

Pre-dawn, on 18 September 2016, four infiltrators of the alleged Pakistan-based Jaish-e-Mohammed outfit entered the Uri sector in India and lobbed seventeen grenades in less than three minutes. Seventeen Indian soldiers lost their lives and nineteen were injured. Ten days later, India conducted a 'surgical strike' on Pakistan. The director general of military operations, Lieutenant General Ranbir Singh, an alumnus of Sainik School, Kapurthala, my own school, gave the news of the surgical strike in his brief three-minute statement. India claimed to have entered Pakistan territory and killed thirty-eight soldiers.

Delhi-based newspapers reported, debated and fought over the genuineness of the surgical strike. A Rajasthan civil services officer ran a Twitter campaign that polled the number of people willing to opt for a nuclear strike as retaliation to this attack. The nation erupted into cheers. The probable war soon became a middle class video game.

Look up the Wikipedia entry titled the '2016 Uri attack'. Panjab has not made it to the narrative. Neither Panjab nor I are surprised. This is passé. Panjab is accustomed to not being acknowledged. Not only in this episode, but even in independent India's earlier wars with Pakistan, and even before that, for three millennia when it served as a gateway to the subcontinent and was invaded countless times. When the surgical strikes took place, with a chest-thumping right-wing Hindutva government, the attention to Panjab was even lesser. Yet, this probable war and earlier wars are part of Panjab's cultural memory.

The India-Pakistan border is marked with white milestones. But in Panjab one can't see them. What one sees are tall barbed wire fences. From a space shuttle, it is said you can see the 150,000 floodlights on 50,000 poles along the 553 kilometres of the Indo-Pakistan border that cuts across Panjab in both countries—India and Pakistan. This is the border India built in the 1980s a few acres inside the nation's territory to prevent Pakistan-trained militants from entering India. It created a new issue—farmers had land on the other side of the barbed wire fence. They were given special identity cards and allowed limited entry to their fields through special gates. They were instructed to work facing India and never looked towards Pakistan in their time on the fields. This is how India maintains one of the most militarised zones in the world which runs along the haphazard borderline drawn through villages, fields, ponds, homes and hearts by the British lawyer Cyril Radcliffe in 1947. Radcliffe had never seen India before he drew the line and never returned to India after he drew it.

Immediately after the surgical strike, the Centre asked the Panjab government to get the Panjab border vacated ten kilometres deep. It was the paddy harvest season and the villagers did not have alternatives. Still the government pushed its plans on them. If anyone was tangibly discomfited by the surgical strike, it was Panjab.

When travelling to Panjab, it is impossible to avoid the border, and I sensed life there could never be lonelier than now. Call it serendipity, a newspaper featured a story of a place I had been to before—Ghanike Bet.

Ghanike Bet is a tiny village, with not more than seventy-five houses, within Indian territory, between the border and the transborder river Ravi. The only way to cross the few-kilometres-long dried-up Ravi is on a pontoon bridge about 300 metres long. In the monsoon, when the waters fill up in this shallow river, the military dismantles the bridge and boats take over.

A few months earlier, in early 2016, I had visited a school in Ghanike Bet. My guide, an ex-smuggler, wanted to interview the teacher for a local newspaper. The school shared its premises with a gurdwara. We reached late. The teacher had left for the day. To teach the eleven children of different ages in her school, each day she travelled 200 kilometres, easily six or seven hours up and down, all the way from Pathankot.

'The government job gives her security. Her next posting won't be a punishment,' said one of the older boys, dulling our concern for her.

'Punishment?'

'What else is our village?' asked the boy rhetorically. Then he added, 'I cross the Ravi every day. To study at Dera Baba Nanak.'

I could spot the military bunkers across the fields—a mere 300 metres behind the village. While talking to the villagers about their issues—lack of potable water, lack of doctors for both humans and cattle—I spotted an old man looking at us intently. Eighty-three year-old Gurmail Singh, the oldest man in the village, was tending to an injured pigeon's wings. He left the bird on the ground and brought me water from his ramshackle hut with mud walls and a straw roof. I asked him if he came from the other side of the border.

'Yes.'

'Then why did you stop at the first village in India?'

'My sister was married here. She kept me.'

'Do you want to visit Pakistan?'

'Yes.'

'Have you tried?'

'The military said they could allow me to cross over.'

'Why didn't you cross?'

'They would have allowed—twice.' He smiled vacantly, his soda glasses slipping down his nose. Then he said, 'The third time they would have shot me dead.'

'Why?'

He turned serious. 'They want to keep up their numbers.'

'Of what?'

'Of smugglers killed.'

I paused. 'How does it feel, Baba? To be here? The military watching you all the time? All your life?'

'I don't think even God watches me as much.' There was a long pause. 'Naked. It feels naked.'

He got up to leave the pigeon back in its cage but left the cage gate open. He knew homing pigeons wouldn't fly away. From the newspaper I learnt that Mohinder Singh, a contractual labour with the Panjab government public works department had been rowing the boat across the Ravi non-stop to ferry the villagers of Ghanike Bet, Lallowal, Mansur, Gunia and other villages across the river. Mohinder Singh was the fifth generation of his family to serve as a boatman on the river Ravi.[151] His father had run the same errand in the 1965 and 1971 wars. With heavy rains and floods destroying the BSF pontoon bridge every monsoon, his boat was the only option.

Now, with the evacuation orders, the newspaper story said that people were ruing the fact that they could not take their cattle with them, and of course, their paddy was standing in the field, ready to be harvested. I remembered seeing Mohinder Singh during my visit. I had wanted to speak to him but had no excuse to do so, because then, in the summers, the pontoon bridge was good enough to carry our small car across. I now wanted to know if Gurmail Singh had left his village. I wanted to learn how Panjab dealt with a war-like situation. Or an actual war. On the ground. Far away from a TV studio.

To check, I called Ravinder from Ghanike Bet whom I had met

on my earlier visit and exchanged numbers with. *Kithe ho?* I asked. 'Where are you?'

'Where will I be? Sent family away. But some of us men are here. Cattle is here. Paddy stands in the fields. We can't leave.'

'Can I come over?'

'Come! I have some stuff ready.' I liked this Panjabi spirit. A war was imminent. But this guy wanted to drink. Then he paused and said, as if realisation had dawned on him, 'But the security won't allow you. Even the boatman is hardly there.'

'What if there is war?'

'Then there is war. We'll see.'

'See what?'

'Maybe swim across? After all, the army would need to send forces here. They will do something.'

'*Achha,* tell me, if Baba Gurmail is also there …'

'Of course he is. Here, right next to me. He is Baba Bodh (a banyan tree). He won't leave. Shall I give him the phone?'

'No,' I said. I did not know what to say to Gurmail Singh. 'But give him my *fateh* (regards).'

'Will do. Do call sometimes. *Changa lagda e, kise ne yaad taan kita.* (I like it that someone remembers.) Come if you can …'

I couldn't. I knew I couldn't. Not because I was far. In fact, I was close by, at Dera Baba Nanak. Yet, I knew the BSF wouldn't allow me to get to Ghanike Bet. I had learnt how things were at the village and been assured that Gurmail Singh was fine. Though I did not know if it was a good thing or a bad thing, he had stayed put. I reckoned that had been his life, just inside India's border, but never so entrenched that he could cross the river Ravi and feel at home. For home was also very near to him, just across the border. A home he would never visit because he did not trust the Indian security forces, or the Pakistani ones, for that matter. That was where reporting from Panjab differed so much from the reporting from Delhi—people in Panjab did not only die for the nation, they also died to save their fields and their families.

At Dera Baba Nanak, the BSF sentry allowed me entry to the border point only when I showed her my fake press pass. Not sternly, but cautiously, she forbade me from climbing the post from where the gurdwara was visible. I noticed the sentry's name tag; she was Sikh, and asked, '*Kithe pind?*' (Where is your village?)

'Nearby. Delhi has started its television war, our family had to vacate home.'

'You didn't go with them?'

'Duty. So their TV channels can run.'

'No army movement here?'

'How can I tell you? See for yourself. Now go!'

The otherwise well-visited border post was almost empty. From this border post, on a clear day, one could see the gurdwara at Kartarpur Sahib in Pakistan. Next to the post was a huge board which read: 'Sikhs are petitioning the government to construct a bridge three kilometres long across the river Ravi so the community can have unhindered access to the site from where Baba Nanak departed for his heavenly abode.'

Sikhs had not just been petitioning. For the last seventy-one years, in every *Ardas*, done multiple times a day, the Sikhs prayed that they would be able to visit the birthplace of Guru Nanak at Nankana Sahib, and his last home where he lived for seventeen years, at Kartarpur Sahib in Pakistan.

The prayers might have registered with God almighty, but not with politicians on both sides of the border. This, in spite of Pakistan twice making an overture to let Sikh pilgrims walk down those three kilometres a few times a year, at least once or twice on Guru Nanak's birth and death anniversaries. For Delhi, for India, for right-wing Hindutva, Pakistan was the worthy enemy who earned them votes and kept them in power. So why would they want Pakistan to show its human face? For the Congress, Pakistan was the foreign hand, only out to destabilise India. How could they allow a message that it was benevolent to Sikhs whom they had earlier accused of wanting to create Khalistan?

A day later, I went down to Amritsar, an hour's drive from Dera Baba Nanak. Sandeep, a photographer, painter and editor, wanted me to talk at the school where he taught. He joined me from the outskirts of the city. We soon arrived at the school. The principal, I noticed, was Bengali. In my rusty Bangla, I asked the principal if he got enough fish there. The Amritsari *machhi* was a delicacy but coastal people have a whole ecology of fish. He sensed a kindred heart and told me the many varieties he missed. I asked why the school was open. Weren't there orders to evacuate? He told me it was open because it was twelve kilometres from the border and not less than ten kilometres. I was amused. Nuclear radiation or even tank shells would care little about the distance.

When I went to the classroom to address the children, I started by asking them if they supported a war. They were overwhelmingly against it. I asked if their families had to move away from border villages. Yes, some of them had to do that. I asked if they watched television. They did, and over the last few days they were getting increasingly scared about the warmongering. The more Delhi rabble-roused, the more scared the children became. The more this generation's counterparts in the rest of the country began to hate the enemy, Pakistan, the more cornered these children at the border felt.

I asked them why they didn't write to the newspapers about their fears or why they didn't call up television studios about their concerns. They told me they had never thought about it and didn't know how to do that. For the television channels the TRP ratings were more important than the psyche of the next generation. The neo-nationalist market was huge, their pseudo-testosterone high and the lure of money immense. Why would they try to understand Panjab and its border issues? They had no incentive. The nation's hormones were boosted and Pakistan was the perfect enemy. The nation celebrated the fifty-six-inch chest of its supreme leader. The Delhi-based media shouted, screamed, and imposed its nationalism on everyone.

In Panjab, every village and town has scores of soldiers, both serving and retired. How many right-wingers or their families had ever served in the defence services, ever been posted at Siachen, in the deserts of Rajasthan, the jungles of Nagaland, or had ever faced the bullets from the enemies is a moot point. Panjab understands. Yet, the nation was once again denying Panjab its geography, its history and its role as a gateway to India.

We came to Amritsar via Ajnala. When I spoke to people in the nearby villages, slightly away from the border, the sentiment was that there would be no war. Every shopkeeper, every friend I met there said it was just a rumour and everything was as usual.

We returned to Amritsar and I waited for another friend to join me near Sultanwind gate, near the Baba Deep Singh Gurdwara, with its huge *khanda*—the Sikh double-edged sword. I crossed the gate to the inner city and looked for a tea shop. An elderly clean-shaven man, probably in his mid-sixties, walked past me. As I stopped him to ask directions to a tea stall, he waved to me to walk with him. We got into a narrow street and he pointed to the tea stall, which, incidentally, was his. I was curious to know from him the Hindu view of Amritsar.

He told me that in 1984 he was freelancing with a printing press that printed local newspapers. He had a special permit and the police would allow him to travel for work. 'All my life I have lived in this narrow city. Look at the streets. How congested! But in those days the

roads were so empty. It was a pleasure to cycle on them.' No traffic
was a new way of remembering the days after Operation Blue Star
which the whole of Panjab even now shudders to remember.

I asked, 'Printing press?'

'Yes, I was a typesetter. You know, before all these computers
came and threw me out of a job and made me sell tea, I used to
make newspaper and book pages. The smell of ink intoxicates me
even now …' He was rambling and I let him. 'I have typeset most
of the classic Panjabi novels. All these big writers Kanwal, Gurdial,
even Batalvi were friends.[w] They would come to check their pages
before printing, treat me to tea and snacks. After them, I was the
most important person. In fact, I was so important, I could ruin their
reputation. I know many stories about all the big writers, good and
dirty …'

I liked his arrogance but he was correct in a manner of speaking.
After all, who more than a typesetter then and a printer today holds
the reputation of the writer in his fingers?

He then suddenly became conscious. 'But who are you? Why are
you asking me these questions?'

Knowing that here was perhaps one person in the whole of
Panjab who understood what it meant to be a writer and not a
journalist, I told him I was a writer. 'Oh! Are you? What language do
you write in?'

Now was the time for me to cut a sorry figure. 'English,' I replied
almost apologetically.

'Oh! Good, good. Write in English. No one reads Panjabi, Hindi
and Urdu these days. Perhaps some people will read English. But
really, you writers are no longer interesting. No one tells *masaledar*
stories anymore. Everyone is stuck up, self-important, their bums
high up in the sky. They think no end of themselves, but frankly, no

---

w. Jaswant Kanwal, Gurdial Singh (Jnanpith awardee) and Shiv Kumar Batalvi, a
poet who died young.

one listens to them or anyone. I have seen it all, all the blood, all the ruin. There is no point writing. Selling tea is better. I get to hear the market gossip ...'

His wife had by then made the tea and he handed me my glass. Then he remembered something and asked me, 'Will you wait five minutes? I have something to give you.'

'Me?'

'Yes, you. I might have to search for it though. It has been years ... wait, drink your tea slowly. I will be back.' He disappeared up the steps to his home above the shop. He returned after a while with an old-looking book in his hand. I could make out the Devanagari script. He said, 'I am giving you this because you are a writer. You may get what this book says. No one else gets it, no one,' and he handed me the book.

I turned it around. It was the seven-decade-old, Saadat Hasan Manto's *Letters to Uncle Sam*, all four of them in one thin volume in Hindi. I looked at the man incredulously. I was travelling to study how Panjab was dealing with a pseudo-war situation and I had received a copy of one of the greatest anti-war texts from the subcontinent. One that saw through the games big nations played, especially with two poverty-struck, desperate new countries, to sell their arms. I received the essays from a stranger, at a ramshackle tea shop.

I was stunned. I forgot to ask the man his name. I forgot even to pay for the tea.

The next day, my friend Kulwinder and I went towards Ferozepur. On the way, I spotted many tractors and trolleys full of people alongside my car. Where were they going? Was this an exodus? Why did they look cheerful? The mystery was soon revealed: it was for a mela at

Gurdwara Beerh Baba Budda Sahib ji, named after the grand old man of the Sikh religion, who anointed five Sikh Gurus and had visions of seven of them and was the first high priest of the Durbar Sahib. I was partly amused and partly surprised. Was this how Panjab looked into the eye of war or was it an I–care–a–damn? The stereotype: *sannu ki*? (How does it affect us?) It was Baba's mela, we just had to go. The nation could sort itself out.

We left the main road to turn to village Naushera Dalla, where stands the tomb of a seventeenth-century saint, Baba Jallan. Kulwinder told me that the border fencing was closest from the tomb. On the way we crossed a village with huge bungalows. While many Panjab villages, especially in Majha and Doaba—from where the migration is highest—had some big bungalows, this one was unique in the way that there was almost no small home here. Yet, we hardly found any human beings in the village. Finally, near a turn, we saw two old women and asked them where everybody was. They told us the village had been evacuated. It was impolite to ask why the houses were big, but we asked the village's name. 'Havelian,' one woman said and giggled. 'Don't you see the havelis here—mansions?' I did not get the joke and Kulwinder patted my hand and urged me to move on. On our way he told me that the village was infamous for drug smuggling. I had no way to corroborate that, but the standard of housing in the village certainly seemed strange and misplaced for a border village.

We were about to cross a dry canal when we realised its one side was way higher than the other. On the tall side were bunkers covered with mud. Migrant labourers were busy cleaning the cement rooms. We stopped to look and entered a few of them. They were cramped in length and breadth but were high enough for an average-sized person to stand straight. They had openings in which the soldiers could place their guns and shoot. The labourers told us that in the eventuality of war, water would be released in the canal and another line of defence would be constructed.

We carried on to the village Naushera Dalla where we spotted the gurdwara. As we stopped near it we realised the tomb was next to the gurdwara. Though Baba Jallan's period coincides with Guru Hargobind's, his writings were not part of the Granth Sahib. Once Baba Jallan's wife, Mai Ramki, said to Baba Jallan that she wanted to go on a pilgrimage. Baba Jallan asked her to sit down and close her eyes. They were transported to Multan where a massive *yajna* was on. While Mai Ramki joined the *langar sewa*, preparing rotis, Baba Jallan started distributing food. That is when some Brahmins came to him and asked for his identity and if he was a Brahmin. They asked him to show his holy thread. Baba Jallan warned them to not put him to the test. When they insisted, Baba Jallan went into meditation and four holy threads adorned his body—gold, silver, copper and cotton. The Brahmins understood he was a realised soul and feared he might curse them, and asked for forgiveness. The Brahmins followed him back to his village Naushera Dalla and he recited his thoughts which they documented.

One day he summoned the Brahmins and told them his time was up. He jumped into the holy pond and disappeared. The pond and the banyan tree he planted still exists. We noticed a small room which was a temple to Baba Jallan. The gurdwara that had come up next to the pond and the banyan tree now included the spot where Baba Jallan used to meditate. This was an instance of the organised Sikh religion usurping a folk saint and smothering a local story with a gurdwara just because the time period of the saint was concurrent with one of their Gurus. The barbed wire fence was indeed merely fifty metres from Baba Jallan's tomb. This too was a religious or faith border transgressed.

After spending some time at the tomb and gurdwara, we took a road parallel to the fence, but about two hundred metres away, and drove to village Khalra near Bhikiwind, from where the wire fence was less than 500 metres away. Close to the village, I spotted an old man on the road. He looked over seventy years of age. I asked him, 'Baba, have you been here all along?' He replied in the affirmative. I stopped the car and got out. 'Can you tell me how many times you have been evicted from your home?' We began counting: Partition, 1965, 1971, Operation Brasstacks, Kargil War, Operation Parakram and now. A few more villagers gathered.

'During which of these was the eviction smoothest?'

'Well, 1971 was the worst,' he said. 'We were moved around for three months and then asked to settle. Indira said no war. Then suddenly there was war.'

'But you supported the army ...'

'Of course we did. We will always do. They fight for us, we stand by them. But *nuksaan* (damage) is of fields, of crops, of homes, schools ... So much is lost,' he said slowly, with pauses.

Another voice came in. 'During Kargil, they planted mines in the fields. The war ended, the army went away. It took them three years to clear the mines. We were compensated for only one crop.'

'And now?'

'This is the most *fuddu* (stupid) operation. Five days and the army is nowhere!'

'But which was the best operation?'

The old man answered, '1965. By around 8 p.m., we had dinner and lay down to sleep. Our eyes opened by 2 a.m. with bomb-*baazi*, the sound of tanks firing. We didn't even realise when the army tanks had crossed our villages. So, we too dug in our heels. Our gurdwaras started preparing *langar* and we started feeding the troops.'

'So ...'

'It is not a lie. Lal Bahadur Shastri was the best prime minister we ever had.'

A man around thirty-five years of age, his legs covered in green and white plastic sacks, butted in, 'Even now I feed the BSF.' I turned to him. 'On 29 September, the gurdwaras asked people to flee. I packed my six-member family off to relatives. I only have a bike, so I did two rounds. Next day, I came back. My cattle were hungry and thirsty. We could not feed them the previous day,' said Sonara Singh.

'Then?'

'That is when the BSF jawans asked me for milk. I told them my cows were thirsty and weren't milking that day. Then they asked me for food. They told me they hadn't eaten in twenty-four hours. Naturally, I cooked for them. Next day, I again came back. My wife had sent *rotis* and *subzi* for the jawans. But you know, even among relatives, these days it is difficult to stay long. Homes are small. Hearts are even smaller.'

'So you came back?'

'After three days. What other choice did we have? Badal says he has set up provisions. He has set up nothing. The stupid thing is, our home does not have a toilet. We all go to the fields. Now the same BSF is not allowing our ladies to go out. I have a mother, a wife and a daughter. What should we do?'

I saw a tar- and gravel-laden dumper approaching. 'So why are you dressed up in these sacks?'

'We are making the road. What if the army finally comes? They would need a road. These leaders are big people. Who knows what they will decide?'

My instinct was to drag down a TV reporter to this village. Show him what to me seemed like the greatest nationalists one could ever find. All of them. All the people in these villages. The nation is not defined in the cosy sofas of India's middle class homes or in the *shakhas* of the right-wing organisations or in the fantastic speeches during election rallies or in parliament. The nation is defined here. On the ground where the border has divided our people from each other.

'Do you know folks across the border?'

Many of the gathered said they did, and even saw them farming every day, even in these days. Our fields are adjacent, our families are near each other, they said. Not so long ago there were no barriers. *Dukh sukh da saanjh hai* (we are together in misery and in happiness).

We moved to Khem Karan, the site of the famous tank battle in 1965. Here, too, villagers sitting on the platform near the gurdwara showed me their paddy standing ripe to be harvested. They cursed Parkash Singh Badal and Narendra Modi in the choicest language. They told me that they were not leaving. The current exercise reminded them of the 1965 War when India had all but abandoned the entire region west of the Beas.

Lieutenant General Harbaksh Singh was the hero of victories in the battle of Asal Uttar where Indian troops with Centurion tanks of World War II vintage took on Pakistani M-47 Patton tanks. The story that folks told was the story that Harbaksh Singh mentioned in his book *In the Line of Duty—A Soldier Remembers.* The general wrote: 'Late at night on the 9th of September, the chief of the army staff rang me up … his advice was that to save the whole army from being cut off by Pakistan's armour push, I should pull back to the line of the Beas river. Pulling back to the Beas would have meant sacrificing prime territory in Panjab including Amritsar and Gurdaspur districts and would have been a far worse defeat than that suffered at the hands of the Chinese in 1962.'

The move would have also resulted in bidding goodbye to the entire state of Jammu and Kashmir. This has been corroborated by Captain Amarinder Singh, aide-de-camp to General Harbaksh Singh, who received the army chief's phone call. He wrote, 'At 2.30 a.m.

army chief, Gen. J.N. Chaudhury called and spoke to the general, and after a heated discussion centred around the major threat that had developed, the chief ordered the army commander to withdraw 11 Corps to hold a line on the Beas river. General Harbaksh Singh refused to carry out this order.'[152]

Some military historians have refuted the general's story about withdrawing, but the people on the ground remember. They knew they had to stay on and might even have to fight. It was their land, after all. If the Indian Army came, well and good. Else, they were ready to resist, repel and perhaps even get annihilated, but they had little hope in the government—whether Centre or state.

'Even if we want to go, where shall we go?' asked an old man. 'There are no camps, no arrangements, no pick-up even. We can't leave our cattle or fields and just go camp at our relatives' and friends' places. What if we go, and Pakistan advances? The military is not yet here; who will save our property? Our livelihood?'

The chant was the same everywhere. The CM was supposed to have directed the chief secretary to immediately release Rs 1 crore to the border districts to meet the exigency. He said that the state may pay if farmers had to stay away from their homes for a longer time. All this was in the news for consumption by the nation. On the ground nothing seemed to have transpired and five lakh or more people had been jostled in and out of their homes for a war that did not seem to be beginning, despite soldiers' leaves being cancelled.

It was clear the government had goofed up big time. The Centre had probably asked the state government to prepare for the army advancing and the state government had crawled when asked to bend.

The Congress MLAs, whether in Dera Baba Nanak, Dina Nagar, Firozepur, Guru Har Sahai or any of the other border constituencies, came and addressed the villagers and asked them to not become refugees of an un-fought war.

We left the main road and through village roads reached Ferozepur. In the cantonment we paused at the Saragarhi Memorial Gurdwara where the Sikh regiment had just commemorated the Saragarhi Day on 12 September. The memorial was historic, though the location was not. The Battle of Saragarhi was fought on 12 September 1897 between Sikh soldiers of the British Indian Army and Pashtun Orakzai tribesmen. My great-grandfather was part of 36th Sikhs (present day 4th battalion of the Sikh Regiment). Though he had not fought this battle, he had been part of the Tirah Campaign whose soldiers fought the battle of Saragarhi. Saragarhi was a small village in the border district of Kohat, situated on the Samana Range in Khyber Pakhtunkhwa, in present-day Pakistan which was attacked by around 10,000 Afghans. The twenty-one Sikh soldiers, led by Havildar Ishar Singh, chose to fight to the death in what is considered by military historians as one of history's greatest last stands.

The details of the Battle of Saragarhi are considered fairly accurate, because Gurmukh Singh signalled events to Fort Lockhart by heliograph as they occurred. The Pashtuns later admitted that they had lost about 180 people and many more were wounded, but some 600 bodies are said to have been seen around the ruined post when the relief party arrived. All the twenty-one Sikh non-commissioned officers and soldiers of other ranks who laid down their lives were posthumously awarded the Indian Order of Merit, the highest gallantry award of that time which an Indian soldier could receive. The battle has frequently been compared to the Battle of Thermopylae, where a small Greek force faced a large Persian army under Xerxes I in 480 BC. In both cases, a small defending force faced overwhelming odds, fought to the last man, and inflicted a disproportionate number of fatalities on the attacking force.

The Sikhs genuinely take great pride in the Battle of Saragarhi but the war itself is in question. The Sikhs were fighting for the British who had conquered them barely half a century back by annihilating Maharaj Ranjit Singh's hard-won Sikh empire. They were fighting against the Pashtuns who sought their own freedom from British imperialism. One can argue that the Sikhs were fighting the Pashtuns because they had previously invaded Panjab a century and a half ago, gone up to Delhi and desecrated the Durbar Sahib.

The point really is the empire: whether of the Mughals, Ahmed Shah Durrani, Ranjit Singh or the British, and its sense of the self. Or even now the way the nation state is constructed by creating enemies. Panjab, and its people—Sikhs, Hindus, Muslims—have been fodder, some glorious, some not-so-glorious, through the ages. What we celebrate depends on which tide of history we choose to stand upon. The real pathos is, after the dynasts, after the empires, after the colonialism, in spite of democracy, Panjab is still at a crossroads with no clear path ahead, as it has been many times earlier in its history.

That evening, we were at the Hussainiwala border near Ferozepur. There was a reason that all this time I had avoided the Wagah border, the more celebrated one, near Amritsar. Many years back, when I was an adolescent, I had seen the Berlin Wall falling. That night in front of our black and white television set, I had promised that one day I would visit the Brandenburg Gate in Berlin and pray for Wagah to be lowered. When I actually reached the site of the now non-existent Berlin Wall, I stood up to pray, but the prayer did not rise to my lips. I realised that my prayer would be empty unless the nation states of India and Pakistan decided to dismantle Wagah. On the other hand, through these years, the nation states had been playing up Wagah. Now it was curated for television as a site of daily bombast, a daily dose of nationalism, aided and abetted by cheering crowds.

I had once taken my American-Jewish teacher who had spent a lifetime trying to build peace between the Jews and Arabs to Wagah. I had got her a special seat in the gallery. After the ceremony she came out with tears in her eyes, 'Horrible, horrible! How can you celebrate this? Look at what Israel has done to Palestine!' I had once taken Lakshmi to Wagah. She came out crying in the middle of the ceremony, 'I can't take it. I can't take this enmity.' We had left and I had sworn I would never go there again. How far I had moved from my adolescent hopefulness!

Those BSF shoes rising 6 feet, towering over humans was a daily assertion that the nation would not see sense and it would not allow Panjab to be peaceful. It would indulge in shady arms deals, but would not build schools and hospitals just so that its mythical enemy could stay alive. Both nations would mutually sabotage dialogue, spark fires in Kashmir, so the rest of India and the rest of Pakistan could continue warmongering.

Hussainiwala is more than a security post. The village lay near the bank of the Satluj river and was named after the Muslim Peer Baba Ghulam Hussainiwala whose tomb was inside the BSF headquarters. It was opposite the Pakistani village of Ganda Singh Wala. So much for Partition! Even the village names were contrary to the idea of the divided nation states. Hussainiwala was where Bhagat Singh, Sukhdev and RajGuru were cremated on 23 March 1931. It hosted memorials from the previous wars but more importantly, it featured the Prerna Sthal memorials to B.K. Dutt and the freedom fighters, and an eternal fire (Amar Jyoti).

The post was empty. Kulwinder and I spent time at the peaceful memorial. Monu, the parking lot contractor, said, 'I paid Rs 6 lakh per annum for the contract and took charge on 25 September. Four days later, the *tamasha* (circus) started. My year is ruined.'

We were getting late and the BSF was not sure they would conduct a full Beating Retreat. 'In any case our ceremony is not like the Wagah one,' said the commandant.

'Wagah is so theatrical, fake, jingoistic and masculine. That is exactly why we came to see it,' I replied. The commandant smiled.

'Come some other time, when all this drama is over.' Even the security forces could see through the hawkish posturing of the government. How the government had squandered the energies of its people, how the nation state had created the hollowness of the other.

In order to catch the light of the setting sun we decided to move on. Further southwards, near Baje Ke, I again stopped and checked with ordinary village folks. It was deep dusk and the street corners smelt of fresh *gobi* and *palak pakodas*. People were unhappy with the eviction orders but they had defied them.

They cribbed to us about how often the police picked them up for questioning. They told us about how they never felt secure, never felt safe, could not trust either the police or their own neighbours. How they were constantly on the edge. They talked about the lack of schools and how teachers did not turn up. They told us how young men and women were collecting multiple degrees but no one offered them jobs. They told us how even when a job was in sight, people from this region were scrutinised extra carefully because their papers said they were from the border. 'Tell me,' they asked, 'what choice do we have? Can we choose our birth?'

They were right. A nation is strengthened when the people on its borders feel secure in it. Not when they are viewed with the lens of suspicion and not allowed to feel equal because they are from the border. The nation that can't build the human index of its borders cannot expect its borders to be saved by guns alone.

The moon had risen. A boy asked me, 'Does it not look the same? From our side and theirs?'

After I had spoken to a cluster of men and was about to open the car door to leave, Rakesh, a thirtyish man with a polio-affected leg stopped me from getting into the car. '*Bhaaji, patrakar hon?* (Brother, are you a journalist?)' I nodded.

'If you can, please get the war started?'

I was like no, no way.

'But see, nothing happens in our lives. So much noise all the time, all this poverty, all this unemployment, and these drugs. If there is a war, at least we will be able to tell our children we saw a war. Would that not be magnificent?'

I burst out laughing and asked what if he died. *Pher khel khatam!* (It will be the end of the game!)

The story of the gate is never the story of the house. While the right wing manufactured its own brand of hooligan nationalism, Panjab, which had been in the crossfire forever and would bear the pain of war on its chest, defined it differently. The homegrown right wingers did not know this about Panjab: the gate did not parrot the house but eventually the house needed the gate. It was really up to them to stay sensible, for if they burned down Panjab, the fire would destroy them, and having never really fought for themselves, they wouldn't even be able to fight the fires.

At Guru Harsahai, Kulwinder told me that earlier they would turn their television antennas to catch Pakistani programmes and now OKCupid, Tinder and Grindr were active in the town connecting people from the other side to the people there. It seemed that people from both nations connected across the border and carried out romantic liaisons without ever entertaining the possibility of meeting each other. If this longing were not so doomed and so laden with the possibility of loss, it would actually be comic. Yet, whichever side of the border, who better than a border area person to understand another border area person?

I left for Fazilka and proceeded to a village about twenty kilometres from Fazilka which was surrounded on three sides by Pakistan and on the fourth side by the river Satluj—Muhar Jamsher.[153] There was only one more village of this kind on the border—Daoke, near Amritsar. Until the bridge on the river was constructed just a few years back the villagers were mostly connected with the mainland by a pontoon bridge or through boats. The issue with this new bridge was that it mostly remained locked by the BSF sentries. I reached the bridge and the BSF told me that the push to evacuate had eased and the villagers were returning home. I was relieved. I hoped Sonara Singh had been able to build the road. It might come in handy another time for the military. Until then, the villagers could use it.

The villagers at Jamsher told me their difficulties. There had been years when they had to evacuate thrice, sometimes because the Satluj had flooded. Now their friends or relatives in other mainland villages were also tired of them asking for shelter for a few days. They couldn't even build concrete homes because they never knew when an attack would happen. They had no help from the government and even the nearest high school and college was in Fazilka. The doctor hardly came to the dispensary, the closed bridge gates at night prevented emergency visits to hospitals.

A young boy showed me the run-down school building that housed around sixty children and told me that the schoolteacher remained absent. Since the BSF used jammers to block mobile phone calls, the villagers were on a wireless local loop. All the 1,500 people of this village had identity cards, and special passes were made to enter and leave the village which made it difficult for even relatives to come and meet them. No one here had an idea why they had to pay such a price merely for being Indian, and that too, charged by their own security forces.

At Fazilka, which I had abandoned when sacrilege had taken place, I connected back with a local historian, Dost. Fazilka was established in the mid-nineteenth century and christened after the original owner of the land, Mian Fazil Watoo. Its favourable position near the Satluj enabled it to capture almost the whole of the export trade from the great desert tract towards Sind (now in Pakistan), and make it a flourishing market town. The first railway line through the town was set up in 1898 on the occasion of the Diamond Jubilee celebration of the accession of Queen Victoria. Before the Partition, Fazilka was the biggest wool market in India, but thereafter, the trade had been hit very hard, with a major portion of the supply area going to Pakistan, and Bikaner gradually attracting the raw wool produced in Rajasthan.

Dost showed me the clock tower and the main market. I had heard that after the Satluj left India at Harike Pattan, it went in and out of Pakistan seven times until Fazilka, before it left one final time to merge with the Indus. We went to see the last stretch. It stank to the high heavens.

Dost told me at this point it had crossed the town Kasur in Pakistan and it reminded me of a great Panjabi folk song:

*Jutti kasuri, pairi na poori*
*haaye rabba ve sanu turna peya;*
*Jina rahaan di main saar na jaana*
*ohni raaheen ve saahnu murna peya ...*

The shoe from Kasur does not fit,
still O Lord, I had to walk;
Walk paths whose destinations I knew not,
negotiate their bends and turns ...

The entire tannery waste from Kasur seemed to be dumped in the river. The slime barely flowed. Here the majestic river Satluj had become the same as the once majestic, now marginal, sewerage-carrying Budda Dariya after Ludhiana. A lonely blue-coloured boat lay anchored on it, its oar dangling on the side.

We went to see the 1971 war memorial, a hall full of photographs of soldiers in action, soldiers winning gallantry awards. Some stories of bravery were etched on the wall, but I couldn't seem to forget that lonely boat on the Satluj.

In the evening we went to see the Flag Retreat ceremony at what is the Sulaimanki border in Pakistan and Sadqi border in India. The site was an open cemented ground with a wire fence going between it. An area for people to sit on both sides. We were about twenty-five Indians and there were about fifteen Pakistanis on the other side. The music was blaring as we waited for the ceremony to start. The song that played was:

*Nafrat ki lathi todo … tum prem ke panchi ho desh premeeyo.*

Break the stick of hate … Oh! Lovers of your nation, you are birds of love.

The lyrics by Anand Bakshi, sung by Mohammad Rafi in the film *Desh Premi*, this retreat was beyond my wildest peace imaginations. The whole ceremony was conducted with such grace, giving each side the right pause and the right space to match their steps. It was a *jugalbandi* of military drill—a perfectly timed melody performed by the two sides. The Indian side gave respect to the Pakistan flag and the Pakistani side gave respect to the Indian flag. The audience on both sides were mesmerised by the performance.

A few jingoists on the Indian side shouted *Bharat Mata Ki Jai* and *Jo Bole So Nihal* but soon feel silent when there wasn't much of a response. What a difference between Wagah and Sadqi, what a difference between jingoistic nationalism and friendly compatriotism. Indeed, it was Delhi and Islamabad that stood between making the two Panjabs one again—one language, one culture, one people, and perhaps someday, again one land of five rivers.

While the national border is a fact of Panjab's geography, hardened by ultra-nationalistic politics, the state's major economic activity also annoys Delhi. Especially in the paddy harvest season. Delhi regularly accuses Panjab of creating pollution by burning paddy straw. After travelling the border I went down to Harjeet's village to see him harvest the crop in his nine acres, of which he owns four and five he farms on *theka*.

When I reached, Harjeet had already been waiting one long week—eyes peeled to the skies, watching out for rain, praying it would not drizzle—to get the combine harvester. September rains can be hard in Panjab. When the combine harvester came, unlike my childhood where labour cut the crop over a week or more, the machine cut the crop in a jiffy, in one and a half days. Yet, the cutting was not as fine as when the sickle cuts the crop. This one left over a feet of stem standing.

The very next day, Harjeet and I took the trollies full of paddy grain to the Moga mandi. All the way Harjeet watched for any slippage or unnecessary leakage. The trollies were his work over the last four months. They could earn money that could help repay his debt to the cooperative bank and the *arthiya*. At the mandi, the cemented floor seems to have turned into a vast desertscape. There were big mounds of paddy piled up like sand dunes.

The *arthiyas* and mandi officials and food inspectors were busy allotting spaces, employing farmers and *palledars* and other workers, mostly migrants, to their tasks. Harjeet met his *arthiya* who scolded him for coming late and alloted him a space on the far side of the cemented floor. We took the tractor and trolley there and unloaded the grain with the help of labour. Once our mounds of grain were ready, the *arthiya* brought a 'meter' to check the moisture in the grain. I understood weights, I understood volume, I understood disease, but I did not understand this meter.

Harjeet explained, 'The maximum limit allowed for moisture in the grain is seventeen. If it is more, we will have to dry the grain and get it re-evaluated.'

The *arthiya* added, 'More moisture will make grain heavy. I would have paid more for less grain.'

Harjeet said, 'But in Haryana they are accepting twenty-two.'

The *arthiya* replied, 'They are accepting, but paying less. Ask your government to increase the limit.'

'But you anyway pay us less,' complained Harjeet.

The *arthiya* retorted, 'Should I pay from my pocket?' Once the grain is accepted, the labour will clean it, load it in sacks, stitch them. Then the *palledar* will load them on trucks. 'I told you, you should have come earlier. Three days back they were all sitting jobless.'

Harjeet didn't expect the harsh response. Scared that the *arthiya* might be angry, he pleaded, 'But the moisture would have been higher. It rained a few days back. We were not ready. Just last evening, we finished harvesting.'

The sale of grain was showing me how the process was servile to a system, to a moisture meter. What if it was tampered? If its reading was wrong? Who could challenge the *arthiya* or the Mandi Board? Certainly not Harjeet, who did not even protest at receiving less than the MSP price. That was what the government had offered. Take it or leave it. There was enough supply in the mandi for this season.

As soon as Harjeet's bill was settled, he walked away from the grain. I pointed to him how some workers were not stitching the jute bags tightly. He did not care. I pointed out that the grain was spilling while being loaded. He did not care. He was keen on a drink. He behaved like any other farmer would behave—deal done, don't care.

The reason Harjeet cut it so close with delivering the crop is another government ruling, this one to save the water of Panjab. The Panjab Preservation of Subsoil Water Act, 2009, though patchily implemented because it is a Band-Aid fix, has still helped conserve a bit of water. The Act mandates dates in June when farmers can plant and then transplant paddy in their fields. This Act came into being to tap into the annual monsoon and the availability of water in the

Gobind Sagar reservoir at the Bhakra Dam. It is another matter that the canal water does not really come to the fields, but it does help with ground water pulled out by tube wells.

The farmers have been more or less following the stipulations and that has led to both, increased acreage under paddy cultivation and at least halting the dip in ground water depletion. The usage of water in Panjab is more than double of what it is in Bihar and Bengal which have been the traditional rice-growing belts of the nation. The ground water depletion has shifted from almost a metre a year before the Act to three-fourths of a metre after the Act. That is a net savings of over twenty centimetres.[154]

However, it has created another issue: the time between the harvesting of paddy and sowing of wheat has now shrunk to about a week or a maximum of ten days. This leads to the complaint Delhi has for Panjab every October: rise in pollution levels because farmers set the paddy straw on fire which creates smoke.

What Panjab saves for itself as water now becomes a calamity of smoke for Delhi which records a huge surge in bronchial disorders and asthma attacks. Around eight deaths are reported each day, from the most polluted city in the world in the harvest season, leading up to Diwali, a festival of smoke, noise and light through firecrackers. Panjab becomes the villain. The National Green Tribunal hauls up Panjab ever so often, demanding that the state comply with its instructions and not allow paddy straw burning. The state government too makes noises, technology is invoked and a solution is promised. Yet, nothing happens.

Traditionally, the gap between crops was longer, the paddy was hand-cut much lower, and there is enough anecdotal evidence that the Panjab Agricultural University itself used to encourage farmers to burn the straw. It was also a fact that the wheat straw used to come in handy to feed cattle. All old homes in villages used to have a huge room near the cattle shed called *toori wala kamra* (the wheat straw room). So, on the one hand the scale of paddy farming has increased so much that the University's own recommendation has now become a bane, and on the other hand the mechanisation and change in seeds has led to farmers not willing to feed paddy straw to their cattle. The situation now is that once the combine harvester leaves more than a foot of straw standing in the field, unless this straw is—with whatever method—removed or mulched into the soil, the wheat planting cannot take place. Time is of essence. The window is only a week to ten days.

The primary solution the state government offers is, upon recommendation of the University, to use a new machine called Happy Seeder. This solution to me is problematic because in typical engineer fashion, to overcome the difficulties posed by mechanised agriculture, one is suggested to use more mechanical devices.

Happy Seeder is a machine with furrows that are extended at the bottom. When you yoke it to a tractor and run it in a farm with standing paddy straw, its furrows reach down to the earth and plough it to plant the seeds. The catch is: it costs money. A small, marginal farmer, who is himself under debt, and hardly makes any money, cannot easily afford to buy a new machine. So, like he does with other technology such as combine harvester, he seeks to rent the machine. This renting charge is what the farmer unions are asking the government to pay per the National Green Tribunal directive. Yet, the government does not pay it. Instead, the government increases surveillance and uses satellite imagery to target farmers who put fire to their fields. The farmer has little choice, so, like Harjeet, at an opportune time, he sets his harvested paddy fields on fire. Like we did.

Yet, the matter is not about this Panjab alone. The post-monsoon winds in Panjab are easterly.[155] If anyone must blame Panjab it is Pakistan. The real issue, however, is not Panjab's paddy straw smoke. The break-up of various air pollutants in north India is—industry 51 per cent, vehicles 25 per cent, domestic 11 per cent, agriculture

8 per cent, and the rest fall under 'others'. Obviously, the major pollution belongs to industry and that too due to its use of petroleum coke.

A report on a website published in 2017 says, 'Petroleum coke is a high carbon residue produced during the refinement of heavy oils. In its raw form, the high carbon fuel can be used as a cheap substitute for coal. In many parts of the world, petcoke is restricted because of its toxicity. In India, however, the fuel is unregulated and burned freely. In this regulatory void, demand has soared, rising 23 per cent a year for the last five years. The country imported 20 times more petcoke in 2016 than it did in 2011.'[156]

Once again, Delhi blames Panjab for what Panjab is not responsible. Even in the 8 per cent bracket, if Panjab's paddy straw smoke is responsible then we must note that Panjab grows it to feed the nation. The solution to this is through Happy Seeders, for which the government must assist the farmer, or through mulching—being adopted by farmers in Panjab in a big way in the past three years—which the Agricultural University must promote. Yet, that is so much hard work, so it is just easy to blame Panjab's farmers while the one who should complain—Pakistan—does not raise the issue.

*Chapter Fourteen*

# *Sikhya* — Education

I was on the road from Barnala to Maur Mandi near Bathinda when I spotted a school named Sant Fateh Singh English Medium School. I stopped to gawk at the gate. I needed to register it. Fateh Singh! The school was named after the head of the Akali Dal and the Panjabi Suba movement when the Centre had agreed to Panjab's trifurcation on linguistic lines—when in 1966, finally, the Sikhs had got their own state out of which Hindi-speaking Haryana and parts of Himachal Pradesh were carved out.

Now—to sell English education—a private school had named itself after an icon of the Panjabi language movement. This was not an isolated instance. There was yet another famous franchise of schools called St Kabir. What does the St stand for—Sant or Saint? If it is Sant, then the term is Hindi and Panjabi, not English. If Saint, then it needs a particular kind of process called canonisation by which a Christian church declares that a person who has died was a saint. This is a deliberate ambiguity for it makes good business sense—selling English. There is another chain called St Soldier. This one from Sant Sipahi—one of Guru Gobind Singh's titles, but whether the St expands to Sant or Saint, no one knows. In Panjab, today, English has a market while Panjabi does not. English means a job, security, and Panjabi means roots, home and nostalgia. English is also hegemony.

The parents of many children told me that their wards were not allowed to speak Panjabi at their private, English-medium schools. The languages encouraged were English and Hindi. One reason was that some staff in these schools, mostly senior, were not from Panjab. They were from Kerala, from Bengal, and instead of them learning Panjabi, they forced Hindi upon the pupils. Another reason was the urban and rural divide—the *shehri* and *pendu*—where the urban was associated with Hindi and English and the rural with Panjabi, which was looked down upon in schools. The issue had taken a form where not only were schools discouraging students from speaking Panjabi but were also flouting state government orders—the Panjabi Language Act, 2008—which mandated the teaching of Panjabi from Classes I to X. This certainly was an inversion of history, the very basis on which the state was created. It was also a cause for alarm, for if a language was not safe in its own land, where would it be safe? In these private schools there were also issues of student uniforms—mandated by school authorities from particular manufacturers; of textbooks—from particular publishers; and of unregulated fee hikes. These too evoked regular protests from parents along with the language issue.

The relegation of Panjabi to the margins, the assumption that the mother tongue is not important for the next generations, that the language of the future is English, is also the message from the skyline of Panjab. Every town, every city, many villages and the highways are dotted with innumerable boards announcing coaching for International English Language Testing System (IELTS) and Test of English as a Foreign Language (TOEFL). There are advertisements on which countries have what kind of visa provisions for student universities abroad, which courses are available or easier to crack, which university one needs to apply to for easier admission, and so on. As of early 2019, there were about five thousand IELTS coaching centres in Panjab and their business turnover was around Rs 1,000 crore.[157]

The tests themselves are very basic: listening, reading, writing and comprehension skills in English further broken down into general and academic streams. The preparation, mostly for one to three months, consists of repeated exams until the student reaches a respectable five plus bands out of nine—six is considered very good—and can take up to a year. The courses are available for anything between Rs 7,500 to Rs 20,000.

I sat through some classes in these institutes, talked to staff and students and it was clear that the reason the preparation time varied was because English remained a language out of context and use in Panjab. The typical Panjabi youngster deifies English, for it is a ladder to prosperity, a visa to a better life, but does not engage with the language to adopt it, internalise it or use it for what a language should do—help in communication.

Any language helps convey the whole gamut of your emotions. Yet, if that be the criteria even with those Panjabis who are adept at English, it remains a functional and not an emotional language. The mistake people make most in sentence structure between Panjabi and English is active and passive voice and that comes from not realising how important it is in English to have a subject, an owner of a sentence. It is cultural: the Gurbani hymns that people hear day in and day out are structured as universal truths, without active subjects. Imbibing that style of language means neo-learners of English need to make a special attempt to assert the subject and the ownership of sentences in English.

The institutes promise help, coaching and preparation for tests and visa interviews. The idea is to attract students who can pay the high fees to study abroad, often in institutions of dubious quality. The students hope that upon completion of the course they would find ways to stay back, converting student visas to temporary work permits and eventually applying for residence status and citizenship.

While talking to representatives of foreign universities, who often conducted day-long seminars to attract students in fancy hotels, it was clear that they needed youth from here because their own governments had stopped funding their universities and they were short on funds. On their prospective list were India and other so-called poorer nations. Within India they looked at Panjab, for they knew that its once-prosperous per capita farmers had not found the system or structure to educate their children. Panjabis seemed to be able to find the money to spend on the next generation.

This system of foreign universities clearly shows how foreign nations, often built on the loot of colonialism, have quickly run out of wealth and are now dependent once again on their erstwhile colonised nations for sustenance. In an open market this actually perpetuates the old order of colonialism. As of 2018, Panjab has spent up to Rs 27,000 crore[158] as fees alone and a total of Rs 60,000 crore by sending about 1.5 lakh students abroad annually.[159]

The rates for visas for those who want to migrate to western countries or to Australia and New Zealand is between Rs 15 lakh and Rs 25 lakh. The rates to migrate to the Gulf countries are between Rs 5 lakh to Rs 10 lakh. Many lakhs of people apply for work permits. There are many professionals also who choose to migrate, and their waiting time is lesser, depending upon how they score on eligibility criteria. The queues at the foreign consulates are at least five to seven years long. Compute the amount of money spent, and that is another huge drain on the state. Since most people who migrate over time take families along, the input to the state through foreign remittances is limited. The scope of wrongs—abandoning wives, re-marriages abroad for citizenship papers, fake marriages between relatives, cases of domestic abuse, abandonments—are infinite and these erode the value system of the society.

While these are candidates who seek to leave legally, there are a number of youth who seek to migrate illegally too. In March 2018, when the Modi government was facing questions on the Panjab National Bank scam and a no-confidence motion was being proposed, the then Foreign Minister Sushma Swaraj chose to declare that thiry-nine labourers, mostly from Panjab, declared missing in the Islamic State (IS) attack on Mosul, Iraq, in 2014 were confirmed dead—shot and killed by the IS.

The news served as a distraction. Questions were posed on why the government had been silent for so long. Some answers were given and the national focus from the PNB scam and the no-confidence motion shifted. Once again, the nation was distracted by a news item from Panjab. The fact was that Harjit Masih, the only survivor of the IS killing in 2014, had escaped, reached India and had already told the Indian authorities about the killing.[160] Yet, he was thrown in jail. Since then the government kept making false promises to the families of those declared missing but did not put out the real news. Two decades ago, 283 youth went missing enroute to Italy through an illegal water channel in an accident that is known as the Malta Boat tragedy. Till date the families are awaiting compensation from a CBI court. In January 2016, about twenty youth were feared drowned in the Panama Canal on their way, illegally, to the US.

There is a difference between going abroad legally and illegally. While governments are responsible for legal citizens, they are not legally liable for illegal ones. Yet, on humanitarian grounds, governments remain responsible. Thousands of young men from Panjab choose to travel illegally, every year. The migration business made up of touts, travel agents and liaison counterparts flourishes in the state. The illegal migrants take routes via Russia and Romania to Europe, via Mexico to the US, and to many other countries. I have met such young men from Poland to Spain, from Boston to Washington. Once in these countries, they try to become *pucca* (permanent residents), mostly through marriage with locals. Until then, they remain cut off from their homeland and their families and relatives. They live in abject conditions abroad but keep sending money home. To families here, that matters a lot.

Early morning in every city of Panjab—Ghumar Mandi, Ludhiana; Labour Chowk, Patiala and Sangrur; Rama Mandi, Jalandhar and scores of other locations—one can see migrant labourers from Uttar Pradesh, Bihar and Odisha standing, waiting to be picked up for daily wage work. Eerily, the scenes remind one of how slave trade used to happen until a few decades ago which has been depicted in books and media. Slave trade has existed ever since human civilisation began. Through all these modern approaches of education and through illegal means, Panjabi youth today want to go and stand to be picked up for labour in the different chowks of the world. The money involved in making them stand at these chowks is leaving the state just because the system has no way of employing them locally.

The reason for parents to send children to private schools is that government schools have failed to deliver. The reason for such an exodus of youth from Panjab is a serious job crisis. A bird's eye view of the education system reveals that in the last decade and a half, there has been nearly a 70 per cent shortfall of teaching staff in government colleges, as lecturers have not been hired. As of 2018, per the education minister's statement in the Panjab Assembly, in the forty-eight government colleges in the state, where 73,421 students study, 1,873 lecturer posts are sanctioned, but 1,292 are lying vacant and are being managed by 251 part-time lecturers and 882 guest faculty lecturers.[161] This, despite the fact that per UGC guidelines, 90 per cent of the teaching staff should be regular across all streams: science, arts and commerce. The last recruitment of college lecturers was held in 2003, which was annulled because of a corruption scandal,[162] and since then no recruitment has taken place.[163] Both the teacher appointment and the civil and judicial appointment cases are still being tried, after over fifteen years. In the meantime, colleges and officialdom suffer with ad hoc appointees serving at lower salaries and in unconfirmed jobs.

Government schools are even worse off. They face a shortfall of thirty-two thousand regular teachers. Around half the posts of headmasters and lecturers are lying vacant. Ironically, around thirty-three thousand five hundred eligible Teacher Eligibility Test (TET) pass outs await jobs.[164] When questioned, the government says it is short on funds. Parents want better education for their children. When the government is not able to provide quality education—over the last few years, each year, at least fifty thousand children in government schools have failed in either English or Panjabi or both—the shift is towards private schools. That is why, in the last five years, Panjab had lost around two lakh students to private schools.[165] Notice the contrast between what Panjab spends privately—by individual parents selling land, homes and assets—and how the state is so poor that it can't recruit teachers. Panjab spends around 88 per cent of its revenues on salaries, pensions and interest payments. Panjab's mainstay is agriculture, which remains untaxed even for big farmers. That is why it does not have the budget to hire permanent staff. Even when it hires them, there are probation periods extending to three years, which are extendable even further. This extends from the teaching profession to all other jobs, which, anyway are seldom notified.

When it comes to working or jobs, as discussed earlier in the chapter *Berukhi, kakajis*—the children of landed Jutts no longer want to touch the land. They have not done so for over a generation since migrant labour became available half a century back. Lands are rented out to tenant farmers or small Jutts. Then there is a huge shortfall in industrial jobs in towns like Mandi Gobindgarh and Batala which were known as iron and steel furnaces, foundaries and rolling mills.

While Batala suffered during militancy and never recovered, in the last decade around 30 per cent of Mandi Gobindgarh's four hundred and fifty factories shut down or went up on sale with no buyers. When I went down to Mandi Gobindgarh, owners of factories blamed the slowdown in the construction industry, shortage of scrap supply, and high rates of power tariff plus erratic supply as the main reasons they were reduced to single shifts or closures.[166]

In Ludhiana, while visiting labour slums and talking to people, a local leader took me to the dilapidated office of a senior functionary (name withheld on request) of the Bhartiya Mazdoor Sangh, the labour wing of the RSS. The gentleman who was around sixty spent a long time with me explaining how he was sworn to secrecy and could not complain about the governments run by their affiliates, the BJP. For the last thirty-five years his work had been with labour and unions. He told me during both the NDA I government under Vajpayee and now again by allowing Foreign Direct Investment (FDI), the BJP had rung the death knell for small-scale industries. He was now torn between his lifelong loyalty to the RSS and his lifelong passion to better the condition of workers. He said while Ludhiana could bear the fall in trade of hosiery items when the USSR split in 1991, the move to defocus from small-scale industries had led to a massive exodus of labour to Baddi in Himachal Pradesh, to Gujarat, and to Kerala and Tamil Nadu. He himself was from central India, yet he bemoaned that Panjab could not provide a permanent home to its workers. Ludhiana had around eight lakh migrant labour who constituted about 70 per cent of its workforce, but now, with production down by around 40 per cent, it was unlikely that the labour that had left would ever come back.[167]

In Jalandhar, once a leading sports goods manufacturer city, a simple lack of a cricket stadium—forever under construction—had caused much damage to industry. Cricket goods manufacturers told me how they were unable to get time with players, unable to get endorsements and unable to get and fulfil contracts. Sansarpur, the village which produced legendary hockey players, was now part of urban Jalandhar, and though some championships did throw up good players, there was no focus or incentive from the government to develop sports goods or sportspersons. Industry, on the whole, that shifted from Amritsar during Partition, had started faltering big time in Panjab, thus reducing their potential for recruitment of the youth. Since 2000, more than twenty thousand factories have shut shop in Panjab.[168]

In my travels, I was lucky to meet someone I had admired for long: former India hockey captain Pargat Singh. In September 2016, he quit the SAD–BJP government over an issue of the government wanting to install a sewage treatment plant in his constituency. This would have increased pollution, not decreased it. He had taken the pro-people step and resigned. With his resignation also went the chances of a leading sportsperson creating a system in which Panjab's talent in sports could be channelised. As of now all the wonderful talent from Panjab is being largely spotted and coached in private academies; the state almost has no role in it except hiring some sportsmen and sportswomen in its departments—mostly police.

Our conversation veered towards drugs and sports. I asked him about his thoughts on what had happened to the body and the physicality of Panjab. Why could he, through his good offices, not help with the issues? Why did the Akalis not make him the sports minister? As a person, Pargat is utterly modest. It was visible even in the lack of paraphernalia, and the ease with security guards around his home and office. His home is also on a side street in Jalandhar Cantonment and he has not moved to a posher area even though he had hit the big league a long time ago.

He told me as director, sports, he had undertaken a massive study of the Olympics, Asian Games and Commonwealth Games champion nations to understand what they did and how they trained to earn so many medals. He studied the plans of over twenty countries and devised a system by which children right from nursery level could be encouraged to take up any one of the three basic sports: athletics, gymnastics or swimming. Then, as they grew, they would be sorted out on the basis of ability and stamina and encouraged to specialise and adopt particular sports per their skills. As they began competing at the school, block, zonal and district levels they could be considered for some relaxation in school grades and marks. In any case, these days there was no detention until Class VIII. All that was needed was good physical training teachers at primary and secondary school levels and infrastructure, which was mostly available through the stadiums the government had created, but which lay overgrown with weeds.

Panjab has over ten thousand schools and he was willing to work with only half that number. Panjab schools already had physical training teachers and all they needed was orientation towards this plan. He told me he did not even need money for the plan; he just needed a buy-in by all concerned departments and he was willing to go down to the people to raise funds for their own village sports infrastructure—making swimming pools and gymnasiums. He was very sure that given how sports was anyway such a part of Panjab's culture, every village and every villager would participate in a grand plan if rolled out.

Pargat repeatedly requested the cooperation of the education minister but never got it. Neither did the Akali leadership give him minister status to be able to negotiate with the education minister on equal terms. His feeling was that if this had been implemented a decade ago, Panjab would not even have plunged as deep into drugs as it had now. As a sportsman he believed that sports could do both: save Panjab from drugs and earn Panjab laurels that the land richly deserved. All that was needed was execution of a good plan on ground. But, he felt, now it seemed like a lost opportunity. I also felt the SAD–BJP government had lost such an opportunity not only in sports development but also in physical development of the younger generation and giving them something meaningful to do so that they stayed away from drugs.

I asked him as a sportsman, as a captain of the India hockey team for a decade, what difference he saw between a team sport and the game of politics where a political party was a team going into elections. He elaborated three differences:

a) in a sport, a game, the whole team was focussed on one goal—winning—which was hardly the case in politics where parties and people were out to sabotage each other's chances;

b) in a match every player was fully assured of cooperation of every other player in the team and they faced the opponents together, which was hardly the case in politics where trust in fellow party members was lower than in the opponents;

c) in a game, whatever be the result—a win or a loss—there was a sense that every player's back was covered and even if something went wrong in team dynamics, in locker rooms, on ground, in strategy, no one squealed on one another, whereas in politics backbiting was the norm, in fact, the practice.

'That trust,' said Pargat, 'is the most important in sports and most missing in politics.' I got a sense that Pargat could have easily retired on his laurels or continued to serve in the Panjab Police or just relocated anywhere in the world and become a coach, but he had a vision for Panjab, for its youth, for its health, which sadly the Akalis did not value, and kept him away from what he could deliver.

Next to the Panjab Police headquarters, on Jan Marg, Chandigarh, is the labyrinthine Panjab Mini Secretariat. On its fourth floor I met a senior bureaucrat with extensive experience both in the state and the Centre. The bureaucrat said, 'The decline in both health and education has been the result of neo-liberal policies we adopted as a nation a quarter century back. At that time the thinking was that the state can withdraw from these essential public services and focus on getting funds to develop industry, provide job opportunities and increase the GDP. The hope was that the private players will be able to step in to take over the essential public services.'

'Well, private players have come in ...'

'Yes, they have, but frankly no economist could ever predict the level of greed with which they have come in. No planner could predict the number of violations that private players are capable of. Our tragedy is we remain individual profit-centred and do not think about society.'

'Is it because we have seen too many social systems collapse? We do not trust them any longer?'

The bureaucrat paused, and said, 'Yes, that is perhaps correct. Since no one has benefitted from the system except by bypassing it, violating it, everyone wants to make igloos out of profits and hide in them. Yet, when the entire society goes down, even these igloos will crumble.'

'So, is there no hope?'

'You see, both health and education are a matter of trust. Actually the whole system is a matter of trust. Now that the system has lost trust, even if we start now, it might take a long time to build it again. Of course, the poor will come because they lack options, but will the middle class and the rich use state facilities?' The reference was to AAP's claim that they had fixed Delhi's schools and started *mohalla* clinics.

The bureaucrat was correct. I was struck by how the bureaucrat had mentioned trust as the core of all interaction of people with the system of the state. If I took an ailing parent of a relative or a friend to a government hospital and their situation did not improve, I would lose trust in the system. The same for education, with its deficit of faculty and with its high failure rates. Most of us and our parents studied in government schools, were taken care of by government hospitals, but the lot of current youth do not have that experience. If the concept of trust arose so easily in understanding the problem, why was it so difficult to keep and build? The core issue was people's inability to place trust in the system. That is why for the youth of Panjab, who have lost trust in the system, the only escape seems to be going abroad, to newer systems which they deem can be trusted a wee bit more easily, and which deliver.

In Rourkela, I was born at the crossroads of four languages: Panjabi at home, Odia with my Adivasi nanny, Hindi on the streets and English at school. On these travels through Panjab, knowing how to speak Panjabi and read and write Gurmukhi was my greatest asset. An added benefit has been the access to social media. Like all other native language social media, I realised the Panjabi social media too is a whole planet unto itself, very far from the English world we live in.

During the last two years, knowing Panjabi, and dealing in Panjabi sucked me in so much that I started feeling, thinking and responding in Panjabi. Until then, since I dealt mostly in English, I had not felt the switch most people who deal in two languages explain: they think in one language and translate it into another before speaking it.

Now, as I travelled in Panjab, the issue of language unfolded in multiple ways, the primary being ease of conversation. Everyone, irrespective of rural or urban, religion or caste, gender or location, deals in the Panjabi language. In fact, it starts from Agra onwards, or even Delhi, but is certainly there full-fledged in Ambala and the rest of Panjab. That is why I remain bewildered by how the Panjabi Suba movement unfolded, with the simple point its leaders were trying to make, but to which the Centre was apathetic.

There are many ways in which a language erodes, and many languages are facing those issues: when literature dwindles, when street signs change, when public instructions change, when official communication stops, when the language is no longer taught in schools, when the language of streets and the market changes, and so on. I remember going to Bangalore in the late 1990s and finding destinations of buses, addresses, vehicle number plates, shop boards, and so on in Kannada. As a north Indian I felt odd because all that militancy had achieved on ground in Panjab was a bit of Panjabi in Gurmukhi script adorning government offices. I wondered if it was a worthy goal for all that bloodshed.

Karnataka was keeping its language alive, though there were tussles with other state languages feeling threatened—Kodava, Beary, Tulu, Konkani and others. Yet, it was necessary for the state to promote Kannada, to avoid how the nationalistic view of Hindi, Hindu and Hindustan was attempting to change its culture. On my travels in European nations I have often been foxed by the national language in supermarkets and in train stations. Yet, just like language is necessary for a state in India, it is necessary for the states to maintain their identity. I was the one moving to a new place; I needed to learn the languages to manage my being in these new places.

One evening, in a shared tempo from Bharat Nagar Chowk in Ludhiana, I saw four non-Panjabi men climb in, speaking fluent Panjabi. I asked them where they had learnt Panjabi. All four of them were born in Panjab, in Ludhiana. One of them, a Class IV employee, said, 'My Panjabi is better than my Hindi.' I asked if they went back home. 'This is home. We have been here since the 1960s. We have no connection with Bihar.'

'Where do your children study?'

'Here, in government schools.'

As a new generation of children who were born in migrant families settled in the state, they started going to government-run schools. Now children of migrant labourers learnt Panjabi. Often, in block-level and district-level calligraphy competitions, many migrant children win prizes.[169] When you visit such schools, the migrant children charm you with how they grasp Panjabi and remember and sing songs that are fast disappearing from even the rural landscape. The next generation of the migrant labourer has certainly adopted the language, though Panjab is yet to accept and acknowledge this generation, its small shop owners, workers in *dhabas* and businesses, plumbers, *mistries* and workers. Panjabi language, the reason for the state formation, appears to be safe at least among the migrants.

At the same time, across Panjab, I find hotels with names like Skyair, Kosmo, Cabana, Klassic Komfort, Whistling Wuds—a deliberate mocking of the English language. I wondered if Panjabi speakers were cocking a snook on being forced to learn the imperial language English for survival and a better life abroad. However, in the absence of rigour, through earlier false translations, terms from English have also been part of the language of Sikh religious affairs. The ceremony of *Amrit sanchar—khande-de-pahul* is called baptism. Baptism is not the equivalent of *khande-de-pahul*. The word ought to be initiation. At the Darbar Sahib, around the *parikarma*, the circumambulation around the *sarovar*, the holy water tank in the middle of which is located the sanctum sanctorum, there are notices saying: 'Please do not throw the flowers of holy communion into the pool of nectar'. The obeisance that the faithful offer the Granth Sahib is not the equivalent of the 'wine and bread' analogy from the Christian world. These are different religions, different contexts, different theologies, and different traditions. They should not and must not be compared. No doubt English is the language of the powerful and trade and commerce and Panjab feels it needs to catch up with learning it. Yet, by distorting it or using it wrongly, they are doing a disservice to both, the language and themselves.

On the other hand, to me, the crises with jobs and language lies on the border with Pakistan. While language grows in many ways, travels in even more ways, passes on from generation to generation, the only way it can really survive is if it creates a market for itself, if it can support people who only know that one language to survive and thrive and prosper. If a language can feed you, it survives, if it can't, it perishes. One can prop up a language through nostalgia and through special efforts such as education, but they do not last. If the language loses its use in the market, it perishes, sooner or later.

The real question is how to provide a market to Panjabi. Today, in Panjab, if someone knows only Panjabi, they will be able to survive, but not really prosper. For prospering, an individual or a market needs to expand.

Panjab's current population is about 25 million but just across the border is another Panjab in Pakistan, roughly three times the size of this Panjab. In this region, the other half of Panjab, the Pakistan government has imposed Urdu. However, for a while now there has been a growing movement there in favour of Panjabi. If the two regions decide to join hands to promote Panjabi, and open their mutual markets to each other, along with the rest of the expatriate population, Panjabi will become the tenth biggest language in the world, spoken by 120 million people.

In itself, this is a huge market. A far bigger market than what is projected when we look at only East Panjab, the Indian part of Panjab. If this market were to be tapped, through trade and commerce, imagine how many people could find their world complete without having to step into another language, especially by force, by imposition, by desperation that English creates.

Panjabi in east Panjab is written in the Gurmukhi script and in west Panjab—Pakistan—in Nastaliq script, Shahmukhi. A language activist said to me, 'We just want technology to provide us with accurate transcreations from one script to another and you will see the border will vanish.' I smile at his hope. What else does Panjab have but hope? To keep Panjabi alive would mean that the border at

Wagah, Hussainiwala and Sulaimanke would have to be demolished. Trade, exchange and work permits would need to be arranged. People ought to be able to travel back and forth for work and personal reasons. What other solution is available for not only the Panjabi language, but even Panjabi people and the land and region called Panjab?

The question is how to negotiate the border which both countries want to keep as the most burning issue in South Asian politics. How to develop the political will to reunite Panjab not politically but through trade. How to cross the massive barriers the two governments have drawn, how to rise above the bloodlust for the enemy that the people of the two nations consider each other. Opening up to Pakistan means Panjab's trade joins, through Afghanistan, with Central Asia and Russia, through Iran and Turkey, with Balkans and Europe, and through the China One Belt One Road project, with the Chabahar and Karachi ports to trade with the world.

It was in the slums of Chandigarh that I met students from Panjab University who were engaged in helping the dwellers arrange their papers to fight the union territory authorities over a recent demolition of slums. Pali, who showed me the movement of slums on a map, also told me he was part of a university student group called 'Students For Society' (SFS). Later, I met more students at the manicured and sprawling lawns of the university and at the cylindrical Students' Centre. Most of them were from SFS. They told me that Pali had, in fact, founded SFS in 2010.

Panjab has had a culture of students' groups. We earlier learnt about the Naujwan Bharat Sabha (NBS). In 1943, the Akali Dal created its students group called All India Sikh Students Federation.

It played an important role in spreading the message and recruiting new cadre during the Panjabi Suba movement. In the 1980s, the body tilted towards an armed struggle under Jarnail Singh Bhindranwale and many of its members fought against the Indian Army during Operation Blue Star and Operation Black Thunder. Later, many of its members joined militancy, especially the Khalistan Commando Force and the Khalistan Liberation Force. They were banned in 1984 and college elections were suspended in Panjab.

When the ban was lifted in 1985, the AISSF split into two factions, one more radical than the other, but both focussed on Sikh issues. AISSF also underwent a change of name by dropping All India and calling itself the Sikh Students Federation. In the early 2000s it ran campaigns in colleges to awaken the political consciousness of the students. When the Akalis came back to power in 2007, they curbed the organisation. Still, its leaders, Karnail Singh Peer Mohammad and Daljeet Singh Bittu have gained a voice in Panjab politics.

On the other hand, in 1968, the French students' protest ignited a lot of movements around the globe. In Panjab, influenced by Left parties, the students created the Panjab Students Union. In the early 1970s, issues like black marketing of cinema tickets at the Regal theatre in Moga and the hike in price of bus tickets, became flashpoints between the students and the government. In 1974, along with the NBS, the PSU stood in solidarity with farmers at the Moga Sangram Rally and even with policemen agitating for their demands. PSU opposed the Emergency and its leaders were arrested or went underground. In the late 1970s, a prominent leader Prithipal Singh Randhawa was gunned down by goons. Randhawa's murder weakened the PSU but it kept its presence in Panjab's colleges through the years of militancy and until now.

However, though the ban on AISSF has been lifted long ago, student elections have still not been held in Panjab. Since Panjab does not allow elections at college and university level, student organisations are nebulous. They are formed on lines of caste and class. There are those whose members come from working class families, Dalit and the poorer Jutt families: PSU (Panjab Students Union), the PSU Lalkar, the PSU Randhawa, the Bharat Naujwan Sabha, the Democratic Students Union in Panjabi University, Patiala, who represent students' issues.

Then there are those students who can be called *kakajis*; they come from landed Jutt or middle or upper class Hindu families and believe in pomp and show-off and are backed by political parties: Students for India which is the Akali Dal youth wing, National Students Union of India which is the Congress students' wing, the Akhil Bhartiya Vidyarthi Parishad which is the BJP youth wing. In all these organisations youth are groomed and used for local political purposes by the political parties. They come in handy during elections as volunteers and muscle men and also to be used against groups that seek accountability and freedom from college and university administrations. There is also a group called Gandhi Group Student Union which is a standalone formation that does not represent anyone—a self-styled power unto itself. The founder died in a gang war.

The scene in Panjab University, Chandigarh—a Union Territory— is different. The University holds regular elections and has a number of student bodies which are traditionally not directly affiliated to political parties but are, to some extent, funded by political individuals. It started well in 1977 as Panjab University Students Union (PUSU) which won its first elections in 1978. In 1997 came the Students Organisation of Panjab University (SOPU). Both these parties have won in turns and while they are unaffiliated to any political party, they do provide a microcosm of Panjab politics where the Akalis and the Congress have rotated power between themselves. As political parties started taking interest in the university politics and the SOI and NSUI entered the arena, they recruited cadre from the PUSU and SOPU. The elections were about money and muscle power. The very class to which the student leaders belonged was representative of the dominance of the Jutt discourse in Panjab and glorified the same feudal and patriarchal culture that is celebrated in Panjab.

Amidst these groups, SFS distinguishes itself by being inspired by Bhagat Singh's ideology and follows the path laid by Banda Bahadur. These days, such a group is often called Left-oriented, but it is not regimentalised like the Left. In SFS I noticed the same inclination to bring a synthesis between socialist thought and the Gurbani—the very instinct that had created the Ghadar Party a century ago in North America. Just that this was completely home-grown and came from understanding the futility of the struggles Panjab had undergone in the last five decades or more. In the rooms of its members you will find Bhagat Singh rubbing shoulders with Sant Ram Udasi, the Dalit poet who traversed the route from Naxalism to a pro-Khalistan stance because what he had been keeping alive was the deeper tradition of Panjab—rebellion against power hegemony and the call for equality.

The SFS has eschewed money and muscle and stands for issue-based politics. The major SFS stances—against the fee hike; ban on four-wheelers and loud music; removal of night curfew in women's hostels; demand for new hostels—reveal a particular emphasis that has been missing in student politics until now, but reminds us of the student politics of the 1970s, an emphasis on people's issues.

Worldwide, students' movements stand for greater freedoms. When seen from that point of view, some SFS stances on the surface (ban on four-wheelers and loud music) might seem contrary to freedoms, but they are deeply entwined with real freedoms. By raising issues of fee hikes—a move by all governments since neo-liberalisation—SFS demonstrates that it has its finger on the gravest aftereffect of the open door policy the Indian government practises by withdrawing from its commitment to universal higher education. SFS's call is against the move to sign pacts like the General Agreement on Tariffs and

Trade (GATT) which leads to privatisation of education by turning it into a commodity and which takes education out of the reach of poorer and hence needier sections of the society.

GATT disadvantages India because we have the youngest population in the world. With half our people below the age of twenty-five, India faces the challenge of educating its youth and preparing them for taking up employment both within the country and outside. GATT proposes a level playing field for both Indian and foreign players but the field would be level only for the traders of education, not for society at large. When a large fraction of people are still first-generation learners, it is paramount that we ensure equitable development. Yet, when education is treated as a tradable commodity, social justice fails. The government cannot even continue to subsidise its own institutions or support needy students through scholarships or reservation policies, as those would be interpreted as unfair trade practices. Any disputes that arise in this regime would have to be referred not to the judiciary but to the World Trade Organization's Dispute Settlement Body.[170] The SFS might be a small group in one university in a corner of the world but its politics is targeting the biggest issue of the human development model of the world.

By raising issues of four-wheelers and loud music, the SFS is challenging the feudal culture of universities where *kakajis* rule the roost. These *kakajis*, absentee landlords, will perhaps never go back to farming and are there in the modern city Chandigarh—Panjab's first contact with the West, as anthropologist Harjant Gill says—to have a good time.

They splurge to dress up well, have big cars and SUVs, and their biggest engagement every day is to go and either line up outside the women's hostels in the evenings or go on what is euphemistically called *gerhi* (a drive). The term *gerhi* is a feminisation of the word *gerha* which was an activity of the big landowners of the past when they went on horseback to inspect their vast fields. Within it, the term encapsulates the political economy of large farms where the *malik* (owner) has many *siris* (serfs) working for him, some from landed castes and many from landless ones.

In a modern urban context, it is the same ritual, but this time the prey are women students—a show of machismo, alpha masculinity. To go on a *gerhi* is to drive tailgating women students, whether they are walking or in a vehicle, sipping beer, with music blaring in what in north India is called car-o-bar—drinking in the car. The open source naming of Google Maps even featured the *gerhi* route: starting from the university, going through sectors to Hotel Mount View and returning from there—in essence, a circle. It defines owners who have separated from their lands, moved to cities and changed their means of transportation from horses to SUVs.

Popular Panjabi music (by singers such as Honey Singh, Badshah and Sidhu Moosewala) aids this activity because it celebrates the upper caste Jutts, bemoans their travails as original sons of the soil, expresses dismay at how modernity has corrupted the feudal value system, pitches the degenerate city against the ideal village, holds women responsible for the vagaries of the male—what all a man has to do to woo a woman—and ends up making a martyr out of the male. It is a familiar trope through ages—blame the materialistic, greedy woman for the downfall of man. Now the music celebrates it with guns and alcohol, and by dissing the English language which is associated with urban culture and modernity which a tradition-seeking Panjab views as an attack on itself. Every few weeks there is a new star singer clocking many millions of hits on YouTube.

Many women object to being commodified, painted in one dimension, and the *gerhi*. The SFS protested the music and the *gerhis* of these young men and sought safe spaces for women students and even other university staff. The protests succeeded, the university authorities agreed and they announced that they would ban four-wheelers, but have still not acted on the ban. A male SFS member told me, 'When we came to the university, we thought being *kakas* was great—dress up nattily and woo women. I did that for a year but no woman came to me. Then I heard what SFS was saying, I related it to what I was studying, a professor guided my thoughts and it made sense to support these new ideas. Now we work alongside women, not in relationships but as friends.' Which is great because in Panjab we really do not have inter-gender conversations.

By raising the demand to allow women twenty-four-hour access to the hostel, SFS is attempting to invert the centuries-old patriarchal culture of the land. This is not only because the women students are majors—above eighteen—but because this challenges the normative behaviour of Panjab. By raising this question, the SFS is actually questioning the age-old entrenched behaviour and practice of Panjab and also the very model on which the state has been run for many decades now. It is questioning the infantilising of Panjab by those it elects as its custodians. It is signalling the end of a prescription model of governance and asking for true democracy to be implemented for one half of the land's citizens.

In the conversations I have had with women, especially students, almost every young girl swore that all their parents wanted was to marry them off. Almost every mother had brought them up, saying, *Bas viyah ton baad saada kam muk jayega* (once you are married, our task will be over).

Forever in the land of battles that is Panjab, the women have been seen as a burden, an object on which family honour depends. In earlier times when kings and bandits ruled, no one knew when and how someone could kidnap them and abuse them. However, even after the advent of democracy, the culture did not change in the feudal society. During the militancy days, owing to the fear of militants and the police and their mutual wariness of each other, the streets of Panjab used to be empty by 6 p.m. A quarter century later, even now roads are empty of women by 8 p.m. Many women friends tell me that they can't stay out late unless accompanied by a man. SFS is saying, if we all have individual rights, if we have a modern democratic system, then whose responsibility is it to create a fearless society? Why do we have a government and an administration if we are not going to be able to ensure every citizen can live their life without fear?

This so-called 'women's protection' by locking them in early is not helping anyone's cause except that the crime rate looks reasonable. It does not mean crime disappears, it only means the vulnerable are silenced and hidden away. SFS's basic reasoning is that if the society has to change, then it's men who have to change. Unless men are challenged and pushed to acknowledge women and both are given equal rights, the system of the state is only deferring the issues and is, in fact, aggravating them by keeping the two genders away from each other. By asking for freedom in a safe space like a university, the SFS is challenging the administration to begin closing the gap between the genders. It is asking for a true and not an elusive safe space where everyone, irrespective of gender, can feel free and no one feels discriminated. After all, if a university is not safe, how would the society be safe?

A part of Panjab's feudal patriarchal system manifests in the craze for the male child, snapping of the link to married girls and sons taking care of aged parents. The discrimination also comes from the practice of dowry that crushes every parent through peer pressure from other families, and the trap has led many farmers and labourers to loans and suicide. The gender bias also has links with the work and lifestyle of the farmer—the fact that the so-called Green Revolution has turned farming so transactional. The whole purpose of agriculture now is not the joy of seeding life, of seeing life grow, of nurturing life and of feeling one with nature. Instead, it is the reverse: how to fight nature, manipulate it, avoid natural phenomenon like even rain, push the earth to create a bounty through fertilisers and manage disease through insecticides and pesticides to make a produce which can then be sold for money, even if it is insufficient.

The aim of agriculture has shifted from subsistence to industrial. The farmer then treats his daughters, too, like his crop—cares for her until she can be harvested (married) and then responsibility ceases. This has further alienated women. The farmer thinks of the daughter as his produce, to be loved while it is his, to wash his hands off once she is married. It is the same with animals and equipment too. This is not to say men are hardened and love their daughters any less. It is just that the system of transactions has pushed people towards objectifying one another instead of forging bonds of affection.

This, in spite of the Sikh religion being unisex, formed on the basis of gender and other equalities. Yet, the Sikh religion does not have a woman as a Guru. It hardly has enough women heroes in its legends and histories. While men were fighting battles, what were the women doing? Wasn't running the home and managing the household glamourous enough to become stories? Until recently, Panjab topped the female foeticide charts in the country, perhaps the world.

The government has ordered against parents determining the gender of an unborn child, against the medical termination of pregnancy. The reporting of pregnancies and follow-up after birth, swooping down on erring doctors, has stemmed the fall in numbers but no change is possible unless the society wills it. That mentality is changing now. In middle class families, women like Minnie are coming forward to prove to their parents that they can do as good a job of taking care of them while following their own careers as any son would have done. Increasingly, while *kakajis* struggle, women are coming to the forefront of not just the society but even homes.

The issues SFS picked to protest resonated with me. I was happy to notice that a generation born after the days of militancy had learnt how to fight its battles for democracy, though the older society was stuck in traditional ways. SFS was pushing the envelope of what it meant to be a student from an ordinary background in these challenging times where hegemony was reinventing itself in new garb. It was pushing the youth to think, act, claim their due space in society and not be bulldozed by the powers that be—academic or political. In the process, by envisioning a better society, it was undercutting the old unequal power structures. I made a number of friends from members of the SFS and sometimes they travelled with me.

Amrit and Sona were in the car with me to Sardulgarh, right at the border of Panjab and Haryana. We were going to attend Parkash Singh Badal's famous *sangat darshan* (open house). The area MP, old Akali loyalist, Balwinder Singh Bhunder, member of the Rajya Sabha, and the CM were coming. The MLA wouldn't come because he was from the Congress.

In the last university student council election Amrit was SFS's presidential candidate. Amrit, from a small village in Hoshiarpur, kept an open beard and played the tambourine. His tambourine was such a hit that everyone believed he would be the president. But he lost narrowly. Until now, in its second outing, SFS had not won the elections. However, his and SFS's approach to student issues was changing the way the students functioned—from being outsiders to the culture of money and muscle to now finding more acceptance of SFS ideas. It could be seen when new students enrolled each year and the SFS booths offering memberships were full. It could be seen in the membership increase and the way students attended SFS programmes.

I appreciated their stance but felt their position on women hostel timing was fairly dramatic and also very edgy. Any idiot could compromise it by attacking a woman and derail the struggle. It was a usual tactic these days, especially with trolls, or even how Kejriwal's odd-even traffic scheme was sabotaged in Delhi. Sona, sitting next to me, replied, 'But our women are out early morning and late night. Any other time it is risky because of the Jutts.'

That is when the gravity of what the students were attempting dawned on me. The SFS position made complete sense. No entrenched caste or class would see this, it was a blind spot like the *gerhi* was a blind spot. We reached the gurdwara, the programme venue. Our contact, a journalist with a leading English daily, had asked us to enter. He would be late, he said. We got down from the car and proceeded towards a tent set up on the side of the gurdwara.

We noticed two gates and took the one closer to us. The police at the gate stopped us. By now I had a fake Press card. Though I had been filing stories for various media outlets and had requested them for a letter or some identity card which said I was a freelancer, no one had helped. I asked a friend who reported from Bastar. She showed me her fake Press card and said it cost her Rs 75 for four cards. I got them made, the front side with my picture on a white card and a bold red line saying Press. Since then, police checks in Panjab, and there are a lot of them, had been a breeze. When they turned the card to find my PAN number given as if it was a registration number and looked at my previous rented home address that said New Delhi, the gates opened wider.

I told the police that I was a journalist from Delhi and that Amrit and Sona were with me. They did not check their cards and waved us to an enclosure right next to where the chief minister would take his seat. We observed the layout. There was a low stage in front and a wide path in the centre of the tent, opening to the stage. On the left of the path were the petitioners. On the right, next to the press enclosure, were the officials. The general crowd was in the back of the tent. We were the only three in the press enclosure until then, waiting for the CM to arrive.

An inspector walked up to us from behind. One could see that he had his hair cut and shaved too, but now he had tied his turban and sported a stubble. The inspector asked me who I was. I replied in English. He was a bit taken aback, and left. Soon after that, an Indian Police Service officer, a tall uniformed Sikh, came up to us and put his hand on my shoulder. I rose and he asked me which paper I was from. I reached for my wallet to pull out my fake identity card but he stopped me. '*The Hindu*,' I said.

He asked, '*The Hindu?*'

I said, 'Yes, *The Hindu*, published from Chennai, India-wide newspaper.'

'Oh!' he said, '*The Hindu!*'

'What happened?'

He said, 'My men did not understand. They thought you were from some Hindu party, the BJP.'

I assured him, 'No, not from a party. A journalist from Delhi. I am travelling to get a sense of where Panjab stands right now politically. Elections are coming ...'

He passed on his card to me. 'Contact me if you need any help. But may I make a request? Are these two young men on assignment with you?'

I said, 'No, but we are travelling together. They are showing me around.'

'Can I request you to send them to the next enclosure? Behind? You know CM Saab ...'

I nodded. I did not have a choice. I asked Amrit and Sona to comply. They moved back. I sat alone wondering why the Akali leader would be wary of their partner, the BJP. Was it because there was some talk of them splitting? Was it regular—this lack of trust even between alliance partners? I did not notice, but another Sikh man came and sat next to me. 'Do you write regularly?' he asked.

I looked at him. He looked to be in his mid- or late-fifties. He wore a grey turban, grey trousers and a light blue shirt, tucked in, and a blazer. I knew better than not to answer. 'I am in editorial but I do special stories. We are planning a feature on Panjab.'

'Can I get your visiting card?'

Luckily Parkash Singh Badal arrived. The whole audience, the tent which was more than half filled up now, got up. I didn't. The Sikh man next to me looked at me quizzically. I did not move.

He carried on talking to me, trying to ask questions. I told him I had come to cover the *sangat darshan* and I needed to pay attention to Badal Saab. He went silent. The stage was being managed by Bhunder, the local MP, who had a list in his hand. The officials were gathering close to the stage. Badal was about ten metres from me and I could hear his avuncular tone. I disliked the way Bhunder was calling people onto the stage. Someone had a hole in his overhead tank, someone had a fight with a neighbour, someone had a marriage coming up and someone had a land dispute.

Badal was hardly adjudicating. All he did was to call the respective official and let Bhunder call the shots. Bhunder remembered one petition from another, remembered who had come a third time. He even rejected some petitions rather crudely, saying, 'How many times will you come? Don't you know Badal Saab is a busy man? Go to your village panchayat.'

This was in vast contrast to how people were treated at the Simarjit Singh Bains office or even how common people met Pargat Singh. No one from the back crowd came forward. The police were blocking their way. Television cameras were recording the crowds but this was hardly a *sangat darshan*. It was just a mobile chief minister office.

The Sikh man next to me had his hand on my thigh. He was patting it, in full public view. It reminded me of how, when I was a young boy and would travel in public buses, older men used to pat my thigh. 'Your friend, does he not know how to tie a turban? As if he never saw the mirror today morning.'

I thought Amrit tied a great turban, wholly original, not with pleats like the Patiala style made popular by the armed services. His was a turban with subtle pleats, more rounded than boat-shaped. I was uncomfortable but remarked, 'As if Badal Saab ties a better turban.' It was a well-known joke: Badal tied his turban, then twisted it to an angle to make it look unkempt, to give the impression that he was an ordinary man and had no airs.

'But he is the CM,' the man defended.

To ease the sarcasm I said, 'It is good the CM makes time to meet people.'

My positive statement assured him. By now the man perhaps realised I was not a risk. He leaned up to me and said, 'I am from intelligence.'

I asked with a smile, 'You are spying on me?'

He said, 'What to do, it is our job.'

I spent another five or seven minutes gawking at what was going on on the stage. By now two officers had been hauled up. They were giving some kind of dictation to stenographers. It was business as usual. I got up. The Sikh man asked me, 'Leaving?'

I replied, 'Yes, I got what I needed.'

He shook hands with me, told me his designation and name. As a matter of security but projected as courtesy he came up to the tent gate to drop me. I waved to Amrit and Sona to get up. We walked to the car. A man and a woman approached us as we were leaving. 'Our case is not listed. Can you help us?'

I answered, 'We? How can we help?'

'You were sitting in front. You might have some connection ...'

I was embarrassed, 'No, no, we don't. We are just ...' I did not complete my sentence. I couldn't lie to them about being a journalist. What if they wanted me to do a story? 'Excuse us,' I murmured.

Of course there was a story. The whole *sangat darshan* drama was a sham. I was livid. Was this how the chief minster's security was arranged? Every citizen was a suspect?

As we drove off, Amrit said, 'Baiji, you don't know what happened with us.'

'What?'

'They put a camera on us.'

'Camera?'

'Yes, all the time we sat there. The police repeatedly asked us our names, our university name, what we studied, where our villages were. It was a full inquiry.'

'But why? What is this scrutiny?' I asked.

Sona replied, 'Because Amrit is wearing a black T-shirt and yellow turban.'

Amrit joined in, 'So the police thought we were from AAP. A constable told us, what if for even thirty seconds you had removed your T-shirt and waved it? The news would be the Badal *sangat darshan* faces black flags!'

My jaw fell. '*Hai Rubba*, I never could have thought of it!' I replied.

'It is like this, *ji*, the rein of absolute power is the scariest for those who wield it,' replied Sona wisely. 'Once they compare the pictures, they will know who they missed.' All newspapers had carried Amrit's pictures during the student elections.

Amrit replied, 'What difference does it make? My name is already in police records for earlier protests.' He burst out into song:

*Jo na jaane haq ki taqat, Rubb na deve us nu himmat …*

Those who do not know the power of their rights,
may God not give them strength.

All that was missing was a tambourine.

## Chapter Fifteen

# *Lashaan* — Corpses

'Be ready to count the corpses,' Satpal Danish had said. Throughout my travels in Panjab, talk and acknowledgement and the counting of corpses was a part of almost every conversation I had with people and the news I read on Panjab. In a state that had one-fifth of all the national arms licences, the gun was often not very far from most conversations.[171] I could often make out the gun sticking out from the pyjama pocket or the holster of the person I was meeting. Upon my noticing the gun the person would give a sardonic smile. I would ask if the person had been part of the movement (Khalistan) and had killed someone. Many would admit to sympathy for the movement, or tell me they were part of it for a while, or they had even done jail for some months, and I was ever thankful no one said they had killed anyone, even if it were a lie. I do not know how I would have behaved with someone who had admitted to a killing.

Corpses also framed much of my travels. When I was looking at Dera Radhaswami Beas, a friend asked me to meet his uncle to learn how his father i.e. my friend's grandfather, was killed. The son of a former Congressman, Ravinder Kalia from Rayya, told me how during the peak of violence, pretty much their entire small town would empty out into the *dera* for the night. 'It started with small incidents and moved towards greater plunder. Those who didn't have cycles suddenly owned motorcycles. In Rayya, there would be one or two gang-related kidnappings every year. The only place we all had to go for the nights was the *dera*.' Indeed, there is no news of the *dera* having ever been under attack or even threatened by the militants.

Kalia then proceeded to relate the incident. 'That day there was no warning. They landed up in the mandi. There must have been a thousand people there. They came on a motorcycle, pointed the gun to the back of my father's head and shot him point blank. I was at the rice sheller. My brother was at our *arthiya* shop and he called me.'

When Kalia learnt of the news and rushed home, the father's body was still in post-mortem. The telephone rang. The militant on the other end said coldly: 'You are not allowed a public funeral.'

In the next day's issue of the *Ajit* dated 14 January 1990, there was a news item that the militants took responsibility for the killing, saying my father was a Congressman and an anti-Khalistani.

'When he was killed, my father was chairman of Markfed. My younger brother had been sarpanch for two decades. I had been an elected member of the municipality and its president. But after my father's killing, the erosion started. People started leaving. Businesses stated moving out to other cities, Jalandhar, Amritsar, even Delhi and out of the state. In 1991, when the Census took place, we discovered that the population of the town had decreased.'

In spite of knowing the SSP and getting immediate police protection, the family could not cremate the body in the cremation ground. Under cover, late evening, the family had conducted the last rites in a corner of their rice sheller. 'But we did not leave. I reckoned that we had spent all our lives here, where would we reach if we were to start all over again? Most of the families that moved suffered bad times.'

'But how was life here?' I asked, sad at the killing, sadder at the denial of cremation, but with admiration for the Kalia family standing its ground.

'Threats started coming over the phone. Mostly about children. We sent away all the kids to boarding schools in Shimla. Most villagers came back to town but those who left town took a long time to recover. We went back by a quarter century. In those days the *dera* earned a good name.'

What Kalia told me was the regular critique of the militancy movement and its anti-Hindu and anti-Congress narrative. He added that in those days there was regular exchange of fire between militants and Hindu families, in many villages of Amritsar and Gurdaspur. Many families migrated, some came back later but some stayed away too. Yet, was that the complete story?

On my journey along Budda Dariya, after the Neelon Bridge, at Katani Kalan, I stopped for directions at a cloth store. The shop owner, Satish, sounded urban and I asked why he had his shop here, on a state highway when perhaps Ludhiana would be good for business. He told me he was from Ludhiana and travelled twenty-five kilometres a day to run his shop there as the city was too crowded. I was struck by this reverse migration for work and asked him since when he had been running the shop. He said for more than three decades.

This brought me to a sensitive question, but since he had offered me tea, I dared ask it. 'But wasn't it risky in those days?' He understood the implication. He was a Hindu.

'In fact, no. This was Rashpal Singh Chhandra's area.'

I was a bit taken aback. Not only because the name of the militant was also Baba's name, but because Satish was agreeing that the militants had marked areas. 'Rashpal never let us be looted like other *khadkus* (militants). He was very clear; people should not be affected.' The saga of militancy is layered and entwined, but this was a very different version, from the most unlikely angle—a Hindu man talking good about a militant who had made life hell for law enforcement agencies for about eight years.

'But it was a reign of fear, no?'

'Not under Rashpal's protection. One morning we saw two bodies of young men lying on the road, not far from here. Next to them was a note by Rashpal: the men were looting from ordinary people. This is the lesson to anyone who dares do that.' He used the word *sodha* (rectification). 'You know how people had spontaneously assembled to gather his body after the police tortured and killed him. They didn't allow police to cremate him anonymously.' From the early 1990s, I remembered people talking about him—legs torn apart, body with torture marks. I later checked with a few police officers from those days. Privately, they agreed.

'Still, I was attacked. Two boys walked in one evening to demand ransom. One shutter was down, the smaller one was open. As I bent down to open my cash counter to pull out cash, I surprised the boy closer to me by grappling with him. You know, head on, like wrestlers. The gun in his hand went off. The bullet went through my chin; luckily it came out from my neck. Else it would have gone to the brain. See,' he raised his chin for me to show his entire stitched-up jaw. 'But I didn't realise, I kept holding the boy.'

'Then?'

'I do not know what happened. I woke up in hospital eleven days later. It took me six months to recover.'

'Why did you still come back?'

'Because of Rashpal. When I came home from hospital his father came to see me. He took my assurance that I wouldn't leave my business and would keep coming to the shop. I owe it to them.'

Rashpal Singh Chhandra was an ordinary farmer who had turned to militancy to avenge Operation Blue Star. He was once picked up, but no policeman recognised him and he escaped. After this the police brutally tortured his father and the rest of the family. This strengthened his drive and he started targeting policemen and made life hell for them.

I checked with others too, enroute on my Budda Dariya adventures and never got a negative story about him from anyone.

That is why, as the shop owner said, upon his death through brutal police torture in June 1992, ordinary villagers gathered in thousands. They did not allow the police to secretly cremate his body. They conducted an honourable cremation themselves.

These two stories, placed next to each other, depict a complete contrast about what militants did, how they operated and what their goals were. This contradiction has lasted in Panjab since the days of militancy and now extends to support for or against Bhindranwale and the question of whether Khalistan was a worthy goal or not.

In late September of 2016, I travelled from Bathinda to village Bhagtuana in the nearby district of Faridkot. As I crossed the railway track between the villages I saw the small enclosed space in front of the school. The brick walls had a red obelisk, like at village Kishangarh which marked the Muzara movement. On this pillar was written: 'In Memory of the Sewewala Episode, Inquilab Zindabad'. A red flag flew high.

I had instructions to turn left from there towards a pink house with a balcony. Bindu, a resident of the village and the leader of the women's front of the Pendu Mazdoor Union, was waiting for me at the gate. On the walls of the home were lines from a poem by someone who was once considered a Naxal poet and was now considered a people's voice, Avtar Singh Pash. '... *the most dangerous is the dying of dreams,*' it said, and there was a picture of a handsome, sharp-eyed, turbaned man. Bindu asked me for tea which I refused because I was eager to hear her. She settled down to tell me the story.

Bindu told me her grandfather was a Leftist. He came from village Longowal to Bhagtuana to join his brother Hardev Singh during the Muzara Leher which took place in the 1950s to free the land from the big landlords and give them to the landless tillers. It was the same movement that my Dadaji had also spearheaded in our ancestral village Manawan. The government had announced an award for the capture of Hardev Singh. Her father grew up in that environment and right from school he was known as Megh Raj 'Baghi' (rebel)— someone who fought for the right causes.

Megh Raj protested against the shortage of fertilisers, resisted the Emergency and was involved in many other such people's movements. He owned ten acres of land and grew vegetables. He had five sisters, all of whom he found grooms for. In the day he worked in the fields. In the nights he taught children at the *dharamsala*. He was part of the Naujwan Bharat Sabha and organised celebrations of Bhagat Singh's anniversary and other functions. His closest association in the village was with the families of labourers. While he was a revolutionary against power structures, he was also a great advocate of resolving issues among people.

Post the assassination of Indira Gandhi in 1984, when militant activity intensified, he turned a full-time activist and formed the *Zabar te Firkaprasti Virodhi Front* (Front Against Repression and Communalism). Front members travelled across villages spreading the message of peace and vigilance against both the state and non-state actors since people were subject to both state as well as militant oppression. Bhagtuana was soon on the hitlist and Megh Raj's and the labourers' home became fortresses. Students from Ludhiana, the youth, teachers, even electricity department employees lived at Megh Raj's home. While the militants and police both had rifles, the activists had stones and petrol bombs.

Among other things, militants would often eat at people's homes and the police would then target such homes. ZFVF would protest it and spread the message that it was a question of the villagers' dignity and urge whole villages to rise up against such tyranny. They wanted people to get organised and fight militant rules like: keep your house lights off, wear such and such clothes, don't smoke, don't organise big weddings, sow such and such varieties of crops, and so on. They opposed all such restrictions as these rules were injunctions on basic freedoms. The ZFVF believed that the government ought to take care of its people. Equally, they also held that the fight of the militants was with the government and not with the people. The ZFVF was thus an irritant to both the militants and the police.

Bindu told me that they would get messages at home from militants, 'Megh Raj, what will you gain from this? Give it up.' Many times the militants confronted him in buses. Megh Raj had to change appearance and carry out his work under the shadow of being chased. Many times he never returned home, on one occasion for up to six months. Family life in his absence was also a fight. Bindu's brother was sent from one relative to another. But Megh Raj used to say, 'Even if you are kidnapped or tortured, you will never cry. You will ask for the bullet on your chest. Even if you get a message that Megh Raj is dead and his corpse is lying here, none of you will go to collect my body. The organisation will go and none of you must lose your cool. Or cry about what will happen next.'

Megh Raj was protecting his village and villages like his own. He would assign duties to his activists. Young children would note down registration numbers of vehicles that entered the village. They would notice every outsider who would step in. That is why the Khalistanis never dared to enter the village and attacked the ZFVF in village Sewewala and not in Bhagtuana. That too with support of the families of Charna Singh Fauji and Sadhu Singh Boriya.

In those nights that no longer belonged to the people of Panjab, when even the police did not venture out to protect people, the one light was a travelling theatre group helmed by Gursharan Singh (Gursharan Bhaji). Between the state discourse of militancy and the militant discourse of freedom, Bhaji represented the third voice of Panjab—a voice which raised issues. It was a voice that focussed on the failure of the state in addressing people's issues and sought to prevent society from spiralling into further violence. At one point, Bhaji's group was supposed to perform Ajmer Aulakh's play, but the event was cancelled. That is when Megh Raj and Jagpal decided to host another event on 9 April. When the event was arranged, a labour woman noticed militants staying at Fauji and Sadhu's home and tried to warn the family, but before she could reach, the militants entered the *dharamshala* through a narrow lane.

The play *Anhe Nishanchi* (Blind Shooters) was being performed by Amolak Singh's team. The play was a curated set of five one-act plays, published individually, which depicted social issues: *Flaming Rage* was about Bhagat the tenant and Madho, his sharecropper, who found their situation so unbearable that they decided to kill the landlord and the moneylender; in *Anhe Nishanchi*, members of the exploiting classes were shown engineering communal killings in 1947; *The Straight Path and the Crooked Man* was a critique of civil officials abusing their power; *Wayfarer* had three characters—an old man, a young girl and a wayfarer, symbolising three generations—toiling under difficult conditions for the attainment of an ideal life; and *Divine Feast* was a new version of the well-known legend connected with Guru Nanak Dev—a child rejected the delicacies of a rich man as blood-soaked and relished the rye loaf of a poor household which he described as sweet as milk.

As the play ended and Amolak took the mike, seven to eight militants attacked. They had AK-47s and ZFVF members had one .12 bore rifle, stones and kirpans. When the firing started, an old woman, Sada Kaur, who had always attended the plays shouted at the militants, 'Dogs, why are you killing them? If you have to kill, kill me. Not my sons.' Her chest was pumped full of AK-47 bullets. When the whole place became bloody, the militants left, Megh Raj snatched the double-barrelled gun from a ZFVF member, ran behind the terrorists and shot at them. One bullet missed and the other hit one of them on the shoulder. When he tried to reload his gun they rained bullets on him. Then they picked up his rifle and danced near his corpse.

Eighteen people died and twenty-two were injured. The family found a letter allegedly signed by Gurjant Singh Budhsinghwala, the chief of the Khalistan Liberation Force. It stated that anyone who wanted to conduct a programme like this would be dealt with in the same fashion.

Bindu added, 'That is why, to challenge them, a big crowd conducted the final rites. After that, we acquired guns and licences from the state. The state even taught women how to use guns. We stood watch for many years.'

We sat in silence, for a long time. I pointed at the turbaned man on the wall and Bindu said, 'Yes, he was Megh Raj, my father.' Megh Raj was born Hindu, a Brahmin. In his deeds he was an aware citizen of the country who gave his life to uphold the code of being a citizen in an enlightened society.

'I must get you some tea,' said Bindu. 'It has been long.'

'Yes.'

'But you know, our pain is personal, the loss of my father is personal, but many Left-oriented families and friends, comrades, fought against the militants in many villages of Panjab,' Bindu concluded.

After I left Bindu's home, I wondered about the letter being signed by Gurjant Singh Budhsinghwala whose name I had read in a different context, associated with the killing of SSP Gobind Ram appointed at Batala. Gobind Ram's list of crimes against humanity was long, but the most provocative was what he called Operation Shudhikaran—a cleansing drive in which he encouraged those working under him to rape Sikh girls. 'If the seed is changed, the revolutionary spirit will leave their homes,' he would say.

On the night of January 1989, he went to village Gora Choor to arrest a very ill Patloo Singh of the Daleep Singh Babbar faction. He accused the village of giving shelter to militants, insinuated that the village's women slept with militants and said that he wanted his men to sleep with them. He took away the host family, including women and children, and kept them at the police station for five nights. The women were raped and the men were beaten. Ten days later Gobind Ram's men came to village Gora Choor again and assembled people from neighbouring villages Kotlee, Bhangali and Kasakre at the village centre. The fearful villagers were forced to sloganeer against women Akali leaders who were in jail. Again the women were humiliated and the men were beaten. A retired major from the Sikh regiment who had fought three wars for India and objected to what the police was doing was taken away and his body returned the next day.

At village Dalaer Khurd, Gobind Ram's men—with orange turbans and Kalashnikovs—came to loot a home where a marriage was being arranged. It was a police trick to defame the militants. The father gave them the jewellery but when they tried to rape the young bride her brother resisted. When he was shot, the militants who had gone into hiding nearby came in and killed Gobind Ram's men. When the police looked upon the ordinary people with distrust, and themselves tried to exploit people, they created a vacuum which the militants filled. The people felt that it was not police but the militants who were upholding their honour and life. The police hit back by picking up people, torturing the men and raping young girls.

In another case, Gobind Ram arrested the wives of militants, Mehal Singh Babbar and Kulwant Singh Babbar on 21 August 1989. Gurdev Kaur and Gurmeet Kaur had not seen their husbands in years. They worked in a bank, supported their children and had never engaged in any untoward activity. Yet, they were wives of militants and the police wanted to get their husbands through them. The police took them to an abandoned factory which now served as a police interrogation centre.[172] For three days and three nights they were beaten with belts, sticks, rods; crushed with solid logs with men mounted on them; tied upside down and whipped. The press got wind of it and the news spread and so Gobind Ram had no choice but to get them medical treatment. Gobind Ram was soon posted out of Batala.

Militants once attacked Gobind Ram's convoy in Amritsar. He escaped but his young son Rajan Bainsson was killed in the attack. This was not unprecedented. In June 1986, DSP Raj Kishen Bedi's son, Ashok, who had just graduated, was killed in Ludhiana. In November the same year, Ravneet Singh, the nineteen-year-old son of H.S. Kahlon, SP (city), was shot dead in Amritsar. A month later, Arun Kumar, the school-going son of Inspector Brahm Dev, was killed in Amritsar. The father died of a heart attack soon after. Gurmeet Singh, the twenty-two-year-old son of Harpal Singh, DSP Baba Bakala, was killed along with his father in February 1987. In the same month Dr Manjit Singh, the newly-married son of IG D.S. Mangat, was killed at Patiala.[173] The militancy phase was a full-blown low intensity war in Panjab. The police then decided to move all the high risk policemen and their families to the police lines in Jalandhar.

At that time one of the most active militant outfits was the Khalistan Liberation Force (KLF) led by Gurjant Singh Budhsinghwala. KLF's Jugraj Singh Toofan took the responsibility of punishing Gobind Ram. He was aided by Gurnam Singh Babbar, chief of the Majha Zone, and Mehnga Singh Babbar. The three of them opened a tea stall near the Jalandhar Police Training Centre. One evening their spy in Gobind Ram's office informed them about him being away and all the sentries being busy with a young girl they had found. That is when Jugraj Singh Toofan fitted a bomb under Gobind Ram's seat in his office. When Gobind Ram returned later in the evening and entered his office, the mole relayed a torch light signal. The Babbars exploded the bomb and Gobind Ram was killed.[174]

This is how the Khalistan militancy period throws up enmeshed narratives. A nationalist, anti-militancy position would contend that Budhsinghwala or Toofan were wrong, but it can't possibly justify Gobind Ram's tortures and the so-called Operation Shudhikaran. This web of narratives makes it difficult for anyone to draw a line through the movement to understand what really was going on, which side to support, and since those years no one can sort out Panjab's complex recent history under neat labels like national and anti-national. I remember during my adolescent years—in the late Eighties and the early Nineties Panjab—one did not know whom to fear more: the police or the militants.

In March 1986, with militancy spiralling out of control in Panjab, Julio Ribeiro, a Maharashtra-cadre IPS officer, was brought in as the director general of police. To take the militants head-on he framed the 'bullet for bullet' policy—though in his book, *Bullet for Bullet* (2000), he says he never uttered the phrase. But still he did use it as the title of his book.

In his interview with Teesta Setalvad for *Communalism Combat*, he talked about how the then Akali CM Surjit Singh Barnala had accepted the status quo: the police ruled in the daytime and the militants ruled at night.[175] Ribeiro asked how that could be allowed. How could people live with the police harassing them in the day and militants harassing them at night?

He explained that Panjab was different from the Bombay underworld. In Bombay, he said, the police and the underworld believed in the framework of the state and the underworld never picked up guns against policemen. However, in Panjab, the police reported to him that when they went to villages and were fired upon, they could not make out whether the bullets were from militants or from ordinary farmers. They needed to be given permission to go around with guns in plainclothes. Ribeiro reluctantly gave the permission for plainclothes policemen with guns but worried about how the ordinary villagers would make out the policemen from the terrorists. For him, it was a choice between his men and the militants, and he had to keep up the morale of his forces.

Ribeiro talked about when K.P.S. Gill was brought in from Assam after president's rule was imposed in Panjab in 1987. No other officer was willing to come to take charge. He confessed, he was 'happy to be kicked upstairs as advisor to the governor' when Gill took charge in April 1988. Gill was removed by the V.P. Singh government in December 1990 and reinstated in November 1991. He retired from Panjab in 1995.

For perspective, there was a precedent to the Panjab Police's excesses. More than a decade before militancy, during the time of Naxalism, under CM Parkash Singh Badal (in his first tenure from March 1970 to June 1971), the Panjab Police had killed around a hundred Naxalites in the same fashion they adopted during militancy.[176] Even those killings were never probed and were hushed up. This time under Gill the police had the backing of the supercop through Operation Night Domination when the police sought to reclaim the nights in the border districts.

Per a Right to Information response, the Indian government put the number of innocents killed during militancy at 11,694,[177] the number of militants killed at 8,049[178] and the number of policemen killed at 1,761. There are two ironies here: one, the proportion of innocents killed to the militants is 1.4:1. That is either a very poor strike rate on the part of militants or it points to something else—that the police killed more innocent people than real militants. Second, the number of innocents and militants killed are very close to the number of farmers and labourers who have committed suicide in the last two and a half decades.

If the first deaths were from a struggle against the state and the victims were ordinary people, this second killing is structural and aided and abetted by the state where again the victims are ordinary people. When the numbers are almost the same I can't help comparing the noise around each: the first killings dominated all headlines for a decade and a half, created a *dehshat*, altered Panjab, and since then has been used to flog Panjab, but the second does not even warrant a whimper, and no attempt has been made to find a solution. No wonder Satpal Danish asked me to count the corpses to understand Panjab.

Yet, there is also a huge number of corpses that continue to haunt Panjab—waiting for a death certificate. These corpses point to why the overall system has failed in Panjab. It goes back to the time of militancy when the state collapsed. That is when the three arms of the state—legislature, judiciary and executive—all but vanished. Everything was handled by a one-legged horse—the police.

This police, whose job is to uphold justice and whose motto is Guru Gobind Singh's words: *shub karman te kabhu na tarun* (never shall I flinch from doing the righteous deed) exercised such a heavy hand through enforced disappearances and extrajudicial killings that it caused the breakdown of the system of justice in the state. These killings—to keep up scores for medals and promotions—added to the already ruptured trust between the state and the people, through Operation Blue Star and the 1984 pogrom and the after-effects of the Green Revolution. This was the black hole in the centre of Panjab and as I learnt of it I realised it was the gap in my understanding and knowledge of Panjab. The extrajudicial killings created the corpses that remain a phantom presence in my life.

In the early 1990s, when militancy was ebbing away, Jaswant Singh Khalra was earlier a panchayat member and later director of a cooperative bank who turned into a human rights activist when he went searching for some of his colleagues who had gone missing in the militancy period. Under president's rule, the police were empowered to detain suspects for any reason, ostensibly as suspected terrorists. Most of those arrested usually went 'missing'.

Khalra discovered files in the Amritsar municipal corporation which contained the names, ages and addresses of those who had been killed and later cremated by the police. His research revealed more cases in three police districts in Panjab—Amritsar, Majithia and Tarn Taran. Even as Khalra went about his work, the then police chief K.P.S. Gill, in his patented manner, conducted a press conference, where he claimed that the human rights folks were not doing anything on human rights. In his view, they had only one motive, to prop up their agenda so that there was no peace in the state and that Pakistan-based ISI agents and human rights activists were hatching a conspiracy to discourage the police machinery and re-incite militancy. Gill went to the extent of claiming that the missing individuals whom the human rights organisations were claiming had disappeared were actually abroad.

Khalra computed 2,097 cases of enforced disappearances and unmarked killings and submitted them to the National Human Rights Commission. The NHRC later released a list of some of the identified bodies that were cremated between June 1984 and December 1994.[179]

Khalra had gathered his data painstakingly, often by visiting cremation grounds and speaking to employees who spoke of, among other things, truckloads of bodies coming in at times. Eventually, his search led him to the municipal corporation which had provided the firewood for the mass cremations and the records maintained for purchase of the firewood.

On 6 September 1995, Khalra was allegedly abducted by Panjab Police DSP Jaspal Singh on the instructions of SSP Ajit Singh Sandhu in front of his house. Khalra went missing exactly the way he had found others had gone missing—an enforced disappearance. The police denied having arrested him and claimed to have no knowledge of his whereabouts. Later, witnesses gave statements implicating the police chief K.P.S Gill as having cleared the abduction.[180]

In 1996, the Central Bureau of Investigation (CBI) found evidence that Khalra had been held at a police station in Tarn Taran and recommended the prosecution of nine Panjab Police officials for murder and kidnapping. Six Panjab Police officials were convicted and sentenced to seven years' imprisonment. Later, a division bench of Panjab and Haryana High Court extended the sentence to life imprisonment to four more accused. On 11 April 2011, the Supreme Court of India dismissed the appeal filed against the sentence to life imprisonment for four accused while scathingly criticising the atrocities committed by Panjab Police during the militancy years.

In May 1997, fearing arrest, the officer who had ordered Khalra's abduction, Ajit Singh Sandhu, threw himself in front of a running train at my hometown Rajpura.[181] He left behind a note: 'It is better to die than live in humiliation.' The statement was proof of the frustration of police officers who stepped in to contain militancy but in the process made a mockery of the law. At the time of his death, Sandhu, a twice-decorated police officer, had fifty-two cases logged and sixteen cases opened against him, including one of land grabbing, and extortions, kidnappings and killings. These included two high-profile cases, one of Khalra and another of the abduction and killing of Kuljit Singh Dhatt, the son-in-law of freedom fighter Bhagat Singh's sister, Prakash Kaur.

While the Khalra and Dhatt cases were public because of their nature, most other cases had come forward because, faced with the increasing number of lawsuits, the state police had set up a separate litigation wing under an inspector general (IG). Over 1,500 petitions were filed against the police in different courts, implicating about

4,000 police personnel. At one point, the police faced eighty-five CBI and ninety-one judicial probes. Besides, thirty policemen were in jail, around 100 were out on bail and 140, including seven SPs, were facing prosecution. Such cases were also lodged against three-time gallantry award winner Narinder Pal Singh and Mohammad Mustafa.[182] Yet, over two decades later, except for a high-profile case like Khalra's which also remained incomplete because it could not be established whether Sandhu and Gill had given orders from top, not much action has taken place on these cases.

Sukhwinder Singh Bhatti's case did not even reach as far as Khalra's. Bhatti was a defence lawyer from Sangrur. He was fighting cases of individuals accused of crimes under the Terrorist and Disruptive Activities (TADA) Act, 1987. He was litigating 131 TADA cases at the time of his disappearance on 12 May 1994. In 1993, the Panjab Police started to apply for and receive production warrants that allowed them to remove individuals accused in TADA cases from jail. Fearing extrajudicial killings, Bhatti secured orders from the Panjab and Haryana High Court, which prevented the superintendent of the jail from removing his clients without the high court's permission.

An inquiry by the CBI collected evidence directly implicating then senior superintendent of police (SSP) Jasminder Singh and deputy superintendent of police (DSP) Surjit Singh in Bhatti's detention, torture and disappearance in an unofficial interrogation centre at Bahadur Singh Wala Qila in Sangrur. Yet, in 1997, the CBI recommended the closure of the case, concluding that Bhatti was untraced. In 2017, the government of Panjab promoted Jasminder Singh to director general of police (internal vigilance cell).

Justice not being served in those cases has led to, in Panjab, a culture of impunity and throwing away the law book. It can be seen in no one being held accountable for the firing in Behbal Kalan in 2015 (Chapter *Rosh*), in how police officers are fighting in court with each other, how reports surface, of them being engaged with the drug mafia, how they illegally detain drug addicts on the same pattern as once militants were detained through copy-paste of FIRs, in how they conduct nightly raids and pick up farmer leaders and other protestors when a call for protest is made, and how they side with the powerful, whether it is Jutts denying Dalits panchayati lands or property brokers squabbling over rates. In fact, at every level in society.

A very good example of this culture of impunity is Sumedh Singh Saini, the police chief transferred after the Behbal Kalan killings. He was once K.P.S. Gill's blue-eyed boys and later Congress CM Amarinder Singh's blue-eyed boy. After that Saini became deputy CM Sukhbir Badal's blue-eyed boy superseding various officers senior to him and being appointed the DIG. He had earned a reputation for anti-militancy work, earned the nation's highest gallantry award and even escaped an attack by Gurjant Singh Budhsinghwala.

On 15 March 1994, an automobile businessman, Vinod Kumar, his brother-in-law Ashok Kumar and their driver Mukhtiyar Singh never returned home after being picked up by the police in Ludhiana or Chandigarh. On the orders of the Panjab and Haryana High Court, the CBI registered a criminal case against Saini. In 2004, the Supreme Court transferred the case to Delhi. All these years, Vinod Kumar's mother Amar Kaur had been fighting the case, even in the last stages of her life from her hospital bed. In 2017, aged hundred, she died. The case has still not been decided upon.

Panjab has not only seen enforced disappearances and extrajudicial killings but also what became notorious in Kashmir in 2017, and split the discourse on anti-terrorism methods—the usage of human shields. As a young researcher, Preetika Nanda, tells me, on 8 June 1992, in village Behla, near Tarn Taran, a large mixed force, comprised of the Panjab Police and CRPF battalions 91 and 102, led by SSP Ajit Singh Sandhu and Khubi Ram, SP (Operations), surrounded the old and abandoned house of Manjinder Singh, a former member of the Panjab Legislative Assembly.

The house was being used as a hideout by militants associated with Surjit Singh Behla, deputy chief and lieutenant general of Bhindranwala Tiger Force of Khalistan (BTFK). One of his associates was Sukhdev Singh Maddi who, after graduation, had started working in a sugar mill at Sheron. The police had illegally detained and tortured his elder brother Kulbir Singh. Sukhdev Singh was unable to tolerate this injustice done to his brother and decided to become a militant. Later on, the police had abducted his father Santokh Singh. The third associate of Surjit Singh Behla was Harbans Singh, from Sarhalli in Tarn Taran district.

Before storming the house, the police officers decided to round up seven or eight villagers to walk in front of the police force and to act as human shields. The selection was random and had little to do with militancy. One of the shields was Ajit Singh, a sixty-year-old man who owned a horse-driven cart and was employed by a brick kiln owner to transport bricks to his customers. He had no political or militant association, no criminal background and no enmity with anyone in his village. That morning, Ajit Singh had carried a cartload of bricks to the house of fifty-five-year-old Niranjan Singh when the police came and forced him along with Niranjan Singh and his sons to be part of the front column. Twenty-five-year-old Sakatter Singh was Niranjan Singh's son. Twenty-year-old Lakhwinder Singh was watering his fields when the forces picked him up and compelled him to walk in front of them as a human shield. Sixty-two-year-old Kartar Singh also had no record of a political or criminal past but was forced to join the others as a human shield.

After entering the house, the security forces discovered that it had a basement but no door to enter it from the inside. They started demolishing the floor that was also the cellar's roof. When the militants holed up inside opened fire, the police pushed these six villagers to the front, and using them as cover, fired back. All of the six persons died in the firing. The encounter lasted around thirty hours. The two militants and Harbans Singh who were holed up in the cellar also died.

On the evening of 9 June, the police extricated nine bodies without bothering to separate the militants from those whom they had used as human shields. Later, in a report published in *The Tribune,* SSP Ajit Singh Sandhu claimed that they had killed nine militants. Two days later, the same newspaper said that only two amongst the killed were militants. Embarrassed by the adverse publicity, the Panjab government later announced an inquiry which was never carried out.

The police cremated all the bodies at Tarn Taran on 9 June 1992, labelling them as unidentified/unclaimed, though the family of Ajit Singh attended the cremation. Other families were not allowed to attend. The body of one person killed in the encounter remains unaccounted for.

A quarter century after the Kuljit Singh Dhatt case had become public, after a commission was set up to probe it, after the family had tirelessly struggled for justice, when the verdict came, all the five high-profile police officers were held guilty. While Sandhu and Sardul Singh were already dead, the other three, S.P.S. Basra, SHO Jaspal Singh and SI Sita Ram were awarded a sentence of five years each. This after Sita Ram had, during the course of his career, gone on to become and retire as an SSP and enjoyed all the perks of the job.

The fact is, in those days, the police had cultivated around 300 personnel as 'cats', a nickname for informers and those who conducted unmarked killings. Many of the cats were former militants who had turned approvers and many of them were later helped to escape abroad and assume new identities. A few years back, a senior journalist Kanwar Sandhu interviewed one of them at length.[183] His name was Gurmeet Singh 'Pinky' and he gave a chilling description of how fake encounters were routinely used by Panjab Police units to quell militancy. 'In (the) name of fighting terrorism, utter falsehood was enacted day after day. Suspects were picked up in one place, taken to a second, kept in a third, and the encounter shown in yet another place.' Pinky has gone on to dissociate himself from the interview but his testimonial is on record in the public domain. His president's medals are proof of his activities.

Within a week of Sandhu's suicide, fearing the sinking morale of the state police, Gill wrote to the then prime minister I.K. Gujral, marking copies to the chief justice, the speaker of the Lok Sabha and the chairman of the Rajya Sabha.[184]

He made a case for his officers, stating:

> Having served the national cause, are they now simply to be forgotten? Or worse, to be persecuted with impunity? ... Thousands of men in uniform stood as a bulwark of democracy ... when every other branch of Government demonstrated their abject surrender before terrorism.
>
> The victory over terrorism was not merely a military victory, it was a moral victory. It must, nonetheless, be recognised that the situation that prevailed in Panjab for over a decade was a state of war—a proxy war, perhaps; 'low intensity conflict' as others prefer to term it—but war, nonetheless. The Panjab Police and various central forces were engaged, not in simple law enforcement activities, but in a battle to retain control over large areas of the sovereign territory of the Indian Union, against an utterly unscrupulous and heavily armed enemy who recognised no constraints.
>
> It is for your government and for the nation's Parliament to debate on, and define, the appropriate criteria to judge the actions

of those who fought this war on behalf of the Indian State and
people. ... It is imperative that we should define a systematic and
proactive strategic response to this challenge.

The issue with the letter is not that it is by a senior officer who seeks
to protect his juniors. That is the loyalty which builds and binds a
force and keeps up its morale. The issue is also not that Gill points
fingers at the judiciary and the political set-up. He is correct that all
other pillars of democracy collapsed. In his interview even Ribeiro
mentioned how judges told him not to bring militants in front of
them as they feared for their lives. Operation Black Thunder I and II
were even on camera but no judge passed any judgement on those
who were arrested.

What tickled me was the claim almost explaining away some
inadvertent lapses on the part of the police. As we have seen in the
last few pages, it certainly was not that. What amused and irritated
me was the claim that the victory over militancy was a moral victory.
K.P.S. Gill is often credited with having ended militancy in Panjab,
but the real question is: what does it mean for a state to employ any
degree of force and provide impunity to its forces to achieve peace?
What about the consequences of such an action? Does peace really
return?

Looking at Panjab today and all that we have discussed until now
in previous chapters, it is clear that peace has not returned. Instead,
there is a great disquiet in every section of society. If Gill's letter
celebrates the fact that police action eliminated every trace of the
idea of Khalistan, then what has been going on for the past quarter
century? Why do politicians, the latest being Sukhbir Badal, raise the
bogey again and again for the past quarter century?

As usual, a response such as this letter attracted public opinion in
its time, was celebrated briefly and soon the nation moved on. But
what happened to Panjab? In Panjab, both the militants and the police

remained trapped in a quagmire, and the state which was supposed to create processes did not play its role. The model of police injustice continued to perpetuate itself. Manipur asks the same question, as do Bastar and Kashmir. These days the questions are being asked about Gujarat and Uttar Pradesh. The model everywhere is Panjab.

To solve Panjab, we need to look again at the letter and see how Gill defines the period of militancy as a low-intensity war. Even during Operation Blue Star the Centre and the army treated Panjab as an enemy state. The Operation followed by Operation Woodrose or later Gill's Operation Night Dominance were all states of war. What Panjab then needs is certainly not that the police officers who conducted these enforced disappearances and extrajudicial killings be feted with medals, given increments and promoted. What Panjab really needs is a healing touch. Panjab needs a post-conflict approach to human rights, to systems of justice and towards truth and reconciliation.

This was a popular demand in the 1997 elections when the Shiromani Akali Dal under Parkash Singh Badal made a bid to capture power in Panjab in partnership with the BJP. In that campaign, in his speeches, Parkash Singh Badal promised an enquiry into police excesses which was forgotten about once he came in power. The reason given was that disappearances couldn't be probed since uncovering them could disturb communal harmony.

Khalra's list of 2,097 people disappearing led to the formation of the Committee for Coordination on Disappearances in Panjab which analysed 900 cases and produced a report called *Reduced to Ashes*, co-authored by Ram Narayan Kumar, Amrik Singh, Ashok Agarwal and Jaskaran Kaur. The report led the NHRC to order

Rs 27.94 crore relief for the families of the disappeared, though only 1,513 victims have been identified, while 584 bodies remain unidentified. Compensation is just one part of the process of restorative justice. It helps the family, provides some succour, though the one disappeared will remain a gaping wound for friends and family. The real solution would be to identify the ones who killed these innocents and then carry out some sort of a process of justice even though it is now fairly late. When the RTI activist P.S. Kitna sought details of the cases, he drew a blank and his complaint languished with the Panjab State Information Commission.

Jaskaran Kaur who was co-author of the CCDP report is now co-director of Ensaaf, a US-based human rights group. Till date Ensaaf has mapped 5,234 victims of enforced disappearances and extrajudicial killings in Panjab from 1981 to 2008. These include 4,393 fake encounters and 841 forced disappearances.

Ensaaf's rigourous and very well-catalogued website provides details of victim demographics, incident information, and the identity of the perpetrators. Whether those killed or abducted were combatants or non-combatants, their marital status, their religion (besides the vast majority of Sikhs, some were Hindu, Muslim and Christian), their caste (besides the majority Jutts, there were other castes too), urban or rural, employed or not, where they were picked up, where they were killed, whether the body was returned or not.[185]

The number of those tortured is even higher and have not yet been entered in the study.[186] The website also lists senior police officers along with their alleged crimes. Most of them are now in top positions in Panjab Police. The searchable website also has films on victim families and their court cases.

The lawyer who features most often in the films has been in the forefront of human rights movements in Panjab for the last quarter century—Advocate Rajwinder Singh Bains. He was on an evening walk when I reached his place one evening in Chandigarh. While

I was seated in his office he came in and apologised for having forgotten the time he had given to meet me. This itself was unusual in Panjab where the clock is best forgotten. I noticed he smiled easily, listened carefully, spoke with care and never sermonised.

He told me how he was a young student when Operation Blue Star took place and had gone a few weeks later to the Durbar Sahib. Until then he was not very religious-minded and did not take interest in Sikh or Panjab politics. Yet, he was moved on seeing the devastation. Something changed in him when he acknowledged that a state had attacked its own people. He sought to help and to uphold the law. For he knew a society that does not uphold the law is doomed.

Being the son of a sitting judge, Ajit Singh Bains was another reason why he took up law. He has been pursuing cases of enforced disappearances and extrajudicial killings relentlessly, but the state does not budge, the witnesses turn hostile, the families crumble, but he takes it all in his stride. He knows it is an uphill, almost impossible, battle, but he braves on.

The topic shifted to his father. Bains told me that after Operation Blue Star, when the Akali government won the elections, Justice A.S. Bains was tasked with compiling the list and verifying the antecedents of over three thousand prisoners who were locked up in Jodhpur. Since it had been already over a year since the detainees had been incarcerated, Justice A.S. Bains took up the matter with urgency. He compiled and submitted his report in a few months, proposing the release of most of the detainees. The Akali Dal government under Surjit Singh Barnala panicked. Bains told me that they had asked his father why he could not have taken more time and why he could not keep the matter as an election plank. Justice A.S. Bains was flabbergasted. The matter did not end there.

In 1992, after he retired and was head of Panjab Human Rights Organisation, he made a speech from the ramparts of Keshgarh Sahib Gurdwara on Holla Mohalla on 18 March. By this time he had been raising the issue of police excesses for a few years. On 2 April, when returning from the Golf Club, the police intercepted his car near the governor's house. He was handcuffed and taken into custody.[187] Under arrest he was treated shabbily, not at all with the respect due to a judge, but like a petty criminal, short of beatings.

The family was sent on a wild goose chase while the police raided his residence in R.S. Bains and his brother-in-law Col. G.S. Grewal's presence. The police found nothing incriminating but kept Justice Bains under arrest. On the afternoon of 5 April, Justice Bains was produced before Karam A. Singh, Deputy Commissioner of Ropar. The Deputy Commissioner ordered his police remand for two days while confiding to him that his name did not figure in the FIR (First Information Report) on the basis of which he had been arrested.

This is how, in spite of not figuring in the original FIR, not being mentioned in the case diary, Justice Bains was booked under Sections 12-A, 153-A and 505(1)b of the Indian Penal Code and under Sections 3 and 4 of the TADA and confined to Burail Jail for over two months. On 9 April, the newspaper *Ajit* reported that according to the Panjab chief minister, Beant Singh, the arrest was made with his approval. Beant Singh said that his government had no intention of releasing Ajit Singh Bains, and recalled that during the Barnala Ministry, Justice Bains while heading a committee to review the cases of those under detention, had indiscriminately released nearly 3,000 persons. Upholding the law was Justice Bains's fault. When Gill targeted the judiciary in his letter to the prime minister, he confirmed Ribeiro's statement that judges were recusing themselves from cases on militants, but in his broad sweep, he also held as wrong the fact that the judiciary was following due processes, like Justice Bains had done.

Like Ensaaf, for the last seven years, England-based lawyer Satnam Singh Bains and his team have toiled hard to bring out their study: *Panjab—Identifying the Unidentified*. Panjab Documentation and Advocacy Project (PDAP) presents compelling new evidence on 8,257 cases of enforced disappearances and extrajudicial killings which took place across Panjab. The group has also made a film *Panjab Disappeared—Disappeared, Denied, But Not Forgotten* which is now being screened abroad after a couple of shows in north India.

Khalra had famously said that there were at least 25,000 cases of enforced disappearances and extrajudicial killings. No one really knows the figure but Ensaaf and PDAP's work shows that the figure is at least in the range of the militants killed per government statistics (8,000) and could even be in the region of the number of innocents killed (11,000), or how many farmer and labour suicides (16,000) have taken place over the last two decades in Panjab.

Both Ensaaf and PDAP are based abroad but their research personnel and fields of study are here in India. Over the last quarter century many Panjab-based writers too have written about the Khalistan movement and the army's role in Operation Blue Star or the anti-Sikh pogrom or police excesses—mostly in Panjabi. The Indian state might not have censored them but it has created a sense of fear around them which was visible when I brought up names of such books in book shops in Chandigarh, Ludhiana and Amritsar. Shop owners asked me to pipe down, lest they and I be accused of engaging with Khalistan literature, and pass on the list to them. They fetched any such book they had from deep inside the shop, from sections inaccessible to the ordinary customer. Almost all of them said, 'The police does not allow us to keep them. We could be arrested.'

Yet, there are thousands of such stories in the form of books, pamphlets, blogs, websites and now on social media. There are movies being made now which seldom get a censor certificate, or get it with cuts, or do not find distributors, or simply do not come to India. Yet, screened abroad, available on YouTube, they reach audiences.

The stories of the excesses of the Indian state grow in the diaspora, in the gurdwaras abroad, and remind a newer generation of the atrocities of the Indian state. On Facebook, each day of the year, Ensaaf puts out the pictures, names and details of people who were abducted or killed in police encounters on that day. Each short description ends with, 'The security officials did/did not return their bodies to their families.'

The stories fit the Sikh ethos of over three hundred years of martyrdom and bravery. They build a case against India, in favour of Khalistan. What do we do with stories? What do we do when people find themselves in these twisted narratives? The Khalistan movement has been crushed, but the stories grow, and continue to evoke mixed responses from the people.

If the state believed that the stories would fade away with time, then it is not happening. A generation has passed, the ones who directly suffered the atrocities are passing away or will pass away, but families remember their grandfathers and grandmothers, uncles and aunts. Those abroad raise their voices because they are in relatively safer conditions, in societies where the freedom of speech and protest is intact. The popular discourse that the Indian state creates—on the basis of these demands—is that those people are pro-Khalistan. Yet, the Indian state has never looked critically at itself.

All that happens with every annual pro-Khalistan parade in London, New York, Toronto and other places is that India—known the world over as a peaceful, secular and just country—loses face. If not to bridge the gap between the people here and abroad, if only for the sake of its own reputation and to correct the system which has been compromised for way too long through impunity to perpetuators, India needs to accept Panjab as a post-conflict region and provide closure.

It is the same with those who are in jails for crimes related to their political ideology and have served their sentence, for those abroad who are blacklisted over the Khalistan movement. India needs to treat the period of militancy as an internal war and follow the post-war processes of bringing peace through restorative justice.

Not to shy away from the brutality of the years of darkness due to militancy—both militant and police—but the call for Khalistan was a non-movement to begin with. There were reasons:

- It was disorganised. There were many factions and groups often working at cross-purposes. Then, and even now, it is impossible for anyone to say which militant was devoted to the cause of Khalistan, who was betraying it, who was undermining it, who was aiming for personal gains, and so on. Some were pro-Khalistan but many indulged in making money, settling scores and even hiring themselves out as mercenaries.
- The police, too, did its best to inject moles ('cats' or 'agencies' in popular parlance) to disrupt the movement. And this seems to have taken place both before and after Operation Blue Star. Within two years of Operation Blue Star through which the Indian Army and the Panjab Police had gained control of Durbar Sahib and other gurdwaras, Operation Black Thunder I and II took place in the summers of 1986 and 1988. Also the Sarbat Khalsa at Darbar Sahib in January and April 1986 took place and openly proclaimed the formation of Khalistan. How could hardline Sikh groups gain access to institutions without the government being complicit? In fact, even before Operation Blue Star, who allowed the weapons to come in as brazenly as they did into the Durbar Sahib?

- It had no clarity of purpose. Was Khalistan—a Sikh nation—truly its goal? The core Sikh philosophy is *sarbat da bhala* (blessings for everyone). How could a call for a nation built on this foundation target any other community, especially the Hindus? How did killing innocent bus passengers, random bomb blasts, and targeting of migrant labour help in the cause of Khalistan? Did it actually advocate the killing of minorities? The very reason such a movement began was on account of Sikhs feeling unacknowledged, deprived and a misused minority in India. In any case, by the time the movement petered down, an equal number of Hindus and Sikhs, perhaps more Sikhs, had died at the hands of the militants.

- A movement needs the semblance of a state system to back it up. It needs the people on whose behalf it claims to fight to repose trust in that nascent state-like formation over the state which has colonised them and oppressed them. That is how the movement could have gained its feet. The movement did not build a system of a state. Perhaps there was no time, perhaps there was no focus, but justice in a system like Khalistan was about what the panchayat or the local big man decided. In some cases, militants like the Babbars did step in to safeguard the villagers from the police, but that in itself was just a small part of building an alternative system which never really happened.

- The fight was not conventional and the terrain was not conducive to guerrilla warfare. Except for the Mand area, the marshy wetland at Hari Ke Pattan near Amritsar, there was no other part of the undulating Panjab plains where the militants could engage the police. The Kandi area—the hills of Shivalik—did not really form part of the battlefield. The battle was mostly in vast, plain fields, sometimes in villages, occasionally in urban spaces. A small number of semi-trained youth could not take on a mighty, armed opponent in such a terrain. It showed up in the casualties recorded on both sides.

• There was no buy-in from the many layers of the Sikh society. While the Jutts fought with Jutts, where was the engagement with the Dalits, the Khatri and Arora Sikhs, the Ramgarhias and the other sects of the Sikh faith? How would the movement play out in mostly Khatri families, some of whose members were Hindus and others Sikh? Women were one half of the society and there was hardly any engagement with them in the movement. The larger issue was the entire Sikh community was deeply hurt by Operation Blue Star and the anti-Sikh pogrom, but the severe militancy phase did not carry that whole voice of anguish with it. Where did they lose the community?

Finally, besides the severe reprisal by the police, what really succeeded in turning the tide against militancy was the Hindu-Sikh *nau-mass da rishta*. The two communities are mixed like milk and water and militancy could not tear them apart.

K.P.S. Gill believed that some cultural input could entice Panjab away from militancy. In that, too, he did not use arts and music and literature to probe into people's angst, or help them articulate their discontent, voice their opinion, but forced a top-down 'happy Panjabi' idea. He conducted shows in which Bollywood heroines marked their presence. He encouraged singers such as Gurdas Maan to sing songs that reminded people of their happy legacy and sing, *Apna Panjab howe, ghar di sharab howe* (Reclaim our Panjab, enjoy home-brewed alcohol) and other songs that listed the virtues of the simple, rural life. This was again a Band-Aid fix for the deep discontent of Panjab. The irony is that home-brewed alcohol is now illegal and its absence is pushing the youth towards synthetic drugs.

If there was an event that can be called a semicolon if not a hard full stop to enforced disappearances and extrajudicial killings in Panjab, it was in the year 1995 when the CM of Panjab was assassinated by a human bomb in front of the Panjab Secretariat. The 1992 polls, with minimal turnout, boycotted by the Akalis had led to the formation of a Congress government in which the Police Raj was perpetuated. Balwant Singh Rajoana and his colleague Dilawar Singh, both constables in the Panjab Police, along with others including the Babbar Khalsa member Jagtar Singh Hawara, Jagtar Singh Tara and Paramjit Singh Bheora, conspired to assassinate Beant Singh.[188] They wanted to shock the state machinery.

On 31 August 1995, a coin was tossed and Dilawar Singh was chosen to act as the human bomb in an explosion in which seventeen others died. Balwant Singh was the stand-by, scheduled to go into action if the first attempt failed (which it did not, and so, while he was involved in the conspiracy, he didn't actually commit the deed). He was arrested in December 1995. His stance was, and since then has been, that the murder was an act of conscience. At his trial, Balwant Singh refused to contest the prosecution's charges, challenge the evidence, engage a lawyer or accept a court-appointed lawyer. He spoke from the dock and from the prison through statements to the courts and letters to the judges. He described the deep wounds on the Sikh psyche caused by the state's despoiling of the Durbar Sahib during Operation Blue Star and the 1984 anti-Sikh pogroms. He demanded that the chief justice first determine who were the terrorists: those who committed these acts or those who had defended the victims?

When convicted by the court, Balwant Singh refused to appeal the death sentence and instructed his friends and family not to petition the government for mercy. He also turned away similar offers from social, religious and political groups. In an open letter to the media, Balwant Singh proclaimed: 'Asking for mercy from them (Indian courts) is not even in my distant dreams. I also dissociate myself from the blue-turbaned ones—the Akalis.'

Today, after almost a quarter century, Balwant Singh Rajoana is on death row and Jagtar Singh Hawara has been sentenced to life imprisonment until death. In the 2015 Sarbat Khalsa, Hawara was nominated as the *jathedar* of the Akal Takht. The split in the community on whom does one side with, the SGPC or Hawara, pro- and anti-nation state, continues to divide the Sikhs.

During the course of my travels I met scores of mothers and some fathers who had lost their sons. Either the sons had joined militancy and lost their lives, or they were victims of enforced disappearances and extrajudicial killings. I found it voyeuristic to go into details of such families especially when no one had helped them in the last quarter century.

The ones who joined militancy did so because of the rhetoric of the times or a religious purpose or a sense of bravado or from hurt or a sense of revenge—a near one abducted, killed, tortured by the police or a sense of injustice. Their religious and cultural cosmos as Sikhs primed them to fight injustice. They might not have considered what dying meant but were responding to their times, their hearts and the politics. If the state has won against them, does it not owe it to them to bring them back into the mainstream and rehabilitate them? What was the fault of their parents? Or does the state trust itself so less that it needs to keep them as pariah? The question becomes even more drastic in the case of those who were mysteriously abducted, killed and those who remain unmarked. Many consider the authorities to be behind such actions.

As I went to meet these families with a TV anchor who has taken it upon himself to raise funds for them from the diaspora, I learnt that there had been some paltry compensation for very few of them from the authorities but neither had the SGPC nor any political party or business house or any social group stepped in in the last quarter century to ameliorate their physical conditions or psychological wounds. They had been left orphaned by the movement that the state curbed.

It is in this context that I find it important to discuss the upcoming Sikh Referendum 2020 being sponsored by a fringe Sikh group, Sikhs for Justice (SFJ), based in North America and run by Gurpatwant Singh Pannun. Pannun is a maverick leader who, using US law, has managed to serve notices to Congress president Sonia Gandhi, called for opposition to former Indian prime minister Manmohan Singh and kept Captain Amarinder Singh out of Canada at one point by claiming that Canadian law did not permit any foreign individual to conduct a political campaign on Canadian soil. These were symbolic gestures which played out in recent years but did not amount to much.

Referendum 2020 has still not been conducted though the bogey term is invoked ever so often by SFJ and the Indian government. It calls for the Sikhs from around twenty countries and regions in the world, especially Panjab, where two-thirds of the community lives, to vote on whether they want the right to self-determination and establish Panjab as a nation state—Khalistan. The referendum statement baffles me. A referendum is a vote by an electorate on a single political question. How do Sikhs living in twenty countries, geographically dispersed around the world, become one electorate? Notwithstanding this flaw in the very idea of a referendum, the move for the referendum, with posters coming up in various places in Panjab, has caused considerable consternation in India, especially in the political class and the Delhi-based media.

I believe that despite the politics of nation states, the questions on the viability of such nation states, any ethnicity, community or religion should have the freedom to decide on the constitution of its nation state. Nations are imagined communities and there is no point in living in a nation in which one does not feel that he or she belongs or where they feel their dignity, self-respect, sense of justice, and resources for a better life are not met. Khalistan is an aspirational nation state and there is no harm in conducting the referendum.

However, a new nation state does not depend solely on the desire of people. Will the demand for Khalistan succeed, and will a real Khalistan be possible, is open to the praciticalities of how the nation state will be implemented. It also depends on geo-politics and whether such a nation state would be able to secure itself and provide its citizens basic amenities, scope for growth, justice and dignity.

Each of the previous chapters of this book outlines issues that the state of Panjab has with the nation state. The issues are huge and urgently need to be solved, not only because Panjab is disquiet but also because in most cases Panjab was the laboratory where social and economic experiments failed, but were still implemented across India. Panjab is where religion and language defined its boundaries twice in the last century, both resulting in unhappy tidings for the state, and have still become the raison d'être for right-wing fascist parties to rise in India. Solving Panjab's human rights and economic issues is in the best interest of the Indian nation state. That is why, on the issue of the formation of Khalistan, I have the following thoughts:

- What will be the physical boundary of a nation called Khalistan? If we have to look at Maharaja Ranjit Singh's Sikh empire, then Lahore was its capital. Will the physical boundaries extend to Pakistan as well?
- Sikhs are 56 per cent of current east Panjab. Even among them there are Bahujan populations. The remaining 44 per cent are mostly Hindu with Bahujan populations and also Christians and Muslims. Will they too find a home in Khalistan, considering the Sikh religion asks us to treat everyone as equal?
- What would the fate of Sikhs who live outside Panjab but within the Indian nation be? Will they be pushed into Panjab like the exchange of populations during Partition which resulted in so much mayhem and chaos?

- What would the economic basis of Khalistan be? The land used to be fertile and still produces bumper harvests of paddy and wheat but how will it export them without a port city? All landlocked nations are severely dependent on their neighbours. Will the people of the newly formed Khalistan have the guarantee that India, which could possibly have a hostile view on Khalistan's creation, would open up its airspace to allow Khalistan to trade with the world? Would Pakistan allow that? Panjab has no mineral wealth. Its gravel and sand too has been extracted and sold by the mafias.
- In the event of secession from India, it is possible that India will stop the river Satluj from flowing into Khalistan. Already headworks are coming up in Himachal Pradesh. What would Khalistan do then, without water, when its own water tables have fallen so drastically?
- A nation state such as Khalistan cannot exist without acceptance of other nations in the world. What is our reasonable estimate that after what Britain did in the Middle East in the last century—create theocratic states—the world will accept yet another theocratic state?

To me it is critical to ask these questions because not only the last decade but for considerable lengths of time in the last fifty years—ever since the state was carved out—the Akalis who are a Sikh panthic party have been in power in Panjab. It was Sikh rule and we see the devastation it has wrecked on the state and its people. Any idea of Khalistan needs to propose how exactly its government will be oriented towards the betterment of Panjab. Do we have a model code of law?

There is no doubt that the people of Panjab and the Sikhs have to find ways in which they address their myriad problems. As earlier in our history, we are still saddled by the twin issues of being a miniscule community and having limited political weight. We need to find new ways of engaging with the central government.

How do we do that is an open question.

## Chapter Sixteen

# *Janamɗin* — Birthday

On the evening of 8 November 2016, I was at a friend's father's place. Bhaji had just poured me Black Label whiskey in his drawing room in Jalandhar when he got a text message on his mobile phone: *notebandhi* (demonetisation)—watch television, the prime minister's address. We rushed to change the channel on television. The PM had finished speaking but the address was being re-telecast. The PM laid out the objectives for removing all Rs 500 and Rs 1000 notes in circulation with immediate effect and providing a window to exchange the currency notes within fifty days as: sniffing out black money (rumoured to be huge), ending corruption (rampant in India) and ending terrorism (especially in Kashmir, by closing hawala channels).

Both Bhaji and I were stunned. 'Wow!' I said. 'Is this what we expected from a strong leader? This is truly a massive step.' We went back to drinking, and as I retired for the night I checked my email on my phone. I had multiple messages from the US. My teacher, some friends. Each message was almost a distress call: 'Donald Trump has won the elections!' I slept with mixed feelings: did India do right? Did the US do wrong?

Bhaji is a cricket coach and has coached some famous players. Next morning, as we started for his cricket academy, a strange sight greeted us in the markets. All shops, except jewellers, were closed. Was the market late in rising? But how come jewellers had big cars parked outside? Bhaji told me, 'Most trader Hindu families (*khatris* and *banias*) have plenty of cash at home. Some of it is undeclared. How will they deposit the currency notes in banks?' Sure enough, Bhaji received news that people were carrying cash to jewellers and buying gold. It was trading at double the price.

I had some cash in my pocket and the fuel tank of my car was full. Bhaji told me the going market rate for Rs 500 was Rs 400 in hundred rupee currency notes. A black market had already opened up and offered to get my cash exchanged. The government had asked for two days and said that the ATMs would be dispensing cash by then. I did not take up Bhaji's offer. However, both these instances gave me the first hint of how the *notebandhi* I had tentatively lauded last night would go down—people would find ways to beat the system. If a leader, a party and a government does not know this about the people it governs, then such a drastic step amounts to folly and can't be appreciated for intent.

The next day I left for Tarn Taran. On the way I intended to stop at Kapurthala to see the grand Moorish Mosque built on the lines of the Grand Koutoubia Mosque of Marrakesh in Morocco by Maharaja Jagatjit Singh and later in the day at Goindwal, considered the axis of the Sikh religion. Though the mosque was run down now, its sparse, austere, angular structure did evoke the lesser-known beauty of Panjab. The mosque also had an elaborate but understated gate. It was built with stone but lined with marble, its windows decorated with glass and latticed wood and a wooden ceiling. Its uniqueness lay in the fact that unlike other mosques in India it was built without any external domes or minarets but had a tall minaret at one end of the edifice. The red mosque's doors were green and the interior was varnished black and red.

When the maharaja built the mosque, the British ruled India and the viceroy questioned him about the extravagance. The maharaja had stated that over half of the people in his kingdom were Muslims and deserved a mosque. Since then, Partition had taken place, the Muslims had left, but the mosque remained—an edifice of memory and beauty. I stood in the mosque remembering that Ibn Battuta—the one who had named the entire region Panjab—too was from Morocco. It was sad that neither could this Panjab retain what the name meant, nor could it maintain the physical beauty of an idea that had travelled the oceans to reach this land.

I proceeded to the man-made Kanjli wetland just outside Kapurthala. This lake and wetland are sourced by the Kali Bein rivulet—that the religious leader, Balbir Seechewal, had cleaned. The maharaja of Kapurthala, Randhir Singh, father of Jagatjit Singh, had, in the latter half of the nineteenth century, made the Kali Bein headworks to create the lake and the wetland. While the descendants of the royal family now lived in a villa near the lake, for ordinary mortals like me, the only place to visit was the tourism department-developed canal side with boats stacked on dry ground and some game stands in the park nearby.

It had been a few years since Balbir Seechewal's enterprising clean up and water hyacinth had once again grown in the Kali Bein. Neglect, apathy and degradation had won once again. On my mobile I read about the multitude of flora and fauna in the wetland, aided by pictures of rare birds and some animals. In front of me, on the ground, I saw decay and pestilence. Neither the tourism department nor the people were even trying to salvage what had been recovered.

Driving onward, I started to feel a familiar sadness envelop me. Encountering Panjab's multiple tragedies, enmeshed in how no issue had been resolved over the past many decades, had been a downward spiral for me. Demonetisation was a step further into darkness. In any society money is itself just as valuable as the paper it is printed on, plus printing expenses. Money is used between citizens as a promissory note of trust. In a nation it is authorised and put in use by the highest bank. In India, the signature is of the head of the Reserve Bank: 'I promise to pay the bearer the amount of ...' With demonetisation—a decision taken by a select few and not as in a democracy through parliament—the prime minister had rendered this solemn promise of the top bank null and void. The bank head had broken a promise made to the people of the land.

It reminded me of the earlier promise the Centre had broken in Panjab, as discussed in the chapter *Rog*. The promise that the state would protect the life and faith of all its citizens. It reminded me of the promise broken by the police, as discussed in the chapter *Lashaan*, by conducting enforced disappearances and extra-judicial killings. It reminded me of the promises the state had since broken in not providing the essential services it needed to provide its citizens: health, education, roads, drainage and food. It reminded me of the promise the state had broken even in the affairs of agriculture as discussed in *Berukhi*, where farmers were supposed to get good seeds and chemicals that did what they promised—whether insecticides, pesticides or fertilisers. It reminded me of the sacrileges discussed in *Rosh*. Panjab was already a casualty of trust and faith in governance and now demonetisation had eroded even the faith in the banking system in the country.

As the sinking feeling in the pit of my stomach was enhanced, I suddenly felt a great hunger pang. I knew I could get *langar* at Goindwal Sahib. Yet, I remembered what Baba used to say on our journey from Rourkela to Rajpura, when we used to wait at Nizamuddin station for a train to Panjab. '*Langar* is both a necessity and a blessing. If you can afford food, you must look at it as a blessing so that someone else who needs it more than you can have it. But if you can't afford food, in all humility bow to the one offering *langar*.'

I wondered now, with demonetisation, if I could afford food or not, at least for the time being. Notionally, I had currency in my pocket, but the currency was suddenly not valid. I chose to look for food and so I could consider *langar* as a blessing.

Short of the bridge on the Beas, I stopped at a small *dhaba*. A lady was running the place. I asked her if she would accept a Rs 500 currency note. She refused. Now I was in a dilemma. I just had another Rs 50 and a Rs 10 note. I asked for tea. She said it was lunchtime. Tea would take a while. I said I just had Rs 60. Could she offer lunch? She nodded and disappeared. As I waited on one of the cots in front of the *dhaba*, I wondered if what I had assumed for so long was true.

In 1989, when I was an adolescent and the Berlin Wall was pulled down, the Cold War ended. When *glasnost* and *perestroika* took place in the USSR in the late 1980s, when Yugoslavia crumbled in 1991, and when apartheid ended in South Africa in 1994, I had believed that the world had changed for the better. The centres of power had shifted, countries were liberated and maps were realigned. In 1991, India liberalised its economy, and with the advent of foreign companies and brands, the world started looking like a global village. Militancy in Panjab also ended around that time and we all marched on, assuming we were making the world a better place. Yet, through my travels in Panjab, I had seen how this new economic policy of liberalisation had reduced the activities of the state and replaced it with crony capitalism and devastated the land.

Now, with Trump winning in the US, a rising right wing in Europe, our own right wing in power in India, the indications were that right under the nose of the glossy global village and the nice-sounding universal concern headlines, people were actually becoming deeply anxious and were choosing to protect their own subsets of ethnicity, religion, language and culture. They were supporting factionalism, even fascism. Was I living in a chimera, a fantasy?

The lady returned with food. There were five rotis, one daal, one subzi, pickle and onions. I told her again I just had Rs 60. She told me to let her know if I needed more and also informed me that the tea was getting ready. My eyes turned moist. Before I finished my food, a big glass of tea arrived. I relished the tea. When I got up to pay her, she took only Rs 50. 'Keep the ten rupees. Who knows where you may need it,' she said.

I was numbed by her grace and kindness. This, and the hospitality and warmth Panjab had bestowed upon me through my travels, clearly showed people were people, and if you met them as an equal, they responded with kindness and grace. However, it was clear to me now how leaders, political parties and their pursuit of power had gamed us—especially those who touted a cause, whether development or religious—by banking on our faith and belief in their declared agendas. The greater the grandstanding, the bigger chances of the politicians betraying the people.

Before Amritsar and later Anandpur Sahib became the pre-eminent Sikh centres, through the period of the third, fourth and fifth Gurus, Goindwal was the axis of the Sikh religion. When Sher Shah Suri built his grand trade route (the Grand Trunk Road or the GT Road), the ferry point at Goindwal gained importance. However, there were rumours of evil spirits inhabiting the land. The trader Goinda approached Guru Angad to relocate here from Khadur Sahib, inhabit the land and drive the spirits away. Guru Angad sent his disciple Amar Das, later the third Guru, who stayed in Goindwal for thirty-three years and established the centre of the Sikh religion. The place, too, was named after the trader, Goinda—Goindwal Sahib.

Since a major part of Guru Amar Das's service to Guru Angad was providing him water from the river Beas, Guru Amar Das decided to dig a well at Goindwal. The stepwell attracted pilgrims from far and near. Guru Amar Das also started celebrating Baisakhi in Goindwal and made the *langar* an integral activity of the community, insisting that anyone who wanted to see him had to first partake of food at the *langar*. Guru Amar Das also developed the *manji* and *piri* system of propagating the faith in far-off places. The *manji* (cot) and *piri* (stool) were seats of authority and also represented a zone of religious administration with an appointed chief called *sangatia* or *masand* to spread Guru Nanak's message, provide spiritual guidance and be responsible for the offerings of each *sangat* (the *dasvand*), which they made as a symbol of their reverence to the Guru. This system was later expanded by Guru Har Gobind, and when the *masands* became corrupt, it was abolished by Guru Gobind Singh. Bhai Gurdas who later compiled the Adi Granth was also born in Goindwal.

Emperor Akbar once visited Guru Amar Das in Goindwal and partook of the *langar*. He was impressed with the tradition and granted land in the name of Bibi Bhani, the daughter of the Guru. The Guru's son-in-law and successor, Guru Ram Das, then founded Amritsar on that newly granted land, and that is how the Darbar Sahib in Amritsar came into existence.

Today, the contrast between Amritsar and Goindwal is all too apparent. In Amritsar, Sukhbir Badal has created a 'Heritage Street' at the entrance to the Durbar Sahib. The architects have used red stone from Rajasthan and made uniform the shop signs of all the stores there except for McDonald's and Subway which obviously are bigger corporate entities than the SGPC. The government has erected a wailing mother statue borrowed from Christian symbolism in front of the Jallianwala Bagh. The whole front of the sacred precincts has been opened up. The four-century-old living museum—the Mai Sewan Bazar—was demolished after Operation Black Thunder and packed off into a three-storey mall to the left of the Heritage Street. Sandeep, whom we met in chapter *Bardr*, said, 'The flyover which brings in tourists directly to the parking lot has taken the Durbar Sahib out of Amritsar. The sanctum sanctorum has become accessible to tourists and visitors, but we, the people of the city, have lost access to it.'

In contrast was the gurdwara at Goindwal, standing next to the Baoli with eighty-four steps, white against the chequerboard courtyard. The simple, unpretentious and serene gurdwara with four rounded domes, echoing the main dome and the facade of turrets, elliptical cornices and projected windows. I am glad the axis of the religion, its sense of *piri* (spirituality), is a little less affected by tourists, markets and corporatism. I entered the *langar* and partook of tea before visiting the gurdwara and walking down the well. I sensed a certain calmness in the place—perhaps this was spiritual. I sat there a long time, amidst the strains of kirtan, not thinking, just at peace.

As I rode towards Tarn Taran, from afar I spotted the new thermal plant near the Beas and thanked heavens that it hadn't yet been commissioned. Once it started operations it would risk the Harike wetlands, one of the biggest migratory bird destinations at the confluence of the rivers Beas and Satluj, where, a few years back, nature lovers and wildlife enthusiasts had spotted a family of river dolphins.

I drove through the town of Fatehabad which hosted an old *serai* (medieval resthouse) that was now completely built over by residents and hardly distinguishable from its urban surroundings. In this reduced Panjab, merely a few hundred kilometres from east to west and north to south, history wrote and rewrote itself as if a painter had run out of canvas and kept painting a new series on top of earlier paintings—a palimpsest.

In recent times, with the attention of the community moving to Amritsar, Goindwal and Sultanpur Lodhi associated with Guru

Nanak, Khadur Sahib associated with Guru Angad and Baba Bakala associated with Guru Tegh Bahadur have been overshadowed by the lustre of the gold plates of Durbar Sahib. At Tarn Taran, waiting for Sunny near the historic gurdwara also called the Darbar Sahib, I looked around the ramshackle town and noticed, unlike how earlier when the Majha was considered prosperous, now it too resembled the comparatively poor and dusty Malwa towns. The same withered shops, half-empty, the old tractors and trollies, the people, too tired and fatigued—the landscape of Panjab had steadily faded.

I reached Tarn Taran to spend a night with Sunny, someone I only knew through social media. Sunny had studied medicine at AIIMS, then decided to leave allopathy. He had trained in various traditional Indian schools of healing, started producing music and films and moved to France where he practises healing. When Sunny arrived, I remarked on the dilapidated, tired look of the town and he asked me, 'Why do you think I have moved to France?' We went to his *kothi*, which was now up for sale, to spend the night there.

The next day the ATMs were supposed to work. I rose early and reached the market which had three ATMs in a row. The crowd in front of them was huge and impatient. The shutters to the ATMs were all down. Sentries stood with guns. I waited for an hour but the shutters did not open and I left for Amritsar with only the Rs 10 in my pocket still carrying any value, hoping to find an ATM.

On the way, near Chabba, I spotted Gurdwara Naud Singh. The gurdwara had been under construction for a few years and had been an informal octroi post for many years before that. Every passing vehicle—car, jeep, motor-bike, private buses, state buses, trucks— handed over some money to the Nihangs on the road. While Baba Deep Singh Gurdwara in Amritsar was under the SGPC, this one was not. It was independent, and the Nihangs ran it. No one had ever challenged the money collection. It was assumed that people gave out of free will. However, today was an exception. Owing to demonetisation, the Nihangs were not on the road. A year ago, this was the gurdwara that had facilitated the Sarbat Khalsa. I decided to visit.

At the gurdwara I asked for the *jathedar* and was guided to a room. On one side of the floor many Nihangs were sitting in a circle counting currency from a huge mound in the middle. On the other side, about fifteen small children, dressed as Nihangs in their blue uniform, were studying. When I asked for the *jathedar* he pointed to a young man who spoke to outsiders. I asked him how things had been since the Sarbat Khalsa. He smiled a bit apologetically and said, 'You can see. It happened, it is over.'

'But you would have some stake in it?'

'We are the defenders of the religion, of the people. We go by what the community wants. They asked us to organise the Sarbat Khalsa, we did that. After that, it is again up to the community.'

'Yet you were not arrested for sedition?'

'No one dares to touch us. The SGPC can't, the government doesn't and neither can their paid stooges, the police. We walk in the tradition of Sahib Sri Guru Gobind Singh. That is how it has been. That is how it shall remain.'

'I see so many young children here. What do you teach them?'

'*Shabd* (the word). *Bani* (the text). We are engaged in research on the *shabd*.' He pointed to many notebooks with jottings. I looked at them. Panjab had many traditions and knowledge systems. Yet, what it lacked was action to follow the word.

The gap between the word and the action has been growing vast and now it seemed the whole of Panjab would fall into the abyss. The danger of the lack of political will to implement the word threatened to subsume every issue of Panjab: the water crisis, the agrarian crisis, the industrial crisis, the casteism, the drugs menace, the high rates of unemployment, and so on. This lack of political will survived by creating distraction after distraction over religious and other emotional issues so that the people found no respite to strategise on how to make political power accountable. In the absence of a justice-oriented system, an ethical core to governance, and a decayed administrative system full of loopholes and internal pecking orders, the people were forever entangled in either how to exploit it or how to survive it. Panjab does bleed through a thousand cuts.

'Do have *langar* before you leave,' said the young Nihang. I nodded.

I drove through the streets of Amritsar, not finding a single open ATM. I returned to Tarn Taran, and the next day, anticipating that the ATMs would now be functional, I went even earlier, at 6 a.m. They were still down. An old man, his white beard tied up, sporting a smart turban and looking like a retired army officer, for some reason screamed in my face: 'This is an emergency, a financial emergency. I have never seen anything like this.'

In the newspaper there was news of the first forged Rs 2000 currency note found in Tarn Taran.[189] I eventually managed to swipe my credit card at a petrol station and get some money in exchange. I proceeded to Ludhiana learning on my way that farmers had no money to buy wheat seeds and that the wheat plantation time was running out. I spoke to Bhola and Harjeet, both of whom said they were finding it impossible to get seeds and fertilisers. In the next week, the seed crisis peaked. Without hard cash, the farmers had no options. Modernisation, corporatisation and industrialisation of agriculture had already robbed them of their centuries-long tradition of saving seeds for the next crop. Now seeds had to be bought from shops and from companies. No bank, no co-operatives, no seed outlets and no fertiliser companies were willing to part with what the farmers needed until they were assured by the *arthiyas*.

Finally, it was the reviled *arthiyas* who helped the farmers. This was the farming ecosystem of Panjab. However draconian, exploitative and unjust it was and however much correction it needed, it was finally this *arthiya*-farmer system that averted the season's crises and the nation's food gap.

Given demonetisation and the difficulty to withdraw money, I returned to Bangalore for a few weeks until the situation eased a bit. Meanwhile, the Election Commission announced the poll dates. I noted that the Panjab elections were slated to be held on my birthday. It was pure serendipity, and yet it was a landmark of sorts in my journeys: was I on my coming birthday going to be at any different place than my earlier birthdays—in terms of how I understood the world, understood Panjab? Where did I stand on my birthday—on which party's side, if at all, or with people's issues?

Once the Assembly elections were declared, the intent of demonetisation became acutely clear. It is common knowledge that in Indian elections political parties rampantly indulge in bribing the voters, luring them with freebies and intoxicants. The EC-mandated ceiling on expenses by candidates is a mere formality. Demonetisation robbed the Akalis in Panjab, but more importantly, it robbed the Samajwadi Party and Bahujan Samaj Party in Uttar Pradesh of their most potent weapon—money to indulge their followers and buy votes.

Given the anti-incumbency in Panjab and the SAD–BJP government having lost favour over non-development, corruption, the incidents of sacrileges and the drugs issue, their not being re-elected was almost a foregone conclusion. Though the Akalis had partnered the BJP for a quarter of a century and had played second fiddle to the national party, the central BJP leadership did not care about them. The key state in the BJP's view was Uttar Pradesh.

Implementing demonetisation broke the back of both the incumbent
Samajwadi Party (SP) and the opposition Bahujan Samaj Party (BSP).
That is where BJP believed it could open up the turf and score, like
it had in the Lok Sabha elections.

I came back to Panjab a few weeks before the elections. I wanted
to travel as much as I could to assess the people's mood. Late winter
is the best season to travel in Panjab. As the sun rises, the fog lifts; the
fragrance of wood smoke tickles your nose while *saag* and *makki di
roti* slow-cook on earthen fires. Gurdwaras, *jatheras*, temples, mosques
and brick-walled homes reveal themselves amidst the green wheat
and yellow mustard fields. One such weekend morning, Jasdeep
and I started for a village and a famous gurdwara not very far from
Chandigarh—Bindrakh. The village was the native village of Surjit
Bindrakhia, well known for his bhangra songs.

The journey through the *kandi* region—a sub-mountainous zone
that stretches in a thin belt along the north-eastern border of the
state—village roads was nothing short of hell. The totally broken
down road showed the ravages of the gravel being smuggled through
these roads day and night. A forty-five minute drive took nearly two
and a half hours. We also briefly stopped at villages to check the
election pulse. Hardly any banners or flags were up and the slogans
on some walls were even blackened, supposedly by the EC. We were
surprised that people were almost not interested in the elections. All
that people wanted was a good road and a ban on the roads being
abused by trucks carrying gravel. The sentiment was: 'But smuggling
is a mafia activity; leaders earn from it. Who will stop it?'

At Bindrakh, the gurdwara was discernible from its distinct colour
scheme: the marble facade was not all uniform white. It was lined
with blue and yellow tiles. The floor was patterned after flower petals.
Inside the gurdwara, instead of one seat, there were nine seats with
the Granth Sahib installed in each of them. Within the boundary
wall of the gurdwara, opposite the main building, were stone shrines.

Jasdeep and I were intrigued on how a gurdwara could follow both practices: Granth Sahib as well as idol worship.

The story was that when Kashmiri Pandits had approached Guru Tegh Bahadur to request the Mughal king Aurangzeb to allow them to practise their religion, they had also settled in areas near Anandpur Sahib. While Guru Tegh Bahadur was martyred, Guru Gobind Singh had continued to protect the Pandits. Baba Amarnath, a Pandit of the Nathpanthi tradition, had escaped to the jungles near Ropar to meditate. This is where he had met Guru Gobind Singh. The Baba had asked the Guru to spend a little time on this land. The Guru had taken a bath in the sarovar nearby and the village had been established in his name. *Bind* (a moment in time) and *rakh* (placement)—where the Guru had placed himself. Since then the gurdwara had been named after the pandit, and both types of prayers—Sikh and Hindu—took place here. Near the *prasad* counter we met an elderly lady who told us that she regularly came to the gurdwara to do service. I asked her if the SGPC had not staked claim to this historic gurdwara.

She replied, 'It does, but every time they come, the villagers chase them away. The village is clear that it is not surrendering its gurdwara to the SGPC.'

'That is very nice, but Bibiji, whom will you vote for in the coming elections?'

'Of course, for the Badals. We are old Akalis. The whole village.'

Jasdeeep said, '*Sing phas gaye* (the horns are entangled).' I too was amused but wanted to know what the lady thought. I said, 'But Badal is SGPC! How can you vote for him and also oppose him at the same time?'

The lady was taken aback. 'Is he? Is Badal SGPC? I did not know that. No one knows that. You are lying.'

'No Bibiji, why would I lie? Just check who controls the SGPC.'

'Yes,' said the lady pensively, 'I will have to talk to my family about this. But we are not giving the gurdwara. Do have *langar* before you leave.'

We took the lady's leave and sat down for *langar*. The *langar* at this gurdwara, named after a Pandit, served peas and paneer. It was true—Panjab was indeed entangled!

On my way to follow the journalist Kanwar Sandhu who was contesting the election on behalf of the AAP from Kharar, near Chandigarh, I saw a dystopian image unfold: the city encroaching upon the villages. It was one straight road, its partition dotted with withering palm trees, on both sides of the road farmlands bought and colonies created, empty plots that stretched on for kilometres in what was being touted as New Chandigarh. In the midst of this empty field stood one structure—a tall building with black glass on its facade, which belonged to Omaxe, a real estate company.

Sandhu was well known to English newspaper readers, was the head of AAP's *Bolda Panjab* team and contesting from Kharar, one of the largest constituencies—184 villages and 1.75 lakh registered voters—many of them migrants to whom he was an unfamiliar face. Sandhu's quandary was instructive in understanding the depth of the language divide in India, Panjab, and the gap that those from the English-speaking, largely urban press must bridge to communicate with locals. On the day I was with the campaign team, Sandhu spoke at a rally in Chahar Majra—a village located less than ten kilometres from Chandigarh.

In his speech Sandhu rattled off a litany of the hydra-headed problems that had been plaguing Panjab for the past few years. He referred to the rising farmer suicides; the necessity of loan waivers and compensation for crop loss; the need to eradicate drugs; and the multiple incidents of the desecration of holy texts. Sandhu also offered a list of the promises that the AAP would fulfil if it came to power. These included: the revival of public schools with additional staff; provision of free check-ups at local dispensaries, which would be equipped with laboratories and the requisite medicines; the creation of more jobs; state support for dairy farming; compensation for the old, infirm and disabled; and the settlement of the dispute over the SYL canal.

He ridiculed the seven star Oberoi Sukhvilas hotel that Sukhbir Badal had built in the new Chandigarh area by diverting a sanctioned road to his resort. In fact, by emphasising its illegality, Sandhu was reinforcing fears that the odd jobs the people of the village got at the hotel would go away if the AAP came to power. He made no mention of the havoc that illegal gravel mining had wrecked on the people and roads in Kharar. At both Chahar Majra and a subsequent rally at Paintpur, he refrained from targeting either Jagmohan Singh Kang, the Congress candidate and the current MLA from Kharar, or Ranjit Singh Gill, the real estate businessman—locally, such barons are called 'coloniser' which I thought was an exact turn of phrase—who was the Akali Dal's candidate.

Sandhu's campaign was being managed by his son who told me the number of people volunteering with the AAP had increased over the past few weeks. 'Yet, there remains a shadow of the ruling powers on our campaign. People are hesitant to support us openly,' he said. That was indicative of the fear of the Congress and SAD in case Sandhu lost and later AAP volunteers faced retribution.

While the lady at Bindrakh was confused, I met a lot of older Sikh men near Ludhiana. They were traditional Akali voters. Their response to my question on who they would vote for this time was, '*Tin aaye tan tilkan ho gayi* (now there are three parties and the turf has become slippery).' They told me most of them were ex-army men and suddenly started praising the Congress for how in its tenure their pensions had risen. I was quite amused by how the traditional Akali voter was looking for reasons to slip away from the party.

Though Panjab is a Sikh-dominated state, the fact is that the key to Panjab elections lies with two non-Sikh groups: urban Hindu voters who earlier went with the BJP and the Dalits and other Bahujan communities who earlier went with the Congress. This time, with a third player (AAP), the dynamics looked different. In the past few months, the AAP had focussed on discrediting the Akalis, but the question was if they had projected themselves as a worthy choice.

At Bhaini Sahib village, the nerve centre of the Namdhari Sikhs, whose matriarch Bibi Chand Kaur had been murdered in April 2016, Harjot Singh Bains—the twenty-six-year-old president of the AAP's youth wing in Panjab and its candidate from Sahnewal—was speaking to an audience of about 250 members. He brought up the attack on the Sikh preacher Ranjit Singh Dhadrianwale and focussed on *chitta*—the colour white and how it was culturally a colour signifying purity and also how it was their party colour. Yet, now, under the Akalis, *chitta*, the drug, was consuming the youth and destroying families.

When the AAP appointed Gurpreet Singh Ghuggi, a comedian in cinema and television, as their state convenor to replace Suchha Singh Chhotepur, the first thing Ghuggi did upon being nominated was to change his surname back to Waraich. It was both an attempt to erase his identity as Ghuggi (meaning dove), which had served his film comedy career, and assert his Jutt identity. Though the AAP had a Dalit manifesto, had promised a Dalit deputy chief minister, they had not touched the panchayati land issue which could have been a draw. Having goofed up on Panjab's water issues earlier and numerous about-turns on the issue over the past year, their inability to take a stand on a core land issue also betrayed their fears. I asked an AAP leader about it and he answered, 'In the land of Jutts, you are talking of Dalits?'

While the urban Hindu voters could have come to them easily, a lot of funding from the diaspora also brought with it the legacy of Khalistan. It was exacerbated when Kejriwal came to campaign and spent a night at the home of a former Khalistan sympathiser. The Akalis and the Congress milked the news to create a fear in the minority Hindu population that bringing in the AAP would be the return of the Khalistan movement. That worked to an extent and the urban Hindu vote that used to go to the BJP switched over to the Congress. Though the diaspora was not rooting for a separatist state, the perception was created and the AAP's association with the diaspora cost it a very clear vote bank. The AAP's conundrum was: without funding, the party would not have grown, with funding they lost a core vote bank.

Dr Sarika Verma, an ENT specialist, was the joint secretary of the AAP Panjab and the head of the *Chalo Panjab* movement, aimed at Indians living abroad. According to her, around 5,000 NRIs and hundreds of people from across India had come to Panjab to campaign for the party. Many more NRIs campaigned over phone calls to family and relatives. I met many of those who came down, and every time their reason to help the AAP was not Khalistan but the simple fact that they had experienced a life different from how it was in Panjab or India. They wanted to join hands with a party they thought could best achieve that goal. In some ways, though, I was a mere observer. I sensed that their concern for Panjab was the same as mine, as I too did not live in Panjab.

Yet, having peaked early, the AAP was poorly exposed. Its woes too did not seem to end. There were fresh accusations of corruption, allegations of the lack of transparency over donations, the problems of unwise candidate selection, and overall, a lack of cadre to support the momentum of the election. The AAP explained its reasons to not display the list of donors—to save them from being targeted by the Congress, the Akalis and the BJP. This was true because traditional parties did have their muscle power, but it did not cut much ice with people, and once again showed how the AAP did not understand the turf in which it sought to create a revolution.

Talking about the issues of the lack of intra-party democracy and transparency that were plaguing the AAP, a volunteer from Texas said, 'When the Chhotepur issue came up, we went into a huddle. We discussed and debated and some of us wanted to pull back. Then we realised that the AAP's final aim is good: a functioning democracy. Kejriwal had to be a bit of a dictator. Until now it was still too early for party elections. We needed to stabilise. If the AAP wins Panjab, then it will be time for transparency and the AAP better do it. Else, it will be like the right wing.' If the party came to power, he continued, 'They will face immense challenges in dismantling the current official and contractor nexus, managing the police and the Mandi boards. There remains a hostile centre, and there will be a loud clamour for positions and benefits inside the AAP ranks.'

I was not convinced. I found it strange that a Panjab known for resistance and rebellion had become so servile to Kejriwal and his diktats. I wondered if they won the elections, with all the power getting to their heads, how they would stay true to their promise of inter-party democracy and transparency.

The Akalis were busy drumming up support for themselves through the politics of memorials and showpieces. The most absurd they could come up with was a water bus. A few months back Sukhbir Badal had bombastically announced that he would turn Panjab into a place where buses would ply on water. He had been roundly ridiculed on social media. He became serious about his desire and finally in December executed an amphibious bus project at the Harike wetland, the confluence of the Satluj and the Beas, the extremely sensitive ecological bounty space of the state.

Obviously, no study on the effect of such pseudo-tourism had been conducted, no one knew the risks, the danger to aquatic and riverine life, including the miraculous dolphin family, but the project was pushed to completion anyway. Finally, one winter morning, extra water was released from Bhakra dam, flooding fields in more than a hundred nearby villages, and Sukhbir Badal climbed the yellow amphibious water bus whose bottom looked like a boat but had wheels which could move on roads. The bus entered the confluence, with Sukbir Badal and his entourage waving green flags. This was supposed to be the highlight of the last decade of the SAD–BJP rule in Panjab. It became a joke. People called it a *ghaduka*—a travelling contraption.

By now, the Congress—which had been lying low all this while when AAP was working hard to draw people away from the Akalis— suddenly came up from behind and began to enter the discourse. The Congress had gamed the AAP and picked up steam from mid-December onwards. The Congress also fumbled with the usual: lack of clarity on contestants. Around one-fourth of the seats remained undecided until the last three weeks before the elections. Around one-fourth of the seats were also contested by rejected Congress candidates who stood against chosen Congress candidates.

The Congress banked on their leader Captain Amarinder's promise to waive off farmer loans, end the menace of drugs, provide jobs to forty lakh youth, and so on. I was amused by how they used a century-old slogan—*Pagdi Sambhal Jutta*—completely divorced from its origin during the farmers's agitation in the canal colonies at the turn of the twentieth century. The main theme of their manifesto was to regain the honour of Panjab.

It was clear that there was no wave, no visible gravitation towards any party except that everyone recognised that the Akalis, and with them, the BJP, should not come back to power. An interesting development was of Navjot Singh Sidhu and his wife Navjot Kaur Sidhu quitting the BJP a few months before the elections. While Navjot Kaur had been a big critic of the SAD–BJP government, releasing regular videos of its irregular functioning, while she remained part of the BJP, Navjot Singh was their big ticket face in Panjab. Having quit, Navjot Singh, along with former Akali leader Pargat Singh, and the Bains brothers, formed the Awaaz-e-Panjab. Speculation about which party they would support tied up the state for a few weeks. However, soon, Awaaz-e-Panjab split. Navjot and Pargat joined the Congress and the Bains brothers chose to go independent, with outside support from the AAP.

As I traversed Panjab, what struck me was the impassive and immense presence of camouflage-uniformed central security forces in every town and big village. When they stopped vehicles in Doaba, the drivers were polite. In Malwa, from where the Akali and Congress chief ministers hailed, the commuters were aggressive: 'We stopped. What else do you want?' In Majha, once Panjab's power centre, drivers asked: 'Did you ask us to stop?' These responses were quite indicative of how people from these regions behaved even otherwise.

I believe all exit polls and all opinions that we form about how people will vote have a huge gender tilt. Whatever be the sample size, the fact is that women's voices and opinions are hardly recorded. It is assumed that women will vote where the men of the family are voting. That is why on my Malwa leg I asked a woman friend to accompany me. Amandeep Caur was my namesake, a PhD student then about to submit her dissertation, but more importantly, she was an ex-presidential candidate from SFS in Panjab University.

My reason to invite Aman was deeper than exit polls. It was personal. Having travelled through Panjab for over a year now, I was aware of the barbed wire that patriarchy draws to enclose women and keep me away from them. I had repeatedly tried to go beyond the pale but met with limited success. I sensed the gap in my understanding and attempted to close it one more time with Aman's help.

As we entered Malwa through Patiala, we were on the road from Chandigarh to Bathinda, which Sukhbir Badal had said could be used to land airplanes. It was still under construction with numerous diversions. Sukhbir Badal had said one could keep a peg of whiskey on the dashboard and it would stay stable through the journey, but here even our water bottles were clanking so hard that we felt our old Alto had developed a defect.

As we kept checking into villages on the way, at tea stalls by the road, the sense was clear: the men were no longer sure the women would vote where told. Yet, when Aman asked women, they were silent. Only after Sangrur was there some sense of an election, with Akali and Congress billboards claiming, 'Panjab is for Panjabis'. It was clearly a negative campaign against the 'outsider' AAP. In Barnala Mandi, we stopped at a rally of those engaged in the panchayati land movement. Among them the opinion was that they should vote NOTA. It was no time for me to engage with what I understood about NOTA. Any protest takes various forms and this was ZPSC's stance. Outside Barnala, going towards a friend's village, we found ourselves caught in Simranjeet Singh Maan's (Akali Dal [Amritsar]) long rally full of tractors and trollies. Late in the evening, the mist was blocking our vision and yet our journey seemed surreal, as if we were driving through clouds.

Next day, outside Bathinda, we stayed at a big home, with the joint family of an uncle of a cousin, and travelled to a few adjacent villages. Aman kept trying to listen to women's voices but mostly drew a blank. We noticed another trend which cut through Panjab horizontally. The youth were with the AAP while the older folks were confused.

A young AAP volunteer in Jassi Pauwalli village said, 'AAP is gunpowder; it can start a fire across the nation.' I knew he was correct and that the nation was looking at Panjab. Especially at the AAP's performance in Panjab as an alternative to right wing and Congress politics in the country. While the AAP did appear to regain some lost ground and garner silent support from the voter base that the Akali Dal may have alienated, the Panjab elections remained too close to call. If voters did gravitate towards the party, it would be because the AAP was their last resort, not their first choice. Even for the AAP's volunteer base, supporting the party was a leap of faith. I was not sure how good a lesson such negative reasons for the AAP's win would be for the country.

That night, at the uncle's place, I found myself in a rather tricky situation. Uncle had brought a bottle of whiskey, the way Panjabis like to honour a guest, but Aman was nowhere to be found. Neither in our room where we poured ourselves pegs, nor at the dinner table. I messaged Aman and she told me she was in the women's section of the house. She had eaten her dinner which was served to her in her bedroom. I was stunned by how patriarchy operated in Panjabi homes. However, Aman did share that a few women had mentioned that they disbelieved their sons who, until then were addicted to substances, were advocating for the AAP. They wondered about the AAP as a choice.

The Congress pitch was friendly and conversational. Captain Amarinder Singh in his rally at Khanna addressed various issues, cracking jokes about Sukhbir Badal, the deputy chief minister. 'That fat one, what's his name?' he asked. There were multiple prompts. 'Ah! yes, Sukhbir. What did I call him last time? *Baloongda* (kitten)! But that was five years ago. Now he has become fatter. He can't see where he walks. He does not know what he speaks.' He went on to reassure the *arthiyas*. 'When I say loan waiver, I mean the Rs 55,000 crore farmers owe to banks. I know you have elaborate systems of loans and credits with farmers. Don't worry, I won't touch you.'

The Akali campaign was arrogantly listing doles: *Nanhi Chaan* targeted at hygiene and sanitation for girls, the cycle scheme, ambulances, road projects, free pilgrimages and so on. The irony: that the political wooing in what was once India's most prosperous state and its food basket still revolved around roads and drains, subsidies and doles.

In many big houses and havelis we saw flags of all three parties. When we asked, the replies were: 'How can I say no to anyone?' or 'Whatever flags they plant, I will vote for whoever I want.' This response could be one of the secrets of the fortress called Panjab, but it might equally be true that no one really knew: people were splintered; they had either decided already or would decide just before voting. There was also the fear of the *parcha*—the police complaint—and the *goondagardi* of the Akalis if they scraped through again.

Panjab was silent.

Through the elections, 'Save Panjab' became the rallying point for all parties. AAP sought to save Panjab from the SAD–BJP, the Congress, drugs, farmer suicides and loan defaults, and the overall penury in a state that had topped human indices till a few decades ago. The Congress and the Akalis sought to save Panjab from outsiders, *topi-walle*, *bhaiye*, *chawl-kane* (the AAP) who they said did not understand the state.

In rally after rally, the three parties invoked the Sikh *jaikara*: *Jo bole so nihal, Sat Sri Akal*. But in these elections, the *jaikara* alone did not seem enough. AAP added *Inquilab Zindabad*; Congress added *Jai*

*Bharat* and the SAD–BJP added *Jai Bhim*. While the AAP signalled its reliance on traditionally Left agendas, the Congress tried to convey that it would not play to Khalistani sentiments, while the SAD–BJP tried to reach out to the Dalits.

The AAP's slogans were catchy—*Captain–Badal dhoka hai, Panjab bacha lo, mauka hai* (the Captain and the Badals are frauds, save Panjab, this is your chance). Another urged, *Niklo bahar dukanon se, jung lado beimaano se* (step out of your shops and homes, fight the war against the corrupt). A revolution is a very attractive call and the AAP promised to rid Panjab of both the Congress and the Akalis who, for the last half a century, had fortified the state over language and identity issues. The AAP promised to breach the walls and usher in what they said was true governance.

The AAP's false bravado was in declaring that they would field their senior leaders against the Akali stalwarts: Parkash Singh Badal, Sukhbir Badal and Bikram Singh Majithia. So, Jarnail Singh, a Sikh face who had risen after throwing a shoe at P. Chidambaram in 2009 when he announced Jagdish Tytler, a 1984 anti-Sikh pogrom accused, as a parliamentary candidate, took on Parkash Singh Badal; Bhagwant Mann took on Sukhbir Badal; and Himmat Shergill took on Bikram Singh Majithia. This was the equivalent of lining up its own generals for the firing squad. Whoever lost to these veteran stalwarts would automatically be eliminated from the contest for the chief minister's post. Especially Bhagwant Maan who, now, for many months, had almost assumed that his popularity with audiences automatically translated into his being the most eligible candidate for chief minister. Once Manish Sisodia, the Delhi AAP deputy chief minister even tested the waters by declaring there was nothing wrong in Arvind Kejriwal taking over as chief minister. His suggestion met with tremendous resistance.

The reason is, since the 1970s, after Zail Singh, Panjab has not had a non-Jutt chief minister, let alone a non-Sikh chief minister. In case of a win, the AAP was staring at a crisis in deciding its chief minister, but that would come later. For now, the AAP was going into the fight without a leader, which again does not work in Panjab.

At this time, the Akali government decided to drop a long-pending Amritsar Improvement Trust (AIT) land scam case against Captain Amarinder. The Vigilance Bureau filed a closure report before the courts in October on the plea that it had not been able to find enough evidence. The Congress returned the favour by putting up its candidates to make each of the contests that AAP was being brave about three-cornered, thus diluting AAP's impact and luring away voters.

Captain Amarinder stood from Lambi against Jarnail Singh and Parkash Singh Badal, Ravneet Bittu, then Ludhiana MP stood from Jalalabad against Bhagwant Mann and Sukhbir Badal and Sukhjinder Raj Singh Lalli stood against Himmat Singh Shergill and Bikram Majithia from Majitha.

In village Lambi, standing by his fish pakoda stall, the owner said, 'Captain did that to contain Congress votes from going to the AAP.'

I played devil's advocate: it would be sad to see the ninety-year-old Badal lose, I said. The owner came up with a litany of complaints against the Badals. Then I asked, 'Why did you not oust him earlier? Why now?'

The owner said, 'Because we had no choice then. Now we have Jarnail Singh.'

Even before the elections, the tense was already past. The fact about Panjab elections for the last century, that the AAP repeatedly emphasised, was that these were elections between a few influential families: the Patiala royals, the Badal family, the Kairons and Majithias who had married into the Badal family, the families of the Brars of Sarai Naga and the Manns of Sangrur.[190] The era of kings might have gone but their system of consolidation of kingdoms through marriages, with minor additions like the Sidhus and Bajwas and subtractions like Khaira for the Congress, continued to hold sway even in modern democracies.

On 31 January 2017, I reached the biggest rally of the elections at Bathinda. It was a rally of small farmers and landless labourers. The non-political people or non-party people, the farmer and labour unions, had called the rally and decided not to tell anyone to vote for any party. They left the decision to the people. Their slogan was: *votan wele Bapu kehnde, mudke saadi saar na lende* (you plead with us for votes, later you don't even turn to look at us).

This was the response of the poorest and the weakest to the charade of electoral politics.

On our way back, near Sirhind, Aman and I stopped by a rally by a famous Panjabi singer Babbu Maan. It was already dark but hundreds of people had gathered. In typical pop star fashion, Maan made his grand entry to loud cheers from the crowd. On stage he said, 'I am appearing only because the candidate has called me. I do not even know which party he is standing with. I endorse every political party and am ready to appear for anyone who calls me.'

Hearing that, Aman and I drove off, amused at how art and music—the mediums that reached millions of fans who considered the artist their hero and were willing to emulate him—were subservient to political power. What is the responsibility of an artist towards the self, towards the society, and towards Panjab?

Three days before the elections, a bomb blast took place in Maur Mandi near Bathinda at the rally of the Congress candidate, Harminder Singh Jassi. Six people died. Jassi was related to Dera Sacha Sauda head Gurmeet Ram Rahim Singh, whose sect had a hold on the Dalit votes in seats in south Panjab. A day after the blast, Gurmeet Ram Rahim pledged support to the SAD–BJP.

Finally, after a year and a half, as Panjab voted on my birthday, I realised, whatever be its past glory, its magnificent history, Panjab now stood naked and exposed—without the fig leaf of ideas, ideology and religion.

All through my travels I had doubted myself. I had asked myself if there was a secret to Panjab I had not fathomed. So much happens in the state, and questions like what was the deep impulse and how its people's pulse ticked had haunted me. Having seen the representative political parties and the process of elections in a democracy—that is all too literal in terms of the number of votes but deeply lacking in its spirit—I could now recognise the sentiment much more clearly than when I had started my journey. Though this understanding should have shattered me, the reverse happened: a weight lifted from my heart and mind. My self-doubt dissolved.

I learnt that Panjab is an extensive exercise in how to keep one's faith alive. I still do not know where in the human body lies the organ that creates faith but I know that Panjab tests the faith of those who believe in it. The choice is whether one is concerned about Panjab for the sake of Panjab or to further oneself. Sooner or later, Panjab rejects those who try to manipulate it to serve their narrow ends. My journey was a gift I had given myself: learning how to discern between issue and distraction.

My faith was not beholden to someone telling me about Panjab but in my being able to listen to my deepest self. I felt, to create a Panjab seeded in the past but flowering in the future I had to, indeed I must, look for answers to questions of justice, both individual and social. There was simply no other way, no shortcut.

That was the original pursuit that had brought me to Panjab. Satnam had said, 'Panjab is a prism. When light falls on it, the prism refracts it in various colours. People take what colour they see, but seldom does anyone walk into the prism to know what it feels like to be in Panjab.'

If Satnam would have been alive, I could now have told him that I had attempted to walk into Panjab and I wasn't taking any one colour from it with me. Having walked through the fields filled with corpses to which Danish had pointed, having looked at its windows and doors, I had found that the only pillars that stood in the ruin of Panjab were its resistance to power and hegemony. That was, that is, and that will always be Panjab. The dropping of the veil of self-doubt gave me the courage to write this book and place it in the landmine of narratives that we know as Panjab.

# Epilogue

On 11 March 2017, after thirty-five days of suspense, the Panjab election results were declared along with that of Uttar Pradesh and other states. The Congress had won with an overwhelming majority—close to two-thirds of the seats. The Akalis were wiped out. The AAP too had not fared well, though they had ended above the Akalis and become the leading opposition party in the State Assembly.

Though the elections had been too close to call, the result was not an absolute surprise. The immediate reason for Congress's win was the Maur Mandi blast and Gurmeet Ram Rahim's support to the Akalis. It had revealed the absolute volte-face by the Akali Dal when it came to Sikh issues by taking support of the organisation at that time considered most likely to be behind the cases of the *beadbi* of the Guru Granth Sahib. The traditional Akali vote bank, rural Sikh votes, had shifted to the Congress. The blast caused enough fear of revival of Khalistan in traditional BJP voters so that urban Hindus who were tilting towards the AAP also shifted to the Congress. Gurmeet Ram Rahim and the Akali Dal had chosen to lose, but by losing, they had won, by keeping the AAP out of Panjab.

The elections were a turf war and once again the traditional parties who governed the fort called Panjab had managed to keep a third party from entering it. The AAP accused the Congress and the Akalis of rigging the electronic voting machines. There could be some truth in those allegations, but even nationally such accusations have not found acceptance and remain in the purview of rumour-mongering. All said and done, now Panjab was assured of a Congress government for the next five years.

For the first few weeks the people of Panjab heaved a sigh of relief that the earlier government was no longer governing them, even as they watched what a Congress government would do differently from a SAD–BJP government to alleviate the many sufferings of Panjab. Apart from banning red beacons on official cars—a popular mark of the powerful—all that the Congress shouted was, 'The treasury is empty!' There was nothing new in that. The Congress should have known this before making those lofty promises. Yet, we know how politicians behave—suddenly pretending to discover what is already public knowledge. Thus began another era of bluster in Panjab.

I believe a silent government that works effectively solves problems and eases people's lives is a good government. In the last few years, nationally, we have been seeing a government that is always making noise, a ruling party that is always in election mode, with little changes on the ground. In fact, various social and economic indices have slipped. This has been going on in Panjab for way too long. That is why in an earlier chapter, *Berukhi*, I said experiencing Panjab now was to experience India's future. True to form, the Congress government kept some or the other flag flying high, and this served as regular grist for the media. Very soon, people came to regard Captain Amarinder's term as akin to the earlier SAD–BJP government.

In February 2018, what Panjab learnt from the Centre's NITI Aayog was a real issue for its agrarian economy because it considers itself to be the nation's food lifeline. While Panjab pushed for the

C2 formula for calculating the MSP (input cost plus rent of land), Dr Rajiv Kumar, the vice chairman of NITI Aayog, told the state not to bother about national food security, but look for open markets for the sale of produce to secure the income of its farmers, and consider diversification to reduce the pressure on its soil, power and underground water.[191]

While it is clear that the Centre now no longer cares about Panjab being a major contributor to the central pool, the real question such a turnaround begets is if it admits that Panjab can now trade with the world through Pakistan. The answer from a nationalistic BJP government needs no guessing. What, then, is Panjab to do now?

When Phuphadji passed away in August 2018, we took his body to his village Chaklan. While arranging Phuphadji's last prayers—Bibiji had bad knees and couldn't climb the steps to the gurdwara—the *sewadars* were worried about the scourge that has been haunting Panjab for the past few years—*beadbi*. Upon a general consensus, we arranged the *Sehej Path* at an outhouse opposite the road. The fear of possible sacrilege made us anxious and made us imprison the mellifluous Granth Sahib, and turned the simple act of prayer and grieving into a ritual of caution and watchfulness. Thankfully, the *Path* and *Bhog* and *Ardas* passed peacefully.

This came on the back of two developments under the new government:

(a) In April 2016, as a face-saver, the SAD–BJP government had brought in a regressive blasphemy law amending IPC 295 (injuring or defiling a place of worship with intent to insult the religion of any class ...), supported by an even stricter IPC

295A (deliberate and malicious acts, intended to outrage religious feelings of any class by insulting its religion or religious beliefs …), by singling out and adding as IPC 295AA the Guru Granth Sahib to it, and sent it for a presidential nod. It was a farce because 295A already encompassed 295AA. The Centre returned the amendment, saying it violated the secular principles of the nation. Instead of letting the Bill slide by, the Congress passed and returned the Bill, after adding the 'Gita, Koran and Bible' to it, and recommended life imprisonment for the accused. To some extent one can understand the law in the context of monotheistic religions based on the book, like Sikh, Islam and Christianity, but how will it work for polytheistic Hinduism with a hundred Ramayanas, a thousand Mahabharatas and a million other revered texts and icons?

(b) Ahead of the submission of the report of the Ranjit Singh panel formed to inquire into incidents of sacrilege and police shooting in Behbal Kalan in which two people had died, the report was leaked in August 2018. Parkash Singh Badal, Sukhbir Singh Badal and the then DGP Sumedh Singh Saini had not appeared before the panel. Nevertheless, based on media reports, previous testimonies and witnesses, the report revealed how the police had lied, given confusing statements, concocted stories, hidden and destroyed evidence, and bullied and silenced witnesses. The report concluded that the police firing was unwarranted and unprovoked. The report held the Dera Sacha Sauda responsible for the incidents of sacrilege. The leakage of the report allowed the Akalis and the SGPC to dismiss it and the witnesses to recant.[192]

As I was compiling my notes for this book, Paramjeet, a friend from Delhi, came home. He told me that my book would be incomplete unless I included the response of Panjab's farmers to the pollution of the land and water and air. This led me to meet Sukhwinder Pappi in Barnala. A few years back, for personal health reasons, Pappi started transitioning from conventional technological to natural farming. He explained his move, 'We need to start with the kitchen. We need to start producing everything we personally consume by farming them without insecticides and pesticides.'

Over the last few years, all across Panjab, thousands of farmers have, in parts or in all of their land, moved to natural farming mostly under the aegis of NGOs. Pappi says, 'The biggest change is that the fun is back in farming. One no longer treats the land as an industry with fixed goals of production. One is humbled and experiments with what crop will work and what will fail. One learns why a crop failed, innovates and tries to succeed the next time.'

Yet, these natural farmers are few. A handful among the lakhs of farmers Panjab has, especially those who are small and marginal. The reason why small and marginal farmers can't easily move to natural farming is because the soil, abused so much through the dual-crop pattern, takes time to regain its potency, and they have no capital to wait.

For those who can afford to wait, once the soil regains its potency and is nurtured, the results are worthwhile.

The Khalistan issue reared its head in March 2018 when the Canadian Prime Minister Justin Trudeau visited India. Both national parties—the Congress and the BJP—ganged up against him and his entourage over accusations of him being pro-Khalistan. The reason was that his Sikh defence minister Harjit Sajjan's father had once been part of the World Sikh Organisation, an organisation that had called for Khalistan. The media even reported that his transport minister Amarjeet Sohi had been incarcerated under the draconian Terrorists and Disruptive Activities Act (TADA). The fact was that in the late '80s, Sohi was working with Gursharan Bhaji, performing (theatre) in Panjab and Bihar. In Bihar, the police had falsely arrested him and labelled him a Naxalite. Theatre groups fought his case and he was released after twenty-one months as an undertrial, not charged under TADA. He had left for Canada and risen up the ranks through his merit.

In the past, Panjab had pulled back from militancy because the issue of Khalistan had lost popular support. Whatever Khalistan might have meant once, today it stands for the pursuit of justice. With India denying justice, it was sad to see the nation refuse to extend its solidarity to Panjab.

After accusing Bikram Singh Majithia of being complicit in drug smuggling throughout the Panjab elections, when faced with a defamation case, in March 2018, Arvind Kejriwal tendered an apology to Majithia. While Kejriwal might have had his compulsions since he was facing a lot of defamation suits by various politicians, this again betrayed how he did not understand Panjab.

In Panjab, stereotyped for its bravado, an apology has various connotations. None of them imply a withdrawal from a contest. Kejriwal was interpreted to have meekly withdrawn. Panjab's AAP unit president Bhagwant Mann and vice-president Aman Arora resigned. The Bains brothers' Lok Insaaf Party also broke its alliance with the AAP.[193]

Meanwhile, to keep his promise to break the back of the drugs menace in Panjab within four weeks, Captain Amarinder Singh constituted a Special Task Force (STF) and brought in Harpreet Singh Sidhu from Chattisgarh to head it. Sidhu was made ADGP (Border) and asked to report directly to the CM and not through the DGP's office. As the police got activated, instances of abuse reduced or became more surreptitious, and people were relieved. Rates of drugs in the illegal market skyrocketed, a proof that the police and the government were working.

A big case that the STF cracked was seizure of drugs from dismissed police inspector Inderjit Singh. When the name of former Moga SSP Raj Jit Singh Hundal cropped up, infighting within the police began. The STF also locked horns with DGP Suresh Arora and DGP (intelligence) Dinkar Gupta and became a 'parallel power centre'.[194] The STF also nabbed around 20,000 addicts in just the same way the previous SAD–BJP government had done with copied FIRs.

In the meantime, given the scarcity of relatively safe *chitta*, abusers started abusing other forms of drugs including injections used to sedate elephants.[195] On 23 June 2018, Kashmir Kaur found her twenty-two-year-old son, a drug abuser, dead in a garbage dump in Prem Nagar, Kotkapura. Her cry went viral on social media. For once, a mother's lament drowned the disputed Panjab government's statistics on drug abusers, the efforts of the STF, the goings-on in the rehabilitation centres, and shot through the hearts of ordinary people in Panjab. Panjab rose in protest and launched the *Chitte De Virodh Wich Kala Hafta—Maro Ja Virodh Karo* (Black Week Against Drugs— Either Die or Protest) from 1-7 July 2018.

Any such protest is always poised on a razor's edge—after all, ten to fifteen people gathering in any village, locality, town, city and conducting personal raids—even dispensing punishment, amounts to vigilantism. Yet, Panjab displayed remarkable nerve. It was the same during the farmer and labour *rail-roko* and the sacrilege protests in

2015, the violence over Ram Rahim's arrest in 2017, and now. The silent discontent could not have been louder.

The CM fell right back into the discipline-and-punish approach and recommended death penalty for drug peddlers, dope tests for all government officials and banning sale of syringes without prescription. A recent study of the NDPS Act in Panjab by the think tank Vidhi Centre for Legal Policy clearly states, 'The NDPS Act has failed to meet its twin objectives of deterrence and rehabilitation in Panjab.'[196]

When addicts cannot find new syringes, they will likely share the ones they have, directly becoming vulnerable to the other major menaces stalking the Panjab countryside—Hepatitis C and HIV. Senior psychiatrist, Dr Anirudh Kala, says, 'The users will pass on these illnesses to their wives and partners. Are we even equipped to manage that?'

In September 2018 Harpreet Singh Sidhu was removed from STF and appointed special principal secretary to the CM. Mohammad Mustafa was appointed the STF head. Mustafa is a 1985 batch IPS officer and was overlooked when the 1987 batch Dinkar Gupta was appointed DGP after Suresh Arora retired in January 2019.

With poor rehabilitation facilities and a compromised police, the government now realises that it is hard to eliminate drugs from society. The political bluster now sounds like the drug-addled talk of an addict: when sober, every abuser talks about quitting drugs, seeking help, not wanting access to drugs—and soon after, they fail. Sadly, Dr Gandhi's approach to amend the NDPS Act, distinguish between hard and soft drugs and decriminalise addiction, has no takers.

The SYL canal court case continues. As in the past many years, whenever Haryana wants to protest a court decision, it blocks the National Highway and cuts off Panjab from the rest of India.

At the same time, we must acknowledge that while river water rights are a Panjab issue, the water crises is now all over the country, even the globe. We have to radically re-think our priorities.

In the most recent land auction in 2019, the ZPSC demanded that like land for *gaushalas*, they should also get land on a thirty-three-year lease. They haven't been heard yet. This July in village Tolewal in district Sangrur there has been a major clash, and at the behest of Congress strongman Lal Singh Chowdhary, auctions have been cancelled.[197] The Dalits, though, continue to try.

During the elections, when Captain Amarinder would say he would waive off the loans of Panjab's farmers, the understanding was that he would address the entire Rs 69,355 crore loan as tallied in 2016 by Panjabi University, Patiala. As per studies carried out by Panjab State Farmers' Commission and Panjabi University, Patiala, the debt per household, which was about Rs 1.79 lakhs in 2005-06, had increased to Rs 4.74 lakhs in 2014-15.

When the Congress came to power in March 2017, they immediately formed an Expert Group led by Tajamul Haque to assess Panjab famer debt and report back within two months. By the end of May 2017, the government proposed to abolish Section 67-A of the Panjab Cooperative Societies Act-1961 which provides for *kurki* (land attachment).[198] The cooperative banks asked how then they could recover their loans. The nationalised banks said the abolition applied only to cooperative banks and not to them. The Akalis said that *kurki* was already abolished (on paper). Most farmer suicides take place due to fear of *kurki* as we saw in the chapter *Karza*.

By June 2017, the expert group sought another two months to finalise their report but came up with interim statistics: Panjab farmers had a debt of nearly Rs 74,000 crore, of which Rs 9,000 crore was owed to cooperative banks, Rs 12,000 crore to nationalised banks, and the rest to private banks and moneylenders.[199] In an interaction with farmer union leaders, Haque had corrected a leader, saying, 'You should not use the term *karza-muafi*. Someone should seek a *muafi* (forgiveness) only if the person has committed a wrong. You should prefer the term *karza mukti* (salvation from indebtedness).' That was indeed a very noble sentiment.

By the end of 2017, the Panjab cabinet, based on the recommendations of the expert group, approved the crop loan waiver scheme to directly benefit nearly 10.25 lakh farmers across the state.[200] However, the notification capped the waiver amount to Rs 2 lakh and addressed only the amount owed to scheduled commercial banks, cooperative credit institutions, urban cooperative banks and regional rural banks. The government package neither included farm labourers' loans, nor loans from *arthiyas* and private moneylenders which amounted to close to three-fourth of the total amount.

Any relief from loan is a 'salvation from indebtedness', to quote Haque, but to benefit only a section of those indebted and leave the vast majority out, and to not even consider commercial loans by farmers because they are not able to earn enough, is more eyewash than real help. The government once again was found wanting. Though the farmer unions try to chase bank officials away, the *kurki* of lands continues and the suicide toll continues to rise.[201] There has been some talk but the government has not moved to cut the electricity subsidy to big farmers or bring them into the tax slabs. There is no easy relief for Panjab's farmers and labourers.

In July 2018, Imran Khan won the elections in Pakistan. Imran Khan and Navjot Singh Sidhu go a long way back as fellow cricketers playing for their countries, and Sidhu was therefore invited for the oath-taking ceremony. On the occasion, Pakistan army chief Qamar

Javed Bajwa proposed a corridor from Dera Baba Nanak to Kartarpur Sahib. Sidhu, overjoyed, or as Panjabis are wont to do, gave Bajwa a big hug.

The response to that hug by Indian media demonstrated the distance of mainstream Indian politics from Panjabi nuances and gestures. The BJP called Sidhu a traitor, national television show hosts raved and ranted, foreign policy experts expressed deep concerns and even the Akalis opportunistically blasted Sidhu. The cynical propaganda against the corridor showed how far the national narrative is from both east and west Panjab whose people share language, culture and deep bonds.

In line with the promise, the ground-breaking ceremonies on both sides of the border took place in November 2018. The countries intend to start the corridor by the 550th birth anniversary of Guru Nanak in November 2019.

If this project succeeds, it may lead to access to other 194 gurdwaras in Pakistan and to Hindu temples. It may lead to better trade and cultural ties between the two Panjabs and nations. Most of all, it could lead to demilitarisation of two poverty-stricken nations and better spending on education, healthcare and employment. Certainly, those are what the people of both the nations seek from their governments.

In September 2018, Students For Society (SFS) made history in Panjab University when its candidate Kanu Priya won the student elections. This is significant because just the previous year, protesting university students had a skirmish with police over the issue of up to 1,600 per cent fee hike for some courses. Over sixty students, all belonging to the SFS, were arrested, even beaten up in the lockup, and released after a few days. However, the protest resulted in the university senate rolling back the exorbitant hike and recommending only a 10 per cent hike.

Upon her win, in an interview, Kanu Priya remarked, 'Students here have decided that the RSS-BJP can rule other universities, but not the Panjab University.' There was a special thrill watching Kanu Priya and other students rent the night with slogans like 'Patriarchy Down Down'.

True to form, in December 2018, after a forty-eight-day protest by Kanu Priya and students, the university senate agreed to 24/7 free entry for girls in their hostels. The implications are huge: security is the lookout of the administration, not a basis to imprison students (citizens). At the same time the decision also shows that male students can be trusted, they should not be stereotyped as abrasive and out to harm women students. It could be the beginning of re-drawing male-female equations on campus, at least.

In March 2018, Captain Amarinder announced in the Panjab Assembly that after thirty-four years student elections would be allowed in colleges and universities.[202] Over a year later, nothing has transpired on the ground.

In the past few years, the Panjab government had recruited a total of 8,886 teachers on contract under the centrally-sponsored Sarva Shiksha Abhiyan (SSA) and Rashtriya Madhyamik Shiksha Abhiyan (RMSA). In its poll manifesto, the Congress had promised to regularise the services of contractual school teachers and remove pay-related discrepancies.

In early October 2018, the cabinet decided to regularise the teachers' services on a fixed monthly sum of Rs 15,300 per month, which was a drastic cut from the Rs 42,300 or more that they were earning as contract teachers. The teachers rejected the proposal and started a protest under the banner of Sanjha Adhyapak Morcha (SAM), a group formed by twenty-six teacher unions, in Patiala.

Another 5,178 teachers recruited under the Pendu Sahyogi Teacher Scheme in November 2014 joined the protesting teachers because their jobs were to be regularised last year on completion of three years, but nothing had been done so far.

With the teacher unions rejecting the regularisation terms, the department gave the option to teachers to opt for regularisation on government terms—reduced salary—or continue on contract with current salaries. The real reason why the government was pushing for salary cuts was that the Centre had cut down its financial support under the newly integrated Samagra Shiksha Abhiyan, which had replaced the SSA and RMSA.[203]

Considering that it was the Centre backing out, the teacher union strike against the state government was against the wrong government. As always, the government formed a committee to look into the matter, and it remains pending. On Teachers' Day 2018, around 6,000 college teachers also went on strike, demanding implementation of recommendations of the UGC with regard to the Seventh Central Pay Commission report.[204]

Overall, it is sad that the frontline workers of the education system feel dissatisfied and that vacancies of teachers in schools and colleges continue to grow. We can easily infer why the levels of government education in Panjab remain so poor. What choice do students have but to opt for private schools and colleges? They then exploit the students over fees, textbooks, uniform and so on. What is Panjab giving its next generation if it does not give them a decent education?

In early November 2018, army chief, General Bipin Rawat suddenly came up with a warning on Panjab. In a seminar on internal security, he said, 'We have to be very careful. Let us not think that the Panjab (problem) is over. We cannot close our eyes to what is happening in Panjab. And if we do not take early action now, it will be too late.'[205] A few days later, a grenade was lobbed at the Sant Nirankari Satsang Bhawan near village Adliwal, Amritsar. Three people died and twenty were injured. The Jaish-e-Mohammad, whose six militants had been allegedly spotted in Panjab recently, was believed to be responsible.[206] The Panjab Police arrested Avtar Singh and Bikramjit Singh who were supposedly helped by Harmeet Singh Happy, also known as 'PhD', and suspected to be the Pakistan-based KLF chief.

In January 2019, union minister of state for home, Hansraj Ahir said as per available information, the grenade attack has shown the involvement of the Khalistan Liberation Force (KLF) and the International Sikh Youth Federation (ISYF). Replying to a written question, he said, 'A total of eighteen Khalistani terror modules have been neutralised in Panjab during the last two years, wherein a total of ninety-five accused persons have been arrested.'[207]

Among those arrested was a British-Sikh activist Jagtar Singh Johal. He was arrested in November 2017 when he was visiting India for his wedding. Johal runs an outfit called 'Never Forget 1984'. He was allegedly involved in the murders of Brigadier (retd.) Jagdish Gagneja, RSS leader Ravinder Gosain and Pastor Sultan Masih, and he is said to have funded and arranged weapons for the banned militant outfit Khalistan Liberation Force.[208]

Among those arrested were also three men from Nawanshaha who got life sentences from a local court for stocking Khalistan propaganda material and for 'waging war against the country', in February 2019.[209] This is bizarre because such material is freely available on the internet and anyone can access it. This case and Johal's case show how, by not solving Operation Blue Star, the anti-Sikh pogrom and the many atrocities of the police during the militancy period, India keeps providing reasons for the diaspora and the local Sikhs to remain agitated. While India blames the diaspora for anti-India activities, the nation also needs to look inward and reconcile the differences between the various narratives of the Sikhs and proactively provide justice to the many who seek it. Until Panjab is treated as a post-conflict region, the state and its people will remain trapped in *84 da geda* (the circle of 1984).

Like in 2014, there was still not much of a Modi wave in Panjab in the 2019 Lok Sabha elections. I had two favourites from Panjab: Dr Dharamvira Gandhi from Patiala and Bibi Paramjeet Kaur Khalra, widow of Jaswant Singh Khalra, from Khadoor Sahib. Both of them were put up by a motley conglomeration of small political parties largely headed by another AAP breakaway leader Sukhpal Khaira. I supported my favourites because Dr Gandhi had worked really hard, using funds at his disposal to build schools, toilets, auditoriums and so on. Bibi Khalra's win would have been a win for human rights, and given the situation in Kashmir, Bastar, Manipur, Mizoram and other conflict and post-conflict regions, there was a real possibility of addressing the state's human rights violations in the parliament. Sadly, both lost. The reasons Dr Gandhi and Bibi Khalra lost was, as my friend Devinder Singh Sekhon said, 'People vote for MPs who will get their work done. They do not vote on ethics, but on pragmatics.' It is both Panjab's and India's loss.

The fact that the Akalis were down, but not out of the game, was proved by the fact that the only two seats they won were those contested by Sukhbir Badal and his wife Harsimrat Kaur, who won from Ferozepur and Bathinda respectively. In spite of the absent governance of Panjab, the Congress won eight seats, second only to Kerala where it won nineteen seats. Through the election campaign and results, it was sad to see Panjab's voters so starved of choices because there was no real opposition—a viable third political party—in the state.

With the BJP's massive win in 2019, the elections showed how strong the Hindutva wave had become in the nation. In spite of demonetisation that had rendered millions jobless, the flawed implementation of the Goods and Service Tax (GST) that pained small and big businesses, agrarian and industrial crises, the BJP's polarisation of society over religious issues, creating a kind of fear among Dalits and minorities, and aggressive nationalism by making noises against Pakistan, won them five more years. More than Modi's win, what was on display was a lack of opposition in the nation. BJP did to India what the Congress had done to Panjab—decimate the opposition.

India, turning towards Hindutva, coming closer to being a Hindu *rashtra*, becoming a dominant centre-run nation, is not good news for any minority, especially for Panjab which has always remained an outlier. I was reminded of the question a friend, a senior journalist, had asked before Modi's first term: if India were to democratically tilt towards Hindutva, what answer would India give the Sikhs who fought against Khalistan?

Over the past few years, Captain Amarinder has run the state from his residence, as did Parkash Singh Badal in his second term, appointing civil servants and police chiefs of his choice, thus signalling a breakdown in protocol and the return of feudal ways of running the state. Over the past few years, Captain Amarinder has also cultivated a friendship with a supposed defence expert from Pakistan. She openly stays with him in Chandigarh and attends official functions, even as he thunders against Pakistan in the media.

Though from the Congress, Captain Amarinder also has been in step with the nationalist Modi government. He was one of the first to praise the flawed GST regime. Harking back to his army career, he even praised the usage of a local as a human shield in Kashmir in May 2017.[210] To keep his new vote bank—the urban Hindu in Panjab— he participates in symbolic poojas and thunders against the diaspora, whether Canadian or British.

In fact, I believe his taking the oath on the *gutka* and not fulfilling the promises has blown away the final frontier of how politicians can make promises to people. It is an abuse of faith and that too is another kind of sacrilege. Perhaps the one event that the whole nation marks as the beginning of the struggle for India's freedom was the 1919 Jallianwala Bagh massacre by General Dyer. This year marked the Jallianwala Bagh centenary. The PM paid homage, the Panjab CM and the nation's vice president visited the site with many other ministers. However, a huge police deployment prevented thousands of farmers and labour from reaching Amritsar to pay their respects. In 1919, this was the message of the British to Indians. In 2012 and 2016, when the Badals stole Banda Bahdur from people, they gave out the same message. In 2019, this blockade on ordinary Panjabis was the message of the current government—a usurpation of people's narratives.

In the run-up to the Panjab elections, Captain Amarinder had declared that this was his last term. I wonder what legacy he is leaving for Panjab. How is this a reclamation of Panjab's honour that the Congress promised?

My wound called Panjab had propelled me on my journeys through its fault lines. My need to make liminal my subliminal blood connection with Panjab had kept me going. Maybe because I surrounded myself with Panjab, not only through journeys but also through media, readings and listening, I began to feel co-dependent with Panjab. My journeys through Panjab evoked a plethora of emotions in me: bewilderment at its events, sadness at its misery, anger at multiple instances of injustice, solidarity with its resistances, humility at its graciousness, happiness when it cheered, at peace with myself driving through its link roads at sunset knowing that an unknown warm meal and bed awaited, and helplessness that Panjab's many issues continued to seek closure.

Yet, nothing had quite prepared me for feeling exasperated the way I felt in the summer of 2019, when Panjab was burning at 45 degrees celsius. One afternoon I called up Bhola. Despite three calls, he did not answer. Concerned, the next day, I called up Bhabi, his wife. She said, 'Oh! There is a twist in Bhola's *jutti* (open shoe). His face has turned towards the skies. Eyes are peeled in anticipation.'

I asked her to explain. She said, '*Kabootarbaazi*—he is betting on pigeons.'

I laughed. In my mind's eye, I could easily see Bhola jumping helter-skelter on the hot roof in the blazing, relentless sun. I realised when news from Panjab comes, most of us living outside Panjab also jump helter-skelter and we have our emotions in a twist. Yet, the people in Panjab continue to function in their own unorthodox ways.

Having thought through Panjab by writing these pages, I cannot still say I know everything about Panjab, especially the silent world of its women. However, I definitely learnt how to cut through the smoke and mirrors and the many distractions that are created to distract attention from Panjab's core issues. Instead of the wound, or black hole, or a phantom Panjab, after three years on the ground, I sensed an empathy growing in my heart. Not only for Panjab—because of Panjab—but also for people's issues anywhere in the world.

There is a clear gap between the reality of Panjab and its representation, but the answers too are at hand if Panjab and the

Centre want to pay attention to them. Panjab's call is for rights on its river waters, greater federalism for all states, local political groups, freedom to trade with whoever wants its produce, the need to re-build institutions, a desire for truth and reconciliation of narratives, and for the state to focus back on the basics: health, education and infrastructure. I see no reason why these can't be closed, provided we have a political party focussed on untying Panjab's multiple knots.

Politically, Panjab realises neither the Akalis, nor the Congress have a plan that addresses its short- and long-term needs. Its people—who have seen one generation lost to militancy, the next to drugs, and the present to exodus—standing on corroded soil depleted of water, are looking skywards for new directions, new voices and new leadership. An indigenous leadership acceptable to all levels of Panjabi society. Someone Panjab can trust to push its issues towards closure. In the past two years, some groups have formed, but also withered without being able to make an impact.

However, I believe that whoever we are, wherever we are, we all live in stories and not in stereotypes. To construct a narrative, Panjab would need a push to bring in a structure where Panjabis not only in Panjab, but also those living in other parts of India, across the border with Pakistan, and in the diverse diaspora, could participate together in re-building Panjab. At the same time, to lift itself from the depression that gnaws at it and erodes it, Panjab needs to rise against patriarchy, feudalism and ritualistic symbolism.

Throughout its long history, Panjab has always been more than its geography and its people. It has symbolised an idea of resistance and rebellion. In the past, in spite of grievous wounds, Panjab has always risen and proved its critics wrong. I believe that someday this Panjab too will rise to its challenges—in its own eclectic way.

As for me, in a world changing rapidly, my journeys through the land of Gurus and Pirs has given me the framework to understand and align with our essential struggle for justice and equality. Not only in Panjab, but also in the big, wide world.

# Post-Script: *Ailaan* — Announcement

When the book went to print in end 2019, I was hopeful one day Panjab would rise. Yet, no one, least of all me, could have imagined that Panjab would rise so quickly and truly in unforeseen ways.

Within weeks of the earlier edition being released, the BJP government passed the Citizenship Amendment Act (CAA). The law was supposed to provide citizenship to non-Muslim immigrants from Afghanistan, Bangladesh and Pakistan, but the right-wing government's moves need to be inferred from how they would apply on the ground. Along with the National Registry of Citizens (NRC),[x] a demand from the days of the Assam Accord to solve the insurgency movement in Assam in the 1980s, the CAA would have potentially thrown up to 20 crore Muslims beyond the pale of citizenship.

At the same time as the passing of the CAA, India's decadal census was due and the government announced the National Population Register. Citizens of the nation, especially the Muslim community which realised it was being targeted, started protesting in Delhi at Shaheen Bagh and subsequently at around 300 places across the country in big and small cities.[211] The protests at Shaheen Bagh

---

x The National Register of Citizens (NRC) is a register of all Indian citizens whose creation is mandated by the 2003 amendment of the Citizenship Act, 1955. Its purpose is to document all the legal citizens of India so that the illegal immigrants can be identified and deported.

were led by older women but the participation was from students, the middle class and workers who joined in the continuous sit-ins at the protest sites. Due to Partition of India in 1947, the exodus of Muslims from India to Pakistan, Panjab has very few Muslims, but the people of the state expressed their solidarity by holding protests. In fact, farmer unions from Panjab reached Shaheen Bagh and organised langar at that site.

The anti-CAA-NRC-NPR protests continued until March 2020 when the government accepted the seriousness of the coronavirus pandemic which it had been denying for a few weeks by then. The government's early response was knee-jerk: a sudden national lockdown with a mere four-hour notice.

Under the cover of the pandemic, the government announced major changes to the economy, all of them suiting the private sector. The limits on foreign investments in power, energy, coal, defence and space sectors[212] were increased to 74 per cent.[213] The government's line was that this was towards making India self-reliant, *atmanirbhar*. Yet, those who can see through the motives know this is a sell-out. The government also began privatising one of the nations' greatest assets— the Railways.[214] By June 2020, the government issued ordinances on changes to laws in the agrarian sector. By September 2020, the government called a special session of Parliament and bulldozed three farm laws through the Rajya Sabha through a hasty voice vote even as the Opposition was protesting them.

When we look at any law, there is always a letter of the law and a spirit of the law, and then there is the timing of the law. There was a sense that the timing of these laws was suspicious and that the government expected to curb any resistance the way it had curbed the anti-CAA protests. The exaggeration in the names of the anti-farmer Farm Laws betrayed their spirit which truly should have been to benefit the farmers and the labourers—those engaged in agriculture, who amount to over 50 per cent of India's population.

Let us look at the laws in brief and how they were perceived:

- The Farmers Produce Trade and Commerce (Promotion and Facilitation) Act, 2020 permits intra-state and inter-state trade of farmers' produce beyond the physical premises of Agricultural Produce Market Committee (APMC) market yards (mandis)—basically a parallel system of private mandis. While traditional mandis in Panjab and Haryana, though the biggest in the world, have many structural issues, the rest of India does not have an elaborate mandi structure. Regulated mandis levy state government taxes needed to build villages roads and other infrastructure. The new law allowed private unregulated mandis which would not benefit state governments. There would be no limit on how low the price of farm produce could drop when private players entered into buying arrangements with farmers. The fear was that private players would prey on farmers with their superior bargaining power. In 2005, Bihar abolished APMCs and since then the farmers of Bihar had suffered greatly.[215]

- The Farmers (Empowerment and Protection) Agreement of Price Assurance and Farm Services Act, 2020 created a national framework for contract farming through an agreement between a farmer and a buyer before the production or rearing of any farm produce. More than 82 per cent of Indian famers are small and marginal.[216] They are trapped in a cycle of debt and agriculture as a profession remains largely unviable. Yet, as far as self-sustenance is concerned, farming is one of their greatest support systems. The argument of many experts is that there is a need for co-operative farming but not contract farming that benefits the corporates. The new law also barred recourse by farmers to the courts. In cases of conflict, the law vested authority with the local sub-divisional magistrate. This would be highly skewed in favour of private entities as the individual farmers would not have the resources to stand against mighty corporations. This model of corporate farming has already failed in Panjab[217] and Gujarat[218] where companies made contracts with potato growers.

- The Essential Commodities (Amendment) Act, 2020 delisted cereals, pulses, potatoes, onion, edible oilseeds, and oils as essential, allowing private players to stockpile as much quantity as they could with no limits. The government could regulate these commodities only in extraordinary circumstances such as war, famine, natural calamities, or a steep price rise—a 100 per cent increase in retail price (in the case of horticultural produce) and a 50 per cent increase in retail price (in the case of non-perishable agricultural food items). When control of supplies is unregulated and in the hands of private players, the fear is that they will cause artificial shortages and increase prices by say 20-25 per cent each time and stay below the radar of regulation. In the end the consumer would be hit. The argument of 'free market' does not apply because there were not too many players who would work as check and balance. The feeling was that there would largely be only one player who would stockpile and another who would sell thus creating a monopoly situation which would harm both farmer and consumer.

Being a predominantly agrarian state, the laws were seen as having the potential to devastate Panjab. Additionally, given that around 67 per cent of India is dependent on the public distribution system for its food needs, the Food Corporation of India was under a Rs 2.65 lakh crore debt, the government's move to cripple the mandi system, begged the question: Where and how would the government procure food for the public distribution system? If these laws were implemented, what would happen to the food security of the nation? As far as freeing the farmer to sell where they wanted, that option had already been available to farmers even before these new laws.

The irony was also that the laws were constitutionally invalid. As per our Constitution, agriculture is a subject of the State List. The central government has no right to make a national law on agriculture. The government has used Article 33 of the Concurrent List 'Trade and Commerce ...' to pass these laws. But this Article applied to traders, not farmers. Here it was important to note that the farmer was always a producer of food, not a trader of food. While the farmer sells food, he does not exactly trade in food. This is a fine legal point but very essential to the understanding of the laws.

As discussed in the chapter *Berukhi* and many later chapters, one major reason why Panjab, the cradle of the Green Revolution, is in crisis is because for the last half century, the Indian state has neglected agriculture. When I travelled Panjab, union leaders such as Sukhdev Singh Kokhri Kalan talked to me in detail about the eighth round of multilateral trade negotiations conducted within the framework of the General Agreement on Tariffs and Trade (GATT), between 1986 to 1993 at Uruguay. The broad mandate of the talks was to extend GATT trade rules to areas considered difficult to liberalize—textiles and agriculture. This meeting led to the creation of the World Trade Organization (WTO) whose mandate India had followed since the 1990s that had led to the decimation of our health and education sector, as discussed in earlier chapters.

Earlier governments had been reluctant to push the WTO policies in agriculture but also remained largely apathetic to the agrarian crises building up all over the country since the Green Revolution in Panjab. A case in point is the Swaminathan Commission, instituted by the Congress but its recommendations never implemented since it was tabled in 2007, though the Congress government was in power for another seven years. Later, during the 2014 general elections, the Bharatiya Janata Party (BJP) promised the implementation of the Commission's Terms of Reference through their manifesto but reneged on them after they formed the government. Now the central government had found its chance to move in the neo-liberal direction mandated by the WTO. The government's alleged corporate sponsors were willing allies. Gautam Adani had already built storage capacity of 8 lakh tonnes of grain and is going ahead with more.[219] In 2006 itself Mukesh Ambani had signed a 'farm to fork'[220] deal with Panjab government which was later scrapped but in the past few years Reliance had established retail chains[221] all over the country. For these corporate houses, with a government willing to help them, the laws were just a matter of time to make the final move—snatch the agrarian sector from the farmers, turning self-respecting farmers into their workers.

They had not considered Panjab.

They had not considered Panjab's centuries-old history of standing up for the sub-continent. Earlier it was to those invading from the outside, but it could do so for those wanting to gain control internally as well. Panjab stood up to stop these designs of the corporates abetted by a populist dictatorial government.

The farmer unions of Panjab began mobilizing support from June 2020 when the ordinances were issued. After the September 2020 Parliament session in which the laws were passed, from early October 2020, Panjab came out onto the streets. For close to two months farmers blocked trains, opened up the toll plazas for free movement on the highways, gheraoed the petrol pumps, malls and warehouses owned by Ambani and Adani.[222] In late October, ten farmer union leaders from Panjab met leaders from All India Kisan Sangharsh Coordination Committee, a pan-Indian umbrella organisation comprising 250 farmers' organisations formed with the integration of 130 farmers' organisations after the death of six farmers in police firing in Mandsaur, Madhya Pradesh in June 2017.[223] As a coal crisis loomed large and thermal plants in Panjab began to run out of coal supplies, because farmers had blocked all trains, the railways minister Piyush Goel met union leaders on 13 November 2020. He tried to broker a deal: lift the blockade on passenger trains so that he could allow goods trains. The leaders refused. That is when the Samyukt Kisan Morcha (SKM)—a collection of thirty-one unions from Panjab—made the *ailaan* (announcement): Chalo Delhi.

November 26, Constitution Day, was chosen as the day the famers from Panjab would proceed to Delhi. On that day, thousands of tractors moved from interior Panjab to the inter-state borders at Shambu, Kanauri and Mandi Dabwali. The Haryana police had erected barricades in anticipation and were prepared with water cannons and tear gas. The restive youth from Panjab, with on ground support from Haryana, broke through the barricades, braved water cannons and tear gas shells, moved huge shipping containers, filled trenches in the roads, and proceeded to Delhi nevertheless. We have discussed the river water issues in the chapter *Paani* and are aware of the deep political divide between Haryana and Panjab. Fifty years of animosity between the states was bridged by this joint action by the farmers of Haryana and Panjab.

This was Panjab's *ailaan* to the nation. It was possible with Haryana's support. A fault line was bridged.

When the government refused to allow protesting farmers to assemble at Delhi's Ramlila crowds, instead asking them to move to the walled Burari grounds, the farmers under the banner of SKM took a smart call—one that would greatly benefit them in coming days, in more ways than one. They decided to set up their morcha at the Singhu on National Highway 44, more popular as the Badshahi Sadak, or the Grand Trunk Road, at one time the life line between north and east India. The setting up of the morcha harked back to the Sikh confederacy of the eighteenth century, when Sikh armies advanced en masse on their enemies. Now the ethos of the sword had changed to one of non-violence, and the tactics of warfare to a blockade of one of India's busiest highways. The morcha between Singhu and Badh Khalsa was permanent with more farmers joining it up to Rai or even Murthal.

Badh Khalsa evoked a deep cultural memory for the Sikhs who dominated the protests. When the Mughal emperor Aurangzeb ordered that Guru Tegh Bahadur be beheaded, he also decreed that no one was to touch the body or the severed head. But Bhai Jaita made away with the head, and left for Anandpur Sahib in Punjab, where the guru then resided. With the Mughal army in pursuit, Bhai Jaita stopped to rest at Badh Khalsa. Here, Bhai Kushal Singh Dahiya, a Hindu Jat, offered his head in place of the Guru's to fool the pursuers, enabling Bhai Jaita to smuggle the Guru's head away.

Another set of farmers, primarily owing allegiance to the Bhartiya Kisan Union Ekta Ugrahan, decided to camp on Tikri border. The firm stance by farmers and their location at Delhi's borders brought about more support—farmers from Haryana in the south and Uttar Pradesh in the east joined the protesting cadres of peasants from Punjab. Three new *morchas* began at Ghazipur, Palwal, and one about a hundred kilometers away at Shajahanpur on the Rajasthan-Haryana border.

One of the great gaps in what happened in Panjab in the 1980s was that media never presented Panjab's point of view to the world. This time, like during the incidents of sacrilege, the farmers were equipped with their own media. In this digital age they even had their own Twitter cells, social media pages, internet television channels, a newsletter (*Trolley Times*) and a women's newsletter (*Karti Dharti*). The farmers remained focussed on building their own narrative. This was 'a war of attrition', said Harjeshwar Pal, a history professor who studies social movements, when I spoke to him. A fierce counterattack was launched by pro-government forces assisted by pliant media to blunt, exhaust, coerce and divide the farmers. The farmers were variously termed 'Khalistani', 'rich farmers', 'foreign hand', 'urban naxals', 'tukde-tukde gang' and so on. The government tried meetings with alternative farmer unions, endorsement by some farmer leaders, and other tactics to blunt the protests. Pro-government media fanned the government's attempts to tarnish the image of the protesters, freely repeating claims suggesting that the farmers were not united and that they were smaller groups serving their own political or economic interests. The media and the government were largely unsuccessful. No label stuck.

Posters emerged in response to the accusation of Sikhs being Khalistan supporters. 'When we save Hindus, we are angels; when we die to save the nation, we are martyrs; when we fight for our rights, we are Khalistani,' said one.

At the Tikri protest site, a youth Sikh farmer we met, said, 'Khalistan in Hindu Rashtra? Ask them first what they have made of the nation.' He continued, 'In Partition, we lost Nankana Sahib and Kartarpur Sahib. If Khalistan becomes a reality, we will lose Patna Sahib and Huzoor Sahib as well. What would we be left with? Look around, everybody is recognising the Sikhs, langars are being served, jaikaras are being shouted. What can be more Sikh than this? The Gurus belonged to the whole world. We are fighting for our dignity as farmers.'

Contrary to what we discussed in chapter *Jaat*, Punjab's peasantry has rarely seen such unity between landowning Jutts and Dalit labourers; despite patriarchal divisions between men and women at home, women in large numbers joined the protests. We met Harvinder Bindu in Chapter *Lashaan*. She is now general secretary BKU (Ekta Ugrahan), a farmers' union. She said, 'Now we have made our place, *Veere* (brother). Now we have shown that we women exist.' Just as in the protests in 2019 and 2020 against the CAA, here too, women had prominent roles. They were visible on stages, in audiences, at tents, at langars—shoulder to shoulder with men. The women farmers saw these protests as the second battle of freedom, after 1947. They were aware of patriarchy and while their struggle against it continued, but for the moment, their attention was on the repeal of laws. It was amazing how the veil I had experienced in Chapter *Janamdin*, the silence of women, had now lifted and the women's voice was loud and clear especially on both Women Farmer's Day in January and Women's Day in March.

More fault lines were bridging. Language and iconography came together, for instance, in the immense output of protest songs—about 400 songs in the first three months. The heart of these protests was the tradition of langar. Farmers had come with two trollies on their tractors—one with people, another with supplies. When middle class India woke up to the reality of protests, some asked how they could help. The farmers said by showing your solidarity. It was an inversion of a well-established route the middle-class society had adopted for decades: providing monetary help. The farmers did not need money, they needed hearts, they wanted the whole society to rise with them. Of course, as the months of the protests increased, the farmers had needs—extreme winter called for better bedding, winter rains called for better cover, advancing summers needed them to put up wood and straw cottages, some farmers needed medical assistance which came from many doctors volunteering, setting up camps, even makeshift hospitals, yet unlike protesters in the past they did not ask for handouts from anyone. After all, these farmers had fed the nation since the heydays of the Green Revolution.

The strength of the protests was that they were bottom up. Looking at the eyes of all those who had joined the protests, looking at their resolve, it was clear they weren't there because of their leaders. They were there because land is Panjab's greatest asset. The protests were driven by the danger of loss of land—big or small; the smaller the land, the greater the danger. The question they asked was: if we lose the land, how will we answer our children? Land plays a big role in the lives of farmers. Land determines their social status in the village, their bargaining power at the political level, their source of income and survival, and cultural reality. For farmers, land is their lifeline and not a commodity like it is for urban folks, who buy and sell flats and plots. It is part of their kinship relations, their organic social life. While the landless do not own land, the new laws were an attack on their stomachs, their livelihood. That is why, they too were part of the protests. While the small traders and arthiyas did not own land or work on land, their existence too was dependent on the farmers whom big corporations could possibly evict. That is why they treated the protests as a battle of existence—*hond di ladai*. That is why, more than the leaders, it was the single mindedness of the protesters that kept the protests going despite attempts to destabilise them.

The mostly Sikh cadre associated with Left-oriented unions saw the protests as a common cause against injustice. The two strands—Sikh and Left—were wires that constantly sparked in competition, creating electricity, running the motor of resistance against the farm laws. This was a fault line, but the friction created energy. While there were Shaheed Bhagat Singh libraries at the protest sites, there was also a Nanak Hut library. There was much debate and discussion about the colours and signs of the flags and badges of the various unions, but everyone was clear, they had a common opponent—the government. The remarkable feature of the protest was the unified message on the lips of every protester: repeal the anti-farmer farm laws, implement Minimum Support Price, repeal Commission on Air Quality Management in NCR and the adjoining Ordinance, and abolish the Electricity Ordinance.

After a few days of the protests starting, when the government opened talks with farmers, contrary to what the government was propagating—that farmers did not understand the benefits of the new laws—the farmer leaders had arguments ready for each and every clause. The government was cornered. In early December, the government announced it was ready to make significant concessions to the farmers in the form of amendments to the farm laws. It was a clear admission that the farmers were right. The farmers remained adamant on their demand for a repeal. On 12 January 2021, the Supreme Court stayed the laws and recommended a committee of four people to examine the laws, all of whom had already publicly spoken in favour of the provisions. Everyone could see the farce that the committee would likely be. Finally, mid-January, the government offered to delay the implementation of the laws by one-and-a-half years. The farmers refused this offer as well. Their question was: what would change by delaying the implementation of the laws?

For 26 January 2021, the Samyukt Kisan Morcha had given a call for a Tractor Parade in Delhi[224] on the Outer Ring Road.[225] This created anxiety in the nation about the farmers intending to disrupt the government's parade on Rajpath—a matter of India's pride and a challenge to the nation. Yet, a perusal of the map of Delhi will confirm that at no point is the Rajpath—the main venue of the parade—closer than 5 kilometers from the Outer Ring Road. In most cases, it is 15 to 25 kilometers away. The intention of the Tractor Parade was not to disrupt the main parade but to assert the agrarian dimension of the society. The pitch was that if the government could celebrate Republic Day with a parade of armaments, provided the government does not repeal the laws, the farmers have a right to celebrate the day in their capital with their tractors and agrarian tableaux. After all, what the jawan does on the border, the kisan does in the field—secure the nation! The protests had shown that the Lal Bahadur Shastri phrase 'Jai Jawan, Jai Kisan' was not a binary but came from the same source—agrarian, rural India. It was that section of society, the rural and agrarian, which was pitted against the government. SKM leaders raised a lot of rhetoric in the run up to the Tractor Parade. For Panjab, this rhetoric is literal. It evokes their history of many centuries of Panjab's battle with Delhi. It reminded the people of the long history of how Panjab had repeatedly laid siege to Delhi and even succeeded in 1783 when Baba Baghel Singh had conquered the Red Fort. Panjab, Haryana, western Uttar Pradesh, the Terai and Uttarakhand responded enthusiastically to the call. While earlier there were around two lakh farmers at the protest sites, around Republic Day the number grow three to four-fold—six to eight lakh farmers joined the protests.

In the rhetoric that built up before 26 January, the government appealed in the Supreme Court to stop the Tractor Parade, which the Supreme Court refused to oblige.[226] Still, three days before the intended Tractor Parade, the SKM did a volte face. Not expecting such a huge response, the SKM agreed to conduct the Tractor Parade on government instructed routes outside Delhi instead of entering Delhi through the Outer Ring Road. The decision did not go down well with protesters.

Now that the protests and the events of that fateful day are a part of history, may I suggest: pull out the road map of Delhi. Look for the Red Fort. Look at the farmer protest sites at Singhu and Ghazipur. You would notice the Red Fort is not on the direct route from any of the sites. The Outer Ring Road is behind Red Fort. From Ghaziabad, a driver needs to take two ninety-degree turns, one left, one right at ITO (Income Tax Office) to reach Red Fort. While coming from Singhu, the national highway touches Outer Ring Road at Mukarba Chowk. A day before the parade, the Kisan Mazdoor Sangharsh Committee (KMSC),[227] not a part of the SKM, declared that they would still march on the Outer Ring Road. A dissenting section in the protests, the panthic oriented youth, also raised their voice a night before the parade from the Singhu stage.[228] The SKM was absent.

The next day, the KMSC's march on the Outer Ring Road seemed too easy. The police stopped them at Mukarba Chowk but it was perfunctory.[229] The tractors broke through the barricades on Outer Ring Road and they proceeded towards Gurdwara Majnu ka Tila. However, the Karnal Road, the older route from Mukarba Chowk, leading onto Red Fort via a turn at Azadpur Mandi was also opened. A group of tractors passed through that. Coming from Ghazipur, police barricaded the Yamuna Bridge next to Akshardam. Tractors broke through the barricades.[230] The question that arises is: how did farmers who had never seen Delhi—I still get lost on its roads in spite of my familiarity—driving their big vehicles on smooth city roads, with no traffic, know exactly how to reach the Red Fort when no direct road goes there?

The farmers coming from Ghazipur and Singhu were enclosed near ITO after a left or right turn depending upon where one was coming from.[231] As the crowd increased at ITO, farmers were getting restive, the police was blocking them, in the push and pull some farmers or unruly elements who had infiltrated the protests destroyed buses and police vehicles. A young farmer on a tractor who was moving towards the Red Fort died when the tractor turned turtle, but the claim was he was actually shot by the police. An act they denied but was allegedly borne out through post-mortem reports.[232] The police sustained injuries and they caned the protesters.[233] The protesters were let out towards the only opening at the right side, towards the Red Fort. On a day when given the national parade, the security at Red Fort should have been tight, the area had very little police and was not barricaded. When the farmers from Singhu and Ghazipur, coming from Karnal Road and ITO, reached the Red Fort, some farmers from Singhu and Ghazipur put up flags of their unions including the Sikh flag, the Nishan Sahib. They did not touch the tricolour which flew above all the other flags. Yet, national media that was already present there flashed the news that the Khalistan flag had been placed on the Red Fort.[234]

This was a hit engineered to exploit Panjab's Sikh versus Left fault line. For a while, it seemed the ploy had worked. The national sentiment that was warming up to the farmers' protest changed to looking at the protests as a move by Khalistan supporters. It took a while for sense to prevail: that the Red Fort was no longer a seat of power; in fact, it has been leased out to a private corporation;[235] that the Sikh flag was not the Khalistan flag; in fact, there was no standard Khalistan flag; and overall, this proved to be an elaborate distraction from the political economy issue of farm laws and minimum support price.

Meanwhile, the SKM leadership panicked. They issued statements against the youth who had reached the Red Fort. They disowned the youth and the KMSC. This was perhaps a mistake. It revealed the leadership vacuum in the SKM and angered the youth who were the energy of the protests. News of more than 150 arrests came in. These were not arrests from Red Fort but mostly innocents rounded up. The SKM again did not demonstrate any leadership in how to free those who had been taken into custody. Though many protesters who had come specifically for the Tractor Parade were leaving, there was an all-pervasive gloom over the protest sites being vacated. Suddenly, the two-month long protests, at least at Singhu and Ghazipur seemed shaky.

As the chasm increased, the government stepped in aggressively. Police began barricading the sites with concrete slabs and concertina wire and nails on the ground. The police presence increased. Internet, water, and electricity was cut off at protests sites. The barricades reminded me of West Berlin in the former East Germany. During the Cold War, West Berlin was surrounded by a 131 km long spiked wall, electric fenced and barricaded. Since the western world was so keen on keeping West Berlin going, they pumped in resources by air. East Germany around West Berlin was under communist rule—a deeply repressive one. At the protests, the barricades sought to keep farmers contained but were open towards Panjab and Haryana and parts of western Uttar Pradesh. The people around whom barricades were set up were free but the rest of the nation was imprisoned by right-wing Hindutva.

On the night of 28 January, when a police team reached the Ghazipur protest site on Highway 24, in the presence of media, Rakesh Tikait, a prominent farmer leader from western UP and the son of Mahendra Singh Tikait, a legendary farmer leader from the 1980s climbed onto the stage. He had sensed the right-wing goondas advancing on the protest site to carry out an armed attack. He knew that the Ghazipur site had mostly Sikhs from Terai and Uttarakhand. He feared a repeat of the 1984 anti-Sikh pogrom. Tikait broke down[236] and called for 'water from his village', essentially a call for help and a call for action.[237]

The news quickly spread.

In the middle of the foggy night, thousands of young men started from their homes in Haryana and western Uttar Pradesh with 'water for Tikait'.

Another genocide was prevented and the farmers protest had executed a mid-race baton change. Tikait emerged as a leader with the turban on his head. In 2013, the BKU headed by Tikait had allowed itself to be appropriated by the RSS which led to riots between Jats and Muslims in Muzaffarnagar. Those riots had changed Uttar Pradesh politics and led to the BJP's win in the area and the nation in 2014. Tikait had in some sense, atoned for it. At the Muzaffarnagar Mahapanchayat the BKU took the 'Lota-Nun pledge'[238]—mixing salt in Ganga Jal, signifying that each oath taker's individual view was subsumed in the community's view and they could never be separated—to fight against the farm laws. This electrified the protests once again and hundreds of mahapanchayats were conducted in Haryana, Rajasthan, Uttarakhand, Uttar Pradesh, even in Panjab, and as far as Bihar, Odisha, Bengal, Karnataka, Maharashtra, and Gujarat and the commitment to the protests reaffirmed.

As the SKM recouped, those in custody were freed. While the pliant media stopped relaying the news of the protests, but subterranean, rural India was waking up. It was clear, this was once again a fight for land which has been Panjab's fight for many millennia. In Panjab, the panthic thinking remained stuck in grudges against the SKM. I wished the panthic leaders had raised other important issues like re-opening the Kartarpur Sahib corridor, opening border trade through Pakistan with Balkans and East Europe. After all, the government had said farmers were free to trade anywhere so why not go international?

The protests then moved out of Panjab to central India, which was a relief given what Panjab had experienced when it opposed Emergency and paid the price through the dark decade and half in 1980s–90s. If these protests were the battle for the soul of India, of its real backbone—agrarian India—and those who wanted to colonise it once again, it had to be fought in central India too and not just Panjab. Panjab's role was to give the *ailaan* and to serve as the bind to hold up the protests. Panjab did that.

Months passed and both sides waited for the other to blink. The government did not resume talks even after elections in Bengal, Assam, Tamil Nadu, Kerala, and Puducherry, for the first time since 2014, the farmers successfully blocked the right-wing propaganda machinery. Finally on 19 November 2021, which was Guru Nanak's 352nd birth anniversary, unilaterally, Prime Minister Modi announced the repeal of the three draconian farm laws. On the first day on the next Parliament session, the laws were formally repealed. On 11 December 2021, the farmer unions suspended the protest and returned home triumphant. The critical matter of guaranteed Minimum Support Price and some other issues like withdrawal of about 55,000 cases on farmers during the protest remained pending but the government assured the protesters that it would follow up on those. Panjab's *ailaan* has resonated through the land though the cost from all sections of society including non-farmers and geographies until date has been over 733 deaths.

Panjab's rise—the farmer protests—needs to be seen in the context of at least half a century of neglect of agrarian India by governments. This government had, by pushing the farm laws, harvested that anger. However, the longest peaceful, non-violent protests since Independence, which have ignited a subterranean India, are also a bright spot in the whole world that is now beginning to understand the consequences of neo-liberalism and pointing fingers at crony capitalism. As is the history of the land, Panjab once again is a beacon of hope not just for the Indian sub-continent, the Indian nation, but for the entire humanity. These protests by the small and poor against the mighty corporations, the international organisations, and the government was proof that Panjab resonates with resistance. The protests have already bridged many fault lines. I dare to believe these gains are here to stay and Panjab will continue to strive for *Sarbat da Bhala*.

Personally, I felt Panjab had turned a new leaf. I felt deeply satisfied that the Panjab of my childhood imagination, that I had been waiting for four decades to rise, rose in my lifetime. Earlier when it rose, it had not been able to build its narrative. This time, it had articulated itself.

This new political awareness, this sense of articulation, reflected in the upcoming assembly elections 2022. Voting at the edge of its political possibilities, to the surprise of many, Panjab overwhelmingly rejected the two traditional political parties—the Akali Dal and the Congress. All stalwart politicians lost. Once again, Panjab exhibited its innate resistance to power and hegemony. Aam Aadmi Party—the party in-waiting—won. It is now up to the new party to handle Panjab, solve Panjab's deep entwined issues, tide over its fault lines. It and everyone else would do well to remember it is impossible to imprison Panjab in a label—to conclude Panjab.

# Acknowledgements

The paperback edition of this book would not have been possible without the generosity and support of my editor Karthik Venkatesh who took the book to Penguin Random House India and Meru Gokhale, the publisher, for accepting the book. Thank you, Kanishka Gupta from Writer's Side, for helping with the contract to re-commission the book.

My intention to write the book was to bring Panjab to all of us. I hope I have succeeded in some measure. However, like all communities painted into a corner, Panjab is a lot about not accepting how anyone understands it. If there are any lapses, misrepresentations or factual errors, they are my responsibility.

Finally, I hear Baba call out: '*Likh ti?*' (Have you written it?)

'*Haanji,*' I say, '*likh ti*'. (Yes, I say, I have written it.)

# Bibliography

*History of the Sikhs*—J. D. Cunningham, Satvic Books, 1849, 1915

*Lions of the Panjab: Culture in the Making*—Richard G. Fox, University of California Press, Berkeley; Low Price Publications, 1990

*Emergency Retold*—Kuldip Nayar, Konark Publishers, 1977

*Sachi Sakhi*—Kapur Singh, Gurmat Pustak Bhandar, 1978

*Robber Noblemen: A study of the political system of the Sikh Jats*—Joyce Pettigrew, Ambika Publications, 1978

*Percussions of History: The Sikh Revolution in the Caravan of Revolutions*—Jagjit Singh, Nanakshahi Trust, 1981, 2006

*Religious Rebels of the Panjab: The Ad Dharm Challenge to Caste*—Mark Juergensmeyer, University of California Press, Berkeley, 1982; Navayana, 2009

*The Panjab Story*—Various Contributors, Roli Books, 1984

*Amritsar: Mrs Gandhi's Last Battle*—Mark Tully, Satish Jacob, Rupa, 1985

*Operation Blue Star: The True Story*—Lt Gen. K.S. Brar, UBSPD, 1993

*The Construction of Religious Boundaries: Culture, Identity, and Diversity in the Sikh Tradition*—Harjot Oberoi, University of Chicago Press, 1994

*The Sikhs of the Panjab: Unheard Voices of State and Guerilla Violence*—Joyce Pettigrew, University of Chicago Press, 1995

*Fighting for Faith and Nation: Dialogues with Sikh Militants*—Cynthia Keppley Mahmood, University of Pennsylvania Press, 1996

*Bullet for Bullet: My Life As a Police Officer*—Julio Ribeiro, Penguin Books India, 1998; Chinar Publications, 2017

*The Other Side of Silence: Voices from the Partition of India*—Urvashi Butalia, Viking, Penguin Books, 1998

*Operation Blue Star: Mighty Murderous Army Attack on the Golden Temple Complex*—Giani Kirpal Singh, translated by Anurag Singh, B. Chattar Singh Jiwan Singh, 1999

*Sikh History from Persian Sources*—Edited by J.S. Grewal and Irfan Habib, Tulika, 2001

*Dreams after Darkness: A Search of a Life Ordinary Under the Shadow of 1984*—Manraj Grewal, Rupa, 2004

*A History of the Sikhs, Volume 1 and 2*—Khushwant Singh, Oxford, 2004

*When a Tree Shook Delhi: The 1984 Carnage and its Aftermath*—Manoj Mitta, H.S. Phoolka, Lotus collection, Roli Books, 2007

*Origin and History of Jats and Other Allied Nomadic Tribes of India (900 BC—1947 AD)*—B.S. Nijjar, Atlantic, 2008

*Sikhism*—Hew McLeod, Cambridge University Press, 1997; Yoda Press, 2010

*Panjab Wich Communist Leher*—Bhagwan Singh Josh, Navyug, 2010

*Khalistan Struggle: A Non-Movement*—Jagtar Singh, Aakar, 2011

*Panjab Bloodied, Partitioned and Cleansed*—Ishtiaq Ahmed, Rupa, 2011

*Debt and Death in Rural India: The Panjab Story*—Aman Sidhu and Inderjit Singh Jaijee, Sage, 2011

*Those Who Did Not Die: Impact of the Agrarian Crises on Women in Panjab*—Ranjana Padhi, Sage, 2012

*Panjab: A History from Aurangzeb to Mountbatten*—Rajmohan Gandhi, Aleph Book Company, 2013

*Fields of Blood: Religion and the History of Violence*—Karen Armstrong, Penguin Random House, 2014

*Non-Congress Politics in Panjab (1947—2002)*—Amanpreet Singh Gill, Singh Brothers, 2015

*The Gallant Defender*—A.R. Darshi, Damdami-Taksal-Mehta, 2015

*Panjab Di Itihasic Gatha (1849—2000)*—Rajpal Singh, People's Forum, 2016

*Master Tara Singh in Indian History: Colonialism, Nationalism, and the Politics of Sikh Identity*—J.S. Grewal, Ocxford University Press, 2017

*Shadow Armies: Fringe Armies and Foot Soldiers of Hindutva*—Dhirendra K. Jha, Juggernaut, 2017

*The Psychological Impact of the Partition of India*—Edited Sanjeev Jain, Alok Sarin, Sage, 2018

*The Great Agrarian Conquest: The Colonial Reshaping of a Rural World*—Neeladri Bhattacharya, Permanent Black, 2018

# Notes

## 1. *Satt* — Wound

1. https://www.tribuneindia.com/2014/20140601/pers.htm
2. Vegetarian India A Myth? Survey Shows Over 70% Indians Eat Non-Veg, Telangana Tops List, Adrija Bose, 14 June 2016, https://www.huffingtonpost.in/2016/06/14/how-india-eats_n_10434374.html

## 2. *Berukhi* — Apathy

3. https://www.dailymail.co.uk/indiahome/indianews/article-4803744/How-Panjab-s-Green-Revolution-1960s-changed-India.html
4. http://investPanjab.gov.in/Content/documents/AgroandFoodProcessing_16Jun2016.pdf
5. http://aercpau.com/assets/docs/Panjab%20Profile.pdf
6. https://www.hindustantimes.com/Panjab/cotton-crop-in-over-3-lakh-hectares-destroyed-in-Panjab-govt/story-lfeakmHWeaZfDaSlMhYQUL.html
7. https://timesofindia.indiatimes.com/india/Whitefly-destroys-2/3rd-of-Panjabs-cotton-crop-15-farmers-commit-suicide/articleshow/49265083.cms
8. https://caravanmagazine.in/vantage/stormed-citadels-badal-rail-roko-Panjab
9. https://frontline.thehindu.com/static/html/fl1826/18260810.htm
10. Julio Ribeiro, 'Dangerous Ploys', *Bullet For Bullet*, (Chinar Publishers, 2017) pages 341-362
11. http://www.thehindu.com/news/national/other-states/the-flaming-fields-of-Panjab/article19934276.ece
12. http://epaper.tribuneindia.com/c/29785946
13. https://scroll.in/article/821052/Panjab-is-set-for-record-rice-production-this-year-but-at-a-heavy-price and http://punenvis.nic.in/index3.aspx?sslid=5758&subsublinkid=4941&langid=1&mid=1

14. https://www.tribuneindia.com/news/nation/fertiliser-overuse-eating-away-Panjab-soil-nutrients/123774.html

15. http://agripb.gov.in/home.php?page=intpu

16. http://indianexpress.com/article/what-is/swaminathan-commission-report-and-how-is-its-implementation-relevant-farmer-protest-madhya-pradesh-4694949/

17. https://thewire.in/politics/badal-roadways-Panjab

## 3. *Rosh*—Anger

18. https://www.indiatoday.in/magazine/society-the-arts/media/story/19840615-despite-threats-from-sikh-extremists-journalists-maintain-their-dignity-803048-1984-06-15

19. https://www.indiatoday.in/magazine/special-report/story/19901231-killing-of-air-official-in-chandigarh-shows-newsmen-too-are-targeted-by-militants-in-Panjab-813465-1990-12-31

20. https://www.indiatoday.in/magazine/indiascope/story/19890815-terrorists-adopt-new-strategy-to-intimidate-media-in-Panjab-816403-1989-08-15

21. http://www.tehelka.com/2013/08/how-cable-cartels-shut-out-independent-views/

22. This time, within the next two years of the incidents of 2015, Gurmeet Singh was sentenced to long terms of imprisonment for two concurrent rapes and then the killing of a journalist Ram Chander Chatrapati. But that was to come later.

23. https://www.dawn.com/news/577448

24. Out of 121 freedom fighters given the death sentence, 93 were Sikh. Out of 2,646 freedom fighters sentenced to life imprisonment in the Andamans, four-fifth were Sikhs—2,147 (http://Panjabnewsexpress com/Panjab/news/3-roads-in-port-blair-to-be-named-after-Panjabi-martyrs-60109.aspx)

25. The Sikh Marriage Act pending since once implemented in 1909, was passed by the Lok Sabha in 2012. It is now being adopted by states.

26. European travellers George Forster and John Malcolm who visited Panjab in 1783 and 1805 left vivid accounts of the functioning of the Gurmata.

27. http://www.sikhiwiki.org/index.php/Gurmata. Through Gurmatas that Sikhs had chalked their response to the atrocities of Zakriya Khan, Ahmed Shah Abdali, recognised twelve misls, confederacies (a misl is a file of

record maintained at the Akal Takht), and permitted them to carry out raids on Mughal strongholds, erect the Ram Rauni fort in Amritsar, to raise the Dal Khalsa, choose Jassa Singh Ahluwalia as its leader, formally endorse the system of Rakhi, guardianship by the ruling Sikh clans

28. Mann is a former police officer who had joined the struggle for Khalistan in the Eighties and was arrested and tortured. He later started a political party and was at the height of his glory in the 1989 general elections when his party won seven out of thirteen seats from Panjab. He then got into disagreements about the issue of the length of the sword allowed in parliament and did not take oath as a member. The sword issue was symbolic and while it mattered, he spent too long agitating about it and squandered the mandate he had received. Since then he has maintained a presence in Panjab politics but was not re-elected until 2022. Mokham Singh was once Bhindranwale's bodyguard who survived Operation Blue Star and now headed a political party which had a small following.

## 4. *Rog* — Illness

29. https://www.tribuneindia.com/news/chandigarh/after-mother-tongue-city-more-proficient-in-english/662470.html

30. http://www.censusindia.gov.in/2011census/dchb/0401_PART_A_DCHB_CHANDIGARH.pdf

31. https://www.hindustantimes.com/Panjab/every-8th-Panjabi-suffering-from-mental-illness-national-mental-health-survey-2016-2017/story-dZPldSU2FAFuvHEMNDOPRP.html. Only 20 per cent of patients in Panjab (4.38 lakh) have access to treatment. The survey found that in Panjab the total lifetime prevalence of mental illnesses was 18 per cent (national level: 13.7 per cent) and the current prevalence was 13 per cent (national level: 10.5 per cent). The survey mentions that treatment gap was 57 per cent for severe mental disorders, 81 per cent for alcohol use disorders and 82 per cent for depressive disorders. Panjab has less than 60 psychiatrists in its government hospitals and medical colleges. There are another 67 private practitioners. 'The ratio of doctor to people is 0.46 per lakh. Panjab needs at least 270 psychiatrists,' says Dr BS Chavan, current director-principal, GMCH-32. Since there are only 13 MD psychiatry seats in four medical colleges, it will take at least 11.5 years for Panjab to meet the deficiency. There is an acute shortage of mental health professionals: 12 clinical psychologists, the number should be at least 226; 32 psychiatry social workers

and 4 nurses. 19 out of 22 districts of Panjab are not running the district mental health programme.

## 5. *Astha* — Faith

32. In the Thirties, Ambedkar considered converting to the Sikh religion as it was premised on the idea of equality. With him, it was understood that many Dalits would convert too. Ambedkar even travelled to Amritsar to meet the Sikhs and Master Tara Singh. But, the plan fell through. The reasons have never been fully analysed, but two possibilities have been posited. Since the Dalit population in India was five times as many as the Sikhs, the Sikh leadership felt the religion's original followers would be reduced to a minority. The other is that Gandhi wanted caste Hindus to undergo internal reformation and eliminate discrimination, not for Dalits to escape to another religion.

33. https://en.wikipedia.org/wiki/Communal_Award

34. https://www.thesikhencyclopedia.com/the-british-and-sikhs-1849-1947/azad-Panjab

35. http://www.frontline.in/static/html/fl2708/stories/20100423270808500.htm

36. http://www.learnPanjabi.org/eos/regional%20formula.html

37. http://www.tribuneindia.com/news/comment/50-years-of-Panjabi-suba-still-no-closure/316966.html

38. http://www.tribuneindia.com/news/Panjab/community/ambedkar-s-role-overlooked/284135.html

39. http://www.learnPanjabi.org/eos/regional%20formula.html

40. The relevant sentence in the working committee resolution was, 'Panjabi speaking areas will be carved out of Panjab.'

41. https://www.sikhiwiki.org/index.php/Betrayal_of_the_Sikhs

42. One of the minor political parties in Panjab in earlier times

43. http://www.satp.org/satporgtp/countries/india/states/Panjab/document/papers/anantpur_sahib_resolution.htm

44. http://byjus.com/free-ias-prep/different-commissions-recommendations

45. https://www.sikhri.org/the_emergency_the_sikhs

46. Jagtar Singh, *Khalistan Struggle: A Non-Movement*, (Aakar Books, 2011) Page 40.

47. At Lahore the Pakistan Special Service Group commandoes neutralised the threat and saved the passengers. The hijackers were put on trial and given the

life sentence.

48. https://indiankanoon.org/doc/74868773/

49. https://www.tribuneindia.com/2014/20140601/pers.htm#1

50. http://www.sikh-history.com/sikhhist/personalities/military/shabeg.html

51. http://dailysikhupdates.com/rare-interview-before-shaheedi-of-general-shabeg-singh-surfaces/

52. http://egyankosh.ac.in/bitstream/123456789/19865/1/Unit-8.pdf

53. Kehar Singh, *Farmers' Movement and Pressure Group Politics*, (Deep & Deep Publications, 1990) Pages 90-120

54. Lt Gen. K.S. Brar, *Operation Blue Star—The True Story*, (UBSPD 1993) Page 31

55. https://www.newhistorian.com/rousseaus-social-contract/1972/

56. https://www.facebook.com/anbPanjabi/videos/1039562086254399/

57. Ramesh Inder Singh, *Operation Bluestar: Who Moved My Army?*, *Hindustan Times*, June 4, 2019

58. https://www.hindustantimes.com/Panjab/33-yrs-on-compensation-for-40-sikhs-held-illegally-from-golden-temple-no-proof-of-announcement-for-civilians-before-op-bluestar/story-LbmSYkl36g00lkUNifeouJ.html

59. https://www.tribuneindia.com/2014/20140601/pers.htm#1

60. https://www.sikhsangat.com/index.php?/topic/78434-amritsar-declaration-1994-akali-dal-and-capt-amarinder-singh-push-for-independent-state/

61. https://www.sabhlokcity.com/2010/12/india-sold-out-by-cpi-congress-and-our-press-to-the-ussr/

62. https://www.indiatoday.in/magazine/special-report/story/19860515-pakistan-involvement-in-sikh-terrorism-in-Panjab-based-on-solid-evidence-india-800879-1986-05-15

63. https://economictimes.indiatimes.com/news/politics-and-nation/442-people-convicted-for-1984-anti-sikh-riots-in-delhi-govt/articleshow/50296105.cms

64. https://www.connectedtoindia.com/new-report-about-british-role-in-operation-blue-star-brings-scars-of-1984-to-light-3001.html

65. https://www.hindustantimes.com/Panjab/the-missing-chapter-of-1984-book-by-book-sikh-library-struggles-to-restore-glory/story-UR8vtp08NrjVpE8eK4ag0N.html

66. https://www.hindustantimes.com/Panjab/the-missing-chapter-of-1984-book-by-book-sikh-library-struggles-to-restore-glory/story-

UR8vtp08NrjVpE8eK4ag0N.html

67. https://www.sikhphilosophy.net/threads/where-are-the-1984-manuscripts.44870/

68. https://www.tribuneindia.com/news/Panjab/gk-rare-copy-of-Guru-granth-sahib-sold-for-rs12-crore/786103.html

## 6. *Mardangi*—Masculinity

69. The set of *Panj Pyara* at the centre of the current crisis were employees of the SGPC. They were granthis chosen from among baptised Sikhs who know the five baanis—Japji Sahib, Jaap Sahib, Sawayae, Chaupai Sahib and Anand Sahib—that are recited during the Amrit Sanchar ceremony that the *Panj Pyara* perform at the temporal seats of Sikhism. Though appointed by the SGPC with no fixed tenure, the *Panj Pyara* draw their authority from the institution itself—they represent the Guru Panth. Besides performing Amrit Sanchar ceremonies, the *Panj Pyara* also lead religious processions.

70. https://timesofindia.indiatimes.com/city/chandigarh/after-decades-shaheedi-jor-mela-turns-non-political/articleshow/62312816.cms

71. The folklore is that Dulla Bhatti was a dacoit hero who fought Emperor Akbar to save two Hindu girls and free the land around his villages from the control of the Mughal Empire.

72. http://animal-symbols.com/bull-symbol.html

73. http://www.tribuneindia.com/2011/20110217/main7.htm

74. https://en.wikipedia.org/wiki/Mardistan_(film)

75. http://www.india.com/news/india/300-killed-in-road-accidents-in-past-2-5-years-due-to-stray-cows-Panjab-gau-seva-aayog-2042699/

76. http://www.tribuneindia.com/news/jalandhar/notification-for-implementation-of-cow-cess-finally-issued/248987.html

77. http://indianexpress.com/article/india/india-news-india/Panjab-gau-raksha-dal-chief-satish-kumar-arrested-2988508/

78. http://www.tribuneindia.com/news/Panjab/community/in-mansa-the-villagers-employ-men-on-horseback-whose-sole-task-is-to-chase-away-stray-cattle-the-protection-money/269353.html

## 7. *Dawa*—Medicine

79. http://www.motorindiaonline.in/commercial-vehicles/not-so-happy-journeys-of-truck-drivers-in-india/

80. Rahul Gandhi was then general secretary and later became Congress

president.

81. https://timesofindia.indiatimes.com/india/70-youth-in-Panjab-take-to-drugs-Rahul-Gandhi-says/articleshow/16772237.cms

82. https://swarajyamag.com/politics/what-are-the-Panjabis-smoking-now-a-tale-of-geopolitics-afghan-heroin-and-manufactured-hysteria

83. https://www.statista.com/chart/11926/poppy-cultivation-and-opium-production-in-afghanistan/

84. https://en.wikipedia.org/wiki/Drug_addiction_in_Pakistan

85. https://india.blogs.nytimes.com/2012/10/12/rahul-gandhis-70-per cent-problem/

86. https://indianexpress.com/article/india/india-others/drug-abuse-another-Panjab-study-too-pegged-it-at-70/

87. https://www.outlookindia.com/website/story/how-different-is-your-imfl-from-desi-daaru/298074

88. https://en.wikipedia.org/wiki/Panjabi_Kabaddi

89. https://www.sportskeeda.com/kabaddi/circle-of-dope-indian-kabaddi-team-players-being-caught-for-doping

90. http://indianexpress.com/article/cities/chandigarh/25-players-test-positive-for-drugs-at-ongoing-kabaddi-world-cup/

91. https://www.sundayguardianlive.com/news/1440-Panjab-cops-claim-kabaddi-route-drug-smuggling

92. http://hillpost.in/2011/11/the-desi-boys-of-Panjabs-kabaddi-world-cup/34415/

93. https://www.sundayguardianlive.com/news/1440-Panjab-cops-claim-kabaddi-route-drug-smuggling

94. https://en.wikipedia.org/wiki/First_Anglo-Sikh_War

## 8. *Paani*—Water

95. In 1977, Parkash Singh Badal had merely followed what the previous Congress chief minister Zail Singh had started. Haryana had paid Panjab Rs 1 crore to undertake the acquisition of the land. Zail Singh had thanked Haryana through correspondence but opposed the canal in court and the matter had come under litigation. https://www.indiatoday.in/mail-today/story/Panjab-haryana-lock-horns-over-syl-canal-as-Panjab-de-notifies-land-acquisition-312880- 2016-03-11

96. http://www.india-wris.nrsc.gov.in/wrpinfo/index.php?title=Main_Page

97. https://indiankanoon.org/doc/933499/

98. http://www.tribuneindia.com/news/Panjab/mp-moves-court-seeks-rs-80-

000-crore-as-river-water-cost/568999.html

99. https://www.youtube.com/watch?v=wy_Vvrtmxyc

100. http://www.tribuneindia.com/news/sunday-special/perspective/unearthing-the-saraswati-mystery/81447.html

101. FINAL ASSAULT | Save Panjab Waters, minute 47 to 51, https://www.youtube.com/watch?v=-2_Viws3Ang.

102. http://indianexpress.com/article/india/sustainable-agriculture-Panjab-has-a-new-plan-to-move-farmers-away-from-water-guzzling-paddy-5064481/

103. https://www.youtube.com/watch?v=DSX3ifL64YA&t=618s

104. http://www.tribuneindia.com/news/Panjab/community/toxic-metals-in-water-should-make-govt-sit-up-says-nuclear-physicist/389750.html

105. https://yourstory.com/2017/11/paddy-Panjab/

106. http://www.tribuneindia.com/news/jalandhar/khassan-village-gets-national-award-for-water-conservation/230875.html

107. https://timesofindia.indiatimes.com/city/chandigarh/mansa-village-chosen-for-national-award-for-water-conservation/articleshow/59078021.cms

108. http://www.postconsumers.com/education/water-conservation-quotes-6/

109. https://www.smithsonianmag.com/innovation/is-a-lack-of-water-to-blame-for-the-conflict-in-syria-72513729/

110. High electricity bills were one of the main issue there were huge farmer protests in Chandigarh in 1984.

111. https://www.tribuneindia.com/news/Panjab/in-Panjab-rampant-abuse-of-power-subsidy-by-well-off/788454.html

112. http://www.tribuneindia.com/news/Panjab/won-against-landlords-but-lost-out-to-debt/189214.html

113. https://timesofindia.indiatimes.com/city/chandigarh/praja-mandal-movement-record-now-unavailable/articleshow/63889078.cms

## 9. *Zameen* —Land

114. http://erenow.com/exams/indiasinceindependence/36.html

115. https://www.tribuneindia.com/news/Panjab/won-against-landlords-but-lost-out-to-debt/189214.html

116. https://asmmag.com/features/feature/6474-land-disputes-make-up-50-per cent-of-india-court-cases-in-Panjab.html

117. https://www.bbc.com/news/world-asia-21171262

118. https://ejatlas.org/conflict/gobindpura-thermal-power-plant-Panjab-india

119. http://www.tribuneindia.com/2011/20110823/Panjab.htm#1

## 10. *Karza*—Loan

120. https://timesofindia.indiatimes.com/city/chandigarh/its-clash-of-stats-over-Panjab-farm-suicides/articleshow/63405424.cms?from=mdr

121. https://www.business-standard.com/article/economy-policy/big-rise-in-farmer-suicides-in-four-states-during-2016-says-ncrb-data-118032300025_1.html

122. https://www.tribuneindia.com/news/Panjab/report-16-606-farm-suicides-in-15-years/526766.html

123. D. Singh, I Dewan, A.N.Pandey and S. Tyagi, *Spectrum of unnatural fatalities in the Chandigarh zone of north-west India—a 25 year autopsy study from a tertiary care hospital*, Journal of Clinical Forensic Medicine. 10 (3): 145–52 doi:10.1016/S1353-1131(03)00073-7. PMID 15275009, 2003

124. https://thewire.in/agriculture/the-facts-behind-the-bodies-mangled-in-the-bhakra-beas-canal

125. https://www.thehindu.com/news/national/other-states/Panjabs-farming-sector-in-crisis/article7815262.ece

126. https://ageconsearch.umn.edu/bitstream/204788/2/07-Sukhpal%20Singh.pdf

127. https://thewire.in/politics/Panjab-commission-agents

128. https://scroll.in/article/828159/in-Panjab-farmers-angry-with-system-of-commission-agents-find-hope-in-aaps-manifesto

129. https://archive.cpiml.org/liberation/year_2007/october/Sardaar_ajit_singh.htm

130. Prakash Tandon, *Panjabi Century*, (University of California Press, 1992)

131. https://archive.cpiml.org/liberation/year_2007/october/Sardaar_ajit_singh.htm

132. https://en.wikipedia.org/wiki/Panjab_Land_Alienation_Act,_1900

133. https://www.jatland.com/forums/showthread.php/30379-Legendary-Legal-Works-of-Ch-Sir-Chhotu-Ram

134. http://www.thehindubusinessline.com/opinion/sidestepping-Panjabs-farm-debt-crisis/article8835745.ece

135. http://www.sikhiwiki.org/index.php/Benipal_assault_case

136. https://indianexpress.com/article/india/india-others/where-the-armed-forces-recruit-from/

137. https://www.indiatoday.in/magazine/indiascope/story/19970804-

i.k.-gujral-writes-off-outstanding-rs-8500-crore-debt-Panjab-accumulated-since-1984-831853-1997-08-04

138. https://www.dailypioneer.com/sunday-edition/sunday-pioneer/town-hall/Panjab-seeks-24813-cr-debt-relief.html

## 11. *Jaat* — Caste

139. http://Panjabrevenue.nic.in/pvcomlact961(1).htm
140. http://www.business-standard.com/article/beyond-business/the-ekta-club-comes-of-age-114062701093.html
141. http://www.dailymail.co.uk/indiahome/indianews/article-2634329/Sangrur-village-landlords-hold-Dalits-ransom-cutting-water-land-row.html
142. http://indiatoday.intoday.in/story/dalits-communal-farming-collective-crusade/1/464831.html
143. https://www.businesstoday.in/magazine/the-hub/the-baba-singh-brothers-and-the-squandered-rs-225000000000/story/281437.html
144. https://www.livemint.com/Companies/qtfOwrskdEFz1TTfU7Ci6K/How-the-Singh-brothers-squandered-their-business-legacy.html
145. https://timesofindia.indiatimes.com/india/Amrit-Bani-Granth-installed-at-Ravidassia-shrine/articleshow/11750558.cms

## 12. *Patit* — Apostate

146. H.S. Bhatti and D.M. Michon, *Folk Practice in Panjab*, Centre for Sikh Studies, University of California, Journal of Panjab Studies Fall 2004, Vol 11, no. 2
147. https://www.jatland.com/home/Sindhu
148. The word Khalsa is derived from Arabic *khalis* (pure) and Perso-Arabic *khalisah* (lands directly under government). The term khalisah was used during the Muslim rule in India for crown-lands administered directly by the king without the mediation of jagirdars or mansabdars. https://www.sikhiwiki.org/index.php/Khalsa
149. https://www.youtube.com/watch?v=t5oP0XGk4Cw
150. A Hindu theological school that specialises in learning Vedic and traditional texts.

## 13. *Barðr* — Border

151. https://timesofindia.indiatimes.com/city/chandigarh/5th-gen-boatman-evacuates-last-Gurdaspur-village/articleshow/54628926.cms
152. http://www.rediff.com/news/special/the-general-who-saved-Panjab-in-the-1965-war/20150907.htm

153. https://timesofindia.indiatimes.com/india/Crossing-over-to-a-new-life/articleshow/30497032.cms
154. https://timesofindia.indiatimes.com/city/chandigarh/water-table-decline-slowed-by-20cm-post-2009-act-in-Panjab/articleshow/59624160.cms
155. https://www.weatheronline.in/weather/maps/city
156. https://www.climatechangenews.com/2017/09/28/us-exports-tar-sand-waste-fuelling-delhis-air-pollution-crisis/
157. https://www.tribuneindia.com/news/business/foreign-dreams-make-ielts-coaching-rs-1-100-cr-industry/733521.html

## 14. *Sikhya* — Education

158. https://www.tribuneindia.com/news/Panjab/cost-of-foreign-dreams-for-parents-in-Panjab-rs-27-000-cr/628584.html
159. https://www.tribuneindia.com/news/Panjab/our-kids-our-money-given-away-on-platter/628681.html
160. https://fountainink.in/reportage/the-one-who-got-away-
161. https://timesofindia.indiatimes.com/city/chandigarh/48-Panjab-colleges-face-68-shortage-of-regular-lecturers/articleshow/63494838.cms
162. In 2002, the Panjab Public Service Commission job-for-cash scam caused a scandal in both civil and judicial recruitment. A certain Ravinderpal Singh Sidhu was chairman of the commission when it was alleged that candidates bribed their way past the recruitment process between 1999 and 2001 and between 1996 and 2002. Sidhu hijacked the entire commission, himself appointing examiners and running the racket through touts. More here: https://www.outlookindia.com/magazine/story/in-Panjab-another-decade-another-scam/299521
163. https://timesofindia.indiatimes.com/city/chandigarh/48-Panjab-colleges-face-68-shortage-of-regular-lecturers/articleshow/63494838.cms
164. https://www.hindustantimes.com/Panjab/testing-times-the-case-of-missing-teachers-in-Panjab-govt-schools/story-uG7xaOsWRSjpkzrBwtKJAP.html
165. No reference.
166. https://www.tribuneindia.com/news/Panjab/community/mandi-gobindgarh-s-steel-business-faces-slow-death/126738.html
167. https://www.tribuneindia.com/news/business/ludhiana-industry-grapples-with-labour-shortage/783698.html
168. https://www.indiatoday.in/magazine/the-big-story/story/20140317-

industries-in-Panjab-centre-and-failure-of-local-entrepreneurs-800447-2014-03-07

169. http://www.tribuneindia.com/news/Panjab/education/migrants-outdo-natives-in-Panjabi-calligraphy/128477.html

170. https://www.thehindu.com/opinion/columns/will-the-gats-close-on-higher-education/article8042337.ece

## 15. *Lashaan* — Corpses

171. https://timesofindia.indiatimes.com/city/chandigarh/Big-on-guns-Panjab-holds-Indias-20-licences/articleshow/51099899.cms

172. Similar interrogation centres were at Mal Mandi in Amritsar where today the India-Pakistan bus service halts, at the old palace of Maharaja Duleep Singh and at many other places across Panjab.

173. https://www.indiatoday.in/magazine/indiascope/story/19891015-terrorists-in-Panjab-increasingly-target-policemens-families-816601-1989-10-15

174. https://www.sikhfreedom.com/how-the-singhs-punished-gobind-ram adapted from *Tay Deevaa Jagdaa Rahaygaa* by Amardeep Singh Amar

175. https://www.youtube.com/watch?v=8W62BeQmero

176. https://countercurrents.org/2017/06/from-naxals-to-taxals

177. https://timesofindia.indiatimes.com/city/meerut/11694-lives-lost-in-Panjab-militancy-RTI-response/articleshow/48257377.cms

178. A people's forum report, *The Bleeding Panjab: A Report to the Nation*, a joint publication of Surkh Rekha and Inqualabi Jantak Leeh, edited by Amolak Singh and Jaspal Jassi, published in 1992 provides a partial list of people killed during militancy but places the number of fatalities at 20,000. https://b484.wordpress.com/2012/04/10/the-bleeding-Panjab/

179. https://www.tribuneindia.com/2004/20040730/nhrc1.htm

180. http://panthic.org/articles/5512

181. https://www.indiatoday.in/magazine/states/story/19970609-top-officers-suicide-indicates-crisis-in-Panjab-police-force-831520-1997-06-09

182. https://www.outlookindia.com/magazine/story/after-the-highs-the-lows/201800

183. https://www.outlookindia.com/magazine/story/confessions-of-a-killer-cop/296046

184. http://www.satp.org/satporgtp/kpsgill/terrorism/97pm.htm

185. Ensaaf.org

186. https://timesofindia.indiatimes.com/city/chandigarh/rights-group-maps-forced-disappearances-extra-judicial-killings-in-Panjab/articleshow/66000889.cms?utm_campaign=andapp&utm_medium=referral&utm_source=native_share_tray

187. https://www.indiatoday.in/magazine/indiascope/story/19920515-Panjab-government-puts-ajit-singh-bains-behind-bars-766252-2013-06-18

188. http://sikhchic.com/1984/the_man_from_rajoana_part_i and http://sikhchic.com/people/the_man_from_rajoana_part_ii

189. https://www.hindustantimes.com/Panjab/2-men-arrested-with-fake-rs-2-000-notes-in-Panjab-s-tarn-taran-planned-to-use-printouts/story-y68tqdt6br05SaXzgWqGzN.html

190. https://epaper.timesgroup.com/Olive/ODN/TimesOfIndia/shared/ShowArticle.aspx?doc=TOICG%2F2019%2F05%2F04&entity=Ar00809&sk=E110BDA8&mode=https://www.indiatoday.in/magazine/special-report/story/20120123-Panjab-polls-six-clans-dominate-the-political-and-social-landscape-756975-2012-01-14

191. https://indianexpress.com/article/chandigarh/niti-aayog-Panjab-rajiv-kumar-niti-aayog-national-food-security-5074662/

192. https://www.thehindubusinessline.com/blink/know/Panjabs-sacrilege-law-unholy-haste/article24829185.ece

193. https://www.business-standard.com/article/politics/kejriwal-s-meek-surrender-to-majithia-apology-to-jaitley-next-10-points-118031600150_1.html

194. https://www.hindustantimes.com/Panjab/rows-marred-drug-stf-s-working-during-harpreet-singh-sidhu-s-tenure/story-5gRcxN9wqdT7THD6V1Ol1L.html

195. https://www.tribuneindia.com/news/Panjab/drug-deaths-trigger-panic-addicts-seek-help-on-own/613627.html

196. https://vidhilegalpolicy.in/reports/2018/8/23/from-addict-to-convict-the-working-of-the-ndps-act-1985-in-Panjab

197. https://indianexpress.com/article/india/two-groups-clash-during-auction-of-shamlaat-land-for-dalits-in-sangrur-5810424/

198. https://www.tribuneindia.com/news/Panjab/-kurki-to-go-cabinet-nod-to-amending-act/415367.html

199. http://www.Panjabtoday.in/Panjabtodayin/Panjab.php?comment&entry_id=1497623291&title=farm-debt-waiver-expert-group-fails-to-submit-report-gets-2-months-extension-interim-report-on-monday

200. https://economictimes.indiatimes.com/news/politics-and-nation/Panjab-cabinet-approves-crop-loan-waiver/articleshow/60766923.cms

201. https://indianexpress.com/article/india/when-the-field-is-no-longer-theirs-Panjab-farmers-loan-kurki-auctions-5603832/

202. https://www.hindustantimes.com/Panjab/after-over-30-years-student-union-elections-to-take-place-in-Panjab-varsities-capt-amarinder/story-VIAqaVshF0JUBSyNbrskxI.html

203. https://www.hindustantimes.com/Panjab/ht-explainer-why-schoolteachers-are-up-in-arms-in-Panjab/story-GNHhkhU3BA2DgUJT gevqYN.html

204. http://www.newindianexpress.com/nation/2018/sep/05/Panjab-6000-college-teachers-go-on-mass-leave-over-pay-hike-1867942.html

205. https://www.sbs.com.au/yourlanguage/Panjabi/en/audiotrack/indian-army-chief-warns-militancy-returning-Panjab?cid=inbody:three-men-get-life-sentence-for-possessing-prokhalistan-literature

206. https://www.business-standard.com/article/current-affairs/grenade-attack-on-nirankari-religious-congregation-in-amritsar-kills-3-118111800207_1.html

207. https://m.economictimes.com/news/defence/18-khalistani-terror-modules-busted-in-Panjab-95-arrested-in-two-years-government/articleshow/67347680.cms

208. https://en.wikipedia.org/wiki/Arrest_of_Jagtar_Singh_Johal

209. https://www.sbs.com.au/yourlanguage/Panjabi/en/article/2019/02/11/three-men-get-life-sentence-possessing-pro-khalistan-literature

210. https://indianexpress.com/article/opinion/columns/i-applaud-major-nitin-gogoi-jammu-kashmir-man-tied-to-jeep-human-shield-4664413/

## Post Script: *Ailaan* — Announcement

211. https://www.timesnownews.com/india/article/sharp-upsurge-in-shaheen-bagh-model-291-protest-sites-emerge-across-india-in-60-days-mha-to-states/562131

212. https://scroll.in/latest/962130/centres-economic-package-centre-raises-fdi-in-defence-to-74-allows-commercial-coal-mining

213. https://www.hindustantimes.com/india-news/govt-picks-defence-coal-among-key-reform-areas/story-WfmVUFdaOop31Jg7uUue9H.html

214. https://www.hindustantimes.com/india-news/the-story-of-indian-railways-and-its-tryst-with-privatisation-101617724857901.html

215. https://www.outlookindia.com/website/story/india-news-nitish-kumars-govt-scrapped-apmc-act-14-years-ago-but-farmers-in-bihar-still-languishing/378104
216. https://www.fao.org/india/fao-in-india/india-at-a-glance/en/
217. https://www.downtoearth.org.in/blog/agriculture/contract-farming-is-yet-to-make-a-mark-in-punjab-here-is-why-83454
218. https://www.thenewsminute.com/article/pepsico-loses-rights-over-lays-chips-potato-variety-which-it-sued-gujarat-farmers-158375
219. https://www.adaniports.com/-/media/Project/Ports/Media-Release/2018/Silo-storage-of-foodgrain-gathers-momentum.pdf
220. https://economictimes.indiatimes.com/r-companies/reliance-industries/ril-signs-mega-farm-to-fork-deal-with-punjab-govt/articleshow/1833122.cms
221. https://www.relianceretail.com/our-business.html
222. https://thewire.in/agriculture/farmers-punjab-protest-central-farm-laws
223. https://www.hindustantimes.com/india-news/six-farmers-were-killed-in-the-june-6-police-firing-in-mandsaur-mp-govt/story-oXPWt7C0PP9PrHNc1sDvlO.html
224. https://indianexpress.com/article/india/farmers-protests-tractor-march-republic-day-7150314/
225. https://www.thehindu.com/news/national/we-will-hold-parallel-tractor-parade-on-republic-day-say-farmer-unions/article33479027.ece
226. https://www.thestatesman.com/india/will-not-fight-celebrate-republic-day-rakesh-tikait-1502947169.html
227. https://www.youtube.com/watch?v=6dAdVNe_rq8, accessed 30 August 2022
228. https://www.youtube.com/watch?v=NKJmYDNvC7w, accessed 30 August 2022
229. https://www.youtube.com/watch?v=j8hXz7BhYIw, accessed 30 August 2022
230. https://www.youtube.com/watch?v=YBXIMNqwOAg&t=564s, accessed 31 August 2022
231. https://www.youtube.com/watch?v=lSRwCwnApow&t=582s, accessed 30 August 2022
232. https://thewire.in/rights/autopsy-doctor-told-me-hed-seen-the-bullet-injury-but-can-do-nothing-as-his-hands-are-tied
233. https://www.youtube.com/watch?v=2UVMG9R7q6U, accessed 30 August 2022

234. https://www.youtube.com/watch?v=NpsbPlvDkXY, accessed 30 August 2022
235. https://www.indiatoday.in/india/story/red-fort-adopted-by-dalmia-bharat-group-congress-objects-to-privatisation-of-heritage-1222339-2018-04-28
236. https://www.ptcnews.tv/water-from-village-made-rakesh-tikait-cry-en
237. https://www.newindianexpress.com/nation/2021/jan/30/villagers-bring-food-water-for-rakesh-tikait-as-bku-digs-heels-at-ghazipur-border-2257246.html
238. https://www.groundxero.in/2021/01/30/thousands-of-farmer-took-the-lota-noon-oath-at-muzaffarnagar-mahapanchayat-for-a-social-boycott-of-bjp/